WRITINGS AND TRANSLATIONS

OF

BISHOP COVERDALE.

# The Parker Society.

## Instituted A.D. M.DCCC.XL.

### For the Publication of the Works of the Fathers and Early Writers of the Reformed English Church.

# WRITINGS AND TRANSLATIONS

OF

# MYLES COVERDALE,

BISHOP OF EXETER.

CONTAINING

THE OLD FAITH.
A SPIRITUAL AND MOST PRECIOUS PEARL.
FRUITFUL LESSONS.
A TREATISE ON THE LORD'S SUPPER.
ORDER OF THE CHURCH IN DENMARK.
ABRIDGEMENT OF THE ENCHIRIDION OF ERASMUS.

---

EDITED FOR

The Parker Society,

BY THE

REV. GEORGE PEARSON, B.D.

RECTOR OF CASTLE CAMPS,
AND LATE CHRISTIAN ADVOCATE IN THE UNIVERSITY OF CAMBRIDGE.

*Wipf & Stock*
PUBLISHERS
*Eugene, Oregon*

Wipf and Stock Publishers
199 W 8th Ave, Suite 3
Eugene, OR 97401

Writings and Translations of Myles Coverdale, Bishop of Exeter
Containing The Old Faith, A Spiritual and Most Precious Pearl,
Fruitful Lessons, A Treatise on the Lord's Supper,
Order of the Church in Denmark, Abridgement of the Enchiridion of Erasmus
By Coverdale, Myles
ISBN: 1-59752-472-7
Publication date 2/16/2006
Previously published by Cambridge, 1844

# CONTENTS.

|  | Page |
|---|---|
| Advertisement | vii |
| The Old Faith | 1 |
| A Spiritual and Most Precious Pearl | 84 |
| Fruitful Lessons upon the Passion, Burial, Resurrection, Ascension, and sending of the Holy Ghost | 195 |
| A Treatise on the Sacrament of the Body and Blood of Christ | 422 |
| The Order of the Church of Christ in Denmark and other countries for the Lord's Supper, Baptism, and Holy Wedlock | 467 |
| Abridgement of the Enchiridion of Erasmus | 489 |
| Fac-simile of Title-page and Colophon of the second edition of the Treatise on the Lord's Supper | 529 |
| Additions to the Translator's Preface, from the second edition | 530 |
| Index | 537 |

# ADVERTISEMENT.

The following is a brief notice of the personal history, and of the works of Bishop Coverdale, as far as we are acquainted with them: a fuller account will be supplied in the succeeding volume.

He is said to have been born in the year 1488, and to have been a native of the district of Coverdale in Richmondshire, from which district it is probable that his family took their name. He received his education in the Priory of the Augustines at Cambridge, of which the celebrated Dr Barnes was the head. It is probable, that from this eminent man he derived those principles which led him to take so great a lead in the Reformation, and especially to devote himself with so much energy to the great work of presenting the scriptures to his countrymen in their native tongue. Bishop Coverdale subsequently shewed his gratitude to his instructor by composing one of his ablest treatises in his defence. The situation of Coverdale having become unsafe from the conspicuous part which he had taken in defence of the new doctrines, he left England for a few years in the latter part of the reign of Henry VIII., during which time he was in the Netherlands, Denmark, and the north of Germany. During the period of this absence, besides assisting Tindal in his translation of the New Testament, he completed the translation of the Bible, which was published October 4th, 1535, besides other works calculated to advance the cause of the Reformation. On the accession of Edward VI. in 1547, he returned to England, and was appointed chaplain to the Queen Dowager. In 1548, he accompanied the expedition of lord Russell for the suppression of the rebels in Devonshire. He was subsequently appointed coadjutor to Veysy, bishop of Exeter, and finally, in 1551, consecrated bishop of that see on the resignation of Veysy. On the accession of Mary, in 1553, he was deprived of his bishoprick; but at the intercession of the king of Denmark he was allowed to leave the kingdom, from whence he went to Denmark, and was at length appointed to the parochial charge of Bergzabern in the dutchy of Deux-Ponts; where he remained till he went to Geneva, at which place he appears to have lived till the accession of Queen Elizabeth in 1558, when he returned to England; and on the 17th of December 1559, he officiated at the consecration of Archbishop Parker. He was collated on the third of March 1563 to the living of St Magnus, London Bridge, by Bishop Grindal, which in the course of the year 1566 he resigned. He died in February 1569 at the advanced age of eighty-one years, and was buried on the 19th of that month in St Bartholomew's Church, behind the Exchange. Although he was not restored to the bishoprick of Exeter after his return from exile, nor promoted to any other bishoprick, it is evident that he never relinquished his episcopal character, (as some have asserted that he did,) as he always signs himself—" Myles Coverdale, quondam Exoniensis."

With regard to the works of Bishop Coverdale, much uncertainty has existed respecting them, from the circumstance that so few of them have been reprinted since the close of the century in which they were first published: one of them however, THE OLD FAITH, was reprinted with a different title in 1624, and another, THE SPIRITUAL PEARL, twice in the present century. They are to be found almost entirely in the libraries of public bodies, or in the collections of private individuals. Even of those works which are best known, few copies are to be met with; while of others the numbers are reduced to two or three copies, and in more than one instance, so far as is yet ascertained, to a single copy. With regard also to the different editions of his works, much uncertainty exists, the earlier editions apparently having in many instances entirely disappeared. These considerations, at the same time that they enhance the interest attaching to the writings of this eminent man, proportionably increase the difficulty of presenting them to the world in as complete a state as could be wished.

The works of Bishop Coverdale are partly original, and partly translated, chiefly consisting of the latter; it being a remarkable characteristic of this great man, that he did not disdain to employ the labours of others, when he thought them likely to be more effective than his own. It has been considered that any collection of his writings, which did not include these, would be incomplete. Even in these works he has shewn the hand of a master; and in his original works, for instance his defence of his friend and preceptor Dr Barnes, he has brought to his subject considerable powers both of learning and argument. It does not appear that any of his works were printed before the completion of his Bible in 1535; and they probably appeared, for the most part, between that period and the time of his elevation to the bishoprick of Exeter.

The following is given as the most complete list which at present can be made out of his writings.

I. The Old Faith; an evident probation that the Christian Faith hath endured since the beginning of the world. (Translation from H. Bullinger.) 1547.

II. A Spiritual and Most Precious Pearl. A translation from Otho Wermullerus. 1550.

III. *Treatise on Justification. From the same.

IV. The Book of Death. From the same.

V. The Hope of the Faithful. From the same.

VI. Fruitful Lessons upon the Passion, Death, Resurrection, and Ascension of our Saviour, and the giving of the Holy Ghost. 1540—47.

VII. Abridgement of Erasmus's Enchiridion.

VIII. A Confutation of that Treatise which one John Standish made against the Protestation of Dr Barnes in the year 1540.

IX. Christian State of Matrimony.

X. Faithful and true Prognostication on the years 1536—48—49.

XI. Translation of Luther's Exposition of the Twenty-third Psalm. 1537.

XII. *How and whither a Christian ought to flee the horrible plague of the Pestilence. Translated from Osiander. 1537.

XIII. Acts of the Disputation in the Council of the Empire holden at Ravenspurg, set forth by Bucer and Melancthon. Translated by M. C.

XIV. (1) The Christian Rule and state of all the world. (2) A Christian Exhortation unto customable Swearers. (3) The Manner of saying Grace or giving thanks to God.

XV. Defence of a certain poor Christian man, who else should have been condemned by the Pope's law. Translated from the German.

XVI. Ghostly Psalms and Spiritual Songs drawn out of the Holy Scripture.

XVII. (1) Exposition of the Magnificat. (2) The Original and Spring of all Sects.

XVIII. (1) *A Christian Catechism. (2) Cantus usuales Witeburgensium. (3) The Apology of the Germans against the Council of Mantua.

XIX. A faithful and most godly Treatise concerning the most sacred Sacrament of the body and blood of our Lord Jesus Christ, translated from Calvin; whereunto the order that the church and congregation of Christ in Denmark doth use at the receiving of Baptism, the Supper of the Lord, and Wedlock, is added.

XX. *The Supplication that the Nobles and Commons of Osterick made unto King Ferdinand. Translated by M. C.

XXI. The Testimony and Report, which Eccius gave and sent in to the Council of those Princes, which name themselves Catholic. 1542.

Prefaces, Letters, &c.

Some other works have been attributed to Coverdale; but the evidence is not sufficient to warrant our ascribing them absolutely to him. Those works which have as yet escaped the researches of the Editor are marked with an asterisk. In conclusion, the Editor begs to express his thanks to those persons who have allowed their scarce copies of Coverdale to be transcribed for the press; of which due acknowledgement will be made in the proper place.

*November*, 1844.

# THE OLD FAITH.

[This work is a translation of a Treatise of Bullinger, of which the title is: "Antiquissima Fides et vera Religio: Christianam fidem mox a primis mundi exordiis usque ad hæc tempora durasse, eamque veram et indubitatam esse, Heinrychi Bullingeri Apodixis, sive clara et evidens demonstratio, e Germanico in Latinam linguam traducta per Diethelmum Cellarium Tigurinum. In hoc Enchiridio, candide lector, habebis brevissimam historiam, cum temporum supputatione, sacrosanctæ nostræ fidei, deque illius præcipuis et operibus et professoribus: habebis hujus item incrementa et defectus ac calamitates jam inde a prima mundi origine ad hæc usque tempora. Brevissima ergo periocha est utriusque Testamenti, et probatio, quod per solam fidem in Christum veram omnes pii Deo et placuerint et salutem fuerint consecuti." Copies of this work of Bullinger are contained in the Bodleian library at Oxford, and in the library of the Archbishop of Canterbury at Lambeth.

It does not appear certain in what year this work of Bishop Coverdale first appeared. An edition of it appears to have been published in 1541, and another in 1547. Another edition was also published in 1624, under the following title: "Look from Adam, and behold the Protestants' faith and religion, evidently proved out of the holy Scriptures against all Atheists, Papists, loose libertines, and carnal Gospellers: and that the faith, which they profess, hath continued from the beginning of the world, and so is the true and ancient faith. Herein hast thou a short sum of the whole bible, &c."

The present edition is printed from a copy of the edition of 1547, which was formerly in the possession of Mr Brand, and afterwards of the late Sir Francis Freeling, Bart., and which now belongs to John Matthew Gutch, Esq., of Claines, Worcestershire, who obligingly granted the use of it to the Parker Society.]

# THE OLD FAITH.

[COVERDALE.]

# The old faith, an evident proba-

cion out of the holy scripture, that the christen fayth (which is the right, true, old and undoubted fayth) hath endured sens the beginnyng of the worlde.

Herein hast thou also a short summe of the whole Byble, and a probacion, that al vertuous men have pleased God, and were saved through the Christen fayth.

1547.

## Myles Coverdale.

## ¶ MYLES COVERDALE TO ALL CHRISTIAN READERS, WISHETH GRACE, MERCY, AND PEACE FROM GOD THE FATHER THROUGH OUR LORD AND ONLY SAVIOUR JESUS CHRIST.

LIKE as the almighty eternal God, three in persons and one in substance, of his tender mercy and love, not only created man at the beginning after his own similitude and likeness, but also, when he was lost, most graciously redeemed him and brought him out of bondage; even so, when man, neither regarding his wonderful creation nor his most dear redemption, gropeth in darkness, in vice, and blindness, lieth in the devil's prison, and goeth in the way of damnation, God alway setteth up his light before him, sendeth the message of his word unto him, sheweth him what case he is in, giveth him warning, openeth the prison door, calleth him out of the devil's service, telleth him what danger it is to be his bondman or servant unto sin: this doth God alway, afore he punish and plague the world. This, I say, hath been the property of God since the beginning, as the stories and prophecies of all the holy bible do testify. And though we had no writing of God's acts in times past, yet hath he practised this same his wonderful work of mercy upon us. So that like as we must needs confess, that we are created of God and redeemed by his only mercy in his dear Son Jesus Christ; so can we not deny, but we have heard his holy message, had no less preachings and warnings of dangers to come, than other have had afore our days: yet even the same merciful God, that sent Noe to preach righteous unto the wicked world, and converted the Ninevites by his word in the ministration of

*The accustomary goodness of God.*

*God hath shewed no less kindness to us than he did to the old world.*

the prophet Jonas, hath done even so with us in every condition. And some (thanks be unto him therefore!) hath he brought out of darkness into his wonderful light, and out of the devil's service into the kingdom of his dear Son.

But alas and woe to this unthankful world! For like as a great number that be in prison of Satan will not come forth, when they are called and the door set open, but go on still stumbling in darkness, when the lantern of light is offered them; even so, if any play a wise man's part, and do as he is warned by God's word, he shall have a sort of apish[1] people, a number of dizzards[2] and scornful mockers, which, because the man will not dance in the devil's morrice with them[3], nor keep their company in the bondage of sin and vice, neither run with them unto like confusion, as St Peter calleth it, laugh him to scorn, and blear out their tongues at him, even like fools and coxcombs of the world. And like as when a poor wretch cometh out of prison, he shall have more to stand gazing and gaping upon him, than to do him good, or to help him to his fees; even so now that God of his mercy hath called us out of Satan's prison, and from the school of false doctrine, my lord's fool with his companions standeth staring upon us, and mocketh us, because we sit not still with other prisoners. There goeth a fellow of the new learning, saith one; there is one of these new-fangled gospellers, saith another; that is one of the new brethren, saith the third; he followeth the new faith, &c.

Wherefore, in consideration hereof, I have here set forth this book: partly, because it sheweth the antiquity and ancient age of our holy Christian faith, and partly, to give occasion unto all such as have received it, not to be ashamed of it,

*They that follow God's word are laughed to scorn.*

[1 Pet. iv. 4.]

*The doctrine of Christ's faith is no new thing.*

[1 Apish: trifling. Todd.]
[2 Dizzards: idle fellows, blockheads. In the original *desertes*.]
[3 The *Morrice* or *Moorish dance* is said to have been first brought into England in Edward the Third's time. The word is found in Milton, Comus, 116.]

nor to shrink from it for any opprobrious mockage or scornful derision in this world. The apostle saith, that the preaching or word of "Christ's cross is foolishness to them that 1 Cor. i. perish," and that "the thing which appertaineth to the Spirit 1 Cor. ii. of God is foolishness to a carnally minded man." Whereby, like as we may learn, that it is no new thing to be mocked and stared upon for holding with the doctrine that maketh so much of Christ's death and the true worshipping of God in the Spirit; even so may we see, to the singular comfort of our conscience, that no man mocketh us for it, but such as perish and are carnally minded; and that, for all their derision and scorning, it is yet the power of God, (1 Cor. i.), and be- *To us which are saved it is* longeth to his holy Spirit, (1 Cor. ii.), and is not our own *the power of God.* doctrine, neither of any other man's making. This is now to us a comfort and consolation.

But because the world is angry with us for our faith, and giveth us so evil report for teaching it, it shall be expedient for us to declare, what faith is, and what faith we mean, when we make mention thereof. First, because we may not describe it after our own judgment, we will rehearse the words of the apostle, which, writing to the Hebrews, saith after this manner: "Faith is a substance of things to be *What faith is.* hoped for, an evidence, or certainty, of things which do not appear." By the which distinction it is manifest, that when we set forth or teach this faith, we mean no vain faith, no false opinion of faith, no fond imagination of faith, no dead faith, no idle faith; but a substantial thing, even a sure belief of things that are to be hoped for, and a proof, experience, or knowledge of things that are not seen. This faith then is the instrument, whereby we feel and are certain of heavenly things, that our corporal eye cannot see.

Now, because none other virtue can so apprehend the mercy of God, nor certify us so effectually of our salvation, as this living faith doth; therefore hath the scripture imputed our justification before God only unto faith; among all other virtues; not without other virtues following, but without any other work or deed justifying.

This is the faith of Christ, which all the scripture speak-
<sub>Ad Romanos.</sub> eth of. This is the faith, that St Paul preacheth to justify in
<sub>Galat. Ephes.</sub>
<sub>James ii.</sub> the sight of God; as St James teacheth, that works justify in the sight of men, and that it is but a dead faith, which
<sub>Heb. xi.</sub> hath no works. This is the faith, without the which "it is
<sub>Rom. xiv.</sub> impossible to please God," and of the which "whatsoever
<sub>Acts xv.</sub> proceedeth not is sin." This is the faith, whereby God
<sub>1 Pet. i.</sub> "purifieth our hearts," and whose end is salvation. This is
<sub>Gal. v.</sub> the "faith, that worketh by charity" or godly love, and is of value before God. This is the faith, whereby the
<sub>1 Cor. x.</sub> holy fathers, which were afore Christ's incarnation, did in spirit eat and drink, and enjoy the same mercy of God in Christ that we are partakers of.

To be short: this is the same faith, whereby God saved
<sub>Heb. xi.</sub> those his elect, of whom St Paul maketh mention in the foresaid epistle to the Hebrews, and rehearseth many godly fruits of the same in their conversation.

This then is no new-fangled faith, no strange faith, no faith invented by man's brain; but even the same that God's holy Spirit teacheth in the infallible truth of his scripture, and that Adam, Abel, Enoch, and all the other servants of God were saved in. Why do men therefore either call it a new-fangled faith, or report evil of us for setting it forth? Why? I fear me, this is one cause: The old faith, that all those servants of God had, whom the apostle nameth in the eleventh chapter to the Hebrews, had a life and conversation joined unto it, which was rich and full of all good works. Therefore seeing there be so many babblers and prattlers of faith, and so few that bring forth the worthy fruits of penance, it giveth to the world occasion to report of us, that our faith is but new-fangled. They see us not fall to labour and taking of pains, as Adam did; they see not the righteousness and thankfulness in us, that was in Abel; they see us not walk after the word and will of God, as Enoch did; they see us not take God's warning so earnestly, as Noe did; they see us not so obedient to the voice of God, nor so well willing and content to leave our friends, to forsake our own wills, our own lands and goods, at God's calling, and dwell in a strange country, to do God's pleasure, as Abraham did; they see that we choose not rather to suffer adversity with the people of God, than to enjoy the pleasures of sin for a season; they see us not esteem the rebuke of Christ, or trouble for his sake, to be greater riches than all the treasures of this world, as Moses did. To be short, they see not in our garden those sweet flowers and fruits of God's holy Spirit, which were in them that had the old faith.

Ashamed may we be therefore, as many of us as either write, teach, preach, speak, or talk of the old faith, if we endeavour not ourselves to have those old heavenly virtues, that were ever plentiful in all God's true servants; in every one, I mean, according to his calling. Not that it is evil to teach or talk of the true old faith; but this I say, because that, according to the doctrine of St James, they are but deceivers of themselves, that are not doers of God's word, as well as hearers thereof. And through such slender receiving of Christ's holy gospel it is now come to pass, that like as we have need of such an apostle as was holy St Paul, to rebuke this vain confidence that men put in their works, and to tell us that no work of our doing, but faith of God's working, doth justify us in his sight; even so have we no less need of such another apostle, as was holy St James, to rebuke this horrible unthankfulness of men, that, professing themselves to be Christian and to hold of Christ's old faith, are yet dead unto all good works, receive not the word of God in meekness, cast not away all uncleanness and maliciousness, are swift to speak, to talk, to jangle, and to take displeasure, are forgetful hearers of the word, and not livers thereafter; boasting themselves to be of God's pure and undefiled religion;

*James i.*

*Would to God we had many such as James the Apostle was!*

and yet refrain not their tongues from evil, visit not the poor, the friendless, and the desolate in their trouble, neither keep themselves undefiled from this world. Read the first chapter of his epistle.

<small>O unthankful world!</small>
What occasion might such an apostle, as holy Saint James was, have to write another, yea, a sharper epistle, seeing so many pretending to be of Jesu Christ's old faith are yet so partial, have such a carnal respect of persons, are not rich in faith, despise the poor, practise not the law of godly love, talk and jangle of faith, not having the works thereof, clothe not the naked, help not the poor to their living, regard not their necessity, have but a dead faith, declare not by good and godly works the true and old faith of Christ, are but vain believers, have not the effectuous, the working and living faith, that Abraham and Rahab had. Read the second chapter of his epistle.

<small>St James could not fail to rebuke such.</small>
How would holy Saint James reprove these bringers up of strange doctrines, blasphemers, backbiters, beliers of good men, false teachers against God's truth, dissemblers with the same; carry fire, as they say, with the one hand, and water in the other; pretend to be learned, and yet bring not forth the works of good conversation in meekness out of God's wisdom, but in frowardness, and out of carnal doctrine! How would he take up these, that delight in malice and strife, belie God's truth, are given to earthly, fleshly, and devilish wisdom, are unstable, full of all evil works, are not in the school of God's wisdom and learning, are not given to unfeignedness of heart, are not peaceable, are churlish, uneasy to be entreated, &c.! Read the third chapter of his epistle.

What would such an holy apostle say to this wicked world, wherein a great number, pretending to be christian men, are given so to quarrelling and fighting, to voluptuousness and inordinate lusts, to envy and indignation, to unlawful spending and consuming of that they may get, to adultery, to the despising of holy wedlock, to shameful un-. cleanness, either not willing to marry, or else putting away their wives for light occasions and for satisfying of their own trifling lusts, falling in love with the vain friendship of this world, taking part against God; yea, whereas by their profession, oath, and allegiance which they owe to their most high sovereign, the king of heaven, they should in a virtuous conversation maintain all godliness, are become even enemies, suppressors, and overthrowers thereof, as well through their obstinate and cruel resisting of God's word, as by other wicked examples of their vicious and filthy living. What would holy St James say to such unthankful bellies, that, knowing the truth, live of such a sort? Would he spare them, though they were never so rich and wealthy? Read the fourth chapter of his epistle, and the first part of his fifth chapter, and ye will judge the contrary.

Wherefore, most dear readers, whosoever of you hath been slack to follow the good life and godly conversation, that St James and all the other scripture beside requireth to be in them which profess the old faith, let him take better hold, turn again to the truth, and follow that loving exhortation, which holy St James maketh in the latter end of his epistle. And if he have at the first not inclined to God's word, nor received it unfeignedly in meekness, nor submitted himself to be ordered thereby, and to cast away all uncleanness, &c.; but hath haply suffered it, promoted it, set it forth, or taken a pretence of favour and love to it, for some other purpose, as to obtain any carnal profit, gains, or liberty by it, let him not put holy St James, or any other true messenger of God, to the pains of rebuking him for so doing; let him rather enter into himself, reprove his own fault and abuse in that behalf; abhor it in any wise, be angry, displeased, and discontent with himself; sorry and repentant for it; shame not to ask God mercy, and by good works from henceforward to labour, that the glory of God and worship of his truth may be pre-

*Let every man take the pains to rebuke his own fault.*

ferred and set up; which he, by such his unchristian living, hath in times past caused to be hindered.

In conclusion, though there be never so many that recant and deny God's holy word, either in their living and conversation, or in their words, writing, or preaching; yet, as many of us as are entered into the school of that wisdom which is from above, let us be true scholars of the same; and deed[1], *We must put on the nature of God's doctrine.* let us even enter into the nature and kind thereof; which, as St James saith, (Jaco. iii.) "is pure, peaceable, gentle, and easy to be entreated, full of mercy and good fruits, without judging and simulation." Which thing if we do, then shall we follow no filthy doctrine nor counterfeited wisdom; then shall we be no breakers of peace; then shall we be as glad to forgive, as we would be forgiven; glad to be reformed; rich and plentiful in the works of mercy and good fruits of the old faith; then shall we be no quarrel-pickers or dissemblers with any man; then shall we not only be found the maintainers of peace and all good order, but peaceably also and in all gentle manner shall we, both in word and deed, sow, spread abroad, and shew the fruit of that righteousness, which cometh only of God through Jesus Christ.

If any of them that are gone, of high or low estate, pretending to be maintainers, favourers, setters forth, or scholars of Christ's doctrine, hath in any condition dissembled therewith, fallen from God, misbehaved himself in the affairs of his prince, misgoverned his household, maintained riot, vice, and sin, or brought the good word of God into any evil report by his ungodly conversation, as I fear *Let the works of God, which are past, be a warning to us.* me it to be too true; let us beware by such men's fall: let us not receive the grace of God in vain: for like as they that harden their hearts at God's word, and spurn wilfully against it, are sure of their damnation, except they repent; even so they that dissemble withal, shall find their

[1] [Deed: indeed.]

judgment. Wherefore let us, that have received the old true faith of Christ, not only be content to abide any storm or trouble for it; yea, to be mocked, scorned, persecuted, and put to death therefore, if it so please God; but also unfeignedly, every man to his power, in his heart by fervent prayer, in his mouth by good words, and in all his body by virtuous conversation and good christian works, help and labour, that the blessed word of God may have the due honour belonging thereunto; and that the same, which it hath lost through the ungodly behaviour of some, may, through the grace and goodness of God, be won again in our good living; that God may have of us better servants, our prince truer subjects, and our neighbours more unfeigned lovers, than many have been before us. Amen.

*Here endeth the Prologue.*

## TO THE READERS.

For your better instruction, gentle readers, ye shall understand, that whereas in this book there be many whole sentences of the bible alleged and rehearsed, always for the most part at the beginning of every such sentence ye find this cross, and such a star at the end thereof; to the intent that the text of holy scripture in this book may the better be noted and known.

# AN EVIDENT DECLARATION OUT OF THE HOLY SCRIPTURE, THAT THE CHRISTIAN FAITH HATH ENDURED SINCE THE BEGINNING OF THE WORLD, AND THAT THROUGH IT ONLY ALL VIRTUOUS MEN PLEASED GOD, AND WERE SAVED.

## CHAPTER I.

I SUPPOSE plainly that many simple christian men will not *The Christian faith is elder than 1500 years.* a little wonder at this mine enterprise; they are so persuaded and think, the christian faith did first begin under Tiberius the emperor: forasmuch as out of the gospel of Luke it is certain, that in the fifteenth year of Tiberius John the Baptist began to preach the gospel; and all histories say with one accord, that in the eighteenth year of Tiberius Jesus Christ did suffer.

Now it is true, that all the prophecies were then first fulfilled, and the true salvation performed; yea, from that time forth were all the glorious treasures of Christ so richly declared and poured out among all people, as they never were afore. Notwithstanding the same salvation in Christ Jesu was promised long afore, and so opened to the holy old fathers, that they have had no less sight of Christ Jesus in the spirit than we, and put their trust in him as well as we; though among us it be clear and open, or performed and fulfilled, that among them was somewhat darker, and therefore looked for with heart's desire, as a thing for to come. Moreover, it is not I that first bring forth this meaning concerning the antiquity or oldness of our christian faith. For the holy bishop Eusebius Cæsariensis, which lived above eleven hundred years ago, and likewise many other christian doctors, hath also taught and written the same more clearly before me. For Eusebius, in the first book *De Ecclesiastica His-* *Eusebius.*

*toria*[1]: saith plainly : "All they that in their estate are noted according to their generations, to reckon backward from Abraham unto the first man, though they had not the name of christian men, (for at Antioch, certain years after the ascension of Christ, was that name given to the faithful, Acts xi.) yet, as pertaining to the religion and substance, they were all Christian."

<small>Acts xi.</small>

For if this word Christian be as much to say, as one that putteth his trust in Christ, and through his doctrine fastened unto faith, unto the grace and righteousness of God, doth cleave with all diligence to God's doctrine, and exerciseth himself in every thing that is virtuous; then verily those holy men, whom we speak of first, were even the same that christian men boast themselves now to be. All these are the words of the foresaid old christian doctors. But to the intent that no man shall think, how that we build upon men, and upon a strange foundation, therefore will we first declare our mind out of the scripture, and allege somewhat more for the better understanding of the matter.

## CHAPTER II.

### OF THE GOODNESS OF GOD, AND WICKEDNESS OF MAN.

GOD, which hath ever been sufficient to all perfection, and needeth nothing of the creatures to his perfectness, only of his own kind and nature, which is good, that is to say, of his own grace and mercy, yea, even because he would do good, created man for himself. But before he created him, he provided first for him wonderfully, and furnished him with unoutspeakable riches of his goodness. For when he devised the creation of man, and the time was now come, which his

<small>The first creation of heaven and earth.</small>

[1 Eusebii, Eccl. Hist. Lib. I. c. iv. (P. 15. Ed. Reading.) πάντας δ' ἐκείνους δικαιοσύνῃ μεμαρτυρημένους, ἐξ αὐτοῦ τοῦ Ἀβραὰμ ἐπὶ τὸν πρῶτον ἀνιοῦσιν ἄνθρωπον, ἔργῳ Χριστιανοὺς εἰ καὶ μὴ ὀνόματι προσειπών τις, οὐκ ἂν ἐκτὸς βάλοι τῆς ἀληθείας.]

godly wisdom and providence had ordained, he first of all appointed a wonderful lodging for man, and garnished the same yet much more wonderfully. At the beginning, when the goodly and clear light was made, the Lord prepared the instruments, which he afterward sundered one from another, and ordained every one to some purpose. Over the deep, that is, over the water and earth, which yet was in the water, made he a firmament, and spread out the heaven above as a pavilion. Afterward out of the water he called and brought forth the earth, as much as served for the habitation of men, and appointed the water his bounds and marks, which it may not overpass. And these three things, the water, the earth, and the firmament, that is to say, the air and clearness above us unto the height of heaven, are the essential and substantial parcels of the world, and serve as an house for the habitation of men. Nevertheless, as yet all this was but rough and unfinished, and nothing garnished at all. Therefore did the wise and faithful Master put forth his hand wider, to perform and pleasantly to garnish that wonderful work; yea, not only to garnish it, but also to make it fruitful and profitable for man, which was the guest and inhabiter for to come. *The garnishing of heaven and earth.*

And first, inasmuch as man should inhabit the earth, he garnished it aforehand, and clothed it with a goodly green garment; that is, with a substance, which he decked first with flowers and all manner of herbs, which not only are pleasant to look upon and wonderfully beautified, of a pleasant taste and goodly colour, but also profitable for food and all manner of medicine. To the same also did he first add sundry trees and plants. Then watered he the earth with fair springs, rivers, and running waters. And the ground made he not like on every side, but in many places set it up pleasantly. And hereof have we the valleys, plains, mountains, and hills; which things all have their due operation, fruit, and pleasantness.

After this also began he to garnish the heaven and firmament, and set therein the sun and moon, the planets and stars; which things all are goodlier and more wonderful than men's tongue can express. As for their office, and the cause why they are set in the heaven, it is to give us light, and with their up and down going, or motion, to declare *The office of the creatures in the firmament.*

the times, years, months, and days, dividing the days and nights asunder.

*Fishes.* Thirdly, he laid his hand likewise in the water, in the which he hath wrought no less wonders than in heaven and upon earth. For in the water, and especially in the sea, do the wonderful works of God appear in the fishes and marvels of the sea, if a man consider the nature and disposition of them.

*Fowls.* And in the air also hath he created and ordained great tokens of his goodness, power, and wisdom; even the fowls, that pleasantly, according to divers commodities, do sing unto man and refresh him.

*Beasts.* At the last endued he the earth yet more richly, and filled it with all kind of profitable and goodly beasts, and sundered one from another pleasantly.

*The creation of man.* When the Lord now had prepared this goodly and rich pleasure, then first after all these he made man, that he might be lord of all these things. Him also endued he above all other creatures, and created him after his own image. He made him of body and soul, which should have endured for ever, if he had not fallen into sin. Now hath he a frail body, and an immortal, everlasting soul: but the first man made he altogether perfect and without blemish; so that verily he was called the image of God, not without cause. The Lord also was not sufficed in garnishing the earth goodly; but first also builded upon the earth a special garden of pleasure, even a paradise; and therein he set man, his dear beloved creature. And forasmuch as he, being solitary and alone, could not conveniently dwell without a mate, he appointed him first to plant and keep the garden of pleasure,

*The creation of woman.* and provided for him a wife, even out of the bones of his own body, that she might be the man's help. Thus would the goodness of God finish and make man perfect, to the intent that he should lack nothing, which served to a right, wholesome, and perfect life.

Therefore was it equal, that man, which was endued with reason and high understanding, should shew thankfulness and obedience unto God for such high gifts. Yea, God himself, which is not only good, but also righteous, requireth the same of him, and that by the means of the commandment, that he might eat of all the trees of the garden of pleasure, only he should eschew the fruit of knowing good and evil. And this commandment was not grievous nor unreasonable: only it requireth obedience and love of God the Maker, unto whom only the creature, even man, should have respect, and look for all good at his hand, and not to take the form of good and evil out of himself; but only to hold that for evil and forbidden, which God inhibiteth as evil, and to count that as good and righteous, which God alloweth or forbiddeth not. For a representation, visible token, and sacrament, God shewed him a right visible and fruitful tree in the garden of pleasure, and forbad him with earnest threatening, that in what hour soever he did eat of the same tree, he should die an everlasting death. But untruly dealt man with his faithful God, transgressed his commandment, and gave more credence to the persuasion of the woman and of the serpent, than to the true word of God: which was nothing else but even as much as to take the form of good and evil out of themselves, or elsewhere, rather than of God; and not to cleave and be obedient only unto him, as to such one as wisheth good unto every man. For man, being deceived through the woman and the serpent, did believe that God was not indifferent, and that he had withdrawn from him some of his godly wisdom. And forasmuch as the mind now was departed from God through infidelity, and looked not for all good at his hand, therefore took the hand the noisome apple, and the mouth did eat the forbidden meat. And thus thought he to help himself to God's majesty by another means rather than by God, and so to repair his necessity, which he thought he had. And so with infidelity, unfaithfulness, disobedience, and unthankfulness, he wrought[1] life, and died the death; that is, he offended against God, and fell into the punishment of everlasting damnation. Yea, he made himself bond unto the devil, whom he was so diligent to believe, to follow, and to serve. Contrariwise he forsook God, and so came he utterly into the bondage of the devil and darkness. And thus have we now the goodness and faithfulness of God; again, the wickedness and great unfaithfulness of man.

*The request of the commandment.*

*The unthankfulness and wickedness of man.*

[1 Perhaps used in the sense of *wrought for*, as in John vi. 27. Wicliffe renders, "Work ye not meat that perisheth." Or possibly the right reading may be *raught*, the old preterite of *reach:* he reached, or reached after.]

## CHAPTER III.

### THE FIRST AND RIGHT FOUNDATION OF OUR HOLY CHRISTIAN FAITH.

*The right-eousness and mercy of God.*

*Gen. ii.*

*The way of satisfaction before God is Christ.*

HERE now had the just God occasion and right to expel man, to destroy him, to damn him, and to leave him utterly to the devil; and the same also did his righteousness and truth require. For he had said, "In what day soever thou eatest of the fruit, thou shalt die the death." Contrariwise, the goodness and mercy of God required not utterly to suppress man, a poor and naked creature. In the mean season was there found a way, whereby the righteousness and truth of God should be satisfied, and in the which the mercy of God should specially be exercised and declare itself; that is to say, Christ Jesus, which is given us by the manifest grace of God, was offered for our sins, satisfied and recompensed the righteousness of God, and so delivered us out of the bonds of the devil. For he died for us all, inasmuch as God said, "In what day soever thou eatest thereof, thou shalt die the death:" therefore died Christ for us all, that through his death we might live, and be taken out of the kingdom of darkness, and be set in the kingdom of the dear beloved Son of God.

*Sin.*

This device of God's wisdom, which no doubt was determinate from everlasting, was also directly opened unto Adam after the fall, in manner following. When man had eaten of the fruit of the forbidden tree, immediately his eyes were opened; insomuch that he was ashamed, when he saw that he was naked. Hitherto had he lived in innocency; therefore began he now to cover himself, but with simple clothing, which they trusted not much to, like as it is all unprofitable that man of himself will cover his sin withal, saying, that they fled from the Lord, and hid themselves from him. But the Lord followed upon the fugitive, put him in mind of his decay, misery, and the life that he was fallen from, and said, "Adam, where art thou?" or, Knowest thou what misery thou art fallen into from great felicity? Now should man have knowledged his fault, but he shewed himself stiff-necked. And the Lord moveth him still, to see if he will knowledge his sin, and said, "Who told thee that thou art naked?" Yea, to help him in the matter, and to make him confess his sin, he saith moreover, "Hast thou not eaten of the tree, of the which I forbad thee that thou shouldest not eat?" But man was loth to knowledge his sin, and laid it first upon the woman his companion; and the same did he with so froward and unadvised words, that a man may easily see, that secretly in his heart he wickedly and unreasonably laid the fault upon God. For he said not only, "The woman gave me of the tree to eat;" but added proudly thereto, "The woman, which thou gavest me," &c. As though he should say, "Thou thyself art in the fault; if thou hadst not given me the woman, I had not been deceived." And yet the righteous God gave not him the woman to deceive him, but to be an help to him. Therefore appeareth it here again, that the sin of man was the more wilful and grievous. Yet for all this did the gracious God proceed further, and would prove whether he might find any knowledge of the sin with the woman, the beginning and occasion of the sin;. but nothing at all could he find. The one person was as the other, and they both had no power: therefore, like as Adam put all the fault to the woman, even so laid the woman all the fault upon the serpent, that is, upon the devil. Which nature doth yet to this day cleave in man. But what man, which hath well considered this foresaid matter by himself, would now say, or durst think, that any part of the promise of righteousness and salvation of man were to be ascribed to his own power and deserving? Forasmuch as it is so manifest, how unable and lost man is of himself, which doth nothing but heapeth sin upon sin, and disobedience upon disobedience. Again, who is so blind, but he seeth that all salvation is to be ascribed to the only mere grace and mercy of God? For now followeth it first, how God handled in this matter.

*The frowardness of man.*

*Why God gave the woman unto man.*

*Grace.*

*We all are loth to knowledge ourselves guilty.*

Now when all the complaint was made upon the serpent, the Lord asketh and examineth the serpent nothing at all; for the deed was open, neither was the serpent created of God to speak, and with the devil was there no truth. Therefore doth the Lord righteously curse the serpent, the devil. Unto the bodily serpent also, whom the devil used as an

*Punishment.*

Gen. iii. instrument, he giveth a sore curse, and saith, "Upon thy belly shalt thou go, and earth shalt thou eat all the days of thy life." When this was done, it was ordained now first for man, that, according to the righteousness and truth of God, he should be punished also with the curse and with eternal death; but for the causes expressed in the beginning of this chapter, the curse was directed unto Christ, who also with clear words was promised, and so was life in him promised likewise.

Therefore saith not the Lord now, "And cursed be thou, man, because thou hast done against my commandment;" The promise. Gen. iii. but, "And I will put enmity between thee and the woman, between thy seed and her seed;. the same shall tread thee on the head, and thou shalt tread him on the heel." Which is thus much to say: "Thou hast used the woman to the destruction of men, so that from henceforth they bring death, and by kind and nature are damned, when they are born. Therefore will I also use the woman, but to salvation; for of the woman shall a seed or child be born, which shall break The serpent's head. thy head, power, and kingdom, sin, damnation, and death; howbeit in his manhood he shall be trodden down and bitten." That is, "Man with his transgression hath deserved eternal death, so that, after the rigour of my justice, he should perish and belong to the devil for ever: nevertheless I will have mercy upon him, and receive him to grace again. But to the intent that my truth and righteousness may be satisfied, I will cause my Son to take the very nature of man upon him. Then will I that he take upon himself the curse and damnation, and die; and with his innocent death to take away that noisome death and curse, and so to set the generation of man out of death into life, out of the dominion of the devil into The sure foundation of our faith. his own kingdom, out of darkness into light.". Thus the right foundation or ground of our holy faith continueth fast and unmoved; insomuch as all the generation of man is whole and cleansed from sin, and delivered from the curse, from the devil and everlasting damnation, only through the mercy and mere grace of God by Jesus Christ.

As touching this, Paul said, when he wrote to the Romans, Rom. viii. in the eighth chapter: "God sent his Son in the similitude of sinful flesh, and through sin, that is to say, through the sin-offering and willing death of Christ, he condemned sin in the flesh[1]." And in the first epistle to the Corinthians, the first chapter, the same Paul saith : "Christ Jesus is appointed of God to be our wisdom, and righteousness, and sanctifying; and redemption; that, as it is written, Whoso glorieth and rejoiceth, let him glory and rejoice in the Lord." 1 Cor. i.

But forasmuch as this is the first promise, and the first sure evangelion, I will now speak of every word in especial. First, God calleth his Son, our Lord Jesus, the seed of the woman; a seed, because of the very nature of man, and because that our Lord should not take upon him a fantastical[2], but a very true body.

But to these words there is added, "Of the woman." For our Lord was not conceived and born of man's seed, but of the Holy Ghost out of the virgin Mary. Therefore cannot this sentence be understood of Eve, but of the virgin Mary. Now whereas she is called "a woman," it is done because of the kindred. For even the daughters also, and maidens, are reckoned in the women's kindred, and yet continue undefiled virgins. God also hath spoken here distinctly, and said not, "I will put enmity between thee and this woman, but between thee and (*haischah*[3]), *the* woman :" understand some special woman, no doubt even such one as he afterward set forth clearly by Esay, saying: "Behold, a virgin shall conceive and bear a son," &c. And this word; The gospel of Jesu Christ.

Isai. vii.

[1 Rom. viii. 3. Ὁ Θεὸς τὸν ἑαυτοῦ υἱὸν πέμψας ἐν ὁμοιώματι σαρκὸς ἁμαρτίας, καὶ περὶ ἁμαρτίας, κατέκρινε τὴν ἁμαρτίαν ἐν τῇ σαρκί : which, in conformity with this place, is translated by Coverdale in his bible: "God sent his Son in the similitude of synfull flesh, and by synne damned synne in the flesh." With respect to the quotations from scripture, which are found in Coverdale's writings, it may be observed that he does not appear, either in his translated or his original works, to have adhered strictly to his own version of the Bible.]

[2 This was the error of the *Docetæ*. On the nature of the opinions entertained by these heretics, and the history of the persons by whom they were supported, see Irenæus, Lib. III. cap. ii. Clemens Alexandr. Strom. Lib. VII. in fine; Tertullian de Præscriptione Hæreticorum, cap. xxxiii. &c. Much valuable information on this subject may be found in Bull. Defens. Fid. Nicen. sect. III. cap. vi. Judicium Eccles. Cathol. cap. ii. 4, 5. Primitiva et Apostolica Traditio, cap. i. sect. IX.; and in Bishop Pearson, *On the Creed*, Art. III. IV.; and particularly in his *Vindiciæ Ignatianæ*, Part II. cap. vii. viii.]

[3 הָאִשָּׁה.]

*seed*, was alway afterward, in every renewing of this promise concerning Christ Jesu among all the patriarchs and prophets, rehearsed, used, and expressed, until the time of David, of whom the Lord afterward was called a flower, the root, sprouting, or blossom of David[1]. The holy apostle Paul expoundeth this word *seed* clearly and plainly, and saith it is Christ, Gal. iii. Moreover, it serveth to the praise of the Lord's mother, that God saith: "I will put enmity between the woman and thee;" for he meaneth the difference of both their natures. The devil is proud, subtle, wicked, false, and untrue; but the mother of Christ is lowly, simple, virtuous, faithful, and upright, chaste, and clean. And the same pure virgin and gracious mother hath borne unto us him that trod down the serpent's head. The head of the serpent is the power and kingdom of the devil, even sin, the curse, and damnation. All this hath that blessed Seed broken for his faithful. All which things the holy apostle Paul also hath taught with these words: "The Lord is become partaker of our flesh and blood, that he through death might take away the power from him which had the lordship over death, that is to say, the devil; and to deliver them which through fear of death were all their life-time in bondage. For he took not upon him the angels, but the seed of Abraham took he upon him[2]," &c. And to the same meaning doth this also serve that followeth: "And thou shalt tread him on the heel." The heel is the lowest part in man; and here it signifieth the most inferior thing in Christ, even his flesh. This hath the old serpent, the devil, persecuted and trodden down by his members, Caiaphas, Annas, Herod, and Pontius Pilate. For Peter saith, "Christ hath suffered for us in the flesh." The godhead is impassible, and the soul immortal. But by this treading down of the Lord hath God trodden down the kingdom of the devil; that is to say, by his death hath he

*A praise of the virgin Mary.*

*Heb. ii.*

*Gen. iii. Christ's heel.*

*1 Pet. iv.*

[[1] Compare Isaiah iv. 2, xi. 1; Jer. xxiii. 5, xxxiii. 16; Zech. iii. 8, vi. 12; Rom. xv. 12; Rev. v. 5, xxii. 16.]

[[2] Heb. ii. 16. Οὐ γὰρ δήπου ἀγγέλων ἐπιλαμβάνεται, ἀλλὰ σπέρματος Ἀβραὰμ ἐπιλαμβάνεται. Coverdale's version is: "For he in no place taketh on him the angels, but the sede of Abraham taketh he on him:" and with this agrees the marginal translation of the authorised version: "He taketh not hold of angels; but of the seed of Abraham he taketh hold."]

destroyed death, and brought life again to all them that believe. Hereof cometh it that Christ saith himself, John xii.: "Now is the judgment of the world; now shall the prince of this world be thrust out. And I, when I am lift up (that is to say, crucified) from the earth, will draw all things to me." {margin: John xii.}

At the last saith the Lord, that he will put enmity between the serpent and the woman's seed. This may we see in the devil, and his members and acts, how they are contrary to Christ, and his members and deeds. But how strong soever the serpent is, yet shall he be trodden down through Christ and his faithful. Hereof cometh it that Paul spake so comfortable to the Romans, Rom. xvi.: "The God of peace shall shortly tread down the devil under your feet." {margin: Rom. xvi.} And herewithal is the duty also of the faithful in Christ shortly comprehended. For as touching them that say, "It is[3] enough then, and is all well, when I knowledge that I am a sinner, and saved through the blessed Seed only?"—to them it is here answered and clearly given to understand, that all they which put their trust in the blessed Seed, take upon them the kind of the Seed, and hate the kind of the serpent, that is to say, sin and blasphemy; and fight alway more and more against the world and the devil, as long as they live; yea, and occupy themselves most faithfully about that which is God's will. {margin: Object. Answer.} And hereto now serveth it that followeth after. For when the Lord had taken away the everlasting death, he laid upon man a temporal punishment, correction, and discipline, in the which he should be exercised as long as he lived upon earth. And upon the woman he laid cumber[4], sorrow, and pain, when she should bear and bring forth children; subjection also and service, with fear and obedience, which she oweth to the man. To man he enjoineth labour; for the Lord cursed the earth, and said: "With sorrow shalt thou get thy living all the days of thy life; yea, in the sweat of thy face shalt thou eat thy bread." {margin: Gen. iii.} Moreover, he laid temporal death upon them both, and saith: "Earth thou art, and to earth shalt thou return." Of the first doth Paul speak also, 1 Tim. ii.: "The woman shall be saved by bearing of children, if she continue in faith and {margin: Gen. iii.}

[3 Is it, Ed. 1624.]
[4 Trouble, Ed. 1624.]

love, and in holiness, or cleanness, and nurture[1]." Of the second speaketh the same Paul likewise to the Ephesians and Thessalonians: "Let no man undermine or deceive his brother in occupying[2];" and "whoso hath used falsehood and deceit, let him do it no more, but let him rather labour with his hands some honest thing, that he may have to distribute unto such as have need." And as touching death, Paul also saith to the Hebrews in the ninth chapter, how that "it is appointed unto men once to die; and that even so Christ Jesus was offered up and died once for all."

*1 Thess. iv. Eph. iv.*

*Heb. ix.*

## CHAPTER IV.

### OF THE FIRST FAITHFUL CHRISTIAN, ADAM AND EVE.

*The sum of the christian faith.*

AND hitherto I trust we have had in the first promise of God the foundation and the whole sum of our holy christian faith: namely, that the whole generation of man was but lost through his own fault and wickedness, and fallen into death and damnation; so that there remaineth nothing in man, but it is displeasant to God. Hereof cometh it, that there is nothing to be ascribed unto the power and deserving of man, save sin and malediction. But God of his abundant mercy had compassion on us, and of very grace promised he life unto us again in his Son our Lord Jesu, whom he would to become man, and to suffer death in his flesh, that thereby he might tread down the devil, death, sin, and hell. Item, he would put enmity between the woman's seed and the serpent: that is, he would endue us, which are the seed, that is to say, the children of Adam, if we believe, with another heart and power; that we might become enemies unto the devil's works, resist his suggestion, and hold ourselves fast by the blessed Seed, labouring and suffering whatsoever God enjoineth us to

---

[1] 1 Tim. ii. 15. σωθήσεται διὰ τῆς τεκνογονίας. So Coverdale's Bible: "Notwithstandynge thorow bearing of children she shal be saved."]

[2] 1 Thess. iv. 6. ἐν τῷ πράγματι. Cov. Bible: "In bargayninge."]

work and suffer. Who is it now, which seeth not herein all that is written in the whole scripture, of belief, of love, and innocency; that is to say, of a christian life and faith? Whoso is disposed, let him look upon the second, third, and fourth chapter of Paul to the Romans, the first and second to the Ephesians: let him compare those chapters toward this sum, and he shall find it none otherwise.

Forasmuch then as Adam and Eve had faith in God, and stood so toward God, that they knowledged themselves to be sinners, and trusted to be saved only through the blessed Seed, giving themselves over willingly into the discipline and nurture, travail and trouble of this time; no man can say contrary, but it followeth that our first elders were christian. Nevertheless we will declare the same yet more clearly by Moses' words following: "And Adam called his wife Heva, because she should be the mother of all living." For as soon as he was now strengthened through the promise of God, and believed that he and his posterity, which else were children of wrath, of the devil, and of death, should live through the blessed Seed, he turned his wife's name, and called her Heva, for the remembrance of the matter and practising of his faith: for he believed that she now living in the power of the blessed Seed should bring forth not only quick men temporally, as pertaining to this natural life, like as we call other creatures living, but living, that is to say, children of salvation. For Adam had lost eternal life from himself and from us his posterity; but the same is given unto us again through Jesus Christ our Lord. Adam, forasmuch as he believed, changed his wife's name, like as we find, that for great weighty causes the names of certain places, cities, and men were changed. Thus was Jacob called Israel; Simon, Peter; Luz, Bethel. Eve had now a name of life; for *Haiah* in Hebrew is as much to say as life[3]. Afore was she called *Ischa*, that is to say, woman, because she was taken from out of the man, which in the Hebrew is called *Isch*, Gen. ii. And thus is it manifest, what faith Adam had; whereby we may well suppose that Eve had none other faith.

But God used his mercy and loving-kindness yet further-

Gen. iii. Adam's faith.

Gen. ii.

Comfort,

[3 Heb. חָוָה.]

*help and loving-kindness in the midst of correction.*

more, even in the midst of all correction : for when he would now expel man out of paradise into misery, he doth unto him in every condition even as a faithful father, which for some misdeed putteth his son away from him; notwithstanding, leaveth him not utterly comfortless, but provideth him a garment, and comforteth him with friendly words, and then first sendeth him away from him. Even thus doth God the Father of heaven also. For first he clotheth Adam and Eve against the frost and tempest of weather; inasmuch as by the means of sin, the weather, the earth, the air, and all creatures were no more so subject, tame, and obedient unto man, as they were afore the fall. Therefore, even now at this present time, whatsoever inconvenience and harm is in the good creatures of God, it cometh by the means of our sins. Afterward doth the Lord comfort the miserable, wretched man with very loving words, after this manner: "Behold,

*Gen. iii.* Adam is become like one of us;" or, "Lo, Adam shall be as one of us, and it shall happen unto him as to one of us, and he shall know good and evil." This doth God speak, which is one in substance and three in persons: he prophesieth here unto Adam, that he shall know or have experience of good and evil; that is to say, that upon earth he must feel prosperity and adversity, misery and trouble, sour and sweet,

*Comfort and patience in Christ.* and must suffer necessity, pain, and affliction. Yet in all this must he be constant and patient; forasmuch as nothing shall happen unto him, save even the same that shall happen to one of them : and he meaneth the Son, our Lord Jesu Christ, the second person in the holy Trinity. With this his passion, and through the same, doth he comfort Adam: as though he would say, "Let the pain, sorrow, and trouble, which thou must suffer upon earth, not vex thee; and consider that one of us also shall take upon him the kind and nature of man, and that the serpent, as it is said afore, shall tread him on the heel; that is to say, he shall die, he shall be oppressed, and have much affliction and trouble all the days of his life." In the same meaning also did the holy apostle

*1 Pet. ii.* Peter say: "Christ suffered for our sakes, and gave us an ensample, that we should follow him, and go in his footsteps."

*Adam's faith.* Out of all this is it easy to understand, what faith and knowledge Adam had of our Lord Christ; namely, that he knew in him very godhead and manhood, and that he saw in faith his passion and cross afar off: moreover, that the passion of Christ, once done for all, breaketh the kingdom of the devil, and bringeth life again to such as faithfully believe. Secondly, that it is to our living an ensample, at the which we ought to learn patience in adversity, and daily to die from all evil. And hereto now serve all doctrines of patience, of bearing of the cross, of despising the world, and mortifying or putting off the old Adam: which thing is contained, and with many and godly words handled throughout the prophets and apostles. As for Adam and Eve, they lacked none of these things, though they had not the matter in writing: for God spake it all to them himself, and wrote it in their hearts. Moreover, our first elders had no church, rites, nor ceremonies, save only the bodily offering, a representation of the sacrificing of Christ, and exercises or tokens of thankfulness. For how should Cain and Abel else have known any thing of sacrifice, if they had not received the same at the custom of their father? who, with his wife Eva, the mother of us all, was saved by none other work or merit of man, but only through and in the blessed Seed, our Lord Jesu Christ.

## CHAPTER V.

### THAT THE HOLY PATRIARCHS ALSO WERE CHRISTIAN AND SAVED BY CHRIST.

Such faith in Christ Jesu as we now have spoken of, did the holy father Adam, no doubt, teach his children, that they also might plant into their children the promise of God, his mercy and device concerning the Messias or Saviour that was for to come. And truly Abel had such a notable faith in God, that the holy apostle Paul wrote of him after this manner: "Through faith did Abel offer a greater sacrifice[1] than did Cain, and thereby obtained he witness that he was righteous; for God bare record to his gifts." Inasmuch then

Heb. xi.

[1 Heb. xi. 4. πλείονα θυσίαν: "A more plenteous sacrifice." Cov. Bib. "A better sacrifice." Authorised version.]

as it cannot be denied, but that all they which are just and righteous be made righteous through the blessed Seed, and Abel was justified; it followeth that he was made righteous through faith in Jesus Christ. In that he did sacrifice, it is a token and fruit of a heart that was thankful and feared God. It was no such enterprise, that he would cleanse and make himself acceptable unto God through that outward sacrifice. For certain it is, that no outward oblation purifieth man within; but the grace of God, granted unto us through Jesus Christ, purifieth us aright. And the outward sacrifices of the old fathers, beside that they were tokens of thankfulness, praise, and magnifying of God, as it is said afore, were figures of the only perpetual sacrifice of our Saviour Christ: and in this behalf they were even as much as sacraments of things to come. Thus also, and in like understanding, have our first fathers done sacrifice, as hereafter it shall follow more largely.

*Sacrifice was a token of thankfulness.*

Now like as in Abel there is set forth unto us an ensample of God's seed, and of a regenerate, true, faithful, christian man; so is Cain a seed of the serpent, a child of the devil, which despised the inspiration of God, and hearkened to the deceitful serpent. And in these two brethren we may see what God meaned, when he said: "I will put enmity between the seed of the woman and thy seed." As though he would say: "There shall be two manner of people: the one shall cleave unto Christ, the blessed Seed; the other shall cleave unto the devil: and these two generations shall in no wise agree, but be at variance in faith and religion. I will endue my seed, that they shall cleave only unto me, fear me, honour and worship me, seek all salvation in me through the blessed Seed, live virtuously, honestly, and soberly. Then shall the serpent tempt their seed with hypocrisy, not to love me, nor serve me right; not to hold of me as they should, not to trust in me, but to love the world, and to follow the lusts and temptations thereof." All this find we here in these two brethren, in whom beginneth the first difference of true and false believers. For Abel was simple, godly, and of a constant faith in God: and inasmuch as he took God for his refuge, he brought him gifts of his best substance; no doubt, because he had first given over his soul and all his power unto God, at whom alone he sought all good, without any

*Cain the father of wickedness.*

hypocrisy. He was also innocent, virtuous, and friendly, and
followed not his own tentations[1]. And for this faith's sake
did his sacrifice please God. But Cain's pleased him not;
for his heart was not right with God: he was a dissembler,
greedy, and unfaithful person, which set his heart and mind
upon earthly things, alway despising God's word, and following his own tentation. Which thing was evident in
this, that he, having no cause, only of a wilful heart and
through the temptation of the serpent, murdered his own
brother; whereby he hath obtained to be the archfather of
all murderers, which persecute and murder the seed of God,
that is to say, the true believers, only for their faith's sake.
Thus became Abel the first martyr and instrument of God *Abel the first martyr.*
and of Christ in the holy church. For these two brethren
have set forth before us the whole battle and strife, which
the world, the city of the devil, the children and citizens
of the cursed city, wherein the serpent is head and master
and hath the dominion, shall make against the city and
citizens in whom Christ is the head, unto the end of the
world. The freemen of the city of God and of Christ do *The difference of true and false faith.*
cleave only unto God, serve him with all their heart, build
only upon Christ. The citizens of the serpent despise God;
and yet they boast of God, to whom also they offer and
do service, but not as they ought to do. Now when they
perceive that their faith is not right, and that their hypocrisy
is espied and misliked; then fall they to murdering, to the
which God is an enemy, and forbiddeth it with his word.
For Cain also exhorted he from his purpose, and said:
"Thou needest not to arm thee because of thy brother,
for thou hast none occasion to be angry with him. For
if thou doest right, thou shalt find it, and have joy thereof;
but if thou dost not right, then is thy misfortune, sin, and
trespass open, and thou shalt shame and destroy thyself.
Thy brother goeth on without fault, he shall do thee no
hurt nor harm: he shall also not be lord over thee, nor
minish thy right; yea, he shall have respect unto thee,
and thou shalt have dominion over him, and so keep thy
birthright, and still remain the firstborn, although his sacrifice be acceptable unto me, and not thine. Cease therefore
from thy wicked purpose, and offend not against thy brother."

[[1] Tentation: an essaying; or inclination tempting him.]

But Cain did as all ungodly do; for he went forth and slew his innocent brother. And afterward, when the Lord would have brought him into the knowledge of his great sin, and pardon him, he despised the voice of the Lord with craking and facing. For the which cause the Lord was wroth with him, and cursed him. Then despaired he first, and went forth, and became yet more wicked, dealt altogether ungodly, set first his mind upon earthly things, thought to exalt his name upon earth, and builded the first city, which he called Hanoch. He begat sons and daughters; but little fear of God was before their eyes, insomuch that the scripture saith, "Adam lay with his wife again, and she bare a son, whom she called Seth: for God, said she, hath given me another seed for Abel, whom Cain slew. Seth also had a son, and he called him Enos. And then began men to call upon the name of the Lord." Out of the which words it is easy to understand, that, as touching holy Adam, he held no more of Cain, than as though he never had had child. For Adam feared God: Cain with his progeny despised God, and became the serpent's generation. Wherefore, when Adam had gotten another son, he was of a good hope, that in Abel's stead God had given him another son, which should do right, and of whom the root of the blessed Seed should spread out afterward. For the which cause also he called him Seth, which by us is called "a plant;" meaning, that God had set and planted him as a branch, out of which the Messias should be born. For, as for Cain, he doubted of him. And from the same Seth proceeded the generation of the righteous until Noe, and from him to Abraham, and so unto David; and from thenceforth unto Christ. This Seth repaired our holy faith, which received great hurt at the death of Abel. This did Seth, I say, forasmuch as he, being taught inwardly of God, and by mouth or outwardly of Adam, learned his children and their seed to put their trust in God, and to comfort themselves in the blessed Seed, and to cleave unto the same. For it is written manifestly: "And then began men to call upon the name of the Lord.[1]" Till this time was Adam,

[1 With this agrees the text of the authorised version. In the margin it is translated: "Then began men to call *themselves* by the name of the Lord." And the passage, thus translated, admits of a

with Heva his wife, only a true friend and server to God. *Adam's life.*
The generation of Cain was now well spread abroad, and come to two hundred and fifty years, and above; but the more part lived without the fear of God, unrepentant and ungodly. Wherefore, inasmuch as the generation of Seth now increased, and the fear of God and right belief was among them, the scripture saith well: "And then began men to call upon the name of the Lord." And by this calling upon, doth the scripture mean the true right belief and God's service, that he most alloweth. Of the progeny, therefore, of righteous Seth sprang the servants of God, and presidents of our christian faith. As for the cursed generation of Cain and of the ungodly, it was destroyed and drowned with the flood. *To call upon the name of God, what it is.*

To the holy genealogy of the true believers pertaineth the patriarch Enoch; of whom it is written, that "he walked before God," that is, he ordered his life and conversation altogether after the will of God, being constant and upright, no doubt, in all that which God had spoken unto Adam. Therefore became he also an ensample of the immortality of the soul and resurrection of the body; and that all God's servants shall be saved after this life. For thus saith the scripture: "And inasmuch as he applied himself to walk after God, God took him away, and he was no more seen." The holy apostle Paul also, in the eleventh chapter to the Hebrews, speaketh very excellently of Enoch's faith; so that no man may doubt, but that he had respect to the blessed Seed, and pleased God through Christ. *Gen. v.*

Moreover, the enmity between the children of God and of man, that is, the issue of the serpent, grew ever more and more; so that, on the one side, the multitude of God increased, and on the other side, the multitude of the devil. Yet at the last the multitude of the wicked was greatest. For when the children of God withheld not themselves from the children of the world, but took wives and husbands among them; they begat rough people, which had no faith *The number of the wicked ever greatest.*

meaning similar to that which is here given to it by Coverdale: "Then began men, i. e. the children of Seth, to call themselves by the name of the Lord; i. e. the servants or worshippers of the Lord, in distinction from the Cainites, and such profane persons as had forsaken him." See Bishop Patrick, ad locum.]

at all, and lived only after their own lust and temptation, forgat God utterly, and regarded not the hundred and twenty years, which God gave them to amend. Therefore was God constrained so to punish the unfaithful world once, that all posterities, unto the end of the world, might have a terrible ensample of the just wrath of God; whereby they might learn, how ungodliness and unrighteousness displeaseth God. Thus the Lord brought the flood upon all the earth, overthrew all that stood up, and destroyed every thing that had life, when the world had stood now a thousand six hundred and fifty-six years[1]. For so many years find we in the fifth and seventh of Genesis, where it is written, that Noe was six hundred years old, when the flood came upon the earth. Now if we reckon the years of the old fathers, in the fifth chapter, until Adam, we shall find the foresaid sum. And thus the issue of the serpent had an end, and all ungodly and unrighteous living was mightily suppressed and destroyed of God.

*The wrath of God upon the wicked.*
*Noah's flood.*

And in this horrible destruction of the ungodly was faithful Noe saved, he being the eighth, and preserved in the ark, through the grace and mercy of God. Here our holy true christian faith had the victory and triumphed. For Noe was of our faith, even of the seed of God, and put his trust in the blessed Seed, our Lord Jesus. Yea, the ark or ship of Noe was a figure of Christ, as we may easily understand by the words of St Peter. Seeing then that Noe was preserved through the ark, it followeth that he was saved by Jesus Christ; therefore is it manifest, that he first believed in Christ. Noe also was he, with whom God first renewed the covenant made with Adam. For it is but one covenant only, even the foresaid promise and end, made by God unto Adam. Howbeit, the same covenant was afterward at certain times renewed by reason of certain occasions. Here might Noe have thought that all the world and all men should utterly have been undone; forasmuch as the Lord said, "I am determined to destroy all flesh." Therefore immediately he addeth moreover, and saith: "But with thee will I set up my covenant," that is

*The first triumph of faith in Noah.*

*1 Pet. iii.*

*The renewing of the promise concerning Christ.*

*Gen. vi.*

[1 Coverdale here follows the chronology of the Hebrew text. With respect to the chronology of the Samaritan text and the LXX. see Shuckford's Connection, Vol. I. p. 30, &c. Ed. Oxf. 1810.]

to say: "Whatsoever pertaineth to my covenant, and what I have promised Adam already, the same will I surely and constantly make good; and though I now destroy the world, yet will I perform my truth through thee. For I will preserve thee alive, that the blessed Seed promised afore may hereafter be born of thee in his generation." To this did Noe trust, and was preserved of God through Christ. Moreover, when he was come out of the ark, he did sacrifice; and thereby declared the thankfulness of his heart, and belief, how that he knew that he had all good of God; which should also give him a Seed, that with sacrificing of himself should reconcile and pacify God. For thus saith the scripture: "Noe builded an altar unto the Lord, and took of all manner of clean beasts and fowls, and offered burnt sacrifice unto the Lord; and the Lord smelled the sweet savour, and said in his heart, I will no more curse the earth for man's sake," &c. So saith Paul in the fifth to the Ephesians: "Walk ye in love, like as Christ hath loved us, and gave himself for us an offering and sacrifice of a sweet savour unto God." Whereby every man may learn and see, that the sweet smell of the outward sacrifice of Noe did not chiefly pacify God, and was pleasant; but rather that through the bodily sacrifice was figured the sacrifice of Christ, and for his sake was he merciful unto the world. For over Christ he said at Jordan, when Christ was baptized: "This is my dear beloved Son, in whom I am pacified or reconciled²."

*The sacrifice of Noe.*

Gen. viii.

Ephes. v.

*Outward sacrifices the figure of Christ's oblation.*

Matth. iii.

Besides this, the Lord gave unto Noe certain laws; but none other than even such as he had given to his forefathers, and written in their hearts. The first pertaineth to marriage and bringing up of children; in the which is comprehended all that is written concerning nurture, cleanliness, and temperance, of care, and bringing up children in the fear of God, virtue, obedience, and learning. The second forbiddeth violence and deceit; namely, that no man shall eat blood. For it is a figurative precept, commanding that no man get his living by murder, by oppressing the poor, by usury, by extortion, by falsehood and deceit. Moreover, all things living were subdued unto him, and all meats were permitted him. In conclusion, whatsoever concerned to love God and their

*The commandments given unto Noe.*

[² Matt. iii. 17. "In whom is my delight." Cov. Bib.]

[COVERDALE.]

neighbour, the same is here renewed unto Noe and his children, and required of them.

*Through Noe was the world replenished.*

Of Noe came afterward all people; yea, among his three sons, Japhet, Sem, and Cham, he had both the seed of God and of the froward serpent; that is, such as had respect unto God, and them also that regarded the devil. Of Cham came the Egyptians, Assyrians, Babylonians; by and from whom sprang idolatry, offering to images, and from whom false religion came up first, and was brought in among other nations by the help of the old serpent, as among the Greeks, Romans, and other people.

*Cham, the first idolater after the flood.*

By this it is good to understand, that our holy christian faith is elder than any other. For here may we see clearly, that after a thousand and certain hundred years (almost in the eight hundredth or nine hundredth year), came up the first beginning of the heathen's belief and offering to images; and yet came it of wicked cursed men. For cursed Cham was the beginning of the Egyptians; and Nimroth, the ungodly extortioner and tyrant, was the first founder of the kingdom of Babylon; which kingdom, with the building of a mighty tower, set forth his pride[1]. Nevertheless, the hand of God declared itself immediately, as it is read in the eleventh chapter of Genesis. Summa, in the generation of Cham had the serpent great power; howbeit in the posterity of Japhet also, of whom the Almaines come, and in the posterity of Som, he had his issue likewise.

*The faith of the heathen is idolatry and worshipping of images. Gen x.*

*Gen. xi.*

Of the progeny of Sem were born Abraham, Isaac, and Jacob, Gen. xi. And, as it is said afore, the sincere faith was somewhat darkened in Chaldea: therefore did God call Abraham out from the idolatry, and renewed with him the old true christian faith begun with Adam, and said, Gen. xii., "Get thee out from thy country, and from thy kindred, and from thy father's house, into a land that I will shew thee; and I will bless thee, and make a great nation of thee, and in thee shall all the nations of the earth be blessed." Item, in the twenty-second chapter speaketh God yet more clearly, and saith, "In thy Seed shall all the nations of the earth be blessed." This doth Paul declare in the third to the Galatians, and saith, "In thy Seed, which is Christ." Therefore

*Gen. xi. Faith darkened after the flood.*

*Gen. xii.*

*Gen. xxii.*

*Gal. iii.*

[1 The commencement of the kingdom of Assyria is fixed by Bishop Lloyd, about B.C. 2234, and that of Babylon rather later.]

was the same now another renewing of the promise of Christ, the blessed Seed. For first was he promised unto Adam; afterward was the promise renewed with Noe, and now with Abraham. And all this now is but one promise, one Saviour, and one faith. Abraham also believed in Jesus Christ, and was saved by faith. For Jesus Christ saith himself in the eighth chapter of John, "Abraham saw my day and rejoiced." What is now the day of Christ, but the clearness of the holy gospel? This light had he not bodily, but saw it with the eyes of faith, and the same made him joyful and saved him. For Christ is the true joy of troubled consciences. Thus became Abraham the father of all faithful believers, Rom. iv. And if we believe and do as Abraham did, then are we Abraham's children, and shall rest with him in his bosom, even in the kingdom of God. Luke xiii. xvi. xix. Matt. viii. Paul also to the Galathians in the third chapter saith: "If ye be Christ's, then are ye Abraham's seed, and heirs according to the promise." Out of this faith in Christ did Abraham christian works: for with a good will left he his own native country, all idols, and all images; all misfortune, hunger, and misery took he patiently; he was not hard against Loth, his nephew, but jeoparded his body and life for the oppressed; he was liberal, merciful, and harborous[2]; he prayed fervently unto God for the poor sinners; he suffered oppression, violence, and wrong; and for God's sake also he thought to sacrifice and offer up his own most dearly beloved son Isaac. Summa, there is no reasonable good christian work, but thou seest it in the life of Abraham. Therefore to us also, for an ensample of our faith and conversation, he is set forth of the Lord himself and his apostles throughout the new testament.

Here also is it manifest, that our holy faith is elder than the Jewish faith. For the Jews do boast themselves of the circumcision, and because they are called Jews and Israel, and that the law, the priesthood, and the God's service was given unto them. And yet, Gen. xv. and xvii. and Rom. iv. it is evident, that Abraham was God's friend, and justified or made righteous, or ever he was circumcised. For when he was circumcised, he was ninety-nine years old, Gen. xvii.

[2 Harborous: hospitable. Harbourage: shelter, entertainment. Johnson.]

Now was the promise made unto him many years afore. The scripture also saith plainly: "Abraham believed God, and the same was counted unto him for righteousness," Gen. xv. So was it many years after, or ever Israel and Judah was born, of whom they have taken their name. The law also was given 430 years after the promise, as Paul made the reckoning, Gal. iii. It followeth therefore, that our christian faith is 2048 years elder than the circumcision, and 2449 years elder than the law, the priesthood, and ceremonies of the Jews. For from Adam unto the flood were 1656 years; and from the flood unto the departing of Abraham out of Chaldea, 363 years. From that time are reckoned 430 years, until the departing of Israel out of Egypt. And on the fiftieth day after the departing, was the law given unto Israel upon Mount Sina, Exod. xix. xx. And after certain days was the priesthood and ceremonies appointed them. Whereas God then made a covenant with Abraham, when he ordained the circumcision, it serveth more to the confirmation of our holy christian faith, than to the maintenance of the Jewish ceremonies.

Isaac and Jacob were Abraham's children, not only after the flesh, but also after the spirit. For they had the faith of their father and grandfather, Abraham, put their trust only in God through Jesus Christ, and lived a sober and virtuous life. Of this doth the scripture bear them record throughout; yea, Jacob, whom the Lord also called otherwise Israel, (of whom afterward all the people of God received the name Israel,) had many visions of the Lord Christ, as with the ladder that stood upon the earth, the top reaching to heaven. on the which the angels of God went up and down. For herewith was represented unto him the Lord Jesus, which is "the way" unto heaven, "the truth, and life;" without whom no man cometh unto the Father. Upon the vision of Jacob saith he also himself, John i., "Verily I say unto you, henceforth shall ye see the heaven open, and the angels of God going up and down upon the Son of man." And so constant was Jacob in remembering the same, that afterward, at the commandment of the Lord, he set up in the same place an altar, no doubt, as it is said afore, for a figure of the cross and sacrifice of Christ; and there honoured he and worshipped the Lord. He commanded all his people also, that they should forsake strange gods, and give him the idols that they had brought with them out of Mesopotamia, and he buried them under an oak that stood beside Sichem, Gen. xxxv. And when he would now die, he prophesied very clearly of the Lord Christ, how he should be born out of the kindred of Juda, and that he should be born the same time that the kingdom should be taken from Juda; which thing also came to pass in Herod's time. For in the thirty-second year of the reign of Herod, was Christ born at Bethleem in Jewry. Whereof the words of Jacob are these: "The sceptre shall not be taken away from Juda, nor a ruler from his feet, till Schilo come, that is to say, the Saviour, and he in whom all nations shall be blessed; and the people shall fall unto him." This stedfast faith of Jacob did Joseph follow also, which mortified his own flesh, declared patience in adversity and prison, and exercised great justice and equity in his governance. He was a figure of our Lord Jesus Christ[1], who also, being sold of his own unto the heathen, preserved his brethren alive. So that from the beginning of the world until the death of Joseph, the right christian faith endured 2300 years. And thus all holy patriarchs before the law were saved, not through the law, nor by their own strength and deserving, but through the blessed Seed, our Lord Jesus Christ.

*Gen. xlix.*

*The faith of Joseph.*

*Joseph a figure of Jesus.*

*The continuance of faith before the law.*

## CHAPTER VI.

THE LAW OF GOD GIVEN BY MOSES LEADETH UNTO CHRIST, AND MAKETH MENTION OF ALL HIS DOINGS.

THE Israelites, after the death of Joseph, until their departing and deliverance out of Egypt, were in the land 140 years[2]. And like as afore in the time of Noe, the

[1 On this point, see Pearson on the Creed, Art. VI.; also Augustin. Opera, Vol. x. p. 169. De Tempore, Serm. LXXXIV. Ed. 1541.]

[2 One hundred and forty-four years, according to the chronology of Bishop Lloyd.]

dwelling among the wicked became occasion of falling unto the righteous; even so now did the Israelites learn idolatry and all unhappiness of the Egyptians. For the which cause also they were sore oppressed a long season: howbeit there remained yet many excellent men, which kept still the old faith, and hated the abomination of the Egyptians. For of Moses, which was born sixty years after the death of Joseph, saith Paul: "Moses, through faith, when he grew up and was great, refused to be called the son of Pharao's daughter; and chose rather to suffer adversity with the people of God, than to enjoy the pleasures of sin for a season; and esteemed the rebuke of Christ greater riches than the treasures of Egypt; for he had respect to the reward," Heb. xi. Now can no man desire to suffer with Christ, except he have knowledge of Christ's suffering. Therefore Moses, in the midst of all persecution, had knowledge of Christ, and the faith in Christ. So is there no doubt, but more virtuous people had this true faith, which were all oppressed and vexed in Egypt; like as afterward the right faithful believers were somewhat more persecuted; as among the heathen, in the time of the judges and kings of Juda and Israel; under king Antiochus; under the emperors Nero, Trajanus, Domitianus, Maximianus, Julianus, and other. As for the unbelievers, they in such miserable times received the reward of their unthankfulness, disobedience, idolatry, and blasphemy.

*Heb. xi*

*The faith of Moses.*

But when the appointed time came, which God had foreseen and opened unto Abraham, Gen. xv., he brought the people of Israel by Moses out of Egypt, with and through great wonders and tokens. By the which he first declared his power, then his loving kindness and mercy toward his own, and his terrible justice and vengeance against his enemies; whereby all the world might know, that there was none other just and true God, save the God of Israel, in whose hand only consist all things; which also of his mere mercy preserveth his own, and with right judgment rewardeth his enemies. Specially this is most wonderful, that in this great business and work he hath so mightily set forth the redemption performed by our Lord Jesus Christ; yea, and expressed it to be a very mighty redemption. For the same night, when they should depart away and be despatched in the morning, the Lord commanded them to kill a lamb, and with

*Gen. xv.*

*The Easter lamb.*

the blood thereof to sprinkle the doors and posts of the house; so when the angel, that in the same night slew the first-born of the Egyptians, saw the blood, he should do no harm, and slay no man therein, Exod. xii. Now testifieth Paul, 1 Cor. v., that Christ Jesus is our Easter lamb and passover. So saith St John: "Behold the Lamb of *John i.* God, which taketh away the sin of the world." Therefore were not the Israelites spared because of the blood of beasts, but for the blood's sake of the blessed Seed that was promised for to come. And thus the whole deliverance out *The deliverance out of* of Egypt was a figure of the true redemption, by the which *Egypt a figure of our* we are delivered from the power of the devil and from ever- *redemption by Christ.* lasting death through Jesus Christ, and brought into the land of promise, even to eternal joy and salvation, which God promised unto our fathers, Adam, Noe, Abraham, Isaac, and Jacob.

Now when the Lord had carried his people out of Egypt, and brought them through the Red Sea dry-shod, and had drowned Pharao with all his people, he commanded his folk to prepare and cleanse themselves at Mount Sina. For he *The giving of the law.* would bind himself unto them, receive them as his own people, and gave them his law and ordinance; which thing he also did, and appointed his law himself, spake it with his own mouth, and wrote it with his own fingers in two tables of stone. In the one and first table he ordained four com- *The first table.* mandments, concerning the worship and love of God; namely, that we should take him only for the true and right God, and none else beside or except him: that we should worship and honour him only, and in no wise to have any other God, comfort, nor hope: item, that we should in no wise make any image or picture of any things, and neither to worship them nor serve them: moreover, that we should not take the name of God in vain, or lightly; and that we should hallow the Sabbath day. In the other table ordained he six commandments concerning man. And like as the four first are comprehended in these words, "Thou shalt love the Lord *Matt. xxii.* thy God with all thy heart," &c.; even so are the six contained in these words following, "Thou shalt love thy *The second table.* neighbour as thyself." The commandments are these: "Thou shalt honour father and mother. Thou shalt not kill. Thou shalt not break wedlock. Thou shalt not steal. Thou shalt bear no false witness. Thou shalt not lust." In all these commandments is comprehended all that serveth for a godly life, and that any where is written of God, of true serving of God, and of right virtue towards this world.

<small>The law written in stone is no new thing.</small>
Whoso now doth well ponder these ten chapters or commandments, and compareth them to the doings and works of the holy patriarchs and old fathers, which had no law in writing, he shall find that the Lord now with this his written law began no new thing, neither aught that was not afore in the world, but rather renewed the old; and the law that he hitherto had written in the hearts of holy men, now, when the people had gotten them stony hearts, he wrote the same in tables of stone.

<small>The first commandment.</small>
For that we ought to worship and serve God only, and to have none other Gods, the same did the holy fathers so believe and keep, that all their conversation and doing beareth record thereof.

<small>The second commandment.</small>
Concerning images or idols, it is evident, that Jacob buried the idols of Mesopotamia under an oak beside Sichem, Gen. xxxv.

<small>The third commandment.</small>
We may perceive also by the oaths of Abraham, Isaac, and Jacob, how the name of God was had in reverence among them of old, and not taken in vain.

<small>The fourth commandment.</small>
The sabbath did not the Lord ordain here first, but on the seventh day of the creation, Gen. iii. The same did the fathers keep aright, no doubt, John vii.

<small>The fifth commandment.
The sixth commandment.
The seventh commandment.</small>
Whereas Cham had not his father Noe in reverence, he was cursed for it, Gen. ix. Adulterers did the heathen rulers forbid under pain of death, as we may see, Gen. xxvi. Whereby it is easy to understand how the blessed friends of God kept holy wedlock.

<small>The eighth commandment.</small>
How contrary the holy men of God were unto theft and deceit, it appeareth in the parting of Abraham and Loth, Gen. xiii., and in Jacob's faithfulness and handling with Laban, his father-in-law, Gen. xxix. xxx. xxxi. Lying and false dealing was so far from the holy fathers, that for keeping their credence and truth they obtained very great commendation. Notwithstanding, they were tempted with evil, as all men be, but they resisted the wicked lusts.

<small>Gen. xxxix.
The law written in stone was fulfilled afore.</small>
For manifest is the chaste act of Joseph, which would not touch his master's wife, nor desire her. Wherefore in these commandments is nothing written or required, that was not also required of the fathers afore the law, and performed

through true faith in Christ. The Lord therefore began no new thing with his people, when he delivered them the tables of the law. Only he would bring into a short sum and set in writing all the law that the fathers had, but not together nor comprehended in a sum, to the intent that they should the less be forgotten of the people, which through their dwelling in Egypt among idolaters and false believers, were brought into sore offence and slander. This must now be rectified again after this manner. As for all the laws and ordinances which afterward were added unto these two tables, they were not joined thereunto as principal laws, but as by-laws for the declaration and better understanding of the ten chapters or commandments. For the perfect sum of all laws, the very right rule of godliness, of God's service, of righteousness, of good and evil conversation, is comprehended already in the two tables. The laws given after the ten commandments were by-laws.

But here might some men make objection and say, If all truth be contained in these ten commandments, how happeneth it, that by no token there is mention made of the blessed Seed promised unto the fathers? Hitherto is it declared and promised unto the holy fathers, that they shall be saved through the blessed Seed, out of the very grace of God, and for none of their own deservings; but now are written laws, which command and forbid us, as though we through our own works and deserving, as namely, if we keep these commandments, should be saved and accepted unto God. Where is now Christ? Where is the faith of the patriarchs? Here is nothing heard of faith, but much, yea, only of works. Objection.

Answer. This objection hath deceived many, that they have had no right opinion and faith of the grace of God and our righteous-making. Therefore will we now give no answer out of ourselves, but set forth holy Paul, and let him answer, that the answer may be the most sure and the better esteemed. Paul, in the third chapter to the Galathians, writeth after this manner: "Dear brethren, I will speak after the manner of men; when a man's testament is confirmed no man doth lightly regard or despise it, nor addeth aught thereto. Now were the promises made unto Abraham and to his seed. He saith not, In the seeds, as in many, but as in one, And in thy Seed, which is Christ." All these are Paul's words, Answer. Gal. iii.

and the meaning of them is: Forasmuch as the testaments or works of men are of such reputation in the world, that when they are made, ordained, and confirmed, no man dare add aught to them, or minish any thing from them, but every man must let them be as they are of themselves; it is much more reason that God's testament or bequest remain still, and that nothing be added to it, or taken from it. Now did God make a testament or bequest with Abraham, and promised him therein, that he would give him a seed, in whom he and his children should be saved. And the same salvation did he expressly appoint in one, and not in many. Wherefore we must add nothing unto God's bequest, seeing that he hath promised us salvation in Christ only, and not in many; that is to say, in no creature, not in our own power and works of the law: neither must we think that the law was afterward added, to the intent as though Christ were not able to save us, or as though we might obtain salvation by our own works out of the law. For thus followeth it in Paul, word to word: "This testament, I say, which afore was confirmed to Christ-ward, is not disannulled or made of none effect by the law, which was given beyond four hundred years thereafter. For if the inheritance be gotten by the law, then is it not given by the promise. But God gave it freely unto Abraham by promise." These are Paul's words, out of the which every man may understand, that to the generation of man salvation is given only of the grace of God through the promise, and through no deserving at all; and that the law of the promise, that is to say, the bequest and testament of God, is nothing minished, but that the sum remaineth without blemish, namely, that salvation is given us freely.

But here might one ask, Seeing that the salvation is clearly enough expressed afore the law, and is ascribed only unto the grace of God, why would God then add the law? why was he not content with the testament alone? Therefore followeth it now in Paul: "Why then serveth the law? It was added because of transgression, till the Seed came that was promised." These are Paul's words, which are thus to be understanded: The law was not given because of the promise, to make it of none effect, and to teach that men are saved by works, and not through the grace and free liberty

*God's Testament.*

*Gal. iii.*

*Salvation by grace, not by desert or works.*

*Objection.*

*Answer.*
*Gal. iii.*

of God; but it was given because of transgression; that is  *Why the law was given*
to say, because that the people of God in Egypt had transgressed the way and truth of their fathers, and knew no more what was sin, right or unright, wherein stood salvation or damnation; for they were corrupt through the long dwelling among the idolaters of Egypt. Therefore did God ordain them the law, out of the which they might learn the will of God, what sin, right, or unright is; and to know themselves, to go into themselves, and to consider, how that the holy works which God requireth are not in their own power; for the which cause all the world have great need of a mediator. And thus the law was given to further the promise; namely, that we through the law might be led only unto Christ. For thus followeth it in Paul's words: "And it was given of angels by the hand of the mediator. A mediator is not a mediator of one only; but God is one. Is the law then against the promises of God? God forbid. Howbeit, if there had been given a law which could have given life, then no doubt righteousness should come of the law. But the scripture hath shut up all under sin, that the promise should come by the faith on Jesus Christ, given unto them that believe. Before faith came, (that is to say, Jesus Christ in whom we believe,) we were kept and shut up under the law, unto the faith which should afterward be declared. Thus was the law our schoolmaster unto Christ, that we might be made righteous by faith," &c. By these words of Paul may every man understand now for what cause the law was given, and how it is not contrary to the promise of the foresaid Seed, but rather bringeth us from ourselves and from all creatures only unto Jesus Christ. The law, therefore, confirmeth the first promise concerning the blessed Seed, and teacheth that we obtain all salvation in him only. Howbeit it is also a rule of our life, informing us what we ought to do, and what we ought to leave undone. Yet on our side is all unfruitful, where faith is not: but where faith is, it ceaseth not through love to work good according to the law; all honour and praise being referred unto God, to men nothing but unperfectness.

*The law was given to further the promise. Gal. iii.*

*The law is the rule to live by.*

God also among his people wrought many things, whereby he set the cause of Jesus Christ clearly afore the eyes of the people, as it is expressed afore by the lamb of the passover. Likewise is it, where as Moses hanged up a serpent in the wilderness, that all they which were stung and poisoned of serpents should behold the brasen serpent hanging, and not die, but be saved alive: whereas doubtless the outward beholding of the brasen serpent saved not them that were poisoned, but it was God, which would so declare that his Son should be hanged upon a cross, to the intent that every one which were poisoned and defiled by the old serpent and sin, should believe in the Son of God, and live in him.

<small>Wisd. xvi. The brasen serpent a figure of Christ.</small>
For so is it written, Sap. xvi. "They had a token of health according to the commandment. For whoso converted, was not made whole by the outward thing which he saw, but by thee, which art the restorer of health and Saviour of all."

<small>John iii.</small>
And yet saith Christ more clearly, John iii.: "And like as Moses set up the serpent in the wilderness, even so must the Son of man be lift up, that whosoever believeth in him should not perish, but have eternal life."

<small>1 Cor. x.</small>
And as touching this, the holy apostle Paul bringeth in another sentence, 1 Cor. x., and saith: "Brethren, I would not have you ignorant of this, that our fathers were all under the cloud, and all passed through the sea, and were all baptized under Moses[1] in the cloud and in the sea, and did all eat one spiritual meat, and drink of one spiritual drink. But they <small>Christ is the rock.</small> drank all of the spiritual rock that followed them, which was Christ."

Besides this, if we consider the declaration of the laws of the first table, which teacheth how we shall behave ourselves right toward God, to love, worship, and honour him, to serve him and to cleave only unto him, we shall find in the same first table the whole cause of Christ. For all that afterward was ordained and appointed concerning the tabernacle, the priesthood, and the oblations, pertaineth to the sum of the first table; forasmuch as the scripture and the mouth of God calleth it his law, precept, commandment, use and statute, ordinance and service.

<small>Question.</small>
And if thou ask, How can God, which is a spirit, be served with outward, visible, and fleshly things, as the foresaid ceremonies of the Jews are?

<small>Answer.</small>
I answer, Such outward rites of the people of God were sacraments and tokens of

---

[1 1 Cor. x. 2. εἰς τὸν Μωϋσῆν, "*under Moses.*" So Cov. Bibl. "*Unto Moses,*" Authorised Version.]

heavenly invisible good things, and were not the heavenly riches themselves. Wherefore they neither served nor pleased God, that used and did such service, without faith and lifting up of the mind. But they that put their trust in God, cleaving only unto him, and lifting up their hearts higher, and remained not in the visible thing, those pleased God. Whereas they had but one altar and one place appointed, where they should do sacrifice; it signified the cross of our Lord Jesus Christ, and that he should be offered up but once, and that in one place, for the sin of the world. Therefore, whereas the high priest also every year went into the inward tabernacle with blood, it signified, that our Lord Jesus should come into this world, and shed his blood once for all, to forgive and cleanse our sins, and so to ascend unto heaven. Yea, all oblations and all sheddings of blood in the sacrifices of the old fathers signified the death of our Lord Jesus Christ. Nothing was cleansed among them without blood: which signifieth, that all the purging of our uncleanness is done by the blood of Jesus Christ. And all the priesthood, which was ordained for to teach, to pray, and make intercession, to offer and do sacrifice, represented the office of our Lord Christ; which came into this world to teach us the truth and righteousness; then to offer himself to the Father for our sins, and, after the sacrifice done, to rise up again from death, to ascend unto heaven, there to sit at the right hand of God; and even there as a true high bishop to appear alway in the presence of God, and to pray for us. This is the sum of the rites and ceremonies of the old fathers, the understanding of the figures, and the spirit of the letter; whereof holy Paul hath written much in the most excellent epistle to the Hebrews.

*One altar, what it signified.*

*Note this well.*

Out of all this is it easy to understand, how that these rites and ceremonies of the fathers were sacraments, and given to the people of God. Not that they, with the letter and outward, visible, and corporal thing, should sufficiently serve God, which is a spirit; but that they should lift up their minds above the same to the spiritual things, pondering the mercy of God; out of the which he being moved, is become gracious unto us. And when he might have damned us for our sins and misdeeds, he spared us

*Why the ceremonies of the law were given.*

for his Son's sake, whom he gave unto death; and his innocent death hath he accepted for our sins. Such a faithful consideration, which is the true belief, pleaseth God, and with such a faith is God served; and such a faith would the Lord have taught and planted in with the foresaid rites and ceremonies. Therefore all they that pleased God among the old fathers, pleased him not for the letter's sake, but by reason of the spirit.

<small>The godly consideration of the fathers.</small> When the sacrifice also and ceremony was executed after the ordinance of God in the congregation, the beloved friends of God had not only respect unto the outward thing, but much rather beheld they Christ with the eyes of faith, and thought thus: Behold, the will of God hath ordained to do sacrifice for sin: now are we all sinners and debtors unto God; insomuch that he hath power and right over us, that, like as the beast which is now slain and offered dieth, and hath his blood shed, even so might God now also kill us all, and condemn us for ever. Nevertheless he hath taken us to his mercy and promised us a Seed, which should thus die on the cross, and cleanse us with his blood, and with his death restore us unto life: which thing no doubt shall as surely come to pass, as this beast is slain and offered now afore our eyes. And like as the blood is sprinkled over the people for the bodily cleansing, so shall the blood of Christ be sprinkled upon our souls, &c. And out of such a thought and faithful consideration of the sacrifices grew repentance and sorrow for their sins, a gladness, praise, comfort, and thanksgiving unto God the merciful Father. And to this do serve certain psalms, which were made concerning the sacrifices. To this also serve all the rebukings of the holy prophets, and the refusings of the oblations. For the exterior pomp and shew of the offerings, without faith in God and the blessed Seed, is nothing worth; yea, it is rather abomination unto God, as thou seest in the first chapter of Esay.

<small>Question.</small> Thou wilt ask: Might not God have taught and shewed his people the cause of Jesu Christ and of true belief, none other way than through and with such cost, pomp, and glory of sacrifices, and other gorgeousness of the church?

<small>Answer.</small> I answer: If the people had not fallen to more wicked-

ness in Egypt through their dwelling among the idolaters, but had constantly and stedfastly remained, as did their fathers, Abraham, Isaac, and Jacob, then might they well have continued by the old, short, simple form, as it was among the holy fathers. But now had they seen in Egypt an outward costly God's service, with temples, altars, sacrifices, priesthood, holy days, ornaments, &c. Likewise the idolatry increased daily in all the world; so that now there was utterly no people which had not their own outward ceremonies, wherewith they served God.

To the intent then that God might retain his people within the compass of faith in one God, and in the blessed Seed promised afore; to the intent also that they should shew no outward service to any other gods, or take upon them to serve God after the manner of the Egyptians, or any other heathen; he appointed an outward God's service, and commanded to do the same unto him, and else to none; and in the same pleased it him to set forth all the cause of the foresaid Seed, till he came and performed all things in deed, that they had figurally in their sacrifices. *Why God ordained such a long service among the Jews.*

Moreover God, according to his wisdom, of his special mercy and good heart that he hath unto man's generation, would with these outward tokens tender our weakness; which of spiritual heavenly things hath better understanding, when they are shewed unto it by corporal visible things. God therefore, through such corporal representations, laboured to shew unto that gross and fleshly people the heavenly cause of his Son. Nevertheless the corporal visible things were given for no longer, but until the time of the fulfilling. But now that Christ hath appeared, and fulfilled and performed all that was written and figured of him in the law and the prophets, the figure ceaseth, and the outward sacraments of Moses' law are of no more value, to be exercised and used. Thus much be said of the ceremonies. *God tendereth our weakness.*

Whereas, beside the ceremonies, there is much written also in the law concerning civil policy, ordinance, judgment, to live peaceable and well in city and land; of buying and selling, of war and peace, of inheritance and properties, of laws matrimonial, of punishment of the wicked, of the judgment and council, of lending and borrowing, &c.; it is *Laws judicial.*

no news at all, and serveth altogether for the declaration of the six commandments of the second table, and is com-prehended in the words of Paul, Rom. xiii.: "Love thy neighbour as thyself;" and in the words of Christ: "That thou wouldest not have done unto thee, do not thou to another." Matt. vii. Such laws and rules to live in peace, in a civil order and virtue, have also the good holy fathers had from the beginning of the world written in their hearts by God himself. Now hath God also caused all to be comprehended in writing by Moses, to the intent that the world might have all more clearly and perfectly, and that no man might excuse himself of ignorance.

Rom. xiii.<br>Matt. vii.

## CHAPTER VII.

### THE ORIGINAL OF THE HOLY SCRIPTURE AND FAITH THEREOF.

*The five original books of holy scripture written by Moses.*

THIS matter, which I have hitherto treated upon, have I not feigned of myself, but taken it out of the mouth and word of God. For God stirred up Moses to write and leave behind him all the matter, for our learning and knowledge. This did now Moses with great faithfulness, and comprehended all in four books. The first is called the book of the Creation, from the beginning of the world unto his time, of the creation of the world, beginning of all nations, and of the patriarchs and old righteous servants of God, of their faith and conversation, of the promises and works of God. The same wrote he, as he was inspired of the Holy Ghost, and as he had received of old fathers, and somewhat as he found in the books of the Egyptians. For Moses was excellently well "learned in all wisdom of the Egyptians," as Steven doth witness of him, Acts vii. The other three books wrote he of his own time, according as he himself was present, saw, and knew; and specially the second book, concerning the departing out of Egypt, how the people of God were oppressed in Egypt, how the

*The first book of Moses.*

Acts vii.

*The second book of Moses.*

Egyptians were punished, how Israel was delivered, received the law, and set up a tabernacle with a gorgeous serving of God. In the third book, which is called Leviticus, are written the spiritual laws, namely, such as concern the priests and the priesthood, their office, living, knowledge, sacrifices, solemn feast-days, rites, ceremonies, and such like. In the fourth, which is called Numeri, he writeth at length, how they went through the wilderness and came to Jordan, with a rehearsal of their order and number, of their murmuring also and punishment, and of certain victories, with a remembrance of certain laws and statutes. Besides all this, he made yet an enchiridion and sum of all the acts of his time and of the law of God, which is called Deuteronomium: the same commanded he to be laid in the ark at the motion of God, and that it should be read unto all the people, as it is mentioned, Deut. xxxi. And in these five books, given us of God by Moses, is the whole ground of our holy faith. For all the prophets afterward grounded themselves upon the same, and wrote thereout; like as afterward our Lord Jesus and the apostles point unto Moses. Neither did ever any righteous man of understanding and that feared God, doubt any thing or blaspheme such scriptures. And from such true servants of God, have we hitherto received our matters in writing.

*The third book.*
*The fourth book.*
*The fifth book.*
*The original Scripture of our faith.*

Thus much have I said concerning the law, how it is no new thing, but even the only will of God, but now comprehended in writing: moreover, that all the law pointeth unto Christ, and that all men of right understanding which lived under the law, were christian. For manifest is it that Paul said, Rom. x.: "Christ is the end of the law to justify every one that believeth." And Galat. iii.: "Or ever faith, that is to say, Christ, came, we were kept and shut up under the law unto the faith which should afterward be declared. Thus was the law our schoolmaster unto Christ, that we might be made righteous by faith." All this, I suppose, will be new and strange in many hearts; nevertheless I trust that all they which have understanding, do see and knowledge that this is the true, old, right, and godly divinity and theology, which ascribeth all honour unto God the Father through our Lord Jesu Christ in the Holy Ghost. To whom be glory and praise for ever. Amen.

*The law written is no new thing.*

[COVERDALE.]

## CHAPTER VIII.

### ALL VIRTUOUS KINGS, AND THE PEOPLE OF ISRAEL, TRUSTED UNTO CHRIST, AND NOT UNTO THE LAW.

*Josue was a figure of Christ.*

AFTER that the law was given, and God's service set up, Moses the servant of God died, being an hundred and twenty years old; and, at the commandment and commission of God, he left God's people to be ruled and guided by the faithful valiant Josue, which also was a figure of our Lord Jesu[1]. For like as it was not Moses, but Josue, that brought the people into the land of promise, even so are we brought into the eternal rest, not by the works of the law, nor through our own deserving, but by the grace through Jesus Christ; like as it is also with many words expressed of holy Paul, Heb. iv. This Josue no doubt did keep, maintain, and defend God's faith and religion, with the spirit and understanding thereof, and taught other to keep the same; like as he, through God's inspiration, received it of the fathers by Moses. Which thing though it be evident in many points, yet is it manifest specially by this, that he would not suffer the children of Ruben and Gad and the half-tribe of Manasse to set up and have another altar, besides the only altar that the Lord had appointed them. For herein, as it is mentioned afore, was figured the virtue and perfectness of the only cross, death, and sacrificing of Jesu Christ. Therefore would not Josue that anything should be set checkmate[2] with the cross and oblation of Jesu Christ, but that all honour of cleansing and forgiveness of sins should be ascribed only unto him.

[1 See this subject pursued and illustrated with great learning from the writings of the Fathers, by Bishop Pearson on the Creed. Art. II.]

[2 To check-mate: to defeat, overthrow. Spencer. But here to be " set checkmate" seems rather to bear the sense of " set equal to," in which sense it is still in provincial use. So in King Henry's Primer: " Neither was it meet to make them *check* with our Saviour Christ, much less to make them *checkmate*."]

Whereas Josue now and other judges, rulers, princes, and kings of Israel after him, used sore and great war, stroke many horrible battles, destroyed much land and people, and shed men's blood without measure, he did it as a chief head, and as an instrument and vessel of God, at the commandment of God, which would so punish the idolatry, the great sin and blasphemy of the ungodly, which he had long suffered, and exhorted them to amendment, but for all his patient abiding they would not convert. Those now did he root out through the sword of his beloved friends; sometime delivered he his people with the sword of the righteous, and saved them from the hand of their enemies. For because of the sins of his people, he gave them over sometime into the hand of their enemies, to nurture and correct them with the rod: then fell the people of God, and fled before their enemies, and were subdued and oppressed of the ungodly, till they knowledged their sins, called upon God and amended, putting their trust in God only through the blessed Seed; worshipping him only, calling upon him, and honouring him according to his word, casting away strange worshipping of God, service of idols, that shameful, blasphemous, and ungodly living. Then sent he them his help, and delivered them in his power, by the ministration of his appointed captains. And such warring, delivering, and punishing, was no fleshly unfaithful work, whom no man ought to follow, as some being wrapped with the unsteadfast spirit of the Manichees and Anabaptists, do mean[3]. For Paul expresseth clearly: "And what shall I say of Gedeon, Barach, Samson and Jephthae, David and Samuel, and the prophets? which

*Josue fought at God's commandment.*

*An heresy of the anabaptists.*

[3 Amongst the various extravagant opinions attributed to the Manichees, there is no mention of this particular error, either by Augustine, or Eusebius, (Hist. Eccles. Lib. VIII. cap. xxxi. p. 365. ed. Reading), or Socrates, (Hist. Eccles. Lib. I. cap. xxii. p. 54, ib.) Lardner, who has examined at great length all the principal authorities relating to them, does not mention their having held any such opinion, (Credibility of the Gospel History, part II. chap. lxiii.); nor does Mosheim, (De rebus Christianorum ante Constantinum Magnum, pp. 728, &c.), who has investigated the subject with great industry and learning. See also Beausobre, *Hist. de Manicheisme.* But it is probable that the Manichees and Anabaptists are here mentioned toge-

through faith subdued kingdoms, wrought righteousness, obtained the promises, stopped the mouths of lions, quenched the violence of fire, escaped the edge of the sword, of weak were made strong, became valiant in battle, turned to flight the armies of the aliens." Heb. xi. All which works the holy apostle praiseth and commendeth, as excellent works of faith. Therefore are they no works of the flesh; neither is it now contrary to the holy faith, if christian rulers deliver their innocent people, whom God hath subdued unto them, from wrongful violence, and defend their liberty, righteousness, house, and land, or punish the shameful blasphemers, idolaters, and persecutors of the holy faith, and not suffer them to have all their malicious will. Nevertheless, this must be done by them to whom God hath committed the sword. For thus saith the Lord: "Whoso taketh away the sword, shall perish through the sword." Matt. xxvi. But specially in the battles of God's people and of the unfaithful, it cometh to pass, and is expressly set before our eyes, that God said to the serpent at the beginning, Gen. iii.: "I will put enmity between thy seed and the woman's seed." For the righteous are the seed of Christ, the unrighteous and unfaithful are the seed of the devil. Between these now we see great discord; but specially this, that the faithful do alway tread the serpent on the head, though they themselves also be bitten in the heel. For the right faithful believers afore the birth of Christ, in the time of the promise, had no less trouble and persecution, not only because of sin, but also for righteousness and faith's sake, than the faithful after Christ's birth in the time of grace and perfectness. Therefore have they small knowledge of the doings of the faithful, which say that the people of old were a victorious people, and governed corporally, but that the people after Christ's coming are born to suffer, and to no victory or governance. Nevertheless, in these wonderful times, in the which God's

*Rulers must punish.*

*An error.*

ther, on account of their agreement in other fanatical opinions, which they held in common. For an account of the German Anabaptists, to whom allusion is here made, see particularly Seckendorf, Histor. Lutheranismi, Lib. I. Sect. 48, § cxviii. pp. 192—194. Lib. II. Sect. 4, § iv. pp. 10—14; also Mosheim, Cent. xvi. Sect. i. chap. iii. § xi., and Sect. xii. Part ii. chap. iii.]

people had no victory, and anon were subdued and oppressed, the true faith continued upright and unblemished from Josue forth throughout all the Judges, until the time and reign of David.

David also was a man that suffered much through diverse and long trouble, through miserable distress and vexation, and through sore persecution, without ceasing, being proved, tried, and provoked, afore he was king. Whereof the books of Samuel and the more part of the Psalms beareth record. But after that he was promoted unto the kingdom by God, which said, "I have found a man after mine own heart," he advanced, set forth, and magnified the true faith right diligently. Here also, to the honour of our Lord Jesu Christ, will I shortly and by the way declare, what knowledge and faith this noble king and prophet had of our Lord Jesu. This will I do with the declaration of the hundred and eleventh Psalm, whose words are these: [Psal. cx.]

"The Lord said unto my Lord, Sit thou at my right hand, till I make thine enemies thy footstool."

In the first verse David knowledgeth the persons in the holy Trinity, the godhead also and the eternal kingdom of Christ. Thus likewise did our Lord Jesus Christ understand and allege this verse in the gospel, Matt. xxii., knowledging two of the persons in the one only Godhead. For he saith: "The Lord said unto my Lord." Now is it certain and undeniable, that he which speaketh, and he to whom aught is spoken, are not one, but two persons. Yet is there but one Lord and God; and they both, the Father that speaketh, and the Son to whom is spoken, are the Lord: therefore they are one, of one substance and being, the very true God. Neither is the Son less than the Father. There can also none be a father, except he have a son or child. Now is the everlasting Father God; therefore is the Son also everlasting. There is also but one only everlasting without beginning. Both the Father and the Son are eternal without beginning: therefore are they one only true God with the Holy Ghost. Like as John also saith: "In the beginning, that is to say, from everlasting, was the Word, and the Word was with God, and the Word was God." And immediately thereafter saith he, that

*Of king David.*

*Acts xiii.*

*The holy Trinity.*

*John i.*

the Word is Jesus Christ our Lord. For it followeth: "The Word became flesh." Therefore doth David also call the Son of God specially his Lord, saying: "The Lord said unto my Lord." And therefore calleth he Christ his Lord, because he confesseth and believeth, that he is his very natural Lord and God, as Thomas also did knowledge: "My Lord and my God." John xx.

<small>The faith of David in Christ.</small>

Afterward calleth he him his Lord, because that after the nature of man he should be born out of his loins. For throughout all the scripture is our Lord Jesus called the Son of David. And thus doth David knowledge two natures in Christ, the nature of God and the nature of man.

That the kingdom of Christ shall last for ever, and that the kind and nature of man shall be exalted above all heavens, as Paul saith, Heb. ii., David testifieth with these words: "Sit thou at my right hand, till I make thine enemies thy footstool." For Mark saith in the sixteenth chapter: "The Lord was taken up into heaven, and sitteth at the right hand of God." Of this also find we, 1 Cor. xv. Now must he needs be very God in deed, which reigneth for ever, and to whom all enemies must be subdued, yea, cast utterly under his feet. Now followeth the second verse:

"The Lord shall send thy mighty staff out of Sion: thou shalt be Lord even in the midst among thine enemies."

Here speaketh he of the preaching of the holy gospel, and how the world should be converted unto Christ, and Christ to reign in the midst of the world. In the first verse is spoken of the eternal kingdom, that he is very God, living and reigning for ever, not only in this time, but also after this time eternally. But here speaketh he specially of the kingdom, where as he reigneth here beneath through the gospel. For the staff, the sceptre, the rod of Christ, is the holy gospel, even the power of God, which saveth all that believe, Roma. i.; which maketh Christ's enemies friends, and smiteth them down that will not convert: so that Christ hath dominion and victory even in the midst among his enemies. It is he, that with the spirit of his mouth slayeth the antichrists. This his word also and preachings of the gospel

<small>The spiritual kingdom of Christ.</small>

came forth first from Sion or Hierusalem, as Esay, Micheas, and Luke, doth testify. Now followeth the third verse: <sub>Acts i.</sub>

"In the day of thy battle, or army, shall thy people be well willing; the dew of thy birth is unto thee in an holy majesty, out of the womb of the clear morning[1]."

Herewith doth David describe the glorious and victorious faith of the Christian. For when the gospel is preached, there ariseth a conflict between faith and infidelity, between the seed of Christ and the serpent, between idolatry and true godliness. And the unbelievers persecute the Lord Christ in his members, that is to say, the faithful; but they are well content utterly to give over body, honour, and goods, their blood and life, for God's truth's sake. For the martyrs and they in the primitive church, being gathered together of the apostles and after the apostles' time, have thus kept truth and faith towards the Lord Christ, and were willing to die for knowledging him. Afterward describeth he also in the foresaid verse the pure and holy conception and birth of our Lord Jesu Christ. And this doth he with a goodly similitude, and saith: "Thy birth shall be holy and very excellent, not unclean as the birth of other men. For like as the dew out of the clear heaven and out of the fair morning, is born as it were out of a mother's womb; even so also shalt thou be born holy and clean of an undefiled virgin." Whereof thou findest more instruction, Luke i.

*A battle.*

*The birth of Christ.*

"The Lord hath sworn, and it shall not repent him: Thou art priest for ever, after the order of Melchisedech."

<sub>Psal. cx.</sub>

In this fourth verse describeth he the office of Jesu Christ, how that he is ordained of God to be one only Priest for ever, which should offer up himself for the sin

*The office of Christ.*

[[1] This verse is thus translated by Coverdale in his Bible: "In the daye of thy power shal thy people offre the frewill offeringes with an holy worship, y<sup>e</sup> dew of thy byrth is of the wombe of the mornynge." This passage is referred also, as it is here by Coverdale, in its mystical interpretation, to the immaculate conception by Tertullian, adv. Marcionem, Lib. v. cap. ix.; although in its literal meaning he understands it of the birth of Christ in the night. "*Ex utero generavi te*, id est, ex solo utero, sine viri semine, carni deputans ex utero Spiritus:" which passage is thus explained by the editor Rigaltius: "Spiritus sanctus in eo Psalmo verba hæc, *ex utero*, carni significandæ deputavit."]

of the world, and alway appear in the sight of God the
Father, and to pray for us. All this doth holy Paul declare
at large to the Hebrews, in the fifth, seventh, eighth, ninth,
and tenth chapters. And specially in this verse is grounded
all that is read throughout the scripture, of the merits of
Christ, of the forgiving of sins, of righteous-making, of
being Mediator, and that he alone is the only salvation,
advocate, satisfaction, and righteousness of the faithful.

"The Lord is at thy right hand: he in the time of his
wrath shall wound even kings."

<small>Christ's cause shall forth.</small> This fifth verse teacheth, how God will ever more and
more stand on his Son's side, further his cause, and bring
down and destroy those kings, princes, and lords, that will
not amend and believe in Christ, but will rather provoke his
wrath than desire his grace. Which thing Herodes, Nero,
Domitianus, Maximinus, and Julianus, have proved. Yet
followeth the sixth verse declaring the fifth:

"He shall judge among the heathen, and fill all full of
dead bodies, and smite the head on the wide ground[1]."

<small>Christ shall destroy his enemies.</small> Christ is also preached unto the heathen, and reigneth
among them; but many withstand Christ, and them doth he
judge. And like as a king overcometh his enemies with
a battle, and covereth the whole plain with dead bodies,
visiteth also and smiteth the head of the war, and the head
city of the enemies; even so doth Christ to his enemies,
and destroyeth their power and kingdom. All which
things we have seen in the old unchristian empire of
Rome, and in many other potentates and powers. But
specially he breaketh the head of the old serpent, according to the promise, Gen. iii. And at the last shall he
come to judge the quick and dead, and destroy his enemies
for ever.

[1 "He shall smite the head on the wide ground." Heb. מָחַץ
רֹאשׁ עַל אֶרֶץ רַבָּה. Cov. Bible: "He shall smyte in sonder the
heades over dyverse countres;" and so the Bishops' Bible, and the
Version of the Psalms contained in our Liturgy. The Authorised
version has: "He shall wound the heads over *many* (marg. *great*)
countries." Chald. מְחָא רֵישֵׁי מַלְכַיָּא עַל אַרְעָא סַגִּיעִין לַחֲדָא:
"he shall smite the heads of kings over the land of very many
(people).")]

"Out of the brook in the way shall he drink, therefore shall he also lift up the head."

Finally, and in the seventh verse, he describeth the passion of Christ and his glory. "In the way," saith he, that is, in his life while he is in this misery, "he shall drink out of the brook," that is, he shall suffer and be overcome. For to drink out of the cup is as much as to suffer: but to drink out of the brook, is to be altogether full of trouble, to be vexed and tormented without victory, and utterly to be overwhelmed with a brook and strong stream of troubles. Thus was it his mind to declare the passion of Christ. After the passion followeth the glory, with the resurrection and ascension. Paul, Philip. ii., speaketh of both, and saith: "Christ humbled himself, and became obedient unto death, even the death of the cross. Wherefore God hath exalted him, and given him a name which is above all names," &c.

Thus much be spoken of this Psalm and of David's understanding which he had of Christ Jesu and of the christian faith.

Upon this I marvel if, after so evident testimonies, there be yet any man, which perceiveth not that David's faith and understanding of Christ was even one faith and understanding with the faith that we knowledge and say: "I believe in one God, Father Almighty," &c., as it is in the twelve articles of the Christian faith. For the holy Trinity in one Godhead doth he knowledge, not only here, but also in the thirty-third Psalm, saying: "Through the Word of God were the heavens made, and all their power through the Spirit of his mouth." For certain it is, that there is but one only God, maker of heaven and of earth: but here is the Trinity called Lord or God, Word and Spirit. Neither is there any thing in the articles of the Belief concerning the Godhead and Manhood of Christ, of his conception, birth, passion, cross, and death, of the resurrection, ascension, and judgment, but it is clearly comprehended here in this Psalm. The articles of the holy church, of forgiving of sins, resurrection of the flesh, and everlasting life, are contained in this psalm, and are treated upon yet more clearly, and with many more words very substantially, in other psalms of David. Therefore had he our holy faith, and knowledged the same, was saved

*The article of the Holy Trinity.*

*David was called Christ's father.*

therein, and of all holy men was called the Father of Christ, with high commendation, because of the promise that was made unto him. Moreover, all the holy prophets following had respect unto David, as to another Moses, and took many things out of his writings. For there is scarce any other, that so clearly wrote of the cause of Christ as this prophet David, and therefore hath he honour and praise above other in Israel; of whom thou readest also, Eccles. xlvii. Such faith and confidence in God through Jesus Christ had David out of the Holy Ghost, and out of the doctrine of his prophets Samuel, Nathan, and Gad, and of other his priests, which also had the same of God, and of the holy fathers, specially of Moses. And no doubt he desired the honour of God and of his Son, not to keep it only himself, but also much rather to require it of all his people. Wherefore no doubt he set up and furthered this his faith and religion among all his men of war, kinsfolk, in all his court and dominion, before the whole congregation, and in all his kingdom, so diligently, earnestly, and fervently, that afterward certain hundred years, they which believed right and lived well were praised for walking in the ways of David their father. They also that did evil, and set not forth the true faith, of them it is written: "They walked not in the ways of David their father." Of this hast thou many ensamples in the books of the Kings and in the Chronicles. Many things also were forgiven the kings and all the people of Juda for David's sake, that is, for the promise sake made unto David, even for Jesus Christ's sake, whom Ezechiel calleth David. In the third book of the Kings, the fifteenth chapter, it is written thus: "The heart of Abia was not right towards the Lord God, as was the heart of David his father. And for David's sake did the Lord give him a light at Hierusalem, so that at Hierusalem he set up his son, and preserved him. For David did it that was right in the sight of the Lord, and all the days of his life did not he shrink from anything that he commanded him, except in the matter of Urias the Hethite." Thus readest thou also of Ezechias, 4 Reg. xviii. In the fourth book of the Kings, the twenty-third chapter, saith the prophet: "Afore Josias was there no king that was like him, which turned himself so unto the Lord with all his

[margin: The ways of David.]

[margin: [Ezek. xxxiv.] [1 Kings xv.] King Abia.]

[margin: [2 Kings xviii.]]

[margin: [2 Kings xxiii.]]

heart, with all his soul, and with all his power, according to all the law of Moses. And afterward came there none like him." But in the second book of the Chronicles, the thirty-fourth chapter, standeth the declaration of the foresaid place after this manner: "Josias reigned at Hierusalem one and thirty years, and did that which pleased the Lord, and walked in the ways of his father David, and declined neither to the right hand nor to the left. For in the eighth year of his reign, while he was yet but young, even sixteen years old, he began to seek the God of his father David."

Thus much be spoken concerning this, that Israel and all the virtuous kings of Juda trusted unto Christ, and not to the law of Moses. Whoso desireth the number of the years, he findeth (3 Reg. vi.) even 480 years from the departing [1 Kings vi.] out of Egypt until the fourth year of the reign of Salomon; and from that time until the captivity of Babylon, are reckoned 419 years, or thereabouts. Altogether make 899 years[1].

## CHAPTER IX.

### ALL HOLY PROPHETS DO POINT UNTO CHRIST, AND PREACH SALVATION ONLY IN HIM.

SOMEWHAT yet will we now declare farther concerning the times of the kings of Juda and Israel, which in a manner were even as the times of the Judges of Israel. For like as in the first years of Josue God gave great victory and honour, and afterward rest and peace; even so were the Israelites very victorious and triumphant under David, and had great rest and peace under Salomon. But like as after

[1 The period of time which elapsed from the fourth year of the reign of Solomon to the first captivity, is (from A.C. 1012 to 606=) 406 years, and to the final captivity A.C. 588, 424 years, according to the chronology of Bishop Lloyd.]

*The departing of Israel from Judah.*

the death of Josue the honour of Israel decreased, and the departing away from God followed with one persecution upon another; (though in the meantime they had peace and deliverers, as Othoniel, Ehud, Barak, Gedeon, Jephthae, Samson, &c.); even so did the worship of Israel decrease after Salomon's time. For the ten tribes of Israel fell away from the house of David: only Juda and Benjamin held Salomon's son Roboam for their king; the other made Hieroboam king. And so of one kingdom were made two, the kingdom of Israel, and the kingdom of Juda. The kingdom of Israel, through the persuasion of Hieroboam, chose them another manner of serving God. Not that they utterly denied and refused the God of their fathers; but they served him after a strange heathenish manner of their own imagining. But afterward they fell the longer, the more, and farther into gross idolatry, so long, till the Lord suffered them to be rooted out and carried away by the king of the Assyrians, and scattered abroad among all the heathen. The kingdom and the kings of Juda were somewhat better; howbeit they had some also which excelled the kings of Israel and of the heathen in ungodliness. For they likewise went forth so long in unrighteousness, till Nabuchodonosor the king rooted them out, and carried them away unto Babylon. But afore, we see that there was a wonderful cumbrance in the civil policy and in the religion. Sometime was all righteousness and true religion oppressed, and violence and idolatry used. Sometime gat righteousness up again, and the right true faith had the victory, all unright and idolatry being put down. This came to pass also in

*King Jehu.*

Israel under Helias and king Jehu. Yet was the idolatry and wrong rather punished, than any amendment following. Like as it came also to pass after the birth of Christ that there were virtuous kings and emperors, which, according to the prophecy of Esay in the forty-ninth chapter, did all righteousness, set up the faith of Christ, and put down all idolatry: again, there came other that set up all unrighteousness and idolatry, persecuted the truth, and at the last received their reward convenient. So weighty a matter is it to have good or evil rulers.

*God always sendeth his prophets.*

But in these wonderful alterations, and throughout all the time of these governances of both the kingdoms, God alway sent his servants the holy prophets, to rebuke wrong and idolatry, and to teach all righteousness and true serving of God. And first after the time of David and Salomon, under whom there was a great multitude of learned and holy prophets, (for David also and Salomon were excellently endued with the spirit of wisdom and prophecy above other men,) these were the chief, most famous, and oldest prophets, of whom the Bible maketh mention with worship: Semeias, which lived under Roboam king of Juda; Ahias the Silonite under Hieroboam; Azarias the son of Obed, which lived under Asa king of Juda; and Jehu the son of Anani, whom Baasa the king of Israel slew; Helias the great prophet, and Micheas the son of Jemla, lived under Achab and Josaphat.

Now, like as in the time of David there was a great number of learned men, even so testifieth the second book of the Chronicles in the seventeenth chapter, that in the time of Josaphat there were many learned Levites and prophets. Heliseus was in the time of king Jehu, and Zacharias the son of Joiada was under Joas, under whom also he was stoned. Nevertheless we have no books written and set forth by these; only we have the prophecy of Abdias, which wrote his prophecy under Achab. Afterward under Usia, Jothan, Achas, and Ezechias, kings of Juda, lived the most part of them whose books are abroad: for under these preached and wrote Jonas, Oseas, Isaias, Johel, Nahum, Amos, and Micheas. Afterward under king Manasses wrote Abacuk. Under the holy king Josias wrote Sophonias, Baruch, and Hieremie; in whose days Israel had such misfortune, that Hierusalem with the temple was destroyed, and the people that remained over and perished not, were carried away captive into Babylon. In the same captivity did Ezechiel and Daniel write their prophecies. And after the captivity, when Israel was delivered again and came home to Hierusalem, then preached and wrote Esdras, Haggeus, Zacharias, Malachias, and Nehemias. Beside these prophets no doubt there were other more, of whom no mention is made. But these are the chief, by whom it pleased God to open unto us all that appertaineth to our salvation. And though we had also the writings of the other, yet should we read no other thing in them, than we find in our own prophets, forasmuch as these whom we have agree so together all in one.

*The prophets preached the old faith.* Now whether they be our own prophets, whose writings we have, or the other whose writings we have not, yet have they all preached the sum of the doctrine, and knowledge the faith that we spake of afore, and wrote in one sum; which faith Adam, Noe, Abraham, Moses, and David had. And this did they the more evidently, because they applied themselves to open the law, and to drive away the misunderstanding, which was risen up among and in the people: therefore point they everywhere from the letter unto the spirit, from the outward sacrifice unto Christ Jesus, from all idolatry unto the only God, which saveth us through his mercy only in the blessed Seed, and through none of our deservings. This did Paul see, and therefore said he, Rom. iii.: "Through the works of the law shall no man be justified in the sight of God. For through the law cometh the knowledge of sin. But now is the righteousness of God declared without the law; forasmuch as it is allowed by the testimony of the *The law and the prophets allow the righteousness of God that cometh by faith.* law and the prophets. The righteousness of God cometh by the faith of Jesus Christ, unto all, and upon all them that believe." So saith Peter also in the third of the Acts: "All the prophets from Samuel and thenceforth, as many as have spoken, have told of these days." And in the tenth chapter: "To this Jesus Christ give all the prophets witness, that whosoever believeth in him, shall through his name receive forgiveness of sins."

Whoso now is learned in the writings of the prophets, knoweth well, that there is nothing read concerning the Lord in the New Testament, which the prophets have not prophesied of afore. He that is then anything instruct in the prophets, hath no doubt considered this in the New Testament, that the apostles prove all their doctrine of the Lord Jesu out of the law and the prophets; yea, that the Lord himself confirmeth his own doings with the scriptures of the prophets, and that the evangelists throughout the holy gospel set unto the doctrines and miracles of Christ these words: "And this was done, that it might be fulfilled which was spoken by the prophets." Nevertheless, for their sakes that are not yet instruct, I will now declare the principal articles of our Lord Jesu Christ out of the holy prophets.

As touching the true Godhead and manhood of our Lord  {The godhead and manhood of Christ.}
Jesu Christ, and that he should be born at Bethleem in
the land of Jewry, of a pure virgin and maid out of the
kindred of David, the prophets testify after this manner.
Esay in the seventh chapter saith: "Behold a virgin shall
conceive, and bear a son, and shall call his name Emanuel,
that is to say, God with us." Micheas saith in the fifth
chapter: "Though thou, Bethleem Ephrata, art too small to
be reckoned among the principal cities of Juda, yet out of
thee there shall come one unto me, which shall be ruler in
Israel, whose forthgoing is from everlasting." In the ninth
chapter of Esay it is written: "Unto us is a child born, and
to us is given a son, upon whose shoulders the kingdom shall
lie, and he shall be called after his own name, even the
wonderful counsel-giver, the mighty one of Israel, the eternal
Father, the Prince of peace: his kingdom shall increase, and
of his peace there shall be no end, and he shall reign upon
the seat of David his father." In the twenty-third of Hie-
remie it is written thus: "Behold the time cometh, saith the  {The righteous blossom.}
Lord, that I will raise up the righteous blossom of David: he
shall be king, and reign, and prosper; judgment and righteousness shall he execute upon earth. In his time shall Juda
be saved, and Israel shall dwell without fear; and this is the
name wherewith he shall be named, even God our Righteousness."

Concerning the coming of John the Baptist, which was
the forerunner of our Lord Christ, and prepared the people
for him, hath Malachi written in the third chapter after this
manner: "Behold, I will send my messenger, which shall  {John Baptist.}
prepare the way before me; and the Lord whom ye long for,
shall shortly come to his temple, and the messenger of the
covenant whom ye would have. Behold, he cometh, saith
the Lord Zabaoth." And afterward: "Behold, I will send
Helias the prophet afore the coming of the great and fearful
day of the Lord."

Of Christ's preaching, of the grace of God, of the forgiving of sins, of the wonders also and tokens of the Lord,
speaketh Esay in the sixty-first chapter after this manner:
"The Spirit of the Lord God is upon me, and therefore hath  {The office of Christ.}
the Lord anointed me, to preach the gospel to the meek-
hearted hath he sent me, to heal the broken-hearted, to

preach deliverance to the captive, to open the prison of such as are in bonds, to proclaim the year of God's gracious will, and to bring consolation to all them that are in heaviness." In the thirty-fourth chapter of Ezechiel it is written thus: "Over my sheep will I raise up one only shepherd, which shall feed them, even David my servant, which shall feed them, and he shall be their shepherd. I the Lord also will be their God, and David shall be their prince: even I the Lord have spoken it." In the thirty-fifth chapter of Esay it is written thus: "Say unto them that are of a feeble heart, Be strong, and fear not; behold, our God cometh to take vengeance and reward; God cometh himself, and will deliver you. Then shall the eyes of the blind be opened, &c. Then shall the lame man leap as an hart, and the tongue of the dumb shall give praise."

<small>Christ is called David.</small>

<small>The miracles of Christ.</small>

Of the kingdom of Christ, in the which he himself alone is king, all the world being subject unto him, declaring his dominion and royal majesty, writeth Esay thus in the second chapter: "And it shall come to pass in the last time, that the hill of the house of the Lord shall be exalted upon the height of mountains above all little hills, and all nations shall come together unto him: the people shall go to him, and say, Come, let us go up to the mount of the Lord, even to the house of the God of Jacob, that he may show us his way, and we will walk in his paths. For the law shall come forth from Sion, and the word of God from Hierusalem." In the seventh of Daniel it is written thus: "I saw a vision in the night, and behold there came one in the clouds of heaven like the Son of man, which came to the old aged, and they brought him before his presence. And he gave him power, glory, and the kingdom; and all people, nations, and tongues must serve him; his power is an everlasting power, which shall not be taken from him, and his kingdom shall not perish." Esay saith in the sixty-second chapter: "And the heathen shall see thy righteousness, and all kings thine honour, and he shall call thee by a new name, O Sion, and the mouth of God shall give the name. And thou shalt be a crown of glory in the hand of the Lord, and a royal crown of the kingdom in the hand of thy God." And soon after it followeth: "Make ready, make ready the way,

<small>The kingdom of Christ.</small>

gather up the stones out of the street, and hang out the banner unto the people; behold, the Lord hath caused it to be proclaimed unto the end of the world. Tell the daughter Sion, Behold, the Saviour cometh; lo, his treasure and his reward bringeth he with him, and his deeds go before him. And they that are redeemed of the Lord shall be called the holy people." Zachary saith in the ninth chapter: "Rejoice, O daughter Sion; be glad, O daughter Hierusalem: behold, thy King cometh unto thee, even the righteous and Saviour; meek and simple is he, he rideth upon an ass, and upon a young colt of the she-ass. He shall preach peace unto the heathen; his kingdom also shall reach from the one sea to the other, and from the river unto the uttermost part of the earth."

Of the death and passion of Christ speaketh Daniel in the ninth chapter after this manner: "And after two and sixty weeks shall Christ be slain and put to death; and yet shall they have no true testimony that he is guilty of death." Esay in the fiftieth chapter saith thus: "The Lord God opened mine ear, and I refused it not, neither went I backward; I gave my body to the smiters, and my cheeks to the nippers, and my face have I not turned from their shameful entreating and spitting upon me. The Lord God also shall help me; therefore shall I not be confounded. And therefore have I hardened my face like a flint-stone, and am sure that I shall not be confounded." In the fifty-third chapter there is written of Christ after this manner: "He shall have neither beauty nor fairness; we shall look upon him, but we shall have no desire unto him. He is despised and contemned of men, a man of trouble, and one that hath had experience of infirmity. He is so despised, that we shall hide our faces from him, and have him in no estimation. And yet hath he borne our unperfectnesses, and felt our sorrows. We also thought, that he should be wounded, smitten, and punished of God. But he was wounded for our sins, and slain for our wickedness' sake. And the punishment whereby we have peace, is laid upon him, and through his wounds are we made whole. All we have gone astray, like sheep, every one of us hath had respect unto his own way, and the Lord hath laid all our sins upon him. Violence and wrong was done unto him; he hath been evil entreated, and yet opened he not

*The death of Christ.*

[COVERDALE.]

his mouth. He shall be led as a beast to be slain, and as a sheep dumb before the shearers, so shall he not open his mouth," &c. The whole chapter describeth all the cause of Christ so clearly, that holy Hierom said not in vain: "Esay is not only a prophet, but also an evangelist[1]." Zachary describeth the priesthood and sacrifice of Christ, and testifieth, that with the same only oblation he hath obtained grace for all sins; and therefore seven, that is to say, all eyes shall have respect unto him, and shall seek peace and rest of their consciences in him, and shall find it: "Hear now, O Josue, thou high priest, thou and thy companions that sit before thee, seeing ye are men of ensamples. For lo, I will bring my servant, even the blossom. For behold, the stone which I have laid before Josue will I bring: to the same only stone shall seven eyes look. Behold, I will dig it up and disclose it, saith the Lord Zabaoth, and the sin of the earth will I take away in one day. And in that day shall every man call his neighbour under his vine and fig-tree."

*The sacrifice of Christ.*

*Zech. iii.*

The burial and resurrection of our Lord Jesus Christ hath the prophet Jonas figured very excellently. For thus saith our Lord Christ himself: "Like as Jonas was three days and three nights in the whale's belly, so shall the Son of man be three days and three nights in the heart of the earth."

*The burial and resurrection of Christ.*

Of the ascension of Jesu Christ, and sending of the Holy Ghost, hath Joel also written in the second chapter; and it is alleged of St Peter, Acts ii. Of the calling and gathering together of the heathen, and of every thing pertaining to the holy church, doth Esay write in the forty-ninth chapter, and so forth to the end of his prophecy.

*The ascension.*

*The vocation of the heathen.*

[[1] The passage which the author had in view, is found in the Prooemium in Esaiam Prophetam ad Eustochium virginem: "Si enim juxta Apostolum Paulum CHRISTUS Dei virtus est Deique Sapientia, et qui nescit scripturas nescit Dei virtutem ejusque sapientiam, ignoratio scripturarum ignoratio Christi est. Unde orationum tuarum fultus auxilio, quæ diebus ac noctibus in Dei lege meditaris, et templum es Spiritus sancti, imitabor patrem-familias, qui *de thesauro suo promit nova et vetera*, et sponsam dicentem in Cantico Canticorum, *nova et vetera, fratrualis meus, servavi tibi;* sicque exponam Esaiam, ut ILLUM NON SOLUM PROPHETAM, SED EVANGELISTAM et APOSTOLUM doceam." Hieronym. Opera, vol. iv. Ed. Par. 1643.]

Thus hast thou, that the prophets also in their time did preach Jesus Christ, and pointed not the people to trust unto the works of the law and their own deserving, but unto Christ, of whom they prophesied every thing that followed after. Therefore did Peter speak right, 1 Pet. i., saying: "Ye shall receive the end of your faith, even the salvation of your souls. After which salvation have the prophets inquired and searched, which prophesied of the grace that should come unto you; searching when or what time the Spirit of Christ, which was in them, should signify; which Spirit testified before the passions that should happen unto Christ, and the glory that should follow after. Unto the which prophets it was also declared, that not unto themselves only, but unto us they should minister the things which are now shewed unto you by them which have preached unto you the gospel through the Holy Ghost that was sent them from heaven," &c. In the which testimony the holy apostle Peter had a special respect to the prophecy of Daniel, which did not only record the passion and glory of Christ, but also pointed to the time in which Christ should come. For like as God in the greatest perils, dangers, and alterations, hath alway renewed and more clearly expressed his promise concerning the blessed Seed; as in the time of Noe, when the world was destroyed; in the time of Abraham, when God would prepare himself a new people; in the time of Moses, when God received his people and carried them out of Egypt, to bring them into the land of Canaan; in the time of David, when all things stood so well, and it must needs be avoided, lest any man should think David were the blessed Seed; before the captivity of Babylon also, and in the time of the prophets, which, as it is said afore, preached and wrote, that no man should doubt in God's promise, as who say they were given up and cast away, though the temple were broken, the city burnt, and though the people, of whom Christ should be born, were led away into captivity: even so now also in the captivity, when the faithful might almost have thought, that the promise of God concerning the Messia were clean gone, even then did God shew his servant Daniel a more clear vision of Christ, after this manner: "The people shall be let go again out of captivity, and shall come home to Hierusalem, build the temple and city again, but with a sore time. And after that the city is builded, unto the time of Christ, shall be sixty-nine weeks," that is, 483 years. And even so was it from the thirty-second year of Darius Hystaspis or Artaxerxes, in the which the city was builded, (Nehemie v.), until the forty-second year of the empire of Augustus, under whom Christ was born. Luke ii. The angel also gave Daniel farther information of Christ; how that his own people should slay him, and find no fault in him, and how that the sacrifice with the ceremonies should cease. "And a strange people," saith he, "shall come from far, and make the temple with the city an horrible abomination, yea, they shall destroy and break down altogether." All which things were afterward fulfilled in the last weeks, that is, within seventy years, or thereabout. For within thirty years did the Lord grow to teach and to suffer. For when he was thirty years old, John baptized him; afterward within three years was he put to death, and within forty years followed the destruction of Hierusalem by Titus and Vespasian. All the time now and years from the captivity of Babylon to Christ's birth are 626 years. For the captivity of Babylon endured seventy years. In the first year of Cyrus were they delivered, in the second year began they to build the temple, and builded forty-six years, even until the sixth year of Darius. In the thirty-second year of Darius was the city finished; which maketh 143 years: add now hereto the 483 years out of Daniel, and thou hast the foresaid sum, even 626 years[1].

*The number of the years.*

*Faith assailed and religion suppressed.*

In the said years had our holy faith sore conflicts, and the seed of the serpent pressed sore upon the seed of God, as the Babylonians at Babylon, and the Persians, when the people of God was come home again. Nevertheless the

[[1] With regard to the general question relating to the period of time which elapsed between the commencement of the Babylonian captivity and the birth of Christ, as well as to that which is connected with the interpretation of this prophecy of Daniel, it will be observed, that the opinion here adopted by Bishop Coverdale differs from those which are maintained by many eminent persons. The principal opinions relating to this prophecy of Daniel will be found detailed by Dean Prideaux, Connection of the Old and New Testament, Part I. Book v., and by Bishop Chandler, Defence of Christianity from the Prophecies of the Old Testament, Chap. II.]

## ALL HOLY PROPHETS POINT UNTO CHRIST.

truth had ever the victory, and was the more clearly testified by Daniel, Haggeus, Zachary, Esdras, Nehemias, and Malachi. Afterward were they specially oppressed by the ungodly king Antiochus, in the time of the Machabees. When as the times were ever the longer the more full of perils and adversity, until Aulus Gabinus, Pompeius, and Crassus, captains of Rome, conquered the land, and the true old religion was utterly gone; insomuch that out of the old serpent there arose in Israel all manner of sects and simony, whom our Lord Jesus Christ with his coming into the world resisted, and called them the serpent's generation, as the holy evangelists testify. Notwithstanding in the midst of such mischiefs in Israel, there were also godly virtuous people, which sought God and his Anointed, though the error was great. Among whom no doubt was specially the priest Zacharias, the father of John Baptist, Elizabeth his wife, and godly Simeon. When Zacharias had knowledge of the Lord's coming, he said with a joyful heart: "Praised be the Lord God of Israel, for he hath visited and delivered his people, and set up the horn of salvation in the house of David his servant, according as he had promised afore by the mouth of holy prophets," &c. For his words are read, Luke i. Simeon, when he saw the child Jesus in the temple, and had taken him in his arms, he said: "Now, Lord, let me die in peace, according to thy word. For mine eyes have seen thy Saviour, whom thou hast prepared before the face of all people, that he might be a light to give light unto the heathen, and the glory of thy people Israel." Luke ii.

*Antiochus.*

*God had ever some virtuous men.*

*Zachary.*

*Simeon.*

Lo, thus the hearts of all righteous in the Old Testament from Adam unto Christ, even 3974 years[2], have stood only upon Christ: in him was their comfort, upon him they trusted, it was he whom they longed for, and in Christ Jesu were they saved. Therefore hath our christian faith endured since the beginning of the world, and is, and continueth still the only true, old, undoubted, and fast-grounded faith.

[2 In this Bishop Coverdale differs from the common calculation.]

## CHAPTER X.

OF THE TIME OF THE GRACE OF CHRIST, AND HOW THAT HE HIMSELF TESTIFIETH THAT THE SALVATION OF ALL THE WORLD STANDETH ONLY IN HIM.

HITHERTO have I set forth the time of the promises, in the which God through the promised Seed, our Lord Jesus Christ, comforted, cleansed, and preserved all his servants and dear friends. There have we learned and seen, that the christian faith, which hath endured since the beginning of the world, is the eldest, undoubted, right, and true faith, which all holy patriarchs had, and in the which they served God, and pleased him, as Adam, Seth, Enoch, and Noe; item, Abraham, Isaac, and Jacob; likewise the excellent and highly-endued prophet, yea, the father and foregoer of all the prophets, even great Moses, his brother Aaron, the holy priest Eleazar, and Phinees; the excellent dukes also and judges, Josue, Gedeon, and other more; even so likewise the kings, David, Ezechias, Josaphat, and Josias; the dearly-beloved of God and excellent prophets, Samuel, Helias, Isaias, Daniel, Zacharias, and all the other. This holy faith also had all righteous, and such as were of godly understanding in all the congregations of Israel from the beginning. In this were saved all they that from the beginning were preserved and ordained to salvation. Wherefore whatsoever they can allege against this faith, whether it be concerning holy men, old age, multitudes, learned men, general councils, convocations or parliaments, fathers, acts, statutes, tokens, and wonders, it is all nothing worth, and is not to be reputed in comparison of our holy faith, as every one that hath understanding may see in this treatise before. And though my purpose be now finished, even declared out of the scripture, that the christian faith hath endured since the beginning of the world, yet will I add a short instruction concerning the time of grace and performing of all promises; and I will declare, that God now also through the appearing of his Son would bring into the world and set forth none other religion, none other faith, neither any other salvation, than even the same which was shewed to the old fathers;

*All God's elect were saved by Christ.*

saving that all things are more evident, more clearly practised, accomplished, fulfilled, and performed; for the which cause also all figures, sacrifices, and ceremonies do cease: for in Christ is all perfection. Yet shall we not therefore cast away the Old Testament, as some ignorant, unlearned, and foolish people do, but have it in greater reputation; forasmuch as we know now through Christ, what every thing signifieth, and wherefore every thing was thus and thus ordained, used, and spoken. Now shall every man first have a courage to read the law and the prophets, when he seeth whereupon every thing goeth. And thus also at the beginning did the holy apostles preach Christ unto the Jews out of the law and the prophets, as it is ofttimes mentioned in the Acts of the Apostles. And our Lord himself, when he went with the two disciples toward Emaus, and preached so unto them, that their hearts burnt within them, he began at Moses, and went through all the prophets, and opened unto them the old scriptures, and shewed them that so it behoved Christ to suffer, and to enter into his glory. This is the cause also that the scriptures of the New Testament hang all together and refer themselves to the scriptures of the Old Testament; so that these cannot be right understood without the other, no more than the gloss without the text. The text is the law and the prophets, the exposition are the evangelists and apostles. Now will we see what the work of grace of the New Testament is.
*The Old Testament is not to be refused.*
*Luke xxiv.*
*The New Testament declareth the Old.*

In the two and fortieth year of the empire of Augustus, after the beginning of the world 3974 years, was Jesus Christ, the blessed and promised Seed, born of the undefiled virgin and maid Mary, at Bethleem, in the land of Jewry. And though he as a very man was wrapped in clothes, and laid in the crib, yet appeareth the angel of the Lord in great clearness unto the shepherds, and saith: "Fear ye not; behold, I bring you tidings of great joy, which shall happen unto all people. For this day is born unto you the Saviour, even Christ the Lord, in the city of David." The first news and tidings of the coming of our Lord Jesus Christ must the angel bring and give, to the intent that it might be the more accept of all the world. All the holy men from the beginning of the world did hitherto long sore after the promised Seed. Therefore saith the angel now, that he bringeth them
*The birth of Christ.*
*Tidings of Christ's birth.*

tidings of great joy, no doubt to them that were gone, dead, and past, to them also that now lived, and to them that were to come afterward. The joy is this, that Jesus Christ the Saviour is born, even the promised Seed, which should save all the world from the power of the devil, cleanse them from sin, and deliver them from damnation. Therefore saith the angel moreover: "Which shall happen unto all people." For unto Abraham it was said: "In thy Seed shall all nations of the earth be blessed." The same, saith the angel, is born in the city of David, even out of David's kindred, out of the which the prophets testified that he should be born; which prophets also for the same cause called him *The grace of God.* David, and the blossom of David. And this is now the grace of God, that whereas we poor sinners belonged unto death, and were in the devil's bonds, he sent his Son to loose and deliver us out of captivity. This is the new testament. For Hieremy also testifieth hereof, and saith: "This is the testament that I will make, I will be their God, and they shall be my people. I will be merciful to their unrighteousness and sins, and will think upon them no more." Hier. xxxi. *Note well.* This full and perfect forgiveness is not therefore called the new testament, as though there had been no remission of sins among the old fathers; but because the promise made long afore unto the fathers is now confirmed and renewed, and the old figures that represented the same are abrogate[1]. *Christ the only salvation of all the world.* Thus the Lord Jesus alone is set forth for the only salvation of all the world; so that not only we, but all they which before or after his appearance or incarnation believed on him, were saved. And at the birth of Christ there cometh to the foresaid angel the whole heavenly host, which praised *Luke ii.* God and said: "Glory and praise be unto God in the height, and peace upon earth, to men a good will." And by this they teach us, what the duty, thankfulness, and knowledge of men is or ought to be in this behalf, that God hath done so great good for man; namely, how that they ought to

[[1] This is the reading of the edition of 1624; in the original edition of 1541, the sentence is as follows: "This full and perfect forgiveness is not therefore called the new testament, as though there had been no remission of sins promise made long afore unto the fathers, is now confirmed and renewed, and the old figures that represented the same are abrogate."]

# X.] THE SALVATION OF THE WORLD STANDETH ONLY IN CHRIST. 73

praise God, to have a sure trust in him, and to be friendly <small>The duty of us.</small>
and loving one to another. And "the fulfilling of the law
is love from a pure heart, out of a good conscience, and
of an undissembled or unfeigned faith." 1 Tim. i.

In the fifteenth year of the empire of Tiberius (from the
beginning of the world 4004 years) came the word of the
Lord to John, the son of the priest Zachary, in the wilder- <small>John Baptist.</small>
ness, and he went and preached unto the people of Israel
amendment of life and forgiveness of sins in Jesu Christ:
to whom he bare record, that he was the fulfilling of the
law and the prophets, very God and man, the only and
ever-living Saviour, which with the sacrifice of his own body
should cleanse the world from sin: yea, he pointed unto him
with his finger, and said, "Behold, this is the Lamb of <small>John i.</small>
God, that taketh away the sin of the world." And so per-
fectly and wholly hangeth he all salvation only in Christ
Jesus, that he saith plainly: "Out of his fulness have all <small>John i.</small>
we received grace," &c. John i. Item: "Whoso believeth <small>John iii.</small>
in the Son of God, hath everlasting life; whoso believeth
not in the Son, shall not see life, but the wrath of God
abideth upon him." Therefore did he also send all his
disciples from him, and commanded them to cleave unto
Christ. He maketh no mention at all of any ceremonies, <small>Matt. xi.</small>
figures, or oblations, as necessary points to salvation, but
preacheth Christ purely and clearly. This is manifest,
John i. and iii. Matt. iii. and Luke iii.

The Lord himself also came unto John, and was bap- <small>Matt. iii.</small>
tized. And when he had received baptism, the heaven
opened, and the Holy Ghost appeared in the form of a dove,
and there was a voice heard from heaven, saying: "This is
my beloved Son, in whom I am pacified:" to the intent that
all the world should have witness of Christ the true Saviour,
not only now by the angels, and by John the holiest man of
all, but also from heaven and of God himself; and that we
might be the bolder to commit ourselves wholly unto him.
When he had received the testimony, he went into the wilderness. And like as our disease began in paradise by temptation, even so at the temptation in the wilderness began the
Lord our health: and like as the father of us all did eat the
forbidden meat, so did the Lord not eat the meat that he <small>Matt. iv.</small>
might have eaten, but fasted forty days and forty nights.

Afterward came he among the people, and began to preach salvation, saying: "The time is fulfilled, and the kingdom of God is at hand; repent, and believe the gospel." Herewith hath he healed all sores, driven out devils, and raised up the dead, testifying so by his acts, that he is Lord of all things, and the true Saviour. And of them whom he healeth asketh he nothing: he commandeth them not to build him a temple, neither to give him block or stock; he requireth no bodily thing, but only stedfast faith and confidence. And to them whom he hath healed he saith: "Go thy way, and sin no more; take heed that a worse thing happen not unto thee." And herewithal doth he teach, in what thing the substance of true religion lieth, even in a right true faith, and in an innocent life, that in all our conversation we keep ourselves from all filthiness: yea, the thing that some man taketh for God's service, refuseth he, as long babbling prayers, vainglorious fasting, and like almsgiving. He nothing regardeth men's traditions, diversities of sects, long garments, outward appearance, their cleansing, nor all their hypocrisy. He goeth into the temple, overthroweth, casteth down, poureth out everything that is to be sold in the temple; he driveth the buyers and sellers out of the temple with a whip. For the temple was ordained for general prayer, thanksgiving, and preaching, and not for chopping and changing, or other such like things. These three points doth he teach us diligently to observe: First, that we obtain remission of sins, true righteousness, and everlasting life, only through him and by his passion and death, and else by none other mean. For he is the only mediator, priest, intercessor, comforter, the only righteousness, satisfaction, ransom, sanctifying, the only perpetual sacrifice, the surety of grace and salvation. Special testimonies hereof hast thou, John iii. vi. xiv. and xvi. Secondly, that we cannot serve and please God with exterior sacrifices or any outward pomp, but with such works as proceed of love and mercy. And thirdly, that all the children of God are bound to keep themselves from the works of darkness, and to apply them to live in righteousness and in the light. And herein also is comprehended all godliness, that is, all right good christian works.

So when he had taught all righteousness, and disclosed

and overthrown all hypocrisy in religion, he offered up him-  *The patient suffering of Christ.*
self upon the cross for the remission of all our sins. For
willingly and patiently put he himself into the hands of his
enemies and of his betrayer, suffered himself to be taken, to
be bound, to be led from one judge to another, to be laughed
to scorn, cried out upon, to be spitted on, and at the last to
be adjudged unto death, to be scourged, and to be crowned
with a crown of thorn. He himself bare his own cross to
the place of execution, where he was crucified, and hanged
up between two murtherers. Then lived he in great pain
from the sixth hour until the ninth. At the last he cried:
"It is finished; Father, into thy hands commend I my spirit."
Thus offered he himself for our sins, and died that we might
live. But soon after followed the things, whereby the fruit  *The fruit of Christ's death.*
of Christ's passion might be perceived. For the veil, which
in the temple separated the Holy from the most Holy, did
rent from the top till the bottom: whereby Christ testified,
that now with his death all ceremonies and figurative things
were at an end, and no more of value; that the way to
eternal salvation was opened; that all things significative in
the tabernacle, in sacrifices, rites, and observances, were now
fulfilled and abrogate; that now the bare and only cross of
our Lord Jesus Christ is altogether unto the faithful; that
the heel of the virgin's Seed is well trodden upon, and his
flesh well rent and slain; but that yet also in the mean
season he hath trodden the serpent upon the head. Therefore did the dead also arise, and appeared unto certain at
Hierusalem. For the death of Christ is our life. The earth
quaked, the stones burst asunder. For the preaching of
the death of the Son of God hath altered the whole world,
and many hard stony hearts are moved to repentance, faith,
and good works. But when the side of the dead body of
Christ was opened with the spear, and the rock, as Zachary
saith, was digged up, there ran out water and blood; de-  *Water and blood.*
claring manifestly thereby, that unto us out of the death of
Christ followeth life and purifying. For water cleanseth, in
the blood is the life of man, and with the blood of Christ is
all blood stanched; and now is Christ's blood only available,
being sprinkled through faith in our hearts. This oblation
and passion of Christ, the ransom for the sin of the whole
world, was done in the eighteenth year of the empire of

Tiberius, reckoning from the beginning of the world 4007 years, the 25th day of March.

*The burial of Christ.* So the whole body of Jesu was taken down from the cross, and honourably buried; and on the third day after he rose up again, so that his soul came again to the body, and his very flesh was raised up from death, howbeit now no more mortal and passible, but glorified. For he is the first in the resurrection of the dead. For like as by one man came death, so by one man must come the resurrection of the dead; and like as in Adam we all died in body and soul, so shall we be all together restored again to life in Christ Jesu. This hope unto life would the Lord print substantially in us with the resurrection. And therefore after his resurrection he continued forty days with his disciples, that he might well instruct them of his resurrection, and that they should have no doubt therein. So when he had shewed and declared unto them his very resurrection diverse ways, and had performed all that the Father commanded him to finish, he ascended up unto heaven with body and soul from mount Olivet in the sight of his disciples, and is set on the right hand of God, there to remain corporally until the last day, in the which he shall come again bodily, to judge the quick and dead; and all such as have walked in faith, shall he take to him with body and soul into heaven, like as he himself is received into heaven; and shall with body and soul condemn all them that have walked in the way of the old serpent, and have not converted from unrighteousness to the righteousness in Christ. And thus shall salvation be perfectly finished, and God's children shall live eternally with God, through Jesus Christ. To whom be praise for ever. Amen.

## CHAPTER XI.

THAT ALSO THE ELECT APOSTLES PREACHED THIS OLD FAITH, AND DECLARED THAT ALL SALVATION IS ONLY IN CHRIST.

THUS through Christ Jesus is all fulfilled that the prophets prophesied of him afore: thus is he become the salvation of all faithful believers, even the Lamb of God, which hath been sacrificed since the beginning of the world: that is, this is he, whose power and deliverance hath cleansed all them, that ever put their trust in God through the blessed Seed. Herein now is the right true salvation; this is the sum of the right and perfect religion. Whoso perverteth this, from him shall God turn himself; whoso addeth ought unto this, to him shall God add his wrathful hand; whoso taketh therefrom, his life shall God minish. But blessed are they, which walk in this simplicity and cleanness, and continue so unto the end; even they that hear God's word, and do thereafter, whose only hope is Jesus Christ. This only true and everduring salvation would he to be shewed and declared to all nations, which came to save all nations; but he would it should be declared by the preaching of the holy gospel, and through the ministration of the holy sacraments. And therefore by his life-time he did choose apostles, whom he received to be witnesses of all his doctrines and miracles, informing them diligently, and held nothing back from them. For he saith unto them: "Ye are my friends, if ye do all that I command you. I will henceforth call you no more servants, for a servant wotteth not what his lord doth. But I have called you my friends; for all that I have heard of my Father have I opened unto you." But forasmuch as they yet lacked understanding and were forgetful, and had ever strange imaginations of the kingdom of Christ, therefore when he now ascended unto heaven, he charged them not to depart from Hierusalem, but to wait for the Holy Ghost, whom he also gave unto them upon the fiftieth day after his resurrection, that is, upon the tenth day after his ascension, even the fifteenth day of May: by the which Holy Ghost they being illuminate spake with all manner of languages, and

*The power of Christ saveth all.*

*Christ held nothing back from his apostles.*

*John xv.*

were mindful of all that the Lord had commanded them afore. For the Holy Ghost did not endue them with a new doctrine: but it that the Lord had taught them out of the law and the prophets, the same did he bring to their remembrance, and elucidate all things, and printed them more clearly in their hearts. For so saith the Lord in the gospel: "The Comforter, even the Holy Ghost, whom the Father will send in my name, he shall teach you all things, and bring all things to your remembrance that I have said unto you." Therefore so long as the Lord was with them, and told them all the matter of his passion, they were sorry, and could not bear away all that he said unto them; but after that he was taken up from the earth into heaven, he sent the Holy Ghost, even him, whom the prophets also had before, and that led them into all christian verity.

So when they were endued with the Holy Ghost, they began, according to the Lord's commandment, to preach in all the world the foresaid matter of salvation, purchased and obtained only by Christ, and gotten by true faith. For he had said: "Go your way into all the world, and preach the gospel unto all creatures: whoso believeth and is baptized, shall be saved," &c. And therewith comprehendeth he both the points which the apostles used and practised, even the preaching of the faith in Jesus Christ, and of the ministration of the sacraments. And how the apostles' doctrine was, it is manifest out of the Acts of the Apostles. But shortly and in a sum, they preached amendment of life and remission of sins through Jesus Christ: that is to say, how that the whole generation of man lay in the dominion of the devil and in the bonds of sin, cursed and damned; but God had mercy on us all, and sent his Son into this world to die, and with his death to restore us unto life, and to wash us with his blood, that whosoever believeth in him should not perish, but have eternal life. All this declared they out of the law and the prophets, and proved that Jesus Christ whom they preached is the blessed Seed promised unto the fathers. Whoso is desirous to have a perfect example of this declaration, he findeth two sermons of the famous apostles Peter and Paul, the one in the Acts of the Apostles, the second chapter, the other in the thirteenth chapter. There doth the holy apostle open the mystery of our holy faith, very excellently declaring it from the time of Abraham unto David, and from him unto John the Baptist. Thereupon sheweth he, how Christ suffered, died, was buried, and rose again from death. All this confirmeth he with the scriptures of the prophets. At the last, he concludeth the sermon after this manner: "Be it known unto you, therefore, ye men and brethren, that through Jesus is preached unto you forgiveness of sins, and that by him all they that believe are justified from all things, from the which ye could not be justified by the law of Moses." To this agreeth now also the sermon of Peter: yea, all the scriptures of the apostles do finally accord to the same effect. Hereout also bring they the doctrine of repentance and amendment of life, the rebuking of sin, consolations, exhortations, and drawing to all manner of good works that follow out of faith. *Acts xiii.*

The special sacraments which the Lord did chiefly institute and command the apostles to practise in the Church, are holy Baptism, and the blessed Supper of our Lord Jesus Christ. Concerning the first, he saith thus: "To me is given all power in heaven and in earth; therefore go your way and teach all people, and baptize them in the name of the Father, of the Son, and of the Holy Ghost, and teach them to keep all that I have commanded you." The other did he institute at the last supper. For thus it is written in the holy gospel: "When they were eating, he took bread, and when he had given thanks, he brake it, and gave them, saying, Take, eat; this is my body which shall be given for you: this do in remembrance of me. So took he also the cup when they had supped, and said, Drink ye all out of this: this is my blood of the new testament, which shall be shed for the remission of sins." With such sacraments through outward visible forms, for our infirmities' sake, pleased it the Lord to shew and set before our eyes his heavenly and invisible grace; not that we should continue still hanging in the visible thing, but that we should lift up our minds, and with a true belief to hold fast, to print sure in our minds, to worship, and to enjoy the things that faith sheweth us by the outward sacraments. With these outward sacraments also hath it pleased him to open, declare, and shew unto us his grace and lovingkindness; namely, how that he giveth unto us himself and all his riches; cleanseth *Baptism. Matt. xxviii.* *The supper of the Lord.* *Matt. xxvi.*

us, feedeth, and moisteneth our souls with his flesh and blood; that he is at one with us, and we with him, so that we use and practise the sacraments with a true faith. For the outward enjoying of the sacraments of itself alone doth not reconcile us with God; but if they be used with faith, then, as St Peter saith, Acts xv., through faith doth God purify the hearts. With the sacraments pleased it him to leave behind him a remembrance of his gifts and benefits, to the intent that we should never forget them, but praise and thank him therefore. Moreover with visible sacraments was it his will to gather us together, and to mark us in his church and people, and to put us in remembrance of our duty, how we are one body together, and ought to apply ourselves to all righteousness. All which things are found at length in the scriptures of the apostles.

<small>The fruit of the sacraments.</small>

As for the apostles, they ministered the sacraments diligently, purely, and simply, and so, without any addition, distributed them unto the people of God. Touching baptism, there are many ensamples in the Acts of the Apostles. The supper of Jesus Christ had the Corinthians somewhat altered: and when Paul pointed them again to the true ordinance and right use, he taketh the simple words and institution of Jesu Christ without any more addition, and layeth those before them, commandeth them to follow the same, and holdeth him therewith well content. And thus did the holy apostles gather together all heathen and people, through the preaching of the gospel and ministration of the sacraments in the church, whose head is Christ, in whom they are builded and preserved. Moreover they did not lade them sore with any ceremonies. For in the Acts of the Apostles, the second chapter, where as a perfect shape of a right christian congregation is described, we have first the sending of the apostles, among whom Peter did first preach the gospel, that is to say, repentance and forgiveness of sins in Christ Jesu. Then baptized he them that were become the people of God. Afterward followeth it, that they which were become Christian, continued in the doctrine of the apostles, in prayer, in breaking of the bread, and in the fellowship. Here are the right substantial points of the Christian Church sufficiently expressed; the doctrine of amendment of life and remission of sins, baptism, the continuing and increasing in Christ's doc-

<small>1 Corinth. xi.</small>

<small>The apostles did not overcharge the people with ceremonies.</small>

XI.]  THE ELECT APOSTLES PREACHED FAITH IN CHRIST.  81

trine, prayer, the holy supper of the Lord, and the fellowship, that is, love, kindness, and works of mercy.

Now whereas Acts xv. it is ordained that the heathen should eat no blood nor strangled, it endured but for a time, and their meaning was thereby to avoid offending of the weak. Otherwise have the apostles everywhere, especially Paul, very earnestly exhorted men, to continue by the doctrine that was shewed and delivered them, and to be at a point in themselves to avoid such learning as was new and brought up by men, because they lead men far from the truth, as we find, Col. ii. Philip. iii. 1 Tim. iv. and vi: and Tit. i. And thus it is manifest, that the apostles taught all nations no new nor strange thing, but even the same that they had received of the Lord.

*The apostles would not offend the weak.*

---

## CHAPTER XII.

A CONCLUSION, THAT THIS FAITH IS THE RIGHT TRUE OLD FAITH, WHICH ALWAY SHALL STAND SURE.

THIS holy undefiled faith, which the Lord planted and set up in all nations by the apostles, immediately after the apostles' decease, was sore attempted by sundry unclean persons, which brought up false customs and misbelievers, and made perilous sects. Besides this also was it sore persecuted with the sword of tyrants. But in all such dangers the truth overcame and had the victory. For though the citizens of the devil's city, according to the disposition of their patriarch Cain, did murther, and although false prophets brought evil counsel, yet the city of God triumpheth, and the blood of innocent Abel and his brethren speaketh yet. But after that the persecution was somewhat ceased, and the persecutors sore and horribly punished for their bloodshedding, (the heresies also being well brought down by faithful shepherds,) in the same rest also was our holy faith not a little hurt. For rest put away fear, brought idle felicity, voluptuousness, and fleshly seeking of riches and dominion; and so through covetousness and ambition, there

[COVERDALE.]

was poured great poison into the church, whereby religion sore decayed. For while the ministers of the word laboured more after riches, than to perform their office and charge, and to edify the church, they were pleased with superstitiousness instead of true religion. Of this then followed it farther, that the singleness of faith was forgotten, new laws made, the old rites and customs either perverted, or else utterly overthrown and abused; whereby men came far from the doctrine and christian ceremonies, from the way of truth into error foolishly, and partly into ceremonies of idolatry. Hereof cometh it, that we have now the abomination of the pope's power of pardons, of masses for the dead and quick, of merits, power and intercession of saints in heaven, of worshipping their bones upon earth, of idols, and vain ornaments, pomp and pride of the church, of hired singing and praying in the temple, and of the whole swarm of idle religious. All which things, with other more like fondness, are nothing but new alterations, pervertings, and contrary to all old ordinances, having no ground in God's word, and are clean against God, though many hard-necked people are yet in a fury and brawl for such things, and will make all the world believe that this their foolishness, alteration, and perverting of God's ordinance, is the old faith. And yet wote they or will not know, that their babbling hath very little ground, and that they, if they considered the matter as it is, are very naked and miserable.

And though this papistical religion hath endured, prevailed, and triumphed certain hundred years, yet hath God alway sent his faithful servants, and had a little holy flock of his own, like as afore time in the days of the Judges, of the kings of Judah and Israel, and in the captivity of Babylon, though it was almost at the worst afore and at the coming of Christ. Like as it is also with us, the nigher the second coming of Christ, the worse is it in the world. Nevertheless, as I said afore, God alway set forth his word, and doth yet. Contrariwise, the pope with his multitude, and Machomet with his, as it seemeth and becometh very antichrists, have hitherto undertaken to suppress the old religion, and to set up his own ordinance, unknown to our fathers of old time, to bring it into possession, and under the name of God and his holy church, to spread it upon all Christendom.

## XII.] A CONCLUSION, THAT THIS FAITH SHALL STAND SURE.

For out of the acts and statutes of the pope and his wanton spirituality, and out of the laws of Machomet, it is manifest, what the one hath taken in hand and done now more than six hundred years, and the other upon a nine hundred years. It is evident yet also even now, whereto his general councils and parliaments do extend. But not regarding how he threateneth and faceth, and how he garnisheth his new and wanton religions with false, but dissembling, titles, boasting of many hundred years, many general councils, fathers, holy men, doctors, universities, cloisters, singing, praying, fasting, almsgiving, displaying, and telleth such like; all his bragging set aside, let us cast his religion from us, and take upon us unfeignedly the true old religion, which hath endured since the beginning of the world, by the which all holy men have ever loved, worshipped, and served God, and knew nothing utterly of the pope's religion. And if we must for this cause be hated and persecuted of the world, well: it happened even so unto all holy prophets before us likewise, and specially unto Jesus Christ our Lord, which shall come shortly to judgment, aud utterly destroy the kingdom of Antichrist, whom he now killeth with the spirit of his mouth. Our possession is not here upon earth; the kingdom of heaven is our native country. From *Phil. iii.* thence look we for the Saviour Jesus Christ our Lord, which shall raise up our mortal and miserable body, that he may make it like his excellent and glorified body; according to the power whereby he may subdue all things unto himself. To him be honour and praise for ever and ever.
AMEN.

*Let us do as our oldest fathers have done long before us.*

*FINIS.*

# A Spiritual

and most precious perle, teachynge all men to loue & imbrace yᵉ crosse as a most swete and necessarye thinge unto the soule: what comfort is to be taken thereof: where and howe bothe consolacion and aide in al maner of afflyccions is to be sought: and agayne howe all men should behaue themselues therin, accordyng to the Word of God.

Math. 10.
He that taketh not his crosse and followeth me, is not mete for me.

Printed 1550.

# A SPIRITUAL

AND

# MOST PRECIOUS PEARL.

[This Treatise is a translation from the German of Otho Wermullerus, or Vuerdmullerus, an eminent scholar and divine of Zurich, contemporary of Bishop Coverdale[1]. Of this we are informed by Hugh Singleton in the Preface to an edition published by him after Coverdale's death, in which he states that in consequence of some spurious editions, which had been published in his name, "he had thought it good to set it forth again according to the true copy of that translation that he received at the hands of M. Doctor Milo Coverdale;" at whose hand he received also the copies of three other works of Wermullerus. The names of these other books are: First, "A treatise on Death;" the second, "Of Justification;" and the third, "Of the Hope of the Faithful."

This work was first sent forth under the especial patronage of the Protector Somerset in 1550, on the conclusion of his troubles at that period, and under the circumstances stated in the Preface prefixed to this edition by the Protector himself. This fact is also mentioned in the title-page to this edition; in which it is said to have been "sett forth by the moste honorable Lorde, the duke his grace of Somerset, as appeareth by hys Epystle set before the same." But no mention is made either of Wermullerus or Coverdale; the fact of its being a translation from the former being, as far as appears, first noticed in the edition of Hugh Singleton.

Copies of this interesting edition are found in the Library of the British Museum, and in that of the Dean and Chapter of Peterborough. This volume contains, in addition to this treatise, a form of prayer composed by the Protector's chaplain, Thomas Becon, which was used daily in his family at Shene during his disgrace. These prayers will be found in the third volume of the works of Becon, (Park. Soc.)

The present edition is taken from the reprint of a subsequent edition of the same year, which appears from internal evidence to have been corrected by Coverdale himself. It has been collated carefully with the Peterborough copy throughout; all the important variations have been noted; the marginal notes have been added from the Peterborough copy; and the scripture references, which are made in that copy according to the division of the chapters employed in Coverdale's bible, have been adapted to the present mode of division into verses. For the opportunity which has been thus afforded of making this edition more conformable to this valuable original edition of the author, the Editor is indebted to the kindness and liberality of the Dean and Chapter of Peterborough.

[1] The following account of this learned person is given in Simler's Bibliotheca, p. 537: "Otho Vuerdmullerus Tigurinus scripsit de dignitate, usu, et methodo Philosophiæ moralis, quam Aristoteles ad Nicomachum conscripsit, lib. 2. Hieron. Curio excudit Basileæ, 1545: item Commentarium perquam eruditum in orationem Ciceronis ad equites Romanos antequam iret in exilium, editum sub nomine Myliandri Tigurini, Basileæ apud Rob. Vuinter, 1539, una cum aliorum lucubrationibus in omnes orationes Ciceronis, et Parisiis apud Mich. Vascosan, seorsim, an. 1540; item Tiguri apud Froschoverum in 8. ex recognitione auctoris, et Basileæ apud Oporinum, anno 1553, cum diversorum in omnes orationes commentariis. Idem scripsit de officio concionatoris Christiani sermones 3. excusos Tiguri a Froschovero in 8. Item Germanice edidit De Justificatione, lib. 4. Summam Christianæ fidei. De morte libellum. De afflictionibus. Scripsit etiam commentaria in epistolam ad Galatas, quæ nondum sunt edita. Librum de similibus ab animantibus desumptis, impressum Tiguri apud Gesneros. Item librum de bonis operibus. Obiit Tiguri anno 1551."]

# THE CONTENTS

## OF THE

## SPIRITUAL AND MOST PRECIOUS PEARL.

|  | PAGE |
|---|---|
| PREFACE | 91 |

## THE FIRST PART OF THIS BOOK.

### CHAPTER I.
That all trouble and affliction cometh from God .................. 95

### CHAPTER II.
That trouble, and affliction, and adversity, are sent unto us of God, even for the punishment of our sins .................. 97

### CHAPTER III.
All manner of troubles and afflictions, whatsoever they be, are always much less and lighter than are our sins .................. 100

### CHAPTER IV.
All manner of afflictions are sent and come from God, of a loving and fatherly mind toward us .................. 103

### CHAPTER V.
That only God for Christ's sake, and that of very mere love and favour, doth correct and punish us .................. 105

### CHAPTER VI.
Similitudes and comparisons declaring how and after what manner God doth plague and chasten us of very love, mercy, and favour towards us .................. 108

### CHAPTER VII.
Trouble and afflictions do serve to prove and to try us withal... 116

## CHAPTER VIII.

Trouble and afflictions do help and further us to the knowledge of ourselves, and of God also, and specially to wisdom .................................................................. 119

## CHAPTER IX.

Trouble and afflictions do help and further us to the right knowledge of our sins, and to perfect sorrow and repentance for them............................................................... 121

## CHAPTER X.

Trouble, affliction, and adversity, do help and further us to the exercising and increasing of our faith .......................... 123

## CHAPTER XI.

Trouble and adversity giveth us occasion to pray unto God, and to laud and praise him .................................................. 127

## CHAPTER XII.

Trouble and adversity do further us to virtue and godliness...... 129

## CHAPTER XIII.

Sorrow and affliction do help and further us toward the fear and love of God........................................................... 134

## CHAPTER XIV.

Trouble and affliction is good and profitable to teach men patience, meekness, and lowliness...................................... 136

## CHAPTER XV.

Trouble and adversity is good to teach men pity, compassion, and patience towards other............................................ 138

## CHAPTER XVI.

Trouble and adversity maketh men hard and strong, and teacheth them soberness and temperancy................................. 139

## CHAPTER XVII.

Trouble and adversity teacheth men to contemn, despise, and defy the world, and to be diligent and fervent in all godliness and virtue ......................................................... 140

## CHAPTER XVIII.

Trouble and adversity is also an occasion and help of much transitory quietness and commodity in this world ........... 142

## CHAPTER XIX.

Trouble and adversity is a furtherance to eternal life ............ 145

## CHAPTER XX.

How and in what respect trouble and adversity can be so profitable and of such virtue, seeing that the unfaithful do wax more obstinate and perverse through trouble and affliction... 146

## CHAPTER XXI.

Fellow-companions in trouble and adversity ........................... 150

---

# THE SECOND PART OF THIS BOOK.

## CHAPTER XXII.

By what natural means or ways trouble and adversity may be qualified, eased, and overcome ..................................... 153

## CHAPTER XXIII.

The best and surest succour and comfort in adversity resteth only in the might, power, will, and goodness of God ........ 156

## CHAPTER XXIV

Examples of the help and aid of God.......................................... 161

---

# THE THIRD AND LAST PART OF THIS BOOK.

## CHAPTER XXV.

We must direct our faith, hope, and confidence towards God ... 164

## CHAPTER XXVI.

Of prayer in trouble and adversity ............................................ 166

## CHAPTER XXVII.

Repentance and amendment of life in trouble and adversity is necessary............................................................................. 168

## CHAPTER XXVIII.

Christian and godly persuasions and examples out of the word of God to move men unto patience in affliction and adversity... 169

## CHAPTER XXIX.

Examples and causes, taken out of natural things, and of heathen men, whereby a man may be moved to patience in adversity  174

## CHAPTER XXX.

By what means patience may be obtained and gotten, and once had how it may be kept and increased .................  182

## CHAPTER XXXI.

The fruit, profit, and commodity of patience, as well corporal as spiritual .................  188

# THE PREFACE.

EDWARD, by the grace of God, duke of Somerset, uncle to king Edward the Sixth, his excellent majesty, &c., to the christian reader greeting.

If they be worthy praise, who for a zeal and desire that they have to do their neighbours good, do write and put in print such things as by experience they have proved, or by hearsay of grave and trusty men they have learned, or by reading of good and ancient authors they have understanded, to be a salve or medicine to a man's body, or to a part or member of the same; how much more deserve they thank and praise, that teach us a true comfort, salve, and medicine of the soul, spirit, and mind! The which spirit and mind, the more precious it is than the body, the more dangerous be his sores and sickness, and the more thankworth the cure thereof.

For a well-quieted mind to a troubled body yet maketh quietness; and sickness of body, or loss of goods, is not much painful to him that esteemeth it not, or taketh it patiently.

But an unquiet mind, yea, to a most whole body, maketh health unpleasant, and death to be wished; and an unsatiable mind with desire of more maketh riches poverty, and health a sickness, strength an infirmity, beauty a deformity, and wealth beggary; when, by comparing his felicity with a better, it leeseth the grace and joy of that it hath, and feeleth the smart of that it hath not.

Now then, sith to amend this in wealth, and to take away sorrow and grief even thence, where in very deed is no apparent cause of grief, through our weakness, is no less than the work of a very great master of physic, and deserveth much commendation; what is he worthy, that can ease true grief indeed, and make health where a very sore resteth? I mean, that can ease a man set in affliction, take away grief from him that is persecuted, loose the prisoner yet in bonds, remove adversity in adversity, or make grievous sickness not to be felt, and extreme beggary to be rejoiced at.

Divers learned men heretofore, by reasons grounded of man's knowledge, wrote and invented great comfort against all kind of griefs; and so among the gentiles' and philosophers' books be books of comfort.

But whosoever followeth but worldly and man's reason to teach comfort to the troubled mind, he can give but a counterfeit medicine; as the surgeon doth, which colourably healeth, or the physician which giveth medicines that do but astonish the sore place, and so deceive the patient. But the true healing of grief and sorrow they had not, for they lacked the ground; they lacked that, that should heal the sore at the bone first, that is, true faith in Christ and his holy word. All medicines of the soul, which be laid on the sores thereof, not having that cleanser with them, be but over-healers: they do not take away the rankling within; and many times, under colour of hasty healing, they bring forth proud flesh in the sore, as evil or worse than that which was first corrupt. This man, whosoever he be, that was the first author of this book, goeth the right way to work: he bringeth his ground from God's word; he taketh with him the oil and wine of the Samaritan; he carrieth the

Luke x. 4.

hurt man from thence where he lay hurt, and bringeth him to his right host, where, no doubt, he may be cured, if he will apply himself thereto.

It is read in histories, that the manner among the old Egyptians or Assyrians was, when any were sick, to lay him abroad, that every man that passed by might tell, if he had been vexed with such like sickness, what thing that was that did cure and heal him, and so they might use it to the patient. And by this means it is thought, that the science of physic was first found out: so that it may appear that this readiness for to teach another that thing, wherein a man feeleth ease of grief, is not only christian, but also natural.

In our great trouble, which of late did happen unto us, as all the world doth know, when it pleased God for a time to attempt us with his scourge, and to prove if we loved him, in reading this book we did find great comfort, and an inward and godly working power, much relieving the grief of our mind. The which thing now calling to remembrance, we do think it our duty not to be more unnatural than the old Egyptians were; but rather, as the office of a Christian is, to be ready to help all men by all ways possible that we can, and specially those that be afflicted.

And hereupon we have required him, of whom we had the copy of this book, to set it forth in print, that not only we, or one or two more, but all that be afflicted, may take profit and consolation, if they will; yea, and they that be not afflicted, may either see what they should have done in their trouble, or what hereafter they ought to do, if any like happeneth unto them; knowing certainly, that such is the uncertainty of the world and all human things, that no man standeth so sure, but the tempest of affliction and adversity may overtake him, and, if the grace of God do not singularly help him, cast him down, and make him fall.

Wherefore it is most necessary always to have in readiness such godly meditations and medicines, as may pacify God's wrath beginning to kindle, and defend in part the bitterness of affliction, whereof this book is very plenteous and full. Fare you well.

[In the Peterborough copy is added: From our house at Somerset-place, the vi day of May. Anno 1550.]

# A SPIRITUAL AND MOST PRECIOUS PEARL,

TEACHING ALL MEN TO LOVE AND EMBRACE THE CROSS AS A MOST SWEET AND NECESSARY THING UNTO THE SOUL; WHAT COMFORT IS TO BE TAKEN THEREOF; WHERE AND HOW BOTH CONSOLATION AND AID IN ALL MANNER OF AFFLICTIONS IS TO BE SOUGHT; AND AGAIN HOW ALL MEN SHOULD BEHAVE THEMSELVES THEREIN, ACCORDING TO THE WORD OF GOD.

## CHAPTER I.

THAT ALL TROUBLE AND AFFLICTION COMETH FROM GOD.

I CALL all that trouble and affliction, whatsoever is reputed to be contrary to the desire and appetite of man's nature; as the unquiet suggestions of the flesh, the temptations of the devil, sickness of body, a wicked and froward mate in matrimony, to have disobedient children, unkind and unthankful friends, loss of goods, to be deprived of any old liberty or privilege, loss or blemish of name and fame, the malice and displeasure of men, hunger, dearth, pestilence, war, imprisonment, and death. And in this register do I put all kinds of crosses and afflictions, whether they be bodily or ghostly, our own or our friends', private and singular, or universal and general, privy and secret, or open and manifest, deserved or undeserved.

In all such things, I say every christian man ought first of all to consider the very root, ground, and beginning, after this wise: that all things, whatsoever God sendeth, we ought to take and receive them patiently. For this is once true, that God is our Creator and Maker, and we his workmanship; he is our King, our Lord, and Father; and like as it is not seeming that the pot should murmur against the potmaker, (Isa. xlv. lxiv. Jer. xviii.) even so is it much less convenient that we should murmur and grudge against God's will and judgment. And although trouble and affliction riseth and springeth oftentimes by the wickedness of enemies, and through the instigation of the devil, or else by some other

*Isai. xlv. 9; lxiv. 8. Jer. xviii. 6. Rom. ix. 21.*

mean; yet ought we never to imagine that it cometh by fortune or chance, without the permission, sufferance, determination, and will of God, but by and with the foreknowledge, providence, and appointment of God. Ezek. xxviii. Job i. Matt. x.

<small>Ezek. xxviii. 2.<br>Job i 21.<br>Matt. x. 21.</small>

And to speak properly concerning safeguard, it is all one, so that we tempt not God, whether we live in poverty or in riches, in the fire or in the water, among our enemies or among our friends, seeing that God seeth, knoweth, disposeth, and ruleth all things, as witnesseth the first book of the Kings, ii. "The Lord bringeth to death, and restoreth again unto life; bringeth into the grave, and raiseth up again; putteth down, and exalteth also." And Job also testifieth in his misery: "The Lord hath given it, and the Lord hath taken it again." And Christ saith: "There falleth not a sparrow upon the earth without your Father's will; yea, the hairs of your head are all numbered." Luke xii.

<small>1 Sam. ii. 4.<br>Deut. xxxii. 23.<br>Wisd. xvi. 13.<br>Tobit xiii. 2.<br>Job i. 21.<br><br>Luke xii. 6.</small>

Seeing then that all our troubles and afflictions come from God, we ought to humble and submit our hearts and minds unto the obedience of God, and to suffer him to work with us according unto his most holy will and pleasure. Wherefore, whensoever unseasonable weather shall hurt and perish the corn and fruit of the earth, or when a wicked man shall misreport us, or raise up any slander of us, why should we murmur and grudge against the elements, or go about to revenge us of our enemies? For if we lift not up our minds, and consider that God layeth his hand upon us, and that it is he that striketh us, we are even like unto dogs, and no better, which, if a man do cast a stone at them, will bite the stone, without any respect who did cast the stone.

And again, no man ought to be unwilling or discontent to render again that talent or pledge that was committed to him only to reserve and keep. Matt. xxv. It is that God, that giveth us life, health of body, strength, wife, children, friends, riches, honour, power, authority, peace, rest, and quietness for a time, so long as pleaseth him. Now if the same God will take again some of these things, or all, he taketh nothing but his own, and even that which we did owe unto him. For the which cause, to murmur against his will, and to strive against his judgment, it cannot be but a heinous and grievous sin.

<small>Matt. xxv.</small>

## CHAPTER II

THAT TROUBLE AND AFFLICTION AND ADVERSITY ARE SENT UNTO US OF GOD EVEN FOR THE PUNISHMENT OF OUR SINS.

Now what thing moveth or causeth God to send home unto us and visit us with affliction, trouble, and vexation? Concerning this point, mark this well. Whatsoever any man hath merited and deserved, that ought he to bear, and to suffer willingly and gladly.

Let every man appose and examine himself, whether he hath not deserved to be correct and chastened of God, if it be not for any special thing at the present instant, yet for other sins committed at other times? Now will our Lord God, in all manner of punishments and visitations, declare the order of his righteousness, and his heavy wrath and indignation against sin and wickedness. (Rom. v. vi. Num. xiv. Nahum i.); for he saith in the second commandment, "I, the Lord, which am thy God, am a jealous and earnest God, and I will visit the sins of the fathers upon the children, even until the third and fourth generation, if they hate and contemn me." And in the fifth book of Moses are all the plagues rehearsed, one after another, which shall be poured out upon the wicked and ungodly. And in Luke, chap. xiii., it is said thus: "If ye do not amend, ye shall all perish." And that we may perceive even before our eyes evidently, how that punishment and plagues are the due reward unto sin, God tempereth and frameth the punishment even like unto the sin, so, that they do both agree together as well in form and likeness, as in proportion and quality. As for an example: like as David defiled Urias' wife, even so were his wives defiled unto him again. He caused Urias to be slain and destroyed, and therefore did his son destroy his own brother again, and stirred a sedition and uproar, and hunted and drove his father out of his kingdom; so that no man can sufficiently express the great misery and punishment, that David and his people suffered, for the shameful wicked-

[COVERDALE.]

ness and abomination that he had committed. 2 Sam. xiii. xiv. xv. xvi. xvii. xviii. xix. xx.

Now consider and weigh, as it were in a true balance, the righteousness which God requireth of us on the one side, and again, the whole trade of our life on the other side. If the generation of mankind had been 'conformable unto the law of God, and had not swerved from the same, it had been altogether thoroughly happy and blessed evermore, and should never have rotted and dried away like the fruit and flowers of the field.

<small>Wisd. ii. 23.</small>

But it swerved and fell away at the first, even from the beginning. Our first parents and progenitors did neglect and despise God's commandments; and so we through their fall are corrupt and infected, our reason, senses, and understanding blinded, and our will poisoned. We feel and find in us wicked lusts and affections; we seek in the world lust and pleasure, even against the holy word of God. And like as if an ass were trimmed and decked in a lion's skin, and would needs be a lion, yet his long ears, being always upwards, should easily descry and bewray him; even so if we adorn, garnish, and set forth ourselves with certain glorious, beautiful works never so much, so that no man can say but that we are utterly innocent and inculpable in divers and many points; yet, notwithstanding, we have filthy, unclean, and wicked hearts, full of security and neglect of God, altogether given to the love of ourselves, and to all manner of dissoluteness.

<small>Gen. iii.</small>

Now therefore, if we be assaulted and visited with sickness, poverty, war, sedition, we ought not to ascribe these things, one to the magistrate, another to the preacher and minister of God's word, or to the faith and religion itself, and the third to the elements and stars, or to God in heaven himself, as though any of these were the occasion of such plagues.

Like as no man ought to accuse and blame the physician, as though he were the only occasion of the corrupt humours within the body, notwithstanding that he hath brought and driven them out, that a man may evidently see and perceive them; but the misbehaviour and intemperate diet of the man himself is the very right occasion, and the only root thereof: even so we ought not to ascribe any blame or fault unto God, if he send unto us heaviness, pain, and trouble, but to think that it is a medicine and remedy meet for our sins, and every man to ascribe the very cause and occasion thereof unto himself and his own sins, and to refer the blame to nothing else.

And this example did the holy men, our godly forefathers, in old times shew, declare, and leave unto us, ascribing always the cause and occasion of the cross, and of such heavy afflictions as did happen in their time, even unto their own sins. As Daniel saith, chap. ix. : "By reason of our sins, Dan. ix. 5. and of the wickedness of our fathers, is Jerusalem and thy people destroyed, even of those that dwell about us." For the which cause we ought rather to lament and bewail, yea, Jon. iii. and to cry out, Alas! alas! out, out upon our sins and wickedness! than either upon any infirmity, sickness, or upon any other affliction or tribulation, which we suffer by reason of our sins.

For if we should wail and be heavy without reason or measure, when God doth nothing but executeth justice and righteousness upon his enemies, what were it else but to mislike the righteousness of God, and even to love that thing which God hateth? And what is this else, but only the very righteousness and goodness of God, when he punisheth, martyreth, and utterly subdueth and destroyeth in us, here in this world, his and our greatest enemies, that is to say, our sins?

Therefore, to sorrow and mourn without measure in the midst of affliction and trouble, is nothing else but to shew thyself a friend unto sin, which is thine and God's highest enemy. Wherefore we should rather laud God, and highly rejoice, not specially because of the misery and affliction, but in the righteous and gracious will of God: righteous, I say, because he punisheth sin; and again, gracious and merciful, forasmuch as he doth punish it much more easily than we have justly deserved.

## CHAPTER III.

ALL MANNER OF TROUBLES AND AFFLICTIONS, WHATSOEVER THEY BE, ARE ALWAYS MUCH LESS AND LIGHTER THAN ARE OUR SINS.

WHENSOEVER a man doth give a small and light punishment unto him that hath deserved much greater, it is reason that he receive and take it patiently: as one that hath slain and murdered a man, if he be but beaten and whipped out of a city or town, he taketh it in good part, because he knoweth well enough that he hath deserved to be hanged.

The holy woman Judith thinketh, that all these transitory punishments are much less, and far inferior unto our sins and wickednesses. (Jud. viii.) Wherefore, if thou suffer poverty, sickness, or any other adversity, consider and think with thyself after this manner: Well, thy manifold sins have deserved a thousand thousand times more grievous punishment, more heavy sickness, more horrible war, and more intolerable imprisonment.

*Judith viii. 27.*

And if all the miseries of the world should come together upon one heap unto thee, yet thou hast deserved much worse; for thou hast well deserved the full power and tyranny of the devil and eternal damnation, which notwithstanding God hath kept and taken from thee of his mere mercy, only for Jesus Christ's sake. Item, he that hath received alway good and prosperous things, ought not to marvel and wonder, if sometime he receive also some misfortune and adversity. Even the children of the world can say, that there is never a good hour, but hath also deserved an evil.

Now so merciful is God, that he suffereth no man upon earth unrewarded with one benefit or other: as well before trouble as after, yea, and also in the very time thereof, he giveth him many high and excellent gifts and benefits, as well bodily as ghostly, corporal as spiritual.

As for his benefits before trouble and affliction, we have a notable example set before our eyes in Job, which saith (chap. ii.): "Seeing we have received much goodness of

*Job ii. 10.*

God, why should we not be content also to receive the evil?" Likewise Pliny the second, being an heathen man, as he would comfort a friend of his, whose dear spouse and wife was departed out of the world, among other things he wrote after this manner: "This ought to be a singular comfort unto thee, that thou hast had and enjoyed such a precious jewel so long a time. For forty-four years did she live with thee, and there was never any strife, brawling, nor contention between you, nor never one of you once displeased the other. Yea, but now thou wilt say, so much the more loath and unwilling am I to forbear and to be without her, seeing I lived so long a time so quietly with her. For we forget soon such pleasures and commodities as we have proved and tasted but a little time only. But to answer to this, take thou heed that thou be not found unthankful, if thou wilt only weigh and consider what thou hast lost, and not remember how long thou didst enjoy her[1]."

And again, in the very time and midst of affliction and tribulation, God giveth us grace to consider other good and prosperous things, which we have and enjoy still, that through the remembrance and consideration of them our smart and pain may be eased, mollified, and mitigated.

As for an example: thou art a weak, impotent, and a diseased man in thy body; but yet hath God given thee reasonable and convenient goods and possessions to sustain thee with; or else, if thou hast scarceness and lack of goods and riches, yet thou hast no lack of bodily health.

Now if we will not set and weigh the one against the

[1 The letter alluded to appears to be that of Pliny to Geminus, in which he mentions the affliction which his friend Macrinus had sustained in the loss of his wife. But in this, as also in other instances, the author appears to have quoted from memory: for although there are several letters from Pliny to Macrinus himself, in none of them does he make any allusion to his loss. PLINIUS GEMINO SUO S. Grave vulnus Macrinus noster accepit. Omisit uxorem singularis exempli, etiam si olim fuisset. Vixit cum hac 39. annis sine jurgio, sine offensa. * * * *. Habet quidem Macrinus grande solatium, quod tantum bonum tamdiu tenuit: sed hoc magis exacerbatur, quod amisit: nam fruendis voluptatibus crescit carendi dolor. Ero ergo suspensus pro homine amicissimo, dum admittere avocamenta et cicatricem pati possit; quam nihil æque ac necessitas ipsa, et dies longa, et satietas doloris inducit. —Lib. VIII. Ep. 5.]

other, then are we like unto little children, which, if any man happen a little to disturb or hinder their play or game, or to take any manner of thing from them, they will by and by cast away all the rest also, and will fall on weeping. Even so were it possible enough for us to do likewise, whensoever any misfortune should happen unto us, to wax angry and displeased; and to have no manner of lust nor desire to use nor to enjoy that good that still remaineth and is left behind.

Be it in case that thou wert deprived of all manner of bodily comfort: yet in thy breast and heart thou hast the knowledge of Jesus Christ, which hath redeemed thee out of hell and damnation, that was due unto thee; in respect of the which damnation all plagues upon earth are to be esteemed as one little drop of water against the whole sea. (Rom. v. 1 Cor. v. Col. i. 1 Pet. iii. Heb. ix. &c.)

<small>Rom. v. 1. 1 Cor. v. 7. Col. i. 14. 1 Pet. iii. 18. Heb. ix. 12—15.</small>

Besides this, also through faith thou feelest a confidence and assurance of everlasting and eternal joy. As St Paul doth write of the same, saying: "I suppose the afflictions of this world are not worthy of the glory that shall be revealed unto us." (Rom. viii.) An example have we set before our eyes in the prodigal and desperate son, which did so humble and submit himself, that he desired no more to be taken for a son, but to be put to labour as a day-labourer and an hired servant, so that he might but only remain in his father's house. (Luke xv.) Even so, whatsoever God sendeth ought we to take patiently, so that we may but only dwell in the house of God in heaven with him everlastingly.

<small>Rom. viii. 18.</small>

<small>Luke xv. 19.</small>

Now if any man should think thus, 'God doth not punish others, which have committed much more heinous sins, with so great and grievous plagues and diseases as he doth us;' that were unreverently and unchristianly imagined of God. For what if thou thyself be more wicked than any other? But be it so, that others do live more wickedly and licentiously than thou, what wottest thou how God doth punish them? The greatest and most grievous pains and punishments are the inward sorrows and secret punishments of the mind, which are not seen with the outward eye.

And although they have no special sorrow nor singular grief that appeareth unto thee, and thou knowest not what God meaneth thereby, yet oughtest thou, as a child unto the father, to give unto him honour, laud, and praise, that he disposeth all things with such wisdom and in such order.

And when he seeth time, he will reward and consider all such things as have been wrought and committed heretofore against his most right and just laws, according as they have deserved.

## CHAPTER IV.

### ALL MANNER OF AFFLICTIONS ARE SENT AND COME FROM GOD OF A LOVING AND FATHERLY MIND TOWARD US.

It is not sufficient for us to know, that all manner of affliction cometh by the permission and sufferance of God of his just judgment by reason of our sins. For in extreme temptations, and in great necessities, these are the first thoughts and imaginations that come into our minds: Forasmuch as I have grievously offended God with my sins, therefore is he displeased with me, and now become mine enemy, and hath cast his favour from me.

And if we prevent not, and shift away such fantasies and imaginations in time, they will make us to fly from God, to forsake him, and to abhor and grudge against him; as Saul did, which imagined and fully persuaded himself that God punished him of hatred and displeasure against him: and therefore Saul's heart turned from God, and forsook him, and so he began to hate and abhor him, as a cruel tyrant. (1 Sam. xxviii.)

Wherefore unto such points and articles as are taught heretofore, this admonition doth also appertain: we ought to receive with high thankfulness whatsoever God of a fatherly and loving mind, and not of any indignation towards us, sendeth unto us, whether it be to the flesh pleasant or grievous. The Lord God visiteth us with temporal and transitory misery, even for the very careful and fatherly heart that he beareth toward us, and not of any hatred or indignation against us. (Job v. Hosea vi. 1 Pet. iv. Heb. xii. Rev. iii.) <sub>Job v. 17, 18. Hos. vi. 1. 1 Pet. iv. 19. Heb. xii. 1, 2. Rev. iii. 1.</sub>

For God is reconciled and at one with all christian men

through his Son, and loveth them even from the very ground of his heart.

For the which cause, howsoever or by what manner of mean it be that God punisheth and correcteth us, he doth it not because he hateth us, as though he would utterly refuse and cast us away; but of very pity and compassion, only to receive us as his children; to keep and preserve us, to exercise and practise us, to humble and to bring us down, and to stir and prick us forward; that prayer, faith, the fear of God, obedience, and other virtues, may wax and increase in us, to his honour and our salvation.

Testimonies for this have we, first: "'As truly as I live, I have no pleasure in the death of the sinner, but that he turn and live." (Ezek. xviii.) Here now doth God swear, that he doth punish, not to destroy, but to allure, reduce, and bring us unto penance.

<small>Ezek. xviii. 32.</small>

Item: "Whom the Lord loveth, him doth he chasten, and yet notwithstanding he hath pleasure in him, as a father in his child." (Prov. iii.) This is an evident testimony, that affliction, trouble, and vexation, are no tokens of the wrath and displeasure of God, but rather sure tokens of his grace, mercy, and favour, whereby God assureth us of his merciful will and fatherly heart toward us.

<small>Prov. iii. 11, 12.</small>

Item: "We know that unto such as love God, all things serve to the best." (Rom. viii.) And again: "We are corrected and punished of the Lord, that we should not be condemned with the world." (1 Cor. xi.)

<small>Rom. viii. 28.</small>

<small>1 Cor. xi. 32.</small>

All this mayest thou also mark in the whole story of Job throughout. Likewise Joseph was sold of his brethren, and delivered unto the heathen, of very malice and envy, by the provocation and suggestion of the devil. But the most faithful God turned it to the profit and wealth, both of the house of Israel, and also of the whole kingdom of Egypt: for so did Joseph himself interpret it. (Gen. xxxvii. xlv.)

<small>Gen. xxxvii. 28. xlv. 5.</small>

Again, the church of Christ, that is to say, the christian congregation, which is Christ's spouse, must suffer vexation and affliction here upon earth.

But forasmuch as God loveth this his spouse of his Son, namely, the congregation of the faithful, and mindeth to comfort her, and to be most beneficial unto her; therefore, like as he hath raised up Christ her bridegroom, head, and king, from death, even so will he also deliver her from all affliction, and give her a joyful victory of all such things as do oppress her. But it is the infirmity and fault of our weak eyes, that we cannot espy the merciful and loving goodness of God in and under the rod and scourge.

Whensoever we are visited with affliction and misery, it is our duty indeed, first to acknowledge and remember our sins, and again to consider the yoke and bands of the devil for sin; but we ought not to judge and imagine of such affliction according to the purpose and will of the devil, as he, of a malicious and a mischievous mind that he beareth us, mindeth toward us, which seeketh continually nothing else but the utter destruction and confusion of all mankind; but rather we ought to esteem and consider of all such troubles and afflictions, according as God meaneth, and so receive them[1], which of his mere goodness turneth them to our wealth and profit, working and finishing thereby our perfect salvation.

And wheresoever the heart cannot conceive this comfort, that God correcteth and punisheth for very merciful favour and love towards us, there of necessity must the temptation and grief be much the greater, and the party at length fall to utter desperation.

## CHAPTER V.

THAT ONLY GOD FOR CHRIST'S SAKE, AND THAT OF VERY MERCY, LOVE, AND FAVOUR, DOTH CORRECT AND PUNISH US.

THE very right and only cause of the merciful and fatherly will of God towards us have we in the only merits of Jesus Christ, unto whom we ought to lift up our hearts toward heaven, and to behold and consider him with our minds continually, after this manner.

Our sins and misdeeds deserve hunger, death, war, pestilence, and all manner of plagues. Now hath Christ ransomed

[1 Peterborough copy: and receiveth them.]

*Isai. liii. 4,*
*&c. John 1,*
*28. iii. 16, &c.*
and made full satisfaction for all the sins that we have committed. (Isai. liii. John i. iii. Rom. v. vi. viii. Eph. ii. Col. i. ii. 1 Pet. iii. 1 John iv. Heb. ix. &c.) He hath redeemed, paid, discharged, and made harmless unto us all our misdeeds with his bitter death, victories, and resurrection, and hath satisfied his Father's righteousness, as St Paul doth testify very comfortably, saying: "Jesus is become and made unto us our wisdom, our righteousness, our sanctification, and our redemption." (1 Cor. i.) So then now, if afflictions hurt us only by reason of our sins, and our sins be satisfied and discharged through the death and passion of Jesus, then must it needs follow, that all our afflictions also are likewise harmless unto us, and cannot hurt us.

*1 Cor. i. 30.*

Yea, Christ, with and through his passion and affliction, hath blessed and sanctified all manner of afflictions, that they all should serve and redound unto all faithful Christians for their greatest wealth, by the ordinance and provision of God, their heavenly Father. He is the true physician, which after he perceived that affliction did fear us, took upon himself to suffer all manner of trouble, yea, the most grievous sorrows and extremities, because he would set and appoint a certain measure and end unto our sorrows, and also bless and sanctify, yea, and also make pleasant and delectable very death itself unto us.

Oh! if we could feel, behold, and consider the heart and mind of Christ, when he did willingly hang upon the cross, and suffered himself so cruelly and painfully to be tormented and punished, for no other cause, but that he might utterly take away the whole strength of all our sins, sorrow, and death, and destroy hell, that none of them should hurt us; and again, that he tasted and drank of the cup before us, that we being sick and weak might the rather drink and taste of it after him, forasmuch as no evil mis-happened unto him thereof, but immediately rose up again from death: Oh! if the knowledge and remembrance of this might remain in our hearts upright, and shine continually before us: then should we never sink or faint, nor yet despair of the mercy and goodness of God, although we should labour in never so dangerous and grievous battle, and though we ourselves should taste and feel the due punishment that our sins have deserved: then should we be able to stand stiffly against the gates of hell; and all manner of sorrow, heaviness, temptation, fear, and misfortune, should thereby be utterly consumed and swallowed up.

And even this is the highest and most special comfort that ever was heard or read of from the beginning of the world. He is only alone sufficient, if we consider him and take hold of him as we should do, to plant and graft such a mind in us, that we shall not only not sorrow nor be heavy, but also triumph and rejoice in and of our misery and affliction; as Paul triumpheth excellently and highly, where he saith, "If God hath not spared his only Son, but hath given him up for us all, how should he not give us all things with him?" (Rom. viii.) Rom. viii. 31.

What make we then with our vain fearfulness, care, sorrow, and heaviness?

Wherefore, if we will be right Christians, we must with all thankfulness set forth, extol, and magnify this excellent, infinite, and heavenly grace and benefit of God, and the high and singular comfort which we have by Christ.

For all they that lack the knowledge of the benefit that we have by Christ, and refuse this excellent and high treasure, whether they be Jews or Heathens, Mahometans or Popish, they cannot be able to give any true, perfect, or wholesome comfort, either to themselves or to any other, in any manner of fear or doubt of the conscience, or in any other affliction and necessity.

So long as they are quiet and safe, and neither feel nor consider the pain of death nor any other grief or necessity, they may well live securely and boldly without any manner of fear: but when the evil hour once cometh, that the weather changeth a little, that either through the revelation and opening of the law they feel and perceive the wrath of God over them, or else through the manifest and evident tokens and preaching of the just punishment and vengeance of God, and through the present taste of some plague, they are suddenly taken and stricken with fear, as then doth all their wisdom, counsel, and policy, wherewith to withstand any such evil, utterly fail them, and suddenly deceive them.

Then flee they from God, and cannot tell whither to run, nor where to hide themselves.

And how small soever their temptation or plague is, their

heart is dashed, and as sore afraid, as Moses saith, of the noise of a leaf, as of a thunder-clap. (Levit. xxvi. Prov. xxviii.) And with such manner persons the whole trade of their former life, with all their labour, travail, and affiance in their superstitious serving of God, and in their hard and strait life, is utterly lost and spent in vain.

<small>Levit xxvi. 36.
Prov. xxviii. 1.</small>

Yea, what comfort soever they have sought, beside Christ, it is all nothing else but an augmentation of their sorrowful fear, and a training of them towards desperation. So that, without and besides the Lord Jesus, there is no manner of comfort, aid, nor succour at all to be looked for. (Acts iv. Phil. iii.)

<small>Acts iv. 12. Phil. iii. 8.</small>

## CHAPTER VI.

SIMILITUDES AND COMPARISONS, DECLARING HOW AND AFTER WHAT MANNER GOD DOTH PLAGUE AND CHASTEN US OF VERY LOVE, MERCY, AND FAVOUR TOWARDS US.

WHEN as Almighty God, for the merits of his Son, not of any ireful mind or displeasure, but of a good will and loving heart towards us, doth correct and punish us, he may be compared and likened unto a father, a mother, a master, a physician, an husbandman, a goldsmith, and such like, after this sense: like as the natural father first teacheth his dear beloved child, and afterward giveth him warning and monition, and then correcteth him at last; even so the eternal God assayeth all manner of ways with us, which are well grown and old in years, but young and tender in faith.

<small>God a father.</small>

First, he teacheth us his will through the preaching of his word, and giveth us warning. Now if so be that we will not follow him, then he beateth and jerketh[1] us a little with a rod, as sometime with poverty, sometime with sickness and diseases, or with other afflictions, which should be named and esteemed as nothing else but children's rods, or the wands of correction.

Now if such a rod or wand will not help nor do any good, then taketh the father a whip or a stick. As in case

[¹ To jerk: to lash.]

his son waxeth stubborn, and will spend his money and thrift wantonly and riotously at the tippling-house with evil company, then cometh the father and pulleth him out by the hair of his head, bindeth his hands and feet, and beateth him till his bones crack, and sendeth him into prison, or banisheth him out of the country: even so, when we wax obstinate and stubborn, and care in manner neither for words nor for stripes, then sendeth God unto us more heavy and universal plagues, as pestilence, dearth, sedition, uproar, casualty of fire, murder, war, loss of victory, that, being taken of our enemies, we are led away prisoners and captives, &c.

All this he doth to fear and to tame us, and as it were with violence to drive and to force us unto repentance and amendment of our lives. Now truth it is, that it is against the father's will to strike his child; he would much rather do him all the good that ever he could. But through long sufferance and over-much cherishing the children wax rude, and forget all nurture. Therefore doth he punish them; but yet, in the midst of all his anger and punishment, his fatherly heart breaketh out.

In case that he putteth his son away from him for some grievous fault, yet he sendeth him not away altogether comfortless, but giveth him some garments and some comfortable words, and so sendeth him from him, not to remain for evermore in banishment, but when he is once a little humbled, meekened, and amended, to turn home again. And this is only the father's mind, to turn and keep from his son all such things as might hurt and destroy him, and never mindeth to cast away or utterly to forsake his child.

Even so certainly, when God sendeth misery and affliction upon our necks, there lieth hidden under that rod a fatherly heart and affection. For the peculiar and natural property of God is to be loving and friendly, to heal, to help, and to do good to his children, mankind[2].

Adam and Eve, when they were put into paradise, were they not plenteously endued with all good things? But they could not order nor use them rightly, as none of us all can (Gen. iii.); but as soon as we have all things at pleasure, and lack nothing that we could desire, then forthwith wax we both negligent and slothful.

[2 Peterborough copy: to do good to mankind.]

And therefore God sendeth us evil, that he may do us good: and yet in the midst of all affliction and punishment he sendeth some mitigation, comfort, and succour. And we may take example by our foresaid first parents, Adam and Eve: when as God was fully determined upon the very point to exclude and banish them out of paradise, first he clothed them against the frost and violence of the weather; and he comforted them also with the promise of the blessed Seed (Gen. iii.), which maketh all manner of affliction not only easy and harmless, but also wholesome and profitable unto us.

<small>Gen. iii. 15.</small>

And this same nature doth the immutable God never change, but keepeth it continually; he will not utterly forsake us, but only suffer us a little to smart for the sins that we have committed, and so preserve us from sin afterward, that we run not into the danger of eternal pain.

Furthermore, be it in case, that the father hath two sons, whereof the one behaveth himself wickedly, and yet his father punisheth or correcteth him nothing at all, the other for the least fault that he doth is taken up and corrected by and by: what thing else is the cause of this, but that the father hath no hope of amendment at all of the one, and therefore mindeth to put him clearly from his heritage, and to give him no part thereof? For the heritage pertaineth wholly unto that son that is chastened and corrected.

And yet the same poor son that is thus chastened, thinketh in his mind that his brother is much more happy than he, forasmuch as he is never beaten nor stricken. And therefore he sighs and mourneth by himself, and thinketh thus: Well, my brother doth what he will against my father's will, and without his leave, and yet my father giveth him not one foul word; he suffereth him to take his pleasure, and to run where he will; and towards me he sheweth not so much as a good look, but is ever in my top, if I do but look awry, &c.

Here now mayest thou mark the foolishness and ignorance of the child, which hath respect only unto the present grief, and never remembereth nor considereth what is reserved and kept in store for him. Even such thoughts and imaginations have christian men and women also, when as they suffer much tribulation, and see on the other side how prosperously it goeth with the wicked and ungodly sort; whereas they ought rather to comfort themselves with the remembrance of the heritage that is reserved for them in heaven, which appertaineth unto them, as good and virtuous children.

As for the other, that hop and spring, make merry, and take their pleasure now for a while, they shall be deprived of the heritage everlastingly, as strangers, and shall have no part thereof.

And this proveth St Paul, where he saith, "My son, fear not when thou art corrected of the Lord, but receive his punishment thankfully, and with a good will; for whomsoever the Lord loveth, him doth he chastise and punish, and scourgeth every child that he receiveth. Now if ye be partakers of correction, then doth God offer and shew himself unto you as a father. And if all those that be children be corrected, and ye without correction, are ye not then bastards, and not children?" (Heb. xii.) In these words doth St Paul evidently compare and liken the punishment of the Lord unto the correction of a natural father. Heb. xii. 6—8.

And whom should not these words make to tremble and quake, where as he saith those are bastards, and not right and lawful children, which are not punished? And again, whom should not this thing rejoice and comfort, where as he saith they that are punished are children?

Wherefore, although the Almighty Lord sheweth himself displeased with us, it is nothing else but a displeasure of a most kind and loving father, which seeketh not our destruction and undoing, but only our reformation, amendment, and wealth. Give over thyself, therefore, patiently unto the will of God, thy faithful father. Rejoice in the correction of the Lord, forasmuch as thou art sure and certain thereby, that he beareth a gracious and a fatherly heart, mind, and will towards thee.

Furthermore, God is also in this behalf compared to a mother. The mother feedeth and nourisheth the child; and all the good she can do unto it, that doth she, even of a tender and motherly heart: and yet, through the frowardness and unruliness of the child, is she sometimes so moved and provoked, that she is angry with it, chideth it, rebuketh it, and beateth it. Even so were it the very God taken for a mother.

nature and property of God to suffer no manner of misfortune to happen unto us; but yet through our manifold sins he is provoked to punish and chasten us.

Now as little as the mother denieth, forsaketh, or giveth over the child, though she be angry with it and displease it, even as little doth God forsake or give over us in our need and necessity, misery and affliction, though he seem never so much to be displeased with us. Scripture for *Isai. xlix. 15.* this have we: "If a mother can forget her child, then may I also forget thee, saith the Lord: but if she should forget her child, yet will I not forget thee." (Isaiah xlix.)

*God a schoolmaster.* There is never a schoolmaster, nor handycraftsman, which taketh any scholar or apprentice unto him to teach, but he will make these conditions with him expressly: that the lad shall not be self-willed nor stubborn, nor follow his own brain and mind, but with all possible diligence shall mark and take heed unto that which the master teacheth him; and if he will be negligent, or play the truant, and not give himself unto his business as he ought to do, if he, being his master, should beat and punish him therefore, that he be content to take it patiently and with a good will. Now the master doth not correct and punish his scholar or servant for any intent to hurt him, or for any malice or evil will towards him, but only that he should learn better afterward, be more diligent, and take better heed. Even so, likewise Christ receiveth no scholar or disciple unto him, but he maketh conditions with him most necessary for every christian man, which *Matt. xvi. 24.* are expressed in Matthew, xvi.

The word of God ought to be the only rule, whereby we should be ordered: but we had rather to follow our own head and our own brain, by the means whereof ofttimes we go awry, and miss the right way; and therefore the heavenly schoolmaster knappeth us on the fingers, till we apprehend and learn his will more perfectly.

Likewise, the physician or surgeon must cut away and burn out the rotten and dead flesh with his iron and instrument, that the whole body be not infected and poisoned, and so perish: even so doth God sometimes plague our bodies sharply and grievously, that our souls may be preserved and healed. And how deep soever God thrusteth his iron into our flesh and bodies, he doth it only to remedy and to heal us; and if it be so that he kill us, then will he bring us to the right life. The physician, in making of his triakle, occupieth serpents and adders and such like poison, to drive out one poison with another: even so God, in afflicting and correcting of us, occupieth and useth the devil and wicked people, but yet all to do us good withal.

As long as the physician hath any hope of the recovery of his patient, he assayeth all manner of means and medicines with him, as well sour and sharp, as sweet and pleasant; but as soon as ever he beginneth to doubt of his recovery, he suffereth him to have and to take all manner of things whatsoever the patient himself desireth. Even so the heavenly Physician, as long as he taketh us Christians for his, and hath any hope to recover or to heal us, he restraineth us from our will, and will not always suffer us to have what we most desire; but as soon as he hath no more hope of us, and giveth us over, then he suffereth us for a time to have and enjoy all our own will and pleasure. This similitude and comparison is taken out of the fifth chapter of Job: "If the Lord God doth wound, then doth his hand heal again," &c. *Job v. 18.*

Furthermore, when a horse-breaker giveth unto a lusty fresh young horse too much of the bridle, he is wild and wanton, and goeth not well as he should do, and by chance in a slippery and sliding place he might fall headlong over and over: even so, if our Creator and Maker should suffer us overmuch, and give us too large liberty, we should soon wax wild, and proud thereof; and it might happen that we should undo and destroy ourselves; therefore he giveth us a sharp bit in our mouths, and helpeth us to bridle and to tame our flesh, that the noble and precious soul perish not.

Again, like as the carter or poor man jerketh his horses with the whip, and striketh them sharply when they will not draw nor go forward, and yet favoureth and spareth them also, that he may enjoy them the longer; even so God striketh and whippeth us, when we do not right as we should do, and yet nevertheless spareth us, and will not make utterly an end of us.

[COVERDALE.]

God a shepherd.

Like as the poor shepherd also, when his foolish sheep stray abroad in the wild wilderness among the wolves, driveth them from strange ways into the right way, and hunteth them into their sure sheepfold, where they may be in safe-guard; even so we likewise, forasmuch as we mix ourselves ofttimes among the worldlings, and have fellowship with those that are enemies unto our christian and true religion, therefore God cometh unto us, and driveth us with sorrow and repentance from them, that we should not be destroyed and perish together with them.

The herdman will suffer such calves as are appointed shortly to the slaughter, to run and spring about in the pasture at pleasure; and again, such as are reserved to labour are kept and used under the yoke: even so Almighty God doth suffer and permit unto those ungodly persons, whose destruction is at hand, to have all pleasure and lust upon earth, and to fulfil and accomplish their pleasures and desires; but the godly, whom he will use to his honour and glory, those keepeth he under the yoke, and restraineth them from the pleasant lusts of the world.

God a husbandman.

A wise and skilful husbandman doth not cast nor sow his seed in a field or ground that is not broken, ploughed, and tilled as it ought to be, but he spanneth his oxen, and goeth to the field, and casteth up the earth with his ploughshare, and so tilleth and harroweth it; and then first of all he soweth it, that if any rain fall, the seed may be saved, driven into the earth, and take hold and wax therein. Even such an husbandman is God, and we are his tillage. (1 Cor. iii.) And he bestoweth not his Spirit and truth upon such as are wild, and past all fear of God.

1 Cor. iii. 9.

Moreover, like as the gardener hedgeth his garden round about, and fenceth it with thorns and briers, that no beasts nor noisome cattle hurt it; even so God defendeth, keepeth, and preserveth us from evil company, and from all manner of sin, through thorns and briers, that is to say, through the cross and afflictions, as Hosea saith, (chap. ii.): "I will beset their ways with thorns, and their footpaths will I hedge." If the gardener cut off the knobs and the crooked boughs from the trees in his garden, and loppeth them a little, yet as long as the roots remain, the trees are never the worse, but wax nevertheless, and bring

Hos. ii. 6.

forth fruit: even so doth God lop and hew the crabby old Adam with the cross, not to the intent to hurt or harm us, but to keep us in awe, and to teach us godly manners. And surely, as long as the root of faith remaineth with us, though we be spoiled and destitute of all riches, and of all manner of worldly and bodily comfort, yet shall we bring forth good fruits to the high honour and glory of God's holy name. (John xv.) John xv. 8.

Christian men without the cross are like unto grapes, which hang upon the vines, and have the fruition of the open air, and remain still upon the stock unfruitful, and no man is the better for them.

Wherefore the heavenly vine-man bringeth the Christians unto the wine-press, where they are beaten, pressed, stamped, and broken, not to their destruction, but that they may be delivered from the corruption and infection of worldly lusts, and may bring forth sweet wine, and bear pleasant fruits.

The goldsmith casteth a lump of gold into the oven and into the fire, not to consume it away with the fire, but to purge it from the corruption that is in it, and that all that hangeth about it, and is no gold, should be burnt away with the fire, and consumed unto ashes: even so is God the goldsmith, the world the oven, affliction the fire, the faithful Christians the gold, and the filth and corruption is sin. Now will God purge and make clean those that belong unto him from all manner of blots, blemishes, and corruption, and make them glorious and beautiful unto him. *God a goldsmith.*    1 Pet. iv. 12.

The free-mason heweth the hard stones, and heweth off here one piece, and there another, till the stones be fit and apt for the place where he will lay them: even so God, the heavenly free-mason, buildeth a christian church, and he frameth and polisheth us, which are the costly and precious stones, with the cross and affliction, that all abomination and wickedness, which do not agree unto this glorious building, might be removed and taken out of the way. (1 Pet. ii.)    1 Pet. ii. 5.

Again, as the dyer bleacheth, or the laundress washeth, beateth, lumpeth, and clappeth the foul, unclean, and defiled clothes, that they may so be white, pure, and clean; even so doth God some time handle and deal with us, to make us pure and clean. (Dan. xi.)    Dan. xi. 35.

## CHAPTER VII.

### TROUBLE AND AFFLICTIONS DO SERVE TO PROVE AND TO TRY US WITHAL.

TROUBLE and afflictions do prove, try, instruct, confirm, and strengthen the faith, provoke and stir up prayer, drive and force us to amendment of life, to the fear of God, to meekness, to patience, to constancy, to gentleness, to soberness and temperance, and to all manner of virtues; and are the occasion of exceeding much good, as well transitory as eternal, in this world as in the world to come. By affliction and trouble will God prove and assay, mark and spy, how deep thy heart hath entered with God, how much thy faith is able to suffer and to bear, whether thou canst forsake both thyself and all other creatures in the world for his sake.

<small>Matt. x. 22; xvi. 24. Mark viii. 34. Luke ix. 23. John xii. 25.</small>

In sum, to be short, he will try how thou wilt behave thyself, when he taketh utterly from thee and out of thy sight that wherein thou most delightest and hast any pleasure upon earth. God knoweth well enough before, how thou wilt take it and behave thyself; but he will shew and declare to thyself and to other also, what is in thee: for oft-times people do so extol a man, and make such boast of him, to be the wisest, most circumspect, manly, and honest man in a country; but when the time of trial cometh, there appeareth no such thing in him, as was thought and looked for.

A man cannot learn to know a lusty and a stout man of war in the time of peace, but best of all in the time of war, when the cruel and fierce enemies do invade and assault his captain.

When a great tempest ariseth in the sea, then doth it appear whether the shipmaster be cunning in ruling the stern or no. Again, those are the most honest and most chaste matrons, which being sore tempted, assaulted, and provoked unto wickedness, do nevertheless keep their spouse-faith towards their husbands undefiled. Even so can no man know nor prove perfectly, how the christian church keepeth her spouse-faith and fidelity towards her spouse and bridegroom Jesus Christ, until such time as antichrist assaulteth and tempteth her with false doctrine, tyranny, and persecution.

Such trees as have strong and deep roots and sufficient natural sap, can no violent heat of the sun hurt nor harm; but such as are felled and cut down, are soon dried up with the heat of the sun, like as the grass also that is mown down doth soon wither: even so likewise such faithful persons as are rooted in Christ Jesus, cannot troubles nor afflictions hurt, they grow and wax green notwithstanding; but the unfaithful do betray themselves, and shew what they are, as soon as they see any heat of trouble or persecution coming. With one flail are both the stalks and ears of the corn beaten, and also the corn itself threshed and purged out: even so with one manner of trouble and affliction are the faithful purged and provoked to pray unto God, and to laud and magnify him, and the unfaithful also to murmur and curse; and so are they both tried, proved, and known.

When the corn is threshed, the kernel lieth mixed among the chaff, and afterward are they dissevered asunder with the fan or windle: even so the people in the church do first hear the preaching of God's word; now some stumble, repine, and are offended at it, and other are not offended, and yet they dwell together one with another; but when they are fanned or windled, and when the wind of trouble and affliction beginneth once a little to blow, then is it easy to sunder and to know the one from the other, the faithful from the unfaithful.

Art thou pure corn? What needest thou then to fear either the flail or the wind? In the threshing and in the wind thou shalt be delivered and sundered from the chaff, and shalt be made more pure than thou wast before. Let them fear that are chaff, which are not able to abide the wind, but must be blown away, and so cast out for ever.

A rotten and an old weak house standeth awhile for a time; but as soon as a wind cometh and bloweth, it appeareth unto all men, how feeble the foundation and stay of it was. Even so are there such christian men without ground or foundation, which so long as all things go well and prosper with them, they are good Christians; but in the time of trouble and persecution their dissimulation is known and breaketh out.

"As gold is tried in the oven, wherein it is molten; Wisd. iii. 10. even so hath God tried and purged them." Now if thou be gold, what needest thou to fear the fire, which doth more profit than hinder or hurt thee?

To this purpose doth this true proverb serve: "In need doth a man try which be his friends."

Examples: Almighty God did tempt and prove Abraham, and bade him offer up and kill his only son (Gen. xxii.): then was Abraham in a great distress, perplexity, and heaviness; he had rather have lost all his goods and possessions, and all that ever he had upon earth, than he should slay his dear son. But yet, though it were against nature, and an intolerable thing, yet he carried his son forth three days' journey to kill him with his own hands; he overcame his flesh by faith, and would be obedient unto God. Then said God unto him: "Now I know that thou fearest God, and hast not spared thy only dear son for my sake."

And Moses saith: "Remember all the ways, through the which the Lord thy God hath led and guided thee these forty years in the wilderness, because he would chasten and prove thee, that it might appear and be known what was within thy heart, whether thou wouldest keep his commandments or no." (Deut. viii.)

Set Pharaoh and David together the one against the other, two notable kings: Pharaoh persevereth and continueth obstinately, stubbornly, and perversely in his wicked purpose, notwithstanding the manifold plagues that did fall and lighten upon him. (Exod. vii. viii. ix.) Contrariwise, how soon did David give over and break out with all meekness, submission, patience, and acknowledging of his whoredom, when as he fled from Absalom, Shimei rebuking and reviling him most shamefully! (2 Sam. xvi.)

Job was stricken with many grievous sores, that there was nothing sound or whole in him, from the sole of his foot to the top of his head; not that he had deserved such heavy punishment more than other men, but that God would declare to all the world his patience and faithfulness. But his wife did then shew her weak faith and wicked corrupt nature. (Job ii.)

Who was more faithful and more fervent than Peter? and yet he denied and forsook Christ before a simple woman. (Matt. xxvi.) Who ought not therefore to fear himself, except he hath before in the trial been found faithful, steadfast, and constant?

In like manner, daily experience teacheth us to know the faithful and unfaithful asunder in persecution and affliction. There are some that cleave to the gospel for a time; but when they see they cannot attain that they sought and looked for, then they forsake it, and fall from it again, yea, and in the time of temptation they fall to blaspheming of the holy gospel: but the godly, which have it fixed in their hearts, stand steadfastly by God both in life and death.

## CHAPTER VIII.

TROUBLE AND AFFLICTION DO HELP AND FURTHER US TO THE KNOWLEDGE OF OURSELVES, AND OF GOD ALSO, AND SPECIALLY TO WISDOM.

BESIDES this, it is a profitable and a good thing for a man to know himself well.

Felicity and prosperity blindeth a man; but when he is under the cross he beginneth to mark the frailness of his body, the uncertainty of his life, the feebleness of his understanding, the infirmity and weakness of man's strength and power.

He shall spy and perceive how far he is entered in the way of virtue, how the matter standeth between God and him, whether he be a champion of God or of the devil: for a man thinketh himself oft-times to be well grounded and stablished, but in the time of temptation he feeleth how lightly and easily he is tossed and turned of every blast of the wind.

Item, by affliction and misfortune God will put thee in remembrance, how many thousand perils are yet hanging over thy head, which should lighten and fall upon thee, if he did not keep and preserve thee from them. And the same God saith thus unto thee: 'The wicked enemy with an innumerable and infinite heap of all evils and mischiefs doth assault thee, and lay watch for to subdue thee, and to swallow thee up; but I have appointed him his bounds, over the which he cannot pass.'

*The right knowledge of God.*

The longer thou art under the cross, the better mayest thou learn all the virtues and goodness of God; as his just judgment and strait justice, whereby he sheweth his wrath and displeasure against the wicked and ungodly, and sendeth upon their necks terrible plagues; and the obstinate and unrepentant he condemneth everlastingly.

Item, his infinite power, whereby he can help and comfort thee in most extreme misery and necessity.

Item, his immutable truth, whereby he doth faithfully perform all his promises, and bringeth to pass all his threatenings.

Item, his exceeding mercy and free grace, whereby he preventeth all evil towards us, and will not suffer us to be caught and oppressed with any misfortune.

*1 Pet. v. 7.*

Item, his eternal and everlasting providence, whereby, like a father, he taketh charge and care over us, and governeth all things most wisely. (1 Pet. v.)

Item, his glory, magnificence, and lauds for the foresaid virtues, which do shine most clearly in affliction and adversity; for the which cause St Bernard writeth thus: "Whereby do we know that he that dwelleth above is among us here beneath? Forsooth by this, that we do stick in trouble and afflictions. For who could be able to sustain, bear, and abide them without God[1]?"

*To learn wisdom in adversity.*

A man hath need at all times of wisdom, circumspection, prudence, and soberness. Like as prosperity shutteth and blindeth the eyes of men, even so doth adversity and trouble open them.

Like as the salve that remedieth the disease of the eyes doth first bite and grieve the eyes, and maketh them to water, but yet afterward the eyesight is clearer and more sharp than it was; even so trouble and affliction doth grieve and vex men wonderfully at the first, but afterward it helpeth and lighteneth the eyes of the mind, that it is afterward more reasonable, wise, and circumspect.

For trouble bringeth experience, and experience bring-

[1 "Unde scimus, quod nobiscum sit (Deus scil.) in tribulatione? Ex eo utique quod in ipsa tribulatione nos sumus. Quis enim sustineret, quis subsisteret, quis persisteret sine eo?" Sancti Bernardi Opera, in Psal. xc. (xci.) Serm. xvi. Vol. i. p. 880. E. Ed. Bened. 1719.]

eth wisdom. The rod and punishment do bring wisdom. (Eccles. xxxiv. Prov. xxix.) And of this did these proverbs first spring up: "The more plentiful land, the more foolish and wicked people;" and again: "Adversity causeth men to look well and far about them;" item: "There is no man wise, but with his hurt and loss;" item, "That man may well learn to swim, which hath the water at his mouth." David saith: "O Lord, how good and profitable is it unto me, that thou hast chastened and humbled me, that I might learn thy righteousness and thy commandments!" (Psal. cxix.) Eccles. xxxiv. 9.<br>Prov. xxix. 15.<br><br><br><br><br>Psal. cxix. 71.

## CHAPTER IX.

TROUBLE AND AFFLICTIONS DO HELP AND FURTHER US TO THE RIGHT KNOWLEDGE OF OUR SINS, AND TO PERFECT SORROW AND REPENTANCE FOR THEM.

GOD requireth that the knowledge of our poisoned and corrupt nature and of the wrath of God should wax and increase in us, whereby we might conceive an hearty sorrow and repentance for our sins, and so daily amend and wax better. Now truth it is, that in our hearts naturally sticketh a rough secureness and retchlessness, whereby we do little regard and esteem the inward filthiness of our hearts; and specially, when we feel no manner of taste of the cross and affliction, we do not consider the miserable wretchedness of our sins, nor the just judgment of God, and the terrible punishment due for the same.

But when the hand of God doth humble and pluck down some special persons or a whole congregation, then remember we the greatness and heaviness of sin, that God's wrath and indignation is not so sore without some special and most just causes.

And then break we out into such words as these: "O Lord, we have deserved these plagues a thousand ways. O good and most just God, thou rewardest the misdeeds and transgressions of the fathers in the children, if they follow their fathers' steps, even unto the third and fourth generation." (Exod. xx. xxxiv. Numb. xiv. Deut. v.) Like as the hard copper and tin do melt in the fire, even so in trouble and affliction the hard, rough, and stubborn hearts do melt and fall to misliking and loathing their sins.

<small>Exod. xx. 5; xxxiv. 7. Numb. xiv. 18. Deut. v. 9.</small>

A trespasser doth then first of all perceive his faults rightly, when he is brought unto the judgment to be punished, and is adjudged and condemned unto death. And for this cause doth God use such rough and hard means with us. And both the common and general, and also the particular and special, plagues and adversities may well be called a part of God's law, and, as it were, God's preaching, which testify and declare unto us, that God is heavily displeased against all manner of wickedness and abomination that reigneth in the world; that all men should humble and submit themselves unto God, bewail and lament their sins unto him with a sorrowful and a right penitent heart, and desire his grace and mercy.

For an example: Joseph's brethren in Egypt did then first of all spy their wickedness committed against their brother, when as very need and necessity did vex them in a strange country. (Gen. xlii.) When as the Lord did send into the wilderness among the Israelites venomous serpents, which did bite them and set them on fire; then came they first to Moses, and said, "We have sinned, forasmuch as we have spoken against the Lord, and against thee." (Num. xxi.)

<small>Gen. xlii. 21.</small>

<small>Numb. xxi. 6, 7.</small>

When the pestilence did rage, then said David unto the Lord, "Behold, it is I that have sinned; what have these sheep done?" (1 Chron. xxi.) Now, therefore, if it be so, that knowledge of the sin, and an hearty displeasure against it, be profitable and necessary, then can we not well forbear trouble and adversity.

<small>1 Chron. xxi. 17.</small>

## CHAPTER X.

TROUBLE, AFFLICTION, AND ADVERSITY, DO HELP AND FURTHER US TO THE EXERCISING AND INCREASING OF OUR FAITH.

That our faith is proved and tried through the cross and through adversity, it is declared before. And now shall it be evidently proved, that our faith is then first right stablished, exercised, and augmented, when adversity cometh. The very true christian faith is grounded only upon the grace, mercy, power, and help of God through Christ. Which thing cannot be right comprehended with vain thoughts, imaginations, and speculations; but God cometh upon the miserable sinners with heaps of miseries. Whatsoever they attempt, go about, or take in hand, it goeth backward with them, and their whole life is made so bitter as gall unto them, that they can nowhere find any rest.

And why? forsooth it is done for this purpose, that they should utterly neglect and despise all manner of counsel and comfort of man; that they should be plucked from all manner of trust in the policies and powers of the world; and that they should utterly despair of all help in any creature: and in the stead of that, they should set and fix their hearts and minds only in God, and that nothing at all should else remain in them, but only unspeakable sighing unto God, proceeding out of a true faith, in whose help and mercy only altogether consisteth.

Testimonies of scripture: Moses witnesseth that God suffered the Israelites to be diversely vexed, and to be brought into great distress, and yet preserved them wonderfully, for this cause, that when they should come into the land of promise, they should not say: "Mine own power, and the strength of mine own hands, were able to bring this to pass; but thou shouldest think upon the Lord thy God: for he it is which giveth thee such power, whereby thou art able to perform and bring any thing to pass." (Deut. viii.) <sub></sub>Deut. viii. 2, &c.

And so did God deal afterward with the children of Israel, which of their own brain and wisdom sought help, succour, and maintenance at the king of the Assyrians, and at the king of Egypt, which were the very same that afterward did besiege them, slay them, and carry them away prisoners.

And so after that they felt and proved that there was none that could succour and help them, but only the Lord, unto whom they yielded and gave over themselves at length; as, I looked for no other but that I should die. (Jer. x. Hosea ii. iv. vi.) But it was done for this purpose, that we "should not put any trust in ourselves, but in God, which raiseth up the dead again." (2 Cor. i.)

*2 Cor. i. 9.*

Item: Whatsoever stirreth up and exerciseth our faith, of that ought we not to be afraid, but rather to rejoice in it. When we live in idleness, in all lust and pleasure, the devil snappeth us up, and so blindeth us in our weakness, that we think God doth not regard us, and all things in the world to happen without any working or foresight of God. But as well in special as in general adversities, there is greater matter and occasion to practise and to exercise the faith.

God suffereth thee to fall into poverty, or thy most dear friends to be taken from thee by death, or some other disquietness to happen unto thee. As then hast thou a great occasion to awake and to practise thy faith; and first to call to remembrance the promises of God, contained in his word, and then to call upon him for his grace and assistance, and so to resist and withstand all manner of natural doubtfulness and despair, that hangeth in thy flesh, how grievous soever the necessity seem to be, and howsoever any man doth imagine that God hath withdrawn his face from thee, and will not help thee at all.

In like manner, in all common necessities and general, this is the right exercise of faith, and the most holy service of God, that we first consider and weigh earnestly all manner of perils and assaults of the church and of the commonwealth; and after that, that we pray unto God with a constant and a lively faith, that he will deliver and preserve the church from false doctrine, superstition, and hypocrisy, and that he will graciously rule and govern it: and that he will also preserve the commonwealth in good order and quietness, and will grant wholesome air and seasonable weather, and will also restrain and let the wild and dissolute behaviour and conversation of the common sort of people; and will grant, maintain, and preserve a christian discipline, behaviour, and honesty, whereby his holy and godly name may be lauded and magnified, his kingdom augmented, increased, and confirmed, and the kingdom of the devil subverted and confounded.

And remember this also: whensoever thou considerest thy adversity, forget not to desire of God hope and trust for comfort, aid, and succour; and look that thou strive and fight mightily and manfully against all manner of mistrust, and put away all manner of despair, how grievously soever thy adversity and sorrow doth increase; and thus is thy faith well rightly practised and exercised.

An example: from holy Job was taken all that ever any man might take any comfort in, wife, children, goods, and friends; and one trouble, sorrow, and heavy message came still in another's neck, and he had not one drop of blood in his body, that was not consumed and wasted. And he sat in the sight of all the world, was their laughing-stock, and so exercised and practised his faith, and gave over himself only and wholly unto God. (Job i. ii. iii.)

Unto Abraham was promised a seed, which should be in multitude as the sand of the sea, and as the stars of the sky (Gen. xii. xviii. Eccles. xliv.); and yet was his wife barren and unfruitful, and he also waxen old and aged, that after the judgment of natural reason it was not possible that that promise should be fulfilled and come to pass, by the means whereof Abraham did exercise, try, and practise his faith. *Gen. xii. 2; xviii. 18. Eccles. xliv. 21.*

And thus did Joseph, David, Daniel, all patriarchs, prophets, and apostles, as well in the common and general adversities of the church, as in their own private and peculiar afflictions, exercise and practise their faith; and this was their highest God's service, wherewith they honoured and served God. (2 Sam. xv. Dan. iii. vi.)

Wherefore in our time also God giveth us great and marvellous occasion, through trouble and adversity, to awake, stir up, and to exercise our faith. And by such exercise is the faith increased and confirmed; yea, and shineth more brightly, and is made more beautiful and glorious. For whatsoever a man hath proved and tried himself, that believeth he afterward the more steadfastly. Now he that is a christian man or woman proveth and feeleth in deed, that in the midst of his sorrow and affliction he is ruled, defended, comforted, and preserved of God. For hope cannot be confounded.

<small>Rom. v. 5.</small>

And therefore the Christian and the faithful man, through trouble and adversity, is made more bold and hearty, and concludeth with himself, more than ever he did before, that God hath a special regard and consideration of those that are in trouble and misery, and will graciously help and deliver them out.

Like as one that hath sailed oft upon the sea, and proved and escaped great and dangerous tempests, and hath been sore tossed with the fearful waves, is afterward the more bold and hardy to go unto the sea, forasmuch as he hath ever escaped well, and hath had good fortune before; even so a christian man, whom the cross hath oft assaulted and exercised, forasmuch as he hath always found comfort, aid, and help of God, afterward he trusteth God, the longer the more, though the same affliction and adversity come again unto him, that he had before.

And to this purpose hear and mark two especial and notable examples; one out of the Old, and another out of the New Testament. David, when he prepared himself to fight against the valiant giant Goliah, said these words: "The Lord, which hath delivered me from a lion and from a bear, shall deliver me also from this Philistine." (1 Sam. xvii.) And again, Paul saith: "God hath delivered us from so great a death, and delivereth us daily, and we hope that he will deliver us from henceforth also." (2 Cor. i.)

<small>1 Sam. xvii. 37.</small>

<small>2 Cor. i. 10.</small>

And to the same purpose doth this also appertain, to consider, that the cross assureth those that bear it in the Lord, of the grace and favour of God, whereby they know certainly, that they are of the number of the elect, and the children of God; forasmuch as he looketh upon them fatherly, to reform and to correct them. (Job v. Hos. vi. Prov. iii. Tobit xii. 1 Pet. iv. Heb. xii. Rev. iii.)

<small>Job v. 17.<br>Hos. vi. 1.<br>Prov. iii. 11, 12.<br>Tobit xii. 17.<br>1 Pet. iv. 16.<br>Heb. xii. 1, 2.<br>Rev. iii. 19.<br>Judith viii. 26.</small>

For[1] why thus it is written: "Yea, all those that ever did please God have been proved and tried by many and

[1 Peterborough copy: Forasmuch as.]

divers troubles, and have been found constant and steadfast in faith." Item: "All those that will live godly in Christ Jesus must suffer persecution and affliction." (2 Tim. iii. Eccles. ii. Psalm xxxiii.)

<sub>2 Tim. iii. 12.<br>Eccles. ii. 4,<br>&c.<br>Psal. xxxiii.<br>18, 19.</sub>

## CHAPTER XI.

### TROUBLE AND ADVERSITY GIVETH US OCCASION TO PRAY UNTO GOD, AND TO LAUD AND PRAISE HIM.

EVERY christian man knoweth this, that it is necessary and profitable for him to pray and to call upon God most fervently and devoutly. Now when a man liveth in all prosperity, then he prayeth very little, or very slenderly and coldly; he hath no great affection or mind upon it.

That prayer that is not pressed and thrust out with the cross, floweth not out from the depth and bottom of the heart.

But sorrow, heaviness, and adversity, kindleth the mind and setteth it on fire; driveth, chaseth, and hunteth it unto God, and compelleth it to call upon God fervently and earnestly: for at such time we feel and perceive well, that we can do nothing of ourselves, and what great need we have of God, that he will vouchsafe to govern, aid, and defend us.

Like as the water, as long as it floweth and runneth over the even, plain, wide, and broad fields, it breaketh not out by no violence, but disperseth and spreadeth itself abroad every where alike; but when it is gathered together by cunning and science, and conveyed into a narrow room, as into a pipe or conduit, then it springeth or spouteth out on high: even so the mind of man, as long as it is quiet, idle, and without sorrow or trouble, it walketh and wandereth abroad at large and at liberty; but when it is brought in, restrained, and driven to a strait and a narrow issue through trouble and adversity, it breaketh out aloft to God in heaven with an earnest, hearty, and fervent prayer for grace, aid, and comfort. (Eccles. xxxv. Acts x.) <sub>Eccles. xxxv. 17.<br>Acts x. 2.</sub>

Whereupon there is a common proverb sprung: "Need and necessity teacheth men to pray." "O Lord, when trouble and adversity is at hand; then do men seek thee: when thou chastenest and punishest them, then call they upon thee lamentably." (Isai. xxvi.) Examples: When the children of Israel heard of the coming of their enemies, the Philistines, they were afraid, and said unto Samuel, "Cease not to cry unto the Lord our God for us, that he may help us out of the hands of the Philistines." (1 Sam. vii.) Manasses, which all the days of his life was a very bloodhound and a tyrant, was bound with chains, and led away into Babylon. And when he was in extreme anguish and necessity, he made his humble prayer and supplication before the Lord his God; and God heard his humble prayer, and brought him again to Jerusalem. (2 Kings xxi. 2 Chron. xxxiii.)

When there arose a great tempest upon the sea, insomuch that the ship was overwhelmed with the waves, and Christ slept, then the disciples hasted unto him, and waked him up, saying, "Lord, help us, for we perish." (Matt. viii. Mark iv.)

The example of the heathen woman doth teach thee how the Lord prolongeth and deferreth his aid and help some time for the nonce[1], that we should be kindled up to cry the more fervently, and to continue importunately in earnest prayer.

St Austin writeth thus: "They that are godly are oppressed and vexed in the church or congregation for this purpose, that when they are pressed they should cry, and when they cry, that they should be heard, and when they are heard, that they should laud and praise God[2]."

And like as the cross and adversity doth further and prick us forward unto the first part of prayer, which is to desire and crave of God; even so doth it also further and

[1 Nonce: occasion, purpose.]
[2 The author does not mention from what part of the works of Augustine this passage is taken: the following is probably the place referred to: Videamus ergo hic quid admoneamur, et unde gratulemur, et unde gemamus, et unde auxilium postulemus, unde deseramur, unde nobis subveniatur, quid simus per nos, quid per misericordiam Dei, quomodo nostra superbia conteratur,—ut illius gratia glorificetur. * * * * Et audiamus jam, fratres, quonam ducitur iste populus Dei, quid hic agatur in congregatione omnium gentium redempta per Christum. August. Enarrat. in Psal. cvi. prop. init. Vol. VIII. p. 272, D. Ed. Par. 1541.]

provoke us all unto the second part of prayer, which is to laud God, and to give him thanks.

The almighty power, wisdom, righteousness, mercy, and truth of God, these high and excellent godly virtues, worthy of all laud and honour, do appear in the cross, affliction, and adversity of christian men, when God visiteth miserable sinners, comforteth those that are in distress and misery, helpeth and delivereth them out of all manner of necessity.

At these things do all christian people wonder and marvel highly, and therefore break they out to magnify, praise, and extol God with unspeakable lauds and praises.

"We have such a treasure in earthly vessels, that the power that lieth above, and hath the victory, might appear to be of God, and not of us," (2 Cor. iv.): that is to say, we are weak and miserable vessels, that God's honour and glory should be furthered, and not ours. 2 Cor. iv. 7.

For an example take the story of Daniel, chap. iii.; how the imprisonment and captivity of the Jews did serve wonderfully to the glory and praise of God. Our Saviour Christ sheweth the cause, why the man was blind from his very nativity and birth, namely, that the works of God should appear and be made manifest in him. (John ix.) Dan. iii. 28, 29. John ix. 3.

Moreover, all the prophets, apostles, and elect of God, by whom God wrought wonderful and marvellous things, were contemned and despised, yea, and sometimes slain and murdered, that all men might spy and perceive, that their faith and working, which did not shrink, but continued upright, was a work of God, and no power of man; and, therefore, that God must be lauded and praised above all. (Psalm xliv. Acts iv. v. Rom. viii. 2 Cor. iv. 1 Mac. ii. 2 Mac. vi. vii.)

---

## CHAPTER XII.

#### TROUBLE AND ADVERSITY DO FURTHER US IN VIRTUE AND GODLINESS.

THE cross and tribulation do banish and dry away the former sins, and hinder and resist those that are to come hereafter, and help to plant, exercise, and increase all man-

[COVERDALE.] 9

ner of virtues, that the ungodly may be provoked and furthered to repentance, and amendment, and reformation of their lives; and the godly to further virtue and godliness. For what affliction soever the flesh doth suffer, it grieveth it very sore; it would rather be merry, at rest, and quiet.

Now every one that hath any reason, knoweth this right well, that he through his own lusts and behaviour bringeth much adversity and affliction upon his own neck; and therefore, in consideration of that, he beginneth to beware, and to take heed afterward of all inordinate and dissolute living, as the cause, ground, and occasion of all misery and sorrow, that besides this present affliction he be not plagued also eternally. Which I will declare and prove, first with similitudes; secondarily, with testimonies of the holy scripture; and, thirdly, by familiar examples.

A water that is continually standing, how clear soever it seem, yet it is corrupt and naught; but that water which hath his continual course, the more it rusheth and struggleth over the stones and sands, the more lively, fresh, and better it is: even so a godly man, in the absence of the cross, is sluggish, dull, and litherly[1]; but through the cross and affliction he is quickened and exercised, and increased in all goodness. The rusty and cankered iron through the file is made bright and smooth: even so the old rusty Adam hath need of trouble and adversity to file and purge him from the cankered rust of sin.

A knife, though it be never so smooth, if it be not used, it waxeth rusty, and the same rust fretteth it and marreth it; but the more it is occupied, though it be somewhat worn thereby, yet it is the more bright: even so, although some person hath a good nature and inclination, if he be not occupied and exercised with trouble and adversity, he waxeth rusty, cankered, and rotten; but through the cross and tribulation, though the rust have worn somewhat off him, being a man and weak, yet he shall thereby be made more bright, clear, and beautiful again.

The seed that is cast into the field must suffer the wind, rain, snow, frost, and all manner of tempests, and yet it waxeth and bringeth forth fruit: even so the spiritual seed,

[1 Litherly: indolent.]

which is the word of God, being received of a devout and fervent heart, is not destroyed through trouble, but bringeth forth right good and profitable fruit. A walnut-tree, the more it is beaten, the better it is, and not the worse: even so man, through many stripes and much adversity, turneth from ill, and waxeth good.

For the thick and hard skin of a horse or an ass, is nothing better than a very sharp whip, to jerk him with: even so, for our stubborn and haughty flesh there is nothing more fit and profitable than much sorrow and vexation, whereby it may be stirred and pricked forward. Cloth must be oft beaten and brushed; whereupon there is a proverb: "Thus must woollen cloth be used, that there breed no moths in it." Even so shall spiritual moths and worms, wickedness, sin, and abomination, have the less power to breed in us, if we be well brushed and beaten in time with affliction and adversity.

The flesh that cometh fresh out of the shambles unsalted, waxeth soon unsavoury, and worms breed in it, but the salt with his sharpness keepeth it sweet from corruption: even so doth God cast and sprinkle salt upon us, through divers temptations and afflictions, that they may bite and season us, that we corrupt not, nor perish in sin.

That body that is always idle, and never moveth nor hath no exercise, is easily subject unto sickness and infirmities; but those bodies that have their exercise and labour, are more lusty and sound, and can better continue: even so the soul that is well exercised and occupied with trouble and affliction, hath occasion and cause to be beautiful, sound, and clear.

It is a very true saying, the sharper that the lye is, the cleaner taketh it away all manner of filth: even so our corrupt and poisoned nature had need of a sharp and a biting medicine. The greater and sharper the trouble and adversity is, the more filth and inconvenience it biteth away. For a raw and weak stomach, which is of a naughty digestion, bitter wormwood is very good and wholesome: even so for the weak and feeble soul is bitter trouble and affliction very wholesome and necessary.

Remember this proverb: "After the sick man hath recovered his sore, he liveth worse than ever he did before."

And therefore sickness is more necessary for him, that he wax not worse, and live not more wickedly.

Now will I allege scripture. God threateneth to send a plague sevenfold greater, if any man will not amend at the lighter and easier punishment that he sent first. Whereby the Lord himself declareth, through Moses, that trouble and adversity should teach us an alteration and amendment of our lives. (Lev. xxvi.)

<small>Lev. xxvi. 16, &c.</small>

"Strokes and wounds do purge and cleanse out evil and corruption, and stripes purify the inward parts of man." (Prov. xx.) "No manner of chastening for the present time seemeth to be joyous, but heavy and grievous; but afterward it bringeth a quiet fruit of righteousness unto those that are exercised therein." (Heb. xii.)

<small>Prov. xx. 30.</small>
<small>Heb. xii. 11.</small>

"He that suffereth in the flesh ceaseth from sin, that from henceforth the time that is remnant in the flesh, he may live not after the lusts of men, but after the will of God." (1 Pet. iv. Rom. vi.)

<small>1 Pet. iv. 1, 2. Rom. vi. 6.</small>

And this shall examples make more manifest. Under Joshua had the children of Israel many battles, and were driven to fight against their enemies; and they did never fall nor swerve from the Lord, until afterward that they came unto rest, and had all things plenty. Josh. i. Judg. ii.

<small>Judges ii. 6, &c.</small>

This is an example of a whole multitude. Now take examples of special persons.

The prophet Jonas, being in the whale's belly, remembered his sins, altered himself, turned, and was obedient unto God. (Jon. ii.) The lost and desperate son did then first of all run home again unto his father, when he saw and felt his misery and poverty. (Luke xv.)

Mark the daily experience. We imagine oft-times thus with ourselves: "Oh, if I were once whole and restored again, I would surely behave and order myself well as I ought to do, and would help and serve every man. Oh, if I were rich, I would gladly distribute unto the poor people faithfully." But as soon as we come out of the danger in deed, we have clean forgotten altogether.

As long as we have no manner of need, no man can hinder nor restrain our wickedness.

For an example, imagine two sundry houses, whereof in the one is celebrate and kept a marriage, where there is mirth, joy, and good cheer; and in the other is one sick on his dead-bed. In the bride-house, where is dancing, is used all manner of lightness and dissoluteness, gross and filthy words, bawdy songs and ballads, shameless behaviour and manners, and wanton and light apparel. One leapeth and winceth like a horse, another stampeth like an ass, the third drinketh himself drunk, and the fourth doeth nothing that honest is; so that a man might say the people were become very brute beasts. But by him that lieth on his dead-bed is all still, not a word spoken but honest and seemly. All things are done sadly, demurely, and discreetly.

And at that time not only the men, but also the women and children, and all that are in the house, are godly occupied: they pray, they comfort, and break out into such words as these: "What is man? How transitory and vain are all things that we have here upon earth! but in the life to come it shall be far otherwise." (Eccles. xiv. Job iv. x. xxxiv. Psal. lxxviii. xc. ciii. cxlvi. Isai. xl.)

Again, from the marriage or bride-house goeth many one home heavy and sad, vexed in his mind, and disdainful that he is not so happy and fortunate as other be; and suddenly is ravished with the beauty of some wife or maiden that he saw at the dancing, which hath wounded and stricken him to the heart. And when he cometh home, he looketh sourly on his wife, he is froward toward his children, and testy against all the household, so that no man can please him.

But he that goeth home from the mourning-house, thinketh himself well blessed and happy, that he himself lieth not in any such extreme necessity. If he hath had any sickness or vexation in time past, now he is able to bear it the more easily and patiently, when he compareth it to the grievous and intolerable pain of the man that lieth in pangs of death. By reason whereof he is the more patient, gentle, and friendly toward his wife, children, and his whole household; yea, he taketh occasion thereby to reform and amend his evil life.

## CHAPTER XIII.

### SORROW AND AFFLICTION DO HELP AND FURTHER US TOWARD THE FEAR AND LOVE OF GOD.

TROUBLE and affliction do engender the fear of God in them which suffer it, and in other likewise which do hear and know of it; so that many take example and instruction thereby, and afterward attempt not any thing timorously and rashly against the will and pleasure of God. For he is lawfully to be feared and dreaded, which can bring and lay upon us all manner of plagues, and also hath just cause and right toward us so to do. (Matt. x.)

<small>Matt. x. 28.</small>

Now we, being feeble and weak, are in no wise able to resist and withstand the strong and mighty God. No; we are not able to withstand or put off the least ill day of an ague; yea, we cannot choose but suffer the least and most contemptuous and feeble creatures to plague and disquiet us, as lice, fleas, flies, and such like vermin, which did master and overcome the mighty puissant king of Egypt. (Exod. vii. viii. ix. x. 2 Mac. ix. Acts xii.)

It is a very true proverb, "A burnt hand dreadeth the fire." For in the same sense and meaning spake Moses unto the fearful people: "God is come to tempt and prove you, that the fear of him may be before your eyes, to consider and remember that ye sin not." (Exod. xx. Deut. viii. and xiii. Judg. ii. and iii.)

As for an example: the more the Lord did exercise and hunt about David, the more diligently did he look upon the Lord, and feared him. 2 Sam. xv. And not only David, but others also, when they saw and perceived their misery and wretchedness, they took occasion thereby to fear God more than they did before; and specially when they saw afterward how God punished David's manslaughter and whoredom with sedition, uproar, murder, and with loss of much people. (2 Sam. xi. xiii. xiv. xv. xvi. &c.)

Holy scripture setteth before our eyes divers like terrible examples, that we should not esteem the fear of God for a light thing, but should be afraid of all manner of wickedness, sin, and abomination.

When a trespasser is led out to be headed, hanged, burnt, or otherwise to be punished, others that see him do learn to fear and to beware of that thing which brought him to his last end: even so when God sendeth any plague, either upon some special person, or else upon some whole community, all other ought so to consider the same, as though they themselves were in the place of the afflicted person, as though his trouble and sorrow were their own, that they may the rather fear God, and take heed that they fall not into like vengeance of God. And in very deed, as well the good and faithful, as the wicked and unfaithful, have cause to fear. (Prov. xi.) Prov. xi. 31.

For the faithful can consider thereby, that these transitory plagues are tokens and evident testimonies of the eternal punishments that are to come, which are a thousand thousand times more grievous, and never have end. (1 Pet. iv.) There- 1 Pet. iv. 17. fore both their own and other men's afflictions and sorrows do give them occasion enough to redress and forsake that thing, whereby all men do bring eternal plagues upon their necks.

The wicked and unfaithful, if they be not utterly obstinate and perverse, but have any use of reason at all, do also begin to fear God, and to think thus with themselves: If Jer. xxv. 29; xlix. 12. Ezek. ix. 6. Prov. xi. 31. 1 Pet. iv. 18. Luke xxiii. 31. God visiteth, scourgeth, and assaulteth with trouble and vexation the good and faithful, which are nothing so wicked as we, how shall it then go with us, which have deserved ten, yea, twenty times more grievous punishment than they? Jer. xxv. xlix. Ezek. ix. Prov. x. xi. 1 Pet. iv.)

"Mark and behold. I begin to plague the city whereunto my name is given: think ye then that ye shall escape free and unpunished? ye shall not go quit and free." (Jer. xxv.)

"If this be done in the green wood, what shall be done in the dry?" (Luke xxiii.) "It is time that judgment begin at the house of God. Seeing then it beginneth first with us, what an end shall they have which believe not the gospel of God!" (1 Pet. iv.)

An innocent dog, that hath not offended, is beaten before the lion; that the lion, when he knoweth that he hath angered and displeased his master, should be put in the more fear.' St Gregory writeth thus: "If God striketh those so sore whom he favoureth, how sharply and sore will he strike them which he favoureth not!"

The crucified and afflicted Christians do love God the more fervently, forasmuch as in the midst of the cross they feel the sweet comfort that cometh from their heavenly Father, of whose merciful will they cannot doubt nor mistrust.

A dog that is of a good nature, if his master strike him, yet he loveth his master notwithstanding, and fawneth again upon him. A good child, although it be beaten, yet it loveth the father or mother nevertheless, and desireth to have their favour again: even in like manner are the true Christians minded toward their heavenly Father; but such children as be wicked, and of an evil disposition, when they be a little scourged, they run away from their fathers, and murmur against them.

## CHAPTER XIV.

### TROUBLE AND AFFLICTION IS GOOD AND PROFITABLE TO TEACH MEN PATIENCE, MEEKNESS, AND LOWLINESS.

PRIDE is a dangerous thing, whereof cometh no manner of good. Now felicity and prosperity, all at pleasure, engendereth pride and contempt of other people; but the cross and affliction engendereth meekness and lowliness, that a man is not too proud in his own conceit, but is content that other be esteemed as well as he, confessing himself to have need of their help and counsel.

Like as men use to clip and to cut shorter the feathers of birds or other fowls, when they begin to fly too high or too far from them; even so doth God diminish our riches, possessions, estimation, honour, authority, and power, that we should not pass our bounds, and glory too much of such gifts. Like as the body, when it is wearied and consumed with labour and travail, desireth ease and rest, that it may lie still; even so the soul, being laden and oppressed with trouble and affliction, is brought to a narrow issue, and then it hasteth after rest and quietness, and nothing vexeth it less than pride.

Nebuchadnezzar did glory of his power, victorious acts, and costly buildings, and was wonderfully proud of them; but after his fall and adversity he learned to ascribe all laud, honour, and glory unto God. (Dan. iv.) Paul confesseth that a buffet was given him of the messenger of Satan, that he should not glory out of measure in the abundance of revelations. (2 Cor. xii.) Experience itself teacheth, that when rich, famous, notable, and proud men are robbed and spoiled of their goods, they are afterward more humble, meek, and gentle; for then they perceive the uncertainty and unstableness of temporal and transitory things, and so learn, the longer they live, the less to trust themselves. Therefore trouble and affliction is oft-times as necessary unto men as meat and drink. <sub>Dan. iv. 37.</sub> <sub>2 Cor. xii. 7.</sub>

The cross, adversity, and affliction maketh a man soft, tame, patient, sober, loving and friendly, both towards himself, and towards all other also. <sub>Meekness and lowliness.</sub>

A piece of iron or of silver stricken or beaten with a hammer waxeth broader, thinner, smoother, and softer: even so the stony and hard hearts of men, through heaviness and adversity, are made more buxom and pliant, that a man may wind them, as a man might say, even round about his finger.

A curst wild colt hath a snaffle put in his mouth, that he bite not him that handleth him: even so the snaffle of the cross and adversity doth let and hinder us, being froward, furious, and full of spite, malice and vengeance, that we commit the less wickedness, abomination, and uncharitableness in our lives.

For an example: the furious raging king Manasses was meek, still, and tame enough, after that he was once bound, taken prisoner, and led away captive. (2 Kings xxi. 2 Chron. xxxiii.) <sub>2 Kings xxi. 16. 2 Chron. xxxiii. 11—14.</sub>

Paul before Damascus was stricken down as a raging and raving wolf; but he rose up again a meek lamb. (Acts ix.) <sub>Acts ix. 6.</sub>

## CHAPTER XV.

### TROUBLE AND ADVERSITY IS GOOD TO TEACH MEN PITY, COMPASSION, AND PATIENCE TOWARDS OTHER.

<small>John xiii. 14.
Rom. xv. 1.
Gal. vi. 1.
Eccl. vii. 2.
Matt. xi. 8.</small>

To have pity and compassion of people that are in misery and distress, is a christian and a necessary virtue; but he that never felt temptation, adversity, or affliction himself, can have but little pity and compassion of other. One sick man can tell the lack and necessity of another, one poor man likewise of another; and also one that is in misery and affliction himself, knoweth the better the grief of another that is in like case.

As for an example: why and for what cause can our high priest Christ have such pity and compassion upon us miserable wretches, that we dare be bold to come unto him cheerfully without fear, and to look for succour, help, and comfort at his hands? Forsooth, even for this cause and by this means, as saith St Paul, that he was also tempted, and <small>Heb. ii. 18; v. 7.</small> suffered most bitter pain and grief himself. (Heb. ii.) And very experience doth teach even the self-same thing also. For whosoever hath once lien sick in a spital-house himself, can have the more compassion of other that are in like case afterward, and is ever after the more ready and prompt to help those that be in such case.

The noble and precious virtue called patience hath no place to put her head in in the time of prosperity. When a man hath been a long season healthful and without any manner of sickness, he cannot take sickness by and by so patiently as he ought to do: and likewise he that never felt any affliction or adversity, whensoever any happen unto him, he is sore vexed with impatientness.

But adversity teacheth men patience, and practiseth them therein. First, when a man seeth that all goeth backward and against him, and that it will be no better, but rather worse and worse; what doth he, but of this necessity maketh a virtue, and so is content, and at a point, howsoever it goeth with him?

Secondarily, when a man is continually used to trouble and affliction, this same use and custom maketh it light and easy unto him, especially considering that God will also help, aid, and comfort him. Paul saith, "Trouble or affliction bringeth patience, and patience bringeth experience," &c. (Rom. v.) Rom. v. 3, 4. The desperate and lost son learned such patience in his misery and affliction, that he said to his father, "Take nor use me not from henceforth as a son, but as an hired servant. I desire no more, but that I may remain in thy house." (Luke xv.) Even so ought we also to suffer all things willingly and patiently, whatsoever they be, so that God will not banish and put us out of his house.

Unto that noble heathen man Socrates did his curst and shrewd wife serve for this use and purpose, that he, learning patience at home, might the better suffer, and the more patiently bear the people that he had to do with abroad.

---

## CHAPTER XVI.

### TROUBLE AND ADVERSITY MAKETH MEN HARD AND STRONG, AND TEACHETH THEM SOBERNESS AND TEMPERANCY.

An ox getteth himself harder hoofs upon rough stubble, and crabbed ground, and is able to draw and to labour better, than if he were fed in rank pasture. Those children that are nursed by fremde[1] men's fires, are for the most part more hard and strong than they which are daintily brought up in all excess, and wantonness, and superfluity, in their own fathers' houses. Even so the wits and minds of men, through pleasure and abundance, wax tender and weak, and effeminate and wild; but being restrained through some painful necessity and affliction, they wax harder, stronger, and more manly and sober. For an example: the dear holy apostles, the more persecution and affliction they had, the more bold, strong, and constant were they, as the Acts of the Apostles do testify throughout.

Paul saith, "I am content, and think myself well in infirmities, in rebukes, in persecutions, in anguishes for

[1 frombdc: strange, foreign.]

Christ's sake; for when I am in such weakness, then am I strong." (2 Cor. xii.) The physician, when he perceiveth that his patient will eat over-much, and will wax too fat, he measureth and restraineth him, and by breaking somewhat from him, he restoreth him to his health again, and so saveth him: even so, when we do shamefully misuse wine, corn, bread, and drink, and other gifts and creatures of God, to maintain drunkenness, surfeiting, excess, and riot, then doth God punish us with hunger, dearth, penury, and with other plagues, that we should learn thereby to be temperate, and to keep measure, and to use his benefits thankfully. It is said, the hour of punishment and of correction maketh us to forget all manner of pleasure and lust (Eccles. xi.): as David soon forgot his lusty pleasures and wantonness utterly, when Absalom drave him out of his kingdom. (2 Sam. xiii. &c.)

*2 Cor. xii. 10. Temperancy and measure.*

*Ecclus. xi. 27.*

## CHAPTER XVII.

### TROUBLE AND ADVERSITY TEACHETH MEN TO CONTEMN, DESPISE, AND DEFY THE WORLD, AND TO BE DILIGENT AND FERVENT IN ALL GODLINESS AND VIRTUE.

THE cross and adversity taketh from us the love of the world, and driveth away all manner of dangerous and delicious lusts and pleasures of this transitory life. We would fain be rich, but God giveth us poverty; we desire health of body, but God giveth us sickness; and so nurtureth and nurseth us in misery and with affliction, that we can no more tell what a delicious and tender pleasant life in this world meaneth; and thus begin we to contemn and loathe all transitory things, and to desire another, better, more precious, and an eternal life, where all manner of misery shall have an end.

He that taketh a journey in hand, and goeth into a strange country, when he cometh into a pleasant town, where he meeteth merry company and good companions, peradventure he spendeth away the time, and tarrieth too long among them, and so forgetteth his household and things at home. But if one hard mischance after another happen unto him, then he maketh the more haste home again to his wife and children, where he hath more rest and quietness.

Even so, when these transitory things, as riches, health, beauty, much profit, honour, and dignity happen unto us, if we will once gape upon them and delight so much in them, that we do the less regard and esteem the heavenly life, then will God make the way rough and crabbed unto us here in this life, that we should not take and esteem this transitory life in this world for our right natural country, towards the which we take our journey.

For example: the children of Israel had little lust to sing and to play upon any pleasant instruments, when they sat as prisoners by the rivers in Babylon. (Psal. cxxxvii.)

Psal. cxxxvii. 4.

And this may a man see and prove now-a-days by those that are in any dangerous sickness, or in any hard prison, or in any anguish and misery, who before were too fond upon eating, drinking, gallant apparel, dancing, toying, playing, and gaming, or upon such like worldly felicity. For the cross and its heaviness wipe away and lick off all such things as clean, as the hot sun licketh and melteth away the snow.

Furthermore, they that be poor and in distress and heaviness, are always readier to forsake this world, and are more desirous to depart hence to God, than those that have riches, health, and felicity at pleasure. And therefore St Austin, in his book *De Symbolo*, writeth thus: "Behold, how God hath replenished and filled the world with so many afflictions, and so much troublesome adversity. It is bitter, and yet it is loved; it is ruinous, and ready to fall, and yet it is inhabited. O thou, my dear darling world, what should we do, if thou wert sweet, stable, and permanent, seeing we do thus now? O thou foul and unclean world, if thou art bitter, and yet deceivest and beguilest us, whom wouldest thou not deceive and beguile, if thou wert sweet?"[1]

[[1] Ecce ruinosus est mundus, ecce tantis calamitatibus replevit Deus mundum, ecce amarus est mundus, et sic amatur: quid faceremus, si dulcis esset? O munde immunde, teneri vis periens: quid faceres, si maneres? Quem non deciperes dulcis, si amarus alimenta mentiris? Augustin. de Symbolo, ad Catechumenos. Lib. IV. Cap. I. Opera. Tom. IX. p. 246, G. Ed. Paris. 1541.]

*Diligence and fervency.*

And the cross doth not only drive and set us forward to all manner of virtue, and putteth us in mind of all godliness, but it quickeneth and kindleth also a diligence and fervency in us, to proceed and go forward in all goodness lustily, stoutly, earnestly, manfully, and not litherly or faintly.

Like as a man sometime must spur his horse, although he be a good and quick horse, that he may go and run the faster and speedier; even so we cannot go forward in our vocation and calling so speedily nor so well as we ought to do, except we be pricked forward with sharp spurs and scourges. When the master striketh his slothful, dull, and sleepy servant, then he laboureth the more diligently, and is more profitable unto him: even so we all, for the most part of us, have the nature of such slothful and sluggish servants, which will do nothing well, except we be driven by compulsion, and even whipped and beaten unto it.

Although those be evil servants, which will do nothing[1] unless a man be ever upon their bones with a cudgel, yea, and then will do nothing well either; yet notwithstanding must a man never cease driving and forcing of them, until such time as they begin to amend and to serve willingly and with a good heart: even so, although no compelled service, that is violently wrung out of a man, doth please God, yet the continual inuring and exercising in goodness may make it at length so pleasant and delectable unto us, that we shall have delight therein.

## CHAPTER XVIII.

TROUBLE AND ADVERSITY IS ALSO AN OCCASION AND HELP OF MUCH TRANSITORY QUIETNESS AND COMMODITY IN THIS WORLD.

HITHERTO have we taught of the spiritual profit of adversity, whereby the soul of man is endued and garnished with wisdom and all kinds of virtue: now let us see what transitory commodities do oft accompany or follow after

[1 Peterborough copy: nothing well.]

trouble and adversity. Such as dwell in valleys and in deep and low habitations, are not lightly hurt by any lightning: even so that state of life that is low and mean keepeth and maintaineth itself most sure and with least danger against all manner of storms.

Like as precious and costly spices and odours do smell and savour best, when they are bruised, broken, or set on fire; even so the praise and commendation of virtue, through continual use and exercise and through adversity, is spread wide abroad, and made manifest and known everywhere.

For an example: What an excellent and singular honour, renown, praise, and commendation was it unto Abraham at length, that he went out of his natural country into banishment, and there suffered great trouble and much adversity! The children of Israel were sore kept under and oppressed in Egypt; but they were led out and set free again with such glory and renown, as never was heard nor read the like.

The banishment of Ulysses for the space of ten years, was an occasion unto him to exercise and practise his wisdom and other virtues in the mean time; so that he obtained thereby an immortal name among all the heathen.

And to speak after the common practice and experience, Joy. there is no exceeding joy or triumph, but some sorrow or heaviness goeth before it. The spring-time, following and coming immediately upon the rough and hard winter, is the more acceptable, pleasant, and welcome unto us.

In battle, the sorer our enemies do assault and fight against us, the greater is the joy and triumph at the victory and overthrow of them.

He that hath kept his bed a long time, and lain sick a great season, afterward when he is recovered, health is a more precious treasure unto him, than ever it was before that he felt what sickness was; and also such as mourned and were sorry for his sickness, do receive an infinite joy and an exceeding rejoicing at his restoring unto health again.

Even so doth God deprive us for a time of riches, wealth, prosperity, our natural country, bodily health, and such other transitory benefits, for this purpose, that when he giveth them again unto us, we may the more rejoice and be the gladder of them.

An example have we of the lost sheep and of the lost and desperate son; for the which there was such joy at the finding of them again, as never had been, if they had not been lost; whereas before there was never thought nor sorrow taken for them. (Matt. xviii. Luke xv.) Now in case we never find nor have restored unto us again here in this world that thing which we have lost, yet our conscience is both quiet and also joyful in God: which quietness and joy far exceedeth all the pleasures of the whole world.

*Welfare and felicity.*

In summa, to be short, after trouble and adversity followeth all manner of goodness and felicity: first, forasmuch as God here in this world doth plentifully and richly reward and recompense godliness, patience, and godly constancy; secondarily, forasmuch as this is the nature and property of God, to throw down, that he may raise up again, and to bring unto death's door, that he may restore unto life again.

*Deut. xxxii. 39.*
*1 Sam. ii. 6—8.*
*Psal. cxii. 4.*
*Wisd. xvi. 13.*

(Deut. xxxii. 1 Sam. ii. Psal. cxii. Wisd. xvi.)

Roses, which are the most pleasant flowers, do spring and wax out of thorns: even so of hard and great travail springeth the most pleasant fruit.

The little bee gathereth the sweetest honey out of the most bitter blooms and flowers: even so men of wisdom and understanding receive much utility and fruit of the present sorrow and affliction.

*Gen. xxxvii. xxxix. xli.*

For example: Joseph was hated of his brethren, and sold of them into a strange and foreign country; which banishment of his turned to his great honour, wealth, and profit, forasmuch as he was lord and governor over the whole kingdom of Egypt. The more the great tyrant Pharao went about to oppress and rid the children of Israel out of his land, the more did they prosper and increase to an infinite number. (Exod. i.)

The devil left nothing unto the godly man Job, but deprived and spoiled him of all that he had; but the Lord restored him all again double, even in this world. (Job i. xlii.) He that marketh and considereth well, shall perceive that some time a man, being of no reputation at home where he is known, is banished away, and cometh to other people, which do highly esteem him, and make much of him, yea, and highly honour him; so that oft-times a man's adversity hath turned to his singular commodity and wealth. (Matt. xiii. Mark vi. Luke iv. John iv.)

<small>Matt. xiii. 53—57<br>Mark vi. 1—4.<br>Luke iv. 24.<br>John iv. 44.</small>

## CHAPTER XIX.

### TROUBLE AND ADVERSITY IS A FURTHERANCE TO ETERNAL LIFE.

THE trouble and adversity of the godly do give an exceeding great testimony unto them of immortality, of a general judgment, and also of an everlasting life. For it is impossible that the best creatures only should be ordained and created to all sorrow and travail, and the most wicked and ungodly to escape and remain unpunished. It were directly against the righteousness of God.

Now it is evident, that here upon earth appeareth no difference between Paul and Nero, having respect to the reward of them both; yea, the most godly and virtuous have most commonly worse luck and least reward. Wherefore of necessity there must needs be another life to come, where every one shall receive according to the demerits of his life here upon earth.

And again, the cross way is pointed to be the very right way unto eternal life. (Psalm xliv. Rom. viii. 2 Cor. iv.) Like as the corn is first threshed, fanned, and rid from the chaff, and then laid up and reserved in the barn; even so christian men upon earth are beaten, mishandled, evil entreated; whereby they are purged of many wild and light manners, and so are brought into the everlasting barn of the kingdom of heaven.

Like as no man can triumph or be crowned, except he hath foughten and warred manfully (1 Cor. ix. 2 Tim. ii.); which cannot be without great danger, labour, and travail; even so can no man attain to the crown of eternal life,

<small>1 Cor. ix. 25.<br>2 Tim. ii. 5.</small>

[COVERDALE.]

except he hath first suffered much trouble, sorrow, and adversity. (2 Tim. iv. 1 Pet. v. James i. Rev. ii. iii.)

<small>2 Tim. iv. 8.<br>1 Pet. iv. 12.<br>James i. 12.<br>Rev. ii. 10;<br>iii. 21.</small>

The man that is sick must receive the purgation and medicine, how sour or bitter soever it be, that he may the sooner recover his health again, and not die: even so, when we suffer the hand of God to rule and order us, being content and patient therewith, although it smarteth and grieveth us, yet it shall profit and help us to everlasting health and soundness.

Testimonies and witness of scripture to prove this: "Blessed are they that mourn, for they shall be comforted." (Matt. v.) "Narrow is the gate and strait is the way that leadeth to life." (Matt. vii.) "Blessed are they that weep here, for they shall laugh; but woe unto you that be rich," &c. (Luke vi.) "We must enter into the kingdom of God through much trouble and affliction." (Acts xiv.) "If we be children, then are we heirs, namely, the heirs of God and fellow-heirs of Christ; so that we suffer with him, that we may also be glorified together with him." (Rom. viii.)

<small>Matt. v. 4.<br>Matt. vii. 13.<br>Luke vi. 21.<br>Acts xiv. 22.<br>Rom. viii. 17.</small>

By these words doth Paul evidently declare, that he that will reign with Christ must also run through the fire with him. "When we are judged, we are chastened of the Lord, that we should not be condemned with the world." (1 Cor. xi.)

<small>1 Cor. xi. 39.</small>

## CHAPTER XX.

HOW AND IN WHAT RESPECT TROUBLE AND ADVERSITY CAN BE SO PROFITABLE AND OF SUCH VIRTUE, SEEING THAT THE UNFAITHFUL DO WAX MORE OBSTINATE AND PERVERSE THROUGH TROUBLE AND AFFLICTION.

HITHERTO have we entreated of the corporal and spiritual, temporal and eternal profit and commodity, which christian men receive by the cross, trouble, and adversity. Which is not to be taken after this sense, as though the cross or adversity of itself, and of her own nature, could bring and work such high commodities; for then should Pharao and other wicked persons, in their trouble and adversity, have been converted and so saved also. But the Spirit of God resteth secretly, and lieth hidden in the faithful under the shadow and back of the cross, and purgeth, reformeth, comforteth, and strengtheneth them, and worketh all these foresaid commodities in them.

Now like as the holy scripture attributeth a certain reward unto our good works, which works notwithstanding, it is not we that work them, but the Lord, which useth us as instruments of his; even so is the cross an instrument of God, whereby he subdueth our flesh, keepeth us in the school of correction, and forceth us, as it were by violence, from evil to goodness. (Phil. ii. 2 Cor. i.) *Phil. ii. 2 Cor. i.*

Now, wheresoever the Holy Ghost will take his resting-place, for the most part he sendeth before his purveyors and forerunners, which are sorrow and affliction, trouble and adversity; that they may vex, cumber, humble, meeken, and utterly overthrow and bring down the heart of man, whereby the Holy Ghost may find the more place, and so work all goodness therein.

And therefore whatsoever is hitherto spoken, specially of the spiritual commodities of the cross and adversity, it is and so remaineth all truth; so that it be understood of the faithful and godly, which are endued with the Spirit of God, to whom all things turn to their comfort and salvation.

And now, on the contrary part, for the better understanding of the matter, I will declare and shew what the cross worketh in the unfaithful and ungodly, which lack the Spirit of God. The unfaithful do ascribe their prosperity and felicity to their own wisdom, working, and policy, and not to God; and their misfortune and adversity they ascribe to blind fortune, as though fortune had a certain power to work of herself, without the working of God. *The cross of the unfaithful.*

Take Sennacherib, the lord and ruler of the Assyrians, for an example; which by the sufferance of God brought the whole world in manner in subjection; which thing he ascribed to his own power and policy, and not to God;

for he did both hate and blaspheme the very true God of Israel. But shortly after did God send an angel, which slew in one night an hundred fourscore and five thousand of his men. And here would he not confess that it was God that did it; but peradventure he thought that it was fortune, mischance, or some other thing that was the occasion. For if he had knowledged this punishment to have come and been of God, he would not afterward have worshipped and done his devotion in the idolaters' temple of the false god and idol Nisroch, as he did. In like manner, when any misfortune happeneth to the ungodly, they put all the fault only in the next middle or mean, that they fantasy themselves; or else very wickedly they ascribe it unto all those that are not of their faith and sect.

<small>2 Kings xix. 35.</small>

As for example: when as it rained not for the space of three years and six months in the time of Achab the king of Israel, the king imputed the cause unto the godly prophet Helias. (1 Kings xviii.) Likewise in our time, when any tempest hurteth the corn, wine, and other fruits of the earth, many there are that cry, This may we thank this new learning for, and this new-fangled faith, &c.: as though they themselves were so holy, that God durst not or ought not to punish them. It can be none but the poor sheep that disturbeth the water, that the wolf cannot drink: whereas, indeed, the poor sheep cometh but only to the brink, and at the very brink of the river drinketh.

<small>1 Kings xviii. 17.</small>

Yea, even they also which have some taste of the gospel, cannot well bear adversity patiently, nor confess themselves guilty; but would fain shift the fault from themselves, and would lay it either upon the rulers or the preachers, or else upon some other thing.

And although their sins be an exceeding heap, and that God would fain drive them to repentance by punishing and chastising of them; yet cannot they consider the heavy burden of their sin, nor spy the clear day of the righteousness of God, which can suffer no sin unpunished.

And, therefore, forasmuch as they will not take this small and light punishment thankfully, but would go free, and have no manner of plague at all, if they might choose; for that cause doth God send unto them afterward plagues and painful punishments by heaps; so that it happeneth unto them as it did unto the ass, whose skin being put over a drum or a tabor, as he wished and desired, was beaten and stricken more than ever it was before, as Æsop saith in his fables.

And forasmuch as through incredulity and lack of faith, which is the mother of all blasphemies and abomination, they will not consider nor call to remembrance, who it is that hath laid his hand upon them; or else, knowing that it is the hand of God, yet will not take it in good worth, nor amend no otherwise but as sour ale in summer; by this means they become like unto desperate children, which will neither turn and amend with threatening, nor yet with beating. *Lack of faith is the mother of all blasphemies and abomination.*

And therefore the scripture testifieth very well, that one sharp word of reproach doth more good to him that hath understanding, than an hundred stripes to a fool. (Prov. xvii.) *Prov. xvii. 10.*

As for example: the longer and the sharper that God punished Pharao, the more obstinately did he swerve and decline from him. The wicked and ungodly do not only take no manner of occasion to reform and amend their lives by their cross and sorrow, but also they pour out all manner of impatientness, bitterness, and spiteful poison against the righteousness of God, saying their cross is greater than their transgression, and that they have wrong and are punished too sore.

As for an example of this, we have one of the thieves hanging upon the cross with Christ, which blasphemed Christ very spitefully, saying, "If thou beest Christ, help both thyself and us." (Luke xxiii.) By the which words he declareth, that he judgeth himself even as worthy of help, as Christ the Son of God; even as though God must forget all his righteousness, and help by and by every blasphemous wretch, and look through the fingers upon the wicked world: which is one of the greatest blasphemies unto God that can be. *Luke xxiii. 39.*

When they have tumbled and weltered in their misery, (for God will not help them, because they have no trust nor confidence in him,) and have sought help by creatures both in heaven and earth, and found none; then beginneth their cross and adversity to open their eyes so wide, that they must needs spy and acknowledge the wrath and hand of God over them. And then doth this outward cross and sorrow even kindle in them an inward trembling and doubtfulness, out of the which springeth the highest desperation; insomuch that they cry out to the devil to help them, if God will not. (1 Sam. xxviii.)

<small>1 Sam. xxviii. 8.</small>

For although they be brought to the knowledge of their sin, and also to sorrow and repentance for the same through the cross, as Cain and Judas also were, yet have they no trust nor confidence that the same sin shall be taken from them and forgiven them, but rave and rage and give themselves over to the devil, and so depart wretchedly out of this world. (Gen. iv. Matt. xxvii.)

<small>Gen. iv. 14. Matt. xxvii. 5.</small>

Of whose destruction yet and confusion these commodities do ensue: first, that they must of force cease any longer to make any disturbance by the wicked example of their life in the church and regiment of God; secondarily, that they which remain alive after them may learn by their terrible example to repent and amend by times.

So that by this that we have hitherto declared, every christian man may know in his trouble and adversity, whether he be a martyr of God or of the devil, and what great profit and singular commodity all those that are God's martyrs do receive by the means of their cross, trouble, and martyrdom.

## CHAPTER XXI.

#### FELLOW-COMPANIONS IN TROUBLE AND ADVERSITY.

Why should any man shew and behave him impatiently in suffering the thing, which he can by no policy, counsel, nor lawful mean avoid, alter, turn, remedy, or amend? He that is wise maketh of such a necessity, as can by no remedy be avoided, a very virtue.

Now trouble and adversity doth so happen unto man, that he cannot help nor avoid it, though he would never so fain. Man must needs suffer trouble and adversity upon earth; there is no remedy.

And again, why should any man without measure becumber himself about that thing which is common unto all men, or to the most part, and not to him alone? By natural reason, that burden is lighter which many do bear together.

Now is the life of man a very miserable and lamentable thing. When another man prospereth, so that all things go well with him, yet it fareth with him even as with a bloom or a flower in the field, which flourisheth for a while, and is pleasant and delectable to look upon; within a little while after it drieth up and fadeth away. *Psal. ciii. 15; xc. 5, 6; lxxviii. 40. Isai. xl. 6, 7. Ecclus. xvii. 17, 18. 1 Pet. i. 24. James i. 10.*

As long as we are upon earth, we are, as it were, in a camp or a siege, where we must ever be skirmishing and fighting, and know neither who shall break out and give the onset against us, nor where, nor how, nor when. Sometime a man is attacked and assaulted in his body, in his goods, in his name and fame. Sometime happen unto him common mischances, as dearth, pestilence, war, which sometime continue very long, so that he may well say, no misfortune cometh alone, but bringeth one or other companion with it.

If not at that present, yet hereafter it may; and there is no misfortune so great, but may happen and light upon any of us all. At least ways we must all look for death, as it was said long ago unto our first parents. (Gen. iii.)

To rehearse examples it were but folly and superfluous, forasmuch as there is no man but may lawfully complain of one thing or other; and although some things happen after our minds, yet it is not without some sour sauce.

And specially at this present, how are all christian realms compassed with sorrows, troubles, and miseries on every side! Look but upon our own country: there is neither good nor bad, godly nor ungodly, but hath one cross or other.

And although some there be that can shift for a while, and can make provision for themselves for a time by craft, subtilty, and dissimulation, or by some falsehood in fellowship, as they call it; yet they bring themselves at length into the highest danger, confusion, and shame, both in this world and in the world to come.

And seeing that all the troubles and adversities in this world are a thousand times lighter and easier, yea, nothing in the respect of the eternal unquenchable fire, which is prepared and already kindled for the unfaithful and wicked enemies of God; all faithful and godly persons ought to bear and suffer their transitory afflictions and adversities the more patiently, willingly, and thankfully, considering and remembering all the dear beloved friends of God, which were wonderfully vexed and plagued of their enemies. (Rom. viii. 2 Cor. iv. v. Matt. xxv. Isai. xxx.)

<small>Rom. viii. 18. 2 Cor iv. 17; v. 4. Matt. xxv. 46. Isai. xxx. 33.</small>

Abraham of the Chaldees, Lot of the Sodomites, Isaac of Ismael, Jacob of Esau, Moyses of his people, David of Saul, and of his own son. As for Job, he had not one drop of blood in his body unconsumed. (Gen. xii. xix. xxxii. xxxiii. Num. xx. 1 Sam. xv. Job ii.)

John Baptist, the holiest that ever was naturally born of a woman, was without any manner of form or order of law, right, or reason, beheaded in the prison, as though God had known nothing at all of him. (Matt. xiv. Mark vi.)

We have many thousand fellow-martyrs and companions of our misery and adversity, in respect of whose imprisonment, racking, chains, fire, wild beasts, and other means wherewith they are tormented, all that we suffer is but a wind or a pastime.

But specially this is to be considered above all other in our trouble and adversity, that we have Jesus Christ for a fellow and companion with us therein, which suffered upon earth in his body all manner of smart and pain. (Isai. liii. Matt. xxvii. Mark xv.)

Now is not the servant above the master. What reason were it that the natural Son of God, being utterly innocent, should be so cruelly entreated and mishandled; and we which are his children, not by nature, but by adoption and election, and in all points guilty, should escape quit and free? (Matt. x. John i. Rom. viii. 1 Cor. v.)

<small>Matt. x. 24. John i. 12. Rom. viii. 17. 1 Cor. v. 5.</small>

Therefore now, whosoever is ashamed of the cross, and aggrieved therewith, the same is ashamed and aggrieved to have Christ for his fellow and companion, and therefore shall the Lord Jesus Christ be ashamed of him again at the latter day. (Gal. iv. Eph. i.)

<small>Gal. iv. 6. Ephes. i 5, &c.</small>

# THE SECOND PART OF THIS BOOK.

## CHAPTER XXII.

BY WHAT NATURAL MEANS OR WAYS TROUBLE AND ADVERSITY MAY BE QUALIFIED, EASED, AND OVERCOME.

FIRST and foremost, no man ought to meddle with other men's matters, which appertain nothing unto him, nor to cast himself into peril and danger without any need. For that were as much as to tempt God, and were clean contrary to the examples both of our Saviour Christ, and also of the holy apostles; which by the commandment of Christ did sometime flee and avoid perils and dangers. (Matt. x.) Matt. x. 23. But a man cannot always honestly and conveniently avoid them.

Therefore, for the second point, like as a waterman will never let out his sail so far, but that he may soon pull it in again; even so every man, as long as all things stand well and upright with him, let him foresee and prepare in time for the contrary.

For the which cause the Lord did tell his disciples of his cross, death, and passion before, that they, seeing him suffer anguish and sorrow, might the less quail and shrink at it. In like manner did he also declare before unto them, that they must be persecuted and suffer trouble, that they might look for it, and be the more hardy, bold, and strong in persecution, whensoever it should happen. (Matt. xvi. xvii. xx. Mark viii. ix. x. Luke ix. xviii.) Matt. xvi. 21, 24; xvii. 12<br>xx. 18, 19.<br>Mark viii. 31, 34; ix. 12; x. 32—40.<br>Luke ix. 44; xviii. 31—33.

Thirdly, a great weight and substance of the matter dependeth and hangeth upon this point, that a man conceive a right judgment and opinion of all things that happen and chance. For every thing appeareth so unto us, even as we in our thoughts and minds do fancy, imagine, and conceive it.

If a man esteem worldly goods for a light thing, as they ought in very deed to be esteemed, then can he forbear the same with the less grief and pain. Contrariwise, if he make a god of them, and esteem them highly, then he trembleth, quaketh, and taketh on unmeasurably, when he is spoiled and deprived of them.

In like manner in other things, a man oft-times fancieth and imagineth in himself, that he can abide and suffer no manner of misfortune; when as if it were well considered, that present evil, which he so feared, should soon seem but a trifle and no misfortune, but rather a blessing or a good turn. And though it be not light and small in deed, yet let it be esteemed and taken for light, forasmuch as it cometh alone, and bringeth not two, three, or an hundred companions with it.

For it is a wonder and a singular miracle of God, that among such infinite and innumerable perils as the world and Satan have ready prepared, and even bent over us, we are not utterly headlong overwhelmed, and suddenly destroyed of them all. (1 Pet. v.) And yet God sendeth and mixeth always some goodness and comfort between.

1 Pet. v. 8.

As, thou hast peradventure a sickly and diseased body, but yet thy mind and heart is sound and strong. Or thou art vexed and cumbered in thy mind, yet hast thou an whole and a sound body. Or peradventure thou art robbed, spoiled, and deprived of thy temporal and worldly goods, and other transitory pleasures; yet thou hast many and divers christian virtues and singular gifts of grace; where is a thousand times more felicity than in all health, beauty, strength, riches, friendship, wife, children, honour, dignity, or power; for this is not written in vain: "O Lord, the earth is full of thy goodness." (Psal. civ.)

Psal. civ. 24.

Here should an heart and mind that is vexed and cumbered cease and leave off from the consideration of the present misery and affliction, and call to remembrance what other benefits of God do yet remain, or what other we have had, or at least what are yet to come and to happen to all faithful Christians. And therefore there is an old common proverb, good to be remembered: "In adversity remember prosperity; and again, in prosperity think upon adversity."

Again, oft-times many a loss and mischance weareth lightly away again, and is soon remedied another way. As, if some special friend of thine be taken from thee by death, thou mayest happen upon another as good for him, or else some other benefits may happen unto thee for that loss within a while.

And be it in case that thy misery and misfortune continue a long while, yet is all manner of trouble that we suffer upon earth transitory, ever passing away, and not durable nor perpetual.

The length and process of time doth mitigate, ease, assuage, and lighten all manner of smart, pain, and grief, if the mind be a while used unto it, and somewhat exercised and waxen hard in it. Yet such as be wise ought not to tarry, till smart and grief wear and fret away of itself, but to prevent the time by such means as we have hitherto taught, and hereafter shall follow.

Fourthly, ordinary means are not to be contemned, despised, nor refused. Like as a ship-master being upon the water, and foreseeing a tempest to be at hand, calleth upon God's aid and help; and yet for all that he hath also a sure eye to the stern, to rule that as handsomely and cunningly as he can. (Acts xxvii.)

Even so in all manner of necessities and perils it is lawful, and men ought also to use all manner of honest and convenient means; as physic and medicines in sickness; labour and travail with the sweat of our brows in poverty; the power and authority of the magistrate in wrong, injury, debate, and dissension; battle array against the enemies of our country, and such like: so that no man build nor trust in any manner of thing, saving in the very living God only, which can help, deliver, and remedy all things, without any middle or mean, if there were none at hand. (Gen. iii. Matt. ix. 1 Sam. x.)

Fifthly, when a man waiteth, tendeth upon, and serveth his honest craft, science, vocation, or office, whereunto God hath called him, and studieth to execute, perform, and follow it diligently, as he ought to do, it driveth away many evil and vain fancies from a troubled mind, that is cumbered with any grief or affliction.

Sixthly, like as weak, tender, and diseased eyes are refreshed and quickened with green and fresh pleasant colours; even so cumbered and troubled minds are wonderfully refreshed, revived, and restored to strength through seemly, honest, and measurable mirth and pastime ; as through hearing of instruments of music, by walking abroad, by altering and changing of the air, and by going out of such places as be obscure and dark into such as be very lightsome.

And specially for a man in his trouble to visit his special friends, or to be visited of them, bringeth a double comfort and easement unto his sorrowful and unquiet mind.

First, in declaring thy grief and disease unto thy friend, and opening thy whole heart, and pouring out thy whole mind before him, thou findest a singular easement in thy mind thereby. And again, a true and a faithful friend, through his pity and bemoaning of thee, helpeth thee, as it were, to bear thy burden ; and although he can take away no part of the substance of thy sorrow, yet his good heart and will and friendly words are a great comfort unto thee.

## CHAPTER XXIII.

#### THE BEST AND SUREST SUCCOUR AND COMFORT IN ADVERSITY RESTETH ONLY IN THE MIGHT, POWER, WILL, AND GOODNESS OF GOD.

Now will I open and declare, that God both can, may, and will help and succour sufficiently for Christ's sake, in respect of whom he promiseth us all manner of help, aid, and comfort, and performeth it. And I will also shew by what means, and in what measure he worketh the same.

God seeth and looketh upon us, how we stick and wrestle in peril and danger, and he knoweth best of all how and when to remedy, help, and deliver us, that his glory and our wealth may be most furthered. And he is not one that only knoweth all things, but he is also almighty, and can work and bring to pass all things. And if our affliction and adversity wax and increase from day to day, the longer the worse ; yet is God always a thousand times mightier and stronger than it.

But so mighty cannot God be, but he is as gracious and merciful also, and hath a greater lust and desire to shew and declare his true heart and love toward us, than we can wish or desire. And although he seemeth in our sight to take utterly away all manner of light of his grace out of our eyes, yet he remaineth gracious and favourable toward us privily, and as it were in secret; and certainly he will not forsake us, give us over, nor suffer us to stick and continue in such heaviness and danger.

And it is not our good works, merits, and deserts that move him thereunto, but the infinite and endless merit and desert of Jesus Christ, which hath purchased unto us through his bitter death and passion remission of our sins, the heavenly gifts of the Holy Ghost, and mitigation or easement of all our troubles and adversities.

And it is not possible that any man that taketh hold of Christ and hath him, can be oppressed or overthrown either of sin, the devil, the world, or of all the creatures in heaven and earth; but shall continue and remain for ever under the wing and defence of God. (Rom. viii. Psal. xxxiv. Prov. xxiv.) Rom. viii. 31, 32. Psal. xxxiv. 17. Prov. xxiv. 20.

Furthermore, Almighty God, being pacified and reconciled with mankind through Jesus Christ, hath promised both unto the children of Israel, and to all that be in any distress and vexation, through his ministers, evermore from time to time, help, succour, and comfort. The promise of God to aid and help us.

"The Lord is nigh unto them that are of a contrite and broken heart, and will help them that have sorrowful and humble minds." (Psal. xxxiv.) Psal. xxxiv. 18.

"He desireth me, and hath set his love upon me, therefore will I deliver him. I am by him and with him in his trouble; I will bring him out, and set him in honour," &c. (Psal. xci.) O, how comfortable a thing, and what an high honour is it, to have such a mighty and so faithful a fellow-companion, which will so lovingly stand by us and aid us! Psal. xci. 14–16.

Now as for the time, God will help in due and convenient season, and we must suffer him to take his time and leisure. For like as God seeth the trouble and affliction of his church, how it is vexed, even so hath he appointed a just time, how long he will suffer the wicked to take their pleasure, and how far they shall go and attempt. And when that is ex- When God will help.

pired, no longer nor further can they go. As the captivity of Babylon was appointed to continue seventy years, and then to cease.

> 2 Chron. xxxvi. 20, 21.
> Jer. xxv. 12; xxix. 10.

Yea, when the sorrow and heaviness is at the highest, and every one of us thinketh that God hath utterly forsaken us, then is God most ready to help us, and his aid is most nigh unto us. Yea, and to speak certainly as the truth is, God comforteth us continually in the midst of all our trouble and heaviness, and is never from us. (Psal. xlvi. Matt. xxviii. John xiv.)

> Psal. xlvi. 1.
> Matt. xxviii. 20.
> John xiv.

For the faithful man hath in his heart the Spirit of God, the fountain and spring of the heavenly water, of the which he is evermore moistened, revived, and refreshed, to his singular comfort. (John iv.)

> John iv. 14.

And the more that our sorrow and adversity augmenteth and increaseth, the greater aid and assistance shall we find and perceive. "God will not suffer you to be tempted above your strength, but together with your temptation he will make a way out, that ye shall be able to bear it." (1 Cor. x. 2 Pet. ii.)

> How God helpeth.

> 1 Cor. x. 13.
> 2 Pet. ii. 9.

By these words doth Paul teach very comfortably, that God will not tempt, test, nor assay us harder nor sorer than we may away with, and be able to bear.

"As the afflictions of Christ are plentiful and abundant in us, even so is the consolation through Christ also plentiful and abundant." (2 Cor. i.)

> 2 Cor. i. 5.

For example: the holy apostles were so strengthened, that they rejoiced that they might suffer any thing for Christ's sake. (Acts iv. v.) And at this present day God sendeth more comfort than all devils and all the world are able to send heaviness, sorrow, and discomfort.

Like as a captain in war giveth his soldiers that are under him a great courage, by speaking manfully and comfortably unto them; even so God will have his comfortable word daily to be published and proclaimed abroad, to the intent to encourage his soldiers that fight under his banner. And yet he is not so satisfied, that we should be encouraged with bare and simple words, but he himself is present by us with his Spirit; which Spirit, as a sure warrant and an earnest-penny, certifieth and assureth our hearts of the grace, favour, and aid of God. (Matt. xxviii. Rom. viii.)

> God helpeth and comforteth through his word and Spirit.

> Matt. xxviii. 20.
> Rom. viii. 15.

And thus he comforteth and maketh our hearts rejoice unfeignedly, and giveth us wisdom, boldness, and strength to skirmish and fight against all manner of enemies, as well ghostly as bodily.

Although in winter the trees seem and appear not only unfruitful, but also utterly dead, yet the sun with his coming, when the winter hath taken her leave, doth so mollify, resolve, and warm both the earth itself and the trees, that they bud out again, wax green, and bring forth fruit: even so, when the faithful are esteemed and seem as though they were deprived and destitute of all help, and utterly forsaken, yet doth the heavenly Spirit of God lighten, warm, and strengthen their hearts to all goodness.

Like as the young infant is not able to go of himself for very tenderness and lack of strength, but must be sustained, holden up, and led with the hand of the nurse; and like as a sick woman, weakened with much and long sickness, is not able to go one step, but some whole and strong woman must take her under the arm, guide, and lead her, that she may go with them; even so are we not able to go of ourselves.

There is some kind of sorrow and martyrdom, that we tremble and quake for fear when we do but hear of it, much less were we able to suffer and to bear it; but God with his mighty hand and present power strengtheneth, sustaineth, and preserveth us. The Spirit succoureth and helpeth our weakness and infirmities. (Rom. viii.) *Rom. viii 26.*

And if the devil through his spirit doth drive and move the people, that they are ready and willing to all wickedness and abomination, though it cost them their lives; why should not God, through his Spirit, make us as lusty and willing to all goodness, whatsoever sorrow or affliction we suffer?

Sometime God mitigateth and easeth the punishments, that we may the more easily overcome them. The captain giveth sometime his soldiers liberty to take their rest, ease, and pastime, that they may somewhat refresh themselves, and afterward fight the more manly and freshly: even so our spiritual Captain granteth oft-times unto his Christians a certain recreation, ease, and rest, whereby they may refresh and revive themselves, that they may afterward handle themselves the more valiantly in their spiritual affairs.

And sometime he dischargeth us utterly of all manner of

trouble and unquietness, and restoreth all our losses and hindrances again, and delivereth us, to our singular pre-eminence, praise, and commendation, and keepeth and saveth us from all manner of misery and unquietness in time to come. And to perform this thing, God useth not only his Spirit, but also other means; as the angels, the stars, the elements, beasts, men, and all manner of creatures.

<small>Psal. civ. 4.<br>Heb. ii. 7.</small>

Like as a man of war hath a lust and a courage to fight, having divers valiant servants about him, which will suffer him to take no wrong; even so the holy angels do compass us about and defend us, that in all manner of affliction and adversity we are bold, and able to stand and continue valiantly. (Psal. xxxiv. 2 Kings xix. Josh. v.)

<small>Psal. xxxiv. 7.<br>2 Kings xix.<br>34.<br>Josh. v.<br>13—15.</small>

Heliseus said to his boy, "Be not afraid; for they that are with us are more than they that are with them," &c. (2 Kings vi.) The Red Sea and the flood of Jordan withdrew themselves, that the children of Israel might go over dry, and never wet their feet. (Exod. xiv. Josh. iii.)

<small>2 Kings vi. 16.<br>Exod. xiv.<br>21, 22.<br>Josh. iii.<br>15—17.</small>

The sun and moon stood still for Joshua's pleasure, and never moved until such time as he had slain the five kings. (Josh. x.)

<small>Josh. x. 13.</small>

Helias was wonderfully fed of the ravens. (1 Kings xvii.)

<small>1 Kings xvii. 6.</small>

Through the hand of a woman the Israelites were delivered from a terrible and cruel host of their enemies. And commonly God comforteth and delivereth man through other men. (Esther vii. viii. ix. Judith xiii.)

And specially this is a comfortable thing, that all faithful and holy Christians upon earth have fellowship and participation together in all manner of things, both good and bad, as well one as other; and therefore whensoever I suffer any smart, pain, or sorrow, both Christ and all true Christians suffer with me. For the Lord saith not, "They were hungry and thirsty," &c., but he saith, "I was hungry, and I was thirsty." (Isai. lviii. Matt. xxv.)

<small>Isai. lviii. 10.<br>Matt. xxv. 35.</small>

And furthermore, the whole congregation of Christ doth help me to bear my burden. For they that are the members of one body take care and sorrow one for another: if the sole of the foot be hurt, doth it not grieve the whole body? (Gal. vi.) Now St Paul calleth all christian men one body, and also one bread and one cup. (1 Cor. x.) And therefore all other faithful Christians have compassion, and

<small>Gal. vi. 2.<br>1 Cor. x. 17.</small>

are heavy and sorrowful for me; and whatsoever is light unto them, is also light unto me.

Take a manifest example by the godly prophet Jeremy, which complained so sore, and was in such distress, when he had no other cause, but that the Jews, his countrymen, were so evil handled and vexed.

## CHAPTER XXIV.

### EXAMPLES OF THE HELP AND AID OF GOD.

To this end and purpose ought we to consider and to call unto mind the examples both of the Old and New Testament. If God had ever forsaken his faithful elect in their trouble and need, then might we have a just and lawful excuse to mistrust him: but forasmuch as none that ever sought upon God was forsaken of him (Psal. xxxvii.), ought not that to comfort and strengthen us, that he will also mercifully stand by us in all our need and necessity? Psal. xxxvii. 25.

The godly man Noe with his sons and his sons' wives were preserved of God through an ark or a ship, when as the whole world beside were destroyed with the sin-flood. Now if we with Noe believe in the blessed Seed, so shall we also with him be reputed for virtuous and good before God, and so be preserved as he was. (Gen. iii.) Gen. vii.<br>Gen. iii.

Lot was also delivered from the plague and punishment of the Sodomites. (Gen. xix.)

Jacob was fain to flee from his brother Esau, and to suffer great wrong and injury of his father-in-law Laban; and yet he was nevertheless blessed and preserved of God. (Gen. xxxii.)

Joseph being sold of his brethren, and because he would not commit filthiness and abomination with his master's wife, was cast into prison; but God delivered him, and exalted him to high honour. (Gen. xxxviii. xxxix. xli.)

King Pharao threatened Moyses very sore, and the children of Israel also themselves would have stoned him to death; but God preserved him under his protection. (Exod. xiv. xvii.)

Unto the children of Israel God gave water out of a hard rock of stone, and bread from heaven, and quails and other necessary things for the comfort of their necessity, wonderfully in the wilderness. (Numb. xx., Exod. xvi. xvii.) How graciously did God preserve king David and Ezechias in their trouble and necessity, and also the prophets Ezechiel and Daniel among the heathen; and likewise defended he Judas Machabeus, with other at that time. (1 Sam. xix. xxiv. xxvi. xxviii., 2 Chron. xxxii., Dan. vi., 1 Mac. ii.)

Forty men had made a solemn vow, neither to eat nor drink till they had killed Paul; but God did not suffer it to come to pass. (Acts xxiii.) These and other like examples are written for this purpose, that we should give like judgment, and have like opinion of other like examples, which are not expressed.

<small>Rom. xv. 4.</small>

Beside this, it is also evident, and hath been marked, that some time such as have been the most timorous, weak, and fearful, afterward being strengthened in faith through the might and power of God, have suffered martyrdom, banishment, and death most willingly and joyfully; and also have comforted boldly such as have suffered with them, even against the nature and disposition of the flesh of man. (Acts iv. v. Rom. viii. 2 Cor. iv. Psal. xliv.)

<small>Rom viii. 37, &c.<br>2 Cor. iv. 8.</small>

Yea, there is never one of us all, but have oft felt and proved the help, protection, and aid of God. For who can make his boast that he himself did help any thing at all to the matter, when he was formed in his mother's womb? Of the which matter read David. "Who hath kept us hitherto while we have been asleep?" (Psal. cxxvii.)

<small>Psal. cxxxix. 13.<br>Psal. cxxvii. 1, 2.</small>

Who hath sorrowed and taken care for us, when we have laboured or taken our pastime, or else done some other thing, and never took thought the least moment for ourselves? It may well happen that God may sometime suffer us to swim, but he will never suffer us to sink or to drown.

To be short: if there were not so many examples before our eyes, if we would but look a little backward, and consider how we have passed and avoided the time that is past, which surely hath been always full of great perils and dangers; whether we will or will not, we shall be compelled to confess and grant, that the merciful goodness of God hath borne us in his bosom, and hath preserved us from divers dangerous perils, over and above all that ever we could think, imagine, or devise.

Now if God hath thus holpen and delivered us many and divers ways, without any labour or study of ourselves, yea, without any manner of care or sorrow of our parts, when as we neither knew nor thought that he was present with us; we must needs be very obstinate, dull, and mad, if we do not from henceforth, in any manner of trouble or necessity, cast our sorrow upon him, and suffer him to care for us; but we in such case (oh shame!) begin to doubt and fear lest he hath already forsaken us, or will from henceforth give us over. (Psal. lv. Matt. vi. Luke xii. 1 Pet. v.) *Psal. lv. 22. Matt. vi. 25, &c. Luke xii. 22, &c. 1 Pet. v. 7.*

Item, if God of his natural love, beneficialness, and free liberality giveth here in this transitory life health, strength, riches, wealth, friendship, power, authority, honour, and such like, even unto the wicked and ungodly; why should not we determine and conclude upon the same, that he will deal and distribute a thousand times higher and greater benefits unto the godly and right faithful Christians, although they neither see nor receive those gifts at that present instant?

Besides this, the Lord also comforteth us: "If God take care for the fowls of the air and the flowers of the field, and provideth nourishment and clothing for them; truly he will deal as faithfully with us men, which excel many ways the fowls of the air and grass of the field." (Luke xii. Matt. vi. x.) *Luke xii. 24, Matt. vi. 28, x. 29.*

# THE THIRD AND LAST PART OF THIS BOOK.

## CHAPTER XXV.

### WE MUST DIRECT OUR FAITH, HOPE, AND CONFIDENCE TOWARDS GOD.

HITHERTO hath it been declared, that the very right and true help, succour, and comfort resteth in God through Christ, and for his sake: now shall it consequently be taught, how we should order and behave ourselves again with faith, hope, prayer, repentance, amendment of life, and patience, that God may participate, distribute, and extend his grace and mighty merciful hand toward us.

First of all, although we must utterly despair of all manner of help and succour of man, and can in no wise devise or imagine what way or after what sort God will or may help and aid us; yet notwithstanding we must utterly resist and banish all manner of heavy, sorrowful, and desperate fancies and imaginations of the mind, and give no place unto them, but conceive steadfastly this sure trust and confidence in God, that he both knoweth and will take and hit the right time, measure, and means to help us, and will valiantly and gloriously deliver us.

Let us commit altogether joyfully and boldly without fear unto God, and let his mercy and gracious goodness more rejoice and comfort us, than all the misery and sorrow under heaven, upon earth, or in hell may fear us.

Yea, we need to care and sorrow for nothing so much as for this, that we be not too careful and sorrowful for ourselves, as though God had given over all his care and sorrow for us: for like as the governor, father, or good man of the house taketh all the care and sorrow upon himself, how he shall find, feed, and sustain his family; and the household servants ought to love their masters, to have a good trust and opinion of them, and also to labour and to do such service as they are appointed unto, faithfully; even so all manner of care and sorrow for us belongeth unto God, and our parts and duty is no more but to trust and believe in him, and to serve in that vocation and condition of life, whereunto we are called and appointed of God, faithfully.

Now if God be most victorious and invincible, and his dear beloved Son also an everlasting strength, that can never fail, against the devil and the world; and again, both Christ and God himself, through faith, are ours and dwell in us, (Eph. iii.); then there is no cause why the faithful christian man should fear neither his own feeble flesh and body, nor his weak and impotent age, nor yet the whole power of the devil, though he be armed and weaponed with a thousand thousand crafts and subtleties. (1 Pet. v.) Eph. iii. 17.<br>1 Pet. v. 10.

For if so be that in God be all manner of joy, blessedness, and felicity, and we through faith do prove and find him a gracious and merciful God unto us; then may we lawfully rejoice in God, even in the midst of the highest sorrow and adversity that can be. To witness, Psalm xxv. lv.: "There shall none be confounded and put to shame, that hopeth in thee." "Cast thy care and sorrow upon the Lord, and he shall defend and sustain thee." What can be thought or imagined more sweet or comfortable? Psal. xxv. 3.<br>lv. 22.

For example: the heathenish woman of Canany, all hope and comfort in the remedy and counsel of man set apart, desireth help and succour of Christ; and although the Lord giveth her at first rough and sharp answers, yet she is nothing abashed, nor will not so be answered. (Matt. xv.) Matt. xv. 22.

Even so hold thou on likewise with the heathenish woman, saying and crying still: "O thou Son of David, have mercy upon me." And so shalt thou hear at length this comfortable gospel and absolution: "Thy faith is great, be it unto thee as thou desirest."

St Bernard sheweth very comfortably what a faith he had, in these goodly words: "O Lord, it is much better for me to suffer trouble, so that thou only mayest be by me, than to rule and live pleasantly and costly without thee. It is better and more pleasant unto me to be in a hot, burning, and flaming oven with thee, than to be even in heaven without thee[1]."

[[1] Bonum mihi, Domine, tribulari, dummodo ipse sis mecum, quam regnare sine te, epulari sine te, sine te gloriari. Bonum mihi,

*And who did ever trust in the Lord, whom he at length forsook? Besides all this, Almighty God commandeth that we should hope, trust, and look for help at his hand; which hope bringeth with her a mitigation and easement of the smart and sorrow. "I hope in the Lord, therefore shall I not fall." "Hope thou only in God, so shalt thou be holpen." "Hope is never confounded nor put to shame." (Psal. xxvi. xxviii. Rom. v.)

<small>Hope.</small>
<small>Psal. xxvi. 1.</small>
<small>Psal. xxviii. 7. Rom. v. 5.</small>

## CHAPTER XXVI.

### OF PRAYER IN TROUBLE AND ADVERSITY.

The holy scripture teacheth us, in all manner of necessities, as well bodily as ghostly, to call upon God, and to flee unto him. And here doth it profit very much, if one be mindful of another in his prayer.

But what should a man pray for? First and most specially, for remission of his sins. For when we have once obtained of God pardon of our sins, then certainly shall the sickness, adversity, or punishment either clearly cease, or else, through the gracious will and goodness of God, it shall redound to the furtherance of our salvation.

Secondarily, we must also pray either that God will help and deliver us, not after the device and fancy of our own brains, but after such wise as shall seem unto his godly wisdom; or else that he will mitigate and ease our pain and punishment, that our weakness may not utterly faint and sink down to the bottom.

Like as a sick person, although he doubt nothing of the faithfulness, honesty, and tenderness of his physician or surgeon towards him, yet for all that desireth him to handle his wound, and to dress him as easily and tenderly as is possible for him; even so in like manner may we call upon God, that,

<small>Domine, in tribulatione magis amplecti te, in camino habere te mecum, quam esse sine te vel in coelo.—Sti Bernardi Opera. In Psalm. xc. (xci.) Serm. xvi. vers. 17. Vol. I. p. 883. E. Ed. Bened. 1719.]</small>

if it be not against his honour and glory, he will vouchsafe to give some mitigation and easement of the pain.

And specially let us desire of him to grant us strength, that we faint not, nor be overcome with the fear or greatness of our sorrow and grief, whereby we might forsake him, and fall into some wickedness; but that we may rather, after the example of the holy martyrs, suffer death and most intolerable torments, than either to forsake and deny our faith, or else to do any manner of thing against the will of God. (Rom. viii.) And it is very expedient for us to pray with the lost and desperate son: "I am no more worthy from henceforth to be called thy son; make me as one of thy hired servants." (Luke xv.) I will gladly with all my heart have sorrow and trouble upon earth, even as a labouring servant that goeth for his hire, so that thou wilt but suffer me to dwell and remain in thy house for ever. Rom. viii. 36. Luke xv. 17.

But now how should we pray? St James in his first chapter teacheth us, that we should pray in faith without wavering, and nothing doubt but that God doth mercifully hear us. We must continually look upon the promise of God, and have this always before our eyes, that we do not only seek help and remedy at his hands, but also hope and look surely for it, committing both body and soul with a good will unto him. (Matt. xxi. Mark xi.) James i. 6.

"Call upon me in thy need, and I will help and deliver thee, and so shalt thou praise me." "Let him call upon me, so will I hear him; I am by him in his trouble, I will deliver him out, and bring him to honour." (Psalm l. xci.) Matt. xxi. 22.<br>Mark xi. 24. Psal. l. 15.<br>xci. 15.

And again: "Verily, verily, I say unto you, whatsoever you shall pray for unto the Father in my name, (that is to say, in the trust and confidence upon my merits,) he shall give it unto you." (John xiv.) For example: when Moyses held up his hands unto God and prayed, his enemies, the Amalekites, were overcome. (Exod. xvii.) The two blind men which did cry after the Lord, "O Son of David, have mercy upon us," were heard. (Matt. ix.) Of such like examples are the gospels full. John xiv. 13. Exod. xvii. 11. Matt ix. 27.

Item, in trouble and adversity we ought to praise God, and to give him thanks that he hath not forgotten us, but through his fatherly visitation calleth and draweth us unto him, and graciously helpeth us to bear all manner of burdens. Praise or thanksgiving to God.

<small>2 Cor. i 4.</small> Even so did Paul in his adversity praise God (2 Cor. i.): "Praised be God, the Father of our Lord Jesus Christ, the Father of mercy and God of all consolation, which comforteth us in all our troubles and afflictions."

## CHAPTER XXVII.

### REPENTANCE AND AMENDMENT OF LIFE IN TROUBLE AND ADVERSITY IS NECESSARY.

Now there must go with all this repentance, heaviness, and sorrow for the sins which we have committed in time past, amendment of life, the love of God, the fear of God, all virtue and godliness. Manasses was sorry and penitent for his wicked life and cruel tyranny; and therefore did God deliver him out of the bands and captivity of the king of Babylon, and restored him again to his kingdom in Israel. <small>2 Chron. xxxiii. 12, 13.</small> (2 Kings xxi. 2 Chron. xxxiii.) By Jonas was it preached and proclaimed unto the great city of Ninive, that God should destroy and overthrow it within forty days. The Ninivites believed this proclamation and preaching, and began to repent and amend their lives with a great and a singular humbleness and submission; and so God of his mercy spared them. (Jon. iii.)

Now is God's merciful heart nothing diminished: if we do as the Ninivites did, he both can and will pardon and <small>Numb. xi. 23. Isai. l, 2; lix. 1.</small> spare us, as he did them. (Numb. xi. Isai. l. lix.)

## CHAPTER XXVIII.

CHRISTIAN AND GODLY PERSUASIONS AND EXAMPLES OUT OF THE WORD OF GOD, TO MOVE MEN UNTO PATIENCE IN AFFLICTION AND ADVERSITY.

AMONG all other virtues, in adversity patience is most necessary; not such a patience as to suffer all things to pass, whether they be good or bad, right or wrong, setting all on six and seven; but when we are in trouble and adversity, and can avoid it by no lawful mean, whereas after the desire and lust of our flesh we would murmur, forsake, and give over both God and all manner of righteousness; then to resist and strive against our afflictions and sorrowful thoughts, and, as a man would say, to spear up and to captivate and subdue our natural eyes, wit, and reason under and unto the obedience of God, yielding and submitting ourselves unto him, suffering whatsoever it be with a good and ready will, even though it were most bitter and cruel death, rather than we would swerve from the word of God (Luke ix.); yea, and moreover to praise God, and to give him thanks, that he will vouchsafe so fatherly to visit us, and that he hath not forgotten us. [Luke ix. 62.]

This is called a right christian patience. For it is God's precept and commandment, that we should not murmur or grudge against him, when he chasteneth us; but that we should submit ourselves most humbly unto his holy will, and after a certain manner to wish, that is to say, willingly to suffer and bear such punishment and correction, whereby we remain and continue obedient unto his godly righteousness. "Murmur not, as certain murmured, and were destroyed of the destroyer." (Numb. xxi. 1 Cor. x.) [Numb. xxi 6. 1 Cor. x. 10.]

Wherefore we ought to shew patience in all things, as a point of our duty; and it is a grievous sin to murmur and grudge against the judgment of God, and to resist and strive against God's will. And God doth not only command patience, but also is himself patient and long-suffering; which destroyeth not at once the whoremonger, the extortioner, and other such like wicked and damnable people with a lightning or thunderbolt, although his holy and strait righteousness requireth no less. (Deut. xxxii.) He giveth time and space sufficient for the man to repent, and to return to grace again.

<small>Deut. xxxii. 36.</small>

Hence Paul saith: "Dost thou despise the abundant riches of his goodness, his patience, and long-suffering? Knowest thou not that the goodness and gentleness of God calleth thee to repentance?" (Rom. ii.) According unto this godly example, though it be so that we must suffer somewhat against our will, and contrary to our minds and affections, yet should we not murmur and grudge, but amend our lives, and patiently look and wait for better.

<small>Rom. ii. 4.</small>

And specially the unspeakable fidelity and love of God towards us ought lawfully to move and persuade us, to suffer God to work with us even according to his will and pleasure: for by this means we give God this honour, that he doth us no wrong nor injury, but disposeth all things most wisely, and will direct them to a good end.

On the contrary part, the unpatient man murmureth and grudgeth against God, and is angry with him, as though his judgments and works were not just and right, forasmuch as the wicked and ungodly live in pomp, pleasure, and all dissoluteness, and the virtuous and godly in poverty, sorrow, and misery. He may peradventure fancy and imagine with himself, that God overchargeth his faithful children, and will suffer them to remain in peril, necessity, and danger, and will not hear them. (Psalm xxxvii.)

<small>Psal. xxxvii. 7.</small>

And thus he is so poisoned with bitterness and obstinacy, that he beginneth to hate and to blaspheme God in heaven, and seeketh unlawful means to help and remedy himself: like as Saul did, running after witches and soothsayers. (1 Sam. xxviii.) Wherefore let every christian man take heed, that no such raving fierceness and bitterness come upon him, or at least that it remain not long by him; but in such temptation let him fight manfully, as in the face and sight of the heavenly Captain, which both seeth and knoweth all things, and also most faithfully rescueth his soldiers, and is, as it were, a fellow and one among them, and will recompense all their labour and travail a thousand-fold in the life everlasting.

<small>1 Sam. xxviii. 7.</small>

Moreover, we have an evident and perfect image and spectacle of all patience in our Lord Jesus Christ, as he

<small>An example of Christ.</small>

himself pointed us unto himself, saying: "Whosoever will follow me, let him forsake himself, and take his cross upon his back, and follow me." (Matt. xvi.) When his unspeak- Matt. xvi. 24. able martyrdom and passion began, he prayed: "O Father, if it be possible, take this cup from me; but thy will, and not mine, be done." Where did he ever once murmur or grudge, or cast out so much as one untoward and unpatient word, when he was mocked and scorned, scourged and beaten, and most cruelly misordered and dealt withal? (Matt. xxvi. Mark xiv. Luke xxii. John xviii. Isa. liii.)

Print this well and surely in thy mind, that he did pray upon the cross for his greatest enemies, and said: "Father, forgive them, for they know not what they do." (Luke xxiii. Luke xxiii. 34. Acts vii.) If he through his heavenly and divine might and Acts vii. 60. power had rid himself of all his pain, sorrow, and danger, and that we in our sorrow, anguish, and necessity had not felt any heavenly strength nor power from God, then could we not have comforted ourselves at all with our Saviour Jesus Christ. But he would not put off his bitter passion through his almighty power, but rather overcome it through weakness.

Now then if he, whom all angels and creatures in heaven and earth do behold and look upon, (Psalm xcvii. Heb. i.) Psal. xcvii 9. Heb. 1. 3, &c. yea, whom they all must serve and fear, doth suffer innocently undeserved with all patience and meekness more than ever any christian man was attempted with; it ought lawfully to make even an heart of stone or iron to yearn and melt, and to take these small afflictions well deserved most patiently and willingly, and to suffer and bear them most meekly.

And this practice did the holy elect of God in the old Examples of the holy time not only inculck and teach with words, but also express fathers and saints. and perform in deed. It was an heavy cross unto Abraham to slay and offer up his most dear son; and yet he with all patience shewed himself obedient unto God therein.

And Isaac perceiving, that it stood upon his life, and that he should die, we read not that he did resist, nor once open his mouth against it. (Gen. xxii.)

Joseph, when he was delivered of his brethren unto the heathen, which were fremde and strangers unto him, yet he forgave it his brethren, and did them good for it. Moyses, Gen. xxxvii. 28. xlv. 5. being reviled of the Israelites as a deceiver and a betrayer,

yet had he such compassion of them, that he prayed for them, saying: "O Lord, either forgive them, or else wipe me out of thy book." Here is he willing, and ready to take all the Israelites' sins and offences upon himself, that God should punish him for them. (Exod. xvii. xxxii. Rom. ix.)

<sub>Exod. xvii. 3.</sub>
<sub>xxxii. 32.</sub>
<sub>Rom. ix. 3.</sub>

David was fain to be a banished outcast a long time, and to flee every where from Saul, whom notwithstanding he might once as easily have destroyed and killed, as he might have eaten a bit of bread (1 Sam. xxiv.); and after that he was put to flight of his own son, and yet said patiently: "If I find grace and favour before God, then will he restore me again: but if he say, I have no pleasure nor delight in thee; behold, here I am, let him do with me as pleaseth him best." (2 Sam. xv.)

<sub>1 Sam. xxiv. 10.</sub>

<sub>2 Sam. xv. 25, 26.</sub>

Job, the spectacle of patience, being full of sores in his body, spoiled of his goods, and deprived of his children, said thus: "God gave it, and God hath taken it again; the name of the Lord be praised." Furthermore he saith: "If he should kill me, yet will I put my trust in him." (Job i. xiii.)

<sub>Job i. 21 xiii. 15.</sub>

Mathathias, in the very highest peril and danger of his body and life, at such time as they would have compelled and forced him unto idolatry, made this answer unto the servants and ministers of Antiochus: "We will not swerve nor depart from our faith, neither to the right hand nor the left." (1 Mac. ii.) The apostles did rejoice that they were worthy to be scourged, beat, and reviled for the name of Jesus. (Acts v.)

<sub>1 Mac. ii. 22</sub>
<sub>Acts v. 41.</sub>

We should learn to cry with Paul: "I am sure that neither death nor life, neither height nor depth, nor any other creature, can separate us from the love of God which is in Christ Jesus our Lord."

<sub>Rom. viii. 38, 39.</sub>

After the time of the holy prophets and apostles, many thousand martyrs (among whom were divers notable matrons, chaste virgins, and other young people) did suffer most grievous torments and afflictions for the truth's sake. (1 Mac. ii. 2 Mac. vi. vii.)

But now here might some man object and say, It is no marvel that the holy saints did suffer joyfully and boldly, for they did suffer innocently, unworthily, and without desert: but as for me, I must needs complain that I am a wretched sinner, and that which I suffer is for my deserts and sins, so that I suffer worthily; and therefore my cross and affliction can in no wise be compared or likened unto the cross of the holy saints, &c. This objection may be answered in few words.

The holy saints, every one of them, concerning themselves and their own nature, were miserable sinners; but again they were holy and righteous through Jesus Christ, which had distributed and given unto them also, through true faith, his holiness and righteousness.

Furthermore, these two virtues, true faith and christian patience, are so nigh of affinity, and so annexed and knit in fellowship together, that always the one helpeth the other. *Faith helpeth to patience.*

Faith is stirred up, exercised, put in ure[1] and practice, receiveth increasement and more strength through patience in sorrow and affliction; when as we for Christ's sake do both desire and also wait for help and strength of God against our nature, which can nothing but doubt and despair; and also against the weakness of the flesh, against the temptation of the devil, and against the assaults of the world.

And again, patience is exercised, proved, and made stronger through true faith. For whosoever knoweth and is fully persuaded, that he hath a gracious and a merciful God, with whom after this miserable life he shall live everlastingly, the same shall suffer all manner of trouble and adversity patiently, christianly, and thankfully. Again, through faith in Christ, we are set at one and reconciled with God, and assured of his grace, mercy, and favour for Jesus Christ's sake and the merits of his passion. (Rom. iv. Gal. iv. Ephes. ii.) *Rom. iv. 22—25. Gal. iv 6. Ephes. ii. 14, 15.*

For example: David, forasmuch as he believed truly and steadfastly in God, spake boldly with a courage: "God is our hope and strength, a very present help in all the sorrows and necessities that have assaulted us. Therefore will we not fear, though the world should sink, and though the hills should be carried away in the midst of the sea, &c." (Psal. xlvi.) *Psal. xlvi. 1. &c.* Yea, every christian man, if it were possible, should be content to lose a thousand bodies and lives, if it were for no other thing, but that he hath heard, tasted, and believed the holy gospel.

[¹ ure: use, practice.]

But for any man to be impatient, and so to remain, it is an evident token that the same person never had any true faith; or else, if he had, that it is quenched and gone again. For impatiency falleth unto murmuring and disobedience against God, and beginneth to hate God and to blaspheme him.

<small>Prayer helpeth to patience.</small> Also christian prayer is a great help and furtherance to patience; for in prayer we desire the sanctification of the name of God. Now is the name of God most praised and sanctified, when we, being in the highest danger and necessity, do depend and hang upon God through faith and patience, as upon one that will dispose all things well and to a good end.

Again, in prayer we desire that the kingdom of God may <small>Matt. vi. 10. Luke xi. 2.</small> come unto us. (Matt. vi. Luke xi.) Now, if God will confound and destroy in us the kingdom of the devil and of the flesh, or else would utterly lead and draw us into his godly and heavenly kingdom through the cross, were it not as much as to pray against ourselves, if we should be impatient under the same?

We pray likewise, that "God's will be done." Now if it be God's will that we should have sorrow, trouble, and adversity upon earth, how dare or can we resist or grudge against his will?

## CHAPTER XXIX.

EXAMPLES AND CAUSES TAKEN OUT OF NATURAL THINGS, AND OF HEATHEN MEN, WHEREBY A MAN MAY BE MOVED TO PATIENCE IN ADVERSITY.

If there were no holy scripture at all, yet might a man of his own reason take example of brute beasts, of natural things, as of body and soul, and the natural parts unto them belonging; also of heathen men, Jews, and handicraftsmen, and of all manner of states and degrees of men; and likewise of the angels, and of the devil: whereby they might conclude and learn, that they ought to behave themselves patiently, boldly, and manfully in adversity and misfortune.

A lamb or a sheep is led unto the slaughter, and never crieth nor openeth the mouth, but suffereth and abideth it patiently and meekly. Even so ought the holy elect of God, when they are cursed and reviled, not to curse or revile again; when they are smitten, not to smite again; but to suffer all manner of smart and pain, and not once to blear or to open their mouths against it. *Examples of brute creatures and natural things.* *Matt. v. 44.*

Our body is but very worms' meat; and if we could bestow the same to the honour of our Redeemer and Saviour Christ, ought we not to be glad and rejoice, if we might so do?

Like as they that are sick and diseased can be content to suffer and abide any of the members of their body to be cut off and to be burnt, so that they might be anything relieved and eased thereby of their great smart and continual pain, which is yet but transitory, and be made whole and sound again; even so ought we gladly and willingly to suffer our Lord God, and to be still and quiet when he sendeth us adversity, whereby we may be relieved and discharged of eternal pain, and obtain health, bliss, and salvation for our souls.

If thou canst consider the order and course of nature, that is naturally written in thy heart, thou shalt thereby learn and conclude, that a man ought to be so strong and steadfast, that he should not be moved by any smart, pain, or other temptation, to do any thing that is unseemly or against honesty.

And out of this honesty, wrought and planted in nature, sprang the learning and examples of the wise and notable heathen men, which we call philosophers, among whom this was a common proverb and sentence: "Bear and forbear[1]." The first word whereof teacheth us, that we should suffer the cross patiently, and to be still and meek when we are visited therewith: and the second signifieth, that we should hate, flee, and avoid all manner of examples, words, or deeds, that might give any manner of occasion to any evil. Aristotle in his Book of Manners teacheth, that felicity and blessed- *Examples of the heathen.* *Bear.* *Forbear.*

[1] ἀνέχου καὶ ἀπέχου.

ness consisteth not specially in health of body, in abundance of goods, or in worldly honour, dignity, and estimation, but rather in the exercise and practice of virtue[1]. Out of the which it followeth, that a man that is virtuous may be blessed, though he have never so much trouble or adversity; and he reckoneth and taketh trouble or adversity for the very matter and occasion, whereby virtue is most stirred up and exercised, and wherein it doth most shine and appear[2].

And the same Aristotle also compareth an honest and virtuous man unto a good captain: for like as a good captain leadeth and ordereth his host, according as the occasion requireth; even so a virtuous man behaveth himself patiently and well in adversity, and maketh the best of it.

The Stoics did teach plainly, that it was not to be reckoned for an evil thing for us to live in poverty, sickness, and misery; but this only to be evil, to forsake virtue, and shew any point of dishonesty. Cicero, one of the most notable and excellent Romans, writeth thus: "Remember and

[1] The author appears to state the substance of the opinion of Aristotle on this subject. In the first book of his Ethics, Aristotle thus states his opinion with regard to happiness: Λέγωμεν... ἐπειδὴ πᾶσα γνῶσις καὶ προαίρεσις ἀγαθοῦ τινος ὀρέγεται, τί ἐστιν... τὸ πάντων ἀκρότατον τῶν πρακτῶν ἀγαθόν.—'Ονόματι μὲν οὖν σχεδὸν ὑπὸ τῶν πλείστων ὁμολογεῖται· τὴν γὰρ εὐδαιμονίαν καὶ οἱ πολλοὶ καὶ οἱ χαρίεντες λέγουσι.

The subject of c. 5. is, ὅτι ἡ εὐδαιμονία οὐκ ἔστιν ἡδονή, ἢ τιμή, ἢ πλοῦτος: which proposition he proves, after his manner, in each particular; and then in the tenth chapter arrives at this conclusion: κύριαι εἰσὶν αἱ κατ' ἀρετὴν ἐνεργείαι τῆς εὐδαιμονίας: and again, τί οὖν κωλύει λέγειν εὐδαίμονα τὸν κατ' ἀρετὴν τελείαν ἐνεργοῦντα; out of all which the statement in the text appears to be extracted. Aristoteles Ethic. Nicom. Lib. I. cap. 4, 5, &c.]

[2] The learned author appears here to have had in view the following passage, of which, according to his manner, he has given the substance, without any attempt at accurate citation: τὰ δὲ μεγάλα καὶ πολλὰ (scil. events of life) γινόμενα μὲν εὖ, μακαριώτερον τὸν βίον ποιήσει... ἀνάπαλιν δὲ συμβαίνοντα, θλίβει καὶ λυμαίνεται τὸ μακάριον... ὅμως δὲ καὶ ἐν τούτοις διαλάμπει τὸ καλόν, ἐπειδὰν φέρῃ τις εὐκόλως πολλὰς καὶ μεγάλας ἀτυχίας.... τὸν γὰρ ὡς ἀληθῶς ἀγαθὸν καὶ ἔμφρονα πάσας οἰόμεθα τὰς τύχας εὐσχημόνως φέρειν, καὶ ἐκ τῶν ὑπαρχόντων ἀεὶ τὰ κάλλιστα πράττειν. Ethic. Nicom. Lib. I. cap. 10.]

persuade this with thyself, that besides sin and dishonesty nothing can happen to a man, whereat he ought to be astonied or abashed[3]." And according to this example did one heathen man often comfort another by all manner of circumstances of things, as these following and other.

It beseemeth not a man to weep and wail like a child or a woman. And Seneca writeth thus: "It is easier to subdue and overcome a whole nation, than one only man." Item: Thou art no more a child of a year, but thou hast age and years, and therefore more is required of thee than of a child. Thou hast been brought up and instruct from thy youth in godly wisdom and knowledge; the same must thou now practise and shew forth.

Before this time thou couldest comfort and give good counsel unto other: do not now therefore like the evil physicians, which boast and pretend that they can help other men, and cannot help themselves. Before this time hitherto thou hast shewed and behaved thyself manfully: therefore be now like unto thyself, and go not backward. It were an unseeming thing to wax from day to day worse and weaker; and such like.

Although this doctrine of the heathen men in this and such other points is to be commended, yet the stories do make mention of many unseemly acts that they did: as this, that Coriolanus for desire of revenge did war against his own natural country; also Cato and Antonius for sorrow and heaviness did kill and murder themselves. But the

[3 The sentiments contained in the above statements are of frequent occurrence in the philosophical writings of Cicero. The substance of them is found, amongst other passages, in the thirteenth chapter of the second book of the Tusculan Questions; where having stated the celebrated axiom of the Stoics,—"nihil bonum, nisi quod honestum; nihil malum, nisi quod turpe,"—he proceeds: Optare hoc quidem est, non docere. Illud et melius et verius: omnia, quæ natura aspernetur, in malis esse; quæ asciscat, in bonis. Hoc posito, et verborum concertatione sublata, tantum tamen excellet illud, quod recte amplexantur isti, quod honestum, quod rectum, quod decorum appellamus, quod idem virtutis nomine amplectimur, ut omnia præterea, quæ bona corporis et fortunæ putantur, perexigua et minuta videantur: ne malum quidem ullum, nec si in unum locum collata omnia sint, cum turpitudinis malo comparanda.—Tuscul. Quæst. Lib. II. cap. 13.]

[COVERDALE.]

very reason of man can discern and judge, that such things are against nature, and against all virtue and honesty.

But the very right and the most notable heathen men have commended and set forth patience, not only with words, but also have shewed the same in example and deed. Among the Grecians, Aristides, an excellent virtuous man, being banished out of his country, did take and suffer his misery very manfully and patiently. Among the Romans, Camillus and Attilius Regulus were highly commended and praised for their excellent patience and stoutness, which they shewed in adversity.

Scipio could have defended and revenged himself of the seditious rebels with force and strong hand: but of an excellent princely heart he went out of the sight of his enemies for a time, and suffered much trouble and injury of them, for the profit of his land, lest he should give them occasion to more bitterness and fierceness. Yea, we read of certain women, as of Cornelia, which in affliction and adversity did shew manly hearts and great stoutness.

But we must always mark the right difference between the heathenish and the christian patience. As Socrates in his adversity did wonder of the unrighteousness of men, and thought that it was but a chance and fortune that he was afflicted; but David knew and confessed that his visitation and affliction came from God. (2 Sam. xxiv. 1 Chron. xxi.)

<sub>2 Sam. xxiv. 10.</sub>
<sub>1 Chron. xxi. 8.</sub>

Socrates, forasmuch as he suffereth innocently and without a cause, he cannot find by his reason that we should wish and desire punishment and affliction: but David, after a certain manner, wisheth and desireth the cross; for he knoweth that it is God's will to testify and to open manifestly through the cross and adversity his wrath and displeasure against sin.

<sub>2 Sam. xxiv. 14.</sub>

Socrates, in his manly sufferance and patience, neither desireth nor looketh for any help, comfort, or mitigation of his afflictions from God. Yea, the notable Cato, hearing that Pompeius, being a good man, was overcome and subdued of Julius, which was a wicked man, he began to doubt and despair. But David in his patience and obedience calleth upon God for help and deliverance, and is certain and sure that the Almighty Lord doth assist him for the holy and blessed

Seed's sake, whereof the heathen have no knowledge nor understanding. (Psal. v. Gen. iii.) <small>Psal. v. 1. Gen. iii. 15.</small>

Thus by comparing the one to the other we shall find and perceive, that the doctrine of the gospel is more pleasant and acceptable, and moveth us unto more thankfulness towards the gospel of Jesus Christ; through whom and by whose means we obtain an whole and a perfect comfort. Now from the old ethnics and heathen men let us descend and come to the Turks, Jews, and to other degrees of men. Many a Turk and Jew would suffer himself to be martyred and tormented most cruelly, rather than he would deny or forsake Mahomet's religion, and his perverse and naughty faith; and why should not a Christian then much more be content to suffer stoutly, if need should require, for the christian religion and faith's sake?

A merchant-man maketh far voyages and great journeys, and ventureth body and goods, and nothing is too hard and sour for him, only for worldly and transitory gain and lucre. And yet his hope is uncertain, whether his chance shall be good or evil. And though he happeneth never so well, yet he bringeth home nothing but frail and transitory goods which shall have an end.

Now all we have a long voyage to make also, even from earth to heaven. And should not we be as well content, as prompt, glad, and willing to suffer all manner of perils and dangers that may happen by the way, seeing that we have an infallible and sure hope of eternal and everlasting riches for Jesus Christ's sake?

A wayfaring man that goeth from home, although he passeth many pleasant houses and goodly meads, yet minding altogether homeward again, all such things do nothing tempt nor grieve him: even so, whensoever we have not all our pleasure and delight here, let us stablish our comfort, and delight ourselves with our country and habitation in heaven. (2 Cor. v. Phil. iii.) <small>2 Cor. v. 1, 2. Phil. iii. 20, 21.</small>

When a man of an high and noble birth is contemned and mishandled in a strange land, where he is not known, it grieveth him nothing so much, as if the like should happen unto him at home in his own natural country. Now is our natural country in heaven; upon earth we are but strangers and pilgrims. Therefore we ought the rather to suffer all things patiently here, only that we may have rest among the inhabitants in our right eternal land and country. (Heb. xiii. Phil. iii. 1 Pet. i.)

<small>Heb. xiii. 14.
Phil. iii. 20.
1 Pet. i. 3, 4.</small>

A man of war preparing himself with all manner of things appertaining to warfare, though his enemy be never so strong, yet he forgetteth all fear, and never once thinketh upon the strokes and wounds, but only upon the victory and triumph, and goeth his way and fighteth manfully like a giant against his enemies, only for worldly glory and lucre: which thing may redound to the great slander and shame of christian people, if they for the honour, glory, and pleasure of God should not as promptly, willingly, and manfully fight against their ghostly enemies for higher and greater triumph, lucre, and commodity.

A ploughman or an husbandman goeth to the field, dungeth, plougheth, soweth, and harroweth his ground, and hath much sorrow therewith, and waiteth for fruit and profit <small>James v. 7, 8.</small> thereof. By the same example doth the holy apostle St James move and exhort us unto patience.

Turn a four-cornered stone how thou wilt, and it will always stand right up: even so, howsoever a right Christian be tempted and assaulted, he will ever notwithstanding remain upright. When a man playeth at the tables, he cannot always cast what he would have, but whatsoever he hath cast, he must make the best of it. To this game doth Plato liken our life, wherein happen many things contrary to our will, which we must take and turn all to the best, and never despair.

When a little child, that can scarcely go, chanceth to stumble upon a stone, he falleth down by and by in the same place, and there lieth still, weeping and crying till somebody take him up. But people of reason and understanding must not do like children, but must use and endeavour themselves, what sickness or inconvenience soever happen, by and by, so far as is possible, to heal, ease, and remedy it.

A virtuous child will not forsake his father in his need or trouble, nor an honest wife her husband and spouse, nor yet a faithful servant his master. And why then should we forsake God our father, or Christ our spouse and heavenly lord and master, in trouble and adversity?

Such as are money-merchants, ambitious and vain-glorious, fornicators, whoremongers, and murderers, care neither for shame nor for any thing else, and spare no labour or travail, so that they may bring to pass their wicked lust and desire; and yet oft-times they miss also. And why then should not a right godly man be constant, painful, and patient in honest and good things? as St Bernard writeth very well, saying: "What a faintness, sluggishness, and dulness is this, that such as are wicked and ungodly should be more fervent to wickedness and abomination, than we should be to honesty and goodness; yea, that they should run more swiftly to the devil and to death, than we should to God and to life[1]!"

Furthermore, thy fearfulness and impatiency is a great pleasure and comfort to thy foes, and a great heaviness and discomfort to thy friends. For doubtless all that wish thee good, do rejoice in thy strength and constantness. Think *The angels.* also that thou fightest in the presence of the holy angels, which by the provision and appointment of God do dwell with thee, and move and exhort thee to steadfastness; and they rejoice when thou continuest steadfast in goodness. (1 Cor. iv.) *1 Cor. iv. 9.*

And again: we should to the uttermost of our power *The devil.* flee and abhor all such things as might delight and rejoice the devil; for he is the deadly arch enemy of God and of all mankind. (1 Pet. v.) *1 Pet. v. 8.*

Now this is the very purpose of his temptations and suggestions, and all that he seeketh; that we, when we are poor, should steal; and when we are sick, that we should murmur against God; and in war, affliction, and adversity, that we should forsake our christian faith and religion. Constantness, faithfulness, and steadfastness toward God and the

[[1] The following passage exhibits the substance of the quotation: Quid? eorum qui avaritiæ serviunt, aut amatores sunt voluptatum, seu vanas sectantur hominum laudes, nonne et ipsorum insatiabilia desideria arguunt nos negligentiæ et tepiditatis? Pudeat certe spiritualium nos bonorum minus cupidos inveniri. Erubescat anima conversa ad Dominum minori affectu sectari justitiam, quam iniquitatem antea sectaretur. Est enim causa quoque valde dissimilis. Stipendium quippe peccati mors; fructus autem Spiritus vita æterna. Pudeat proinde negligentius nunc in vitam, quam prius in mortem ire, et minori studio salutis acquirere quam perditionis augmentum. S. Bernardi Epist. cccLxxxi. Vol. I. p. 344. F. Ed. Bened. 1719.]

christian church doth grieve and displease him. Therefore we, to rejoice the angels, and to grieve the devil, ought the rather to be constant and patient in the midst of all adversity.

## CHAPTER XXX.

#### BY WHAT MEANS PATIENCE MAY BE OBTAINED AND GOTTEN; AND ONCE HAD, HOW IT MAY BE KEPT AND INCREASED.

NOTWITHSTANDING that we know and perceive that patience is so profitable and fruitful a thing unto us, yet we feel in our flesh a certain misliking and grudge toward the cross. Who can be content and glad to see himself deprived of his life, honour, estimation, goods, children, or wife? The remembrance of the pleasure and prosperity that we have had in times past, doth so grieve us, that with Lot's wife we <sup>Gen. xix. 26.</sup> sighten and look back after Sodoma. (Gen. xix.); and with the children of Israel we lust after the flesh-pots in Egypt. <sup>Exod. xvi. 3.</sup> (Exod. xvi.) And like weakness do we also find in the noble king and prophet David, as he himself saith: "Many say unto my soul, He hath no God: my soul would receive <sup>Psal. lxxvii. 2, 3.</sup> no comfort, my spirit is waxen weak and feeble." (Psal. lxxvii.)

Item, our Saviour Jesus in his innocent flesh did shew and declare the fearfulness and anguish of the flesh, when as he, kneeling upon the mount Olivet, considered his passion and martyrdom that was coming and at hand, and sweat for sorrow and anguish, so that the drops of his sweat gushed upon the earth like drops of blood, and he prayed unto his Father, that if it were his will, that cup might be taken from <sup>Luke xxii. 44.</sup> him. (Luke xxii.) In like manner, being upon the cross, he said, "My God, my God, why hast thou forsaken me? <sup>Psal. xxii. 1. Matt. xxvii. 46.</sup> how long will thou thus deal with me?" (Psal. xxii. Matt. xxvii.)

But it is not to be understood, as though Christ did <sup>Mark xiv. 36. Luke xxii. 42. John xviii. 11. Gal. v. 17.</sup> doubt of his Father's favour and grace; but the weakness of his flesh could have been content to have suffered no more. (Mark xiv. Luke xxii. John xviii. Gal. v.)

Now like as the spirit forepasseth and overcometh the flesh in Christ; even so must it do in us also, that we have more respect unto God and unto the life everlasting, than unto this worm-eaten flesh. And therefore now will we declare by most sure and infallible reasons, by what means and ways a man may master and overcome his flesh in the time of the cross and affliction, and so shew and declare true and perfect patience.

Which virtue, like as all other, hath her first beginning and increase of the grace, power, and Spirit of God, without whom we can work nothing that good is, neither yet resist or overcome any evil.

It is written: "The victory consisteth not in the multitude of men; but the power and strength cometh from heaven." (1 Mac. iii.) <sub>1 Mac. iii. 19.</sub>

Item: "I am able to do all things through him that maketh me mighty, which is Christ." (Phil. iv.) Wherefore, although my fleshly reason sinketh, wavereth, and faileth never so much, yet doth God continually preserve and uphold my spirit, that it do not utterly faint, but continue prompt and willing till such time as it may be delivered and eased. <sub>Phil. iv. 13.</sub>

But now, how should we order and behave ourselves, that God may grant us his strength, and true patience, and boldness? Forsooth, through faith, hope, prayer, love, truth, faithfulness, virtue, and godliness, we may obtain it of God.

First, we must furnish and comfort our hearts and minds with faith toward God. For whosoever doth know perfectly and is certain, that God, which is the Lord of all haps and mishaps, of prosperity and adversity, is pacified and reconciled with him, and that he for that cause cannot be deprived of eternal salvation; the same shall be able to contemn and to defy all worldly honour, pomp, and lusts. And again, there can be no pain so bitter, sharp, and grievous unto him, that can bring him out of patience. <sub>Faith worketh patience.</sub>

In our christian faith we confess and believe an holy universal church, and that we have fellowship and participation with all saints and elect of God; and also we confess and believe remission of sins, resurrection of the flesh, and life everlasting. And Christ giveth unto every one that hath faith this absolution: "Whosoever heareth my word and <sub>John v. 24.</sub>

believeth him that hath sent me, the same hath everlasting life, and cometh not to judgment, but passeth through from death to life." (John v.) Wherefore through faith a man obtaineth power, strength, patience, constancy, and steadfast-ness in all goodness. (Rom. v. viii. Heb. x. xi.)

Rom. v. 1—5;<br>viii. 26.<br>Heb x. 22;<br>xi. 1, &c.

If strong and mighty enemies should come upon thee, assault, and besiege thee, and thou hadst on thy side one whom thou knewest certainly to be lord, and to have power over all thine enemies, thou mightest lawfully be bold and without fear. Now have we, through faith, Christ on our side, which is Lord over all lords, which hath full power over all fortune and misfortune, prosperity and adversity.

Therefore thou must not long think and look upon the weakness of thy flesh, but thou must stir about with thy faith; that is to say, thou must earnestly and diligently consider the mighty and true love of Jesus Christ, which both can and will comfort and rejoice thee more, than all misfortune is able to discomfort thee, or to make thee heavy.

It is said to us: "Your enemy the devil goeth about like a roaring lion, and seeketh whom he may devour; whom resist ye steadfastly with faith." (1 Pet. v.) Item, St James saith, that "your approved faith worketh patience." The holy and faithful apostles did evidently declare, that according to the inward man it was a joy and comfort unto them to be beaten and scourged for the Lord's sake. Again: all troubles and affliction are grievous by reason of our weak faith, which is yet but little exercised, and hath not well and fully tasted the riches and treasure of the children of God.

1 Pet. v. 8.<br>James i. 3.<br>Acts iv. v.

Yet notwithstanding no man ought to despair, though he have not a perfect strong faith.

It happeneth oft-times, that the faith, being little and weak, in the time of necessity and affliction draweth back, and is like to a brand and sparkle that hath but a little fire upon it, which the Lord Jesus will not quench, but increase, so that we do but pray with the dear apostles, and say, "O Lord, strengthen our faith." (Isai. xli. Matt. xvii. Mark. ix.)

Isai. xli. 10.<br>Matt. xvii. 20.<br>Mark ix. 23.

But when a man is utterly destitute of faith, as he that knoweth of no other nor of no better life than this, it is no marvel at all though he despair at length.

Yea, the more he trusteth in himself, or in any worldly and transitory thing, the more unable is he to resist and continue in trouble and adversity. (Acts iv. v.) For there is no right comfort nor succour in any manner of thing, besides the Lord Jesus.

There are two kinds of hope; the one is of nature, and the other cometh of faith. The natural hope is a special gift and benefit of God, which after a certain manner doth help and comfort a man that is troubled and vexed, that he do not utterly despair; but in the midst of all adversity, hopeth that in a while it will, within a while, be better, and so waiteth and tarrieth till the adversity be overblown. *Hope maketh men patient.*

Now if this natural hope have such a strength and virtue, should not the other hope, which the Spirit of God doth newly inspire through faith, work a much greater and perfecter patience and strength; that a man in the midst of his cross shall hope and wait for heavenly comfort and aid of God for Christ's sake? And although the natural hope doth often and many times fail and deceive, and is always uncertain, yet this christian hope doth never fail nor deceive.

The husbandman considereth not only his labour and travail, and what tempest and mischance of weather may fortune; but forasmuch as he trusteth and hopeth that the fruit shall wax and come forth when the time is, therefore he laboureth stoutly and with a good will: even so in the spiritual vineyard, under the yoke of the Lord, the hope and trust of honour and reward maketh men patient and willing, and giveth them courage. "If we hope for that thing which we see not, we wait for it through patience." (Rom. viii.) Rom. viii. 25.

Furthermore, we must seek upon God fervently and without ceasing through prayer, that he will give us a bold and a strong spirit to suffer all things, and to continue steadfast unto the end. (Matt. xxiv.) Thus doing, he will surely hear us most graciously according to his promise, and faithfully give us his spiritual gifts most specially. *Prayer helpeth to patience.* Matt. xxiv. 13.

When a man maketh his complaint, and openeth his need and grief unto his special friend, he feeleth a certain ease afterward, so that his pain and grief by the rehearsing thereof is somewhat relieved, remedied, and taken away.

Much more comfort and ease shall we receive by telling and opening our grief and complaint unto God. For man is soon weary and irk of our complaining; but if we should spend the whole day in praying, crying, and complaining unto God, he would love, comfort, and strengthen us the more.

*To hear the word of God helpeth to patience.*
*Luke xviii. 1—8.*

Again, to search, hear, and learn the word of God, and for a man to exercise himself therein, is a great furtherance and help to patience. (Luke xviii.) For God hath not revealed and opened his word in vain unto us, but hath shewed and set before us in the same most sweet and loving promises and comfortable examples; that we might learn thereby his goodness, faithfulness, and great lovingkindness, and so comfort and strengthen ourselves by the same in all manner of trouble and adversity. For an example, the holy word of God saith: "In the world ye shall have sorrow and trouble; but be of good comfort, for I have overcome the world." (John xvi.)

*John xvi. 33.*

Item: "God is our hope and strength. O Lord, thou forsakest not them that seek thee, &c." (Psal. xlvi. Isai. xxviii.) Many such godly promises and excellent comfortable sayings have we, which we ought to seek and to fetch, though it were even from Jerusalem, upon our knees, and never to cease lauding and praising of God, that he in these latter days hath made us partakers of the eternal and infallible comfort of our souls in his word and gospel: which word is nothing but pure virtue and life, as all faithful hearts do feel and perceive; and it ought no otherwise to be received of us, but as though we heard the very voice of God himself from heaven, speaking all such things as we hear out of the Old and New Testament.

*Psal. xlvi. 1. Isai. xxviii. 16.*

*Love toward God worketh patience.*

Again: the love, which waxeth and springeth out of faith, worketh patience in adversity, and constancy and steadfastness in goodness. Jacob served seven years for the damsel Rachel; and by reason of the hearty love that he bare unto her, the time was but short unto him: and the days that he served for her, seemed but a short space. (Gen. xxix.) Even so whosoever loveth God, shall bear and take patiently whatsoever God layeth upon him; and whatsoever he suffereth for God's sake, it shall be ease unto him.[1]

*Gen. xxix. 20.*

[1 The concluding words of this sentence are wanting in the Peterborough copy.]

Now sickness and other plagues do not happen unto us without the will and providence of God: therefore if we love God heartily, (as we ought to do, forasmuch as he is our merciful Father, and we his children and heirs,) we cannot murmur against his visitation, nor be discontent with it, but we shall rather run after him through all manner of ways, be they never so rough; and shall contemn all things, be they never so hard and grievous; and evermore press unto him through thick and thin, until such time as we come to perfect rest in him, according to the example of the holy apostles and martyrs, whose love toward God did mitigate and ease all their sorrow, cross, and adversity. (Acts iv. 2 Cor. xi. 2 Tim. iii. 1 Mac. xii. 2 Mac. vi. &c.)

Item: to give alms, and to exercise all kinds of virtue and godliness worketh patience, and that specially for these two causes: first, because God doth increase his spiritual gifts in them which do well use and bestow them; for to him that hath shall more be given: (Eccles. xxxv. Matt. xiii.) and secondarily, whosoever behaveth himself godly and virtuously, the same hath a better and a more quiet conscience, and so much more boldness and confidence, but yet only building and staying upon the righteousness of Jesus Christ. (2 Tim. ii.) *The exercise of virtue worketh patience. Ecclus. xxxv. 2. Matt. xiii. 12. 2 Tim. ii. 10.*

Item: like as a soldier, (first, for fear of prison and of the shameful death which he should suffer, if the battle should be lost; and again, in hope of the high reward and excellent honour and renown, if the victory go on his side,) will fight the more boldly and lustily; even so every true Christian is stirred and provoked to more faithfulness and patience, when he considereth the exceeding profit and commodity of patience; and again, the great hurt and discommodity of impatience. (Job i. Rev. ii.) *Job i. 21. Rev. ii. 25, 26.*

## CHAPTER XXXI.

### THE FRUIT, PROFIT, AND COMMODITY OF PATIENCE, AS WELL CORPORAL AS SPIRITUAL.

LAST of all, patience serveth to the honour and glory of God, and to the wealth and profit of man, both in soul, body, and in transitory goods and possessions, and also in worldly honour and commendation. For the faithful do resist and withstand their pain and smart, and patiently without any grudging suffer the Lord to deal with them according to his own will; not for any vain-glory, nor for any worldly or transitory gain or lucre, but only and specially to shew themselves obedient to God, and to laud and praise him.

*By patience God is glorified.*

As for example: God was as highly praised and glorified, when the three companions of Daniel suffered themselves so patiently and manfully to be cast into the hot burning oven, as he was by the excellent wisdom of Daniel, which he declared in that he could open unto the king his dream.

*Patience is profitable for the body and goods.*

Furthermore, the patient is less sick, and when he is sick, he is sooner whole again: whereas through impatiency the heart is pressed, vexed, gnawen, consumed, and eaten up. A merry and a quiet heart is an help and furtherance to health; but a heavy and sorrowful mind maketh the natural strength to consume. Like as the moths do hurt the garments, and worms the wood, even so doth sorrow and heaviness hurt the heart of man.

When a child, being corrected and punished of his father, suffereth it patiently, his father hath the more pity upon him, and holdeth his hand, and ceaseth the sooner; but if the child shew himself froward, cry any thing loud, or murmur and grudge against him, then is the father the more angry and fierce over him, and beateth him the more sharply: even so the heavenly Father punisheth the patient man the more easily, and healeth him the sooner; but toward them that murmur against him he sheweth himself sharp and fierce.

The patient man Job obtained his goods double again, and was plentifully recompensed of the Lord even here in this life. The faithful have experience and proof in very deed, that it is good for them to be patient, and to suffer the Lord to work his will. And again, many by reason of their impatiency and murmuring, do lose that thing that they should else have enjoyed[1].

Sufferance and patience is a token of wisdom; unmeasurable heaviness is a token of foolishness, when we weep and complain like children, saying, I would never have thought, I would never have believed, that it should have come thus and thus to pass, and such like. *Patience is profitable to the soul and mind, and a furtherance to all virtues.*

Item, impatiency entangleth and ensnareth the mind, and maketh a man sometime dull and at his wit's end. When a man submitteth and giveth over himself humbly unto the will of God, although his adversity cannot be remedied, yet it shall be easier and lighter unto him; yea, there is nothing so bitter, sour, hard, or terrible to a man, but by this means shall be easy, sweet, light, and unto him comfortable.

And again, so long as a man doth not utterly give over and yield himself to the good will of God, and will not suffer him to work his pleasure with him, content whatsoever he sendeth, his grief is the worse, and the more sharp is his pain; his mind never ceaseth gnawing and fretting, and of one sorrow he maketh three or four. Like as the bird that is caught with the lime-rod, the more it striveth to deliver itself, the more do the feathers cleave and hang to the lime; and in like manner, the more the fish that is caught in the net seeketh to come out, the more it windeth itself in; and as he that is bound with chains or fetters of iron, the more he strayeth abroad, the more harm doeth he to himself; even so such as are froward and unpatient in adversity, do increase their sorrow, and hurt themselves the more.

He that hath a heavy burden upon his back, the more he shuttleth and moveth the same, the more doth it grieve him: even so the more froward and unpatient a man is under the cross, the more grievous and painful is it unto him. It is not unwisely spoken of the heathen man, Pliny, which saith: "A good heart in adversity taketh away the half of his misery;" and it is a common proverb of the heathen men: "The fear

[[1] Enjoyed. Peterborough copy: had.]

of adversity and pain, before it cometh, is worse than the pain itself, when it is come."

All manner of punishment and adversity, which, according to the merit and desert of man, should be unto him a taste and beginning of everlasting pain and damnation, the patient man taketh and useth it for an occasion to exercise thereby all kinds of virtue; whereby the spiritual gifts of grace do wax and increase more and more. For they that are patient do keep the true faith toward God, cry and call upon God through fervent prayer, honour, laud, and praise God, not only for that he ruleth and disposeth all things, but also that he bringeth all things to a good end and success, and that he will so continually do. And thus through patience is patience increased.

And contrariwise, the unpatient man decayeth daily in all kinds of virtues, and is daily more and more spoiled and deprived of all goodness. For whosoever is content and can suffer himself to be provoked of the devil and of the flesh, and giveth place unto them, the same forsaketh faith, prayer, and obedience toward God, and suffereth them to depart, and so is unthankful unto his true and faithful God; whom he cannot be content to suffer, and to commit himself unto him for a while, that he may the more defend and preserve him afterward.

He thinketh that God doth not regard him, and that it is in vain to trust and to wait for help, comfort, and deliverance of God; he imagineth with himself nothing else, but that God is utterly wroth and displeased with him; and can find in his heart to curse and to blaspheme God, as though he were a cruel, unmerciful, and an unrighteous God, shewing more love and favour, and doing more good, to the wicked than to the godly: and by this occasion he seeketh for aid, help, and comfort of creatures, and maketh vows unto saints and to pilgrimages, that is to say, to chapels of idolatry and of false gods, and maketh wicked covenants, agreements, and promises against God.

Some for fear do forsake and deny the christian faith, and receive the wicked popish religion, consenting to manifest idolatry, and make God a liar, as though he could not or would not help any more in this or that thing, according to his manifold promises in the Old and New Testament.

Furthermore, unquietness is augmented and increased through impatiency; so that a man that is unpatient is every day more sorrowful and desperate than other; fleeth, where he should steadfastly continue; and findeth neither rest, ease, nor quietness in his heart: and many one, because he will not suffer and abide poverty and other like extreme necessity, falleth to naughtiness, murder, whoredom, lying, stealing, extortion, riot, cutting of purses, and to such other detestable abomination.

Item, they that be unpatient do envy and disdain at other men's wealth and prosperity: for they imagine that to be the cause of their cross and sorrow, and they fret against it, envying, disdaining, and hating oft-times the innocent without any cause; yea, they rage and rave, running headlong to revenge themselves. By the reason whereof ofttimes, as many stories do testify, contention, hatred, war, uproar, shedding of blood, decay and destruction of the church, of religion, and of the commonwealth, have risen; as Coriolanus, to revenge himself, as an enemy did procure war against his own natural country. Besides this, it is an high honour and commendation before men, before the angels, before the holy saints, and also before God himself, when a man sheweth patience, boldness, and strength in adversity. *Patiency is a commendation and honour before men.*

And again, when a man behaveth himself unseemly, unpatiently, and desperately, it is a shame and a dishonour for him both before all creatures, and also before the Creator himself. For it is no high nor hard thing for a man to shew a bold and a strong heart, and to be content with God's working, when all things happen prosperously and according to his mind; but this is a virtue and a point of cunning, when a man's mind is not moved nor broken in adversity and misfortune. Like as in a school or place of fence, he that hath shewed the most manly touch, and hath won the victory, hath the greater commendation and higher honour; even so is it much more commendable and a greater honour, to overcome and to subdue our spiritual enemies, and to have the victory against the assaults of the flesh and the devil.

He that forsaketh his bodily master without a just cause, is taken before the world for a man that lacketh faith, truth, and honesty: and should it not then be a greater point of dishonesty and of unfaithfulness, in the time of affliction under the cross, to forsake Christ and his word, and through impatiency to work and to do against the same? He that subdueth the temptations of the mind, is to be preferred, and more to be commended than he that hath besieged and overcome a strong city. For the which cause, as well among the Christians as among the heathen, divers notable persons have gotten high commendation and praise for their trustiness, fidelity, and excellent constancy, which they have shewed at an hazard and at the time of need.

*Prov. xvi. 32.*

And specially the example of our Saviour Jesus Christ is to be considered, whereof Paul maketh mention, saying: If Christ, after his affliction and obedience even unto death, were exalted to high honour and glory, it shall be a furtherance likewise unto us to great honour, if we take our cross daily upon us, and follow him boldly and manly.

Experience teacheth also, when a man will shift away the cross from him by unlawful means, oft-times he is compelled and driven by force to suffer as much or more with shame and dishonesty[1].

*[Wisd. xvi. 5—12.]*
*Patience is profitable for the lengthening of a man's life.*

Judith saith: "They that have not taken their cross and temptation in the fear of God, but through murmuring and grudging against God have shewed themselves unpatient, they were destroyed and murthered of serpents[2]."

Item, whether a man do suffer worthily or innocently, if he continue in murmuring and is unpatient, it serveth to his eternal damnation.

*Patience may further a man to everlasting life.*

And again, whether a man suffer worthily or innocently, if he take it patiently as he ought to do, it will be profitable[3] unto him, and a furtherance to everlasting life. And all the sorrows and pains upon earth, in respect of the bliss and salvation that is prepared for us, is but the biting of a gnat or a flea, which is easy to overcome.

When men in warfare lying in camp will play the sluggards and be slothful, and not resist the enemies stoutly and manfully, their fields are destroyed, their houses spoiled,

[1 The Peterborough copy reads in addition: "for the devil's sake, and to have great dishonour and confusion thereby."]

[2 This paragraph is different in the Peterborough copy; in which also the reference to the book of Judith is erroneous.]

[3 The Peterborough copy has "meritorious."]

their villages set on fire, their dear friends and neighbours murdered and slain, and their wives and daughters defiled and ravished, and all goeth to havoc, and is full of misery; even so in the spiritual warfare and field, if we yield unto the flesh and the devil, and resist them not manfully and constantly, we cast ourselves into perpetual danger, misery, and unquietness. But if we fight against Ephes. vi. 12. the ghostly enemies stoutly and patiently, we may the sooner attain to perpetual rest and quietness.

He that is sick, if he will not receive the medicine, because it is bitter and sour, it is no marvel nor wonder, if the same man perish in his sickness or disease; but if he would suffer himself to be handled after the mind and counsel of the physician, he might overcome the smart, and have good hope to be restored to his health again: even so all right and faithful Christians, that are patient in adversity, may conceive a much more stedfast and sure hope, that they shall attain to everlasting rest of body and soul: whereas contrariwise, they which remain and continue in their frowardness and impatiency against God the heavenly physician, must smart for it everlastingly, both in body and soul. Scripture, to confirm and prove this, have we: "Happy is James i. 12. Job v. 17. that man which suffereth in temptation; for after that he is Prov. iii. 11, 12. proved, he shall receive the crown of life." But no man Hos. vi. 1. 1 Pet. iv. 12, may gather or conclude upon this, that we merit or deserve &c. Heb xii. 1, eternal salvation for our patience, which thing only Christ &c. alone hath done.

Last of all, patience is profitable, and bringeth singular commodity, not only to him that hath the same virtue, but also to other; for when another perceiveth thee to be constant in the truth, he taketh occasion to exercise like patience and stedfastness. It is manifest by divers credible stories, when as the Christians have died boldly for the christian faith's sake, that certain of the persecutors have wondered so sore thereat, that they by that and no other occasion were converted to the faith of Christ[4].

Item, patience and stedfastness have wrought quietness in commonwealths, in the church, in many nations, cities, and towns. Scipio, a noble ruler, chose rather to leave Rome, than to subdue and oppress his enemies with force of arms;

[4 Peterborough copy: faith and religion of Christ.]

[COVERDALE.]

the doing whereof turned to the singular commodity of the whole commonwealth: and contrariwise, a bitter, cruel, and unpatient mind bringeth, worketh, and occasioneth infinite harm and destruction[1].

Also through our unpatientness in adversity[2] we give occasion to them that be weak in the faith to doubt, whether our faith be the true faith or no, when we confess of God, that he is our comfort both in this world and in the world to come, and yet shew ourselves so desperate in adversity, as though God had utterly forsaken us[3].

Wherefore we ought to prepare ourselves for all adversity in time of prosperity, and not to hang upon transitory things, that when need shall require, we may be content to forego them, and continue stedfast in the true faith, wherein "whosoever shall continue unto the end, shall be saved[4]."

Matt. xxiv. 13.

[[1] To these words is added in the Peterborough copy: "in commonwealths, and heresies in the church of God"; and this sentence is succeeded by the following paragraph. "For Marius, as he came again to Rome, and could not refrain himself through his unpatientness, wrought great tyranny, and shewed much cruelness, causing divers principal people of the contrary part that held against him most cruelly to be murdered and put to death, whereupon did follow and ensue much inconvenience. Also Arius, because he could not obtain his purpose, nor bring his device to effect, for very frowardness and impatiency he vexed and disquieted the church of Christ with horrible heresies. In like manner through our unpatientness," &c.]

[[2] "Unpatientness in the cross and adversity," Peterborough copy.]

[[3] To these words is added in the Peterborough copy: "and as though there were no better life after this."]

[[4] This concluding paragraph stands rather differently in the Peterborough copy: "Wherefore we ought to arm and prepare ourselves to all manner of adversity in time, while we are here in good wealth and prosperity, and not to depend and hang overmuch upon transitory goods and prosperity, that whensoever need shall require, we may be content with patience to forego and forbear them, and continue stedfast in the true faith, wherein whosoever shall continue unto the end shall be saved." Matt. xxiv. 13. Amen. To God only be all honour and praise.]

# FRUITFUL LESSONS

UPON THE

PASSION, BURIAL, RESURRECTION, ASCENSION,

AND OF

THE SENDING OF THE HOLY GHOST.

# Fruitfull Lessons VPON THE PASSION, BV-RIALL, RESVRRECTION,

Ascension, and of the sending of

the holy Ghost.

## GATHERED OVT OF THE FOVRE

Euangelists: with a plaine exposition

of the same.

### By MILES COVERDALL.

JOHN 14. 6.

I am the waie, the truth, and the life, no man commeth vnto the Father but by me.

[TABLE OF CONTENTS.

|  | PAGE |
|---|---|
| The Author to the Reader | 199 |

CHAPTER I.

The Passion of Jesus Christ out of the holy Evangelists . 209

CHAPTER II.

The Burial of Jesus Christ out of the holy Evangelists . . 315

CHAPTER III.

The Resurrection of Jesus Christ out of the holy Evangelists 322

CHAPTER IV.

The Ascension of Jesus Christ out of the holy Evangelists . 379

CHAPTER V.

The sending of the Holy Ghost . . . . . . 387]

[The idea and plan of this Treatise are borrowed from one by Huldric Zuingle, entitled, "Brevis commemoratio mortis Christi ex quatuor Evangelistis per H. Zuinglium in unam seriem concinnata; sequitur historia resurrectionis et ascensionis Christi:" but the learned writer has so far improved upon his model, that it is justly entitled to the character of an original work.

There is no table of contents in the original work, nor are the different passages of the Evangelists mentioned, from which the extracts are taken. It has been thought right, for the sake of clearness and the convenience of the reader, to supply both these omissions in the present edition. In all other respects it is exactly conformable to the original copy.

An edition of this work is said by Tanner to have been published at Marpurg, 1540—47, in 8vo. The present edition is taken from a copy of the original in the Rectorial Library at Milden in Suffolk, printed by Thomas Scarlet in 1593; the use of that copy having been kindly permitted for the purpose by the authorities to whom the present charge of the Library belongs.]

# THE AUTHOR TO THE READER.

SINCE our human imperfections are such, as one sin driveth out another, and the frailty of our natures is so great, as having touched the brim of the ocean thereof, we never cease till we are overwhelmed and drowned in the bottom of the same; since of ourselves we are but grafts of a corruptious tree, children of eternal darkness, infidels who bow the knee to Baal, having uncircumcised hearts and lying lips, whose minds are fixed on the world and fastened on mammon; I thought good, christian reader, considering the self-love in us, which have converted the angels into devils,—which, as Augustine witnesseth, hath builded the very Babylon of contempt of God[1],—to level out a way for all men to tread, a glass for all men to see, an adamant, wherewith all souls may be drawn to the beholding of their vices, the loathing of the same, and finally the amendment and hearty conversion for their misdeeds. And for that it most evidently appeareth, that the justest man falleth oftentimes a-day, and they that discern errors in themselves; and seeing then that they are in the next step to amendment, it behoveth us to consider the weakness which is in us, how far we are fallen and do fall from the protection of the just; so that in the end we

[[1] The following passage seems to be that referred to: Videte nomina duarum istarum civitatum, Babylonis et Hierusalem. Babylon *confusio* interpretatur, Hierusalem *visio pacis*. . . . Possumus tamen et aliquid afferre, quantum Dominus donat, unde distinguantur pii fideles, etiam hoc tempore cives Hierusalem a civibus Babyloniæ, Duas istas civitates faciunt duo amores. Hierusalem facit amor Dei, Babyloniam facit amor seculi. Interroget ergo se quisque, quid amet, et inveniet unde sit civis; et si se invenerit civem Babyloniæ, extirpet cupiditatem, plantet caritatem. Enarratio in Psalmum LXXIV. Opera, Vol. VIII. p. 144, A. B. Ed. 1541. See also Expos. in Apocalypsim Joannis. Hom. XVI. Opera, Vol. IX. p. 148, E. F.]

may in the spring of repentance wash away original and successive sins, which have defiled our souls, and cleaving to the true corner-stone, whereon our faith should be builded, withstand the perils of perdition, which our ghostly enemy hath raised against us.

And for that truth is never known but by his contrary, and our nakedness is not disclosed, unless our eyes be opened; let us examine ourselves, and we shall find that these are inseparable errors in us, from which the justest are not exempted, namely, blindness and corruptness of judgment, pride in spirit, mistrust in God, to be slack and weary in God's service, defacing of God's truth, not to have God before the eyes, surmising, vanity of heart, curiosity and niceness, grudging in our hearts against the enemy, bitterness, desire of vengeance, a man's good intent, greediness to be seen and praised, vain-glory, ambition, proper election, maintaining of our own evil, a disdainful, false, unfaithful, wicked eye, and such like pharisaical points and feats, wherewith the devil tempteth the good men that keep themselves from the gross vices. These and other innumerable vices shall every one, how good soever he be, find in himself, if he search himself uprightly and throughly to the bottom.

Seeing then, that we find ourselves so vicious, altogether sick, poisoned, and wounded unto death, we ought day and night without ceasing to complain and lament before God, to watch and pray unto God for remission of our sins; yet should we not despair of life. The true Physician of our souls came down from heaven, and through his passion hath he made us a plaister for our wounds; only let us use it and lay it to the sore. The faithful Samaritan poureth oil and wine into our wounds, taketh us up to cure and to heal us; only let us follow him, and fashion ourselves after his image. He is the brasen serpent without sin, whom with the eyes of faith we must behold hanging and lift up upon the cross for us: he taking our sins upon himself, giveth us his own innocency.

If the burden of sin now oppresseth and grieveth us, we ought to run unto him: he shall ease us and give us rest; for his blood washeth away our sins. Him hath the Father given unto us to be our righteousness and redemption.

Besides this great treasure that God hath given us in

Christ, he is set forth unto us, especially in his passion, for a pattern or example, whereby we may learn to die from sin, and find a preservative against vices to come. For self-love and high esteeming of a man's own self is the well-spring of all vice. Consider that Christ was not proud himself of his own highness, but took upon him the shape of a servant, and came to serve us, humbled him most lowly, loved not himself, sought not his own, desired not his honour, but the honour of his Father; all despite and reproach fell upon him. If we ponder this by faith, all greedy love of ourselves shall fall away.

The obedience of Jesu in true belief considered expelleth and healeth our disobedience, and the idolatry of our own carnal heart. With his obedience covereth he the disobedience of all men, so far as we abide in the obedience of faith, that Christ be dearer unto us than the whole world; for the which cause we freely give over ourselves into his obedience, suffering all things for his sake. Pride and vain-glory is healed through Christ's humility and contempt, which he suffered for us manifold. "Learn of me," saith he; "for I am meek and lowly of heart." Why are we so greedy of temporal things, when Christ, the Lord of heaven and earth, became for us so poor, hanging bare and naked upon the cross? The chaste pure life of Jesus Christ expelleth in us all uncleanness of the flesh. Also his martyrdom, anguish, and trouble, which in his flesh he suffered for us, quencheth the lust and concupiscence of the flesh.

Oh, how evil doth it become a believer to be ireful and greedy of vengeance, when his forerunner, being in most humility like unto a sheep, prayed for his enemies!

Envy and hatred is highly expelled, if we consider the excellent deep love of Jesu towards us. Gluttony and excess of life shall fall away from us, if we well remember that Christ for us drank vinegar mixed with gall.

As it is here shewed in certain points, even so against all vices and blemishes of the soul there may remedy be found in the passion of Christ, if it be rightly used in the contemplation of faith. The old Adam ought we to lay aside, to mortify the members upon earth, and to put on Christ the Lord, as the new wedding-garment. In the cross ought to be our exercise, our joy, comfort, and life.

Hereunto also helpeth us our heavenly Father, who unto us his children, whom he most entirely loveth, suffereth manifold passions, afflictions, troubles, and anguishes, sickness, poverty, and persecution to come, to keep us upon the cross, lest we as negligent people gape for temporal earthy things. And if we will needs follow our own lusts, he hedgeth our way with thorns, nurturing and humbling us through trouble; that we, being tried and purified as the gold in the fire, may cry and call unto him, and that we may give our earthly things, seeing we find no quietness in them. He bringeth us into the land of promise, howbeit through the wilderness, through much travail and labour. Blessed are they that in patience, without murmuring, suffer the Lord to work, and do faithfully follow him.

All this, and more than I can say, ought to be the consideration and exercise, when we celebrate the supper of the Lord Jesu, that we so sprinkle the blood of Christ in our hearts, and drink it into us, that it may work in us, and bring forth fruit. Our eyes and hearts we ought to lift up into heaven, and consider what the bread and wine pointeth us unto, namely, unto the body of Christ, that was offered up upon the cross for our sins, and to his blood, that was shed for the washing away of our offences; and that we fashion ourselves unto his image, and practise also such love one towards another. This is the proof that Paul speaketh of, with the which a faithful believer ought to exercise himself before and in the Lord's supper, examining well his faith and love, which out of the love of God towards us is kindled and increased. First, ought a man to consider the excellent love of our Lord Jesus Christ, who so loved us, that he died for us. And seeing that he biddeth us to so high a feast of his grace, we ought also to ponder the same in such sort, that we be thankful unto him, and prepare ourselves thereafter.

St Paul saith, that there is a feeding with milk, and a feeding with strong meat, which is to be observed according to the nature and property of those that receive the meat. And in the church of God there be three sorts of men, as the same by the high illuminated good wise teacher Augustine and by others is written[1].

[[1] This classification of the members of the christian church does not appear in any single part of the works of Augustine, although it

First, there be men, which having spent their former time past in pastime and wantonness of the world, and con-

agrees with his general opinions on the subject. 1. With regard to the first class (who are described under the character of *Penitents*), the opinions of Coverdale will be found to harmonize in general with those of Augustine, as they are detailed in his general works, where he treats on the subject of repentance. 2. With regard to the second, who are described by him under the character of *Reformers*, the doctrine of Augustine is contained in his Treatise De Trinitate, c. 16, 17. Opera. Vol. III. p. 99, I. p. 100, A. B. Ed. Par. 1541. 3. Of the third class of persons, namely, those who are called *Perfect*, Augustine speaks in different parts of his writings, but more especially in his discourse, " De perfectione justitiæ contra Celestium ;" and in the following remarks on those passages of the old and new Testament, which speak of the attainment of holiness, and contain exhortations to it; e. g. Deut. xviii. 13; Matt. v. 48, &c.: " Horum testimoniorum aliqua currentes exhortantur, ut perfecte currant, aliqua ipsum finem commemorant quo currendo pertendant. Ingredi autem sine macula non absurde ille dicatur, non qui jam perfectus est, sed qui ad ipsam perfectionem irreprehensibiliter currit." Augustin. Opera, Vol. VII. p. 307, L.

The expression τὸ τέλειον is also used with reference to the Eucharist,* as it is frequently called in the canons of the ancient councils. (Concil. Ancyrani Canones. Can. 4, 5, 6, apud Routh, Rel. Sacr. Vol. III. pp. 405, &c.; Suicer. Thes. p. 1259; Bingham, Orig. Eccles. Lib. I. c. iv. 3.) But the terms τέλειος, τελειόω, τελείωσις, are also used by some of the Fathers, and particularly those of the Alexandrian school, to denote the religious condition of the more advanced Christian, (Suicer. Thes. pp. 1256—9; Routh, Vol. III. p. 227); as may be seen in the writings of Clemens Alexandrinus, in whom the following passage occurs, remarkably illustrating the opinions of bishop Coverdale in this passage: ὁ δὲ ἐν τῷ σώματι καθαρισμὸς τῆς ψυχῆς πρῶτος, οὗτός ἐστιν, ἡ ἀποχὴ τῶν κακῶν· ἥν τινες τελείωσιν ἡγοῦνται· καὶ ἔστιν ἁπλῶς τοῦ κοινοῦ πιστοῦ, Ἰουδαίου τε καὶ Ἕλληνος, ἡ τελείωσις αὕτη· τοῦ δὲ γνωστικοῦ, μετὰ τὴν ἄλλοις νομιζομένην τελείωσιν, ἡ δικαιοσύνη εἰς ἐνεργείαν εὐποιΐας προβαίνει· καὶ ὅτῳ δὴ ἡ ἐπίτασις τῆς δικαιοσύνης εἰς ἀγαθοποιΐας ἐπιδέδωκεν, τούτῳ ἡ τελείωσις ἐν ἀμεταβόλῳ ἕξει εὐποιΐας καθ᾽ ὁμοίωσιν Θεοῦ διαμένει. Strom. Lib. VI. pp. 464, 5. Ed. 1616.]

---

* Is. Casaubonus Exercit. XVI. 48. adv. Baronium : " τὸ τέλειον, *perfectio* aut *consummatio*, est ipsa Eucharistia, quæ etiam Dionysio dicitur τελείωσις, ut ante observabamus : quia conjunctioni nostræ cum Christo, cujus instrumenta sunt verbum Dei et sacramenta, veluti colophonem imponit participatio corporis et sanguinis Christi in cœna Dominica : nullus enim restat alius modus, quo in terris versantes arctius cum Christo capite nostro conjungamur."

sidering the careful end thereof, as they be inwardly moved by the grace of God, have undertaken to cease and refrain from sin, and from all occasions of sin; and in most diligent wise, as near as they can, with the assistance, grace, and help of God, to be circumspect and wary thereof; albeit they are yet weak, and have not so strong a spirit, as to lay aside and despise all worldly things out of hand. And these are the right true beginners of repentant and *penitent* persons: though they be not new beginners, yet are they unto God the Lord so dear, that all things cannot sufficiently commend and praise it.

This is witnessed unto us by the holy gospel of the unthrifty son; who, when with shameful riot he had wantonly consumed his inheritance, did in time of his extreme hunger convert and turn again to his loving father, and received not only gracious forgiveness of his trespass, but also special tokens of his father's love; as the garment, the kiss, the fat calf, the sweet minstrelsy and melody. This is the first anchor of true repentance. This is the first state concerning the blessed swine-herd, who forsaking the hogs with the cods[1], draff, or swillings, that he sometimes greedily filled his belly withal, and returning to his loving father, is now in his first coming again to his merciful father graciously taken up, received, and rewarded.

Whoso now with this unthrifty son forsaketh his sins, and coming again in true and hearty repentance unto God, his most loving and gracious Father, saith meekly, "O Father, I am not worthy to be called thy son, for I have sinned against heaven and before thee; O make me one of thy hired servants;" to him shall the Father deny nothing. Whoso now with an unfeigned heart and mouth may speak this unto God, and truly and unfeignedly seeketh Jesus, assuredly he findeth him and hath with him a cheerful supper. Look unto whom God in his great mercy giveth such a taste of his grace, let him render thanks and praise unto Almighty God: let him now look for it, that the Father who hath received him, will also nurture him in his own school, and through manifold adversities furnish him, prepare him, and make him more perfect. He hath been fed with the milk; he must learn also to know what hard meat

[1 cods: husks.]

meaneth. Through adversity and troublesome chances he must be tempted and proved, whether he have ought in him of the blessed seed that groweth upwards unto eternal life: which thing shall well appear and be made manifest, if in time of temptation and troubles he be not choked with the thorns, nor trodden down by the high-way-side, nor withered among the stones, but found fruitful in a good and fertile ground.

Other men there be, which are called *reformers*, to whom belongeth somewhat more than there doth unto the other. For like as it appertaineth to the first repentant or penitent persons, that they continually and fervently, with the confession of their sins unto God, with sorrow and lamentation, with prayer, watching, and chastising of the body, do break out away from their old sins, harnessing and arming themselves against others for to come, and earnestly withstanding and forsaking their own evil and naughty customs, if they mind to bring forth fruit, and not to fall away again; even so the reformers in the second order and manner, after the hard rooting out of vice and wickedness, must still exercise themselves in the will of God and in good works, seeking diligently experience thereof in holy scripture, and of those teachers, who by reason of long practice, and by the scriptures, can declare and teach the same way. When these men in such a stedfast purpose to walk and practise themselves in the will of God with his grace and power, do go unto the supper of the Lord, they inwardly with joy and fruit of the godly feast are nourished and refreshed. For whoso desireth to cleave unto virtue, and to a godly life, shall nowhere find the same so evidently and plain, as in Christ's passion, whereof he is mindful at the supper with faith and thanksgiving.

The third sort of men are called *perfect*: not that any man here in time may be perfect, as to lack nothing, or to have no sin in him; but therefore are they named perfect, because their exercise is such, that after long accustomate doing of virtuous deeds, after many spiritual fruits brought forth by them in patience, after many temptations, which they with the help of God have overcome, they have so wholly humbled and cast down themselves before God, being reconciled with him, that they are become one spirit with

Christ their head, whom they cleave unto, whose cross and holy passion they follow without fainting, so far as their wit and power may suffer; being dead from the world and the flesh, following only the Lord Jesu Christ, suffering with him, and living with him. These with their minds and hearts step somewhat higher than the others, having their dwelling in heaven, in the sweet contemplation and beholding of God's almightiness, wisdom, and goodness, with fervent devotion. Which men also, by enjoying of the said feast according to their belief and fervent love, receive the more excellent rites, whereby they may expel the temptations that they like not. For the devil keepeth no holy day; he sleepeth not, runneth about as a roaring lion, he ceaseth not; and therefore these men continually get them to their weapons, with the consideration of the passion of Christ. Abraham, the good friend of God, must still drive away the ravenous birds from the sacrifice, till the sun go down, and till a man cheerfully say: "In peace will I lay me down and take my rest," &c.

This probation must be well taken heed unto; for many men not justly considering themselves, neither right discerning this meat from others, receive the food of life unto death. Not that this holy bread was instituted and ordained of Christ, to hurt any man; but because the evil man doth wickedly receive that which is wholesome, and abuseth it through unbelief, therefore justly doth Paul exhort, that there be first had a diligent examination of a man's self, and that then he eat of this bread, and drink of this cup. Thus let every man take good heed to his own state and vocation, that this banquet may set him forward, not unto his hurt, but to eternal life.

Whoso taketh not heed unto this difference, and to himself, as, alas! carnal people do, which are not spiritually instructed; the same faileth oft in many things, and undertaketh to fly high, yea, higher than his knowledge and power may attain. Hereof then it also proceedeth, as we see before our eyes, that so few folks come to stedfast amendment, namely, even hereof, that when men are not exercised in discerning of God's matters from others, a mad heady notion of sensuality provoketh them inordinately to sit highest at the table, whereas yet they are not worthy of the lowest place; and so will they forthwith possess the seat royal, afore they have found the asses, or kept the sheep, as of David and Saul in figure it is read. But thus ought it not to be: for though the grace of the Holy Ghost use not long fetches about, yet cometh no man suddenly to the happiest step. I speak after the common course, as it beseemeth us to talk and do in the church of God, namely, after the ordinance which he hath appointed us.

Behold St Paul, being so perfect in the law, that the world could not accuse him; being also chaste, earnest, fervent, and well exercised in all virtues; whom God, that had separated him from his mother's womb, would call to his service. Though he was taken up into the third heaven, and saw secrets that no man can express, yet doth he not trust so much thereto, as by reason of that great grace to magnify himself, and to take upon him the office of preaching, before he being taught at Gamaliel's feet, and baptized and instructed of Ananias, had perceived in himself and proved that same, which he afterwards out of the perfectness of the Spirit might distribute abroad unto all Christendom. This is peradventure laughed to scorn of the unexpert, proud, worldly-wise: but whoso hath ears circumcised with the fear of God, will think more upon the matter.

He that will sit now at the table of the high King, let him diligently consider what he receiveth in his soul through faith, namely, the body and blood of Jesus Christ, which feedeth and nourisheth him to eternal life, and draweth him to God, altereth him, and maketh him stedfast, which the outward bread taken with the mouth doth point and lead unto: yea, let us ponder, how great love, and what an example Christ there setteth before him, that he also must prepare the like; that is, that he to his power must follow the love, life, and passion of Christ, to the intent that he, being wounded with Christ's love, and fastened with him upon the cross, may abide in him unto the end.

For in the passion of Christ is the instruction of the way which we ought and must follow unto eternal life. There also is information, where and how the same way and the everlasting truth is shewed and found. Thus the penitent findeth the way, the reformer the undoubted unwandering truth; the perfect the very life eternal, which is Christ Jesus, and there is eternal peace. God grant that all they which read this little book, and consider this matter, may so burn in love and fervent devotion, that they continue and live in Christ, and he in them for ever! Amen.

## [CHAPTER I.]

### THE PASSION OF CHRIST OUT OF THE HOLY EVANGELISTS.

[Matthew xxvi. 1—9. Mark xiv. 1—25. Luke xxii. 1—19. John xiii. 1.]

THE feast of sweet bread, which is also called Easter, drew nigh, namely, after two days. Then said Jesus to his disciples: Know ye, that after two days shall be Easter, and the Son of man shall be betrayed and crucified. At the same time were the chief priests and council gathered together in the palace of the high priest, whose name was Caiphas; and there they counselled, how they might craftily apprehend, take, and kill him. Howbeit they feared the people. Therefore said they together: Not on the holy day, lest there be an uproar among the people. But Satan was entered into Judas called Iscariot, one of the twelve, who went out to the high priests and rulers, intending to deliver him unto them: therefore how he would deliver Jesus unto them, he told them, and said: What will you give me, and I will deliver him unto you? When they heard that, they were glad, and agreed with him, promising him thirty pence. Then promised he them, and sought from thenceforth opportunity, how he might deliver Jesus unto them handsomely and without any uproar.

But afore the feast which is called PASSAH, Jesus, knowing that his hour was come, and that he should depart out of this world unto the Father, while he loved his own that were in the world, he loved them unto the end.

On the first day of sweet bread, when they offer passah, the disciples came to Jesu and said: Where wilt thou that

[COVERDALE.]

we go and prepare passah for thee? Then sent he two of his disciples, namely, Peter and John, saying: Go and prepare for us, that we may eat passah. They said: Where? Then said he: Go into the city to one: behold, when ye enter in, one shall meet you bearing a pitcher with water; follow him into the house that he entereth into, and say unto the householder, The Master saith unto thee, My time is now here, that I will eat passah with thee. Where is now the place where the multitude shall be kept? Where is the parlour, that I shall eat passah in with my disciples? Then shall he shew you a great parlour that is paved; there make ye ready.

So the disciples went, and found as the Lord had told them; and they made ready the passah. At even came Jesus with the twelve, and when it was time, he sat him down at the table, and the twelve with him.

Now when he sat at the table with his disciples, and they did eat, he said: I have greatly longed and heartily desired to eat this passah with you afore I suffer. For I say unto you, that now from henceforth I will not eat of it, till it be fulfilled in the kingdom of God.

Now as they did eat, Jesus took the bread, gave thanks, and brake it, gave it to his disciples, and said: Take, eat, this is my body, which shall be betrayed and delivered for you; do this in remembrance of me. Likewise also when they had eaten, he took the cup, rendered thanks, and gave unto them, saying: Take and divide among you, and drink ye all thereof. This is my blood of the new testament, which is shed for you, and for many, to the forgiveness of sins. I say unto you, that from henceforth I shall not drink of the fruit of the vine, until the day that I shall drink it new with you in the kingdom of my Father. And they all drank thereof.

## NOW FOLLOWETH THE DOCTRINE AND MEDITATION.

HERE should we children of belief diligently ponder and consider, what Christ hath done for our sakes; namely, that he, when he had fulfilled his ministration committed to him of the Father, and now would offer up himself upon the cross for the sins of the world, and with his own death deliver mankind from the captivity of Satan, and from eternal death, declared, how he loved his own until the end, and with what desire he longed to eat the Easter lamb with his disciples, before he suffered. 1 Cor. v. Isai. liii. John i.: giving them thereby to understand, that he was the true paschal Lamb, which, being slain for us, should take away the sins of the world, that the figures of the old testament might be reduced into the truth; that like as the Jews, to whom with a prescribed ordinance it was commanded yearly to eat the Easter lamb, did the same for a memorial of their deliverance out of Egypt; so we believers also might in the new testament have a remembrance and exercise of the gracious redemption, whereas we by his death are delivered from the power of darkness, of the devil, and of sin, and brought to eternal life. *John xiii. Luke xxii. Exod. xii.*

And to the intent now that the remembrance of such excellent benefits, grace, and merits of the passion of Christ, might ever be fresh and new with his disciples and all believers, our Lord Jesus Christ, when he now would go unto death, and pay the ransom for the sins of all the world, he then did eat the Easter lamb with his disciples, to finish the shadow of the old testament; and that he might be remembered thereby, he instituted the bread and wine for a sacrament and memorial of his holy body and blood.

Seeing then that we are cleansed, delivered, and redeemed with so dear and worthy a treasure, namely, with the precious blood of Jesus Christ, the undefiled Lamb; we ought never to forget such an high benefit, but at all times with thankfulness to remember, that Christ our paschal Lamb was slain and offered up for us upon the cross, that we from henceforth should walk in pureness, singleness, and innocency of life; and that, when we in the supper by true faith do eat his body, and drink his blood, we might through him be so strengthened and fed to eternal life, as to abide and *1 Cor. v. 1 Pet. i. 1 John i. 1 Cor. xi. 1 Cor. x. 1 Pet. ii.*

live in him for ever. For he is the bread of life that came down from heaven, to nourish and strengthen our weak and hungry souls, yea, to make us dead to live again.

But then eat we his flesh, and then drink we his blood, when we through true belief do ponder and consider, what he hath done and suffered for our sakes; then are we partakers of his supper and feast, when we for his sake do live, as he did for his Father's sake. He gave himself whole unto us: so ought we to give ourselves whole unto him, and to our neighbour; to him through belief, to our neighbour through charitable love. Through faith we abide in him; by working love he abideth in us. The more we love, the more enjoy we of this meat; the more we believe, the more we love. In this shall all men know that we are his disciples, if we love one another. God is love; and he that abideth in love, abideth in God, and God in him. What greater love can there be, than to give his own life for us? The death of Christ ought never to come out of our hearts; that we may do and suffer all things for his sake that died for us.

## THE SECOND PART.

[John xiii. 2—17.]

WHEN supper was ended, after that the devil had put in the heart of Judas Iscarioth, Simon's son, to betray him; Jesus knowing that the Father had given all things into his hands, and that he was come from God, and went to God, he rose from supper, and laid aside his upper garments, and took a towel and girt himself. After that poured he water into a bason, and began to wash his disciples' feet, and to wipe them with the towel wherewith he was girt. Then came he to Simon Peter: and Peter said unto him, Lord, dost thou wash my feet? Jesus answered and said unto him, What I do thou knowest not now, but thou shalt know hereafter. Peter said unto him, Thou shalt never wash my feet. Jesus answered him: If I wash thee not, thou hast no part with me. Simon Peter said unto him: Lord, not my feet only, but also my hands and my head. Jesus said unto him: He that is washed needeth not save to wash his feet, but is clean every whit; and ye are clean, but not all: for he knew who should betray him; therefore said he, ye are not all clean. So after he had washed their feet, and received his clothes, and was set down, he said unto them again: Wot you what I have done you? Ye call me Master and Lord; and ye say well, for so I am. If I then your Lord and Master have washed your feet, ye also ought to wash one another's feet: for I have given you an ensample, that ye should do as I have done to you. Verily, verily, I say unto you, The servant is not greater than his master, neither the messenger greater than he that sent him. If ye understand these things, happy are ye if ye do them.

### DOCTRINE AND FRUIT.

HERE ought we diligently to consider the unspeakable Love. and fervent love of our Lord Jesus Christ, who until the end leaveth nothing undone that may serve for our welfare. Likewise also should we ponder and regard the meek lowli- Humbleness. ness of him, in that he the King of heaven doth humble himself, even to wash his disciples' feet, which thing is accounted base and vile amongst men; yea, even unto the man that betrayed him, is not he ashamed, neither refuseth to shew such lowliness and work of love.

By this we learn to declare all works of charitable love unto our neighbour, and not to be ashamed, how high soever we be, meekly to do our neighbour service, though he be poor, base, and small in reputation, yea, albeit he hath already hurt and betrayed us. We ought to learn with Christ our head to do good, not only to our brethren and friends, but also to our adversaries, enemies, evil willers, and such as love us not; even unto them should we shew friendship, serving them, being gentle, mild, and loving unto them. We must pray unto the Lord, that he will grant us grace to fulfil and do that we hear and read of him.

Furthermore, considering that we daily perceive in ourselves spots and blemishes of sin, so that our feet, that is to say, our affections and desires, while we walk in the miry way, are still continually defiled and stained; we ought therefore incessantly to watch and to call unto God, that he with the water of his grace will vouchsafe to make clean our feet, and wash away the mire of earthy and carnal spots, that we in the pureness of faith may abide in Christ our head, and he in us.

## OF THE SERMON THAT CHRIST MADE UNTO HIS DISCIPLES AFTER THE SUPPER.

[Matthew xxvi. 31—35. Mark xiv. 18—21. Luke xxii. 31—34. John xiii. 18—38.]

*The exhortation and warning of Christ.*

THEN said Jesus unto his disciples: This night shall you all be offended because of me. For it is written: I shall smite the shepherd, and the sheep of the flock shall be scattered. But when I am risen again, I will go before you into Galilee. Peter answered and said unto him: And though they all be offended because of thee, yet will I not be so. Then said Jesus to him: Verily I say unto thee, that this night, before the cock crow twice, thou shalt deny me three times. Upon this spake Peter further: Though I should die with thee, yet will I not deny thee: and so said all the disciples likewise. But Jesus said: I speak not of you all, I know whom I have chosen. He that eateth bread with me, shall lift up his heel against me. This I tell you aforehand, ere it come to pass; that when it is done, ye may believe that I am he. Verily, verily, I say unto you, he that receiveth him whom I send, receiveth me; and whoso receiveth me, receiveth him that sent me.

*The presumption and rashness of Peter.*

*The dignity and worthiness of the disciples.*

*The foreknowledge of Christ.*

When Jesus had spoken this, he was troubled in spirit, and protested, and said: Verily, verily, I say unto you, one of you shall betray me, yea, even he that eateth with me. The disciples looked one upon another, and doubting of whom he spake, they were very sorry and dismayed, and began to say one after another: Lord, is it I? Then said Jesus: One of the twelve, even he that dippeth his hand with me in the platter, he shall betray me. The Son of man goeth, as it is written of him: but woe unto him, by whom the Son of man is betrayed! Better it were for him, that he never had been born. Then said Judas that betrayed him: Lord, is it I? Then spake Jesus: Thou hast said. *The presumptuousness of Judas.*

One whom Jesus loved among the disciples lay upon Jesus' lap. To him beckoned Peter, and said: Who is he, that he speaketh of? Now when he leaned on Jesus' breast, he said unto him: Lord, who is it? Jesus answered: He it is, unto whom I shall reach the sop. And when he had dipped in the bread, he gave it unto Judas Simon Iscarioth; and after the sop entered the devil into him. And Jesus said unto him: That thou doest, do it quickly. None of those that sat at the table, perceived why he spake this: some thought, seeing Judas had the purse, that Jesus had commanded him to buy something necessary at the feast, or to give something unto the poor. Now when he had taken it, he went out immediately, and it was night. *Treason cometh of the devil.*

Now when he was gone forth, Jesus said: Now is the Son of man glorified, and God is glorified in him. If God be glorified by him, then shall God glorify him in himself, and shall straightway glorify him. Little children, I am yet a small time with you. Ye shall seek me, and as I said unto the Jews, whither I go, ye cannot come. And now I say unto you: A new commandment I give you, to love one another; as I have loved you, that ye even so love one another. Herein shall all men know and perceive, that ye are my disciples, if ye have love among yourselves. Then said Simon Peter: Lord, whither goest thou? Jesus answered him, and said: Whither I go, thou canst not follow me now, but thou shalt follow me hereafter. Then said Peter unto him: Why may not I now follow thee? I will jeopard my life for thee. Jesus answered, Wilt thou jeopard thy life for me? Verily, verily, I say unto thee: afore the cock crow, thou shalt deny me thrice.

### DOCTRINE AND FRUIT.

Good virtuous children should hearken most diligently unto the words of their father, and fasten them in their hearts; but specially those words which he speaketh and committeth unto them, now when he mindeth by death to depart from them, and to take his leave of them. For the same words, being the last, pierce very deep into the heart, and are never forgotten. Seeing then that we are God's children, and Christ here nameth us so to be with his disciples; we ought very diligently to ponder and consider all his words and doctrine, but specially such as he uttered unto them when he now would go to his passion. For there shall we find an ardent, earnest, and fervent doctrine, full of most excellent, godly, and inestimable love, proponed[1], and thrust into their hearts, with words sweeter than honey. In this oration bringeth he forth specially that same, which most of all concerneth his disciples. First, the Eternal Wisdom declareth, that he is ignorant of nothing, that unto him there is nothing hid. He knoweth what shall happen unto them through weakness of the flesh and fear of men: albeit our feebleness and imbecility doth always break forth, presume, and brag more than we are ever able to perform, as we have example in Peter. Such heady rashness the Lord rebuketh, admonishing us of our own weakness and fall.

Moreover, we ought to consider in Christ our head and forerunner, how earnestly and lovingly he mentioneth and warneth the traitor, setting his great offence before his eyes, and always touching him, to remove him from his wicked purpose. Yet maketh he mention of him, and of the vice, in such sort, that he never desireth his hurt, but only his conversion and amendment. His desire is, that he were reformed, not that he should be bewrayed, or that any harm should happen unto him by him or others. Such lenity and gentleness ought we also to shew and declare unto our ene-

[1 Proponed: propounded.]

mies, and those that hurt us; if it only concern us, we should not be desirous of vengeance. And though we all ought sore to mourn in the church, that is to say, in the christian congregation, if there be transgressors and naughty people, applying our diligence the best we can, that such be not therein; yet where as their vices be secret, and as yet not opened, we ought in love and patience to bear and suffer them until the harvest, when the Lord shall purge and cleanse his floor. Besides this, we ought not to cease with warning and advertisement, with correction and doctrine, that they may leave off from their obstinate wickedness.

And when the congregation of God through his grace is quit of such evil people, and discharged of such wicked blemishes, God must be thanked, and diligence applied, that no wicked thing breed therein again.

But above all things must we regard that principal and new commandment, which Christ giveth us; namely, upon the love, that he after a new sort hath declared and performed; by the which love he reneweth those that are his, and plentifully endueth them through the Holy Ghost, whom he giveth in their hearts. Love comprehendeth and fulfilleth all laws: therefore Christ leaveth all other commandments, and admonisheth us only of love. Love.

Love hath he himself shewed us aforehand; of him must we learn to love. Love is the assured and unfailing evidence of the children of God. Whoso hath not it, though he had all other virtues, yet hath he nothing, neither is it profitable to him that he hath. If he have love, then hath he all things that are necessary for his health and salvation. Therefore ought we to regard nothing so much as love. There is nothing more acceptable, nothing more perfect, nothing better in heaven and earth, than love: for it is of God, and may rest nowhere else but in God. Only love maketh us godly, and shapeth us likest unto God; namely, that love which springeth and groweth out of a pure heart, out of a good conscience, and of an unfeigned faith. Nevertheless we must love one another, not with words only and with tongues, but with the deed, and in the truth, even with our whole hearts, as Christ loved us.

[John xiv. 1—14.]

Jesus said unto his disciples: Let not your hearts be troubled. If ye believe in God, believe in me. In my Father's house are many mansions. If it were not so, I would have told you. I go to prepare a place for you. And if I go to prepare a place for you, I will come again, and receive you even unto myself, that where I am, ye may be also: and whither I go ye know, and the way ye know. Then said Thomas: Lord, we wot not whither thou goest; and how is it possible for us to know the way? Then said Jesus: I am the way, the truth, and the life. No man cometh unto the Father, but by me. If ye had known me, ye had known my Father also. And now ye know him, and have seen him. Philip said unto him; Lord, shew us the Father, and it sufficeth us. Jesus said unto him: Have I been so long time with you, and yet hast thou not known me, Philip? He that hath seen me, hath seen the Father; and how sayest thou then, Shew us the Father? Believest thou not, that I am in the Father, and the Father in me? The words that I speak unto you, I speak not of myself; but the Father that dwelleth in me, is he that doth the works. Believe me, that I am in the Father, and the Father in me. At least believe me for the very works' sake. Verily, verily, I say unto you, he that believeth on me, the works that I do, the same shall he do also; and greater works than these shall he do, because I go unto my Father. And whatsoever ye ask in my name, that will I do, that the Father may be glorified by the Son. If ye shall ask any thing in my name, I will do it.

### DOCTRINE AND FRUIT.

When the disciples of Christ heard of his death and departing, what trouble should fall upon them, and what should happen unto them through the weakness of the flesh,

they were very heavy and dismayed; for they had great *Adversity.*
love unto the Lord, and loath were they to depart from
him, and yet might they not follow him at this time.
Therefore lovingly doth the Lord comfort and strengthen
them, saying: Be not afraid, let not your heart be
troubled. This comfort is spoken unto us all; for while
we live here, we must look for much trouble and adversity, whereof springeth many times heaviness, fear, and
unpatiency in our flesh. Therefore Christ, who corporally *Patience*
is absent from us, but present among us with his grace,
speaketh unto us inwardly by his Spirit in our hearts, or
outwardly by his word and exhortation, comfortably strengthening and mightily comforting our feebleness; giving us
gladness also in sorrow.

To be without adversity, if it please God otherwise,
is not good for us; to be rash and heady is hurtful.
Therefore bringeth he us in between fear and hope, that
we should turn neither to the right hand nor to the left.
Much adversity suffereth he to come unto us, so that ofttimes fearfulness and sorrow falleth on us: but this keepeth
us in his awe, cutteth our comb, bringeth down our pride, *Meekness.*
and humbleth us. Out of this we learn, that if any human
infirmity and feebleness fall upon us, as it did upon the
disciples in the Lord's passion, we shall not utterly despair,
nor fall away through fearfulness; but remember, that in
this time it happeneth so of course, that we must suffer
and bear much trouble and adversity, to the intent that the
glory and power of God may be opened in our weakness:
and yet in all our adversity must we be manly and stout,
valiantly fighting for his name's sake. And though of weak- *The fear of God.*
ness we be fallen in the field, yet will he have compassion
upon us, and graciously forgive our fall. For who would not
be afraid to fall, when the earnest and fervent apostle Peter
fell so sore, and all the other disciples fled from the Lord?
If this chanced to the beloved disciples, no man need to think
the contrary, but the like may happen unto him. He that
standeth, let him stand fast in the fear of God, and look that
he fall not.

Christ unto his own that stand in this conflict and dan- *Faith.*
gerous battle, giveth the shield or target of faith, which they
cast up, and receive all strokes and shot therein. Believe

ye in me, saith he. Whoso believeth in Christ, believeth in God; for Christ is God. This faith giveth strength, and overcometh all adversity. As if Christ would say: Be not afraid by reason of my bodily absence. Though ye see me no more from henceforth with bodily eyes, yet with my grace and comfort will not I forsake you, but be with you until the end of the world. I will alway remain with you; only look that ye believe in me, continuing and cleaving fast unto me with the belief of the heart; so will I defend, deliver, and save you for ever. Be not afraid for *Eternal reward.* any adversity; put your confidence in me. After your trouble, there is prepared for you an excellent great joy, and an exceeding unspeakable reward. For in my Father's house are many dwellings, which from everlasting have been prepared for all the elect, that believe in me, and follow me under the cross. I will not deceive you, I will shew you no unfaithful touch; I will not disappoint you, into no fool's paradise nor false hope will I bring you. If the mansions were not prepared for you in my Father's house, I would tell it you: but doubt ye not in my promise; fall ye not off from faith and hope; stay your belief and affiance stedfastly upon me; hope undoubtedly for the dwellings to come, which are ordained and prepared of my Father for you. Here is nothing but misery and trouble; here is no abiding, no dwelling, but a pilgrimage. Here ye are among strangers: but in my Father's house are many dwellings, not only for me, but also for you. And forasmuch as now through my death I will furnish and perfectly open and make an entrance into the same dwellings, which were prepared for you of my Father afore the creation of the world; be not you therefore *Christ's death our life.* dismayed by reason of my death. My death shall be your life and salvation. Through my death go I before you, and make you a way unto heaven. Look what the Father of his gracious goodness hath ordained for you from everlasting, that will not he give you, but through me; therefore must I die, and with my death open you the entrance unto life.

*The fruit of the death of Christ.* And albeit that through my death and ascension I shall corporally depart from you; yet will I not fail you, neither forsake you. Like as by my death I open unto you the entrance into the heavenly mansions, so will I send you my holy Spirit, who shall furnish you, and make you meet for such dwellings. That I go from you, it is done for your wealth; therefore be not sorry, that I open the dwellings unto you. I will come to you again, and receive you to myself; that ye may always be with me in my Father's kingdom. For he that serveth me, shall also be eternally with me in my Father's house. Thither will I bring you through my power and grace; fear ye not, and believe in me. Thus ye know whither I go, namely, unto the Father, to work your welfare: ye know also through what way ye must follow me, even through faith and adversity. Abide ye stedfast in faith, and put your trust in me; so will I be your faithful mediator and attorney in the presence of God my Father.

And if we would say, as Thomas did, that we know not the way, the Lord Jesus instructeth us further, and saith, that he is "the way, the truth, and the life." This ought we poor sinners well to fasten in our hearts, that Christ is the only way which bringeth us unto God, and that no man may come unto the Father but by him. We should not therefore erect or choose unto ourselves any other way. Only by Christ must we come unto God: this hath he spoken, that is the truth itself, and cannot lie. In the way is he our guide, and by it he leadeth us unto himself, and so by himself unto God. Through this way we come to life, and though we must die in adversity for his sake, yet in him we find eternal life; for he is the life and resurrection. Whoso believeth on him cannot die, but cometh out of death into life; and though he die, yet shall he live in him everlastingly. *Christ is the only way.*

Furthermore, we must take sure hold upon Christ's promise, which in life and death shall strengthen and comfort us; in that he promiseth us, he will give us all that we desire in his name. Wherefore in all our necessity and trouble we ought to have recourse only unto him, or unto God his Father in his name. And then do we pray in his name, when we desire that which may serve to the honour of his Father, that the Father may be honoured through the Son, and in the Son, when we desire such wholesome good things, as the Spirit of Christ moveth us unto.

All this doth stir up in us patience, peace, joy in the Holy Ghost, belief in Christ, who is our God and head; whom by his doctrine and wonderful miracles we have learned to be very good in deed. The holy scripture also, both of Old and New Testament, doth sufficiently declare the same; as Esa. vii. ix. xlii. xlix. lxii. Hier. xxiii. xxxiii. Mich. v. Zach. xiii. Mala. iii.

What doth he else in his whole gospel, but evidently and strongly prove that Jesus is very God? as in the i. ii. iii. iv. v. vi. vii. chapters; yea, in all.

Christ calleth himself the Son of God, and teacheth every where, that we ought to believe on him. Now if he were not very true God, then had he deceived us, then had he taught us wrong, and then were he himself a false teacher; for we must believe in none, save only in God. If Christ now were not God, how should we believe in him? If he were a false teacher, then would not the Father have commanded us to hear him; then had not he spoken from heaven these words; "This is my dearly beloved Son, hear him:" then had not he also confirmed his cause with miracles, raised him up from death, taken him up into heaven, and set him on his right hand: for he hateth all liars, and hath no pleasure in the wicked.

John viii. : "Afore Abraham was, I am." Christ saith, that "the Father hath given him all power in heaven and earth." Matt. xxviii. Which sentence alone were sufficient and strong enough, to prove that Christ is God; for God giveth his glory and honour to none other. Esa. xlii. He saith also, that "what the Father hath, it is his." John xvii. And, John xx., saith Thomas unto Christ: "My Lord and my God." By him were all things created. John i. Col. i. Then must he needs be God; for no creature is the maker or creator of all things. Paul saith: "He is the wisdom of God." 1 Corinth. i. The wisdom of God is eternal. Prov. viii. Eccles. xxiv. Rom. i. ix. In the Epistle to the Hebrews, what doth Paul else, even from the beginning, until he come far within it, but bring in testimonies, that Christ is [1 John iv.] very God? John saith: "Every spirit which confesseth, that Jesus came in the flesh, is of God." Out of the which it followeth, that as concerning his divine nature, he was from everlasting, afore he came in the flesh. Item: Paul to the

Hebrews saith: "God took upon him the seed of Abraham:" [Heb. ii.] then must he needs be eternal God, before the humanity was. As also John saith: "The Word was God, and the Word became man." Item: "No man hath seen God at any [John i.] time. The Son of God which is in the Father's bosom, he hath opened it unto us." John iii. Saith Christ: "No man ascendeth into heaven, save he that came down from heaven." Now canst thou not say, that he came down, as touching his human nature; for that took he first upon him in the Virgin Mary. Luke i. Then must it needs be true, that he came down concerning his Godhead; as he oft saith: "I came [John xvi.] forth from the Father;" and Paul, Phil. ii.: "He took upon him the shape of a servant." Who? God. Also, John xvii., he saith: "Glorify thou me, O Father, with the glory and honour, which I had with thee afore the world was created." And, 1 John v.: "We know that the Son of God is come, and hath given us understanding to know him, who is the true God: and we are in him that is true, even in his Son Jesus Christ. The same is the true God, and the eternal life."

Seeing then that God hath given us his Son to be our righteousness, our sanctification, saviour, redeemer, ransom, life, light, and head, to believe and trust in him, and finally by him to be saved, he must needs then be the true living God; else might not, neither should our heart trust nor cleave unto him. This ought a believing heart fully and well to take hold of, and stedfastly to stand thereupon.

---

[John xiv. 15—24.]

If ye love me, keep my commandments; and I will pray the Father, and he shall give you another Comforter, that he may abide with you for ever; even the Spirit of truth, whom the world cannot receive, because the world seeth him not, neither knoweth him; but ye know him, for he dwelleth with you, and shall be in you. I will not leave you comfortless, but will come to you. Yet a little while, and the world seeth me no more, but ye see me; for I live, and ye shall live. That day shall ye know that I am in my Father, and you in me, and I in you. He that hath my commandments and keepeth them, the same is he that loveth me; and he that loveth me, shall be loved of my Father, and I will love him, and will shew mine own self unto him. Judas said unto him, not Judas Iscariot: Lord, what is the cause that thou wilt shew thyself unto us, and not unto the world? Jesus answered and said unto him: If a man love me, he will keep my sayings; and my Father will love him, and we will come unto him, and will dwell with him. He that loveth me not, keepeth not my sayings: and the words which ye hear, are not mine, but the Father's which hath sent me.

### DOCTRINE AND FRUIT.

CHRIST promiseth his disciples, that is, such as believe on him, that he will give them whatsoever they make petition for, or desire; yea, if they love him. For faith without love is dead, and hath no strength. Where there is faith in man, there followeth love. Many of us say, We believe in Christ, and we love him, yet we keep not his commandments. <small>He that loveth worketh.</small> Such men ought well to note the words that Christ here speaketh: "Whoso loveth me, keepeth my commandments." The disciples thought that they loved Christ right, because they were sorry for his departing; but Christ teacheth us, that love consisteth in the keeping of his commandments. If we will declare our love towards God, it must not be done only with word and tongue, but with keeping of his precepts. <small>Psal. xxxiv.</small> "The eyes of the Lord behold the righteous, and his ears consider their prayers." God will not that we, whom he through his grace hath admitted for his own children, and purified through faith, should go idle. Faith, which God giveth us in our heart, standeth not idle: we have for this purpose <small>God's commandment.</small> received it, even to keep his commandments. Now is it his commandment, that we deny and mortify ourselves, hate and despise the world, take up our cross upon us, and follow him, stoutly and manfully confessing and acknowledging him before the wicked world, loving one another, as he hath loved us; innocently and godly leading our lives, whereby we may daily receive the more gifts at his hand. For if we keep not his grace that he giveth us, if we do not continually and daily reform ourselves, and with all diligence fashion our lives after his life, it is but right that we lose again what we have received.

And if any man saith, it were unpossible for man to keep God's commandments, (as it is true indeed,) yet unto us that believe in Christ are all things possible, not in ourselves, but in Christ our head. If we abide in him through faith, then hard and unpossible things are light and possible unto us; for in him that strengtheneth us we may do all things. And if we love God, then for his sake that is beloved we may do and suffer all things; for there is nothing but love overcometh it. Our Lord Jesus Christ fulfilleth the commandments and will of his heavenly Father. So far as we now are his members incorporated with him, and abiding in him as our head through faith, our daily exercise, ferventness, and diligence shall be in undertaking to perform and keep his commandments. And if we out of a true belief do apply such diligence to keep his precepts, then may it be perceived that we love God. *[marginal: All things possible to believers. Love overcometh all things.]*

And if that, after such diligence in keeping God's commandments, there be aught lacking, (as we shall ever here want something,) we must cry unto our heavenly Father, and pray: "O Father, forgive us our debts and trespasses." And then have we with him a faithful Mediator, even Jesus Christ the righteous, who maketh intercession for us, and taketh our faults upon himself; and what we are not able, that fulfilleth he for us. Thus is it his first and highest commandment, which he earnestly requireth of us, that we believe in him. Where the same faith is right, it brings with it love, which keepeth all the commandments. Now when we begin to break our minds off from earthy worldly things, and to set them upon godly heavenly things, which Christ calleth us unto; then take we in hand to be obedient unto God the Father, after the example and pattern of Christ; for he loved us first. If we now also love him, and practise ourselves in his love, then shall he help us to keep his commandments. *[marginal: Faith, love, keeping of the commandments.]*

And to the intent that we may be able to put our trust

in him, to love him, and to observe his precepts, he promiseth us his holy Spirit, to work all such things in us.

He comforteth also his disciples and all his elect in this world; as if he would say: "Be not ye afraid, neither sorrowful, by reason of my departing. Albeit I now die, and go corporally from you unto the Father, yet will I always have a fatherly love, faithfulness, and care for you; neither will I leave you friendless, as those that are utterly destitute of all help and consolation. I will pray unto the Father, so that he shall send you another to succour and comfort you. While I have been with you myself, I have instructed and taught you in all things that were necessary for your welfare. Unto all such works as are acceptable unto my Father, have I exhorted you; unto all good things have I moved you; from all evil have I defended you; in all trouble and adversity have I comforted you. I have been your teacher, your exhorter, your attorney, your advocate, and mediator; so that ye have lacked nothing, neither hath any man hurt you. Seeing now I have hitherto never failed you, I will also from henceforth not forsake you, but pray unto my Father, who shall send unto you the Holy Ghost.

*The office of God's Spirit.*

The same shall perfectly bring to your remembrance, and be your teacher in all that I have shewed you; he shall exhort and admonish you, aid, succour, and comfort you; so that ye shall not be without consolation. He shall be your tutor and defender; neither shall he be with you only for a time, as I have been, but even in your hearts shall he dwell with you, and never depart from you.

*Comfort and strength in adversity.*

Of this helper, comforter, teacher, and tutor, shall ye also have need; for great trouble and persecution shall the world move against you. To overcome the same, is your flesh too feeble: therefore will I send you down from heaven a power, whereby in all adversity ye may be able to stand fast, and to have the victory.

O the unspeakable love of our Lord Jesu Christ, who taketh such diligent care for us, and endueth us with so excellent a gift, namely, his own holy Spirit! With what modesty and soberness, with how pure and honest behaviour ought we to walk, seeing that God hath into our hearts given his holy Spirit, who utterly abhorreth and loatheth all vice and all filthiness of sin? Great diligence ought we therefore to apply, in keeping clean and undefiled our bodies and souls, which God through his holy Spirit hath purified and consecrated to be his own dwelling place and temple, lest we expel the chaste Spirit of God. For in no froward soul abideth he, neither dwelleth he in that body which maketh itself slave and thrall unto sin. The ears of our mind ought we to open, and to hearken whereof this Spirit admonisheth us, and what doctrine he in our Saviour's words doth teach us; and his motion ought we to follow. Afraid ought we not to be: he that is in us is stronger than all our enemies.

This Spirit hath Christ by his prayer and merits obtained of his Father; for he prayed with weeping and tears, and was heard for his worthiness' sake.

He is called also the Spirit of truth, because he proceedeth of the truth, teacheth the truth, and maketh us true: we are else of our own nature altogether liars, inconstant, untrue, and dissembling hypocrites; and whatsoever the world speaketh and doth, it is nothing but vanity and lies. Blessed therefore are they, unto whom God giveth the high gift of his truth.

The world, that is to say, fleshly men and children of the world, receive not this Spirit; for they despise the word of Christ, and laugh it to scorn. Therefore God sheweth not himself unto them, for they love him not; which thing they declare, in that they refuse his word. But whoso receiveth his word, sheweth thereby that he loveth Christ and God: him will God love again, and open himself ever more and more unto him. This is a high reward, which God giveth unto his lovers; that he cometh unto them, maketh his dwelling, and abideth alway with them, working all good things in them and by them. Therefore ought we earnestly to hear his word, to love him, and to keep his commandments. And so even the same, his own Spirit, which he gave us at the beginning, shall he still grant unto us more perfectly from time to time. Thus shall that Spirit pour out love in our hearts, and endue them with more perfection. The love of the world, which is not of God the Father, shall this Spirit root out and daily consume; but the love of God it shall continually plant and increase. The more love there is, the more groweth the knowledge of God; yea, the more God's knowledge increaseth, the more fervent and perfect is love. Grant us, O gracious Father, thy holy Spirit, to take possession of our heart; that it may only trust in thee, love thee above all things, keep thy commandments, and cleave still unto thee for evermore. Amen.

---

[John xiv. 25—31.]

THESE things have I spoken unto you, being yet present with you. But that comfort which is the Holy Ghost, whom my Father will send in my name, he shall teach you all things, and bring all things to your remembrance, whatsoever I have taught you. Peace I leave with you, my peace I give unto you. Let not your heart be troubled, neither fear. Ye have heard that I said unto you, I go, and come unto you. If ye loved me, ye would verily rejoice, because I said, I go unto the Father; for the Father is greater than I. And now have I shewed you before it come, that when it is come to pass, ye might believe. Hereafter will I not talk many words with you; for the ruler of this world cometh, and hath nought in me. But that the world may know, that I love the Father; as the Father gave me commandment, even so do I. Arise, let us go hence.

## DOCTRINE AND FRUIT.

THE Lord Jesus continueth his oration in comforting his disciples, and in telling them what the office of the Holy Ghost should be. Whereby we learn, that all reading and hearing, yea, and all doctrine, bringeth utterly no fruit, if the Holy Ghost do not give us understanding, and teach us the word of God. For the disciples were ignorant and forgetful: many things that Christ had told them, they understood not; many things had they forgotten; in many things they doubted. Such like happen also unto us. Therefore ought we at all times to pray unto God, that he will send us his holy Spirit, to admonish and provoke us, to comfort and strengthen us, to instruct and teach us all things that are necessary for us

*We must all be taught of God, which is done by the Spirit.*

to salvation. He is the right heavenly schoolmaster: when he cometh into us, he expelleth all ignorance away.

But forasmuch as there remaineth much trouble and adversity unto all faithful believers, while they live in this time, Christ doth therefore promise them his peace against the turmoiling, unquietness, and trouble of this world. In the world are many hurley-burlies and adversities; in Christ we find true peace and quietness. And Christ unto those that are his giveth such a peace, as surmounteth all understanding; in the which peace they being coupled and knit, are able valiantly to overcome all enemies and adversity. For inasmuch as they know, and be undoubtedly assured through faith, that their sins are forgiven and taken away by Christ, that the Father of heaven is favourable and gracious unto them, that they be his own children and inheritors, they do little pass what thing outwardly happeneth unto them. All adversity and trouble that outwardly is laid upon them, is through the inward joy and peace which they have in God clean swallowed up, and so forgotten. They settle and stay their hearts upon salvation and eternal peace. *The peace of Christ through the Spirit. Phil. iv.*

The peace of the world seeketh quietness and rest of the body, throweth away the cross, and flieth from it: the peace of Christ rejoiceth in the midst of adversity, and overcometh the cross. For faithful believers look unto Christ, who went before them unto the Father, and after his passion and death took possession of so high honour and glory, and hath carried their nature up so high unto the right hand of the Father, where he now ruleth as a mighty king of heaven and earth. Oh, how great comfort, how sure a hope giveth it unto us, when we see our own nature, our own flesh and bones, incorporated unto Christ, the only-begotten Son and eternal word of God, in so high honour and glory! How can it be otherwise, but we must needs hope, that our weak flesh also shall be taken up? *Worldly peace. Our nature exalted in Christ. Comfort in adversity.*

Look what is past in the head, the same shall assuredly be fulfilled in the members; for without the members cannot the head be. Which thing considered, and through true belief printed in the heart, maketh a man patient and cheerful in all adversity, giveth peace and joy in all trouble. Let the prince of this world, through his ministers and members, stir up all vexation against us, yet hath he no vantage of us, *The devil hath nothing in the faithful.*

if we be in Christ. Easily might he find somewhat in ourselves, but in Christ nothing; such innocency doth Christ make us partakers of. Tempt us he may, and thrust at us; but to overcome us he is not able, so far as we abide in Christ. In us is death a punishment of sin; in Christ it is obedience and love. For seeing the Father loveth the Son, and of very love gave him unto death for us, the Son would of love obey the Father; and as he also loved us, so would he willingly and obediently suffer death for us, that all the world might see his obedience, and that we might learn of him to obey our heavenly Father, even unto the death, and faithfully follow his precept; and that likewise, whereas it toucheth his glory, we should be afraid neither of adversity nor death, considering how obediently he died for our sakes.

*We must suffer, that we may be obedient unto the Father.*

---

[John xv. 1—8.]

I AM a true vine, and my Father is an husbandman. Every branch that bringeth not fruit in me, he taketh away; and every branch that beareth fruit, he purgeth, that it may bring forth more fruit. Now are ye clean through the words which I have spoken unto you. Abide in me, and I in you. As the branch cannot bear fruit of itself, except it abide in the vine; no more can ye, except ye abide in me. I am the vine, ye are the branches: he that abideth in me and I in him, the same bringeth forth much fruit; for without me can ye do nothing. If a man bide not in me, he is cast forth as a branch, and withered; and men gather them, and cast them into the fire, and they burn. If ye abide in me, and my words also in you, ask what ye will, and it shall be done unto you. Herein is my Father glorified, that ye bear much fruit, and become my disciples.

### DOCTRINE AND FRUIT.

UNDER this fair similitude doth Christ teach his Church, that without him we can do nothing, but in him all things.

Now forasmuch as he through his grace hath incorporated us unto himself, we ought with great diligence to apply ourselves, that we may abide in him, and bear fruit. For as long as we are in him, we live, that is, we receive lively virtue and sap of him, namely, his Spirit. For whoso cleaveth unto the Lord, and is incorporated unto him through faith, the same is become one spirit with him. 1 Corinth. vi. For hereby know we that we are in him, and he in us, in that he hath given us of his Spirit. 1 John iv. For why? In the vineyard the branches are of one nature and kind. Thus the only-begotten Son of God took our nature upon him, is become man, and giveth us of his Spirit, and maketh us to be of a godly mind and spiritual nature. Out of the same pith and sap do all manner of godly virtues and good works break forth. Gal. v. Psalm lxxxv. (lxxxvi.) For through his grace are we his operation and work in Christ Jesu, created unto Eph. ii. good works, wherein we are bound to walk. And seeing we Col. ii. have received Jesus Christ of God the Father, we ought to walk in him, that in him we may be well rooted and stand fast.

But hereby know we that we are in him, if we walk as *What it is to abide in* he hath walked. For whoso saith, that he abideth in him, *Christ.* then even as he walked, so must we do. 1 John ii. But if we would say, that we were in him, and had fellowship with him, and yet would walk in darkness, (seeing he is the light, wherein is found no darkness at all,) then were we liars, and went not about with the truth. But if we walk in light, as he is light, and we children of light, then have we fellowship and company with him, and the blood of Christ purgeth us from all sin. 1 John i.

In Christ Jesu may no man be idle and without fruit. 2 Thess. iii. Whoso now is unthankful to the grace of God, *Punishment of unthank-* and doth not practise himself in good works to God's glory, *fulness.* the same is cut off, and as an unfruitful dry branch, thrown into the fire and burnt. Faith grafteth us into Christ; love declareth that we are planted in, and it knitteth the members with the head. Where the Spirit of Christ followeth from the head into the members, from the stock into the branches, there are fruits of the Spirit; for by the fruit is the tree Gal. v. known.

Christ through his word and Spirit hath pacified[1] us, that *How the faithful are*
[1 An error probably for *purified*.] *clean.*

is, he hath called and separated us from the world and from the filthiness of the flesh unto good works. And into his own service and school of godly nurture hath he admitted us, and written up our names. He hath begun to purge and cleanse us from carnal lusts, and from all uncleanness of the world, accepting us into the number of those that die from the world, and that now from henceforth will live unto him, and bring forth fruit. But that is not enough; we must also obediently wait upon the grace that he hath placed us in, applying our diligence, watching, and praying, that from so high a vocation, from so excellent grace and honour, we fall not away again. 1 Cor. x. It is not enough to have begun, there must be a stedfast continuance. He that forsaketh the head again, hath neither spirit nor virtue; for without him we are able to do nothing. Therefore through faith and love ought we to abide in him, having respect unto him in all things; so shall we bring forth much fruit unto him. Then abide we in him, when we do that he commandeth us, and love that which he promiseth us. Howbeit, these fruits that we bring forth are not ours, but the Father's; to him ought we to bring them forth, unto his honour must they extend. Matt. v. xxviii.

*1 Pet. i.*
*Faith bringeth fruit.*

*The good works are not open[1].*

For when God's light doth appear and shine in our conversation, and many folks thereby are drawn unto God, the Father of heaven is honoured, his name is hallowed, and then are we his disciples. For we have learned of him, how Christ was obedient unto the Father, and sought his glory in all things; and so do we likewise.

*What we ought to pray.*

Hereunto ought all our prayers to extend, that we may bring and win much unto Christ. Therein is the Father praised, when we bring unto him much fruit; but that might we not, if God had not given us his Son, that we might be his branches, and he our vine.

Where faith is, there is the Holy Ghost, which teacheth to wish and pray for that only, which may serve for God's honour; and that is the cause, why he that prayeth, obtaineth all his desire: for God may not give over his glory. Whoso undertaketh to further that, him doth he assist and help.

[1 Qu. *ours.*]

[John xv. 9—17.]

As the Father hath loved me, so have I loved you. Continue ye in my love. If ye keep my commandments, ye shall abide in my love, as I have kept my Father's commandments, and abide in his love. These things have I spoken unto you, that my joy might remain in you, and that your joy might be full. This is my commandment, that ye love together, as I have loved you. Greater love than this hath no man, that a man bestow his life for his friends. Ye are my friends, if ye do whatsoever I command you. Henceforth call I you not servants, for the servant knoweth not what his Lord doth. But you have I called friends; for all things that I have heard of my Father, have I opened unto you. Ye have not chosen me, but I have chosen you, and ordained you, that ye go and bring forth fruit, and that your fruit remain: that whatsoever ye ask of the Father in my name, he may give it you. This command I you, that ye love together one another.

## DOCTRINE AND FRUIT.

OH, how excellent great consolation is this to us all, which believe in Jesus Christ, and are undoubtedly assured in ourselves, that Christ loveth us as his own children and disciples, howsoever the world judge us to be forsaken of him! If this love came right into our heart, oh, how earnest and fervent should we be to love him again, to further his honour, to keep his commandments, and in charitable love to serve our neighbours! Then should all good works and keeping of God's commandments flow out of faith; namely, when we believe that God is favourable and loving unto us, yea, that he is our Father, and his Son Jesus Christ our king, head, and brother. This faith worketh through love: for we could not love God, if he had not loved us first. His grace, love, and mercy preventeth us.

Therefore doth Christ ever still set forth his love before us, as a light torch, to kindle us in love towards him and our

*Entirely doth Christ love those that are his.*

*1 John iv.*

neighbours. If we believe this grace, committing us cheerfully unto his love, which he hath declared, and continually doth practise towards us, if we still abide therein; then shall this faith upon the love of God work great things in us and by us, and shall move us with good will gladly and cheerfully to observe his commandments. And if we keep his commandments, every man shall have an assured token, that we be and continue in the love of God; that is, that we keep ourselves unto his love.

<small>Love is an evidence of faith.</small>

Seeing then that he loveth us exceeding much, and we finding the same in our hearts, through faith, do comfort ourselves thereupon, there must needs follow love to our neighbours, joy, peace, softness of mind, gentleness, patience, &c. Gal. v.

<small>What followeth out of the love of God.</small>

Now that Christ doth not slenderly, but most notably love his disciples, and all in them, he proveth it himself divers ways. First, in that he giveth his life for us, and dieth for us upon the cross; for greater love hath no man, than to die for his friend. Thus Christ with his death and blood sealeth his love towards us.

<small>Tokens of God's love.</small>

Secondly, in that he counteth and esteemeth us, not as servants, but as dear friends, brethren, and heirs with him. And the same declareth he in this, that all things which he hath heard of his Father, and sucked out of that fatherly heart, he openeth them unto us, and writeth the same through his holy Spirit in our hearts. All his secret, his godly will he giveth us to understand. For we which be in Christ do know through an undoubted faith, and feel it also in our hearts, that God is our Father through Christ, and that in him he hath admitted and chosen us, that he is reconciled with us through the blood of his dear Son, that he loveth, preserveth, and defendeth us. Therefore do we also patiently and cheerfully bear all adversity in this time for his sake, considering we know, that so is the good pleasure of our dearest Father.

<small>John i.</small>

<small>1 Cor. ii.</small>

<small>Rom. v</small>

Thirdly, Christ declareth his excellent love towards us, in that he did choose us afore the world was created, and loved us when we were yet his enemies, calling us by his word, and appointing us to bring forth fruit unto him.

<small>Eph. i. Rom. v. We are chosen to bring forth fruit.</small>

Fourthly, in that we obtain at the Father's hand all that we pray and desire in the name of Jesu.

Are not these sure tokens of an exceeding love of God towards us? After that we once have perceived such love, oh that we always remained therein! Which cometh to pass, when we apply ourselves unto his commandments, and when we in obedience and patience are content to be at his will, as he for our sake was obedient unto his Father, even until the death of the cross. Now that we might know what his commandments be, he concludeth them in a short sum, and saith: "Love ye one another together, as I have loved you." As if he would say: Seeing I have declared my love so worthily, so notably, and with so great faithfulness towards you, that I have not refused to die for you; therefore is it my will, and so is it reason also, that ye likewise shew such love one towards another; for I have given you example afore, that ye should do as I have done, and follow my footsteps. This shall not only be very seemly unto you, but much profit also and great honour shall it bring you. For like as my Father, as ye shall shortly see, shall after my passion bring me unto glory, so shall he also do unto you, so far as ye endure stedfast in adversity, and continue in love one towards another. Like as I with great travail and labour have shewed you the way and will of God my Father, and therefore go now unto death to make you living; so ought ye also to be minded one towards another. Look that ye serve one another in love; lead all men unto God; and the grace of God, which he giveth unto the world through me, publish ye unto all men, though ye must lose your life therefore.

*We ought to endure in love.*
*Phil. ii.*
*The commandment of God is love.*
*John xiii.*
*1 Pet. ii.*

---

[John xv. 18—25.]

If the world hate you, ye know that it hated me, before it hated you. If ye were of the world, the world would love his own. Howbeit, because ye are not of the world, but I have chosen you out of the world, therefore the world hateth you. Remember the word that I said unto you, The servant is not greater than the Lord. If they have persecuted me, so will they persecute you. If they have kept my sayings, they will also keep yours. But all these things will they do unto you for my name's sake, because they know not him that sent me. If I had not come and spoken unto them, they should not have had sin; but now have they nothing to cloak their sin withal. He that hateth me, hateth my Father also. If I had not done works amongst them which none other man did, they had not had sin; but now have they seen, and have hated both me, and also my Father: even that the saying might be fulfilled, which is written in their own law: They have hated me without any cause.

### DOCTRINE AND FRUIT.

LIKE as Christ in the aforesaid words hath given unto his disciples, and to us that believe in him, an excellent consolation in his love, which is infinite great towards us; so doth he now comfort us against such trouble and adversity to come, as outwardly happeneth unto us, and against the hate and persecution, wherewith the children of the world recompense us for our love and well doing. Love ought we to have towards all men: such godly love shall move us earnestly to further God's glory, to bring all men to the knowledge and love of God, and to withdraw them from fleshly lusts and worldly vices. When we now of a godly zeal begin thus to rebuke vice, and to reprehend the carnal lusts of the children of the world, then they that are drowned in the shameful vices of the world and the flesh, may not suffer it, but hate, trouble, and vex us, molest, persecute us, and put us unto death, contemning and despising the word which we offer them from God, whereby they might be saved, and going about by all means to root it out.

*Exhortation to patience.* But all this ought not to drive us back, or discourage us; for in this world must we seek no high honour nor praise, but willingly humble and submit ourselves under the *1 Pet. iii. John xiii.* rebuke and cross with Christ our head. Christ also exhorteth us to follow his footsteps, and to do after his example, and not to forsake the truth and love of our neighbour for their hatred; but constantly to proceed and do our best to *Acts v.* guide all men unto God. And if for such our faithfulness

and love there happen reproach and trouble to us, we ought
to rejoice, that God doth us so great honour, as to grant us
to suffer somewhat for his name's sake. If we lived as do
the children of the world, we should not be hated of them,
and happily we needed to fear but little danger. But Christ
hath taken us from the world, and hath chosen and called us
to good works and to innocency of life. Nothing hath he
omitted, that might serve to our welfare; faithfully therefore
ought we to follow his vocation, and not do as the unthankful
Jews, that despise his doctrine and works. He talketh yet
daily with us, provoketh and calleth us; therefore ought we
to cease from sin, and not to fashion ourselves after the world. Rom. xii.
For if we would live to please the world, to serve it, and to
hunt after the favour and praise of it, we should not be
faithful ministers of Jesus Christ. We ought not to look
for worldly honour; but to have respect to the eternal
glory, which we shall have with Christ our head, yea, so
far as we suffer rebuke and dishonour with him. When
he lived in this time, and practised the truth against the
Pharisees, he was reviled, put to shame and death. The
same happeneth also unto us; for we are not above the
Lord. An evil token were it, if the world loved us. Patiently therefore and with joy ought we to bear such rebuke
and shame, as happeneth unto us for his name's sake by
those that hate the truth. For our honour and reward is
great in heaven; but after our trouble shall the same be
first opened, as it happened also unto Christ our head
first after the cross.

---

[John xv. 26.—xvi. 7.]

But when the Comforter is come, whom I will send
unto you from the Father, even the Spirit of truth, which
proceedeth of the Father, he shall testify of me. And
ye are witnesses also, because ye have been with me from
the beginning. These things have I said unto you, that
ye should not be offended. They shall thrust you out of
their synagogues, and excommunicate you; yea, the time

shall come, that whosoever killeth you will think that he doth service unto God. And such things shall they do unto you, because they know not the Father, neither me. But these things have I told you, that when the hour is come, ye may remember that I told you. These things said I not unto you at the beginning, because I was with you. But now I go my way to him that sent me; and none of you asketh me, Whither goest thou? But because I have said such things unto you, your hearts are full of sorrow. But I tell you the truth: It is expedient for you that I go away. For if I go not away, that Comforter will not come unto you: but if I depart, I will send him unto you.

## DOCTRINE AND FRUIT.

FORASMUCH as it is our bounden duty to bear witness unto Christ with our mouth and life, and yet our weak flesh feareth the hatred and resistance of the world; Christ therefore promiseth us here, that he will send us strength from heaven, namely, the Holy Ghost, first in our hearts to bear witness unto Christ, and then to open our mouths, that we may testify the Lord Christ and his truth manfully and without fear. Certain it is, that "all they which will live here godly in Christ Jesu, must suffer persecution." But seeing that to suffer such adversity our flesh is far too slow, cold, and feeble, God giveth us the Spirit of his Son, to move, strengthen, and preserve us in all goodness. This Spirit poureth out love into our hearts, expelleth all fear and terror, as we see in Peter on Whitsunday, and maketh us to overcome all adversity.

*Matt. xxvi.*
*Acts i*
*Rom. viii.*

*2 Tim. III.*

*Rom. viii.*

*Rom. v.*
*Acts ii.*

*John xv.*

We are branches in Christ the true vine, albeit as yet very weak and tender, soon blown away with the wind, or smitten down other ways: but forasmuch as out of Christ we receive yet the sap and virtue of spirit and life, we are in life preserved, that we wither not away. Of this now must we be mindful in all adversity, so that without ceasing we pray unto God for his holy Spirit, who is our instructor, comforter, and teacher. We ought to have respect unto our fore-goer and finisher of our faith; remembering, that we suffer not as thieves and evil doers, but for his sake, yea, 1 Pet. iv. and that of the wicked. This shall make our adversity and cross the more easy and light, when we feel the comfort of the Spirit, and behold how shameful a death Christ suffered for us. Therefore should there no fear make us to shrink from the confession of Christ and his truth. We are not Matt. x. they that speak, but it is the Spirit of the Father which speaketh in us. We may not fear those that kill the body; we may not be ashamed of him: so shall he also knowledge Luke ix. us, and make us honourable in his Father's sight. The John v. honour of this world should not be dearer unto us than the glory of God. And though we die for it, yet ought we not to shrink or stir from the confession of the truth.

This engendereth many times much heaviness and fear in us, that we consider only that which is present, little regarding that which is to come and everlasting; and because we think, that when God thrusteth us into adversity, he is far from us: whereas he then is most of all with us by his grace, comfort, and strength, and trieth us through the cross, standing behind the wall, and looking through the grate upon our Cant. viii. conflict and battle, yea, helping us to fight and to overcome. Therefore must we not always be children, we must not hang 1 Cor. xiv. still at the breast, seeking milk as children do; but grow to a Heb. v. perfect age, learning to know Christ the Lord after the Spirit, as he now governeth, and is a mighty King; under whose banner we must fight valiantly, and endure the cross unto the death; throwing behind us all things in this world, and lifting up our eyes and hearts into heaven, whence our help Psal. cxxi. cometh, and into the which Christ is gone, to prepare for us John xiv. an everlasting dwelling.

---

[John xvi. 8—14.]

AND when the Spirit is come, he will rebuke the world of sin, and of righteousness, and of judgment: of sin, because they believe not on me; of righteousness, because I go to my Father, and ye shall see me no more; of judgment, because the prince of this world is judged already. I have yet many things to say unto you, but ye cannot bear them now. Howbeit when he is come, which is the Spirit of truth, he will lead you into all truth. For he shall not speak of himself, but whatsoever he shall hear, that shall he speak; and he will shew you things to come. He shall glorify me; for he shall receive of mine, and shall shew unto you. All things that the Father hath are mine: therefore said I, that he shall take of mine, and shew unto you.

## DOCTRINE AND FRUIT.

<small>John v.</small>

IN these words doth Christ shew us the office of the Holy Ghost, and what he worketh by his disciples, and by all faithful believers in the world. The whole world is set upon wickedness and iniquity; and when that is rebuked, it hateth and persecuteth those that rebuke it. Whereout it followeth oftentimes, that through imbecility and weakness of the flesh we cease from rebuking of vice and sin.

Now when we find it to be thus, that the infirmity of our flesh, and the terrible threatening of the world, will hinder us or utterly draw us back from the free rebuking of vice; we ought to pray unto God our Father for to give us the Spirit of his Son, that he may pour out love into our hearts, and expel all fear, that with stout stomachs and words we may reprehend the vices of the world, and valiantly resist

<small>1 John iv.<br>Isai. liii.</small>

them. This Spirit shall teach us the thing, that neither our flesh nor the world is instructed in. All we of nature do err, and every one wandereth his own way, that is, every one followeth his own purpose and intent; and if we believe

<small>John iii.</small>

not in Christ, we perish in our sins. And this is the greatest sin of all, wherein the world is wrapt, afore it receive the

<small>Unbelief is the original of all vices.</small>

truth. Not to believe in Christ is a sin, out of the which all vice and wickedness doth grow. How great this sin is, no man is able to know, only the Spirit of God openeth it: therefore the Spirit teacheth us, how far we go astray. And if we come to Christ from this erroneous way of unbelief, all sins are forgiven us through Christ, and not imputed us to our damnation.

Neither is it enough to know that we have erred, or do yet err; but we must know also, which is the right way, wherein, when error is forsaken, we must walk to attain unto godliness and bliss. This right way doth the Spirit also shew to be even Christ, who is our way, our righteousness, and goodness; which way nevertheless the world will not go. To believe in Christ, is the true way to attain unto righteousness and salvation: whoso now departeth not from the erroneous way of unbelief and vice, and will not walk in Christ, the way of all virtue and goodness, which all the world, alas! so abhorreth, the same is convict, that the judgment of eternal pain doth righteously fall upon him, seeing the light is set before him, and he will rather abide and perish in darkness. But is not this a just judgment, that the world should perish in sin, and be punished for ever, considering that God hath graciously sent unto them his own Son, promising everlasting life and salvation in him, who with his blood hath washed away our sins, mightily overcome death, sin, and the prince of this world, delivered us out of his power and heavy yoke, and taken possession of the kingdom and glory with his Father; and yet they will not know, receive, nor honour Christ, as their chief king and Lord, but still serve the prince of this world in vice and sin, and not submit themselves under the easy yoke of Christ, and of his love and virtues?

O dear children, let us depart out of the kingdom of darkness into the kingdom of Jesus Christ the Son of God: let us regard his word with diligence; let us hearken what God speaketh in us; and though there be many things that as yet we know not, many that we do not understand and perceive, we will earnestly pray unto God for his Spirit, who is the right schoolmaster and teacher. He shall lead us into all truth, he shall renew us in the spirit of our mind, and teach us to understand, what the good, acceptable, and perfect will of God is. He shall plant and root us in love, that we may comprehend with all saints, what is the length, the breadth, the height, and depth; that we may also know the exceeding love of the knowledge of Christ, that we might be filled in all godly perfectness. Thus the Spirit teacheth us all truth, when he poureth love into our hearts.

This schoolmaster teacheth all believers here in time, every one as much as he can comprehend, and kindleth spiritual hearts with greater desire. He that now increaseth

[COVERDALE.]

in love, that is, whoso loveth that whereof God giveth him knowledge, and desireth to know that which as yet he knoweth not, him doth the Spirit lead into all truth. For the more that love groweth, the more perfect is knowledge. And in this school of the love which the Spirit poureth into our hearts, the faithful believer learneth more, than all books and all men can teach him: but the more a man learneth and can, the more must he acknowledge and confess, that he can nothing towards that which we shall know, when we shall clearly and perfectly see God face to face. Unto us shall it be enough and sufficient, that we in spirit and in the truth know Jesus Christ, which was crucified, and that he shine and be glorified in our mortal body, in our hearts, mouth, and in our whole life.

<small>1 Cor. xiii.
1 Cor. ii.
2 Cor. v.
John iv.
2 Cor. iv.</small>

---

[John xvi. 16—22.]

AFTER a while ye shall not see me, and again after a while ye shall see me; for I go to the Father. Then said some of his disciples among themselves: What is this that he saith unto us, After a while ye shall not see me, and again after a while ye shall see me; and that I go to my Father? They said therefore, What is this that he saith, After a while? We cannot tell what he saith. Jesus perceived that they would ask him, and said unto them: This is it that ye inquire of between yourselves, that I said, After a while ye shall not see me, and again after a while ye shall see me. Verily, verily, I say unto you, Ye shall weep and lament, but the world shall rejoice: ye shall sorrow, but your sorrow shall be turned into joy. A woman, when she travaileth, hath sorrow, because her hour is come; but when she is delivered of the child, she remembereth no more the anguish, for joy that a man is born into the world. And ye now therefore are in sorrow: but I will see you again, and your heart shall rejoice, and your joy shall no man take from you.

## DOCTRINE AND FRUIT.

An excellent comfort doth Christ give here unto his disciples, who by reason of his departing were in great sorrow and heaviness. But like as the disciples of Christ, because of his passion, abode for a little season in great cumbrance, fear, and trouble, and yet received great joy out of the resurrection, when he shewed himself unto them; even so in adversity ought not we to be faint-hearted, but comfort ourselves in this, that the Lord doth not long leave those that are his. Though he hide himself for a time, he shall shortly shew us his gracious countenance again, and refresh us with rich comfort. The adversities of faithful believers are not only short, but also they end with unspeakable joy. After adversity and death followeth everlasting joy and eternal life. We are here with Christ our head in trouble and on the cross, where the world laugheth at us and rejoiceth. For all this ought not we to be unquiet in ourselves. Very shortly will the matter change and turn upside down; so that their laughter and joy shall be altered into weeping and eternal sorrow: but our heaviness shall God shortly end with great fruit and joy, and the same joy shall no man be able to take from us, when we with Christ our head shall everlastingly be glad and rejoice, when all tears shall be wiped away from our eyes, and we discharged of all travail and labour of this time.

---

[John xvi. 23—33.]

In that day shall ye ask me no question. Verily, verily, I say unto you, Whatsoever ye shall ask the Father in my name, he will give it you. Hitherto have ye asked nothing in my name: Ask, and ye shall receive, that your joy may be full. These things have I spoken unto you in proverbs; but the time will come, when I shall no more speak to you in proverbs, but I shall shew you plainly of my Father. At that day shall ye ask in my name. And I say not unto you, that I will pray unto the Father for you; for the Father himself loveth you, because ye have loved me, and have believed that I am come out from God. I went out from the Father, and came into the world; and I leave the world again, and go to the Father. His disciples said unto him, Lo, now speakest thou plainly, and thou speakest no proverb. Now are we sure that thou knowest all things, and needest not that any man should ask thee any question. Therefore believe we, that thou camest from God. Jesus answered them, Now ye do believe. Behold, the hour draweth nigh, and is already come, that ye shall be scattered every man unto his own, and shall leave me alone; and yet I am not alone, for the Father is with me. These words have I spoken unto you, that in me ye might have peace. In the world shall ye have tribulation; but be of good cheer, I have overcome the world.

## DOCTRINE AND FRUIT.

MANY times doth Christ promise us, whatsoever we pray, to obtain the same of the Father of heaven; whereby he may stir up our hearts faithfully to cry unto God, the gracious and loving Father, whose love towards us is exceeding great, neither can he say us nay, that hath given and bestowed upon us his own Son. Yea, not only hath he sent down unto us his dear and only-begotten Son, to take the nature of man upon him, and to die for us; but hath also into our hearts given his holy Spirit, with whom he hath sealed us, and certified us of his love, pouring the knowledge and love of Christ into our hearts. How can we then doubt of his love and faithfulness? How is it possible, that in all our trouble and heaviness we should not unto him only have recourse, seeking help and comfort at his hand? The Son for our sake came forth from the Father, humbled, and made himself of no reputation, took all reproach, shame, and trouble upon himself for our welfare. To the Father was he obedient, until the death of the cross; and after that he through his blood had washed away our sins, and finished the work of our salvation, he arose again from death through the power and might of his Father, overcame death for us, and with his ascension opened heaven, and prepared an entrance unto God, carrying up our nature and flesh unto the honour and glory which he had from everlasting, and giving us therein a hope and sure comfort, that we also shall with him have everlasting joy and glory for ever.

Seeing then that he came out from the Father, we ought to hearken unto him, and not to despise his word. He is the eternal wisdom of God, he is the truth, no false teacher can he be; forasmuch as he cometh from God, and is his only-begotten Son. To contemn so dear an ambassador and messenger of God, must needs have great punishment; and though we are not able in most perfection to understand his doctrine, truth, and love, (for here in this time is our knowledge unperfect;) yet should we consider that the Father loveth us, and faithfully ought we to cry and pray unto him for his Spirit, that shall teach us all truth, so much as is necessary and profitable for us; which knowledge from day to day shall increase, till we shall see him face to face, and have the perfect knowledge of him. Our nature is weak and feeble, the nature divine is high and incomprehensible. We are full of darkness; God is the clear and far-passing light: but when our dark mist is taken away, then in clear brightness shall the godly light open unto us. *(Heb. i.)* *(1 Cor. xiii.)*

Some first-fruits and beginnings of God's knowledge have we received already. God hath cast and planted a little seed of knowledge in our hearts, which through his grace and moisture shall daily grow, increase, and prosper. Of such knowledge as we have of God, we may not presume, neither of our weak faith, nor yet ascribe too much unto our own strength. He that standeth, let him look that he fall not. We think many times that we are very strong in faith; but adversity sheweth how feeble we be, and how soon we shrink. Therefore in all trouble and distress of this world we ought to comfort ourselves, and trust only in the grace and strength of Christ. In him shall we find peace and quietness, in him shall we overcome all our enemies: for his overcoming is our victory, his power is our strength. The world is not able to hurt and plague us, more than of our gracious Father is permitted unto them for our wealth.

While we live here, we are in misery, affliction, and distress: but seeing that the head hath overcome, the members ought not to doubt of the victory. Let us with stedfast belief look unto Christ, the fountain of life, our foregoer and finisher of our faith; and let us stoutly step forth after him, let us go the way that he is gone, and hath trodden, and made before. Afflictions shall serve us unto high honour, as they served Christ the Lord unto glory. In Christ we find the peace and rest of our consciences and souls; in him we know and find the goodness and love of God the Father; out of him receive we power, strength, comfort, and eternal life; only let us look, that we turn not the eyes of our heart and faith away from him. Our welfare consisteth in the stedfast belief and love of Jesus Christ the Son of God. Though we may many times stumble, fall, and be proved by sundry temptations and afflictions; yet is the same good and profitable for us, that we may the better learn to know our own weakness, and again, the strength and grace of God. If it were not profitable for us, Christ had not suffered his disciples to fall so grievously. But in all distress he putteth his hand under us, and in adversity he leaveth us not alone, as he also left not his own Son alone. Though all men fly away from us, yet have we God with us.

[John xvii. 1—8.]

John xvii.

THESE words spake Jesus, and lift up his eyes to heaven, and said: Father, the hour is come: glorify thy Son, that thy Son also may glorify thee: as thou hast given him power over all flesh, that he should give eternal life to as many as thou hast given him. This is life eternal, that they know thee the only very true God, and whom thou hast sent, Jesus Christ. I have glorified thee on the earth: I have finished the work which thou gavest me to do. And now glorify me thou, Father, with thine own self, with the glory which I had with thee ere the world was. I have declared thy name unto the men which thou gavest me out of the world. Thine they were, and thou gavest them me, and they have kept thy sayings. Now they know that all things, whatsoever thou hast given me, are of thee: for I have given unto them the words which thou gavest me, and they have received them, and know surely, that I came out from thee, and do believe that thou didst send me.

### DOCTRINE AND FRUIT.

CHRIST the true, only, and chief priest, who now would offer up himself to the Father upon the cross for our sins, after that he had loved his own unto the end, comforting and strengthening them, turneth now himself in an earnest and fervent prayer unto his heavenly Father, for an ensample and doctrine unto his disciples and all faithful believers, that they in all temptations and afflictions should with an earnest and fervent prayer have recourse unto the Father of heaven. That he taught afore in words, the same declareth he now in the deed; shewing not only what, but also how, and after what sort, we ought to pray; not only for ourselves, but also for those that are given and committed unto us of God, and whom we have comforted and exhorted. Our eyes and hands ought we to lift up unto heaven, from whence our help cometh; which doing is a token of a devout, humble, and lowly mind: yea, the eyes, not only of the body, but also of the heart and belief. *How we should pray.*

But unto this end principally ought all our prayers to be directed, that the heavenly Father may be glorified. The devil, the prince of this world, through his adherents, causeth the name and truth of Christ, his doctrine and knowledge, to be rooted out and despised. Seeing then that we are God's children, we should in nothing be so earnest, as in saving the honour of our Father, and in furthering his glory. Which thing cometh to pass, when we notify to men upon earth his grace, faithfulness, love, and great mercy, which he by his only-begotten and dear Son hath declared and shewed unto mankind; when we lead men unto God from earthly vices and false gods' service, and when we direct all things to his glory. Thus is Christ also honoured and glorified by us, when we through the gospel do publish unto all men his power and *The sanctifying of God's name should we chiefly desire.* *What it is to honour the Father.*

goodness, his honour and glory; when we know, that he is our Saviour, our righteousness, and sanctifying; when we know, that the Father hath given all things into his power; that to those whom the Father hath granted to him he may give everlasting life. Which life everlasting consisteth in this, that we know the living God, and his Son Jesus Christ, whom he sent into this world. For God the Father cannot be known without Christ Jesus his Son, neither is there any more Gods, but only one, on whom we hope and trust. The way to God is Christ, whom God therefore sent down, that by him the mercy and grace of the Father might be opened and appear unto us. Wherefore if we will have eternal life, that is, the knowledge of God, we must believe in Christ, and know him; and by him as the way and mediator we must know God the Father. Whoso refuseth Christ, cannot have the Father. What should it help thee to think, that thou knowest God, the highest goodness of all, if thou hast not him, by whom thou art delivered from sin and eternal plague?

*John xiv.*

*Christ is the way to God.*

Where as God, the original of all goodness, is known, and our mind through Christ his Son assured of his grace; namely, that he is favourable unto us, and that he therefore hath separated us out of the world, to the intent that by his Spirit he might make us like unto his Son, righteous and blessed; there doth there spring in our hearts a comfortable trust unto God, a love, and such joy, as nothing in this world may be compared unto. There also doth arise in us a diligence to keep his commandments, godly and innocently to live. Thus cometh our health originally out of the grace and mercy of our heavenly Father, who, afore the world was created, did choose us in Christ Jesu his Son unto eternal life, and in the book of life wrote up our names. After the same did the Father grant unto us the Son, and gave him power over all men. Now that we are given unto Christ, he openeth unto us the name of his Father, through the outward word, and through his Spirit in the heart. When we believe in him, which to do also cometh of him, then increaseth the knowledge of God in us. Out of that knowledge groweth an assured confidence in God, the highest good; of this assured trust cometh love towards him; and when God granteth us all this, he saveth us, and giveth us eternal life.

*The knowledge of God, eternal life.*

*The order of our health.*

This is an high worthiness and honour of Christ, in that the Father giveth him all things into his hand, that he may give everlasting life unto faithful believers. No man can have life, but through Christ. Whoso believeth not in Christ, remaineth in death, and the wrath of God abideth upon him. But then giveth he us eternal life, when we receive his word, and know that he came out from God, and that the Father sent him the Saviour of the world. And when we thus are become faithful believers, then keep we his commandments: for faith studieth and is diligent to please God. This honour and dignity of Christ, his power and kingdom, are first opened unto the world, after his death and cross, in the resurrection and ascension. Of the which honour and glory we also in due time shall, after our measure, be partakers, if we suffer with him. For the high Priest, who hath prayed for us, is heard of the Father, and glorified with eternal honour and glory. Wherefore we may not doubt in the remnant that he prayeth for still on our behalf; he shall be, and is for his worthiness' sake heard, and hath his request. Of this we will consider more.

*What it is to keep God's commandments.*

---

[John xvii. 9—23.]

I PRAY for them, and pray not for the world, but for them whom thou hast given me; for they are thine, and all mine are thine, and thine are mine; and I am glorified in them. And now am I no more in the world, but they are in the world, and I come to thee. Holy Father, keep them in thy name, whom thou hast given me, that they may be one, as we are. When I was with them in the world, I kept them in thy name. Those that thou gavest me have I kept, and none of them is lost, but the lost child, that the scripture might be fulfilled. Now come I to thee, and these words speak I in the world, that they might have my joy full in them. I have given them thy word, and the world hath hated them, because they are not of the world, even as I am not of the world. I desire not that thou shouldest take them

*John xvii.*

out of the world, but that thou keep them from evil. They are not of the world, as I am not of the world. Sanctify them with thy truth: thy saying is truth. As thou sentest me into the world, so have I sent them into the world; and for their sakes I sanctify myself, that they also might be sanctified through the truth. I pray not for them alone, but for those also which shall believe on me through their preaching; that they all may be one, as thou, Father, art in me, and I in thee; and that they may be also one in us, that the world may believe that thou hast sent me. And the glory that thou gavest me, have I given them, that they may be one, as we are one; I in them, and thou in me, that they may be made perfect in one; and that the world may know that thou hast sent me, and hast loved them, as thou hast loved me.

## DOCTRINE AND FRUIT.

This prayer of our high Priest and mediator Christ Jesus is fervent, earnest, full of the fire of godly love, full of great secrets and spiritual instructions. Herein may we learn to know, what high honour, dignity, and power, Christ by his obedience and patience, hath obtained with his Father, wherein consisteth our peace, joy, and welfare; what care and love Christ beareth towards those that are his, and how he committeth them unto his Father. First, he prayeth for his disciples, whom he did choose to publish his truth; afterward prayeth he for all such as should come to the faith by their preaching until the world's end. And forasmuch as the disciples had a great weighty matter in hand, full of danger and adversity, (for they must needs procure to themselves great hatred of the world,) he first prayeth for them, that the Father will strengthen, comfort, and preserve them through his power, and defend them from all evil.

*How the ministers of the word should be prayed for.* In this are we taught diligently, chiefly, and specially, to pray for those, unto whom is committed the preaching of the gospel; for a chargeable and great work carry they upon their shoulders, by means whereof, among all others, they have special need of the grace, help, and assistance of God.

But our prayer ought we to frame as Christ hath framed his. First, we must in our prayer to God make special mention of his own grace and mercy; whereby he choosing them to such an office, hath given them unto Christ his Son. Forasmuch then as they are the ministers of him and of his Son, and seeing the Son is so dear, worthy, and beloved unto the Father, our prayer must be, that he for his Son's sake will defend and preserve them, as in him and by him they are worthy.

Secondly, considering that for his sake and his word, which they declare, they are persecuted of the world, it is requisite that God preserve them in his own work. For great need have they of his fatherly protection, while they yet live in the weak feeble flesh, and are mortal men.

Thirdly, their office serveth to many men's health and welfare; their office is necessary and profitable to the whole world, which walketh in blindness and darkness; for they are the light of the world, that through doctrine and living must shine to many men's life; which without the assistance and help of God cannot come to pass. Matt. v.

Thus ought we to pray for the ministers of the word, and to desire, that God through his holy name and power will defend, strengthen, comfort, and preserve them in all adversity; but principally that he will give them grace to be one, coupled together in the band of peace, love, and uniformity; that they may be of one spirit, and of one mind; that in one spirit they may further and plant the honour of God; that like as Christ neither spake nor did anything, but that which was acceptable and well-pleasing unto the Father, they also in their sayings and doings may have respect unto God's glory; and that they, being rooted and fortified in love, be not vanquished nor overcome of the pleasures or threatenings of this world. Ephes. iv.<br>Phil. ii. Ephes. iii.

Secondly, that in all their labour and travail, in all adversity and persecutions, he will put into their hearts his own comfort and spiritual joy. For the world hath manifold mirths, pastimes, and pleasures; much bragging and wilfulness useth it in the riches and fleshly voluptuousness thereof. But the true ministers of Christ, seeing he hath severed them from the world, must and ought to refrain and absent themselves from all worldly joy and voluptuousness; yea, it is John xv.

they that ought to dissuade the world from such wantonness and vanity; by means of whose faithful admonition there falleth much hatred and trouble upon them; neither were it to the furtherance of God's honour and our commodity, to have them utterly taken away out of this world. Therefore doth Christ desire, and so must we with him, that from evil, namely, from the devil the prince of this world, who stirreth the world against them, they may of the Father in the world be defended and kept.

Thirdly, that he will sanctify and cleanse them afore other men, that they may be holy and pure vessels in the house and temple, that is, in the church of God: for they are means and instruments, by whom God ministereth his grace and truth unto men; therefore is it also convenient, that they be pure and holy. This cometh through the truth that God putteth in their mouth and heart by the Holy Ghost, which inwardly purifieth them. But then are they holy, when they teach truth, and live godly. Into the world hath Christ sent them, as the Father sent him into the world. The Father sent Christ into the world, that he should destroy the kingdom of the devil and of the world; that he should declare unto the world the grace and mercy of God towards mankind; that he should bring men from sin and from false idolatrous faith to the true living God, and to a virtuous conversation; that he with the light of truth should shine upon those which sat in darkness; that he should bring the knowledge of God into the world, and exhort men to the amendment of life. Even this hath Christ given in commission to his apostles, and to all ministers of the word to do. This is their office, this is their ministration, unto this have they great need of the grace, power, and assistance of God. Therefore ought we most earnestly to pray for them: for if they fail or fall, it hurteth the whole church; yea, out of the same there groweth slander unto the name of God in the sight of the unbelievers, and an occasion of falling to such as are weak of faith. Therefore Christ also offered himself to the Father for them, and sanctified them, that they might be pure and holy, not in outward appearance, but from the heart, and in the truth; that through their uniformity and love, through the word of truth which they preach, through the holiness of their doctrine and living, all men and the whole world might

*1 Cor. iv.*

*Ezek. xxxvi.*

know and understand, that God hath sent them; yea, that God sent his Son Christ into the world, unto whom they with mouth and life bear record, and who also everywhere shineth out of them with words and deeds.

Not only for them hath Christ prayed, but also for us, as many as hearken and believe the word of truth preached by them. Wherein first we may perceive and see the love, faithfulness, and great care of Christ for us, how earnestly the trusty Shepherd of our souls committeth his poor sheep into his Father's protection, how faithfully our Mediator and Advocate prayeth for us; whereby also he setteth forth a doctrine unto us, how and what we shall pray of our heavenly Father.

First, that he will make us one by his holy Spirit in the truth, in the unity of faith, and in love unseparable, that we may all be of one mind, one body, and one spirit in Christ Jesu our Head, and to keep the unity of the Spirit in the bond of peace; that we all being illuminated by his Spirit, may in word and deed, yea, in our whole life, seek and further the glory of our heavenly Father, that we may all be one among ourselves and with God; whereby all the world may spy, see, and perceive, that we are God's children and Christ's disciples. *Phil. ii. Ephes. ii. John xiii.*

Secondly, that of his fatherly goodness he will defend, save, and preserve us his own poor sheep, which be in the midst among wolves and manifold dangers, and seeing we be yet in the world, do not live after the world; that it will please him to keep us from the evil, namely, from the prince of this world, that though the same our enemy doth tempt and plague us, he never yet have power to prevail against us. *Matt. x.*

Thirdly, that inasmuch as we, being in sin conceived and born, have hitherto lived in sin, and seeing that albeit we are cleansed already by his word and faith, yet the uncleanness of the flesh and of the world doth daily defile us, it will please him through his truth to purge and sanctify our bodies, our souls, and our whole lives, that we may become an holy temple of his grace, pure, clean, and holy vessels, consecrated and sanctified to God's own use. He hath once purified and hallowed us through the blood of his Son, and unto the Father hath Christ sanctified and offered up himself an holy acceptable sacrifice for our sins; but the devil, the world, and our *Psal. l. 1 Cor. vi. 2 Cor. vi.*

flesh, is ever busy to lead us away again from God and from true holiness. Therefore must we daily pray unto him, that through his holy Spirit, and through his holy truth, he will continually purge, cleanse, and sanctify us, that we be not dissembling hypocrites, but godly and unfeigned even from our hearts, and that we be not stained in the filthiness of this world, but to refrain from all uncleanness, through the assistance of his grace; that we may also offer up our bodies an holy acceptable sacrifice to God the Lord, as he offered up himself upon the cross for our sakes.

James 1.

[John xvii. 24—26.]

John xvii.

FATHER, I will, that they which thou hast given me, be with me where I am, that they may see my glory, which thou hast given me; for thou lovedst me before the making of the world. O righteous Father, the world also hath not known thee, but I have known thee, and these have known that thou hast sent me. And I have declared unto them thy name, and will declare it, that the love wherewith thou hast loved me, may be in them, and I in them.

### DOCTRINE AND FRUIT.

AFTER that Christ had committed his unto the Father, that he will care for them, defend, and keep them, while they live in the world; he desireth now that it will please him finally also to save them, and to take them to himself into his kingdom. With the which prayer, he giveth a great consolation to his disciples, and all faithful believers, that we might be the more cheerful to serve him, considering the high reward that is prepared for us; that for his sake we should joyfully and stoutly bear all adversity, seeing he will make us, yea, hath made us already, partakers of his glory and of his kingdom.

Oh the great grace and incomprehensible love of God towards us, who through his mercy and great love, whereas we were children of wrath and damnation, hath made us his own children, elect and beloved; and when we were dead in sin, hath with his Son raised us up from death, Ephes. ii. revived us, and made us sit with him among those of heaven in Christ Jesu; to declare unto the ages to come the riches of his grace in kindness and love to us ward, through Jesus Christ.

Forasmuch now as God hath caused the light of his glory, even Christ, to shine into our hearts, and through the light of faith hath kindled and purified our hearts; it is meet that in this time we live as children of light, to the intent that men may see the brightness of those good works Matt. v. which proceed of faith, to the praise of our heavenly Father. And though we be not as yet bodily with Christ, yet our hearts and minds are always above, there as Christ sitteth Col. iii. at the right hand of God: our conversation and being is in heaven; albeit we are in corporal misery, with heart we desire to die, and to be with Christ. We are sure, if this Phil. i. earthly house were fallen and broken down, that we have 2 Cor. v. one everlasting in heaven. We are dead, but our life is reserved with Christ in God. It is not evident yet what we be: but when Christ our life shall shew himself, then shall we also appear with him in glory; even when we shall rise up, and be taken up in the air, and be with him for ever, and see his honour and glory, which the angels delight 1 Thess. iv. to see and behold.

Oh, how great pleasure and joy is it, to behold the eternal light that never quencheth, in the which no darkness hath place; from the which shall be expelled and cast out all they that would not receive and know the light which God hath sent into the world to illuminate them, but are blinded by the prince of this world, lest the light of the gospel should 2 Cor. iv. shine upon them. No wrong doth the righteous Father unto them, when he plagueth them, and taketh the light from them. A righteous and just judgment is it, seeing the gracious Father so mercifully sent them the light of the truth, and they yet so maliciously and stubbornly have despised and refused it. Yea, reason it is, that they perish in untruth, in lies, and in everlasting blindness; forasmuch as John iii. they would receive darkness rather than the light, lies rather than the truth. And considering that they have forsaken the brightness of the truth and of the Son of God, they must needs be cast into utter darkness, and never enjoy the light.

O gracious Father, grant unto us, which through thy Son have known thy name, that in such knowledge and light of the truth we may increase more and more; that the love wherewith thou lovest thy dear Son may be and remain in us; and that thy only-begotten Son Jesus Christ our head, may in us his members, continue still, work, live, and bring forth fruit acceptable unto thee.

---

[John xviii. 1, 2. Matthew xxvi. 36—39. Mark xiv. 32—36. Luke xxii. 39—42.]

AND when Jesus had spoken these words, he went out with his disciples, as he was wont, over the brook Cedron, unto mount Olivet, into a village called Gethsemane, where as was a garden, into the which Jesus went with his disciples. Judas now, who betrayed him, knew also the place: for Jesus used oft to come thither with his disciples. Jesus said unto his disciples, Sit ye here till I go yonder and pray. And he took unto him Peter and the two sons of Zebede, and began to be heavy and sorry. And a fear and terror came upon him. Thus said he unto them: My soul is heavy unto the death; tarry ye here and watch with me. And he went from them as far as a stone's cast. Then fell he down upon his face to the ground, and prayed, that if it were possible, that hour might depart from him. And thus he prayed: O Father, unto thee are all things possible; take this cup from me; howbeit not my will, but thy will be done.

### DOCTRINE AND FRUIT.

AFTER that Jesus hath established his disciples in faith and love, comforting and strengthening them against adversity and trouble to come in this world, promising also unto them the Spirit, love, defence, and protection of his

Father; he goeth now to meet his traitor and enemies, and beginneth the work of our redemption. Awake up now, O thou faithful and devout soul, and go after thy Redeemer; follow his footsteps; gather up diligently the drops of his blood, and sprinkle them with a true faith in thine heart: take up the bundle of myrrh, and lay it at thy breast, O thou noble bride and spouse of Christ; his passion that he suffereth for thee, write then in thy mind; learn to die from all sin, from thyself, and from the world, that thou mayest be crucified unto the world, and the world unto thee.

Death is ugsome, and very terrible unto the flesh; but joyful and welcome is it unto all such as are instructed in the secret science of God, namely, that death unto faithful believers is an end of all trouble, an entrance into a better and eternal life.

Christ, in that he goeth forth to meet death, declareth that he will suffer, not of compulsion, but willingly; whereby he comforteth us. But whereas he is heavy, and trembleth before his disciples, and confesseth how he feareth death; the same is done for our wealth, to declare unto us the weakness and feebleness that our flesh receiveth at the sight of adversity: for in all things, sin except, it was his good pleasure to become like unto us his brethren; he would take upon a true man, who felt our adversity in his own flesh, and so could have compassion on us. Besides this, he sheweth also to whom our weakness ought to resort for comfort and help in adversity, namely, to our Father in heaven, before whom we must fall down with devout and fervent prayer, and unto him disclose and open our anguish and trouble. *Heb. ii.*

To this prayer, he seeketh and chooseth out a place meet and convenient for the same; for prayer is a lifting up of the mind in God, which among the multitude of men and confusion of worldly matters cannot well be done. Therefore Christ sheweth us, what great diligence we ought to use in prayer, when the enemy falleth in, that the mind may cleave unto God constantly and without shrinking: and what gesture the body ought to shew in prayer, Christ also declareth, in that he falleth down to the earth upon his face, and prayeth with the voice and words. God hath no need of our prayer: but unto us is nothing more profitable and better, than oft and fervently to pray. And the greater the adversity is, the more ardent and earnest should the prayer be; as we see here in Christ our head, whose passion is very great in body and in mind: for the which cause also, as a very true man, he sheweth the same his passion and heaviness to his disciples.

The strongest of all is weak; and the comforter of all hearts hath need of comfort himself: he that expelleth all terror and fear, doth himself fear and tremble. But all this cometh to pass for our learning; that when we be in temptations, we should not doubt in the help of God; and that none of us, being in danger and adversity, and feeling himself loath to suffer, or pensive and slow to tame the motions and wickedness of the flesh, should therefore shrink and be fainthearted; but with a constant faith to resort unto God, complaining to him of his trouble, with hearty prayer that he will bring the hard and painful beginning to a blessed and joyful end; that in all adversity we may consider, as well the excellent and great fruit which proceedeth thereof, as also the gracious good-will of our heavenly Father, to whom we ought wholly and perfectly to give over and offer up ourselves; that neither through the multitude of sins, neither through the greatness of adversity, we despair nor fall away; but with his help and assistance manfully to go through.

[Matt. xxvi. 40, 41. Mark xiv. 37, 38. Luke xxii. 45, 46.]

JESUS came again to his disciples, and found them sleeping. Then said he unto Peter, Simon, sleepest thou? Couldest thou not watch with me one hour? Watch ye, and pray, that ye enter not into temptation: the spirit is willing, but the flesh is weak.

### DOCTRINE AND FRUIT.

THE love of Christ towards us is fervent, earnest, and great; but our flesh is so weak, that we not only consider it not, but are also so slow, that we sleep and feel not, for whose sakes Christ hath suffered so great things. Ofttimes is there in us a ready will to take great matters in hand, as

Peter and the other disciples did; but at the last we miss, and have many a sore fall. Therefore Christ, who knoweth us better than we ourselves, willing to expel from us all pride and presumptuousness, teacheth us to be lowly-minded and humble, to be ever watching, and with continual prayer to cleave only unto him, without whom we are able to do nothing, and in whom we may do all things: and even so doth he also in his feebleness, which assaulted him as a very true man, to the intent that we, alway remembering our own weakness, might understand how to tame the rebellious flesh, and in no case to trust it; and that we might be careful and vigilant, lest the subtle enemy in temptations come behind us, fall upon us, and oppress us. It is no time to sleep: the battle is yet a fighting, the enemy is yet alive, and as yet besiegeth he our castle, that Christ hath in keeping. All is full of snares and dangers, which no man is able to escape, save only he, which in fervent belief and prayer doth earnestly watch and stoutly fight, yea, and that continually unto the end.

Neither the present anguish and trouble, nor yet Christ's exhortation, can bring so much to pass in the disciples, as to keep them from sleep; so little it helpeth, where the Spirit giveth not life. Nevertheless Christ's talk and admonition unto his disciples is not utterly unprofitable; for that they now understand not, the same afterwards, when the Spirit cometh, is made plain and evident unto them, and then are they fervent and earnest in godly prayer. Wherefore we should never cease from comforting and exhorting the feeble and weak: for though it help not at this present, the hour shall come, that the Spirit will make it to have life, and to be fruitful in them.

---

[Matt. xxvi. 42—46. Mark xiv. 39—42. Luke xxii. 43, 44.]

He went forth the second time, and prayed like as afore: My Father, if this cup may not pass, except I drink it, thy will be done. Then came he again, and found them sleeping, for their eyes were heavy; and they knew not what answer to make him. So he left them again, and went and prayed the third time like as afore, and kneeled down and said: Father, if thou wilt, take away this cup from me; nevertheless not my will, but thine be done. And there appeared unto him an angel from heaven comforting him: and when he was in the agony, distress, and conflict, he prayed the longer, and his sweat was like drops of blood trickling down to the ground. And when he rose up from prayer, and came to his disciples, he found them sleeping for heaviness, and he said unto them: What? sleep ye? Sleep on now, and take your rest. It is enough: up, and pray, that ye enter not into temptation. Behold, the hour approacheth, and the Son of man is betrayed and given into the hands of sinners. Up, let us go: behold, he that betrayeth me is at hand.

### DOCTRINE AND FRUIT.

In the perfect example and mirror of our life, Christ Jesus, we find an earnest fervent love, a doctrine how we ought to behave ourselves in adversity. First, we see that Christ of an exceeding great love taketh upon himself all infirmities of mankind, and becometh "like unto his brethren in all things, sin except," being a very true man: he is therefore not ashamed before his disciples to acknowledge his infirmity, sorrow, heaviness, and fear, and to complain thereof unto his Father. A fear, by reason of the death and passion, he receiveth as a very man; for not to feel trouble is not the nature of man, and passion is no passion, if it smart not, if it be not felt. Christ therefore both in his mind and body feeleth the passion; he feeleth the conflict of death, albeit in wrestling withal he overthroweth it. O the exceeding fervent love of our head and foregoer Jesus Christ, who for our health cometh into so great an agony and trouble, that above natural moisture, through the fearful conflicts of the passion and death, he sheddeth his blood and sweateth it! But with hearty desire runneth he to his heavenly Father; to him complaineth he of his weakness and distress; to him giveth he over himself in all obedience and contentation of mind; of him also receiveth he comfort and strength. In the mean season, he forgetteth not his disciples, but cometh to them, exhorteth them to watch and pray, and hath great compassion with their feebleness and sloth.

If we now be the disciples and scholars of Christ Jesu, and have surrendered ourselves up into the school of the heavenly Schoolmaster, we ought diligently to look, what Christ here in himself doth teach and prescribe unto us; that we learning the same of him, and following his footsteps, when temptations of sin, and conflicts of adversity, trouble, and death fall in upon us, may know how to order and frame ourselves therein.

First, that we know ourselves to be poor, full of faults, mortal men, and sinners, having nothing of our own but feebleness. So when the temptation of sin and of the flesh assault us, we must not be ashamed to open such our faults and conflicts unto God our heavenly Father, and to complain unto him of them. God hath not made us to be utterly without temptation, but hath suffered the same to remain in the flesh, that we thereby might be exercised and provoked to seek help at him, and to learn, in how miserable a case we should be, if he withdrew his hand from us. When we now feel that the spirit is willing and the flesh weak, and that the law of the members withstandeth the law of God in us, that the flesh fighteth and striveth against the Spirit, we must not be ashamed to confess our feebleness before our heavenly Father, (yea, though of weakness we had lain under in the battle already,) desiring his help, that we may rise again, and valiantly to fight it out. Thus must we also do, when the cross and hatred of the world for Christ's sake, or that is contrary to our nature, falleth upon us. *Rom. vii. Gal. v.*

The cup which the Father hath filled in, that we should drink it, the same ought we willingly to drink: and if there grow in our flesh a terror and fear to taste it, we must not be ashamed to complain thereof unto our Father; forasmuch as we see here that Christ, for our sakes being in such heaviness and fear, did not yet, for all that, step aside from his Father's will. The patience therefore of Christians standeth not in this, that they feel no passion, or be not fearful, heavy, or sorry; but in this, that no cross be so great, as to be able to drive them away from Christ. Yea, the more the cross that God the Father hath laid upon them doth make them to smart, and the more it presseth them, (so that they yet bear it,) the more precious and more excellent is their patience; which patience we ought to declare, but not as they that suffer or feel no passion at all.

For here we are instructed and certified of the kindness of our loving Father, that he is not angry, neither taketh it in evil part, when we complain to him of our present trouble, so that we give over our will unto his. All they therefore that be in afflictions, adversity, and temptations, must set this example of the Lord directly before their eyes, and ponder it in their hearts. Not only is the Father not angry, when we complain unto him in our necessity; but in all trouble he sendeth us his own help and comfort, either by his angel, or inwardly by his Spirit, or outwardly by some other mean: he sendeth us strength, giveth us his hand, draweth us, delivereth us, and suffereth us not to be tempted above our power; or else, in the midst of our adversity, he giveth us consolation and strength to overcome it.

O how great comfort bringeth this unto us in our afflictions in life and death, if we ponder, weigh, and consider the exceeding love of God our heavenly Father, who giveth his dear Son into so great trouble, that we might be delivered from eternal adversity and sorrow! If we also remember the love of our Lord Jesus towards us, who for our sakes taketh upon himself so great a fear and passion, how cannot we look for all good things at his hand? What thing is so great, that we his members would not suffer for his sake, if we behold the head in such anguish and trouble? And forasmuch as he suffereth all this for the satisfaction of our sins, we ought to apply great diligence, that we fall not again into sin, for the which Christ suffered this, and from the which Christ with so great a passion hath delivered and cleansed us.

We learn here also to love our neighbours, to care for them, to pity them, if they be impotent and slow, to pray for their infirmity, seeing we are all weak and feeble: and unto such weakness must we so have respect, that we be not arrogant, nor hold much of ourselves, when we see that Peter and others are so full of sleep and sluggishness, that all the admonitions and exhortations of Christ could at that time do little with them. But ever in humbleness of mind, and in the fear of God, ought we to stand; to ascribe all good things unto him; to be careful and watch, lest the devil draw us into his temptations.

O merciful Father, give us grace with fervent hearts to consider the unspeakable love of thee and of thy Son, and never to forget the same; that our faith and trust in thee may be strengthened; that love in us towards thee and our neighbour may be kindled; that above all things we may love thee, the well-spring of all goodness.; that we may serve our neighbours in love, care for them, and do them good, according to the love that thy dear Son hath bestowed upon us. O give us patience and stedfastness in adversity, strengthen our weakness, comfort us in trouble and distress, help us to fight; grant unto us, that in true obedience and contentation of mind we may give over our own wills unto thee our Father in all things, according to the example of thy beloved Son; that in adversity we grudge not, but offer up ourselves unto thee without contradiction. Give us strength constantly to subdue the rebellious and stubborn flesh, and to make it obedient unto the Spirit; to cast away all temporal and carnal fear; to resort oft unto prayer; to be earnest and fervent therein; to mortify all our own wills and lusts, and utterly to give them their leave. O give us a willing and cheerful mind, that we may gladly suffer and bear all things for thy sake.

---

[Matt. xxvi. 47—50. Mark xiv. 43—45. Luke xxii. 47, 48. John xviii. 3—9.]

So when Judas had gotten him a company of soldiers of the high priests, and of the Pharisees' ministers, he came thither with lanterns, links, and weapons, yea, the same Judas Iscarioth, one of the twelve, (as Jesus yet talked with his disciples,) and with him a great heap of people, with swords and staves, sent from the high priests, scribes, and elders of the people. Now had the traitor given them a token, saying, Whomsoever I do kiss, the same is he; take him and bring him warily. So Judas went before them, and came near unto Jesus to kiss him. And when he came, he stept unto him, and said, All hail, Master! and with that kissed him. Jesus said unto him, Friend, whereto art thou come? Judas, betrayest thou the Son of man with a kiss? Jesus, knowing all things that were to come upon himself, went forth, and said unto them, Whom seek ye? They said, Jesus of Nazareth. Then said he unto them, I am he. And Judas that betrayed him stood with them. Now when Jesus said, I am he, they went backward and fell to the ground. Then Jesus asked them again, Whom seek ye? They said, Jesus of Nazareth. Then answered Jesus, and said, I have told you that I am he: if ye seek me, then let these depart: that the saying which he spake might be fulfilled: Of them whom thou gavest me I have lost none.

## DOCTRINE AND FRUIT.

CHRIST, the worthy and strong Captain, when he hath wholly given over himself, steppeth forth weaponed, going manfully and stedfastly against the prince of this world and his ministers, yielding and offering himself willingly to suffer for us, as Esay saith, *quia voluit;* for so was it his will. No man had been able to take him, or put him to death, if he had not so willed himself; for he had power to leave his own life. Many times afore did he give place to their fury, and got himself out of the way: but when the hour appointed of the Father was come, he goeth himself willingly, and meeteth death by the way. Here ought we also to learn willingly and stoutly to go into adversity, if it be the will of our Father; if God's honour and our neighbours' welfare so require. For like as the Father suffereth not his Son to die, till the hour of death come, even so standeth our life in his hand. The limits that he hath set unto us, may we neither prevent nor overpass: neither lieth it in the power of our enemies to kill us, when they will themselves. Christ careth for those that are his: the enemies are able to do us no harm at all, no neither in body nor goods, till the Father give them leave. Therefore he saith, "Let these go." The Father, according to his great mercy and gracious will, thrusteth us into adversity with Christ his dear beloved Son,

Isai. liii.

John x.

Job ii.

in such wise, so much, and at what time he will himself. Against his will ought we not to strive, but patiently and with obedience submit ourselves wholly unto it.

Oh, what an unspeakable great love is here! The shepherd dieth, to save the life of the poor sheep; the Lord goeth unto death, to the intent that the servant should not die; the Creator spareth not himself, to save his creature. If the Son of God now doth not abhor to suffer death for us, why should we then be ashamed to suffer and die for his sake?

And though he be very God, and sheweth his enemies the brightness of his godly strength, in that he so throweth them to the ground, yet will not he in the same hour use such his divine power to deliver himself: albeit he admonisheth them thereby to cease from their conceived malice; for his godly strength casteth them down, his mercy and grace lifteth them up again. Out of the which great miracle they should have learned not to lay hand on him maliciously; they should have considered, that if it had been his pleasure, he might well have escaped their hands, so that they had not been able to hold him: but the unbelieving rabble are blinded, indurate, and hardened, that neither miracle nor kindness can move them.

O the high majesty of Christ! How shall unbelievers be able to stand before him, when he shall appear in the judgment, whereas before his weakness and humility, when he was now about to be judged himself, they were not able to stand? If his loving voice, wherewith he speaketh so gentle unto them, and saith, "I am he," doth so fear them, and throw them down; what will then the horrible voice of the Judge do, when he shall say, "Depart, ye cursed, into everlasting fire?" O how innocently and godly ought we to live before him, who is among us, and in us, heareth all our words, seeth all our works, searcheth and looketh through all our thoughts, how secret soever they be! Christ at this time withdrew his high power, and in weakness of the flesh, and in wonderful high patience, stept he forth to suffer. By his ensample must we learn, not to take us to our high estate, but with patience and humbleness of mind to meet the enemy.

Like patience and gentleness useth he also towards his

traitor, whom he goeth to meet, not speaking rough words unto him, brawleth not with him, rateth him not, as he was well worthy; but receiveth him with all softness of mind and gentleness, whereas yet he came to deliver and betray him into the hands of the wicked, and unto death. Neither doth the Lord deny him so much as the kiss, the token of friendship, but lovingly also talketh he with him; albeit he also maketh mention of his feigned and dissembling friendship, telling him of it, admonishing him, if he had not been hardened, to cease from his conceived treason. Wherefore we also must learn of Christ, so far as concerneth our own person and estimation, with all mildness, softness of mind, patience, and greatest love, to meet those that hate us and betray us; if peradventure with such love and gentleness of mind we may bring them away from their malice and wickedness.

Matt. v.
Rom. xii.

Here also with great fear and dread ought we to consider of the judgment of God in Judas; that he, being one of the twelve and elect disciples, doth betray and sell the Lord Jesus, his gracious loving master. Whereby we are taught, how that amongst all men there is nothing throughly perfect and whole, seeing that in so holy and small number there is one man so greatly stuffed with wickedness. Therefore he that standeth, let him look that he fall not. Let covetousness blind no man; let the desire of temporal good possess and rule no man's heart: for out of covetousness, the root of all vice, groweth nothing but treason and despair. No righteousness, no fidelity, no truth, no honesty, can be in that heart, where greedy covetousness hath taken root. Judas for very greediness of money giveth over God and all love; and he that afore was a fellow and companion of the holy congregation of God's children, is become a mate, companion, and captain of the wicked and unbelievers; he that was chosen to the preaching of the gospel, is become an enemy, persecutor, and traitor against the truth. O from how high and great honour, to what shame, dishonesty, and vile state falleth Judas; who, having wolvish conditions under sheep's clothing, doth under the token of love practise treason against the truth! From Jesus, the true health, he separateth himself to the children of the devil; he getteth him amongst the blood-thirsty, yea, even he that hitherto in outward appearance had confessed the truth. Thus goeth it, when temptation breaketh in, when the truth cometh into peril and adversity: then the enemies of the truth declare themselves, and hypocrites get them to the adversaries against Christ; then may we learn to know them.

Of these (the more pity!) there be at this day in the church of God many, which, under the pretence and colour of truth, fight against the truth, and that taking the name of Christ in their mouth, betray Christ, yea, with the sword of their venomous tongues kill Christ, and in sheep's clothing are very wolves, false teachers, and most noisome enemies, whom covetousness and vain glory blindeth. And whereas they are not able to root out Christ with the truth, they undertake to do it with weapons and swords, and set the princes and powers of the world to defend their falsehood and tyranny. Yea, many there be of those that, rebuking Judas' act, do even as he did themselves; feigning the truth, when in very deed they persecute the truth.

O our great slothfulness! whereof we are admonished in the disciples that sleep, when wicked Judas in his ungracious work so diligently watcheth, and earnestly runneth about. O that the love and zeal of God might do as much in us, as the ungracious will in the wicked! O that we which are chosen into the service of Christ, were so diligent to minister unto our Father and Lord, as the children of this world are to wait upon Satan their master! For nothing do they omit, that may serve to the persecution of the truth.

O merciful God, grant us poor feeble men patience in adversity; that sudden wrath overcome us not, and that bitterness and desire of vengeance kindle us not to use uncharitable words, and to do hurt, when enemies fall upon us, and brag against us, telling us our faults, whereof we think ourselves unguilty. Grant us ever lovingly to receive all adversity; and that we may know those to be our best friends, which speak unto us, and rebuke us hardest of all. Let no wicked root of envy, malice, and evil will, grow in us; no tediousness, nor sloth. Give us strength to be willing and patient, and with fervent desire to suffer yet more grievous things for thy sake. Pull up the wicked root of covetousness, and the false shine of feigned spirituality out of us. O save us, that Satan bring us not into temptation. Grant us love towards friends and enemies, that we may follow the nature of thee our Father, and the example of thy only-begotten Son, Jesus Christ. Amen.

---

[Matt. xxvi. 51—56. Mark xiv. 46—53. Luke xxii. 49—53. John xviii. 10—12.]

THEN came they and laid hands on Jesus, and took him. But when they that were with him saw what would come of it, they said unto him, Master, shall we smite with the sword? Jesus answered and said, Suffer ye thus far forth. Simon Peter had a sword, which he drew out, and smote the servant of the high priest, and cut off his right ear. And the servant's name was called Malchus. Then said Jesus unto Peter, Put thy sword into the sheath. Wilt thou not, that I shall drink the cup which my Father hath given me? All they that draw the sword, shall perish with the sword. Thinkest thou not, that I might pray my Father, to send me now more than twelve legions of angels? but how should the scriptures be fulfilled? It must needs be thus. And when Jesus touched his ear, he healed it. Then began Jesus to speak unto the multitude that were come to him, and to the high priests, and to the chief rulers of the temple, and to the elders, and said: Ye are come forth, as to a murderer, with swords and staves to take me; whereas I yet being daily in the temple, sat and taught, and ye took me not. But this is your hour, and the power of darkness. All this cometh to pass, that the scriptures should be fulfilled. Then the disciples forsook him, and fled all from him. There was a young man that followed after, who had a white linen cloth upon the bare, and him they took. But he left the linen cloth behind him, and ran away naked. The multitude, and the captain, and ministers of the Jews, apprehended Jesus, took him, bound him, and led him first to Annas the chief priest;

for he was father-in-law unto Caiphas, which Caiphas was high priest, and was the same Caiphas, which gave counsel unto the Jews, that better it were one man to die, than the whole people to perish. And all the priests, and scribes, Pharisees, and elders, came together.

## DOCTRINE AND FRUIT.

PETER declaring his earnest love which he bare unto the Lord, undertaketh to defend him from malicious violence; but at the same hour it pleased the Lord to declare and shew, not only his own might and power, but also his unspeakable goodness even unto his enemies : therefore is it not his will, that any man on his behalf should have harm; for he was come to bring health, and no hurt; and therefore the uncircumcised zeal of Peter, which was not directed after the will of God, he rejected and reproved, commanding Peter to put up his sword into his sheath; and the servant's ear that was smitten off he set on again, and healed it: for he was ready to be obedient unto his Father's will unto the death, and to drink the cup that his Father had filled for him. Yet doth he shew unto his enemies, that he willingly suffereth, and that if it were not his will, they should not be able to take him. But he affirmed the hour now to be here, that the Father had given him into the power of darkness, and that they shewed such violence unto him, that the scripture might be fulfilled.

The disciples fly from Jesu their Lord, and leave him to tread the winepress alone. In their weakness, fear, and flying, is signified the infirmity of the unperfect members of the Church, which yet, when the Spirit cometh, is strengthened. Let no man build upon his own strength, but pray unto God, that he suffer him not to be led into temptation.

The gracious Lord Jesus is sold unto sinners, that we which were sold under sin, bond, and thrall to the prince of this world, might be redeemed and delivered. He is content to be bound and taken, that we might be quit and free from the snares and captivity of sin.

O Jesu Christ, the mirror of all gentleness of mind, the example of highest obedience and patience, grant us thy servants with true devotion to consider, how thou, innocent and undefiled Lamb, wert bound, taken, and haled away unto death for our sins; how well content thou wast to suffer such things, not opening thy mouth in unpatience, but willingly offering up thyself unto death. O gracious God, how vilely wast thou mishandled for our sakes! O Lord, let this never come out of our hearts: expel through it coldness and sloth out of our minds; stir up ferventness and love towards thee; provoke us unto earnest prayer; make us cheerful and diligent in thy will; bind our stubborn flesh with the cords of thy fear and nurture; yoke us under thy holy work and obedience. Yea, thy bands make quit and free from all sins; thy bands keep us, and draw us in, that we run not at large in curiosity and worldly vanity; they preserve us in thy holy service under continual nurture and blessed perseverance. O grant that it be light and not grievous unto us, to break and yield ourselves; that we do not loath nor abhor to be informed, taught, led, and corrected against our own self-will. Grant that we never become disobedient, unquiet, stubborn, busy, heady, and contentious; that we never be found fighters, neither such as use brawling and scolding. Make thou us quiet, mild, soft-minded, tractable, and meek; ever ready, and not loath to keep thy commandments. Bow down our neck under the yoke of thy obedience; help us, through strait exercises, to tame and overcome our flesh and wicked dispositions, which we are most inclined unto. O Lord Jesus Christ, grant unto us whom thou hast delivered, that fully and perfectly we may yield ourselves unto thee, committing us wholly unto thy Spirit; and to have always before our eyes and hearts, that we are even as sheep appointed to the butchery and shambles; that we defend not ourselves in ire and greediness of vengeance; for thou hast numbered our hairs, and given us thine angels to be our keepers. Wherefore preserve thou our minds from displeasure and desire of revengement; grant us a mild, friendly stomach towards our enemy, that we may love him, speak good unto him, pray for him, recompense him good for evil, that we may be ready to offer the other cheek also. And when we stand in any danger, O grant us, that we do nothing which doth evil become thy children, and that is not agreeable unto thine example.

*Isai. liii.*

[Matt. xxvi. 57, 58, 69—75. Mark xiv. 66—72. Luke xxii. 54—62.
John xviii. 12—27.]

AND Annas sent him so bound unto Caiphas the high priest. The soldiers took Jesus and led him unto the high priest Caiphas, there as the scribes, the elders, and Pharisees were come together. But Peter followed after afar off into the palace of the high priest, and so did another disciple. The same disciple was known to the high priest, and went in with Jesus into the high priest's palace. But Peter stood without at the door. Then the other disciple, who was known to the high priest, went out, and spake to the damsel that kept the door, and brought Peter in. So Peter went in, and sat with the servants to see the end. They had a fire, and coals kindled in the midst of the palace, and sat about it. Peter also sat amongst them, and warmed him by the fire. The other servants also stood round about the fire, and warmed themselves, for it was cold; and Peter, being with them, stood and warmed himself. Now when the high priest's maid that kept the door, saw Peter, and spied him by the light of the fire, she said, Wast not thou also with Jesus of Nazareth the Galilean? Art not thou likewise one of his disciples? Another said, He also was with him. Then Peter denied before them all, and said, Woman, I know him not; I am not he; neither wot I whereof thou speakest. And when he was gone out into the porch, the cock crew. Then there spied him another damsel, which said unto those that were there, This fellow also was with Jesus of Nazareth. Then denied he again with an oath, and said, I never knew the man. After a little while, as it were about an hour, others that stood there spied him, and said, Verily thou art one of them, for thou art a Galilean; thine own speech bewrayeth thee. Then said one of the priest's servants, a kinsman of his whose ear Peter had smitten off, Did not I see thee with him in the garden? But Peter began to swear, and to curse himself, and to make great protestations, that he never knew the man. Immediately while he yet spake, the cock crew again. And the Lord turned him about, and beheld Peter. Then Peter remembered the word that Jesus had said unto him, Afore the cock crow twice, thou shalt deny me three times. And he went forth, and wept bitterly.

### DOCTRINE AND FRUIT.

O THE sudden change! O the great inconstancy of man's weakness! O the unsearchable judgments of God! Not long heretofore would Peter have gone with Christ his master into prison and death: but now he is so afraid of the words of one damsel, that he denieth the Lord. Of the which fall Christ told Peter and the other disciples afore for a warning; but they, believing it not, became presumptuous, and ascribed too much unto themselves: therefore the Lord suffereth them to fall, that they may learn what they have of themselves, and what they have of God; yea, that we all may see what the apostles were afore the receiving of the Holy Ghost, and what they became after the power that was given them from above. Afore they received the Holy Ghost, they were weak, feeble, inconstant, and wavering; but when God had clothed them with power from above, they became fervent, earnest, and stedfast. Grievously doth Peter fall in denying of his Master: which thing yet turneth to the wealth of him and all men; to the intent that thereby we might learn, how hurtful and dangerous it is for a man to trust to himself, to his own strength, and not only unto God, without whom we are able to do nothing that good is. Good godly people do fall many times, and through fear and greatness of the battle they should utterly give over, if they were not fortified and preserved by the power of God.

Therefore the mercy of God, which continually careth for us, hath brought to pass and appointed, that such examples should be noted in the scripture, to teach us and to declare unto us his power and goodness in every thing. Thus the sins and falls of holy and virtuous men are set before us; partly to the intent that if we stand, we should so continue upright, looking well to ourselves, that we fall not; and partly that if we be fallen, we should learn to rise up again, to amend our lives, and to bewail our sins. And so have the holy evangelists perfectly and uniformly described the fall and denial of Peter; not that thereby they thought to deface Peter, or to publish and make known his trespass; but that the power of God in him might be known and praised.

As for such sins as holy men commit through weakness and ignorance, God useth them to his glory and our commodity; that with the wounds of his saints he might heal ours, and that the shipwreck of the godly might be unto us a sure port and haven. Peter's fall serveth, first to the knowledge and praise of the power and goodness of God, in that we see how mightily he setteth up Peter again, and strengtheneth him, how graciously he forgiveth him his sins; that we which are fallen should not despair, but hope for assistance and forgiveness of God, who giveth strength and power unto those that are his. Item, it serveth to our commodity and profit, in that we see a good godly man fall and sin, and afterward rise up again and amend; lest we should say, "Alas! I am lost, I have done this, and I have done that:" but forasmuch as we see that Peter by repentance, weeping, and converting again, doth obtain grace, it is meet and convenient, that we acknowledge our offences unto God, desire grace, weep and complain of our sins before God. For both are here set before us, the fall, and the repentance: and this ensample is good and profitable to those that are in the right way of godliness, and also unto sinners. The godly, just, and righteous learn by this to be circumspect, and not to presume: sinners by occasion of this do learn immediately to rise up again from their fall, and not in any wise to despair.

Yea, our own fall learn we to know by Peter's fall: but, alas! our fall is much more grievous and greater than Peter's. Peter sinned through weakness; many a time do we sin wilfully and advisedly: he once, we daily: he was constrained through fear, we many a time through light occasions fall from the way of truth and righteousness: he riseth up again forthwith, we seldom and slowly: he wept bitterly, we scarce do confess and knowledge the sin. Yea, bitterly wept he: which thing all the elect ought to do, if they have sinned.

[COVERDALE.]

There should nothing grieve us more, than to have sinned against God, than to have displeased God. This do not wilful sinners, which pass little or nothing upon sin; and when they come into the deepness thereof, care not for it, neither confess nor acknowledge their sin, until afterward with despair, as it is to see in Judas.

But Peter, bewailing the grievous fall and wickedness of his denial, without further falling away into horrible desperation, is preserved through the goodness of God; in the confidence of God's oft proved and accustomed mercy, is he lift up unto blessed repentance, and so healed. Christ's look, the true physician, is unto him as much as a word or speech. Wherein we may learn to know the unspeakable love of God; who even in the midst of sin forgetteth not his own, forsaketh them not, but graciously looketh upon them with the eyes of his mercy, admonisheth them, speaketh unto them through the outward and inward word; with the which gracious countenance he dissuadeth them from sin, and calleth them again to himself, provoking them to sorrow and mourning, lamentation and weeping. He spreadeth out his arms and lap of his mercy, and graciously taketh us up again, and receiveth us with the lost son. Therefore let us knowledge, repent, and bitterly bewail our sins; let us wash them away with tears, and endeavour ourselves with great diligence, that negligently we fall not into them again; let us run to the bottomless well of God's mercy, and pray.

O merciful God, give us the well of blessed tears, that from the bottom of our hearts we may with Peter bewail our sins. O with how great and grievous sins are we laden and entangled! O suffer us not to lie under the heavy burden; let us not sink down in heaviness and desperation. Set thou us up again, and convert us throughly: send grace of thy holy repentance into our heart; wash away all our sins and negligence; grant us the light of new graces and gifts; let not the souls perish, for whom thou didst submit thyself into so many pains and rebukes, and at the last didst suffer the terrible bitter death of the cross. Amen.

[John xviii. 19—23.]

THE high priest asked Jesus of his disciples, and of his doctrine. Jesus answered him : I have openly spoken unto the world; I have always taught in the synagogue, and in the temple, there as all the Jews resort together, and in corners have I taught nothing : Why askest thou me? Ask them that heard me, what I said unto them : behold, they can tell what I said. When he had thus spoken, one of the ministers that stood by smote Jesus upon his cheek, and said, Answerest thou the high priest so? Then Jesus answered him and said : If I have spoken evil, then bear record of the evil; but if I have well spoken, why smitest thou me?

### DOCTRINE AND FRUIT.

HERE in the high priest we see an example of those malicious persons, that take in hand to overthrow and condemn the truth, afore they hear it. Great is the arrogancy of man, who dare presume to make himself a judge of God's truth; whereas of more right the truth and word of God should judge our words and works. The understanding of the man and of the flesh perceiveth not the thing that concerneth God; and therefore he refuseth it, and judgeth it unright, and so giveth sentence, afore he know what the matter is. This (the more pity!) do all they that seek their own profit and estimation, and not the honour of God.

Now in such a false and temerarious sentence, how we must behave ourselves towards the unrighteous judges, Christ teacheth us. When the faithful believer is for the truth's sake presented, prosecuted, smitten, hurt, and condemned, he must never hold with the untruth, nor allow it; but disclose their falsehood and contrary doctrine: and as Christ here doth, and Peter teacheth, with softness of mind to give an account of his doctrine, and yet with patience stoutly to bear and suffer what reproach and displeasure soever the wicked do unto him. For albeit that Christ, after the letter outwardly, doth not offer the other cheek unto the stroke, yet inwardly in heart he is after such sort disposed and furnished with love towards his enemies, that he desireth not to hurt them; yea, he is ready to suffer his body to be hanged up upon the cross for them. And yet besides this, he maintaineth and defendeth his doctrine, that it is neither seditious and false, and reporteth himself unto those that heard it. The truth and doctrine he defendeth, not his body: he declareth not his power, but his patience and softness of mind; and yet with valiant stedfastness and truth, not with glosing and flattering the unbelievers.

O God, give thou us patience, when the wicked hurt us. O how unpatient and angry are we, when we think ourselves unjustly slandered, reviled, and hurt! Christ suffereth for us a sore stroke upon the cheek, the innocent for the guilty: we may not abide one rough word for his sake. O Lord, grant us virtue and patience, power and strength, that we may take all adversity with good will, and with quiet silence of a soft mind to overcome it: and if necessity and thine honour require us to speak, that we may do the same with meekness and patience; to the intent that as well the truth and thy glory may be defended, as our patience and stedfast continuance perceived.

[Matt. xxvi. 59—68. Mark xiv. 55—65.]

THE chief priests and the whole council sought false witness against Jesus, that they might put him to death, and they found none. For though there stood many false witnesses, yet did not their testimonies agree. At the last came two false witnesses, and testified against Jesus, and said: We heard him say, This temple made with hands will I break down, and in three days will I set up another again, not builded with hands. And yet their witness agreed not together. Then start up the high priest, and stood there, and demanded of Jesus, and said: Givest thou no answer to this that these testify against thee? But Jesus held his peace, and made no answer. Then the high priest asked him yet once again, and said: I charge thee by the living God, that thou tell me whether thou be Christ, the Son of the blessed God. Jesus said unto him, Thou hast spoken; I am. But yet I say unto you: Ye shall from henceforth see the Son of man sit at the right hand of God, and come in the clouds of heaven. Then the high priest rent his clothes, and said, He hath blasphemed God: what need we further witness? Now have ye heard his blasphemy. How think ye? Then said they all: He is worthy of death. They that had bound him, laughed him to scorn, and mocked him, spit in his face, and blind-folded him, smote him, gave him buffets upon the cheek, and thumps in the neck; and then asked him: Aread[1], who hath smitten thee? and the servants stroke him upon the face, and did him much other villany.

## DOCTRINE AND FRUIT.

O how unjust people come together against the fountain of righteousness! What false witness and sentence goeth against the truth! And yet all their shifting is, that their malice and hatred may have an appearance of justice. They prevent him with false witness, they press him with perlous[2] and subtle questions, and go about to undermine and supplant the eternal wisdom. The enemies are accusers, witnesses, and judges. And whereas they revile and blaspheme God's Son to the uttermost, they will be seen to be the men that are sorry and displeased, when God is dishonoured. But as much as they seek in the innocent Lamb, yet find they nothing, no not so much as any suspicion of evil; so pure and sincere is all his life, so true and constant are his words.

This example ought all faithful believers to set before their eyes, learning thereby so to direct their life, that the enemies not only find no vice in them, but also no suspicion of evil; that unto the evil speaker there be given no occasion nor cause to slander, and that the name of Christ through them be not blasphemed. But where as the honour of God

1 Thes. v.
Ephes. iv.
1 Tim. iii.

[1 To aread, or areed: to judge, to pronounce. Spenser and Milton.]

[2 Perlous: perilous. Spenser.]

Matt. xv.   so requireth, we must openly speak and confess the truth before the ungodly, although they be angry and offended; according as in this place we hear of Christ, who telleth them of his glorious coming in majesty and power, although they take it for a blasphemy. Here ought we also diligently and devoutly to consider, what Christ suffereth for us, what ignominy and reproach he taketh upon himself for our sakes, how vilely he is reputed, and how shamefully in his body and in all the parts thereof he is beaten; and yet in all this, how blessedly he behaveth and sheweth himself; to the intent that it should not grieve us, for his sake to bear vile buffets and all ungentleness: for all this suffereth he for the truth's sake. Even he whom the angels do worship, is blasphemed of unthrifts; he that giveth true answer, is named a blasphemer; the righteous Judge is condemned of the unrighteous, and pronounced to be worthy of death. But the gracious Lord is quietly content to keep silence, and doth suffer: and therefore the more humble he is, and submitteth himself to be misentreated, the more glorious is his victory.

With many wicked evil words is he defaced and scorned, sore beaten and mishandled. That gracious face, which the angels delight to behold, is blindfolded, spitted upon, and buffeted; the head, the face, and neck, beaten with many sore strokes. Christ is become a stranger unto all his friends, forsaken of all his acquaintance and kinsfolks, a mocking and jesting-stock unto all men. Even as if it were a dizzard fool, is he laughed to scorn, that is wisest of all; upon whom the cruel dogs all the night long practise their unsatiable malice and pleasure, with mocking, nipping, pulling, buffeting, spitting, and reviling of him.

In all this doth his swiftness of mind and excellent patience abide still constant and unmoveable: whereby we may justly learn to be ashamed of our presumptuous brags, in our pomp and pride which we use in our soft and costly apparel; whereas Christ for our sakes became most poor and vilely reputed. Very evil beseemeth it us, yea, a shame it is for us, which of Christ are called Christians, and will be his disciples, to seek bodily pleasure and earthly joy and sensuality in all things; whereas the Lord Jesus our head doth bear and suffer all that is contrary thereunto. O how unlike are we to our head and foregoer! How far are we from right and true humility, when for the least wrong and unadvised word we be displeased with our brethren; and whereas we should give thanks for being rebuked to our profit, we are unpatient and miscontent!

O Lord Jesus Christ, grant us so to consider thy holy passion, that it bring fruit in us: make us patient, when hurt and displeasure is done unto us; teach us after thine own living example, not to fear the railing words and persecution of wicked people, neither to be discouraged for any wrongful accusation that happeneth upon us. Teach us to see our own vileness; how justly we are of the people reviled and despised for our sins. Have mercy, O Lord, upon our unperfectness. Thou wast reviled, that thou mightest take from us everlasting shame; beaten thou wast, that from the stripes which we with our sins have deserved thou mightest deliver us; spitted upon and mocked, to bring us from everlasting confusion to everlasting honour. Wherefore strengthen our minds, O Lord, that in lowly shamefacedness we may patiently suffer and bear the hard words and checks that other folks give us for our sins and offences; for many more falser accusations and rebukes hast thou borne with highest patience for us vile sinners.

O let the hard strokes and knocks of thy head be unto us a suaging of all our bodily pains: let that scornful blindfolding of thine eyes be unto us a restraint and keeping in of our sight from all wantonness, vanity, and lightness of eyes: let the vile spitting upon thy holy face expel out of us all carnal lusts; and teach us not to regard the outward appearance, but to hold and keep in honour the virtues of the soul. That carrying about and scornful derision, which happened unto thee undeserved, drive from us all dissolute manners and wanton gestures. Let that refusing of thy worthiness quench in us all desires of temporal honour; let it move us unto things that of the world are contemned and in small estimation. Give us, O Lord, a strong victory in all patience; that from our heart-roots we may acknowledge and confess ourselves to be most worthy of all contempt and slander, of all rebuke, shame, and punishment. Amen.

[Luke xxii. 66—71. xxiii. 1. Matt. xxvii. 1, 2. Mark xv. 1. John xviii. 28.]

EARLY in the morning, at the break of day, went the chief priests and elders of the people to counsel how they might destroy Jesus. And they brought him to their council, and said, If thou be the Christ, tell us. Then said Jesus unto them, If I tell you, ye will not believe me: if I ask you a question, you will give me no answer, neither let me go. But from this time forth shall the Son of man sit at the right hand of the power of God. Then said they all, Art thou then the Son of God? Then said he, Ye say it, I am. They said, What need we any more witness? We have heard it ourselves out of his own mouth. Then arose the whole multitude, as many as were there, and bound Jesus, and led him from Caiphas to Pilate into the judgment-hall. And it was early in the morning. They went not into the judgment-hall, lest they should be defiled, but that they might eat passah. Then went Pilate forth unto them, and they brought Jesus bound, and delivered him unto Pontius Pilate the deputy.

## DOCTRINE AND FRUIT.

SATAN sleepeth not, but watcheth and is diligent to drive his household together, to destroy Jesus Christ, to make him sure, and to bring him to his end. For they thought, if they might have Jesus once dead, then had they rooted out the doctrine of the truth. But foolish and vain is their device, for the truth is immortal: the more it is opprest, the more it breaketh forth again: when men undertake for to quench it, then doth the shine and brightness thereof appear more glorious. Shame therefore and rebuke, yea, eternal punishment bring all they upon themselves, that, withstanding the truth, take it prisoner, bind it, and deliver it to the judge. They think they bind the truth: but the truth and word of God cannot be bound; for it maketh all

2 Tim. ii.
John viii.

things free, and such as are tangled and wrapt in the snares of sin, those it delivereth. Whoso goeth about to bind the truth, doth knit and snare himself with unloosable bands, and casteth from him the band of love, wherewith God offereth to draw him unto himself, and to bind him under his yoke. Wherefore let us be obedient unto the truth, and not strive against it; for if we undertake to condemn it, it shall so appear again in high majesty, that through the beautiful, fair, and clear brightness thereof we shall all perish and be blinded.

[Matt. xxvii. 3—10.]

WHEN Judas, which had betrayed him, saw that Jesus was condemned, he repented so, that he took the money, the thirty silver pence, and brought them to the high priests, and to the elders of the people, and said: I have sinned in betraying that innocent blood. They said: What have we to do withal? Look thou to that. So he cast the money from him in the temple, went his way, and hanged himself in a snare. But the high priests took the money, and said: It is not lawful to put it into the treasury; for it is the price of blood. And they took counsel, and bought with the same money a potter's field, to bury strangers in. Wherefore the same field is called *Acheldema*, that is, the field of blood, until this day. Then was fulfilled that which was spoken by Jeremy the prophet, saying: And they took thirty silver plates, the price of him that was valued, whom they bought of the children of Israel, and gave them for the potter's field, as the Lord appointed me.

### DOCTRINE AND FRUIT.

LIKE as we have had in Peter an ensample of the grace and mercy of God, so have we in Judas a fearful and terrible ensample of God's righteousness. In Judas are described unto us all unbelieving desperate persons, whom the gracious God of his bottomless mercy calleth to his goodness and service; but they despise it, and follow Satan, who blindeth them, and enticeth them through manifold wickedness, which they consider not; but when they are come into the deepness of vice, they force not of it. The devil also, to whom they surrender themselves to serve, and that hath taken possession of their heart, blindeth them in such sort, that they ponder not the vileness, grievousness, and greatness of their sins, till they have fully finished the abomination: for if they did consider it, they should repent and amend. How many loving admonitions had Judas heard of the Lord, to dissuade him from his purpose! Yet all could not help. At the last openeth he their eyes that they repent, but a godly repentance they receive not. They behold the greatness and grievousness of the sin and offence, but the greatness of God's mercy in Christ they see not; by means whereof they despair in their sins, and are damned.

In the priests that loathe the blood-money, and yet abhor not to shed the innocent blood, is set forth before our eyes an ensample of all hypocrites, which outwardly appear to be good and virtuous, and yet regard not the godliness of the Spirit. A gnat choketh them, and a camel they swallow up.

But unto us poor strangers and pilgrims there is prepared and bought, through the blood of Christ, a field and churchyard, that we, being washed clean from our sins, might find eternal rest to our souls.

Preserve us, O God, from covetousness and despair, from false hypocrisy, treason, and blood-shedding: O lead us not into temptation. And whereas we have sinned, grant us true and fruitful repentance, that we never forget thy goodness and mercy, but immediately cease from sin, and serve thee continually until our end. Amen.

---

[Matt. xxvii. 11. Luke xxiii. 1—7. John xviii. 29—32.]

Jesus stood before the deputy. Then said the deputy, What accusation bring ye against this man? They answered and said, If he were not an evil doer, we had not delivered him unto thee. Then said Pilate unto them, Take ye him, and judge him after your law. Then said the Jews, It is not lawful for us to put any man to death: that the saying of Jesus might be fulfilled which he spake, signifying what death he should die. Then began they to accuse him, and said, We have found this man perverting the people, and forbidding to give tribute unto the emperor, and naming himself to be Christ a king. Pilate asked him, and said, Art thou king of the Jews? Then answered he and said, Thou hast spoken it. Then said Pilate to the chief priests and to the people: I find no cause nor guiltiness in the man. Then were they more earnest, and said, He hath with his doctrine moved the people to sedition throughout whole Jewry, beginning in Galilee, and from thence hither unto this place. Now when Pilate heard of Galilee, he asked, if he were a Galilean: and when he perceived that he was under Herod's jurisdiction, he sent him unto Herod, who was then at Hierusalem.

## DOCTRINE AND FRUIT.

ALL they that hitherto from the beginning of the world have at any time preached the truth, were of the adversaries noted and accused to be seditious and deceivers of the people; which thing was brought upon them, to rid them out of the way. Hereof find we examples enough in the Old and New Testament. Jeremy xxvi. xxxii. xxxviii; 3 Reg. (1 Kings) xviii; Amos vii. In Christ and his apostles we see it evident. Therefore have we no cause to give over the truth; for we are no better than our Master.

And though we be complained upon for the truth's sake, it ought not greatly to grieve us; forasmuch as we see, that the like happened unto Christ, in whose mouth there was never found guile. He is set forth unto us for an example of most perfect patience. We that be spiritual disciples of Christ must go unto him to school, and learn of him meekness, obedience, patience, and lowliness of mind.

Behold, our Head standeth before an heathenish unrighteous judge; wrongfully and sore is he accused, even our Saviour, our King, and Lord; yea, even he that is Judge of us, and of the whole world. Why should we then be grieved, and refuse for God's sake to obey worldly authority, though they oppress us, and do us wrong? He is innocent: as for us, we are in many things guilty. Never should the patience of Jesus slip out of our hearts.

Have mercy upon our impatiency, O merciful Father, and print in our hearts the image of thy Son: grant us grace to follow his footsteps; expel out of us all fear of worldly accusations and false judgments; give us such a gentle spirit, as when we be wrongfully accused, or unjustly punished, is not soon unquieted. O drive thou out of us all furnishness, indignation, and self-will: let thy love increase and grow in us through the contemning of ourselves; and whatsoever is in us, that striveth or resisteth against thy holy will, let the same be clean extinct and die.

---

[Luke xxiii. 8—12.]

AND when Herod saw Jesus, he was exceeding glad: for he was desirous to see him of a long season, because he had heard many things of him, and he trusted to have seen some miracle done by him. Then he questioned with him many words: but Jesus answered nothing. The high priests and scribes stood forth and accused him straitly. And Herod with his men of war despised him; and when he had mocked him, he arrayed him in white clothing, and sent him again to Pilate. And the same day Pilate and Herod were made friends together; for before they were at variance.

### DOCTRINE AND FRUIT.

THE everlasting Wisdom of God is mocked and jested at, as a dizzard fool; the Truth is belied. Us therefore, that of nature are foolish and liars, it should not grieve to be reviled for God's sake. No answer giveth Christ to the ungodly voluptuous king, who, of a curious desire, would fain have seen or heard some new thing of Christ; for at that hour to answer, it could not edify. It was a time wherein it pleased him to suffer, not to do miracles. Thus the innocent Lord Jesus, for us guilty, is drawn and haled from one unrighteous judge to another. All reproach, shame, dishonour, and derision, taketh he upon himself for our sakes; every where is he grievously accused, in every place is there hurt done unto him, and after many questions and examinations they hang him up upon a cross. Thus the high God is brought low, as if he were most vile; the Almighty is defaced, as if he were most weak of all; the wisest of all is laughed to scorn, as if he were a natural fool; the most unguilty is handled as an evil doer.

This spectacle ought we very diligently to behold: for we are laden with grievous burdens of all wickedness, and have for our iniquity deserved so much, that we are worthy of all rebuke, shame, and confusion; yet are we unpatient, when we be despised. Nevertheless all such vile entreating doth Christ suffer for our sakes, to deliver us from eternal shame and confusion, which we justly have deserved.

O Lord, take from us all wantonness and pride. How evil beseemeth it us, thy servants, wilfully and vainly to deck our bodies; whereas thou, Lord, king of heaven, art scornfully despised in a fool's coat! O Lord, set thou before our eyes and hearts the contempt and derision that was done unto thee: teach us to follow thee through the contempt and hatred of ourselves, and to rejoice when we are despised.

Let us never set our hope upon men, upon praise, upon honour, upon power, upon money; but that from the bottom of our hearts we may be able to despise all temporal things, and love thereof, and firmly and stedfastly to follow after thee, O Lord Jesu, our welfare; that as touching all the rebuke and contempt, which thou for us, poor unworthy sinners, hast suffered, we may bear the same in the perpetual remembrance of our heart, and never forget it. Amen.

[Luke xxiii. 13—22. John xviii. 33—40.]

PILATE called together the high priests and chief rulers with the common people, and said unto them: Ye have brought this man unto me, as one that perverteth the people; and, behold, I examined him before you, and find no fault in this man, of those things whereof ye accuse him; no, nor yet Herod. For I sent you to him, and lo, nothing worthy of death is done unto him. So Pilate went again into the judgment-hall, and called Jesus, and said unto him: Art thou the King of the Jews? Then answered Jesus, Speakest thou that of thyself, or have others told it thee of me? Pilate answered, Am I then a Jew? Thy people and thy high priests have delivered thee unto me: what hast thou done? Jesus answered, My kingdom is not of this world: if my kingdom were of this world, assuredly my ministers would fight for me, that I should not be given over unto the Jews. But now is not my kingdom from hence. Then said Pilate, Then art thou a king? Jesus answered, Thou sayest it; I am a king. For this cause was I born; for this cause came I into the world, that I should bear witness unto the truth. Whoso is of the truth, heareth my voice. Then said Pilate unto him, What is truth? When he said this, he went forth again to the Jews, and said unto them, I find no fault in him. But ye have a custom, that I should deliver one unto you loose at Easter. Will ye that I loose unto you the King of the Jews? Whom will ye that I shall let go? Barrabas, or Jesus which is called Christ? For he knew that the priests had of envy and hatred delivered him up. Then cried they all, and said, Not him, but Barrabas. As for Barrabas, he was a murderer; who because of an uproar made in the city, and for manslaughter, was laid in prison. Then spake Pilate further with them, willing to let Jesus loose. But they cried, Crucify him, Crucify him. Then said he unto them the third time, What evil then hath he done? I find no cause in him. Therefore will I punish him, and let him go.

## DOCTRINE AND FRUIT.

FORASMUCH as the devil knoweth, that Christ and his ministers apply all diligence with their doctrine, that the kingdom of him, who is the prince of this world, might be destroyed, and that the kingdom of Jesus Christ the Son of God, the chief king of all, might prosper; he bringeth to pass, that Christ and the ministers of the word are noted and suspected of sedition; whereas they seek nothing less than worldly power and dominion. Christ flieth away, when they would make him king: now is he noted and accused, as one that seeketh to be emperor. Nevertheless Christ is a true king, whose kingdom consisteth not in corporal things, but in spirit and in power. Christ despised all honour, riches, power, and pleasures of this world: his ministers therefore must of all the world be contemned. But Christ ruleth through his Spirit and power in their hearts, and they also shall rule with him in the resurrection. He is the truth, and giveth witness unto the truth; and whoso is of the truth heareth his voice, and beareth record also unto the truth.

Here likewise we learn the unstedfastness of the world. They that afore ran still after Christ, and would have made him king, crying joyfully, "Hosanna unto the Lord," cry now, "Crucify him, Crucify him." So little worthy is the praise and commendation of the world to be regarded. They that said afore, "Praised be he that cometh in the name of the Lord," the same cry now, "Away with him, crucify him:" and so they chose a murderer instead of the Saviour. Their request is, that the murderer may live; as for the Saviour and well of life, him they desire to be put to death. If we pondered this well in our hearts, that our Saviour, our Jesus, was esteemed worse and more vile than a murderer, there should be nothing that we would not be glad to suffer for his sake.

Now when the world is in hand with us, and casteth many opprobrious words upon us, we must not be overcome with unpatiency; the false accusation and threatening of wicked people ought not to make us shrink: but if we love

Christ with our hearts, we must remember his patience, when he was falsely accused, and reviled for our sakes; and so with stopped ears ought we to let all sharp words pass, yea, to pray for them that speak evil of, or to us.

When our good works and meanings are taken in evil part, our enterprise resisted, our words rejected and refused of every man, we ought patiently to suffer it. For far inferiors are we unto Christ our Lord; over whom goeth so horrible and wicked a cry, "Crucify him, Crucify him."

Hereof should all faithful believers be admonished, yea assured, if they mind to live godly in Christ Jesu, that they must suffer much persecution, and that if they will walk and go forward in the way of God, they must bear many hurtful and noisome things; for no man can please God, that for his sake is not exercised in much adversity. Therefore saith he unto his dear friends: "Blessed are ye when men revile you, and persecute you, and shall falsely speak all manner of evil against you for my sake. Rejoice and be glad: for great is your reward in heaven."

Matt. v.

Wherefore, dear children, let us follow our innocent Lord Jesus; who being refused of wicked men upon earth, but chosen of God the Father, is crowned with eternal glory and godly honour in heaven. No evil saying or curse ought to overcome us, considering that for the same there is so exceeding joy prepared for us of God.

[John xix. 1—12.]

THEN Pilate took Jesus therefore, and scourged him: and the soldiers wound a crown of thorns, and put it on his head. And they did on him a purple garment, and came unto him, and said, Hail, King of the Jews; and they smote him on the face. Pilate went forth again, and said unto them, Behold, I bring him forth to you, that you may know that I find no fault in him. Then came Jesus forth, wearing a crown of thorn, and a robe of purple. And he saith unto them, Behold the man. When the high priests therefore and ministers saw him, they cried, saying, Crucify him, crucify him. Pilate saith unto them: Take ye him, and crucify him; for I find no cause in him. The Jews answered and said unto him: We have a law, and by our law he ought to die, because he made himself the Son of God. When Pilate heard that saying, he was the more afraid; and went again into the judgment-hall, and saith unto Jesus: Whence art thou? But Jesus gave him no answer. Then said Pilate unto him, Speakest thou not unto me? knowest thou not that I have power to crucify thee, and have power to let thee loose? Jesus answered: Thou couldest have no power at all against me, except it were given thee from above. Therefore he that delivereth me unto thee hath the more sin. And from henceforth sought Pilate means to loose him. But the Jews cried, saying: If thou let him go, thou art not the emperor's friend: for whosoever maketh himself king, is against the emperor.

### DOCTRINE AND FRUIT.

HERE in Pilate we learn, how hurtful it is, when every one in his office and vocation looketh not diligently about him, but slenderly letteth the thing slip and pass, that he earnestly ought to bring to effect. Pilate was the deputy of a country, and knew that Christ had wrong; whereof he himself also many times beareth him witness with his own mouth. Seeing then that he was a judge, it appertaineth to his office to judge right, and not to suffer the innocent to die. For though Pilate doth, as if he would discharge Christ, yet he mindeth it not earnestly. He goeth about to let Christ loose: nevertheless so far as he displease not the Jews and the emperor, so far as he lose not the favour and friendship of men.

While Pilate now fainteth in the righteousness that he knoweth and is sure of, and holdeth not on stoutly, as he should, to deliver Christ, God suffereth him still to fall, till he come to this point, that he condemneth the innocent to death against his own conscience. Thus goeth

[COVERDALE.]

it with all those, that for the grace of God lent unto them are unthankful and unfaithful in the little. It is the part of a righteous judge to maintain justice, and to defend the innocent, though it should cost him body, honour, and goods.

The pride also of Pilate, that presumed by reason of his authority, is brought down with the words of the Lord: "There is no power but from above," and therefore should it be godly used; the higher powers are God's ministers. In the which words of Christ the faithful believers that be in adversity are comforted; knowing that no man hath authority nor power over them, except it be given him of God.

Christ is bound, to deliver us from the bands of our sins, and to place us in eternal freedom. He is scourged, to take from us the stripes that we should suffer by reason of our sins; yea, to heal our wounds, is he sore wounded himself. Altogether suffereth he for our sakes; through his stripes are we made whole. "His back," as Esay saith, Isai. l., "offereth he to the smiters, and his cheeks to the nippers," to purge us from all filthiness of sin. He became without beauty, as a leper despised, spitted upon, and mocked, to deliver us from eternal shame and punishment. We had deserved all this, he did nothing worthy thereof; we are the cause of his martyrdom. Oh the great burden of our sins, that the Son of the eternal God must suffer so sore stripes and cruel pains for us, to reconcile us with his Father! Oh the exceeding great love which he declareth unto us, in that he taketh all rebuke upon himself for us! Oh that we considered this with true devotion; so that we might say with Christ and David: "I am ready to be scourged, and my plague is always before me."

O Jesu, kindle us with the fire of thy exceeding love, which thou in so much adversity hast well tried towards us. Grant us the help of thy grace, to the strengthening of our weakness, when the heavy burdens of adversities fall upon us; that through the terrible overcharge of them we be not opprest and thrown down. Give us grace, so to chasten and subdue our body and flesh, that it may be subject unto the Spirit, and obedient unto thy will in all things.

[John xix. 13—16. Matt. xxvii. 12—26. Mark xv. 3—15. Luke xxiii. 13—25.]

WHEN Pilate heard that saying, he brought forth Jesus, and sat down to give sentence in the place that is called the Pavement, but in the Hebrew tongue Gabatha. It was the preparing of the Easter, about the sixth hour. And he saith unto the Jews, Behold your king! They cried: Away with him, away with him! Crucify him. Pilate saith unto them, Shall I crucify your king? The high priests answered, We have no king but the emperor. And the high priests with the elders of the people accused him in many things, but he gave no answer. Pilate asked him further, and said: Makest thou no answer? Seest thou not, in how many and great things they accuse thee? But Jesus moreover gave no answer, so that the deputy marvelled sore at it. At the feast he had a custom, to let one unto them loose, whom they would desire. Now while the people pressed on, Pilate began to ask them, as he always did, and said: Whom will ye that I let loose unto you? Barrabas, or Jesus who is called Christ?

While Pilate sat in judgment, his wife sent to him, and said: Have thou nothing to do with that just man; for this night in sleep have I suffered much for him. But the high priests and the elders persuaded the people, and enticed them, that they should ask Barrabas, and require Jesus unto death. Then answered Pilate, and said unto them: Whom will ye of these two that I shall let go loose unto you? They said, Barrabas. Then said Pilate unto them: What shall I then do with Jesus, who is called Christ? Then said they all, Let him be crucified. The deputy said: What evil then hath he done? Nevertheless they cried yet more, Let him be crucified.

When Pilate saw that he profited nothing, but that the uproar was greater, he took water and washed his hands before the people, and said: I am unguilty from the blood of this just man; look ye to it. Then answered all the people, and said: His blood be upon us, and upon our children. So Pilate, according to their desire, let Barrabas loose unto them: and Jesus, whom he scourged, gave he over unto them to be crucified.

### DOCTRINE AND FRUIT.

PILATE feareth men more than God: therefore doth he against God, and condemneth the innocent, although he thinketh to be unguilty of his blood.

The evangelist maketh mention of the feast of Easter or Passah, to the intent we should consider, that Christ, the true right Paschal Lamb, was put to death and slain for us.

Here we learn what the judgment of the world is: righteousness is refused and condemned; wickedness, ungraciousness, and murder, is delivered and quit. O how lamentably perisheth the righteous, and no man there is that considereth it, or that goeth about to deliver him! The true is given over to the liars; the innocent to the guilty; the godly to the ungracious: the murderer is chosen before Jesus the anointed Son of God: here the wicked is preferred before the just, death before life, night and darkness before the light.

This now in all our troubles, when we are oppressed and false ycondemned, shall comfort and strengthen us, if we set before our eyes the blessed example of Jesus the innocent, who for us was condemned as an evil doer. For we servants are not above our Lord. If the Judge of the quick and dead be wrongfully condemned, how much more convenient is it, that we poor guilty should suffer, when we are judged, whether it be done justly or unjustly!

Christ for our sake was falsely condemned, to take from us the just judgment of eternal damnation, which was gone out upon us for our sins.

Grant unto us, O Lord Jesu, that neither threatening nor slander drive us away from the contemned cross, but that with our whole powers we may gladly follow thee. O give us grace, to fasten our flesh with the temptations thereof, unto the cross; that we, bewailing our former sins, may withstand and overcome the temptations that are behind. Help us, Lord, in the conflict of the spirit; let thy cross, O Lord, be unto us a medicine against all vice; and grant, that we alway cheerfully take up our cross, and follow thee. Amen.

---

[Matt. xxvii. 27—34, 38.  Mark xv. 16—23, 27, 28.  Luke xxiii. 26—33.
John xix. 16—18.]

THEN the soldiers led Jesus again into the judgment hall: and when they had mocked him, they stripped him out of the purple robe, and put his own garments upon him, and led him forth to be crucified. And he bare his own cross himself, and went on towards the place of execution. And as they led him, they caught one that was called Simon of Cyren, who came from the field, and was the father of Alexander and Rufus: him they compelled to carry the cross of Jesus, and laid it upon him, that he might bear it after Christ. And there followed him a great company of people, and women, which bewailed and lamented him. But Jesus turned back to them, and said: Ye daughters of Jerusalem, weep not for me, but weep for yourselves and for your children. For behold, the days will come, in the which they shall say: Happy are the barren, and the wombs that never bare, and the paps which never gave suck.' Then shall they begin to say to the mountains, Fall on us; and to the hills, Cover us: for if they do this in a green tree, what shall be done in the dry? And unto the place of execution, there were led with him two other, murderers, to be slain. And they came unto the place called Golgatha, that is, a place of dead men's skulls, or the place of execution. And they gave him to drink vinegar mixt with gall; but when he had proved it, he would not drink it. And they crucified him, and with him two murderers, the one on the right hand, the other on the left, and Jesus in the midst: that the scripture might be fulfilled: He was counted among the evil-doers.

## DOCTRINE AND FRUIT.

Here ought we with devout hearts to behold our Saviour Jesus; how meekly he taketh the cross upon him for our sakes; and patiently beareth it, to bring the lost sheep again upon his shoulders. Here we see our King bear his kingdom upon his shoulders, as Esay the prophet saith. He is not only led forth, but it is done with great reproach, even as if he were a ring-leader of murderers and unthrifts. Oh, how was the King of glory blasphemed and misentreated for our sakes! He taketh our sins upon him, and dischargeth us of our burden.

<small>Isai. ix.</small>

In the consideration of this reproach, we should not weep over him, but over ourselves. For if this be done to the innocent Son of God, what are we then worthy of? By this also must we learn patiently to bear our cross in following our foregoer; for he sheweth us an example before, that we should follow his footsteps, even to the death. And if we so consider our cross, it shall be light and easy unto us. We have sworn under the cross, from the which we must not shrink, if we will follow the Lord. The love of Jesu Christ shall make all adversity sweet and acceptable unto us. Our joy and comfort ought to be chiefly "in the cross of our Lord Jesus Christ, by whom the world must be crucified unto us, and we unto the world." He shall cause our slothful flesh to be quick and diligent, and shall kindle our cold heart. He goeth before us in the narrow way, and is a companion of our pilgrimage, a helper in all trouble, a comforter in all adversity, a worker with us in the grievous travail that we suffer for his sake.

<small>1 Pet. iii.</small>

<small>Gal. vi.</small>

O Lord, help us to bear the heavy burdens; that we may be diligent and apt unto all good works. Assist us with thy power and grace; help us according unto thy accustomed mercy; teach us to break and utterly to leave our own will. Make us true cross-bearers and followers of thee: take from us all worldly lust and wilfulness, whatsoever hindereth us in thy love; that in obedience and patience we may alway follow thee, and find rest with thee after adversity. Thou, Lord, wast stript out of thy apparel, and spoiled thereof, that we with virtues might be clothed. The same that was put upon thee to rebuke and shame, is unto us become the highest honour. Thou wast lift up from the earth, that thou mightest draw the hearts of thy faithful believers unto thee from all earthly things, and kindle them in the love of high heavenly things; that thou through thy death mightest reconcile and fully restore all that is in heaven and earth.

O ye righteous and faithful, that delight to serve God, behold with the eyes of your heart, how our God, Lord, King, and Redeemer hangeth on the cross for us: let us consider our lover, who for our sakes hangeth naked and bare in great shame and reproach before the world. He spreadeth out his arms, to call and receive unto himself us poor sinners and lost children, saying: "Come to me, all ye that labour and are laden, and I will refresh you." He sheweth his wounds, out of the which floweth the plentiful river and fountain of his precious dear blood, to the washing away of all our filthiness. He boweth down his head, to speak friendly unto us. Boldly therefore, with great comfort and confidence, ought all sinners to resort unto him, where they shall find help and consolation, defence and protection: there should they lay down the heavy burdens of their sins. Unto us must all the world be a cross, and we unto the world; only let Christ the Lord be our life, and to die with him our greatest advantage. Far be from us all rejoicing, save only in the cross of Jesus Christ: far be from us all confidence in our own works and merits; for all our health consisteth in the cross of Jesus Christ, wherein undoubtedly we may well set all our hope. By him cometh forgiveness of sins; out of him floweth the riches of all deserving; with him is the reward of all righteousness. Through the contempt of ourselves, and of all temporal things, let us barely, nakedly, and simply follow the naked and crucified Lord.

Teach us, O God, to have delight in contemning ourselves, and all temporal things; and when other folks are in trouble, to be sorry and pray for them. Grant us grace to wish good unto those that hurt and punish us: let us not trust in men; for there be few faithful and constant friends.

Here also should we learn not to be grieved, if we have few lovers and many enemies; for so happened even unto Christ our head. He had many foes; to whom yet he did none evil, but much good, and received great unthank for his labour. Sweet and acceptable should it be unto us, to suffer reproach of the world, and to be despised for his sake; yea, to avoid all voluptuousness and joy of the world, seeing[1] we are fastened unto the cross with Christ. To seek much pastime and pleasure of the world, becometh not him that must suffer adversity. All this learn we in the passion of Christ, and in the cross. Blessed is he that directeth his daily exercise and his whole life thereafter; he shall enjoy the fruit of the tree of life for ever.

Rev. ii.

Psal. lxxxiv. O God, heavenly Father, look upon the face of thine Anointed, who hanged for us upon the cross: be merciful unto us poor sinners, which be laden with great and grievous sins; forgive us for the most worthy merits' sake of thine only-begotten dear Son, who for our sins was beaten and wounded; let him satisfy thee for all our sins.

He is our surety in thy sight, our faithful Advocate and Mediator; him thou gladly hearest; O Father of mercy, and graciously acceptest his intercession for all sinners.

O gracious Lord Jesu, Son of the eternal God, who of very love towards us tookest upon thee our weak flesh, undefiled from all sin, and didst offer up the same flesh unto thy Father upon the altar of thy cross for the safe-guard of the world; have mercy upon us thy servants, for thy everlasting goodness; and for the infinite merits' sake of thy holy passion. For thy deserving excelleth all men's sins, and much greater is the abundance of thy mercy than all our wickedness. Therefore fly we unto thee under the protection of thy holy cross, and with sighing hearts seek we help, grace, and remedy for our wounds. Receive us that are fled unto thee; heal us that be sick; make us just and righteous, that be sinners. Draw thou us up on high, O Lord Jesu, from all worldly things; bind up our flesh with thy fear; wound us with thy sweet love, that nothing else take hold of our heart, save only Jesus Christ.

Psal. cxx.

Out of the wounds of Jesu, and out of the running out of his blood, do we receive hope; there find we medicine for our souls, abundance of grace, and perfect forgiveness. Whatsoever we receive of sinful vices, whatsoever we commit with bodily sensuality, the same is altogether washed and reformed in the fountain of Christ's blood. O the unoutspeakable love, which the Son of God beareth towards his church; that he

[1 Ed. 1593, *saying*.]

washeth and cleanseth it with his own blood, with the blood Eph. v.
of the new testament, that it may be holy, pure, and without
spot! Not with silver and gold doth God redeem his crea- 1 Pet. i.
ture, but with the precious blood of his own Son. O dear
children, let us not tread under foot the blood of the holy
testament; let us not be unthankful unto our Saviour.

Thy holy blood, O Jesu, make us pure and clean from Heb. x.
all sin, and sanctify us throughout; that our spirit, soul, and
body may cheerfully wait for thy coming, and live with thee 1 Thess. v.
for ever.

---

[Matthew xxvii. 35—37.  Mark xv. 24—26.  Luke xxiii. 34—38.
John xix. 19—24.]

JESUS said: O Father, forgive them; for they know not what they do. Pilate wrote a superscription of the matter, and fastened it above at the head of the cross. The superscription was written in Greek, Latin, and Hebrew, with these words: Jesus of Nazareth, King of the Jews. This superscription did many of the Jews read; for the place where Jesus was crucified was near unto the city, and the superscription was written in Greek, Latin, and Hebrew. Then said the high priests of the Jews unto Pilate, Write not, King of the Jews, but that he called himself the King of the Jews. Pilate answered: What I have written, I have written. The soldiers, when they had crucified Jesus, they took his garments and made four parts, to every soldier one part, and also his coat. The coat was without seam, wrought upon throughout. Then said they together: Let us not divide it, but cast lots for it, who shall have it; that the scripture might be fulfilled, saying: They have parted my raiment Psal. xxii among them, and for my coat they cast lots. And the soldiers did such things in deed. Then sat they down and kept him. There stood also much people, and beheld.

## DOCTRINE AND FRUIT.

The last words which Jesus spake upon the cross, ought all faithful believers well to write in their hearts, and therein diligently to keep them. First, he spake a loving friendly word, a word full of grace and sweet comfort to all sinners, sufficient and enough to break all hardness of heart, and to provoke fruitful repentance: "Father, forgive them." O how great goodness and lovingkindness is this! how ready is Jesus unto mercy! how well willing is he to forgive his lovers, that sheweth himself so mild and gracious unto his enemies! No angry word, no displeasure poureth he out against those that crucified him; no vengeance nor plague desireth he to fall upon that ungracious people, but speaketh most sweet words, full of ardent love: "O Father, forgive them," &c.

In these words appeareth his exceeding great love with unoutspeakable softness of mind, which through no malice might be overcome. They, like mad and blood-thirsty men, cried: "Away with him; crucify him, crucify him." O the wonderful great lenity of our Lord Jesus Christ! They revile and misentreat him to the uttermost; he prayeth for them, that they, being converted from their wickedness, may acknowledge him the very true Son of God to have appeared in the flesh.

*Isai. liii.* Here is fulfilled that Esay said: "He hath borne the sins of many, and made intercession for the transgressors," that they should not perish.

Who now being in sin, will despair in the mercy of God, when the great offenders, that crucified and slew the giver of all remission, found so great grace and goodness?

A stedfast hope therefore ought we to conceive and to be sure of, how great soever our sin be. The hope of life standeth yet open, the bowels of mercy are yet ready prepared. Only unto him let us resort; full graciously will he receive us, so far as we give over ourselves unto him. Here likewise, by the example of our foregoer, we must learn to forgive our neighbour, to pray also for our enemies, and for those that do us harm. If we gladly forgive that little, God will forgive us the great. If we so do, we find grace, and are the children of the heavenly Father. As for the recompensing of all despite, and taking of vengeance, we must commit and refer that unto our Father, who judgeth right- 1 Pet. ii. iii. eously.

O Jesu, thou heavenly schoolmaster, teach us this, and grant us grace to do it. Give us also an assured hope of thy mercy and grace, that we fall into no despair through the multitude of our sins; but with faithful minds to consider, that for to heal sin thou camest into this world, and hast shed thy blood. O grant unto us free refuge and sure defence under the shadow of thy wings, and under the invincible token of thy holy cross. Receive us poor sinners, which utterly trust not in any good deed or merit of our own, but only in thy mercy. Amen.

Very spiteful extremity is shewed unto our Saviour, in that he must behold and see, how the vile unthrifts part his clothes amongst them. By this is there set forth unto us a doctrine, how we ought to behave ourselves, if our temporal goods be withdrawn and taken from us. We must be readier to suffer temporal harm, than to be revenged, or with unquiet suit at the law to require our own. He that created the whole world, hath not a corner where to rest his head. He that beautifieth and decketh all things, hangeth bare and naked himself. Whereby we must learn to be patient, if that which is ours be taken from us: we must learn to be content with few things, and to take in good part things of small reputation, and not to grudge, but with quiet minds to be thankful unto God.

O Lord, grant unto us, that we appear not naked and bare before thee; clothe us with the wedding-garment of faith and love; and when we suffer wrong, give us grace to follow thine example in patience, that no sorrow nor heaviness for loss of temporal goods lead us away from thee. Amen.

---

[Matthew xxvii. 39—44. Mark xv. 29—32. Luke xxiii. 35—43.]

THEY that passed by reviled and blasphemed him, wagging their heads, and saying: Lo, thou that breakest down the temple, and settest it up again in three days, help now thyself: if thou be the Son of God, come down from the cross.

The high priests also mocked him, together with the scribes and elders, and said amongst themselves: He helped others; can he not help himself? If he be Christ, the chosen of God, the king of Israel, 'let him come down now from the cross, and we will believe him.' He setteth his hope and trust in God: let him deliver him, if he will have him; for he hath said: I am the Son of God. The murderers also that were crucified with him, cast the same in his teeth, and reviled him. The people stood there, and waited; and the chief of them mocked him, and said: Hath he helped others, and cannot help himself, and is Christ the chosen of God? The soldiers also mocked him, came, and proffered him vinegar, and said: If thou be king of the Jews, help thyself. One of the murderers that hanged by him reviled him also, and said: If thou be the Christ, help thyself and us. But the other rebuked him, and said: Fearest thou not God, seeing thou art in the same damnation? As for us, we are justly punished, for we receive according to our deeds; but this man hath done nothing amiss. And he said unto Jesus: Lord, remember me, when thou comest into thy kingdom. And Jesus said unto him: Verily, I say unto thee, this day shalt thou be with me in paradise.

### DOCTRINE AND FRUIT.

Jesus for our sake took upon himself the most extreme shame, rebuke, and derision, to deliver us from eternal villany[1], and that we should learn gladly to suffer reproach and shame, and to despise the vain glory of the world. He is mocked and contemned of high and low, of spiritual, of temporal, and of every man. For they, being full of gall, bitterness, and poison, pour it out with their false tongues and outward gestures, casting out wicked slanderous words, and sharpening their venomous tongues against the innocent Saviour. They rather should have bewailed their own great sins: but there is no compassion nor mercy in them; their

[1 Villany: slavery.]

hearts are stopped, Satan hath the leading of them. Yet cannot their malice overcome good Jesus; through their wickedness and despite cannot his patience be vanquished. No opprobrious or vile word might cause him to omit the work of our redemption; but he continueth in love, and performeth it with an honourable end. Even as he teacheth us Matt. xxiv. to endure unto the end, so doth he practise it himself, and declareth it unto us in deed and example.

We therefore that will be followers of Jesu Christ, should set before us this excellent example of our foregoer, and learn to contemn the world, and stoutly to abide in our holy vocation and purpose. It is the work of Christ that we have in hand; and before us we have an high perfect example-giver, of whom we ought to learn, even Christ Jesus, who for our sakes was obedient to the Father until the death of the cross. Phil. ii. Wherefore, seeing we are become children of God through grace, we must be obedient to our heavenly Father, looking to his good pleasure, bidding the world farewell, despising the mocks and scorns thereof, looking up ever diligently unto the crucified Lord Jesus, who waiteth for us with outstretched arms, calleth us lovingly unto him, and for a short travail promiseth us eternal reward, and saith: "If thou suffer with 2 Tim. ii. me, thou shalt reign with me; if thou die with me, thou shalt also be crowned with me."

O Lord Jesu Christ, our foregoer and protector, grant us grace stedfastly to continue in our holy vocation, and to abide in thy service; that through no tediousness or sloth we shrink or cease from the ferventness of good works and holy exercises; that we, being alway ready furnished with watching and prayer, may stedfastly stand, and with a constant mind despise all bodily provocations, shewing patience in adversity, not fearing the slanders and despiteful words of the people, neither desiring the praise and honour of this world; that in the only eternal wealth we may set all our trust, and never to go back from the cross for wealth nor woe; but that under the same banner, through true patience, meekness, and obedience, we may finish our life with a blessed end. Amen.

In the offender that received of Christ the promise of grace, there is set before us a comfortable example of the mercy and love of God. For he that afore had been a murderer, and now was become a penitent and repentant person, as soon as he acknowledged the trespass, and was unfeignedly sorry for his offences committed, confessing Christ the fountain of life, there was promised unto him forgiveness of his sins and entrance into joy. Whereby we see, that no true penitent cometh too late, and that no conversion is unfruitful, if it be done unfeignedly from out of the heart. Here should we learn to go into ourselves, to acknowledge and confess our sins, to complain unto God with lamentation, and to desire grace at his hand; affirming also, that we are well worthy of all rebuke and shame, all punishment, pain, and adversity. Nevertheless, in the consideration of God's eternal mercy, we ought not to despair, but to turn us unto the Bishop and chief Shepherd of our souls; and say: "Lord, remember us in thy kingdom, where thou sittest at the right hand of God thy Father:" so shall we undoubtedly hear this cheerful voice: "To day shalt thou be with me in paradise." This word of consolation, this gracious promise, shall strengthen and comfort our troubled heart in the careful and terrible hour; so that we shall be able quietly to die, forasmuch as Jesus so friendly speaketh to us, and receiveth us so graciously.

Great and unsearchable is the mercy of God, that pardoneth so great a sinner and offender, and doth not cast him off: neither will he reject our fervent prayer, which we in true confidence make unto him. He "desireth not the death of a sinner, but willeth that he convert and live." "So loved he the world, that he gave his only-begotten Son, that whosoever believeth on him should not perish, but have everlasting life;" neither came he to call the righteous, but sinners.

*Ezek. xviii.*
*John iii.*
*Matt. ix.*

O Jesu, be mindful of thy promise; think upon us thy servants; and when we shall depart hence, speak unto our soul these loving words: "To day shalt thou be with me in joy." O Lord Jesu Christ, remember us thy servants that trust in thee, when our tongue cannot speak, when the sight of our eyes faileth, and when our ears are stopped. Suffer not the old serpent and wicked enemy, the devil, to find anything in us, though he subtilely tempt us, and craftily lay wait for us. In thee shall we overcome him; for in thee is our strength. Thou takest all our sins upon thyself; so that he shall find nothing in us, but must depart from us with shame. Let them be turned back, and soon confounded; but let our soul alway rejoice in thee, and be joyful of thy salvation, which thou through thy death hast purchased for us.

[John xix. 14, 25—27.]

It was near hand about the sixth hour. And beside the cross of Jesus stood Mary his mother, and his mother's sister, Mary the wife of Cleophas, and Mary Magdalene. Now when Jesus saw his mother, and the disciple standing whom he loved, he said unto his mother: Woman, behold thy son. Afterward said he to the disciple: Behold thy mother. And from that hour forth the disciple took her for his own.

### DOCTRINE AND FRUIT.

In the passion of Christ, as is mentioned afore, it ought to be considered, that he was most extremely reviled, and suffered most great pain for our sakes. This now appertaineth to the increasing of his pain, that he seeth his mother in all adversity, who might not help him, neither he her. Now doth the sword that Simeon spake of pierce through her heart.

But Jesus, seeing her in sorrow and heaviness, declareth his careful love upon the honour and worthiness of his dearly beloved mother, and giveth her a tutor, such an one as will look unto her. On both the parties may we perceive great love, which we ought to learn of the Lord, and to exercise towards those that be committed unto us. Neither is it written of the evangelist for nought, that she stood; for thereby we see, that though Mary was in very great heaviness and sorrow, yet behaveth she not herself unseemly nor undiscreetly, as carnal men do in adversity many times. She standeth demurely and soberly, being fortified through the strength of the Spirit that stayeth her. Whereby we may learn, when our dear friends die, not to be sorry for 1 Thess. iv them beyond measure and discretion. But chiefly we learn, when adversity cometh, one to have respect to another, to care for our own, faithfully to commit them unto others, that one may brotherly and truly look to another: but specially we ought to be careful for those which are dear unto God.

---

[Matthew xxvii. 45—49. Mark xv. 33—36. Luke xxiii. 44.]

From the sixth hour there was darkness upon all the earth, till about the ninth hour, and the sun was darkened. About the ninth hour, Jesus cried with a loud voice, *Eli, Eli, lama sabacthani?* that is, My God, My God, why hast thou forsaken me? Some standing there, when they heard it, said: He calleth to Helias. Immediately one of them ran, and took a sponge; and filled it with vinegar, and put it upon a reed, and gave him to drink. Other said, Let us see whether Helias will come and deliver him.

### DOCTRINE AND FRUIT.

In all adversity and despite, is all bodily and temporal comfort withdrawn from Christ; that even when he without all consolation doth suffer most grievous extremity, we might perceive his love. The Lord of all creatures, that lacketh nothing, cometh into so great affliction and necessity for our sake, that he complaineth himself to be forsaken of him, who worketh all things in him. This is the voice of the passible mortal flesh, which for us poor sinners crieth upon the cross. His patience is our comfort, his complaint is our help, his sickness is our health, his pain is our satisfaction. The physician came from heaven, that he through great compassion might give over himself into exceeding many torments and rebukes. Therefore with the sick he is sick; with those that suffer he suffereth; with the sorrowful he is sorry; with them that suffer violence he complaineth; for his feeble and weak members he prayeth. And the voice of the flesh and of natural sense is neither rebellious nor desperate. The flesh feeleth great pain undeserved, the innocent holy body suffereth sore punishment: the Godhead nevertheless useth the highest silence; and as for the divine presence, the sensible pain is not minished by it.

But a marvellous stedfastness of patience is here declared, to perform the redemption of mankind. This pain and smart is so great, that even the elements, which have no sense, declare tokens of their compassion. The sun lost his shine, and hid his cheerful light from the wicked rabble, having as it were a displeasure for the death of their Maker. Seeing now that the sun mourneth, and the earth quaketh, much more ought we reasonable men to have compassion, and to consider the death of our Maker.

Behold, O faithful servant of God, how thy foregoer, in all his punishment and sorrowful trouble, endureth still mild and patient, and that there is heard no bitterness out of his mouth. His prayer and complaint sendeth he up unto his heavenly Father, neither nameth he any other, save only God. To him alone he complaineth and openeth his desolation. Even so ought we to do, when adversity, reproach, or any such thing assaulteth us: we must not undiscreetly sorrow, or be angry, but run straightway unto the cross, and at the cross tarry and abide a little while with the Lord. If thou be forsaken, complain of thy trouble unto God the Father; consider, that Jesus also for thy sake was left in great trouble and anguish; learn thou likewise to be soft-minded and patient, without murmuring or cursing; keep thee to the only comfort of God, give over all the joy of this world: so shalt thou not be forsaken of him. All earthly things set apart, turn thou thy mind up into the country of heaven. Take God for thy Father, Jesus for thy brother: thou art of a noble high kindred, namely, a child of the ever-living God.

O merciful Father, we cry unto thee in all trouble, and call upon thee through the crucified Jesus. Suffer us not to sink in great afflictions, give us not over unto our own strength; but the more the enemy presseth upon us, the more be thou our assistance: for in all anguish and trouble thou art the right helper and most faithful friend. If temptation then come upon us by thy fatherly will, grant us grace, O Lord, patiently to bear it, and to lay the bur-

[COVERDALE.]

den upon thy mercy; that in all trouble we, being else destitute of all consolation, may put our whole trust only in thee. Amen.

---

[John xix. 28—30.]

AFTER this, Jesus knowing that all things were now performed, that the scripture might be fulfilled, he saith: I thirst. So there stood a vessel by, full of vinegar. Therefore they filled a sponge with vinegar, and wound it about with hyssop, and put it to his mouth. As soon as Jesus then received of the vinegar, he answered and said: It is finished.

### DOCTRINE AND FRUIT.

ADAM satisfied his lust in the forbidden apple; which noisome lust was occasion of our death. But Jesus, for the reformation of this concupiscence, suffereth also upon his tongue, to restore us again from the fall, and to conquer us in this life. His bitter drink is unto us a blessed medicine. Such great unthankfulness of the Jews was prophesied by king David in the Psalms. To him that fed them in the wilderness with bread from heaven, and gave them water to drink out of the hard stony rock, even unto him for a recompence they give vinegar and gall. O the sour and unnatural fruit that the Lord receiveth of his own vineyard, which he had planted and garnished so fair! To us here is prepared a sovereign medicine against gluttony and all voluptuousness of the flesh, through the love whereof God is forgotten and forsaken.

Now when Christ, who is the fulfiller of the law and all the prophets, had wholly and fully performed the will of his heavenly Father, he saith for a conclusion and end of his life: "It is finished;" as he would say, "Now is finished all that the old law hath written and spoken of me, all that the old testament figured with oblations and sacrifices, with glory and beauty in the God's service. Now are truly fulfilled the holy prophecies of the prophets, and the long

*Psal. lxix.*

*Isai. v.*

wished desires of the holy old fathers. Now is wrought and performed all that belonged and concerned the redemption of mankind. It is all, as it was promised of God, concluded with an honourable blessed end. And look, what is behind shall undoubtedly be fulfilled in due time. I have accomplished the commandment of my Father, who sent me into this world; the work that he gave me to do, have I finished. What could I do more for thee, O my people, that I have not done? Upon the sixth day he finished the work of the creation of the world; and now upon the sixth day and age of the world he performeth the blessed work of man's redemption. Upon the sixth day he created man, and made him of the mould of the earth; upon the sixth day he restored him again, and delivered him with his holy blood. Thus all things are finished: the great work of his mercy and most excellent love is accomplished; the way unto heaven is opened, and the devil's power is broken." John xvii.

In such hope ought we valiantly to travail at this time, in this unconstant world, and not to let fall the work of God that is begun; but by his assistance to bring it unto a blessed end, and stoutly to endure therein. It is well nigh come to the point, that all shall be finished: the evening and end of our life cometh on apace, wherein we may say with glad hearts, as Christ our foregoer did: "It is all finished."

Wherefore, dear brethren, let us ever most diligently and earnestly walk in the way of the truth, and of commendable virtues begun, exercising ourselves in righteousness. We must not think otherwise but to have battle against vice, against the flesh, the world, and Satan. Daily go we on apace towards death, in hope to attain eternal life. O that we might say with Paul: "I have fought a good fight, I have fulfilled my course, I have kept the faith!" We must suffer and have travail yet a little season; the time of our deliverance will shortly be here. 2 Tim iv.

O Lord Jesu, direct thou all our works according to thy good pleasure; illuminate and purify our minds and thoughts. Teach us how we ever, to the praise and honour of thy holy name, may meekly begin, diligently do, and blessedly end all our works and enterprises. O give us grace faithfully to labour in the vineyard of the Lord, that the heat and travail drive us not back, that we faint not; that in the school of heavenly exercise we may stedfastly endure, till we give up the ghost; and that through thy mercy, after many commendable battles and long striving, we may say in the last hour of our life, It is all finished. Vouchsafe thou to be the final occasion of our whole life, and of all our workings: so shall it follow, that thou wilt also be our eternal reward, joy, and salvation.  Amen.

---

[Matt. xxvii. 50. Mark xv. 37. Luke xxiii. 46. John xix. 30.]

AND Jesus crying with a loud voice said: Father, into thy hands I commit my spirit. And when he had thus said, he bowed his head, and gave up the ghost.

### DOCTRINE AND FRUIT.

THE life of all living dieth after the flesh: through the painful torment of death doth Jesus depart. But by his death he openeth unto us the way of life, and taketh from us everlasting death. This is a precious, dear, and victorious death, which hath slain our death, and conquered us life again. Let this death evermore continue in our hearts, and let our death be considered in the consideration of his death. This shall bring us comfortable trust and hope, when our death striveth in us; so that we shall neither be afraid, nor despair, if we stedfastly believe that Christ died for us, and that he through his death hath opened unto us everlasting life.

Let us with devout hearts consider the death of him that hath redeemed us, and restored us again. The gracious innocent Lord Jesus dieth miserable and naked, so poor, so destitute, as no man else; and yet unto God is none so dear, although of men he be most vilely entreated. This is even the reward of the world, to despise the children of God, and to recompense evil for good. If the like happen unto us, we must not think it strange; for the servant is not above the lord. The Lord hangeth on the cross, hard pierced, not only with nails, but also with ardent love towards us; sore beaten and hurt in every place, without succour, without help, without comfort, even as a dead man who is forgotten and out of mind. Ponder well, O thou good servant of Christ, who and how great he is, that crying with a loud voice, giveth up the ghost: verily, even the Son of God, as Centurio likewise doth testify.

O dear brethren, let us consider, how great our sins are, for the which the innocent Son of God dieth. Justly ought all the world to be dead unto us in Christ, and we unto the world. And what is our life but a blessed death? He that learneth not to die in this life, is afraid, when the hour of death cometh. Every day go we one day's journey unto death: therefore ought we so to watch, so to speak, and so to work, as if we would die even now out of hand. Before death we must learn to die; lest he suddenly take hold upon us, and make us afraid. Death, unto those that faithfully believe, is through the death of Christ become the gate to life; for their comfort and strong hope is in the words of Jesus, when he saith: "He that believeth on me, though he were dead, yet shall he live." Item: "Whoso heareth my word, and believeth on him that sent me, hath everlasting life." John xi.<br>John iii.

In this promise ought we to live and die, casting away all impediments, and such things as hinder us from his love; being with heart and mind separated from the world, and undefiled from the filthiness thereof.

Out of the passion of Christ we must pick out unto ourselves comfortable help and medicine; so that obediently in all patience we offer up ourselves unto our heavenly Father, committing our souls into his hands. In life and in death let the death of Christ be our comfort; and let us set it against all fearful temptations, and between the wrath of God and our sins.

O Lord Jesu Christ, who in the feeble nature of man hast suffered death for us unworthy sinners, grant us grace fervently in our hearts to bear the pain and love of thy most bitter death, and through the subduing and overcoming of all vice and wickedness to use and exercise ourselves daily in following thy footsteps, and dying with thee; and when the end of our life draweth nigh, that we then may depart in thy mercy and grace, and receive the joy of paradise. Assist thou us when we die, and defend us from the old enemy, whom thou through thy death hast overcome. O Father, we commit our spirit into thy hand: thou hast redeemed us, O God of truth. Let these be our last words, when we depart hence. Amen.

---

[Matthew xxvii. 51—54. Mark xv. 38, 39. Luke xxiii. 47, 48.]

AND behold the vail of the temple rent into two pieces, from above till beneath; and there was an earthquake; the stones cleave asunder; the graves opened; they that had slept rose up, and went out of the graves, and came after his resurrection into the holy city, and appeared unto many. The captain, and they that were with him, which kept Jesus, when they saw the earthquake, and that he gave up the ghost with such a cry, and other things that there happened, they were afraid very sore, and said: Verily, this was God's Son. Centurio likewise praised God, and said: Verily, this was a righteous man. And all the people that were there and saw it, smote upon their breasts and returned.

### DOCTRINE AND FRUIT.

THE Jews alway required tokens of Christ; and of such there happened many now in the death of the Lord. For the very earth quaketh at their wickedness and blaspheming of God; the hard stony rocks, with their cracking and cleaving asunder, express a lamentation on their Maker's behalf; the vail in the temple rendeth, for a declaration, that the old covered things in the old testament are laid away, and the hid significations of Christ expressed and opened. For he is the holy true oblation, that taketh away the sins of the world: he is the undefiled Lamb of God; he is the true High Priest, that entereth within the vail into the sanctuary; for the way of holy things is opened through his blood: he is the High Priest, that once entered in, and with one only sacrifice doth perfectly cleanse and sanctify. The graves

Heb. x.

opened for an evidence of his resurrection. Centurio knowledgeth that, which the hard-hearted Jews would not confess.

O good faithful believers, let us not be harder than the stones; let our hearts rend asunder in repentance and sorrow for our sins, that we may enjoy the fruit of the Lord's death.

---

[Matthew xxvii. 25, 26. Mark xv. 40, 41. Luke xxiii. 49.]

AND afar off stood all his acquaintances; among whom were many women, that came up from Galilee, and followed him, and ministered unto him: among whom was Mary Magdalene, and Mary the Mother of James the Less and Joses, and the mother of Zebedee's children, with many other that were come to Hierusalem.

The Jews then, because it was the sabbath-even, that the bodies should not remain on the cross upon the sabbath-day, (for that was the great sabbath-day,) besought Pilate, that their legs might be broken, and that they might be taken down. Then came the soldiers and brake the legs of the first, and of the other which was crucified with him. But when they came to Jesus, and saw that he was dead already, they brake not his legs; but one of the soldiers with a spear thrust him into the side; and forthwith came there out blood and water. And he that saw it bare record, and his record is true; and he knoweth that he saith true, that ye also might believe. These things were done, that the scripture might be fulfilled: Ye shall not break a bone of him. And Exod. xii. again, another scripture saith: They shall look on him whom Zech. xii. they pierced.

### DOCTRINE AND FRUIT.

OUT of the side of him that sleepeth upon the cross, runneth the fountain of wholesome water, with the which our uncleanness is washed away, and the whole world sprinkled, purified, and cleansed therewith. The heart is opened and wounded; love floweth out, the blood gusheth forth, to the washing away of all our sins. This is the true stony rock, which, being smitten upon, giveth water unto our thirsty souls: like as Eve was taken and fashioned out of the rib and side of her husband that slept, so is the holy church, the spouse of Christ, shapen out of the side of her husband. This gate is opened wide to all faithful believers; he that hideth himself in this hole, is sure from all hurt and harm. Of this holy and godly fountain whoso drinketh once, or taketh a draught of the holy love, doth forthwith forget all his adversities and griefs, and shall be whole from all wicked heat of temporal lusts and bodily provocations: fervently shall he be kindled in love, and desire of eternal things; and shall be replenished with the unspeakable goodness of the Holy Ghost; and "in him shall be a fountain and well of living water, flowing into eternal life."

Eph. v.

John vii.

By this creepeth the poor sinner into the loving heart of Jesus Christ, which with exceeding great kindness is pierced through; and there findeth he rest and quietness in the stony rock. Here are opened the conduits and well-pipes of life, the way of our health, wherein we find rest unto our souls, and shadow for heat and travail: this fountain of grace is never dried up. This is the well of the godly river, that floweth out of the midst of paradise, to water the whole earth, to moisture the dry hearts, and to wash away sin.

Out of this plentiful well ought we with great desire to draw and drink; that from henceforth we live not in ourselves, but in him who for our sakes was wounded so deep. Our heart must we give wholly unto him, that hath opened his heart so wide. His heart and ours must be all one. Nothing requireth he of us but the heart. "Son," saith he, "give me thy heart." Our heart must we give to the Lord, not to the world; to eternal wisdom, not to lightness. There do the true herdman's sheep find pasture; there are the water-brooks of life; there may they go in and out. Nothing is there upon earth that so kindleth, draweth, and pierceth the heart of man, as doth Christ's love declared upon the cross. When we thus surrender our heart unto the Lord, when we thus wholly and fully give over our heart into the Lord's hands, that he may keep it and possess it for ever, then have we blessed peace.

O Lord Jesu Christ, draw thou our hearts unto thee; join them together in unseparable love, that they may fervently burn; that we may abide in thee, and thou in us, and that the everlasting covenant between us may stand sure for ever. O wound our hearts with the fiery darts of thy piercing love. Let them pierce through all our slothful members and inward powers, that we being happily wounded, may so become whole and sound. Let us have no lover but thyself alone; let us seek no joy nor comfort, but only in thee.

Thus have we the passion and death of our Lord and Redeemer Jesus Christ. Now, as Paul saith, let us go forth of the tents, unto him that for our sake is despitefully crucified without the city of Hierusalem, and let us help him to bear his rebuke, giving him thanks and praise for his great love. In his death standeth our life: for in his death is our death slain; the sting of death and sin is taken away. Here find we true life and eternal salvation; here sin is forgiven, and pardon granted *a pœna et culpa;* here mercy is denied unto no man; for the virtue and merits of the Lord's holy passion is bottomless. Through his shame cometh eternal honour and glory unto us. His passion is the wholesome plaister for all wounds; his cross the overthrow of all enemies, and victory against all vice. Heb. xiii.

From our whole hearts therefore ought we to rejoice in the great and blessed fruits of thy holy passion.

O Lord Jesu, whilst we are in this feeble life, grant us so to live, that we may direct all our works, desires, and intents according to thy godly will and pleasure; that this our temporal course may be found and finished in thy grace; that after the overcoming of all temptations and careful things we may come to the reward of eternal salvation. Teach thou us daily to die, and by the spirit to subdue the flesh; that when the flesh corrupteth, the spirit may be taken to eternal rest. Grant us grace, cheerfully and continually to cleave unto thy holy cross. O give us blessed tears of true repentance, while the door of grace standeth open: grant that we may stedfastly and blessedly finish the thing which commendably is begun.

Let our daily exercise be in the consideration of the passion of Christ; let him be our mirror continually: let us not shrink from the cross, but endure with Christ in life and death; with him on the cross, with him in the grave and death. So shall we continue in rest, peace and quietness; that when Christ our life shall appear, we may rise up with him in glory. God the Father, Son, and Holy Ghost, grant this unto us all! Amen.

# [CHAPTER II.]

## THE BURIAL OF JESUS CHRIST OUT OF THE HOLY EVANGELISTS.

[Matthew xxvii. 57—60. Mark xv. 42—46. Luke xxiii. 50—54. John xix. 38—42.]

Now when it was late, forasmuch as it was the day of preparation afore the sabbath, there came a rich man of Arimathia, named Joseph, such a principal and famous senator, as was just and righteous. The same had not consented to their counsel and doings; for he also was one of those that waited for the kingdom of God; a disciple of Jesu, but secretly for fear of the Jews. Boldly went he in unto Pilate, and begged the body of Jesu. But Pilate wondered, if he were now dead already. And when he had learned of the captain, that it was, he granted him the body of Jesu, and commanded it to be given him. Joseph had bought a white linen cloth, and took down the body of Jesu, and wrapt it in the fair linen cloth. There came also Nicodemus, who was come to the Lord afore by night, and brought myrrh and aloes, upon an hundred pound, mixt together. So taking the body of Jesu, they wound it with clothes, and prepared it with sweet ointments, according as the manner of the Jews was to bury. And by the place where Jesus was crucified, there was a garden, and in the garden a new sepulchre. There Joseph laid Jesus in his own new sepulchre, which he had caused to be hewn out of a rock, into the which no man had yet been laid. Forasmuch then as it was the Jews' day of preparing, the sepulchre being at hand, they laid Jesus into it; and Joseph weltered a great stone afore the entrance of the sepulchre, and went his way.

## NOW FOLLOWETH THE DOCTRINE AND CONTEMPLATION.

In the former little book we have heard of the passion of Christ. Now if our great sin put us in fear, making our conscience unquiet, and press us with the terror of everlasting death and damnation, we ought to remember, that the Lamb of God being slain, and hanged up upon the cross for our sins, hath himself satisfied for them all, and washed them clean away. This holy sacrifice was offered unto God the Father for our welfare, and even the same it is that hath taken away the sin and wickedness of all the world.

Whatsoever is read and spoken concerning the passion of Jesus Christ, it is altogether done for our eternal wealth and comfort. Now it is described of the holy evangelists, with what honour and glory his holy body was buried; and that not of mean persons, but of noble and famous just men, Joseph and Nicodemus, who, while Christ yet lived, favoured him, and were secretly his disciples. But now after his death they step forth somewhat more stoutly and boldly, begging of Pilate the body of Jesu, to bury it. In the which act is declared their worthy and valiant belief and love unto the Lord Jesu. For their bodies, their estimation, and goods, they must needs put in jeopardy, and procure unto themselves the hatred and displeasure of all the world, if they honourably bury him, who in his life-time was taken to be an evil doer, a deceiver, a seditious murderer, and so was condemned unto death. But thus it pleaseth God, in weakness to declare his own strength and glory. Thus the dead wheat-corn bringeth forth fruit in the death of Christ; and thus appeareth the power of his death. For though he verily and truly died as touching the body, yet after the spirit, and in mighty power, he liveth; yea, he himself is the life of all things.

<small>1 Cor. i.<br>John xii.</small>

This is the power and fruit of his passion, when a mighty and strong spirit doth exercise itself in faithful believing hearts. They that were afore ashamed to go openly unto the Lord, step now forth manfully, all fearfulness set apart, jeoparding their bodies and goods. For besides that they put themselves in peril of losing their life and estimation, they bestow also great cost in linen cloth and in costly sweet ointment. For they bury not Jesus as an evil doer, but as an honourable man and friend of God, according to their custom. Lo, what a thing it is to cleave somewhat unto Christ, how feebly soever it be done; it bringeth alway great fruit in his time. No man therefore ought to be rejected, that cleaveth any thing unto Christ, and earnestly seeketh him. Faith is strengthened in affliction and adversity: the death of Christ giveth power unto the fearful. In death beginneth his honour and glory to appear; there are all things fair and beautiful. Centurio giveth testimony, and maketh an honourable confession, and so do they that were under him.

Necessary it was we should believe and confess, that Jesus verily died upon the cross: therefore do the evangelists describe it so perfectly, how his body was taken down from the cross by Joseph, and was laid in the sepulchre; to the intent that we also might believe and confess, that he hath broken the bands of death, and is from death mightily risen again. For life might not be holden captive in death, neither might death with the rules thereof always bind him that of all things is the life, in whom "we live, move, and have our being."

Here we must learn to know the eternal infallible foresight and providence of God, who for his Anointed appointeth aforehand an honourable sepulchre, and moveth the hearts of his elect to bury the body of Jesu; which else undoubtedly had been vilely cast out, and remained still unburied. Howbeit his burial and rest must needs be honourable, as the prophet saith, Esay xi. For when he by death had finished the course of his life and the work of his Father, this rest appertained to his honour, and the Father heard him, as he prayed afore: "Father, make thy Son honourable, or glorify thy Son." *John xvii.* This began in the burial: there was the fair white linen cloth, the new sepulchre, the honourable men, and excellent dead-buriers, as witnesses of his death; there were the hundred pounds of precious and costly ointment. All these things were evidences of a glorious, new, and immortal life, which Christ had in his body, as the firstling of his dead, and as we also shall have according to our measure. The sepulchre is new, partly to prevent all wrong suspicion; for if any man had lien in that sepulchre afore, it might easily have been suspected or talked, that Christ was not risen again from the dead, but some other; partly to declare the newness of life in Christ, and in those that are his, as it is said afore.

By this also we see, into what poverty Christ submitted himself: he that in his life-time had neither house nor place where to lay his head, is now covered with strange cloth, and laid in a strange sepulchre. In the which thing, though Christ's body was alway uncorrupt, we are taught fruitfully to consider the corruption of our body. We are earth, and to the earth we must yield and pay earth again. Ashes we be, and into ashes we must return. Why brag we then? Why are we proud and high-minded, seeing that shortly we shall become foul dung and carrion? Why have we such desire to the wicked world, considering it casteth us out so vilely? We should alway remember, that within a small short time we shall be laid down into a foul pit. There is the harborough[1] of all flesh; there lie the rich and poor together in one bed. There is no difference between the noble and base of blood; there neither goods help the rich, nor subtle craft the witty. There the tender is worms' meat, and he that a little while ago went bragging up and down in costly apparel, is now an ugly smell to the nose: there the hardy giant is fain to play stout gallant's part; the praise and commendation of such as are puffed up in foolish pride departeth as the dust before the wind. Thus passeth away all mankind, and all flesh falleth to the place from whence he came, being dissolved by reason of original sin.

Wherefore let us learn in this time so to live, and so to subdue the flesh through the Spirit, that when the flesh corrupteth, our soul may be taken into eternal peace and rest.

Rom. vi. "For all we that be baptized into Christ Jesus, are baptized into his death, being buried with him through baptism into death; that as Christ was raised up from the dead through the glory of his Father, so we likewise might walk in the newness of life. For if we be graffed in him through the similitude of his death, we shall assuredly also be partakers of his resurrection: knowing this, that our old man is crucified with him, that the body of sin might be emptied, and that we should serve sin no more; for he that is dead is made righteous from sin. If we now be dead with Christ,

[1 Harborough: harbour. Spenser.]

we believe that we shall also live with him." Look upon the whole sixth chapter to the Romans.

We must die from the world, and from our own flesh, that the world may be crucified and dead unto us, as we unto the world. The old Adam, who in us did live and rule, must be subdued and mortified, that Christ only may live and reign in us. We must bury our bodies with myrrh and aloes, that is, with lamentation and sorrow for our sins, with weeping, with fasting, and with abstinence; which works of repentance are bitter unto the body. But like as those bitter things, aloes and myrrh, do keep the body from corruption; so the cross and adversity sent of God, and borne for his sake, preserveth our flesh from sin.

If we thus die with Christ from the world, and be buried in his death, we shall rise again to a new life, here and in the world to come; and so, as for death, we need not be afraid of it. For the sepulchre is new, and lieth in the garden: which noteth unto us the return to the pleasant garden of paradise, which is opened us through the death of Christ. For he as a guide is entered in before us (John xiv. Heb. ix. x.), that we also after a new sort might escape from death, and rise again to a new life. For in the death of Christ is death killed, overcome, and wholly renewed, and as much as altered into a sleep. For we live unto God; and our bodies, as the scripture testifieth, shall also live again. And this is the cause, that the scripture affirmeth those which are dead in Christ to be asleep. Isai. xxvi. 1 Thess. iv.

Afore-time had death mightily and openly reigned, even over those also that had not sinned like unto Adam, (yet had they put on Adam's image, and were therefore subdued unto the curse:) but when the second Adam, namely, Christ, ap- peared, he purchased life again for mankind, through the death of his flesh, destroying the dominion of death, and rising from death again. Then was death renewed and changed, and became like unto a sleep: for it destroyeth us not for ever, but is a gate and entrance into a better and eternal life. Therefore have we a much more perfect hope of the resurrection in Christ, than they of old; which there- fore buried the bodies so costly and honourably, because they hoped in the resurrection to come. As for us, we must be- stow such cost upon Christ in his members, clothing and

1 Cor. xv.

feeding the poor, and being ready also to lose all things for his sake.

Grant unto us, O God, that as concerning the world and the old life we may die with thy Son our head, and be truly buried in his death; that with him, and in him, we may rise again to a new life; that we, weak and feeble, may with Joseph and Nicodemus grow in virtue and stedfastness, daily laying somewhat to the heap of godly exercises, being ever still renewed in the spirit; that we in our hearts laying up Christ, who died for our sakes, may so in thankful remembrance bury him, to the intent that our body and soul may still remain pure and unspotted until the coming of our Lord. Amen.

---

[Matthew xxvii. 61—66. Mark xv. 47. Luke xxiii. 55, 56.]

MARY MAGDALENE and Mary Joses, sitting over against the sepulchre, beheld where Jesus was laid. For certain women there were, which coming with him from Galilee, and following him, beheld the sepulchre, and how his body was laid. Those returned back and prepared sweet odours; but upon the sabbath they rested, because of the commandment.

The next day after the day of preparation the high priests and Pharisees came unto Pilate, and said: Sir, we remember, that this deceiver said, while he was yet alive, that after three days he should rise again. Cause therefore the grave to be kept until the third day, lest his disciples happily come and steal him away, and say unto the people, that he is risen from the dead; and so shall the last error be worse than the first. Pilate said unto them, Ye have watchmen; go, and keep it, as ye know. They went and kept, and provided the sepulchre with watchmen, and sealed the stone.

### DOCTRINE AND FRUIT.

HERE we learn to have an earnest, diligent, and fervent love unto Christ, hearing with what zeal and ferventness that devout women cleave unto him, and serve him in life and death. Him whom they loved in life, will they not forsake in death; but cheerfully with constant minds they jeopard their life and goods. What availeth us then, that we cannot shew friendship, love, and service unto Christ, as well as these women? Seeing we have not Christ always bodily with us, who now, being in his kingdom, needeth no corporal ministration and service, we ought to bestow the same upon his poor ones, whom we have always with us. Herein ought we to spare neither goods nor money to serve and please Christ, who unto death did jeopard and give his body and life for us.

But like as in the women there was a devout gesture and good mind toward Christ; so in the Jewish priests and Pharisees there was found a great malice and hatred against Christ. They were not satisfied in persecuting him while he was alive, but undertook also to hinder his resurrection. Yet God by his wisdom useth their wickedness to the glory of Christ; that even the enemies themselves, albeit against their will, must bear record of his burial and resurrection, in that they keep the grave with watchmen, and seal the stone. The truth is immortal: the more it is opprest, the more it breaketh forth. Therefore ought we to beware, that we never go about to hinder the truth; for if we should do so, we should both labour in vain, and procure unto ourselves everlasting hurt.

[COVERDALE.]

## [CHAPTER III.]

### THE RESURRECTION OF JESUS CHRIST OUT OF THE HOLY EVANGELISTS.

[Matthew xxviii. 1—7, 11—15. Mark xvi. 1—7. Luke xxiv. 1—3. John xx. 1.]

<small>Mark xvi.</small> AND when the sabbath was now past, even the sabbath-day at even, Mary Magdalene, Mary James, and Salome, bought sweet spices, that they might come and anoint Jesus. <small>Luke xxiv. Matt. xxviii. John xx.</small> The evening when the sabbath is ended, and the first day dawneth after the sabbath, namely, the first day of the week, while it was yet dark, and the sun brake forth and began to arise, the women came to the sepulchre to see it. But there happened first a great earthquake: for the angel of the Lord came down from heaven, and went and rolled back the stone from the mouth of the sepulchre, and sat upon it. His countenance was like the lightning, and his raiment white as snow; and for fear of him the keepers were astonied, and became as dead men. And behold, some of them that had watched the sepulchre, came into the city, and told the high priests all the things that had happened. Then gathered they themselves with the elders, and took counsel, and gave large money unto the soldiers, saying: Say ye, that his disciples came by night, and stole him away while ye slept. And if this come to the ruler's ears, we will persuade him, and save you harmless. So they took the money, and did as they were taught. And this saying is noised among the Jews unto this day.

Now as the women were in the way going, they said among themselves: Who will roll us the stone away from the <small>Matt. xxviii.</small> door of the sepulchre? (for it was a very great one.) And as they looked, they saw that the stone was rolled away. Then went they into the sepulchre, and found not the body of the Lord Jesu; but saw a young man sitting at the right side, clothed in a long white garment: and they were afraid. But the angel said unto them: Fear not; I know whom ye seek. Ye seek Jesus of Nazareth, that was crucified: He is not here, he is risen, as he said: Behold the place where they laid him. But go ye, and tell his disciples and Peter, that he is risen again from the dead. Behold, he goeth before you into Galilee, as he said unto you. Lo, I have told you.

### DOCTRINE AND FRUIT.

The resurrection of Jesus Christ from the dead is very diligently and perfectly described of the four evangelists: for right profitable and necessary is it for the strengthening and stablishing of our belief in Christ. And whereas in the description of this history they speak not all alike, the same happeneth to our wealth, through the ordinance of the Holy Ghost; that we should exercise our faith therein, and apply our diligence, perfectly to learn and comprehend the same resurrection of Christ. For where that is right conceived and believed, there is faith perfect. The evangelists now in describing Christ's resurrection do most of all declare, to what high honour Christ came after death; and that in one order and degree, according as our belief and weakness increaseth and groweth towards perfection.

At the first is faith in us feeble and unperfect; but through the grace of him that hath given it, it daily groweth. Very hard also is it for our natural reason to receive and believe the resurrection of the dead. Therefore do the evangelists right diligently and with many words set forth the same resurrection of Christ, that our belief therein might be assured and stedfast. For whosoever truly and constantly believeth the resurrection of Jesu Christ, is ready and prepared to believe all that concerneth Christ. Neither is there anything that maketh a man more joyful, than when he believeth that at the coming of the Lord he shall rise again, and receive a glorified body after Christ and with Christ. What can be tedious to such a faithful believing man, when he beholdeth so high a reward from God? Diligently therefore ought we to hear, what the holy evangelists write of his resurrection, and to give credence to the witnesses that saw it.

First, we hear again the great zeal and the fervent love and diligence of these devout women, in that they desire to shew honour unto the Lord being dead: but the angel, a messenger of his resurrection, commandeth them to declare this joy unto the disciples, and to get them unto the Lord now being alive. Heavenly is the messenger and proclaimer of the resurrection; for it passeth far all natural reason and all flesh. Therefore are the women also afraid of him, and at the fair brightness of his countenance and apparel. For our feeble flesh is not able to sustain the glorious shine of the heavenly light and godly clearness; but is afraid at it, and feareth. Nevertheless God by his angel doth right soon comfort the women's weakness, taketh from them their fear, speaketh lovingly unto them, maketh them apostles, that is, messengers and proclaimers of the joyful resurrection. So little doth God reject our weakness, that he maketh even women to be the declarers of his resurrection: for he ever delighteth of the last to make the first. Forasmuch then as they were the beginners of death in sin, they are here first, afore the apostles, chosen to be the declarers of that immortal life, which even out of death is come forth unto us in Christ.

As Christ with the earthquake died on the cross, so riseth he with the earthquake; which also was heard in the sending of the Holy Ghost. This signified, that through his death and resurrection, and by the power of the Holy Ghost, when the apostles declare the same in the world, the whole world should be moved and changed; and though the ungracious falsehood of the high priests undertook with their lies to hide and suppress the truth of Christ's resurrection, yet God did direct it another way. Look, wherewith they minded to oppress the truth, even with the same have they helped to set it forth: and thereby was it signified, how the Jewish people should be blinded and refused. And forasmuch as they had no love unto the truth, but rejected it, it was meet that they should be blinded and darkened in lies, and that there should error and blindness enough fall upon them.

*The cross is the glorious* The angel is not ashamed to call Jesus *the crucified:* for the cross is the token of Christ's victory. Through the cross began his honour and glory; through the cross was death overcome; the cross is the glorious token of all Christians; in the cross is the exaltation of Christ the head, and of all his members. We ought not therefore to be ashamed of the cross of our Lord, which was crucified: for therein standeth our health, life, and resurrection, all our rejoicing and glory. Commission is given, that unto Peter before other disciples they should declare the Lord's resurrection; that from the fear, wherein he stood by reason of the denial, he might be delivered, and so comforted.

*and victorious token of the faithful*

He sendeth them to Galilee, (thither will he go before them,) that they might be safe from the fear of the Jews, which at that time raged horribly.

Grant us, O God, an earnest zeal and love unto the poor, in whom we may highly honour Jesus thy Son. And whereas we, through the weakness of the flesh, are inclined to be faint-hearted, and not able of ourselves to behold the bright shine and clearness of his glorious resurrection, strengthen and comfort thou us by thy holy angel, that we may constantly believe the resurrection of thy Son; whereby we receiving an holy hope of the life to come, and of the immortal resurrection of our bodies, may be able also to comfort and strengthen others that be weak. O make thou this hard earth of our flesh to quake and move, through the power of thy Spirit, to holy fruitful penance, amendment, and conversion of our life. Preserve us, that we never resist the truth, nor take part with lies. Grant us love unto the truth; keep us from error and blindness. Let our joy be in the cross of Jesu Christ thy Son, and our life in his resurrection; that we with him, and in him, may truly rise again here to a godly, righteous, and sober life, and in the world to come to the blessed life everlasting. Amen.

[Mark xvi. 8. John xx. 2—18.]

AND the women went out quickly, and fled from the sepulchre: for they trembled and were amazed. Neither said they anything to any man; for they were afraid. Mary

*Mark xvi.*

John xx.
Magdalene ran, and came to Simon Peter, and to the other disciple whom Jesus loved, and said unto them, They have taken away the Lord out of the sepulchre, and we wot not where they have laid him. Then went Peter forth, and that other disciple, and came to the sepulchre. They both ran together, and the other disciple outran Peter, and came sooner to the sepulchre. And he stooped down, and saw the linen clothes lying; yet went he not in. Then came Simon Peter following him, and went into the sepulchre, and saw the linen clothes lying, and the napkin that was about his head not lying with the linen clothes, but wrapt together in a place by itself. Then went in also that other disciple, which came first to the sepulchre, and he saw, and believed. For as yet they knew not the scriptures, that he should rise again from death. And the two disciples went away again unto their own home. But Mary stood without at the sepulchre weeping. And as she wept, she bowed herself into the sepulchre, and saw two angels in white sitting, the one at the head, the other at the feet, where they had laid the body of Jesus. And they said unto her, Woman, why weepest thou? She said unto them, For they have taken away my Lord, I wot not where they have laid him. When she had thus said, she turned herself back, and saw Jesus standing, and knew not that it was Jesus. Then said Jesus unto her, Woman, why weepest thou? Whom seekest thou? She, supposing that he had been a gardener, said unto him, Sir, if thou have borne him hence, tell me where thou hast laid him, and I will fetch him. Jesus said unto her, Mary. She turned herself, and said unto him, Raboni, which is to say, Master. Then said Jesus unto her, Touch me not: for I am not yet ascended to my Father. But go to my brethren, and say unto them: I ascend up unto my Father and your Father, unto my God and your God. Mary Magdalene came and told the disciples which had been with the Lord, and now were weeping and mourning, that she had seen the Lord, and that he had

spoken such things unto her. But though they heard that he was alive, and that Mary had seen him, yet they believed not.

### DOCTRINE AND FRUIT.

The evangelists do most diligently set forth to us the resurrection of Christ, as a thing necessary, profitable, and joyful unto all faithful believers. For in the resurrection we see how Christ is exalted, and what hope we have in him. But this resurrection do the evangelists teach, according as man's understanding may comprehend it. For if Christ had suddenly at once opened himself to his disciples, so that other exhortations and warnings were not gone before, then should they have taken it but for a plain fantasy and vision, as they did when the Lord appeared unto them upon the water. Matt. xiv. Therefore the evangelists describe the matter very distinctly and sundry ways; so that no man can be able to suspect any deceit. First, how the women and men came to the sepulchre, looked, and went in; and how they viewed every thing thoroughly, not once, but oft and many times; the clothes wherein the Lord was wrapped, the headkerchief, every thing folden together in his several place; and how they saw and perceived that the body was not there, that the sepulchre was open, the stone rolled away, and how the angels and heavenly spirits testified that he was risen again. Yet for all this they are weak, and believe it not stedfastly; but be as yet in a doubt. Thus God permitteth them to waver, and to be feeble of belief, and doth not throughly persuade them forthwith, and that altogether for our sakes.

He might well suddenly have certified and assured Thomas and them at the first; but thus is it better both for them and us. For the more a sick man feeleth his own disease and wounds, the more acceptable is the medicine unto him: the weaker that our belief is, the more cause have we to call upon God for the increase of faith; the more weakness we find in ourselves, the farther are we in debt, and the more bound to praise God, when he maketh us strong. And seeing it is his only strength that stayeth us, we ought the less to rejoice in our own. Christ in his life-time had oft Matt. xx. told them afore of his resurrection; but their mind was so dull, that they understood it not, neither perceived they that great mystery. The resurrection of the bodies they could not comprehend, but alway understood it otherwise. There was much written thereof, and that with evident words, in the scripture, as in the sixteenth psalm and in the figure of Jonas; and yet could not they understand it. Which thing nevertheless to believe, Christ had given them occasion sundry ways; as in that he raised up Lazarus, and other which were dead, and made them alive again. In all his preaching and doctrine he declared, that this was unto him in no wise unpossible, by reason of the divine power working in him. For all this the disciples are yet so weak, that they understand it not all.

*John xi.*

Therefore doth the godly wisdom lead them still by little and little, to make them stronger, declaring unto them certain assured evidences; as that the body was not in the sepulchre, but that the clothes lay there wrapt together; for these were undoubted tokens, that he was risen up again. For if any man had taken him out of the sepulchre, as Magdalene thought, he could not have had so much time and leisure, as to loose up the bands, and to undo the clothes from the body; but had taken and carried away the clothes and body together: for the clothes did cleave hard fast to the body, partly by reason of the blood, and partly through the aloes and myrrh, that the body was dressed withal. But for all this they are weak still, and in doubt, until such time as the Lord himself doth strengthen them. Therefore even Mary also, as fervent as she is, judgeth not the body to be risen again, but to be stolen and privily carried away. Thus God openeth himself unto whom, and when, he will. For though we see sometimes many great and wonderful works, though we read and hear much of the scriptures, yet remaineth our heart still ignorant, neither doth the doctrine take effect, till Christ open it, and till he himself be schoolmaster within.

Whoso would rather have another and higher sense or exposition than this, it may be understood, that Christ appeareth unto those which mourn and weep, and stand in death with Christ in subduing of the flesh, in mortifying of the body, in abiding of the cross. For while they be in adversity under the cross, and buried with Christ, the greatness of the trouble causeth them to think that Christ is not risen again; that is, they have nothing but heaviness and sorrow. Notwithstanding Christ appeareth unto them, comforteth and refresheth them, and maketh them partakers of his resurrection and joy.

Here may we perceive and see a great desire and love unto Christ in the disciples that ran, but especially in Mary Magdalene: for seeing that much was forgiven her, therefore was her love exceeding great[1]. Peter also and John, which were more fervent than others in the love of Christ, and drew nearer than others did, when the Lord was taken, although the one fled, and the other denied him; therefore unto them, as to the principal, was this opened before others. Luke vii.

Mary loved Christ very fervently; for many sins were forgiven her, many devils and vices were driven out of her: therefore unto her did Christ first appear. The cross and trouble was not able to bring Christ out of her heart, it could not quench her love unto Christ; the seed of faith was in her heart, it had taken root, although it were not yet ripe. Very earnestly and with great diligence seeketh she him whom she loveth, declaring her ferventness by her weeping, and her zeal by tarrying still at the sepulchre, when the two apostles were gone away already. The Lord therefore forsaketh her not; but instructeth her, and comforteth her by the angel, appeareth unto her unknown, at last talketh with her, and maketh himself known unto her. The number of seven for many. Mark xvi.

The angels, which are ministers for the wealth of the elect, dissuade her from weeping and mourning, and bring her tidings of great joy. For herein now is no just cause to weep, but rather to rejoice; seeing that Christ hath overcome death for us, delivering and setting us free from the

---

[1] The language here used by Bishop Coverdale implies his approval of the opinion, which has been held by many persons, that Mary Magdalene is the person of whom mention is made in that chapter, as having anointed the head and feet of our Saviour. That however they were entirely distinct persons, has been maintained by others, whose opinion is entitled to great respect. See the question stated in "A letter to Jonas Hanway, esq., in which some reasons are assigned, why houses for the reception of penitent women, who have been disorderly in their lives, ought not to be called Magdalen houses." Lardner's Works, Vol. v. pp. 459—464. Ed. 1815.]

power thereof, and placing us in eternal life. Like as the angels at the birth of Christ in this mortal life did bring tidings of joy; so do they here also, when Christ is risen again into an immortal life. And hereunto also serveth the brightness of the countenance, and whiteness of the clothes; for all such are tokens of joy.

But some man might marvel, why Christ will not suffer Mary to touch him, seeing he would afterward be touched of the other women, of the disciples, and of Thomas; yea, he provoketh Thomas and the disciples thereto.

It seemeth that Mary, with the ointment which she brought with her, thought to anoint the body of Christ, as she did afore in his life-time, and to reverence him, and to deal with him as with a mortal man; which thing Christ forbad her to do. Hereafter shall we hear, how he offereth unto his disciples his hands, feet, and side, willing them to touch him. But with this inhibition, and that commandment, he hath respect to one only thing; namely, to deliver Mary and the disciples from unbelief, from weak faith and doubting. Unto Mary he will say: "Touch me not of a carnal devotion, as though thou wouldst anoint me. I need it no more. As for such corporal service, it is not necessary to do it unto my body any more. The cause why I became man was not that ye should alway hang upon my corporal flesh, and honour me with bodily service. Thou shalt now shortly understand, that I have like power with the Father. I am in thy heart not yet ascended up unto the Father: that is, thou hast as yet no right knowledge of my Godhead; therefore canst thou not now rightly touch me."

*2 Cor. v.*

*God is a spirit, with spirit will he be worshipped.*

Thus learn we also to know and honour Christ now no more after the flesh, and to shew no corporal outward service unto his person. In spirit will he be worshipped, with the faith and love of the inward mind. If any thing bodily be done of us, the same should be done unto the poor, and to the neighbour that hath need thereof. Thus may faith and love well use some outward things, not to do service therewith unto God, but unto ourselves or to our neighbour. As when we take and minister bread and wine about in the supper, distributing and eating it, the same is not done principally to the intent to declare a service unto God; but somewhat to provoke our outward senses and flesh by the exterior signs, that we may the better consider and ponder the grace of God declared unto us in the death of Jesus Christ, and that we may lift up our minds unto Christ, the heavenly food and living bread, which inwardly feedeth us with his flesh, and nourisheth us with his blood.

Thereto also hath Christ our Saviour instituted the figurative tokens and sacraments of his grace, to help our infirmity. For sacraments are gracious evidences of the faith that men have, or should have, to God; in the which they comfortably exercise and practise themselves towards God's promises; wherein also they declare the obedience of their inward faith, and that they faithfully believe the words and promises of Almighty God. For the token without belief is nothing profitable, but rather hurtful. All bodily service that the flesh imagineth, pleaseth not God. He sitteth at the right hand of God: there ought we to touch him with the lifting up of a faithful heart, and with the worship which he through his Spirit worketh and directeth into us: for therefore he died, rose again, and ascended up into heaven, that he might fulfil all things, and reign truly and spiritually in our hearts. Our hearts must we lift up there, as Christ sitteth at the right hand of God, and our conversation ought to be in heaven. Col. iii.<br/>Phil. iii.

Whereas the Lord willed his disciples to touch him, it was done to banish their doubtfulness, and to strengthen their weak faith. Which touching was not required of them as a worship, but that their flesh through the outward handling of his body might be quieted and stilled: and so is it a proof and testimony, that he verily rose with the former body, rather than a worshipping or service. Christ did not therefore take upon him his flesh, that we should alway hang and depend thereon; but that we by his humanity should ascend up to his Godhead. For when we know the high and holy mystery of his passion and resurrection, with the which he hath served our turn, we ought to stir up our minds to know the Godhead, wherein he is like unto the Father.

Therefore unto Mary Magdalene also doth Christ speak of ascending up to the Father; which thing he commandeth to shew the apostles, as if he would say: " Now shortly beginneth mine honour, that I, as concerning the humanity received, shall be taken up to the glory which I have had from everlasting; that is, the flesh which I have taken upon me for your sakes, shall sit at the right hand of my Father."

Oh, how great a grace is this! Oh, how high is the glory that here is promised unto us in Christ! The only-begotten Son of God descended and became man for us, that we, so much as were possible for our nature, should ascend up unto his Godhead. He descended down low, that when we are humbled, he might receive and exalt us to his own promotion. He that of nature is the Lord, took upon him the shape of a servant, that of us which naturally were bond-servants, he might make us God's children.

Forasmuch then as he became man, to make us God's and children of godly grace, he took upon him that which is ours, to give us and to part with us that which is his.

<small>Psal. xxii.</small> Therefore calleth he us brethren, and maketh his own Father common unto us; so that he is also our Father and our God: that same which he hath of nature, doth he of grace give <small>Rom. viii.</small> unto us. "For his Spirit beareth record unto our spirit, that we are the children of God: for we have not received the spirit of bondage to fear, but the spirit of adoption, in the which we cry, Father, Father."

<small>John xv.</small> Christ also calleth those that be his, not servants, but friends and brethren: he will be our God, and we his people; <small>Jer. xxxi.</small> our Father, we his children: and his covenant which he hath made with us shall be everlasting: for it is sealed and confirmed with the blood of his only-begotten Son. Now have we fellowship and company with God the Father, the Son, and the Holy Ghost.

<small>The glory of the faithful is hid under the cross.</small> But such grace and glory is inwardly seen with the eyes of faith, and felt in the spirit, being hid here in time under the shape of the cross. For Christ doth not straightway by and by declare himself openly unto Mary Magdalene, as he is in his glory; but standeth there as a gardener, and speaketh unto her, by the which voice she knoweth him: he long deferreth the comfort, permitting her a good while to weep and lament, that the joy and consolation afterward may be the greater. But the cause why he so long delayeth his help and comfort from these that be his own, is, that their inward desires may be the more fervent and earnest, and that he may stir up and kindle their faith. Now when the fire

is kindled enough, then cometh he with his comfort, as it is evident here in Mary Magdalene, and in the woman of Cananee. Matthew xv.

Moreover he sendeth Mary Magdalene from him, to bring the apostles tidings of this glorious exaltation; whereas she doubtless had rather have been longer with him, and to have had the comfortable fruition of the sight of him. Howbeit he directeth her forth, to declare that felicity, and pointeth her to the work of charitable love, to the service of her neighbour. For here in time we cannot as yet come to the beholding and sight of God face to face; it shall first begin after this time. Now while we live here, we must serve our neighbour in charitable love, and do him good.

O God, strengthen thou our weak faith in the resurrection of thy beloved Son; that by it our consciences being examined may well answer: illuminate our minds, and expel out of us all darkness, through the light and brightness of the glorious resurrection: O strengthen our weakness through the power of thy Spirit. Raise us from the death of sin, in the same Rom. i. Spirit and power wherein thou hast raised up thy Son from the dead. Comfort and strengthen us in adversity, and make us constant therein; that we may press through the same in stedfast hope to the joyful and blessed resurrection. Kindle in us the fire of thy godly love, that with earnest and fervent desire we may seek and find thee through Christ. Withdraw our hearts from all earthly love of creatures, and from filthiness, up to heaven-ward, where Christ sitteth at thy right hand, that we may lead a godly and heavenly life upon earth. Set up the spiritual kingdom of Christ Jesu in our hearts, that in us thy name may be sanctified, and thy will performed; that we may become thy virtuous children, and never displease thee, our gracious Father; that we, continuing still in thy merciful covenant, do never fall away from the company and fellowship of thee and thy Son. And 1 John i. whereas thou hast given us such knowledge, grace, and understanding, grant that we may make the same known unto many, being alway ready through charitable love to serve our brethren. Amen.

It followeth now further in the history, how the women that were first with Mary Magdalene at the sepulchre, and being afraid, fled away (no man saying ought unto them), returned now more stoutly and boldly to the sepulchre, to see what would come of that wonderful terrible matter.

---

[Luke xxiv. 4—11. Matthew xxviii. 9, 10.]

WHEN the women came to the sepulchre, and found not the body of Jesu, they were sore troubled in their minds. And behold, two men stood by them in shining garments. And as the women were afraid, and bowed down their faces to the earth, they said unto them: Why seek ye the living among the dead? He is not here, he is risen. Remember how he spake unto you, when he was yet in Galilee, saying, That the Son of man must be delivered into the hands of sinful men, and be crucified, and the third day rise again. And they remembered the words of Jesu; and returned from the sepulchre, and told all these things unto those eleven, and to all the remnant. And as they went to tell his disciples, behold, Jesus met them, saying, All hail. And they came and held him by the feet, and worshipped him. Then said Jesus unto them, Be not afraid. Go tell my brethren, that they go into Galilee, and there shall they see me.

<sub>Matt. xxviii.</sub>

But when the women, namely, Mary Magdalene, and Joanna, and Mary Jacob, and other that were with them, told these things unto the apostles, their words seemed unto them feigned things, neither believed they them.

### DOCTRINE AND FRUIT.

LOVE is not idle, but diligent and zealous: which thing may well be perceived in these women, that ran again to the sepulchre, although they had found it empty afore. Gladly would they have found the body, and done reverence to their Lord whom they loved. This fervent zeal of the women confoundeth our coldness and unmercifulness towards the poor.

Ofttimes do they seek him that is absent, and that with great diligence; we receive him not, when in the poor he cometh unto us. No travail, labour, nor cost grieveth them: as for us, we pity our substance, when we should distribute to the poor, which are Christ's. O that we could rightly consider, how precious a treasure we gather unto ourselves in heaven, when we give of our goods into the hands of the poor, lending the same unto Christ! Then should not we garnish and build timber and stone, but the living temples of God, keeping them from wind and rain, and from decay; namely, that they suffer no extreme poverty, nor be destitute of help. Such a treasure had Tabitha laid up in store: for when she died, it was not stones and stocks that commended her benefits, but the bodies of the widows; they lamented her death, and declared how merciful she had been. *Acts ix.*

Christ openeth and sheweth himself unto those that earnestly seek him, and those he suffereth to touch him; to the intent that, forasmuch as they must declare his resurrection to the apostles, their weak faith must be strengthened, to know and to be assured, that he was verily risen again. For not only the angel, but Christ also himself commandeth them so to do. He comforteth them, and taketh from them the fearfulness and sorrow. Thus we ought not to doubt he shall in all adversity and trouble meet us, he shall cheerfully appear unto us, and with his joyful presence and resurrection shall he comfort and preserve us.

But we lack an earnest and strong faith; our hearts are slow and cold; diligent we be in seeking of temporal things, but godly things we either despise or neglect. Love hath no rest, she ceaseth not to run and seek, till she find him whom she loveth; and when she findeth him, she holdeth him fast, that she loose him not again: glad is she also to make others partakers of the treasure that she hath found.

O God, kindle our cold hearts with the fire of faith and love, that we may earnestly seek thee; and that when we have found thee, we may fervently receive and keep thee, and with a right spirit worship thee. Expel all hardness and ungentleness out of our hearts; make us loving and merciful unto the poor ones. Take from us the terror of all doubtfulness, unbelief, and fear of the world; and comfort us in all adversity. Grant us the faith of thy resurrection; that we, despising all transitory things, may set all our comfort and hope in the blessed resurrection to come. Amen.

Here also we learn, how exceeding weak and ignorant our flesh is to receive and believe the truth, if the Spirit of God give not light and strength. For afore the hearts of the apostles were illuminated and instructed by the Holy Ghost, they esteemed the truth of Christ's resurrection, opened unto them by the women, to be a foolish and feigned thing. Nevertheless Christ forsaketh not those whom he hath once embraced; but still openeth himself unto them more and more, to expel out of them all dubitation and unbelief.

---

[Luke xxiv. 13—24.]

*Luke xxiv.* AND behold, two of them went that same day to a town called Emaus, which was from Hierusalem about a threescore furlongs; and they talked together of all these things that had happened. And it chanced, that while they communed together and reasoned, Jesus himself drew near, and went with them: but their eyes were holden, that they should not know him. And he said unto them, What manner of communications are these, that ye have one to another, as ye walk, and are sad? And the one of them, whose name was Cleophas, answered and said unto him: Art thou only a stranger in Jerusalem, and hast not known the things which have chanced there in these days? He said unto them, What things? And they said unto him: Of Jesus of Nazareth, which was a prophet, mighty in deed and word before God and all the people; and how the high priests and our rulers delivered him to be condemned unto death, and have crucified him. But we trusted, that it had been he which should have redeemed Israel. And as touching all these things, to-day is even the third day that they were done. Yea, and certain women also of our company made us astonied, which came early to the sepulchre, and found not his body, and came, saying, That they had seen a vision of angels, which said that he was alive. And certain of them that were with us went to the sepulchre, and found it even so as the women had said; but him they saw not.

## DOCTRINE AND FRUIT.

The longer the more, is set forth unto us the unoutspeakable love and trusty faithfulness of Jesus Christ our Lord, who forsaketh not those that any thing love to talk of him. For look, whom he admitteth into his school, those he teacheth still continually, how weak so ever they be, until he bring them to perfect understanding, and expel all doubtfulness out of their hearts. Forasmuch now as these his disciples speak of him in the way, he getteth him to them, albeit he holdeth their eyes that they know him not; that by the means thereof they themselves with their own words might knowledge and confess their doubtful wavering and weakness of faith; that they might open their disease unto him, and he to give a convenient medicine for their unbelief; that through the long delay, friendly talk, and opening of the scriptures, their hearts and desires might more and more be kindled and set on fire; that their doubtfulness might be taken away, and their weak faith strengthened. For though they held Jesus for a great and principal prophet, and for an innocent good man, yet speak they uncertainly of the matter, and their heart wavereth; yet were not they assured that he had overcome death, and by his own death purchased life for all the world; that he was risen again into an immortal life, and made us undoubtedly partakers of the comfortable and joyful resurrection and eternal life in himself.

Now forasmuch as they gladly talk and willingly hold of him, how feebly and unperfectly soever it be, yet the gracious and loving Lord approacheth near unto them, and instructeth them. It shall never be unfruitful, it shall never pass without profit, but assuredly do good, where Christ is gladly and with a good heart spoken of. Where two or three be assembled in his name, there is he in the midst among them, and informeth them. That he doth to the disciples in the way by mouth, the same declareth he alway unto us inwardly by his Spirit in our hearts, and outwardly with the scripture and word, and with the teachings of good

[COVERDALE.]

godly men. He that well and faithfully useth the little talent, shall not be denied a greater, if he earnestly desire it.

Wheresoever he is earnestly and fervently thought upon and talked of, there is he present, and instructeth and teacheth the ignorant. For he is not ashamed to resort unto those that lack knowledge and be in error, and to talk with them.

This lowly and gentle condition ought we to learn of our Head, that we shame not to repair unto such as are not yet right instructed, that we may inform them, and commune with them. We should despise no man that with a single heart seeketh God; though as yet we perceive much wavering and weak faith in him. For if the eternal Wisdom was not ashamed to humble himself, and to instruct the ignorant, much more ought we to do it; seeing we are neither sufficiently instructed in the scripture, nor yet diligent and careful to do that which we know.

---

[Luke xxiv. 25—35.]

THEN said Jesus unto them: O ye fools, and slow of heart to believe all that the prophets have spoken! Ought not Christ to have suffered these things, and so to enter into his glory? And he began at Moses and all the prophets, and interpreted unto them in all scriptures which were written of him. And they drew nigh to the town that they went unto; and he made as though he would have gone further. And they constrained him, saying, Abide with us; for it draweth toward night, and the day is far passed. And he went in to tarry with them. And it came to pass, as he sat at meat with them, he took bread and blessed it, and brake, and gave to them: and their eyes were opened, and they knew him; and he vanished out of their sight. And they said between themselves: Did not our hearts burn within us, while he talked with us by the way, and opened to us the scriptures? And they rose up the same hour, and returned again to Hierusalem; and found the eleven gathered together, and them that were with them saying: The Lord is risen indeed, and hath appeared unto Simon. And they told what things were done in the way, and how they knew him in breaking of bread.

### DOCTRINE AND FRUIT.

CHRIST saith (John v.), "Search the scriptures, for they testify of me;" also, "If ye believed Moses, ye should believe me, for he hath written of me." Christ therefore, willing to strengthen the weak, and to teach the unlearned, expoundeth unto them the scriptures, beginning at Moses, and so throughout all the prophets. For whatsoever is written in the scripture concerning the mercy, goodness, and wisdom of God, the washing away of sin, and satisfying for the same, it belongeth properly to Christ. For so worthily and evidently have they described the passion and glory of Christ, that one would think them not to write of a matter which were to come, but done already; as it is plain in the Psalms and Prophets. Psalm xxii. Isaiah liii. 1 Pet. i. &c.

Thus out of the scripture we learn, partly, the testimonies of the passion and resurrection of Christ; partly, by what way Christ came to so high honour and glory of his Father; that we first believing, that Christ died for our sins, and rose again for our righteousness, might by his resurrection be sure of a good conscience, and consolation of the life to come.

Secondly, that we in patience and obedience might learn to be obedient to our heavenly Father, to take up our cross, and to follow our Lord Jesus Christ: if we will have joy with him, we must also suffer and travail with him. Our Head goeth to eternal joy through adversity and trouble; and will we enter into it through the pleasure of the world and lust of the flesh? It passeth the bounds of all humanity, and comeliness, and honesty, for the servant to be sluggish and slothful, when the master taketh upon him such travail and pain. This is the narrow gate that we must enter in at: for through many tribulations, vexations, and miseries, must we come into the everlasting kingdom of heaven; and "all they that will live godly in Christ Jesu must suffer persecution" in this world. He that will possess an inheritance, must bear and suffer all the charges belonging to the same.

The eternal inheritance is appointed us of our heavenly Father through Christ; but with this addition, that we receive the possession of it in such sort as the Son hath done, namely, with and through the cross and trouble. Blessed are they, whom God the Father maketh partakers of the passion of his only-begotten Son: for whoso is a companion with him in suffering, shall have his eternal fellowship in heaven, and enjoy with him everlasting bliss and rest. He that understandeth not this, is a "fool, and slow of heart to believe" the scriptures. Let that man beseech God to open the scriptures unto him, and to make him understand it. Where that cometh to pass, ignorance vanisheth away, and the heart is fervent, and receiveth understanding: for the Lord is the right and perfect schoolmaster, that toucheth the heart, and pierceth it through with the arrows of his words and ardent love.

In breaking of the bread, they know the Lord: for afore in his life-time, when he now would go to his passion and death, he took bread, rendered thanks, brake it, and gave it them, admonishing them, that as oft as they did the same, they should do it in remembrance of him. Whereby they now thinking on the same words, and being admonished of the act, remember that it is he. Thus the breaking of the bread before our eyes in the supper is an admonishing token, that Christ's body was broken, and died for us on the cross; and the drink an admonishing token, that his blood was shed for the washing away of our sins. And so when we break the bread, and drink the drink, we ought thereby to know the Lord; thanking him for his death, which is our life, being mindful of him, and following his great love, wherein he died for our sins.

---

[Luke xxiv. 36—43. John xx. 19, 20.]

As they thus spake, (it was very late the same day, which was the first day in the week; and where the disciples assembled together, the doors were shut for fear of the Jews,)

Jesus came, while they sat at the table, and stood in the midst among them, and said unto them: Peace be with you. But the disciples were afraid, thinking that they had seen a spirit. Then said Jesus unto them, Why are ye troubled? and why do thoughts arise in your head? And he said yet again unto them, Peace be with you. And with that shewed he them his hands, feet, and side, and said: Behold my hands and feet, that it is even I myself; handle me and see, for a spirit hath not flesh and bones, as ye see me have. The disciples were glad, when they had seen the Lord. And while as yet they believed not for joy, and wondered, he said unto them: Have ye any thing to eat? So they offered him a piece of broiled fish, and an honey-comb. The same he took, and did eat before them; casting in their teeth their unbelief and hardness of heart, because they believed not them which had seen that he was risen again from the dead.

### DOCTRINE AND FRUIT.

In that the evangelists describe the true resurrection of Christ, they declare withal, unto whom such a high mystery was opened and shewed. For when we hear how the disciples were minded and behaved themselves, we learn thereby, what becometh us, that we also may believe that Christ is truly risen again; yea, not only to acknowledge the same with the mouth, but also to prove and feel it in the taste of the spirit. So have we heard afore, what the desire and ardent love, which God stirred up in Mary Magdalene, did bring to pass, and what good came of the ferventness and diligence of Peter. This we see now here: for God hath a pleasure to stir up our desire, when he will open himself unto us. And therefore all the same day, from morning early until night, were the disciples still more and more endued with new joy, that the desire to see Christ might be kindled more and more in them. And as they were assembled in love and uniformity, (for those two things please God well,) Christ cometh and appeareth unto them. He openeth himself unto those that, longing after him, are coupled in love and uniformity, and being assembled, do hold themselves together. For where love is, there is God; where discord is and division, there is the devil.

O dear brethren, let us regard charitable love; let us care for our brethren, that the brotherhood be not broken, and that love be not spotted; for else farewell faith. No man needeth to boast himself of faith, that hath not charitable love, but stirreth up and seeketh division.

Moreover, we see here that the disciples of Christ stood in great danger of their bodies and life: for when the Jews had no more power to rage against Christ, they raged against his disciples. Look, what men are partakers of the cross and passion of Christ, they verily shall understand the high mystery of his resurrection. For undoubtedly, God with his own consolation shall visit and comfort those that suffer any danger and harm for his name's sake. Forasmuch then as the good disciples of Christ must still be in conflict and battle with the Jews, the Lord speaketh unto them with this comfortable word, "Peace be with you:" as if he should say, "Be of good cheer; your matter shall stand in good case; in me ye shall have peace, and be safe, and quiet, how hard soever it go outwardly: fear not, be not afraid; howsoever the Jews do rage, ye shall do right well." This salutation was common among the Jews; therefore doth Christ also use it. Such a charge gave he likewise unto his disciples, when he sent them to preach, that entering into an house they should say, "Peace be to this house."

*Luke x.*

And though the disciples were somewhat amazed and afraid at the first blush, yet was their gladness great, when they were throughly instructed that it was the Lord. Now was fulfilled that which Christ had said, and promised unto them afore, John xvi. "Ye shall mourn, and the world shall rejoice: but I will see you again. Your sorrow shall be turned into gladness, your heart shall rejoice, and your joy shall no man take from you." For the joy of a faithful believing heart is constant, and endureth. If the resurrection of Jesus Christ were rightly and truly believed, and the same joy comprehended as it ought to be, all sorrow must needs vanish, all hurt and adversity must needs be little regarded. For what can be grievous unto a man, when by faith and hope he is assured, that he in a glorified and immortal body shall arise again with Christ his head, and have everlasting joy with him?

And this is the cause that Christ appeareth so often unto his disciples, instructing them so much and so perfectly of his resurrection; even to make them stedfast in this faith, and to assure them of this joy. Therefore sheweth he them his body, and giveth it them to handle. The palpable body certifieth them, that it is a true body; the immortal body sheweth that it is glorified, and of highest honour; the prints of the wounds declare, that it is even the self-same body that it was afore. He sheweth them the tokens of victory, as a mighty overcomer of death; and so doth he the wounds that he had gotten for them in the battle; and likewise the side that was opened, declaring his great love. His wounds sheweth he to them, to heal the wounds of their unbelief. As if he would say: "Look upon me, and fight manfully; without a battle shall no man be crowned. But unto him that overcometh in the conflict will I grant to eat of the bread of heaven, and will crown him for ever." 2 Tim. ii. Apoc. ii.

Whereas he eateth before them, it is done for the probation of the true human nature, and not for the great necessity of the body. To them was it very needful, not unto Christ. Even so we, knowing how to further our neighbour's faith, must and ought many times to do somewhat, and to leave somewhat undone, that for ourselves we need not.

O God, grant us true love and uniformity, take from us all schism and division; gather us together through thy holy Spirit; remove all discord and variance out of thy holy church. Give us patience in adversity; send thy godly comfort and joy unto all such as be in distress and trouble for thy name's sake; strengthen the weak, lift up the feeble, establish the doubtful, and in the battle help those which be thine own; that they lie not under, but that in thee they may overcome all danger and harm. Amen.

[John xx. 24—29.]

THOMAS, one of the twelve, which was called Didymus, was not with them when Jesus came. The other disciples therefore said unto him, We have seen the Lord. But he said unto them: Except I see in his hands the print of the nails, and put my finger into the print of the nails, and thrust my hand into his side, I will not believe. And after eight days again his disciples were within, and Thomas with them. Then came Jesus, when the doors were shut, and stood in the midst, and said, Peace be unto you. And after that said he to Thomas, Bring hither thy finger, and see my hands, and reach hither thy hand, and thrust it into my side; and be not faithless, but believing. Thomas answered and said unto him: My Lord, and my God! Jesus saith unto him: Thomas, because thou hast seen me, thou hast believed: blessed are they that have not seen, and have believed.

### DOCTRINE AND FRUIT.

THAT which was spoken afore is here evident and plain, namely, that Christ openeth himself unto those, which are desirous of him, and long after him, associating themselves together one with another in true love, and being partakers of the passion and cross. Forasmuch then as Thomas is less fervent, and therefore absent from the rest, he saw not Christ with the other disciples; but when he obtained a desire to see Christ, and was associate and joined to the other, he became also partaker of the joy that they had.

And here we learn the nature and condition of true belief, (which is an illumination of the grace of God, yea, a very godly property,) that he maketh others partakers of his holy and glorious joys, and that through love, which seeketh not her own profit, neither is disdainful; to the intent that the glory of God may be preferred among all men. Therefore the disciples of the Lord make Thomas their companion partaker of such gladness, as they had received of Christ's resurrection opened unto them; for he was

very faithless, and too stiff in his own opinion. Which
unbelief God suffered to happen unto him, and to continue
somewhat the longer, that his slackness and lack of faith
might serve to our commodity; that through his unbelief
we might be provoked unto faith, forasmuch as we hear
that he, so perfectly proving, seeing, and feeling the thing,
came so to an undoubted faith; that we also might believe,
that the body of Christ, which was hanged upon the cross
for our sins, was of the Father raised again unto life. For *Acts ii.
Rom. x.*
if we believe in our heart, and confess with our mouth, that
God hath raised him up from the dead, we shall be saved.
Yea, believe we must, that Christ, according to his words *John ii.*
afore, hath through his godly power erected up again from
death the temple of his body. Therefore through the doubting of Thomas we learn the mystery of the resurrection of
our own bodies. For Christ hath sufficiently proved, and
Thomas hath confessed, that the body of Christ, which was
hanged upon the cross, is verily risen again from death.
Wherein our faith is confirmed to believe, that our bodies
also shall truly and lively rise again to eternal life.

When Thomas is with the other disciples, Christ sheweth
himself unto him. For they that in the unity of faith and
of undivided love do not associate and accompany themselves
with other faithful believers in the church, shall not be partakers of heavenly joys. Truth it is, that to believe with
the heart justifieth; but the confession that is made with the
mouth belongeth unto health, and serveth unto love and
unity of the Church and congregation of God; without the
which there can be no hope of health. He that saith he
believeth, and doth not join himself unto other Christians, his
faith is vain and of none effect. And therefore did Christ
for his church institute the sacraments, that is to say, exterior signs of his grace; that his people might be associate
together in the unity of faith. The church of God is it
that preserveth us poor ones, as did the ark of Noe aforetime in the flood, and bringeth us through this raging sea
unto the haven of eternal salvation. Not that the grace and
health is therefore to be ascribed to the elements and outward things; but that it may appear, how effectuous faith
is, and what it worketh through charitable love in the
church. Christ maketh mention of the words which Thomas

had spoken afore to the disciples in his absence; namely, "Except I see in his hands the print," &c. Therefore saith Christ, "Thomas, bring thy finger hither, and see," &c. Whereby it is evidently proved, that Christ is God: and even so doth Thomas understand and confess.

The wounds are shewed of Christ, specially to this intent, that his passion might be printed and sealed in men's minds. For a very deep and high mystery it is, that Christ's side is opened, out of the which floweth blood and water; whereby the spiritual and faithful believing minds may well perceive Christ's good loving will towards mankind. Now when we look upon his hands, touching his side inwardly with our desire of inward faith, and considering why and with what love Christ suffered for us, it shall be no hard thing unto us to believe his resurrection. If Christ were dead but even as another pure man or prophet, we could have no hope of the resurrection. Whoso believeth it, cometh soon to this knowledge, that immortal life is given unto us. Now where there is hope of an immortal life, there is the Lord served with great diligence. For if God hath not spared his own Son, but given him for us all, what good thing may we not look for at his hand? If we be only true believers with Thomas, then shall God faithfully perform that he hath promised us. Christ desireth no more of us weak feeble ones, than that we be not faithless, but stedfast believers.

Rom. viii.

Thomas is immediately obedient unto the voice of Christ, and becometh forthwith a new man. The Pharisees could by no doctrine, by no miracles, be brought to give credence unto Christ, and to believe in him, although they saw Lazarus raised again from the dead; malice and hatred did so hinder them: but Thomas acknowledgeth him freely to be his Lord and God. He seeth and handleth man; he confesseth God, whom he saw not. He acknowledged, that he whom he saw was his God and Lord. Through the same faith was his unbelief and sin forgiven him.

O merciful God, grant us love, that we seek not our own commodity nor honour, but the profit of our neighbours and thy glory in all things. Expel out of us all disdain, greediness, ungentleness, headiness, and flattering of ourselves. Preserve us from discord and division; bind us together in uniform love; that we may be one body, and of one mind.

Stablish also our faith; that our minds may be always comforted in the resurrection of thy Son, and immortal life purchased by him. Amen.

---

[John xx. 30, 31.]

AND many other signs truly did Jesus in the presence of his disciples, which are not written in this book. These are written, that ye might believe that Jesus is Christ, the Son of God; and that ye so believing might have life through his name.

### DOCTRINE AND FRUIT.

LIKE as Christ, while he yet lived, did miracles before his death, to declare his godly power; even so after his rising again from death, he worketh many tokens in the presence of his disciples, to prove his resurrection in the flesh. Some of the same are described of the evangelists, not of any curiosity, or for vain-glory, but to confirm our faith therewith. To write all, John thought it not needful; for who could have written all? or who could have fastened and borne them all in mind? Whoso will not believe these few that are written, shall never believe a greater multitude. A faithful believer is well satisfied with these. For these that be written of him are therefore written, "that we should believe that Jesus is Christ, the Son of God, and that we through his faith might have eternal life." Seeing then that all things which are written do extend and serve to this end, that we might believe in him, and be saved by him, what lack we then?. or what can we desire more? So that hereby we learn, with great diligence to read, to consider, and to apply into our own life, whatsoever the evangelists have written of Christ; as they have written nothing but that which is altogether excellent, dear, holy, and godly, and such things as do lively describe, set forth, and print Christ unto us; that our faith, hope, love, patience, meekness, and all good things might grow with blessed fruit; that we in our life might become thankful for such an excellent grace, and in no wise to contemn or despise it.

A scornful thing is it, and the evidence of a great unbelief, whereas some think by these words to prove, that forasmuch as all things are not written in the book, it is lawful for certain men to add the rest, and to devise and ordain what they will. For in these things that are written doth John comprehend the whole sum of faith; which consisteth in this, that Jesus is the Son of the living God, who for our salvation came down from heaven, died, rose again, and purchased for us eternal life. Jesus the Son of Mary is the anointed King and High Priest, the Saviour of the world promised of God, and spoken of afore by the prophets. And even he it is, who being of the heavenly Father anointed king everlasting, was to come after David, and to reign for ever. This king is the Redeemer and Saviour of mankind, and the very true Son of God. If we believe in Christ, we believe in the true God; one only God we honour, one only God we worship. Seeing now that we honour and worship Christ, we worship God; for only God is to be worshipped. Forasmuch now as we worship the Son no less than the Father, it is certain that Christ is of one nature with the Father; yea, this ought we to believe, and that he came down into this world to die for us, to wash and wipe away our sins, and to kill sin in our mortal flesh, when he maketh us partakers of his passion, and mightily worketh in us by his Spirit, in mortifying our carnal desires. We must also believe, that he by his godly power arose again from death to a new, glorious, and immortal life. For if we thought that he died, and believed not that he were risen to life again, we should have no life in him. For us he died, for our sakes he rose again, for our welfare reigneth he for ever. A new godly and blessed life worketh he in us with his resurrection, and after this life have we in him life everlasting.

---

[John xxi. 1—14.]

AFTERWARD did Jesus shew himself again at the sea of Tiberias. And on this wise shewed he himself. There were together Simon Peter and Thomas, which is called Didymus, and Nathanael of Cana in Galilee, and the sons of Zebedee, and two other of his disciples. Simon Peter saith unto them, I will go a fishing. They say unto him, We also will go with thee. They went their way, and entered into a ship immediately; and that night caught they nothing. But when the morning was now come, Jesus stood on the shore; but the disciples knew not that it was Jesus. Jesus saith unto them: Children, have ye any meat? They answered him, No. And he saith unto them: Cast out the net on the right side of the ship, and ye shall find. They cast out therefore, and anon they were not able to draw it for the multitude of fishes. Then said the disciple whom Jesus loved to Peter: It is the Lord. When Simon Peter heard that it was the Lord, he girt his coat unto him, (for he was naked,) and sprang into the sea. The other disciples came by ship; for they were not far from land, but as it were two hundred cubits; and they drew the net with fishes. As soon then as they were come to land, they saw hot coals, and fish laid thereon, and bread. Jesus saith unto them, Bring of the fish that ye now have caught. Simon Peter went up, and drew the net to the land full of great fishes, an hundred and three and fifty. And for all there were so many, yet was not the net broken. Jesus saith unto them, Come and dine. And none of the disciples durst ask him, What art thou? for they knew that it was the Lord. Jesus then came and took bread, and gave them, and fish likewise. This is now the third time that Jesus appeared to his disciples, after that he was risen again from death.

### DOCTRINE AND FRUIT.

We read in the holy evangelists, that at the first Christ called his disciples, namely Peter and the others, from fishing; which they also left, and came to Christ, who told them that he would make them fishers of men. Now, when he will send them out to that office, and depart from them, he appeareth again unto them at their fishing. And, like as he did afore at their vocation, he doth before them a great miracle; in the which he admonisheth them of their office, and chargeth them diligently to care for his sheep committed unto them. But first he proveth his resurrection, to stablish and confirm their weak faith thereby; commanding them afterward, to bring other folks also thereto.

This history in itself is evident enough: therefore ought we first to consider it after the letter; for the letter also teacheth for itself. Christ, like as he appeared unto those that were sorrowful and mourned, so doth he appear unto those that labour and travail. Christ gave his disciples authority out of the gospel, that they preach, to take a competent honest living, as food and necessaries of the body; and yet did he not restrain them, that they should not or might not labour, when occasion serveth. Therefore Paul also used not that liberty at certain times, but laboured with his own hands, and won his meat. So did the disciples of Christ exercise themselves in their labour. For when they were come into Galilee from the feast of Easter, which they had kept at Hierusalem, afore the Holy Ghost was given unto them, they would not go idle, and thereby become a burthen unto other men, (for he that goeth idle liveth upon other folks, eating that theirs is, and overchargeth them,) but undertake to get their own living with their handy-work, which they had used afore. Whereby we must learn to apply ourselves unto labour, and not to be idle; for idleness is the mother of many and great vices. Every man ought to have an honest travail, to be exercised either with the body or with the mind. Whoso laboureth not, must not eat. Man was created to labour, as the bird to fly. Therefore ought every father to bring up his children in honest exercise from their youth up, that the devil get no place in their hearts; which yet cometh to pass, if he find them idle. The first commandment given to our forefather Adam after the fall was this: "In the sweat of thy face shalt thou eat thy bread."

Now when we in true faith and confidence unto God do take in hand the work that he hath committed unto our charge, we ought not to doubt God shall prosper it, and give us his rich and gracious blessing in it; as it is written, Prov. iii. : " In all thy ways remember the Lord, and he shall direct and order thy doing." Eccles. v. ix.

Here is also to be considered, how Christ uttereth his godly power before his disciples, in the great miracle that he did in their sight, to confirm our faith in him. For out of the appearing of Christ groweth faith. Psalm lxxxv. And [Psal. lxxxvi.] his true resurrection will he print in them, in that he appeareth unto them, and eateth with them.

Here we see the ardent desire of Peter, which leapeth into the sea, as soon as he heareth that it is the Lord: he that afore had denied him, maketh now speedy haste again unto him. Though we of man's feebleness and fear, do fall into sin, yet always when we hear God in his word, we ought forthwith to turn again unto him; and so shall he with the Luke xv. lost son graciously receive and embrace us again.

In that Peter covereth himself being naked, we learn nurture and shamefacedness, to walk and dwell with all honesty in the sight of men, specially in the presence of our superiors and governors.

In the corporal works and deeds of Christ, there is nothing in vain, nothing without effect. Besides the outward appearance of the work, there is described somewhat more excellent, whereunto a faithful believer ought to direct the eyes of his mind. As when he maketh the blind to see, it is an outward act, and a declaration of his godly power, and an alteration there is outwardly in the eyes of the blind, in that his sight is restored unto him again: nevertheless over and besides the outward work there is given us to understand, that Christ is the true light of the whole world, which driveth away the blindness of our heart, and illuminateth the eyes of our mind, according to the scriptures. Esay xlii. xlix. John i. ix. xii., &c.

Christ, taking bread and wine, giveth the same to his disciples to eat and drink. This, as no man can deny, was an outward act, and they commanded outwardly to do it, albeit in the remembrance of him. Besides and above the outward eating and drinking, the faithful believer must lift up his heart, and look with the eyes of faith unto that which is spiritual; namely, how that Christ is the true living bread, which feedeth our souls to eternal life; how his body was broken for us upon the cross; how we through his death are made living, and washed away from our sins by his blood. In this is set forth unto us the highest love of all, namely, that Christ gave himself unto the death for us: whereby we are admonished of his grace, yea, not only in this described unto us, but also the Holy Ghost doth mightily and fruitfully work the same in the hearts of the true believers, which in faith at the supper receive the true body and blood of Christ; whereby their hearts are kindled in love towards God and their neighbour, so that they dwell in Christ, and he in them, &c.

So here likewise the outward fishing representeth a fishing spiritual. Like as in fishing it lieth not in the fisher's power or wit to take many or few, but it is the power and blessing of God; and as the labour of the disciples is in vain afore Christ commandeth them, but when they have his commandment, and cast out the net upon the same, they draw up a multitude of fishes: even so cometh it to pass at this present day, that we bring forth no fruit, so long as the Holy Ghost worketh not with us inwardly; but when Christ biddeth cast out the net, that is, when he giveth his Spirit, we are able to draw up many men, and to win them unto Christ. For all the night long had they taken nothing, till Christ came unto them: even so can we do nothing, if Christ be not with us by his Spirit. On Whit-sunday, when the Spirit came upon his disciples, they brought much fruit, and drew many men unto Christ.

<small>Acts ii.</small>

Hereby declareth Christ unto them in this taking of fish, how it should go in their office, and how the time was now at hand, that they should shortly draw many men out of the sea of this world unto him, and that they should prosper and have good success therein. The world is this wild raging sea; the shore is the quietness of eternal life that we have in Christ, unto whom we make haste with Peter and the other disciples; neither do we bring men unto ourselves, but unto Christ, and to the haven of everlasting life. Faith is not idle, but is always occupied in the Lord's business, causing us to contemn all perils, and to speed us apace unto Christ with the clothing of virtues, especially with faith, the wedding-garment; that we appearing not naked, may make haste unto the land of the living, where Christ is, the conqueror of death;

for the faithful believers are not far from the land, when their conversation is in heaven. Without Christ we must begin nothing, without faith may no man please God. In *Heb. xi.* the night of sin our labour is vain and unprofitable; yea, "whatsoever is not of faith is sin." Upon the right hand must *Rom. xiv.* the net be cast out; that is, in the office of preaching must respect be had to the only glory of God, and edifying of the *1 Cor. xiv.* church, and not to our own profit or preferment.

Christ hungereth after our health: this is the meat which he desireth, that we do the will of his heavenly Father, that *John iv. vi.* we put our trust in him and love one another, that we lead a just and innocent life, that we keep ourselves from the filthiness of the world, and bring much people unto God. Such meat is brought unto Christ by the apostles, when they through their teaching do catch men, and bring them unto God. Therefore doth he ask them, whether they have anything to eat. They said, Nay: for afore the receiving of the Spirit they could do nothing; but when he came, they brought many profitable things to pass. The harvest was so great, that they must needs have many workmen.

So when God helpeth the faithful ministers of the word, that they in the ministry of preaching have prosperous success, so that they draw up many men through the net of the gospel, and find much fruit; then the disciples whom Christ loveth, and which love him again, do know that it is the Lord, and that the same cometh not of their own virtue, but of the power of God. And hereof then groweth there in them a great desire to come unto Christ, and to be with him. The office therefore of apostles and of all ministers of the word is this, that when they do what Christ commandeth them, they turn them to Christ again, and ascribe the honour unto him. And if aught would let or hinder them to come unto Christ, they ought to refuse all the same, and to haste unto him with the loss of their life. John knoweth Christ afore Peter; but Peter cometh to the Lord before him: whereby we may note the diversity of ministrations and gifts in the church. Though Peter be more fervent, yet is he not ashamed to learn of John.

The fishers come with the fish unto Christ, the shepherds with the sheep to one manner of salvation. For they are not careful only for themselves, how they may be saved; but

[COVERDALE.]

also for those whom they have caught, to bring the same with them unto the shore of eternal rest. It is our salvation, when we become Christ's meat, yea, when Christ is our food and sustenance. For they that in the sea of this world do faithfully labour to draw the fish unto the haven, shall obtain great fruit, and enjoy an eternal banquet at Christ's table in his kingdom. For Christ prepared them a dinner, wherein he set forth unto the ministers of the word, what they ought to do, namely, to feed the people committed unto them. A great honour is it, to bring much people unto Christ. Great commendation and unspeakable joy shall those teachers have, that faithfully travail in scriptures and word of God.

By the multitude and great number of the fishes that the apostles drew into the net, is figured the multitude of the heathen, who through the preaching in the whole world should be brought into the unity of the faith. And although many schisms and erroneous divisions arise, yet of those that are ordained unto life there shall no man fall out of the net. God "knoweth those that be his;" and they shall alway hearken unto the voice of their Shepherd. Thus shall there ever be one only church, which cannot by us be throughly purged: evermore will hypocrites do all their diligence to continue therein, though the makers of division shall not be without great travail and labour. As for such vices as be manifest, great, and offensive, they that be in authority are bound to suppress them, according unto the ordinance of Christ. Matt. v. xiii. xviii.

First, they that be faithful believers, and ordained unto life, do cleave unto Christ their head, and then to the members, that is to say, all faithful Christians. For they that are faithful believers, be knit together in perpetual unity. And although some at this present day be in contention, yet so far as they are of the number of the elect, they will agree together again one with another, afore they depart hence; that they may die in the unity of God's congregation and church, without the which there is no health.

After the great labour that the ministers of the word have in the raging sea, Christ rewardeth his with a very costly and glorious feast in his kingdom: there will he be the bread of life, that feedeth and satisfieth them for ever.

O merciful God, grant unto us all, that we may faithfully

cleave unto thee, and follow thy commandment. Tame thou our body and members in honest labour, that we loiter not in vices. O draw our hearts alway upward; that, all temporal things set apart, we may haste only unto thee. O gracious Father, give us such faithful fishers, as being true and careful in their office, may with the net of thy holy word draw us out of the raging sea; that we with them, and they with us, may enjoy the everlasting banquet. Amen.

[John xxi. 15—17.]

So when they had dined, Jesus saith to Simon Peter, Simon Joanna, lovest thou me more than these? He saith unto him, Yea, Lord; thou knowest that I love thee. He saith unto him, Feed my lambs. He saith unto him again the second time, Simon Joanna, lovest thou me? He saith unto him, Yea, Lord; thou knowest that I love thee. He saith unto him, Feed my sheep. He saith unto him the third time, Simon Joanna, lovest thou me? Peter was sorry, because he said unto him the third time, Lovest thou me? And he said unto him, Lord, thou knowest all things; thou knowest that I love thee. Jesus saith unto him, Feed my sheep.

### DOCTRINE AND FRUIT.

FORASMUCH as Peter had taken a special grievous fall, Christ lifteth him up with a special comfort; but so, that he setteth forth unto all shepherds of his sheep, what their office is. Peter had many sins forgiven him; therefore was it Luke vii. meet that he should love the Lord the more. And seeing he had thrice denied, he maketh now a three-fold confession; so that now the tongue doth no less service unto love, than it served fear afore. Christ sheweth him, that he is received again unto grace; so that he may safely put his trust in him, seeing he committeth unto him his own sheep. As if Christ would say: "As for thy denial, I will no more remember it. And for an evidence hereof, I put thee in trust to keep my sheep. In no wise do I refuse thee; but a shepherd of my sheep will I make thee." Neither doth he cast him, in the teeth with his denial, but saith: "If thou love me, then take upon thee the care of the brethren. The love that thou hast willed to declare unto me in all things, and wherein I delight, the same declare thou now unto my sheep, whom I so dearly have bought. Thy life that thou wouldest have offered for me, give now for my sheep[1]." Now, to the intent that Peter should not say he were expelled from the apostleship through his denial, the Lord therefore giveth him a new commission to keep his sheep. As for Peter, he was no more so rash and foolish-hardy; but answereth more advisedly than afore, and taketh the Lord to witness. For he remembereth, how it had happened unto him already: therefore standeth he not arrogantly in his own conceit, neither speaketh he against the Lord; so witty and circumspect is he become through the fall.

Arrogant had he been, and high-minded; and therefore through the denial he fell very sore. But his weeping, through faith and sure confidence, purifieth him again; and in love he becometh more fervent, pondering that much is forgiven him; so that where sin was great, grace is more abundant and plentiful. Rom. v.

In Peter is the office of the other apostles, and of all preachers of the word, described: for here may we see, who are meet to be called to guide the people, and what care and diligence they ought to take for them.

But here principally we must note this, that Christ, minding to stablish his special excellent doctrine, did ever first work a notable token and miracle. As when he fed the five thousand men with few loaves, he taught immediately upon the same, how we must be sustained with the bread of heaven; even so here, when the disciples had taken a great

John vi.

[1 The author appears to have had the following passage of Chrysostom in view: Καὶ τί δήποτε τοὺς ἄλλους παραδραμὼν τούτῳ περὶ τούτων διαλέγεται; ἔκκριτος ἦν τῶν ἀποστόλων .... ἅμα δὲ καὶ δεικνὺς αὐτῷ, ὅτι χρὴ θαρρεῖν λοιπόν, ὡς τῆς ἀρνησέως ἐξεληλαμένης, ἐγχειρίζεται τὴν προστασίαν τῶν ἀδελφῶν, καὶ τὴν μὲν ἄρνησιν οὐ προφέρει, οὐδὲ ὀνειδίζει τὸ γεγονός· λέγει δὲ, ὅτι, εἰ φιλεῖς με, προΐστασο τῶν ἀδελφῶν, καὶ τὴν θερμὴν ἀγάπην, ἣν διὰ πάντων ἐπεδείκνυσο, καὶ ἐφ᾽ ᾗ ἠγαλλιάσω, νῦν δεῖξον, καὶ τὴν ψυχὴν, ἣν ἔλεγες θήσειν ὑπὲρ ἐμοῦ, ταύτην ὑπὲρ τῶν προβάτων ἐπιδὸς τῶν ἐμῶν. Chrysostom. in Evang. Joann. cap. xxi. Homil. lxxxvi. p. 566. Vol. II. in Nov. Test. Ed. Paris. 1636.]

heap of fishes at Christ's commandment, and were afterward fed of him, he told them immediately upon the same, what their office is, and that they should look even so to nourish and feed those that are committed unto them. This was spoken unto Peter, and in him to all others.

Christ, who searcheth and knoweth all hearts, doth not ask this question as one ignorant, or as one that first would prove and learn; but to teach faith, and to declare it unto others. Such a question demandeth he, Matt. xvi.: "Whom say the people that the Son of man is?"—shewing thereby, what confession and faith he requireth of those that are his. Even so here the schoolmaster of the whole world, minding to put them in trust, will declare unto them with this question, how they ought to be, and the same will he print sure into them with this threefold interrogation. Here also will the Lord teach, how necessary it is, that he who is to be made a shepherd and teacher of christian people be first well known, proved, and tried, and that in many things aforehand he be found faithful. It is not requisite to take children unto such an office, but such godly and apt men as have been tried and tempted; namely, such men as have proved, suffered, and felt somewhat by experience, whereby they have learned humility and nurture.

The first thing that Christ in his examination requireth of those which must guide the people, is a great, fervent, and a notable love to God. Without this love shall soul-shepherds do no good. This love to God shall bring with it love towards the sheep committed unto them. Forasmuch then as at this day the love of Christ is so greatly quenched, therefore are many curates and soul-shepherds so faint and cold to preach and teach Christ. They burn not in the love of God against vice, they print not virtue and godliness fervently into the people; for there is no love of God's name in them. Seeing then that they have no heavenly zeal unto the glory of God, and to the amplifying of his name, it is no marvel, that their preaching is so cold and unfruitful. Therefore saith our Saviour Christ unto Peter, *Agapas me* (ἀγαπᾷς με)? *Lovest thou me?* For *agapao* (ἀγαπάω) among the Greeks signifieth *fervently, earnestly, and right heartily to love;* yea, to love with a great good will; and this word he useth in the two first questions. In the third question he saith, *Phileis me*, (φιλεῖς με)? *Lovest thou me?* *Phileo* (φιλέω) signifieth so to love, that one be loving to another, and shew him friendship. Therefore doth Peter take the Lord himself to witness. As for the high excellent love, he dare not brag of it, but saith, *Philo se* (φιλῶ σε).: which is as much to say, as: "I have hitherto done all that becometh a friend to do. If any derogation or hindrance be done to thy honour and name, I am heartily sorry; as a friend is justly grieved, if his friend be vilely entreated."

Thus the Lord with the three questions layeth hard unto Peter; for a notable love is it that he requireth of those to whom he committeth his sheep in his absence. Peter had a good conscience, and knew no falsehood or deceit by himself; but bare a fervent and notable love unto Christ. Yet by reason of his former fall, and this oft questioning, he was partly out of quiet, fearing lest peradventure there lay yet hid in him some secret thing, that displeased the Lord, or were against him, or that happily he should not stand in such favour with Christ. Therefore said he: "Lord, thou knowest all things, thou knowest the hearts of all men, and wottest that I bear thee a good heart and friendly mind:" which words proceed of a meek fervent heart. Christ knoweth better how we love him, than we ourselves. Thus a shepherd ought to have an ardent love unto Christ, and yet not to stand high in his own conceit, or to brag of himself, although he love, and be garnished with virtues more than other men.

Wherein may it be perceived, that a soul-shepherd loveth Christ, and is his friend? Verily, in loving his sheep, which Christ hath committed to him. Therefore saith Christ alway upon the same: "Feed my sheep." But Christ useth here two distinct words. First, he saith, *Vosce* (βόσκε), that is, feed them, pasture them, fodder them. Secondly, he saith, *Poimene* (ποίμαινε), that is, be thou unto them a herdman, take thou care for them, as it beseemeth a shepherd; be thou a shepherd unto my sheep, keep them from the wolf, and from all such hurt. First, he requireth of him a fervent love; then committeth he his sheep unto him, a treasure great and dear, redeemed and bought with the precious blood of Christ. As if he would say: "If thou love me, declare the same in care and love toward my sheep, whom I commit to thy charge."

The sheep are Christ's, not the shepherd's. As for such shepherds as keep them so, that they make them hang upon themselves, those love themselves, not Christ. They that seek their own glory, profit, and lucre among them, are not faithful shepherds. Against such doth cry the threefold voice of Christ: "Feed and keep my sheep:" "mine," saith he, "not thine. Feed them, oppress them not, slay them not. Feed them, not thyself; seek my glory, not thine own." For some there be which, as Paul with weeping tears com- *Phil. iii.* plaineth, seek themselves, not the glory of Jesus Christ. Of these spake Paul also afore, 2 Tim. iii. "Men shall be lovers of themselves, covetous," &c. Where the wicked root of self-love is in a curate, there follow all the vices which he in the same place maketh mention of. Whoso now will be a lover of Christ, and a faithful shepherd of his sheep, let him not love himself. This vice, self-love, must Philautia: be abhorred of those that are to be made overseers of the $(\phi\iota\lambda\alpha\upsilon\tau\acute{\iota}\alpha.)$ people. For so fervent and great love ought a soul-shepherd have to Christ and his sheep, that he be ready to die and jeopard his life for the glory of Christ and profit of the people; and that through such fervent love all natural and carnal fear may be driven out of him.

Behold, how worthy and high an office the ministers of the word are put in; how great love, what care, what diligence, what earnestness, what labour and travail they must have, to whom so precious a treasure, and so dearly beloved of Christ, is committed. He maketh not of Peter and his Luke xxii. apostles princes, kings, emperors, but committeth and giveth them a ministration, yea, the most honourable ministry: he commandeth them to become faithful shepherds, willing them to love the people, and to pasture them with the fodder of God's word. He committeth to their charge the sheep, whom as he himself, the true Shepherd, hath with his own death delivered from the pit of hell, so have they a desire to hear their Shepherd's voice. He speaketh not to them John x. of the milk or wool, (which the thankful sheep yet give unto their shepherds,) that they should not have respect to their own lucre; but only with what faithfulness they ought to feed the sheep.

"Feed them," saith he, "kill them not, murder them not; be a shepherd, not a wolf; build, break not down. Peter, if thou love me and art my friend, then put I thee in trust with my best beloved treasure, even mine own sheep, whom I so dearly have purchased. If thou wilt shew me now a friendly part, then take the charge of them, and watch them faithfully. I shall now corporally depart from you; therefore canst thou from henceforth serve me no more in the flesh; but do thou service to my sheep, which hear my voice. If thou faithfully keep them, and take diligent care for them, then shalt thou declare, that thou art my friend, and lovest me; and herein shalt thou do me chiefest service of all."

O gracious Father, grant us to have a fervent love unto thee and thine; but specially provide us with such good faithful soul-shepherds, as earnestly loving thy sheep, and caring unfeignedly for them, may both truly feed them, and valiantly withstand the wolves and all false doctrine. Give grace to those rulers, and unto all such, as by virtue of thy commission do call, choose, and appoint ministers of the word; lest they, being blinded by affection, favour, disfavour, love, hatred, bribes, and such like, prefer unworthy and unmeet men; but to pick out such as be apt, virtuous, godly, and well expert, and that seek thy glory and edifying of thy people. O grant unto all high governors and magistrates, that whereas the goods of monasteries have heretofore served the wicked lusts of unprofitable priests and vain religious, they may, after their decease, be converted by the said rulers into good and godly uses; as provision for the poor, for widows and fatherless children, for bringing up of youth in the scriptures of God, and in honest necessary sciences, that they may be fruitful and comfortable to the whole christian congregation. If this might come to pass, then should there be no lack of wise councillors and active men, profitable to be in common authority; and also amongst christian people there should be found men meet to be made overseers in the ministry of God's word, with which men the people should be well and worthily provided for.

Good virtuous teachers bring forth a virtuous and godly people. And doubtless, the meaning of those that gave such goods to monasteries and churches was at the first that they thought thereby to serve God, and to do good unto the poor. If such goods then, as heretofore have been evil bestowed, be now profitably and blessedly turned to the honour of God and commodity of the whole church, then is the last will and meaning of the founders fulfilled. They also that must pay such rents, tithes, and goods, will be the readier so to do, if they see that the same is well and profitably bestowed. Then shall not they untruly, but faithfully perform and pay all things, when they consider that they do service unto God himself.

Grant us all, O God, to hearken and be obedient unto the voice of true shepherds; and give us hearts to have in great honour, and worthily esteem of such faithful shepherds, as upon earth are thy ministers and stewards, by whom and in whom thou speakest to us and with us: that we, shewing unto them all reverence and honour which they be worthy of for thy sake, may give them honest livings, and consider, how that Christ thy Son our Lord teacheth the same, Matt. x. and Paul thy servant, 1 Cor. ix. Reason it is, seeing they sow spiritual things unto us, that they of us reap things corporal. O Lord, remove away the contempt of thy word and ministers; for the same never escaped without great punishment and harm.

---

[John xxi. 18, 19.]

Jesus said unto Peter: Verily, verily, I say unto thee, when thou wast young, thou girdedst thyself, and wentest whither thou wouldest: but when thou art old, thou shalt stretch out thine hand, and another shall gird thee, and lead thee thither as thou wouldest not. This he said, signifying with what death he should glorify God. And when he had spoken this, he said, Follow me.

### DOCTRINE AND FRUIT.

It is not sufficient to have begun, except the soul-shepherd continue in his office and faithfulness. For to take the cure and charge of the sheep bringeth great danger, loss, travail, and labour with it. Many a time must a faithful shepherd jeopard his life for his sheep. Such peril doth Christ promise unto Peter, namely, that he must die, and with what death. Aforetime, when he was young, he sought that which pertained to the flesh; he might not away with the cross: but now after the receiving of the Holy Ghost, he is stout, and dieth for Christ's sake, and for his sheep. Behold, such an end had Peter, that of love he dieth for him, with whom to die he rashly promised afore[1]. But necessary it was, that Christ should first die for Peter's health, and that Peter afterwards should suffer death for his name's sake.

The presumption and headiness of man would have set the cart before the horse; but the everlasting truth hath appointed this order. Peter thought he would have jeoparded his life for Christ, and have redeemed the Redeemer: but Christ came to give his life for his sheep, of whom Peter was one. Now after that Christ died for those that be his, there is strength given in the hearts of such shepherds and sheep as be faithful, to suffer death for Christ's sake. Death is not now so to be feared of us, that we would therefore go back from the truth; for by death do not we lose life, yea, Christ hath made death to be the way unto life; and by his resurrection he hath set forth unto us an example of another life, which is immortal. Peter was first afraid, and feared death; and would have dissuaded Christ that he should not die. But now that the precious treasure of Christ's blood is shed, he followeth his Redeemer, yea, even unto the death of the cross goeth he after him; therefore is he now no more a Satan, but a Peter.

*Matt. xvi.*

*Petrus of the rock.*

But from whence cometh such strength into a feeble man? Even from God, who dwelleth in the hearts of the faithful: for else is the nature and flesh of man impotent and weak, being afraid of death; which fear, natural heat being abated, is the greater in them that are old. And though we all wish to be with Christ, and be desirous of eternal life, yet would we fain have it without any grief of death, if it might be. Thus came the conflict of death even upon Christ, whereby he declared himself very man; but the will of God

[[1] Eusebius, Hist. Eccles. Lib. II. cap. xxv. p. 83. Ed. Reading, 1720; also Caii Fragm. apud Routh. Rel. Sacr. Vol. I. pp. 168. 179—80.]

had the mastery above man's in the wrestling. Peter also went not with his will to death; but with his will he both suffered it, and overcame it. Christ likewise, to comfort us, was heavy: who nevertheless came upon earth, that he would die; neither was it necessity that moved him to die, but his own good-will and love: for he had power to give his soul, and take it again. John x.

Now though the fear of death be great in nature, yet is it overcome through the strength and greatness of the love 2 Cor. v. which we bear unto him who is our life, even Jesus Christ. And albeit he was the life itself, yet pleased it him to suffer death for us. Seeing then that he alone died for us, we ought not to be ashamed; neither should it grieve us to die also for him, specially considering that the publishing of so excellent grace is committed unto us. When the shepherd dieth for the sheep, it is no great matter if the sheep die for the shepherd's sake. Forasmuch now as the faithful shepherd with his love directeth and encourageth many of the sheep to die for his name's sake; how much more meet is it, that the shepherds be the first which jeopard their lives, striving for the truth, and even unto blood to resist sin, when Christ hath put them in trust to feed his sheep? This is now the occasion, why our Saviour Christ telleth Peter of his death aforehand, and strengtheneth and encourageth him thereunto: for though the will be constant in the saints, yet is the flesh feeble and weak. No man dieth without pain and grief: which thing is appointed unto us by the wisdom of God, to the intent no man should kill himself. For seeing the devil doth now and then persuade some to murder themselves, how should it go, if the soul were not so loth to depart from the body? With these words therefore thought not Christ to make Peter afraid, or to discourage him, but to furnish him and make him ripe. For Peter had a good desire to suffer somewhat for Christ's sake: nevertheless, being yet young, he could not follow. But when he was old, he followed him: therefore will Christ perform his desire. As if Christ would say: "Peter, thou hast hitherto been weak and fearful; but I will strengthen thee: so that henceforth thou shalt deny me no more, but manfully die for me. Thou hast been tender, in that thou wast afraid at one woman's voice: but now shalt thou stretch forth thy hand to Rom. vii. Matt. xxvi.

the cross to be bound." For by the stretching out of the hands, he understandeth and signifieth with what death he should die, namely, upon the cross. Which death aforetime was most shameful: but after that Christ was hanged upon the cross, it is now an honourable and glorious death, with the which the faithful do glorify God; and therefore saith the evangelist, that the Lord would thereby signify, "with what death Peter should glorify God."

For in God's quarrel and for Christ's sake to die is the highest honour, whereof no man ought to be ashamed. This ought all soul-shepherds to ponder and consider, that they, faithfully and constantly following Christ the Lord, go not from that they have taken in hand, but proceed and bring their course to an honourable end, keeping fidelity and trust with their Lord, and being fully appointed in themselves to die for the sheep of Christ. Therefore should they consider aforehand, what things they must suffer for the truth; lest they destroy that, which they have of long time builded and taught.

2 Tim. iv.

O gracious Father, strengthen thou us in thy work and in thy truth; that in the thing which thou hast begun in us, we may stedfastly continue to the end. Expel out of us the fear of death, and stablish us through thy holy Spirit, that we manfully may despise and jeopard this life for the life eternal. Grant, O God, to the shepherds of thy sheep a fervent love to the truth and thy glory. Strengthen them with thy Spirit, that they valiantly standing by the flock, may even with their death confirm thy people in the truth.

[John xxi. 20—25.]

PETER turned about, and saw the disciple whom Jesus loved following; which also leaned on his breast at supper, and said, Lord, who is he that betrayeth thee? When Peter therefore saw him, he said to Jesus: Lord, what shall he here do? Jesus saith unto him: If I will have him to tarry till I come, what is that to thee? Follow thou me. Then went this saying abroad among the brethren, that that disciple should not die. Yet Jesus said not to him, he shall not die; but, If I will that he tarry till I come, what is that to thee? The same disciple is he, which testifieth of these things, and wrote these things, and we know that his testimony is true. There are also many other things that Jesus did, which if they should be written every one, I suppose the world could not contain the books that should be written.

### DOCTRINE AND FRUIT.

The former words which Christ spake unto Peter, "Follow me," were spoken unto him in this meaning; that he should follow the footsteps and passion of Christ, namely, with word and deed to go the way that Christ had gone. But inasmuch as Peter is a figure of the church, Christ spake those words not only unto him, but unto all faithful believers. For the church of Christ, while she dwelleth here temporally in many troubles and afflictions, she followeth Christ her spouse and head, who also delivereth her from all adversity. She loveth Christ, and in the behalf of his truth she striveth until the death; for seeing Christ died for all, it is meet that they which are his do follow his footsteps. To follow Christ is nothing else than stoutly to suffer and overcome despite and poverty in the world for his sake. And God truly, even in his wrath, which we with our sins deserve, cannot forget his mercy. Over and besides the manifold comfort and help which he otherwise declareth unto us, he hath given us his own Son to be our Mediator; by whom, if we put our trust in him, we should be saved and delivered from eternal death; that we living from henceforth still in faith, hope, and charitable love, as pilgrims in this world, and being in all troubles and adversities preserved by the corporal and spiritual comfort of God, might walk innocently before his sight in him who is become our way unto God. It is no vile thing to suffer and to be put to death for Christ and his truth's sake; yea, a man cannot die a more honourable death, than when for the truth innocently he suffereth with a good conscience and with an upright mind. No man ought indeed to put himself in danger arrogantly, wilfully, or for vainglory.

Whereas Peter asketh a question concerning the disciple whom the Lord loved, what he should do, it is a niceness and unprofitable curiosity, that serveth nothing to edification; and therefore it pleaseth not the Lord. Whatsoever edifieth not, that ought not we to desire of Christ. ' Let every man look to himself, waiting upon his own business and office, and not to be curious in another man's matter. Whatsoever is not committed unto his charge, and belong not unto him, let him not meddle withal. Peter loved Christ: so did he John[1] also: therefore asked he what should become of him, and whether he should remain still, or die; for he was very loth and unwilling to depart from him. And so he passed more upon John, than upon the precept and commission of Jesus Christ. Such curious back-looking doth the Lord rebuke.

We many and sundry times do regard and esteem more the thing that we love, than that which God commandeth and biddeth us. But such love is very hurtful, and especially in those that should be soul-shepherds. Christ's will is, that they have respect to his work and commandment, and with a fervent love to perform the same, not meddling with other business not needful.

To inquire curiously of other men's matters bringeth not alway profit, but much rather unquietness. Therefore Christ, removing Peter from such curious questions, draweth his mind unto a better thing, namely, to follow him. As for that which he desireth to know, Christ telleth him, that it is no point of his charge; as if Christ would say: "What hast thou to do with other folks' business? Thou hast heard what I have commanded thee; look that thou faithfully do the same. What inquirest thou after other men's matters?"

Thus looking diligently and faithfully to our own charge, and expelling the affection of the flesh, we should neither desire curiously to ask any thing beyond the will of God, neither to look upon any other men; but uprightly to follow the Lord.

Here also we learn, that in the commission and final departure of the faithful there be manifold differences. Some rest in the Lord blessedly, without any special heavy affliction; but some it pleaseth God to bring through sore travail and exceeding trouble, laying the greater burden upon him;

[1] Ed. 1593, them.

according as it was told Peter aforehand, that he should be crucified, but not John.

They now that are admitted to feed Christ his sheep, prepare themselves, and be always ready, without any curiosity to follow the will of God.

Whereas John, in the conclusion of his book, refuteth the erroneous opinion of some, it is an evidence of his meekness and sincerity. It was not so spoken of the Lord, saith he, that the same disciple should not die: whereby John confessed, that he himself also was mortal. His writing will he have credited; for he hath written nothing save only the truth, whereof he may well testify that which he hath seen; yet saith, he hath not written all, but only that whereby we may obtain eternal life; as we have heard sufficiently afore.

[Matthew xxviii. 16, 17. Luke xxiv. 44—49.]

THE eleven disciples went away into Galilee, into a mountain where as Jesus had appointed them. And when they saw him, they worshipped him; but some doubted. And Jesus said: These are the words which I spake unto you, while I was yet with you, that all must needs be fulfilled, which were written of me in the law of Moses, and in the prophets, and in the psalms. Then opened he their wits, that they might understand the scriptures, and said unto them: Thus it is written, and thus it behoved Christ to suffer, and to rise again from death the third day; and that repentance and remission of sin should be preached in his name among all nations, and must begin at Jerusalem. And ye are witnesses of these things. And behold, I will send the promise of my Father upon you. But tarry ye in the city of Hierusalem, till ye be endued with power from on high.

*Matt. xxviii.*

## DOCTRINE AND FRUIT.

The Lord, minding to make his disciples assured of his resurrection, instructeth them first well in his passion, which he declareth out of the scripture, and printeth it in their hearts. He teacheth them, that it was necessary that Christ should suffer and die, yea, even thus to die, namely, upon a cross, upon a tree. On the tree was the transgression committed, upon the tree behoved it the restitution to be made; upon the tree was death fetched, upon the tree was life given; upon the tree must satisfaction be made for the lusts of the flesh, which on the tree were first conceived. And would God that we rightly knew the passion and cross of our Lord Jesus Christ! Then should the glory of the resurrection be well known and loved of us.

O Jesu, grant us grace right to consider, what, wherefore, and with what love and ferventness, thou hast suffered for us. Then shall our heart feel and profitably enjoy the sweet fruit of thy resurrection; then shall our life become new and of another sort, if we take upon us true penance, being sorry for our sins, converting us unto thee, amending and changing our conversation, which with the gracious forgiveness of our sins is declared and promised unto us in the gospel, according to thy commandment.

<small>Isai. ii.<br>Psal. cx.<br><br>John iii.</small>

O what a joyful message is this, that such great grace should out of Sion be shewed unto us, which come of the heathen! From this grace is no man shut out: it is common unto every man, unless the unthankful exclude himself; as do they that love darkness more than the light, and they that disdainfully inclose thy grace, and hedge in thy church, which thou, by the preaching of repentance and forgiveness of sins, hast commanded to be gathered unto thyself in the whole world, not only at Hierusalem, but also in Samaria and Galilee, even unto the end of the world. O God, suffer us not to be subject unto vain-glory and headiness; remove all contention and strife out of thy holy church. Preserve us from schisms and all dissensions; knit us together in uniform love, which is an undoubted token of thy children.

It behoved Jesus Christ to suffer, not for himself, but for our sakes, to become the sacrifice for our sins; that he, so satisfying the justice of God, might make amends for our trespass, and deliver us from death. It behoved him also to rise again, that he by his power might raise us up from the death of sin to a new life, and by his own resurrection to make us assured of ours, and of immortal life.

---

[Matt. xxviii. 18—20. Mark xvi. 15—18. John xx. 21—23.]

Jesus came to his disciples, and said unto them: To me *Matt. xxviii.* is given all power in heaven and in earth. As my Father *John xx.* hath sent me, so send I you. And when he had thus spoken, he breathed upon them, and said, Receive ye the Holy Ghost. Whose sins ye forgive, they are forgiven; and whose sins ye retain, they are retained. Go therefore, and teach all people, *Matt. xxviii.* baptizing them in the name of the Father, and of the Son, and of the Holy Ghost, teaching them to observe all things whatsoever I have commanded you. And, behold, I am with you every day until the end of the world. Go ye therefore into the whole world, and preach the gospel unto all creatures. Whoso believeth and is baptized, shall be saved; but *Mark xvi.* he that will not believe shall be condemned. The tokens which shall follow those that believe are these: In my name they shall cast out devils; they shall speak with new tongues; they shall take away serpents; and if they drink any venomous thing, it shall not hurt them; they shall lay hands upon the sick, and they shall be whole.

### DOCTRINE AND FRUIT.

When Jesus with many evidences had certified his disciples of his resurrection, he sheweth them now, to what excellent glory and how high power his heavenly Father had brought him, whereby their hearts might be established; and how that all things are justly subdued unto him, who through the cross hath overcome, gotten a glorious victory, and suppressed the prince of this world. And though some

[COVERDALE.]

now declare themselves contrary to his kingdom, and are not obedient unto his power, but persecute and kill him in his members, saying, "We will not have him to reign over us," resisting and gathering themselves together against God and his anointed King; how mighty soever they be, yet shall he bruise them with an iron rod, and as an earthen vessel all-to break them; yea, they must become his footstool, and he shall reign for ever.

*Luke xix.*

*Psal ii.*

*Psal. cx.*

As if he would say: "In most perfect humility, in highest patience, and being in greatest contumely, I have hitherto served you and all mankind; but now is the time come, that my Father will glorify me, and bring me to high honour, which I had afore the world was made, that in my name all knees should bow; for I am set above all power and dominion, having all things in my hand. From henceforth shall I be worshipped and honoured of the angels in heaven, and of all men upon earth. And forasmuch as I have received a whole power over all flesh, I send you, not only unto the Jews as afore, but unto all nations in the whole world; for in myself have I sanctified the whole nature of man. Look therefore, that ye declare this joyful and gracious message unto all men, and plant them in with baptism unto the Father, to the Son, and to the Holy Ghost. And those whom ye baptize, see that ye teach to observe and keep all that ye have received of me. Ye must also be stout, and not faint-hearted. Many afflictions, much evil-will, great persecution, shall happen unto you: but consider how mighty a Lord ye have, unto whom is given all power in heaven and earth; he is able enough to defend and save you from all enemies. And albeit that I go now from you, as touching corporal habitation, yet will I be still remaining with you with my power, grace, working, and protection, until the end of the world. Wherefore go your way, set your whole delight in me, keep yourselves unto me alone; so can ye not miscarry."

*John xvii. Phil. ii.*

*Matt. x.*

O how excellent and great consolation is this unto all faithful and believing hearts! O how mighty a strength is it in all adversity and dangers of this world, to hear and consider, that all power in heaven and earth is given unto Christ our Lord and King, under whose protection and wings we are safe and well preserved! And who cannot understand, that this promise reacheth not only unto the twelve disciples, unto whom it was then made, but unto all faithful believers, which through their doctrine are come unto Christ? For those twelve did not continue in this life until the end of the world; and yet he saith: "I will be with you until the end of the world." Wherefore we may well perceive, that Christ, until the end of the world, will be with all the faithful believers; that is to say, with his holy church, to instruct, teach, strengthen, comfort, defend, and deliver it against all malicious violence of this world. In his hand they are safe and well kept; and no man is able to pluck them out of his hand. Although the world rage, and the devil, the prince of the world, set all his power, great as it is, against the church of Christ; yet are not the gates of hell able to do anything against it; for it is founded and strongly builded upon Christ the rock; and he that is with it unto the end of the world is mightier than all enemies. John xvii. John x. Matt. xvi.

Now, forasmuch as the disciples of Christ should bring the heavenly doctrine throughout the whole world, man being yet of himself unable to comprehend the doings of God; he therefore first expounded and declareth the scriptures unto them, as Luke mentioneth; and seeing they were simple unlearned men, he opened to them their understanding. But to the intent they might not think, What should we poor simple bodies do against so many learned and wise men? who will arm us against those that are so mighty? therefore he breatheth upon them, and saith, "Receive the Holy Ghost," whom he there giveth them, and therewith strengtheneth them inwardly; but with much more power and might upon Whit-Sunday. Whereupon he commandeth them to wait at Hierusalem, where he will send them the promise of the Father; clothing the weak with heavenly strength, as with a garment, and arming them as with a shield. Joel ii.

What good thing then can he lack, or what evil thing can hurt him, which is his messenger, that hath all power in heaven and in earth, and with whom such a king is ever abiding?

But when Christ would send out his disciples, he saith unto them: "As my Father hath sent me, so send I you." Whereunto did the Father send his Son into the world?

Even that he should open the glory of the Father unto the world; that he should declare the will of the heavenly Father; that he should offer health unto the world. This to do, Christ also sent forth his disciples. He sent them not to seek after vain-glory, after power and riches, after bodily pleasure and worldly pomp; but to do as he himself did. Christ sought the lost sheep, brought men unto the knowledge and love of the true living God, taught them to lead a virtuous and honest life. He was a physician, went to the sick, helped them, and healed them; he was not come to do his own will, but the will of his Father; he was not come to condemn the world, but to save it.

<small>Luke xv.</small>
<small>Matt. ix.</small>
<small>John vi.</small>
<small>John iii.</small>

In all this ought the ministers of the word to follow Christ, and to do as he did. Unto this new, heavenly, and godly life and work, Christ giveth them the Holy Ghost. For like as he himself was risen into a new life; even so through his holy Spirit will he grant and give a new life unto those that are his. Therefore breatheth he upon them, to declare, that it is he, who at the beginning made man, and now by his death had quickened him, and renewed him; and that even he is the fountain and giver of the Spirit. Thus unto his disciples he gave the firstlings of the promised Spirit, and with it a taste of more and greater perfection, as an earnest-penny.

All this declareth, what belongeth to true apostles and ministers of the word, which are sent of Christ, (for no man sendeth himself;) what their office is; and that they which seek the pleasures of the body, honour, praise, and riches, are not followers of Christ and successors of the apostles. Wherefore ought we most diligently to pray unto God, that he will give us faithful ministers of the word, which, looking truly to the work of Christ, may lead us unto God.

But forasmuch as without the Holy Ghost nothing can be fruitfully done, we must nevertheless pray for his holy Spirit, who may in us stir up holy thoughts and devout desires, directing and moving our will, and so giving power and strength to accomplish the works of God, and stedfastly therein to continue; and that the same Holy Spirit may illuminate and kindle our minds, and provoke them unto all good and godly works. Considering then, that the keys which were promised unto Peter, and in him to the whole church (Matthew xvi.), are here given of Christ, we shall also entreat somewhat thereof.

These keys are nothing else than the gospel. Christ now deduceth his oration from the common custom of men. Like as things corporal are shut and opened with the key; so be the consciences of men shut or bound with the gospel. Thus are these the keys which Christ giveth unto the apostles, unburdening of consciences and souls. And that cometh to pass, when the Holy Ghost illuminateth the mind, that it understandeth the mysteries of Christ, and committeth itself thereunto. To be discharged or unbound is, when the mind that hath despaired of health or salvation, is lift up to an assured and undoubted hope. To bind is to leave the obstinate and unbelieving mind unto itself. Jesus therefore sendeth forth his disciples, to publish this health unto the whole world, and to exclude and separate no man from this grace.

*Of the keys.*

But first he giveth them the Holy Ghost, as John saith; that is, he openeth their minds, that they may understand the scriptures, as Luke saith; for what is it else to open the understanding, but to give the Holy Ghost? Meet is it also and convenient, that they which by the gospel should bear Christ throughout the whole world, should receive the Holy Ghost. For if they should preach Christ, it was necessary they had Christ's Spirit, seeing that they and Christ had one manner of thing in hand. As Christ was sent of God, so were they sent of Christ. Without fruit verily should the ministers of the word preach the gospel, if they were not endued, illuminated, and inspired with the Holy Ghost.

"Preach," saith he, "the gospel;" that is the key, wherewith the gate of heaven is opened. Whoso believeth the gospel, when he heareth it preached, and understandeth it, feeleth comfort in his conscience, that he is delivered from sin.

Now doth the gospel set before us, not only the grace of God by Christ, through the which grace our sins are forgiven us; but also it teacheth and requireth a new life. Neither doth any man begin a new life, unless he first be ashamed of the former old and wicked life. Therefore saith Luke, that Christ "opened the minds and understanding of the disciples, that they might perceive the scriptures," namely, that he

*Luke xxiv.*

might thus and thus suffer, and rise again; and that in his name, that is, in his commandment and power, conversion of life and forgiveness of sins should be preached and declared among all people.

Therefore when the poor sinner through the preaching of the Holy Ghost heareth his wicked and sinful life, (for the holy gospel rebuketh the world of sin,) he beginneth to know himself a sinner, and to be displeased, repentant, and sorry for his sins; he considereth also, that he is well worthy of eternal punishment and damnation: by means whereof, through the multitude and greatness of his sins, he utterly despaireth in his own power and righteousness, and eternal salvation. But therewithal he heareth also, that Christ, by reason of his sins, came down from heaven, and died for him upon the cross, washed away all his sins with his blood, hath reconciled him with God, made him God's child, and an eternal inheritor of his kingdom; and this he stedfastly believeth. I pray you, doth not such a man's heart leap for joy, when he heareth, that through Christ he is discharged of all the sins that so sore pressed him?

The keys, therefore, are the pure word of God; which teacheth men to know themselves, and to put their trust in God through Christ. With that word, with those keys, do the ministers of the word open. For they that so are taught and instructed by the word of God, that they put all their confidence in God through Christ, those verily are loosed and discharged of their sins. But he that either will not hear, or when he heareth, will not receive and believe this grace declared to the world through Christ, and offered unto him by the ministers of the word, him do the ministers bind, that is, they leave him still in his error; according as Christ commandeth his disciples, (Matt. x.) that from such as will not receive and hear their word they shall depart, and shake off the dust from their shoes upon them. Thus did Paul bind, Acts xiii. xviii.

To bind then with the word, is nothing else but, when the word of the grace of God is preached, and not received, to leave such impenitent people, and to have no fellowship, neither aught to do with the despisers of the truth and grace. For in the day of judgment it shall be easier unto Sodom and Gomorrha, than unto such.

Now, although the word that the Apostles preach is not their own, but God's, and no man may cleanse, unbind, and discharge from sin, but only God; yet Christ of his grace, and according to the property of the scripture, ascribeth such unto the apostles. For the gracious Father, of his abundant love and kindness, and by reason of the covenant that he hath made with us, doth oft ascribe unto us many things which can properly belong unto none, save only to himself. Neither is this any marvel, seeing he hath given us his only-begotten and most dear Son to be our own; for "how cannot he give us all things with him?"

Notwithstanding, we ought not by reason hereof to be high-minded and proud, and to ascribe unto ourselves that which only is God's; but much rather be thankful for his grace, and diligent in our vocation, faithfully to employ and bestow the high treasure and gifts of God, and not to abuse them. This thing therefore extendeth not so far, as that every one man, properly to speak, doth of his own power and authority forgive sins. But forasmuch as the apostles and ministers of the word do publish and declare remission of sins, they bring the keys, and forgive sins ministerially and as ministers. Nevertheless, if herewithal the Spirit of God do not work in the hearer to believe the word when it is preached, then is not the sin forgiven. All the power therefore and working is God's.

Thus the apostles may damn no man, but undoubtedly they may by the word declare damnation to the unbelievers. Where an assured promise of grace is declared, there sins are forgiven. Now when the apostles shew unto sinners remission of sin, they do it out of the Holy Ghost, and are not deceived; for they preach that our sins are pardoned us through Christ, who hath made satisfaction for them. If this faith upon Christ be lively in us, so that we abhor sin, and be desirous of heavenly things, then are our sins forgiven us through the Holy Ghost; for "no man can say that Jesus is the Lord, but by the Holy Ghost." *The Holy Ghost that worketh in the apostles forgiveth the sins.* *Note this condition well.*

The key, therefore, extendeth to this end, that the minister declare remission of sins through Christ. Whoso now believeth the gospel preached, "shall be saved; he that believeth not shall be condemned." And seeing that the faith is an inward thing in the soul inspired of God, the minister cannot know who in the sight of God believeth, or believeth not; for God only knoweth the heart. Howbeit, by the outward confession, which is done with the mouth, and by receiving of the preaching, and by the fruits, the minister may judge. For whoso receiveth the word, openly confessing Christ, and doth not outwardly defile himself with vile deeds, to such the minister openeth with the key, and dischargeth them; that is, he taketh them into the church of Christ, numbereth them among the people of God, and receiveth them into the kingdom of heaven. As for those that will not hear the word preached, or that, when they hear it, do refuse it, not confessing Christ, or uttering their unbelief with foul, gross, and open vices, those the minister bindeth; that is, he shutteth them out of the church, and banisheth them out of the realm of heaven. To him that is in the church is forgiveness of sins promised: whoso despiseth charitable love, hath not faith; upon such one remaineth sin still, and the wrath of God.

Now, what the apostles and ministers of the word do, that do they not in their own name, not in their own power; but as they which are sent of God, and that declare his word, the holy gospel, out of the power of God, even out of the Holy Ghost, who being given unto them, doth work and speak by them. What these bind is bound before God and in heaven; for out of God is it that they judge: and what they unbind is unbound before God; for God will ratify and allow what they do, that being sent of him, keep themselves in exercise, and meddle with in his word and commission. As for him that is not sent of God, and declareth not his word and gospel, but of his own proper power will bind one man, and unbind another, set this man in heaven, and that man in hell; is it any marvel, if such one do many times miss, and be called a wolf, and not a shepherd, seeing his proceedings cometh not of God?

Luke x.
Heb. xiii.

Here also we learn, with what desire and thankfulness we ought to receive the ministers of God, that bring us his holy word, and comfort of our conscience; how we ought to esteem them that have the Holy Ghost, who speaketh unto us by them. For if we despise them, we despise God himself. St Paul, therefore, exhorteth us to be obedient unto them, and to have them in worthy estimation, that shew us the word of God. Worthy they be of double honour; partly, 1 Tim. v. for that through them God speaketh, whose ministers and 2 Cor. v. ambassadors they be, (for the highest king of all sendeth them out unto us with his commission;) partly, for that they be charged with so dangerous and heavy office and travail. For though, as concerning themselves, they live justly, well, and blameless, yet if they regard not the life of their sheep, but neglect them, they must look for great and sore punishment: not only for themselves must they give account, but for all the souls that are committed unto them, if one of them perish through their negligence. We should not therefore have respect to the infirmity or baseness of the ministry, but unto him that sent him, and whose commission he executeth. When a prince or king sendeth out a mean servant with a commission and charge, who will despise him without the wrath and indignation of the prince? How can we then contemn the ministers of the high eternal King without plague and punishment?

This be spoken, not that unworthy and unmeet men should be placed in so high an office, or that we should delight in their evil; but to the intent that malicious judgment may be avoided, and that there be no villany done to the anointed of the Lord. More respect and regard should we have to the word of God, that they bring unto us, than to their living and faults; more to the giver, than to the minister. It is not they that work, but God worketh through his own power; he cannot fail us in his promise. The minister lendeth his hand and mouth, but the Holy Ghost worketh in the hearts of the believers; neither can the wickedness of the priest diminish or hinder that operation. If we ourselves have pure, clean, and faithful believing minds, it is not the uncleanness of the minister can either defile or hurt us.

This is now the story of the resurrection of Christ; wherein we see, how the goodness of the Lord wonderfully striveth with the weak faith of those that are his. For when the angels could not persuade them that he was risen again, he himself appeareth unto them alive, and proveth by many evident testimonies, that he is of a truth risen again and revived, talketh with them, eateth with them, offereth himself unto them, that they may see him and handle him; sendeth the women and certain disciples for witnesses, and leaveth nothing unattempted that may persuade them. For in the faith and belief of the resurrection of Jesus Christ lieth all our welfare. We must therefore beseech Almighty God to establish in us this faith, and by his Spirit mightily to work, that we from sin may truly rise again to a new and godly life, and afterward with our bodies to enter into an immortal and everlasting life. Hereunto help us God the Father, the Son, and the Holy Ghost! Amen.

Here endeth the Sermons upon the Resurrection
of Jesus Christ, according to the true copy
of the Author; and now followeth the
Sermons of the Ascension.

# [CHAPTER IV.]

### THE ASCENSION OF JESUS CHRIST, OUT OF THE HOLY EVANGELISTS.

---

[Luke xxiv. 49—53. Acts i. 4—14. Mark xvi. 19.]

JESUS led his disciples out unto Bethany. And when he had brought them together, he spake unto them of the kingdom of God, and commanded them that they should not depart from Hierusalem; but to wait for the promise of the Father. For John, saith he, baptized with water; but ye shall be baptized with the Holy Ghost after these few days. When they therefore were come together, they asked of him, saying: Lord, wilt thou at this time restore again the kingdom to Israel? And he said unto them: It is not for you to know the times and the seasons, which the Father hath put in his own power; but ye shall receive power, after that the Holy Ghost is come upon you; and ye shall be witnesses unto me, not only in Hierusalem, but also in all Jury, and in Samaria, and even unto the world's end. Now when Jesus had spoken these words unto them, he lifted up his hands, and blessed them, and was taken up, and a cloud received him out of their sight: so that he departed from them, and was carried up in heaven, and sitteth on the right hand of God. And whilst they looked stedfastly up towards heaven, as he went, behold, two men stood by them in white apparel, which also said: Ye men of Galilee, why stand ye gazing up into heaven? The same Jesus, which is taken up from you into heaven, shall so come even as you have seen him go into heaven. So when they had worshipped him, they returned with great joy into Hierusalem from mount Olivet;

which is from Hierusalem a sabbath-day's journey. And when they were come in, they went up into a parlour, where abode Peter and James, John and Andrew, Philip and Thomas, Bartholomew and Matthew, James the Son of Alpheus and Simon Zelotes, and Judas the brother of James. These all continued still with one accord in the temple, lauding and praising God, and making their prayers, with the women, and Mary the mother of Jesu, and with his brethren.

### DOCTRINE AND FRUIT.

John xiii.

CHRIST, who loved his disciples, declareth unto them his love, even unto the end; yea, he never ceaseth to love them.

Matt. xxviii. For though he leave them, as concerning his bodily presence; yet with his love, grace, and power, he is ever still with them. Forasmuch now as after sufficient proof of his resurrection he will depart from them, and go to his Father that had sent him; he taketh them forth with him unto the place, from whence he mindeth to depart from them. And manifestly, before their eyes, he ascendeth into heaven into the glory of his Father; that they might be witnesses, as well of his glorious ascension, as of all other things which they had heard and seen before. O how fervent words spake he then unto them! How deeply entered he into their hearts! How earnestly printed he those his last words into them! The eternal wisdom speaketh nothing vainly, nothing slenderly, nothing without profit. Although the disciples, as men yet somewhat carnal, do ask questions concerning the restitution of a bodily and temporal kingdom, yet maketh he no answer unto their demand, but directeth them unto that which is for their profit, and belongeth to their office; drawing their hearts from the earthly kingdom, from the which they ought to be mortified, unto the kingdom of heaven, even unto the kingdom of God; in the which he himself is king, and into the which they now were received as citizens, that they should declare the same throughout the whole world, and offer it unto all men.

This is the gospel of the kingdom of God, which for a

testimony unto all nations must be preached in the whole world, to witness the grace of God unto the elect; but to the damned and unbelievers, a testimony of their damnation; in that they are convinced of their own infidelity, and shall have no excuse, if they contemn and despise the grace offered unto them. By this ought we also to learn to see such things which are most profitable and wholesome unto us; and which bring us the nearest way to put our trust in God, and to love our neighbours; for that part of the play is ours. As for unprofitable and contentious questions, if we meddle not with them, then the less division, and the more love and edifying in the church of God shall follow. Many times are we too much careful for such things as we desire ourselves; as, what end this thing or that will come unto, when God will set up our prosperity, and what shall be done hereafter, when and how God will punish those that are against us. And this temptation, carnal zeal, and curiosity, chanceth oft even in the hearts of the faithful; as we see here in the disciples of Christ. Sometimes there be froward and wicked minds, which, pretending to be Christians, seek out of the gospel nothing but honour, lucre, and profit: but such be both false and feigned. Notwithstanding, all these set apart, we ought to commit and refer all things unto our merciful Creator and gracious Father, who can right well order and dispose them, how and when he will, as he thinketh best to further his glory, and to edify his elect children. Our care ought rather to be, how we may lead a godly life, and beautify the faith of Christ with good works. We must look, that we be neither ungodly nor hypocrites; but to live virtuously and innocently in his sight, and patiently at his hand to wait for our deliverance. The kingdom of Christ, that is published and offered through the gospel, is not a corporal, but a spiritual kingdom; neither consisteth it in outward things, but in a pure and faithful believing heart: and yet reacheth it throughout the whole world, and amongst all nations. In the hearts of all faithful believers doth Christ reign through his Spirit, and there overcometh he the devil, sin, and death.

And to the intent they should well understand this kingdom, he commandeth them to wait for the Holy Spirit, whom he had promised them; as if he would say: "Now go I to my Father, now enter I into my kingdom, that I may mightily reign upon the earth. . This thing ye understand not; but when the Spirit is given you, ye shall perceive it well. All things in heaven and in earth are given into my power. In those that are mine shall I reign, and make them righteous through faith; yea, invincible shall I make them against all enemies: hereof shall ye bear witness, when ye are baptized through the Holy Ghost. This my kingdom shall ye publish in all nations, from one end of the world to another. Thus shall I reign from sea to sea; of the which my kingdom the prophets spake so much before."

Of this kingdom doth Christ take possession through his ascending up to the Father, at whose right hand and in this kingdom he sitteth; reigning much more mightily in his church, and working more effectually in those that be his, than he did before, when he lived yet corporally with them.

Thus taking his leave, he giveth them loving words, comforteth them, and admonisheth them of their office; that they all may be diligent therein, that they continually direct and lift up their hearts into that kingdom; and that they take in hand to bring all men to the same into the obedience of Christ. His blessing he giveth them, saluting them, wishing them good, and praying heartily unto his Father for them.

Thus was he taken from them, and carried into heaven. By the heaven we understand the incomprehensible light in the which God dwelleth, and which no mortal man can attain unto. From thence came Christ unto us; and thither is he gone again, even into the invisible glory and clearness of God. For the eternal Word and Power of God, dwelling in God's incomprehensible light from everlasting, became man, and had his conversation upon earth in all parts, sin except, as a very true man. But when he had fully finished and throughly ended the work that was given him in commission of his heavenly Father, and had obeyed him even unto the death; forasmuch as in all things he had honoured and glorified his Father upon earth, it was convenient that the Father also should glorify his Son. And therefore raised he him from death, and took him up into heaven; not after the Godhead, (for so was he always in heaven,) but after the manhood. For his true human nature, which he took upon him for our sakes, is carried and taken up out of this world into the invisible honour and glory, into the highest incomprehensible, and into the perfect fruition of the Godhead.

In this honour and glory Christ dwelleth and reigneth; and yet amongst those that are his doth he finish and perform all things by his Spirit, having governance in the hearts of the faithful through belief, through love, through patience, and innocency of life.

To the intent now that this kingdom might be erected in the hearts of men, it was necessary that he should give his disciples commission to publish the same, and to prepare men's minds thereunto through the preaching of the gospel. But first he made the minds of his disciples ready and apt to receive the Holy Ghost, whom he afterwards poured into others by them; and therefore he commanded them, until the Spirit appear and open the work, to wait still at Hierusalem; from the which place the kingdom of Christ was afterwards planted in all the world. Of the promise of the Spirit read Isai. xliv. Jere. xxxi. Ezek. xxxvi. Joel ii. John xiv. xvi.

Considering that the mystery of Christ's ascension is great and excellent, and that there is notable power contained therein to those that be faithful believers; the evangelists do therefore describe very perfectly the time, the place, the persons, with all circumstances and assured testimonies thereof. He ascendeth up before his disciples, that they might openly and evidently see it with their eyes: there did appear angels, as messengers and witnesses from heaven, even two of them, that in the mouth of two all truth might be established. The white apparel signifieth the evident glory, into the which Christ is taken up, as a noble, royal, and mighty King and Conqueror, entering into his heavenly kingdom.

Thus the high and glorious King, clothed with our nature, is entered into our royal palace, as one that mindeth faithfully to despatch our matters. He is our own mediator and advocate in the presence of the Father; notwithstanding our sins committed, we have a free entrance unto God by him. Our flesh hath he in himself carried up, and exalted our nature unto the right hand of God the Father. Wherefore we that are bones of his bones, and flesh of his flesh, do justly conceive a comfortable and assured hope, that our mortal bodies shall also be taken up, and have immortal and eternal joy.

The earnest-penny of his Spirit hath he given and left behind him unto us, and contrariwise he hath of us taken an earnest-penny and pledge, namely, our sinful and wicked flesh, which he in himself hath carried up into the kingdom of heaven. Now where the parcel is, there shall also be the whole sum.

By this we that are flesh and blood have a comfortable and assured trust, that in Christ we shall have the possession and inheritance of heaven. Our sins in him are recompensed, heaven in him is opened, in him is the hope of immortal life sealed and made sure unto us; Christ, the victorious and glorious conqueror, is able to defend his church: so that from henceforth no man shall have power to condemn his elect and faithful believers. Rom. viii. Heb. v. vii. viii. x.

That his flesh is withdrawn from us, and taken into heaven, it is our great profit; to the intent that all our devotion and God's service may be directed upwards in the spirit, and that the minds of faithful believers may be drawn from earthly unto heavenly things, even unto the place where Christ sitteth on the right hand of God the Father.

When the disciples saw that their schoolmaster was taken away from them into heaven, they perceived and considered the thing that they knew not before, although Christ had told it them, John vi.; namely, that by the ascension they should receive understanding. Therefore they worshipped Jesus Christ, and according unto his commandment they returned to Hierusalem, where they kept themselves until the time that the Spirit came: neither were they idle, but continued in the holy fellowship and godly exercises, with prayer and devotion, preparing and making themselves ready unto the coming of the Spirit.

By occasion hereof (all niceness, curiosity, and contentious questions, all pride, vain-glory, and fond affections and desires set apart) we ought with upright minds, and with the eyes of faith, to be alway taken up into heaven, and there to have our dwelling, where Christ our head sitteth at the right hand of God, King and Lord of all things, our faithful advocate and mediator. Then shall true godliness increase, then shall virtue blessedly grow and bring forth fruit in us, if we with stedfast faith do consider, that our Lord Jesus Christ died for our sakes, rose again from death, and is exalted at the right hand of God, reigning mightily above all things in heaven, and finishing our salvation, if we in spirit and in the truth worship and honour him as the eternal God; confessing with a true faith, that all power is given unto him of God the Father, that he careth for us, and that for our health's sake he ruleth and shall reign, until all things be brought under his feet. In the meantime he daily in his church purifieth all his members by his Spirit, cleansing them still more and more from all their sins. And when he shall have rooted out all sin in his elect, overcoming death the last enemy, so that God shall be all in all; then shall Christ also give up his kingdom unto God the Father, namely, the mediation for our sins, the purging of the same, defence against the devil, and deliverance from death. For then shall there be no more sin in the elect; so that he shall not need to be mediator for them, to purge from sin, to defend against the devil, or to deliver from death.

O merciful Father, grant us perfectly to know the[1] blessed and glorious kingdom of Christ thy Son: draw up our hearts in such sort, that we with all obedience may yield ourselves into this kingdom, seeing and regarding only those things that are above, and wholly applying ourselves unto this end, that the same heavenly kingdom may be far spread abroad and known unto all men; to the intent, that as for all worldly things, wherein many foolish people set all their salvation, but in vain, men may utterly refuse them, and heartily with body and soul, and with their whole life, may give over themselves perfectly unto the only Lord Jesus Christ, the true God. For thy good pleasure it was, O God, that in him all perfectness should dwell, and that by him all things towards thee should be reconciled and pacified through his blood, whether they be in heaven or in earth. Grant us, O God, unity and brotherly love in thy holy church; kindle our hearts to fervent and devout prayer; make us diligently to watch, and circumspectly to wait for

[1 Old edition, *thy*.]

[COVERDALE.]

the coming of thy beloved Son, that we neither be drunken in excess and bodily lust, nor entangled with the snares of this world; but that we, having always the eyes of our heart open, and praying with upright minds, may cheerfully meet our Redeemer, and joy with him for ever. To him be eternal praise and honour. Amen.

# [CHAPTER V.]

## THE SENDING OF THE HOLY GHOST.

[Acts ii. 1—4.]

WHEN the fifty days were come to an end, they were all with one accord together in one place; and suddenly there came a sound from heaven, as it had been the coming of a mighty wind, and it filled all the house where they sat. And there appeared unto them cloven tongues, like as they had been of fire, and it sat upon each one of them; and they were all filled with the Holy Ghost, and began to speak with other tongues, even as the same Spirit gave them utterance. *Acts ii.*

### DOCTRINE AND FRUIT.

HERE the evangelist Luke describeth, how that after Christ entered into his glory, the gospel, even the heavenly doctrine and grace, was opened unto the world down from heaven by a glorious and great miracle. For though the law, which is the will of God, and also the gospel, that is his grace, hath from the beginning been always in the world, namely, in the hearts of God's elect children; yet was each one of them at several times gloriously uttered unto the world by manifest and apparent miracle. And like as the Holy Ghost was in the hearts of the faithful believers, (for after the resurrection he gave the Spirit unto the disciples;) even so here he giveth them the Spirit with an open miracle, and with a more perfect working and power. For the Spirit which Christ gave them after his resurrection, when he breathed upon them, was given this day with more perfection; that is to say, his operation and strength declared itself more evidently and more perfectly, and shewed his presence by the visible miracle.

Thus it is here described, how the promises of Christ and of the prophets made as concerning the Holy Ghost were fulfilled, and how the same Holy Ghost, who is the teacher of the truth, the earnest-penny of salvation, the wedding-ring of grace, and joy of the mind, was given. Now when it is said that the Holy Ghost is given unto men, the same may be understood of the gifts and operations of the Holy Ghost; for though God may be comprehended of man's mind, yet can he not be included or shut therein. Nevertheless, his gifts, according to his will and pleasure, are poured and measured into our hearts, unto every one so much as may serve to his welfare and profit.

<small>1 Cor. xii.</small>

Whoso is desirous to know where the Holy Ghost is promised unto faithful believers, let him read Ezech. xxxvi. xxxix. Joel ii. Matt. iii. Now look, what God the Father hath promised by his ministers, the same also doth Christ his Son promise: whereby we may see that the Son hath like power with the Father, and that there is but one only Spirit of them both, as we may read, Luke xii. John vii. xiv. xv. xvi. xx.

But before we come to the sending of the Spirit, we will first substantially and well peruse the story, and look what may be gathered thereof: for here is nothing written or set down in vain.

The evangelist doth here make mention of "the fiftieth day," upon the which this great wonder was done. In the which there lieth hid a notable mystery. The Jews, from the day that they offered the Easter lamb, told fifty days, and upon the fiftieth day was the Feast of Weeks; in the which feast they kept holiday, offering unto God a willing sacrifice of the first-fruits, when they cut them down. We begin to number from the resurrection of Christ, our Easter lamb, who also was offered up. Upon the fiftieth day, when the fruits began now to be ripe and ready to be reaped, the harvest also being great, and the labourers few, then sent God his Spirit to prepare and furnish the disciples, that they from amongst the heathen might gather fruit together unto the Lord. And like as before time, when the children of Israel was departed out of Egypt, the law was given of God

<small>Exod. xii.
Deut. xvi.</small>

<small>Matt. ix.</small>

<small>John iv.</small>

unto the people upon the fiftieth day; even so was it convenient that upon the fiftieth day the Holy Ghost should be given to the disciples; which Holy Ghost is both an interpreter and fulfiller of the law. The place where the Holy Ghost was given is Sion: for there Christ commanded his disciples to wait, and from that place should the law of God, according to the saying of the prophets, proceed forth into the whole world. Therefore like as aforetime the law was given upon mount Sinai, even so was the Spirit given upon mount Sion. Upon Sinai did God at that time with some terrible things declare his might and power, his plague also and vengeance, which should fall upon those that despised his law; and therefore was there such fearfulness through lightnings, thunderings, and other like terrible things. Here there is heard a noise, mighty and vehement, but not horrible and fearful; in the which wind is signified, that the doctrine of the Spirit should speedily and with power break in through the world, and bring fruit; and that no man should be so mighty as to hinder the strength thereof, even as the wind in his course can by no man be kept back.

*2 Cor. iii.*
*Luke xxiv.*
*Isai. ii. Micah iv.*
*Note.*

Whereas fiery tongues do appear and are seen, it signifieth the manifold speeches and instruction, which the Spirit giveth to Christ's disciples; the zeal also and ferventness that he worketh in their hearts, making them altogether fire, and kindling them in such sort, that even their words are fervent, and pierce afterwards into the hearts of others. All weakness, fear, and coldness removeth he out of them, so that they are not afraid manfully to step forth before all the people; although not long before they durst not abide, but fled from the Lord. Now they confess him to be the Saviour of all the world, whom they before had denied.

Whereas the tongues were divided, it signifieth the diversity of the gifts of the Spirit. Christ promised them in Mark xvi., that they should "speak with other tongues," or with a new speech or language; which promise is now performed unto them. The tongues of christian men ought to be garnished with gentleness and with the Holy Ghost, that no foul or wanton talk proceed out of their mouth. The tongues that pronounce and confess Christ, the eternal Truth, and his sincere Spirit, must not lie, neither talk any unclean, hurtful, nor venomous thing; for unto all such

*Eph. iv.*
*Col. iv.*

is the Spirit enemy. Therefore are they not fleshly, but fiery and spiritual tongues; out of the which the fire of the Spirit hath consumed all moisture of worldly and carnal wantonness, and God with his own love hath kindled them. How could the apostles else have been instructors of the whole world, if the Spirit had not taught them the diversity of tongues? O the great wisdom and grace of God, who at all times for our wealth hath set forth and offered unto us poor men his high, spiritual, heavenly things, under corporal and visible tokens! For how might we carnal men else understand godly matters, if they were not exhibited with visible and bodily things? Therefore hath God always this custom, that he represent unto us his high gifts under those tokens, which are most known of us, and likest unto those things which he offereth us; and so with human things he covereth divine and godly things. Not that God is closed or shut in with things of men; but that celestial and heavenly things, set forth unto us by such as be earthly, might be of us the better understood. For else every man of knowledge wotteth well, that the Holy Ghost is not a dove, neither a wind, a tongue, fire, nor water. For God is not a thing corporal, neither a thing that can be felt or comprehended with outward senses. Notwithstanding, things invisible are the better known and perceived of us, when they be set forth and represented by visible things; namely, by such as have some similitude with the invisible and spiritual things; and so far as natural things may set forth heavenly matters, do perfectly describe before our eyes the nature and property of them. Therefore doth the Spirit appear in the form of fiery tongues, and with a sound; that thereby the two principal senses of men might be moved, namely, his hearing and seeing: for the sound toucheth the ears, and the fire moveth the sight. Like as Christ also in the supper with bread and wine, to move the outward senses of men, thought to represent his body and blood. For by bread is signified unto us the true body of Christ, which died for us upon the cross, and by wine the blood that was shed for our sins; which true flesh and blood they that believe do at the supper eat and drink through faith: by the which food and sustenance their souls are upholden to the gracious and eternal life.

Thus with exterior tokens it pleased the wisdom of God

to guide the outward senses of his disciples into the obedience of faith, and under the same to signify and declare the strength and operation of the Holy Ghost. For like as the wind bloweth through the whole earth, piercing, moving, and altering all privy and secret places; even so the Spirit of God goeth through all things, searching all secret corners and inward minds of men: mightily also he worketh in men's hearts, kindling and changing them. He is the clear, pure, and hot fire, that consumeth all filthiness of sin, inspiring men's hearts, and drawing them upward to God.

Without this Spirit may a man work no fruitful thing, yea, think no good thing: for man is nothing but flesh, neither considereth he of himself aught that is spiritual or godly, but only carnal things. Forasmuch now as the wisest and most gracious God knoweth this so to be; whereas he hath made man his creature, to have fruition of himself, he will not suffer him to corrupt in the flesh, but give him his own holy Spirit.

God the Father, through Christ his eternal Word, did shape man out of the mould of the earth, and created him after his own similitude and likeness. Now is God a Spirit; therefore the image of God in man must needs be spiritual: which image in the inward man is such a thing, as partly doth express and declare God that created him.

But when man, being deceived through the devil, fell into sin, and lost this image; then the proportion of God's pure Spirit, in whom his image was printed, was defaced, and the image of God lost his beauty: so that the noble man, who at the first was of God, so fair and goodly fashioned and beautified in similitude of God, became after sin like unto the devil, filthy and shameful, yea, altogether carnal, having nothing more of the Spirit in him, as the scripture in the book of Creation testifieth. Forasmuch now as the miserable Gen. vi. man was degenerate from the noble, spiritual, and godly nature, to an unclean, carnal, and devilish disposition, becoming altogether flesh; he was able no more either to think or work any spiritual or godly thing.

All his thoughts and imaginations are carnal, in that he is fallen into eternal death, and hath lost the life of the Spirit: "for the affections and lusts of the flesh are death; Rom. viii. but the desires of the Spirit are life and peace. The affections of the flesh are enmity against God; for the flesh is not subject unto the law of God, neither can be: they therefore which are in the flesh cannot please God." Now when man, who had taken so hurtful a fall, was brought down from life unto death, from the grace of God into his wrath, life might not be given him again but by the Spirit of God, whom man by sin hath lost.

Therefore like as the Father at the beginning had created man, so fashioneth he him again by his Son; who overcometh and destroyeth death, and giveth unto us again the way of immortality. "For into a froward soul entereth not the Spirit of God:" therefore is it convenient and necessary, that such foul and corrupt flesh be purged and cleansed again. By Christ the eternal Word were all things created; by him therefore, after the fall, must all things be restored again. For this cause died Christ upon the cross, to banish the sin of the world, and to make satisfaction for it. From death he also riseth again, to give us a certain and assured hope and an undoubted pledge of an immortal and eternal life, and that he hath overcome death and sin for us.

<small>Wisd. i.</small>

Immediately after the resurrection, he breatheth upon his disciples, and giveth them the Holy Ghost; to declare that he is the same, who at the beginning created our nature, and sealed it with his Spirit; and that it is even he, who now, in the beginning of a new life, must by his Spirit renew and restore our decayed nature again; that thus Christ, who is the living and "express image of the invisible God," may be fashioned and formed of the new in us. Now cannot Christ the image of God be right proportioned and renewed in us but by the Holy Ghost. Now like as Christ after the resurrection gave his disciples the Spirit, to print into them a new life, whereby they knew and were assured, that he was the fountain and giver of the Spirit; and therefore he said, "All that the Father hath is mine;" item, "All power is given unto me in heaven and in earth;" even so immediately after the same he ascended up into heaven, to declare unto them, that he was the Lord of all things. Out of the high and real throne, where he sitteth at the right hand of God his Father, Christ the eternal King sent down his holy Spirit upon all flesh, that we by him might obtain the old innocency and salvation again; and that the image of God,

<small>John xx.</small>

<small>Heb. i.<br>Col. i.<br>Gal. iv.</small>

<small>John xvi.<br>Matt. xxviii.</small>

<small>Col. iii.<br>Eph. iv.</small>

stained and defiled by sin, might be restored unto us, and that we thus might become partakers of eternal life. What they be, unto whom God giveth his Spirit, that see we well here; namely, even unto those, that in unity of faith and fervent love are gathered together with one accord; for of all unity he is the fountain and original. In contentious and proud hearts dwelleth not the Holy Ghost: therefore is it meet that we pray:

Come, O Holy Spirit, replenish the hearts of thy faithful believers, and kindle in them the fire of thy love, thou that through manifold tongues hast gathered together all the nations of the heathen in unity of faith. O take all dissension and discord out of thy holy church, and make us to be of one mind in unfeigned love, without the which we cannot please thee.

---

[Acts ii. 5—11.]

THERE were dwelling at Hierusalem Jews, devout men, out of every nation of them that are under heaven. Now when this was noised about, the multitude came together, and were astonied; because that every man heard them speak with his own language. They wondered all and marvelled, saying amongst themselves: Behold, are not all these which speak of Galilee? And how hear we every man his own tongue, wherein we were born? Partheans, and Medes, and Elemites, and the inhabitants of Mesopotamia, and of Jewry, and of Capadocia, of Pontus and Asia, Phrygia and Pamphylia, of Egypt, and of the parts of Lybia which is besides Syren, and strangers of Rome, Jews and proselytes, Cretes and Arabians; we have heard them speak in our own tongues the great works of God.

### DOCTRINE AND FRUIT.

THE eternal Wisdom hath endued all good minds diligently to learn and search the thing wherein they think to find that which they desire: and what can be more worthy to be desired, or more acceptable to the mind of men, than eternal life and salvation, which only consisteth in God the highest good of all? Now was the sacred scripture given by the Holy Ghost, that man thereby might be guided and led unto salvation, and to most excellent felicity. For they that exercise themselves in holy scripture, studying and perusing it, ought thus to do; even to direct themselves and others unto life. Therefore, by the ordinance of God, there hath been ever men in all nations, which to instruct others have applied themselves to the scripture; as among the Jews we find Levi, of whom in the prophet Malachi it is written, that "the law of the truth was in his mouth, and no wickedness in his lips; that he walked before God in peace and equity, and converted many from ungodliness: for the lips of the priests are sure of knowledge, and the law is required at his mouth; for he is a messenger of the Lord of hosts." Thus, as it may well be conjectured, there were at Jerusalem congregations of learned men, that exercised themselves in the holy scripture. For though all wisdom come of God, as the fountain and well, and no man can be learned, whom God himself teacheth not; yet will he not give his grace, Spirit, and knowledge to the idle, slothful, and unthankful, neither to the proud; but unto those that with meekness and fear of God practise themselves in the scripture, and that, applying unto fervent prayer, do not despise the means and gracious gifts granted them of God.

And if any man will say, that all falsehood and destruction, all erroneous doctrine and discord, were come into the church by such as be learned; let him consider, that the thing which in himself is good, ought not for the abuse's sake to be refused. Remove the abuse, and then the thing is good and profitable. Wine is a profitable and wholesome thing, created of God for the behoof of men, and is never dispraised of any witty man to be evil, because many do abuse it, and is drunken: even so is holy scripture and other profitable sciences to be esteemed as high gifts, although many men, puffed up with pride, blinded in covetousness, and entangled with other affections, have misused the same scriptures.

In the papistry, the universities, colleges, cathedral churches, and monasteries, have highly exalted the pope and his false faith, and by false interpretation of the scripture brought him so far, that the doctrine of the faith and Christ is utterly darkened. Now, whereas lewd learning with false science, with wrong understanding of scripture, have brought such high things, great goods, and plentiful riches to pass, drawing so much people unto themselves; we ought not therefore to cease from reading and exercising of the scripture, but to take upon us to further the true religion and faith of Christ, and to set it forth again with no less diligence than they do theirs. If we will that the true faith of Christ shall grow, continue, and increase, then we must bring the same to pass by true understanding of the scripture, by pure, sound, and wholesome doctrine. With the truth must lies be banished, with sound doctrine must false be rooted out, with the light must darkness be expelled. But how can the true understanding of the scripture, the undoubted, wholesome, and sound doctrine, be had, when men do neither exercise and employ themselves, nor apply their endeavour, study, and diligence therein?

All the charges therefore and expenses, which heretofore have been bestowed upon the unprofitable and noisome learned men, ought now to be converted to godly colleges and studies; to the intent that little seeds, which God hath laid up in young wits, may fruitfully grow, be planted, and brought forth. "If thou seek wisdom, as the gold," saith Salomon, "thou shalt find it." Gold is with great travail and labour digged out of the inward and secret veins of the earth, and of the high hills; it raineth not down upon men's heads: even so must knowledge and wisdom be gotten with great travail and diligence, not with loitering and idleness. But when God giveth us his gifts, we must look that we be not unfaithful in them, but use and bestow them to his glory and edifying of his church. Where godliness cometh to knowledge, or where they two are together in one man, God is highly to be thanked for so excellent a gift and grace, and greatly is such a gift to be had in estimation; but where as pride, heaviness, contention, greediness, and self love, is in a learned man, there is not a more hurtful poison found upon the earth.

> O God, thou that of thy grace and fatherly love hast given so good and excellent gifts with singular light of all sciences; grant unto such as be learned a heart and mind, that in all things they may have respect only to thy glory, and, that in all their readings, writings, teachings, and doctrines they may prefer the same. For "knowledge puffeth a man up, but love edifieth." O suffer not thy holy and excellent gifts to be stained, defiled, and marred, with the filthy dirt of men's affections. Grant that our studies be not heathenish, but godly and christian. Preserve the tender and good youth from wicked and ungodly schoolmasters; that the pure hearts which thou hast consecrated to be a temple for thee and thy holy Spirit, be not polluted with vice and filthiness.

1 Cor. viii.

---

[Acts ii. 12—21.]

Acts ii.

They were all amazed, and wondered, saying one to another, What meaneth this? Other mocked, saying: These men are full of new wine. But Peter stept forth with the eleven, and lift up his voice, and said unto them: Ye men of Jewry, and all ye that dwell at Hierusalem, be this known unto you, and with your ears hear my words. For these are not drunken, as ye suppose, seeing it is but the third hour of the day: but this is that which was spoken by the prophet Joel: And it shall be in the last days, saith God, I will pour out of my Spirit in those days, and your sons and your daughters shall prophesy, and your young men shall see visions, and your old men shall dream dreams: and on my servants, and on my handmaids, I will pour out of my Spirit in those days, and they shall prophesy: and I will shew wonders in heaven above, and tokens in the earth beneath, blood, and of fire, and the vapour of smoke; the sun shall be turned into darkness, and the moon into blood, before that great and notable day of the Lord come. And it shall come to pass, that whosoever calleth on the name of the Lord shall be saved.

## DOCTRINE AND FRUIT.

When the truth is published in the church of Christ, and the power of God uttereth itself, there be always some simple people, that of good mind seek to know that which they understand not, and therefore they demand questions: unto those the Lord doth gladly open himself. But again there be others, that despise, slander, mock, and abhor all holy things, as in the old and new testament we have many witnesses of the same. Jerem. xx. xxvi. xxxii. John viii. x. xi. Acts xvii. For the natural man understandeth not the things that appertain unto God. And thus do they most of all, which, being puffed up in the wisdom and science of men, have not yet attained to the spirit and right kernel of the scripture: in the sight of which men the wisdom of God, and preaching of the cross of Jesus Christ, is but a derision and foolishness. But blessed are they, that in the singleness of their heart, with pure minds, in meekness, obedience, and in the true fear of God, submit themselves unto his doctrine. From them cannot God hide himself; but openeth their minds, that they may understand the scriptures. For they that of a good mind do here ask the question, "What meaneth this?" are afterwards converted by Peter's preaching. Peter, the fervent disciple of Christ, the faithful shepherd of Christ's sheep, as soon as he receiveth the Spirit, is bold to step forth, and to confess him whom before he had denied.   *1 Cor. ii. 1 Cor. i. Matt. xi. Matt. xi. Luke xxiv.*

But first he persuadeth that the disciples were not drunken: for if such vice were in the ministers of Christ, and they truly convinced thereof, it should bring unto the gospel and name of Christ great hinderance, stain his doctrine, and make it to be despised and subject. Most diligent therefore ought we to be in keeping us from such vices, whereby our office, ministration, and doctrine might be suspect and set at nought. Yet must we not defer too long in answering such evil reports: for more diligence must we apply in setting forth the name and glory of God, than in defending and maintaining our own estimation.

Thus the apostle Peter, in answering that objection concerning drunkenness, doth shortly pass over, and saith:

"Brethren, these are not drunken, as ye suppose: for why? the time doth not permit; it is yet too early in the morning." Immediately upon the same, he proceedeth forth to admonish them of the excellent graces and gifts, which the God of mercy hath promised before, and now performed them. But this satisfaction concerning drunkenness, and this instruction of the ignorant, is made with all meekness, and yet with sincerity and stedfastness, not lordly or braggingly; although he was highly endued with the Holy Ghost.

Thus we that be ministers of Christ, and teachers of his congregations, ought not by reason of our office or high gifts to take too much upon us, that with bragging or arrogancy we would out-face the weak; but worthily and valiantly, with sincerity and truth of scripture, to instruct such as be ignorant and out of the way. Our mouth is an instrument of the Holy Ghost and of the truth, not of any lightness, bragging, or presumption.

This word "prophesy" is taken not only to tell and shew before of godly and high things, but also to hearken unto the same and to perceive them; and this maketh for the understanding of this place. For the Holy Ghost declareth by Joel, and promiseth also, as he doth by Jeremy, that the knowledge of God should be common in all the world, and that from the least unto the most every one should be instructed in God's knowledge, through the guiding of the Spirit: which knowledge before time was common only to the Jews and scribes, but by Christ is such abundant and plentiful knowledge of God poured out in all the world through his holy Spirit, who worketh in the church until the end; not only in scribes, from whom such high mysteries of God's wisdom are oftentimes hid, but unto simple and unlearned fishers, and to others that in the sight of the world are not esteemed.

Yea, richly poureth he out of his holy Spirit upon all flesh, unto every one his measure, as it best pleaseth him: no man excludeth he from his grace; his knowledge suffereth he to flow over all the earth as a water-flood, unto all those that are his servants and handmaids. This is the dear and excellent treasure, which, instead of it that was given before, by the incarnation of Christ is now offered, that the knowledge of God, which by the Holy Ghost is the preaching of the gospel, is come forth into all the world; whereas before

it was manifest only amongst the Jews. For after the death Ps. lxxvi.
of the Lord finished upon the cross, was the gospel published
in all the world, by the which preaching the children of God John xi.
dispersed abroad are gathered together.  The Holy Ghost  Isai. xl.
also, who was before in the godly, did by his gifts and
operations work much more mightily and strongly after the
death and ascension of Christ, than before: by the which Jere. xxxi.
Holy Ghost the captivity of the law and ceremonies is taken
away, and heavenly freedom given to the children of God.

Forasmuch as to know Christ and his kingdom, it ministereth true godliness and eternal life, Peter in his oration travaileth especially to this end, that the Jews being there present, which held Christ for a wicked doer, and put him to death, might know him to be the true Saviour of the world, and to be risen again from death; and therefore he allegeth the prophecies which in Christ were fulfilled. As if he would say: Behold, Joel told before of the time that these your children should prophesy; now ye see it performed in them. Whereby ye may well perceive, that the kingdom of Messias, which is a spiritual thing, is now begun already. In the which kingdom must be not only Jews, which have the outward temple and ceremonies, but all as call upon the name of the Lord, wheresoever they be in the world. Unto the Jew was promised a Saviour; nevertheless such one as should not only save them, but also the whole world, and whose kingdom should be everlasting; that he also should deliver and bring them, yea, all mankind, from the captivity of the prince of this world. Of these things there were amongst the Jewish people many signs and figures, whereby in bodily and corporal things God did partly set forth these things spiritual: which they also which are spiritual and elect amongst the people of the Jews, understood right well, though darkly; in that they with the eyes of inward faith had a further respect than to gaze only upon the outward corporal things. Thus God the Holy Ghost by visible things led and taught them, (even as a young scholar is first taught by letters and syllables under the schoolmaster,) until the time that the glorious kingdom came, that in Christ the true Messias all things were reformed, and became spiritual.

Thus had the Jews the corporal kingdom of David,

and of other kings; and thus for their sins they were brought unto Babylon into captivity. By the which captivity was figured the grievous bondage and thraldom of mankind under the violent power of the devil. But when they were in captivity at Babylon, God, comforting them by his prophets, promised to bring them thence, and to restore them to their own land; in the which deliverance was figured the redemption of the world by Christ. This custom had all the prophets, that when they told the people beforehand, and promised of God's behalf deliverance out of the captivity before they came into it, they always made mention also of the punishment of the sins that should go before. Prosperity shall come, (said they;) but first there must be an horrible plague for sin, the justice of God must first be satisfied. Thus doth Joel here also: in whom partly we learn, that God will not suffer our sins to pass without punishment; as we see also in the grievous captivity of all mankind, that God will have the sin so worthily satisfied, that even his only-begotten Son, by whom no sin was committed, must therefore die, and by his innocent death pay for our sins. If God now spared not his only-begotten Son, how may we then think that he will suffer our vile and sinful life to pass without punishment? But if we patiently and with good will bear the just punishment of our sins, sent unto us of God; and converting from our sins, do turn us to the gracious Father that beateth us, God undoubtedly shall send us grace, prosperity, and welfare, and help us out of all misery. Once we must either live a godly and innocent life, and throughly amend ourselves; or else sin must be punished, and every unclean thing must in the fire and punishment of God's wrath be consumed. Again, though we were virtuous and godly, yet is God of this nature, that he maketh his chosen to be like-fashioned unto the image of his Son, and by much adversity and trouble he leadeth them unto joy; even as it behoved Christ to suffer, and so to enter into his glory. The punishment of sin is hard, and the judgment of the Lord, as often as he cometh to recompense sin, is sharp; which the prophet partly by bodily things doth describe, as other prophets do also. Isai. xiii. Jerem. xv. Amos viii. "The sun shall be turned into blood, &c.;" and even so is it in the opinion of those, that must bear the judgment of God.

*Luke xxiv.*

Forasmuch now as the apostle Peter, according as the matter required, did necessarily allege testimony out of the prophet, concerning the Holy Ghost, who is given to the good children of God; he thought also to specify that which was written in the prophet, as touching the punishment of the wicked, that despise the grace of God; giving a warning thereby unto the Jews, to cease from their unbelieving and shameful life; declaring unto them, that if they proceed forth in wickedness, it should happen unto them, as it did before unto their forefathers, unto whom Joel opened the punishment of God. Whereby we must learn, patiently to bear it, and to take it in good part, when our sins are rebuked, our vices spoken against, and we told that the punishment is at hand. For this custom had the apostles in their preaching and declaring of the gospel, that they not only made mention of the grace of God offered unto the world by Christ, but therewithal likewise they threatened sore punishment to those, that either despised such excellent grace, or having knowledge of the truth did cleave unto vice; which thing in the word of Peter is yet more evident.

The gospel also preacheth amendment of life, and not remission of sins only through the blood of Christ. But now at this present time there be many dainty Christians, as certain princes and senates in the countries and cities, whose opinion is, that the grace of the gospel is to be preached, yea, and they permit Christ and his grace gently and worthily to be spoken of. But if the false gods' service, as the honouring of images, and all that is crept in and erected up in the papistry against God's word, be reproved; or if the preacher speaks against their tyranny, unjust acts, their malicious violence and wilfulness, whereby they oppress poor widows and fatherless children, doing right unto no man; or if the preacher touch them on the galled backs for their excessive pomp and pride, for their rioting, whoredom, adultery, gluttony, drunkenness, fighting, and extortion; if such vices, I say, wherein they still lead their lives, be touched to the quick, then is all favour gone; then, 'Burn these preachers,' say they, 'drown them, they be seditious fellows; they will set us together by the ears, and bring the common people in our necks.' But such men should consider, that unto this office of the preacher it belongeth to cry against vice, lest

<small>Isai. lvi. lvii.
Ezech. iii.</small> he be called of God a blind watchman, a dumb dog, and lest all the souls which perish through his silence be required at his hands: their wilfulness, pride, and vain life they should forsake, and reform themselves, and so needed not the preacher to cry out against them. Now considering that the prophets used, as I said before, to make mention of the kingdom of Jesu Christ, and of the calling of the heathen to the grace and knowledge of God, especially in their orations when they speak of captivity, and deliverance from the same; Joel in his prophecy doth also keep that order. For seeing that the Jews were ever still continually a stiff-necked, rebellious, and unbelieving people, unthankful to the grace of God; the Holy Ghost foresaw their rejection, declaring it by the prophets, and that another people, namely, the heathen, should be received in their stead. For inasmuch as they despised the grace of God, which first was offered unto them, it was meet that "the kingdom of God should be taken from them, and given to another nation." Seeing they thought scorn to come to the marriage, and to the royal feast whereunto they were bidden, it behoved others to be called unto the same. Therefore is Peter earnest upon this sentence: "Whosoever calleth upon the name of the Lord shall be saved." As if he would say: 'O ye Jews, brag not of circumcision, of Abraham, of the temple, or of other ceremonies; think not that ye only are the people of God; the time is now come, that God will bestow his grace upon those whom ye esteem to be unclean. God is no accepter of persons, but among all people whoso calleth upon him shall be saved.'

Of this sentence doth Peter now take occasion more manifestly to speak of the kingdom of Christ: for much more pithily and with more evidence doth the apostles describe the kingdom of Christ, than do the prophets. Whoso calleth upon God's name must know God. Now can no man know God but by Christ. Therefore in this little word, "to call upon the name of the Lord," is comprehended the whole sum of the christian faith: like as oftentimes in the prophets be these,[1] "to swear by God," is contained his whole religion. But forasmuch as the Jews knew not Christ, by whom cometh the true knowledge of God, therefore beginneth Peter, and

[1 Perhaps *by* or *in* these.]

declareth with strong arguments, how the name of God is to be called upon; namely, through true faith in Christ, who is the true Messias, the anointed King and Son of God, which was promised in the prophets. This doth Peter prove by the ground of the resurrection of Christ from death, by his ascension into heaven, and by that he now sitteth at the right hand of God, Lord and King of all things. First let us hear the text.

[Acts ii. 22—28.]

YE men of Israel, hear these words: Jesus of Nazareth, a man approved of God among you with miracles, wonders, and signs, which God did by him in the midst of you, as ye yourselves know; him have ye taken by the hands of unrighteous persons, after he was delivered by the determinate counsel and foreknowledge of God, and have crucified and slain him: whom God hath raised up, and loosed the sorrows of death, because it was impossible that he should be holden of it. For David speaketh of him: Aforehand I saw God always before me; for he is on my right hand, that I should not be moved. Therefore did my heart rejoice, and my tongue was glad; moreover also my flesh shall rest in hope; because thou wilt not leave my soul in hell, neither wilt thou suffer thine Holy One to see corruption. Thou hast shewed me the ways of life; thou shalt make me full of joy with thy countenance.

### DOCTRINE AND FRUIT.

To the intent now that no man should be offended at the death and cross of Christ, Peter sheweth first, that in the counsel of God it was concluded, foreseen, and determined, that the Son of God, the true Messias, should and must die; and how that the same sacrifice was ordained from the beginning of the world, to be slain and offered up upon the cross for our sins. And that no man should make any stop by reason of his death, Peter therefore declareth that he was no misdoer, which had deserved his death by any transgression; but that he was sent unto us by God the Father, to die for us, whereby we might perceive the love of our Father in heaven. And if they now would think, "Well, if it were so concluded in the counsel of God, then are not we guilty of his death;" he answereth unto the same, and saith: "Unrighteous men brought him thereto, and it is ye yourselves that slew him and crucified him." As if he would say: 'Yea, even so behoved it to be, that the righteousness of God for the sin of mankind might be satisfied. Christ must needs die, to recompense and wash away with his blood the sin of all the world. And yet ye Jews, which have betrayed Christ and brought him to the cross, are not unjustly accused. Ye cannot through the 'fore-ordinance of God discharge yourselves, that ye be without sin, seeing ye have slain the Saviour of the world, he being guiltless.' By this now we learn, that when we do wrong and evil, we may not excuse ourselves with the free ordinance of God; for it is not God, but the devil and our own wickedness, that provoketh us to sin.

And here we see, that when the grace of God through the gospel is offered unto the world, the sin and vice also wherein the world is entangled, must be spoken of and touched: for no man can be justified, and come to the health of his soul through Christ, which doth not first know and confess his sin and wickedness. How can he be made whole, that will not know his own disease and sickness? Therefore doth Peter set before their eyes their great sin, which they had committed against the innocent Son of God, saying: "The Innocent and Righteous, whom God had given unto you, have ye slain and crucified; which is a great wickedness and sin. Now go to, on your behalf it was evil done, and grievously offended; but on his behalf it was so ordained before. Therefore at his death, which in the sight of the world was so shameful and vile, ye ought not to be offended; that ye therefore would hold the less of him, or not receive and know him for a Saviour. For if you look upon his former conversation, the same was innocent, pure, and holy; therefore cannot ye doubt but he was sent of God. Besides this, ye have perceived and seen God to be everywhere in his works: for the tokens and wonders which he shewed and declared amongst you, give evident knowledge that God was in him, and wrought in him presently; for no man had been able to do the tokens that he did, unless God had been with him. Which tokens also were spoken of before by the prophets concerning Christ; and by those tokens must ye know and confess, that he is even the true Messias, of whom the prophets spake. Wherefore considering, that by his former doctrine and godly power ye know that he is the true Messias, ye ought not to be offended that he, as an evil doer, was crucified upon the cross: for it was the special determination of God, that Messias should be crucified, according to the foresayings of the prophets. Consider ye also, that the prophets likewise spake of his resurrection from death; by the which ye may well perceive that he is the true Messias.'

Thus earnest is Peter, beating into them the resurrection from the dead, and that out of the scripture. For Christ's resurrection from death is a strong argument to prove his Godhead; as it is taught, Rom. i. John xx.

"Yea, he died," saith Peter, "for our sins, but now he is alive and risen again from death; death hath no more power over him, for he liveth for ever, and his kingdom is everlasting. Yea, unpossible it was, that the Son of God should corrupt in the earth and sepulchre; namely, he that is the firstling risen from the dead, and that from his own godly power." Seeing that these words of Peter concerning the resurrection and life of Christ were little credited among the Jews, he allegeth the 15th psalm of David, who amongst [Psal. xvi.] them was in great reputation. But now might the Jews say or think : "David speaketh these words of himself, and not of Christ." That weapon, therefore, doth Peter take from them, and proveth, that the same words may in no wise be referred unto David; but that David, as a prophet having knowledge of things to come, spake them of Christ, in whom they be now fulfilled; and thus he saith :

---

[Acts ii. 29—31.]

YE men and brethren; let me freely speak unto you of the patriarch David; for he is both dead and buried, and his sepulchre remaineth with us until this day. Therefore seeing he was a prophet, and knew that God had sworn unto him with an oath, that Christ, as concerning the flesh, should come of the fruits of his loins, and should sit on his seat; he, knowing this before, spake of the resurrection of Christ, that his soul should not be left in hell, neither his flesh should see corruption. This Jesus hath God raised up, whereof we are all witnesses.

### DOCTRINE AND FRUIT.

The prophet David speaketh of one, whose flesh should not corrupt. Now could not he have spoken this of himself, for his flesh corrupted in the sepulchre, which we yet have, and his bones lie yet in the sepulchre: by the which it may well be perceived, that David, as a prophet knowing of things to come, spake of another, which should be born out of his own loins and seed, whom God with a solemn oath had promised to sit upon his seat, and reign after him; not only for a season, but also that his governance, kingdom, and dominion, should be perpetual, and endure for ever. And this king is Christ the true Messias, who as concerning the flesh was born of the seed of David, and is his son.

If this son now of David had after death remained still in death, and not risen from death again, how could he then reign for ever? It is evident therefore, that David out of the Holy Ghost, who had opened this unto him, prophesied it of the resurrection of Christ his Son, the eternal King. For though he as a very man died indeed upon the cross, and was then buried; yet his soul, or life, remained not in death, neither did his body resolve into corruption, as other men's; but on the third day he rose again from death to life. This must we needs testify; for after his resurrection he appeared oft unto us. We saw him, we heard him, we handled him, we did eat and drink with him.

Here we learn, that the saints in the old testament understood and knew by faith the resurrection and eternal kingdom of Christ, seeing they prophesied of it so evidently. Here is also proved, that Christ died in very deed, and yet abode

*Ps. lxxxix.*
*2 Sam. vii.*

not still in death, forasmuch as he overcame it: also, that the power and virtue of his holy passion and death came not only to the living upon earth, but unto all those that died before him.; according as St Peter in his Epistle, and the Article of our Belief, HE DESCENDED INTO HELL, declareth. Whereof in the Catechism upon the Creed there is made mention sufficient[1].

[Acts ii. 33—35.]

SINCE now that he by the right hand of God is exalted, and hath received of the Father the promise of the Holy Ghost; he hath shed forth this gift, which ye now see and hear. For David is not ascended into heaven; but he saith: The Lord said to my Lord, Sit thou on my right hand, till I make thine enemies thy footstool. *Psal. cx.*

### DOCTRINE AND FRUIT.

WE believe that Jesus Christ, our King and Saviour, is not only risen again from death to life, but also is ascended up into heaven, sitteth at the right hand of God, and reigneth for ever. For though he here a season was despised and refused, as the stone of the builders; yet hath the strong hand of God exalted him, and mightily wrought in him. Which thing may well be perceived by this, (as St Peter here valiantly concludeth,) that he sendeth down from on high such an excellent gift of the Holy Ghost upon those that are his. This is a sure evidence, that he mightily reigneth at the right hand of God, and hath all things in his hand; seeing he hath power of the Spirit of God, whom he poureth into the hearts of his, and that sometime in visible manner. For the glorious triumpher, ascending up to heaven with great victory, did after the custom of great kings, and let fall his gifts down upon us, and parted them among us, namely, the gifts of the Holy Ghost, whom he as man received of the Father, but after the Godhead he had him *Psal. cxviii.* *Ephes. iv.*

[1 What Catechism is here referred to, is very doubtful.]

alway; for of the Father and of the Son there is one only Spirit.

Neither may this be applied unto David. For though he, as a just friend of God, be saved and come to heaven; yet did not he immediately after death ascend into heaven with body and soul, that he might be reported to sit at the right hand of God. For his words speak of another, whom he calleth his Lord; namely, in the hundreth and ninth psalm he saith: "God the Father said unto my Lord, even the Son, Sit thou on my right hand."

<small>Matt. xxii.<br>[Psal. cx.]</small>

[Acts ii. 36.]

So therefore let all the house of Jerusalem know for a surety, that God hath made this Jesus, whom ye have crucified, Lord and Messias.

### DOCTRINE AND FRUIT.

WITH these words doth Peter conclude his oration, exhorting them not to doubt Jesus Christ to be the same anointed Saviour and King, who of God the Father was first promised, and then given for the deliverance of the people of the Jews and of all nations.

In this conclusion is comprehended the sum of the whole christian faith; namely, that we believe that Jesus, who was born of the virgin Mary, and crucified of the Jews, is the true Christ, that is to say, Messias, even the king that was ordained and anointed of God, to reign for ever over all faithful believers, Lord of the whole world, and Saviour of all such as put their trust in him. This hath God the Father opened and set forth unto us by miracles, by the resurrection, by the ascension, and by the power of the Holy Ghost, that we might believe it, and not doubt thereof. Therefore saith John, "Whoso believeth that Jesus is Christ, the same is born of God."

[Acts ii. 37—41.]

When they heard this, they were pricked in their hearts, and said unto Peter and to the other apostles: Ye men and brethren, what shall we do? Peter said unto them: Repent of your sins, and be baptized every one of you in the name of Jesus Christ, for the remission of sins; and ye shall receive the gift of the Holy Ghost. For the promise was made unto you, and to your children, and to all that are afar off, even as many as the Lord our God shall call. And with many other words bare he witness, and exhorted them, saying: Save yourselves from this untoward generation. Then they that gladly received his preaching were baptized; and the same day there were added unto them about three thousand souls.

### DOCTRINE AND FRUIT.

This is the fruit and end which followeth out of the preaching of the word of God, that they whose hearts God toucheth, are so sorry for their sins, that it even pierceth them. For God's word is even a sharp two-edged sword, and entereth through to the depth. Blessed are all they which so read and hear the word of God, that they, begin to be ashamed of their sins and wickedness, being repentant and sorry therefore. A blessed and wholesome sorrow is that, which riseth and groweth out of the truth, which is opened unto the heart by the Holy Ghost: which Spirit in the heart giveth hope upon the mercy of God, and driveth away all despair. Then beginneth a man to ask, "What shall I do?" Then inquireth he after the will of God; and such a man that so asketh is easy to be helped. Soon is he healed, that, knowing his disease, would fain be made whole.

Unto such a man doth the faithful minister of Christ give counsel out of the scripture, and sheweth him the fruit of Christ preached and known. He doth not bid him to bestow money on solemnities and dirges, on images, monasteries, or cowls, in buying of pardons; he doth not will to run unto Rome, or to Lauret[1]; but requireth of him the best and most profitable thing of all, namely, amendment and conversion of life. Our minds, our works, and manners must be altered, if we will please God. Whoso saith with his heart, that he believeth in Christ, holding Christ for his Saviour and King, must forsake his evil ways, eschewing evil, and doing good. Jere. vii. xi. Isai. i. Nineve stood still upright, when they took upon them true conversion and amendment. As for Hierusalem, though they offered many sacrifices, and fasted much, it helped not: because there was not true reformation and forsaking of sin, needs must they be destroyed, and miserably perish. To botch or patch the matter it will not help; there is no remedy; we must become godly and virtuous of life. It availeth not to dissemble; God looketh into the heart, which he will have pure and unfeigned. Forasmuch then as we through baptism in the faith of Christ have received Christ, and are marked out for him, having once forgiveness of sins through the grace and gift of Christ, let us be of a virtuous life, walking innocently and in the fear of God. Let us die therefore to the innocency which is restored unto us again through Christ: let us daily remember to hearken and follow the admonishment of the Spirit, which teacheth us all good things. We are they, unto whom God hath promised his grace of the Spirit, yea, and unto our children also, so far as we abide in his covenants. Let us thankfully receive such excellent grace, dear brethren, being ware that we stain not the temple of Jesus Christ and of his holy Spirit with filthiness of the world; that we never make ourselves partakers in the iniquity of wicked and faithless men; but to lead here a pure and clean conversation with a good conscience before God, our most loving Father; and alway lift up our minds unto the place, where Christ our Lord and King reigneth at the right hand of God, from whence he shall come and take us unto himself. At all times therefore ought we to watch and wait for his coming, that we may joyfully receive him, and be partakers with him in eternal bliss.

Col. iii.

Here also we learn, how faithful believers use themselves

[1 Loretto.]

in the outward sacraments. They that, being moved by the inspiration of the Holy Ghost in their hearts, do hear the eternal word preached, giving credit unto it, and gladly receiving it, these do not afterward despise the outward sacraments, which God hath instituted for the welfare of his church, but use the same with all obedience, good-will, and reverence. To use the sacraments without faith profiteth not, but rather hurteth; to be loth to use them declareth a compulsion and unbelief.

For though the water in baptism be an outward thing, and cannot cleanse the soul from sin; yet the faithful do know right well, that Christ, the eternal Wisdom in whom they believe, did not institute it in vain; and therefore will not they contemn or leave unexercised the ordinance of their Head, to whom they as members are incorporated by faith. For they know, that Christ with these outward tokens thought to couple and knit together the members of his holy church in obedience and love one towards another; whereby they knowing one another among themselves, might by such exterior things stir and provoke one another to love and godliness. They know also, that sacraments are evidences of the promise and grace of God, which they after a visible and palpable manner do set forth, declare, and represent unto us. These tokens of grace doth no man use more devoutly and with more reverence, than he that in himself is certified and assured of the gracious favour of God; as we see in Cornelius, in Paul, and in Queen Candace's chamberlain.

What fruit followeth the preaching of the gospel, it is here evidently seen: for in one day at Peter's preaching, by the working of the Holy Ghost, there came three thousand men to the church of God. God suffereth not his word to pass void and unfruitful. Very earnest therefore and diligent ought we to be, and to spare no trouble, cost, and labour, that the pure and sincere gospel, the word of truth, may every where be preached by good and faithful men; not doubting God will give blessed success thereto, that the seed sown by the minister shall bring forth fruit.

[Acts ii. 42.]

AND they continued in the apostles' doctrine, in the fellowship, in the breaking of bread, and in prayers.

### DOCTRINE AND FRUIT.

To endure crowneth and rewardeth all works: "whoso endureth unto the end shall be saved;" without continuance may no good thing be brought to end and fruit. Therefore is it now declared, how the word preached in the church of God bringeth fruit, and what the same fruits be, wherein faithful believers do exercise themselves.

Saint Luke mentioneth four things that proceed out of the faith in Christ; for faith is not void nor idle, but worketh without ceasing in them that believe. Therefore here we find a pattern and mirror, how it ought to go in the church of Christ; for where these four things be, there is Christ's church. First, the church of Christ, which is the fellowship of all saints and faithful believers, endureth, abideth, and continueth " in the doctrine of the apostles;" for every thing is preserved with that out of the which it is born. Now is the church of God born first of the word of truth : therefore in the word of truth also must it endure and be kept; daily must it be planted, nourished, and watered with the word and doctrine; the success and the increase doth God give.

John i.
Mark xvi.
Rom. i.

The doctrine of the apostles is nothing else but the holy gospel, which the Son of God committed unto them, and which they received of him; which also the prophets before Christ spake of by the Holy Ghost. What gospel was preached by the apostles, it is easy to perceive by the aforesaid sermon of Peter, and of others in the Acts, by the evangelists and epistles of the apostles; namely, that " God so loved the world, that he gave his only-begotten Son for it, that whosoever believeth on him should not perish, but have eternal life." Also, he died for us, rose again from death, ascended up to heaven, and sitteth there at the right hand of God, being king and high priest for ever; in whose name all knees must bow, and without whom "there is none other name given unto men, in whom we must be saved;" than the only name of Jesus, whose blood washeth away our sins, and he is the only perpetual mediation between God and us. 1 John ii. 1 Tim. ii.

In this doctrine continueth the church, being builded upon the sure rock Jesus Christ, and is not moved or driven away by every wind of strange and inconstant doctrine. She Matt. vii. xvi. Ephes. iv. hearkeneth not to the voice of any other, but of Jesus her shepherd. In the doctrine of the apostles there is no deceit, no guile, no poison. And in this doctrine is found none of those things, which certain years after the apostles were brought in by Romish bishops, as masses, dirges, cloisters, worshipping of idols, setting up of images, buying of pardons, forbidding of this or that meat.

First now, doth faith in Christ bring forth this fruit in the church, namely, in faithful believers, that it draweth them to the doctrine of the truth, by the which they became believers; and in the same it maketh them to continue, that they neither hearken nor give credit to any false erroneous doctrine. For they do very assuredly know, that such doctrines are not wholesome, but venomous and hurtful. But in the gospel of our Saviour Jesus Christ, and in the doctrine of the holy apostles, they are sure to find the truth, which nourisheth and preserveth them unto eternal life. The church of God abhorreth all untruth, for she knoweth it is of the devil; but of the truth is she desirous, for she knoweth that the same cometh of God, and bringeth unto God again.

This evangelical truth and doctrine of the apostles, in the which the church of God and all the members of Christ must continue, hath been of long time, even from the beginning, comprehended in certain articles, which we call the CREED, whereof there is sufficient mention made in the Catechism[1]. Among the true children and servants of God also there is no schism, doubt, nor division, concerning the head and chief articles, in the which they are well and firmly established, fully persuaded, and of one mind and consent.

And whereas there be some men which overreach and go beyond this mark, willing other men, and compelling Chris-

[1 See above, p. 407.]

tians, as far as in them lieth, thereto, teaching those to be heretics and damned, that cleave to the only doctrine of the apostles; the same cometh and proceedeth of the presumptuous arrogancy of flesh, who esteemeth his own invention more than that which God speaketh: as when they say, that images must be had in churches, that pardons must be bought with money, and such like things, which are not grounded in the doctrine of Christ nor of the apostles, nor mentioned in the articles of the right and true ancient belief, but invented by the fantasy and covetousness of men.

The second thing that must be constantly and inviolably kept in the church of God, is the communion and "fellowship;" namely, that none look unto his own singular profit, that no man seek himself, but that every member, looking one to another what he lacketh, supply the same, helping him and comforting him, and giving him the best counsel he can. This friendly love and loving fellowship ought to be among Christians.

All temporal and outward goods ought to be common among them: not, as some fondly think, that I must defraud another of that which is his, or take it against his will, whether he will or no, or that I should go idly and loitering, eating and consuming that which other men labour and travail for; or to think, that when I do service and am profitable to no man, every man shall give and serve me. Christian love, which groweth out of the belief and doctrine of the gospel, must distribute the goods and make them common; it must not be any man's greedy desire, presumption, nor wilfulness, that shall do it.

All faithful believers are one body. Now, like as in the body one member serveth to the profit and wealth of another, so ought one Christian to help and serve another in love. The eye looketh not to himself only, but unto the whole body; the mouth eateth for the whole body, and for all the other members; the stomach digesteth for all the whole body, and for all the members. Thus ought it to be likewise among the spiritual members of the body of our Saviour Jesus Christ. No man must be wise and learned for himself only; no man ought to be rich for himself; but every man's gifts must serve to the profit one of another, and to the edifying and sustaining of the whole body. Every one is bound to serve the body, according to the gift and measure which the Spirit of God hath distributed unto him.

Among all living creatures, there is none created to a more loving and friendly society and fellowship than man. Hereunto serve all sciences and handicrafts, that men, after a friendly manner agreeing among themselves, may relieve one another's necessity and want, and help to bear one another's burden. Hereunto serve all inward gifts of the mind, as reason, and judgment, will, and remembrance: also the speech given of God unto man, whereby one is known and discerned, and made privy one to another. And therefore is man born into this world without any defence or weapon, bare, naked, and feeble; whereas all other creatures living in this world bring with them every one his weapon and defence. The bear hath his claws and teeth, the horse his hoof, the ox his horns, the hedgehog his pricks, and the serpent his poison, &c. Only man is born smooth and unweaponed, to signify that he must not be mad, furious, and terrible, but mild, loving, and gentle; there must be one mind, one meaning, and one will.

Man also cometh into the world bare, and naked, weak, feeble, and impotent, not able to do any manner of thing to help himself, but must stand unto the courtesy of another: for if he be not helped, relieved, and succoured, he could not choose but perish; there were no remedy. Whereby Almighty God will declare, that there is no man that either may or can live without the help and comfort of another. Thus the poor, wretched, and distressed child, lying upon all four, (whom, if it were not for pity, no man would take up, but let it lie still,) is helped, nourished, and brought up of the mother, nurse, &c. Other folks must cherish it; by other folks' help must it live: for nothing doth it bring with it into this world; it must beg and borrow everything, and therefore it weepeth and crieth.

This teacheth us to do good, to be obedient, loving, and thankful to our parents, and unto those which bring us up and do cherish us, that we recompense them according to our power. By this also we learn to help others, and to have compassion of them when they are in need, remembering and considering, out of what misery and poverty other folks have helped and brought us.

Who is he that is at this present so rich, so mighty, and strong in this world, if he will live, but he must use the help and service of poor and feeble folks, as the husbandman, the miller, the baker, the shepherd, the weaver, &c.? Yea, the higher and greater any man is in office or authority, so much the more must he use and have the help of other people, that are not so great as himself. Therefore doth God set up some so high, that they must make provision and help all those which are under them, seeing that they must have the use of them all. For the poor and they that be under must support and bear up the rich and mighty, as pillars do the house, that they fall not: for without the help and service of such are not they able to live in their dignity and calling one day. Therefore it is ordained of Almighty God in his secret wisdom, that certain countries lack some things, whereof others have sufficient and too much, that one might be sustained by another, and that no man shall be enough to himself.

God hath given unto man remembrance, to the intent that he should never forget the benefits which he from his youth upwards hath received of others, and daily doth receive; without the which he cannot live. And also again remember, and forget not, how and in what manner he ought to behave himself in love, in compassion, in succour, and in faithfulness towards those that have any ways need of his help. To this is he moved when he considereth and pondereth in his thoughts the weakness, feebleness, and necessity of man's corrupt nature, which constraineth us to lack so many things.

Hereof groweth unity, love, and fellowship among men, when we cast and call to our minds thus: either he hath been, or is now, profitable unto us, or he doth good unto ours, of whom we have profit, or hereafter he may do us some good. This to be so, there is not any man that can deny: and whereas we perceive not this, and are not of one mind, friendly, and fellows in love and good-will one towards another, but given unto such variance, dissension, strife, and discord, it cometh through the darkness of our own wicked and froward natures and dispositions.

Forasmuch now as our eyes are so blinded, that we see not God's ordinance and creation in man; our ears are so stopped, that we will not hear the plain and perfect voice of nature; our understanding and remembrance so dull and blunt, that we will not once regard or think any such thing, whereby we might the sooner forsake the division and stiffness of our heart, and in friendly unity and brotherly love to do good one to another; Christ therefore, the restorer of our decayed nature, and the only true and eternal light, came into this world to illuminate and lighten our blind eyes; to cry with his voice unto us that be dumb, and to set that again before our eyes, which we ourselves have made dark and dim. He crieth unto us in his gospel with a loud voice, so that no man can say he hath not heard it. He is the heavenly schoolmaster, the eternal wisdom, the fountain of all knowledge, the only and true teacher, the whole building of his church, the foundation and roof: the beginning and end of all his commandments hath he set and comprehended in only love, exhorting us to love, unity, and friendship, and saying, that "men hereby shall know us to be his disciples, if we love together, and do good one unto another;" and that then we are right and true Christians, when we do love one another, as he hath loved us.

What is a Christian else, but such an one, as being by the grace of Jesus Christ and of his Spirit delivered from the destroyed, poisoned, and wicked nature, is restored again to the original nature and godly disposition, from the which our spiritual enemy the devil had seduced him, taken him prisoner, and overcome him? Thus through Christ is man become the child of God; even he, which through pride, self-love, greediness, envy, hatred, discord, and division, became afore the devil's prisoner. Christ teacheth us love, faithfulness, and friendship; to love our neighbour as ourself, to do good, and help the poor: as in the fifth chapter of Matthew and the seventh verse, and in Luke, the sixth chapter, and in the five and twentieth chapter of Matthew, and in the thirteenth chapter of John, and in the twelfth chapter to the Romans and thirteenth verse, and John in his epistle. The apostles therefore, and faithful believers, at the beginning, as appeareth in the second chapter of the Acts of the Apostles, of very love and ferventness of the Spirit, had all things common, "distributing unto every one according as he had need." And this is the fellowship that is here spoken of, that as oft as the Christians came together, there was collection made and gathered for the relief and sustentation of the poor; whereof it is written in the first epistle to the Corinthians, the eleventh chapter, and fifteenth verse; and also in the second epistle to the Corinthians, the eighth chapter, and ninth verse.

The third thing is the breaking of the bread, the token of the new and everlasting covenant, which Christ upon the cross confirmed with his body and blood. This did the holy apostles and faithful believers use thus after the instruction of Christ. They took the bread; the same was broken, and to every one a portion given, which they did eat, giving thanks unto their heavenly Father, who had purged them from sin through the blood of Jesus Christ his dear Son; and so held they the joyful and glorious memorial of Christ's death.

Thus ought all faithful believers to do likewise: when they come together, as appertaineth, then with the breaking of the bread, and distribution of it among themselves, they must be mindful of the precious death and passion of Jesus Christ, rendering unto him perpetual thanks therefore. For Christ did not institute and ordain this his supper in vain, but thereby to make his church mindful and put them in remembrance of his death; and that over and besides faith, which inwardly liveth in the heart, the outward senses also might have somewhat to stir and draw them unto that, which faith inwardly considereth and looketh upon. These tokens are instituted, to signify and represent unto us high and great things, to gather together and unite the church; that, being dispersed every where over the face of the whole earth, might gather together into one communion and fellowship in Christ, and be made partakers of his promises, and enjoy those comfortable blessings which he hath promised from the beginning, namely, such as be faithful and true believers; and that the exterior and outward sense might from all corporal things be withdrawn to that which is spiritual. For the eyes see the bread, which representeth the body of Christ: they see, as the bread is broken, so was the body of Christ broken upon the cross for our sins; and that as the wine is poured in and out, so was the precious blood of Jesus Christ shed to wash away all our sins. The ears do hear Christ's words spoken by the minister in the person of Jesus Christ; by the which the promise is renewed, by which means those that are his, and of his church, are by a certain feeling and comfort in their souls and consciences refreshed. The taste upon the tongue, the smell in the nose, and likewise the handling, and so each other member in his several office, every one of them hath his delight and operation, in confessing, acknowledging, and doing his service unto faith.

But for what cause our Saviour Christ did specially use bread and wine before any other corporal things, to signify his death and shedding of his blood, it may well and easily be perceived by the nature of faith. With bread is the body fed and sustained, with wine are men's hearts made merry. Forasmuch then as faith, the life of our souls, through the flesh of Christ spiritually eaten is nourished and sustained; and seeing our mind is moistened and refreshed with true and perfect joy through the blood of Christ shed for us; there was nothing more meet, nothing more expedient, nothing more necessary for this sacrament, than bread and wine.

Moreover, through the blood of Christ are all other oblations and sacrifices clean laid aside: and therefore Christ, minding to finish the high sacrifice upon the cross, testified and declared beforehand, that his body being offered up, and his blood shed, should be sufficient to wash away all men's sins, and that from thenceforth there should not need any other sin-offering, in the which there must blood be shed. Therefore would he with evident and plain words testify and say: "This is my body, which is given for you; do this in remembrance of me. This is the cup of the new testament in my blood, which shall be shed for many to the forgiveness of sins." To the intent then that this excellent and worthy propitiation and sacrifice should not [be lost][1] out of their eyes and hearts, he added visible signs, not bare signs, but seals of his covenant, as was the circumcision and passah, and common tokens of love and friendship amongst men, even bread and wine, which have no blood, to declare that all blood for sin is only in Jesus Christ.

Christ's mind was also, in one body to couple and knit together[2] the whole multitude of his church. To signify this,

[[1] A word is here wanting in the original edition.]
[[2] After *together* the old edition repeats *in one body*.]

there[1] was nothing more apt and fit than wine and bread: for like as out of many corns is made one paste and one bread, and like as out of many grapes one wine floweth together; even so by faith and love become they all one body, that eat of one bread and drink of one cup.

And even from the beginning of the world it hath always been the use among men, that with bread and wine they have made and confirmed great friendship and league: and even so Christ with the distributing of the bread among his disciples would establish an everlasting friendship with them.

The fourth thing now in the church of Christ is prayer; namely, as Christ taught them to pray unto the Father of heaven, that the kingdom of his Son might still grow and increase, that his glory might arise and spread itself throughout all the world, that his name might be hallowed, and his will fulfilled, &c.

This is the necessariest thing of all: and if we lack this, in vain are all our good works, in vain are all the honest actions of a civil life, in vain are all godly exercises; nothing prospereth we go about, no oblation is sanctified, all is impurity, that we either do or think. The holy apostle Paul willeth us to pray continually: God granteth not the presence of his Spirit to any thing but unto prayer. Without the presence of God's Spirit, unprofitable is the word preached, unprofitable are the sacraments ministered, unprofitable shall all things be unto us; so that prayer is most requisite. Let us therefore pray unto Almighty God, to increase in us the spirit of prayer, that with our soul and spirit we may pray continually for spiritual gifts, that they may daily increase in us to his glory. Grant this the great giver of all good gifts, for his mercy sake! To whom be all honour, glory, power, dominion, and thanks, for ever and ever. Amen.

[[1] Old edition, *that there*.]

## A PRAYER.

O MERCIFUL God, preserve our hearts from pride, from vain-glory, and from shameful covetousness: give us grace to abide in thy holy vocation, and to be thankful for thy grace; that the fall of thy apostle being always before our eyes, we may walk in thy fear before thee. For if we stand, we must take heed that we fall not, neither despise those that as yet do not stand. Make us to continue [in] thy grace; for nothing have we, saving only that which we have received of thee. And if of weakness we fall, put thy hand under us, O Lord, and suffer us not to despair in sin; but cause us with repentance and sorrow for our offence to resort unto thee. O keep us, that we neither despair, nor betray thy dearly beloved Son, whom thou through thy gospel dost send unto us; for without him is no safeguard, but eternal death and damnation. From which keep us, good Lord, for thy mercies' sake. Amen.

FINIS.

# A FAYTHFVL

and most Godly treatyse concernyng the most sacred sacrament of the blessed body and bloud of our sauiour Christ compiled by John Caluine, a man of no less lernyng and literature then Godly studye, and example of lyuyng. And translated into Lattyn by Lacius a man of lyke excellencie, and now last of al, translatyd into Englishe bi a faythful brother, no lesse desyrous to profite the weake brothers than to exercise ye talent of the Lorde to his honoure and glorye.

)✠(

;'

Wher vnto is added the order that the church and congregacyon of Christ in Denmarke doth vse.

(',')(,',)
(:)

Luke. 19. Chapter.
Be doynge tyll I come.

# A

# TREATISE ON THE SACRAMENT

OF THE

# BODY AND BLOOD OF CHRIST,

TRANSLATED FROM CALVIN.

[The title of this treatise, and the address which is prefixed to it by the translator, contain a full account of its history. The original was published by Calvin in French, A.D. 1540, and stands the first in order of his miscellaneous treatises, in the Latin edition of his works, with the title, "De Cœna Domini."

With reference to the church of Denmark, by which the services subjoined to this treatise were adopted, the reformation of this church began in the year 1521, under Christiern II. It was carried on by his uncle Frederic, Duke of Holstein, who succeeded him on his deposition from the throne; and was finally completed by Christiern III.; who however, as Seckendorf states, contrary to the advice and wishes of Luther, proceeded to great extremities against the bishops, who resisted all the efforts which were made by the sovereign for the reformation of the abuses of the church. These were deposed by him, and in their room he appointed seven superintendents, who discharged the spiritual part of the episcopal office, without sharing any portion of the temporal power and authority formerly possessed by the bishops. A more detailed account of the reformation of the Danish church will be found in Mosheim, Eccl. Hist. Cent. XVI. Sect. I. chap. ii.; and in Seckendorf, Hist. Lutheranismi, Lib. III. Vol. II. pp. 88, 89, 241—243.

There are two editions of this treatise, the first of which is without date; the last was printed (with the epistle to the reader much enlarged) by John Day, between 1546 and 1584. Herbert possessed a copy of both editions: the present Editor has not been able to meet with a copy of the latter. The work is here reprinted from a copy of the first edition in the University Library, Cambridge.]

¶ TO ALL THEM THAT PROFESS THE CHRISTIAN NAME, THE TRANSLATOR WISHETH MERCY FROM GOD THE FATHER THROUGH OUR ONLY ADVOCATE AND MEDIATOR, JESU CHRIST, WHOSE SPIRIT, THE GIVER OF ALL GOODNESS, LEAD YOU INTO ALL GHOSTLY KNOWLEDGE.

---

As the author of this little book, moved with the desire to profit as well the rude and unlearned, as the lettered and professors of knowledge, wrote it in his vulgar tongue; even so I, most dearly beloved brethren, moved also with the desire to profit my natural countrymen, so much as shall be in my little power, have thought it my bounden duty to employ my diligence to the translating thereof.

And because it hath pleased the Lord to give me more knowledge in the Latin tongue than in the French (wherein this book was first written), I have translated it after the Latin copy, putting the faithful reader out of doubt, that I have not in any point gone from the true meaning of the author, but have thoroughly observed the phrases of both tongues, avoiding in all that I might the dark manner of translating after the Latin phrases; to the intent the English reader might have the full understanding hereof, without any knowledge of the Latin tongue. And that the godly mind of the studious readers may be the more stirred to read the matter with indifferent judgment, I shall without dissimulation assure them, that herein is no matter of contention at all; but charitably, without any word of reproach, as well the right use of the sacrament of the body and blood of Christ, as the abuses and errors concerning the same, are set forth so plainly, that no man (unless he will willingly shut up the eyes of his conscience against the manifest truth) can read the book thoroughly, but he shall easily perceive, what great abuses have these six hundred years been, and are at this present day, maintained and defended, as concerning the ministration thereof.

First, for that the popish church have and do abuse it, in offering it up as an healthful sacrifice for the redemption of the souls of the congregation: for in their canon, which they call the secrets of the mass, are these words: *Pro redemptione animarum ecclesiæ tuæ;* that is to say, "For the redemption of the souls of thy church." Where they hold opinion and teach, that by offering up this sacrifice (as they call it) they apply to, or make partakers of the passion of Christ, all them that hear or hire such masses as they have invented, dashed full of whisperings, duckings, and crossings, besides the demure countenance in their turn and half turn. I will speak no more as concerning their fond inventions about the ministration of this most sacred sacrament, lest I should thereby be an offence or stumblingblock to the weak brothers, whose consciences are not yet fully satisfied as concerning the true belief of this holy mystery; I mean, lest I should give them occasion to do, as certain fond talkers have of late days done, and at this present day do invent and apply to this most holy sacrament names of despite and reproach, as to call it "Jack-in-the-box," and "Round Robin," and such other not only fond, but also blasphemous names, not only void of all edification (which ought to be the end of all our doings and sayings), but very slanderous also. For though the thing being so turned from the right use, as it is, be abominable, so that it is lawful for us to speak unreverently of it in the abuse; yet is it not meet for them that profess charity, nothing to refrain for conscience' sake: the conscience, I say, of the weak brothers, not yet strong in the truth; and so much the more, for that many godly-minded persons, which by the persuasions of certain discreet and modest brothers have been made, of Romish idolaters and diligent students of duncical dregs, disciples of great hope in the sincere and true evangelic doctrine, have by the hearing of these names of reproach and despite taken occasion to think, that the knowledge which these men did profess, which would be so outrageous as to mock and jest at the remembrance of our redemption, could not proceed of the Spirit of God; and have through this persuasion returned to their old leaven again; thinking them to be the true teachers of God's doctrine, which offend in the contrary, making it so divine a thing, that it should be of no less importance than the whole Trinity, the Father, the Son, and Holy Ghost: for so they affirm, saying, that forasmuch as it is the body of Christ, and that Christ is in all places at once with his Father, and his Father with him and the Holy Ghost, it must needs follow, that in it is the whole Trinity, the Father, the Son, and the Holy Ghost. For these are not nor cannot be separated.

I will say for these men, that "they have the zeal of God, but it is not according to knowledge." For as the Jews (who were from time to time taught and believed, that God dwelled in the temple that Solomon builded) could not abide to hear that God should not dwell in a temple made with man's hands, nothing considering that he is *immensus*, and cannot be contained, for heaven is his seat, and the earth his footstool; even so these men, through a fond persuasion of the essential presence of Christ in the sacrament, cannot abide to hear, that the whole Trinity should not be really contained under a piece of bread, yea, under every little crumb thereof. I speak not this, as one putting no difference between that sacramental bread and our common bread; but that I may thereby declare and open the great blindness of them, that knowing and confessing the immensurable nature of God, would have him really and naturally contained in so small a thing.

"Heaven is my seat," saith he, "and the earth is my footstool:" and yet will they truss him so short, that they will bring him into a little pix, wherein a man cannot turn his fist.

He filleth all places, and is contained in no place; and yet will they at their pleasure place him in the chalice: he was never visible to the mortal eye, and yet will they make him appear at every knave's request, that will do as other men do, I mean pay their ordinary shot; and so doing he shall not only see him, but also eat him up every morsel.

I would the men would diligently peruse the words of Saint Augustine in their legend on Corpus Christi day, which are these, taken out of the twenty-sixth Treatise upon John: "He that eateth my flesh and drinketh my blood, tarrieth in me, and I in him. To eat that meat therefore, and to drink that drink, is to tarry in Christ, and to have Christ tarrying in us. And by this, he that tarrieth not in Christ, and in whom Christ tarrieth not, no doubt he doth not spiritually eat his flesh, nor drink his blood, although he do carnally and visibly crush with his teeth the sacrament of the body and blood of Christ; but he doth rather eat and drink to his damnation the sacrament of so noble a thing[1]." Here is your transubstantiation utterly denied; for Saint Augustine putteth a plain difference between the sacrament and the thing itself. Again, the same Augustine in the same place addeth these words: "The sacrament of this thing, that is, of the unity of the body and blood of Christ, is in some places prepared every day; in some other places but certain days, as on the Sunday; and is taken of the table of the Lord to some persons to life, to some other to destruction: but the thing itself is to all persons to life, and to destruction to no man that may be partaker thereof[2]." What needeth it to rehearse any more witnesses, seeing these are sufficient, either to prove Saint Augustine an heretic, either else to declare this transubstantiation to be both foolish and abominable; both for that it trusseth together the divinity, and enlargeth the humanity beyond all measure, thruching up into a corner that part which no place can contain, and setting at liberty to be in all places that which must needs be in one place only? If every man will follow his conscience in this matter, I doubt not but they shall soon

[1 Denique jam exponit, quomodo id fiat quod loquitur, et quid sit manducare ejus corpus, et sanguinem ejus bibere. *Qui manducat carnem meam, et bibit meum sanguinem, in me manet, et ego in illo.* Hoc est ergo manducare illam escam, et bibere illum potum, in Christo manere, et illum manentem in se habere. Ac per hoc qui non manet in Christo, et in quo non manet Christus, proculdubio nec manducat spiritaliter carnem ejus, nec bibit ejus sanguinem, licet carnaliter et visibiliter premat dentibus sacramentum corporis et sanguinis Christi: sed magis tantæ rei sacramentum ad judicium sibi manducat et bibit, quia immundus præsumpsit ad Christi accedere sacramenta. Augustin. Expositionis in Evang. Joannis Tractatus XXVI, de Cap. VI. Tom. ix. p. 50. G. H. Ed. 1541.]

[2 Hujus rei sacramentum, id est, unitatis corporis et sanguinis Christi, alicubi quotidie, alicubi certis intervallis dierum in dominica mensa præparatur, et de dominica mensa sumitur quibusdam ad vitam, quibusdam ad exitium. Res vero ipsa, cujus et sacramentum est, omni homini ad vitam, nulli ad exitium, quicumque ejus particeps fuerit. Ib. F.]

be persuaded, how far wide this transubstantiation is from the truth. But now take they hold of the words of the Lord at the first institution of this most sacred sacrament, which are these: "This is my body, which shall be delivered for you. This is my blood which shall be shed for you and many unto remission of sins." What natural, essential, and real presence they build upon these words, is abundantly declared in the Bishop of Winchester and Doctor Smith's books[3].

I shall therefore most humbly desire the reader utterly to shake off all superstitious persuasions of old usages, giving himself wholly to the teaching of the Spirit of God, who teacheth inwardly in the heart all them that give over themselves to his teaching and information. And I, for my part, yielding me to the same Spirit, shall in this case write the thing only, which my conscience shall give me to be of the Spirit of the living God; and my trust is, that the good Spirit of God is my leader.

As concerning the understanding of the words of Christ, you shall know that the manner of teaching is double, that is to say, by words, and by signs. By words we teach, when we declare unto the hearers by words the thing that we would they should know. By signs we teach, when we do something, whereby the beholders may gather our meaning; as Tarquinius Superbus did, when he struck off the tops of the highest poppies, declaring thereby, that his advice was to have the greatest rulers beheaded[4]. We teach also both by words and by signs, when we add unto the words some action, to declare and, as it were, to expound the words withal: as is mentioned in the Acts of the Apostles [Acts xxi. 10—11.] of a prophet, which declared unto Paul the persecution he should endure at Hierusalem, whither he was going; and to make the matter more plain, he took Paul's girdle from about him, and tied his feet withal, saying, "The man whose girdle this is shall be thus bounden at Hierusalem." Even so, good christian brethren, our Saviour Christ, willing to

[3 For a full account of these works, see Strype's Life of Cranmer, Book II. Chap. xxxv.; also Memorials. II. 1. p. 52; also Cranmer's Writings and Disputations relative to the Sacrament of the Lord's Supper; Hooper's Answer to the Bishop of Winchester's Book; Early Writings of Bishop Hooper, pp. 97, &c. P. S. Ed. Bishop Ridley's Works, pp. 307, &c.] [4 Tit. Liv. Histor. Lib. I. cap. liv.]

declare to his apostles the wonderful participation that all faithful Christians, should have in his body and blood, took bread, which is the chief, and in scripture counted the only food of the body of man; and when he had after his accustomed manner given thanks, he blessed, not crossing the bread with the three hinder fingers, having the forefinger and the thumb fast joined together: no, he made no sign of the cross at all: for to make the sign of the cross was in those days none other than it is now to make the sign of a gallow-tree. He blessed, therefore, after the manner that the fathers, the prophets, and patriarchs used; that is, he invocated and called upon the name of his Father, desiring him to accomplish invisibly in all his faithful darlings the thing which he intended to declare unto them by the visible sign. Then said he to his apostles, "Take ye, eat ye; this is my body, which shall be delivered for you." Not meaning that he had changed the nature of bread into the nature of flesh, making the bread that he held in his hand his natural body; for then had he given unto them a mortal and corruptible body to eat; which thing is so much ungodly, that very nature abhorreth it. But he gave them the bread to eat, saying: "This is my body, which shall be delivered for you. I became man for none other purpose, but that my body should be torn and rent to satisfy for your sins, that your souls might be fed, and have like participation thereof, as your bodies have of this bread; and you, which be my faithful, are as this bread is, one body made of many bodies; for every little grain whereof this bread is made is of himself a body, and yet joined together they are but one body. In like manner, you that believe in me, though ye be many, yet joined together by faith, ye are but one body, and I am your head. This mystery can you not understand without some visible sign, which may represent unto you the verity thereof: Take ye this bread therefore; and know for certainty, that like as it is one, so are ye one, if ye remain in faith. And as it nourisheth the body, so doth my passion nourish the soul, which hath no life but in me, and by me." In like manner, when he had supped, he took the cup, saying: "Take ye, and drink ye all of this; this is the cup of the new testament in my blood, which shall be shed for you and many unto remission of sins. Do this, so oft as you drink, in my remembrance." Another sign to declare this mystery by: "This cup of wine is but one body, and yet it is made of many grapes; and so are you but one body, although you be many, so long as you be joined together by faith. It comforteth the heart and the lively spirits of the body; and so doth my blood shed on the cross comfort the soul. By this action have I declared unto you the mystery of the participation you have in me by faith. Use you the same; that this your deliverance by me may never slip out of your mind. We have eaten the lamb, which putteth us in remembrance of the wonderful deliverance out of the captivity in Egypt, which was done more than a thousand years past; so shall you eat this bread, and drink this cup, in remembrance of your redemption and deliverance out of the spiritual Egypt, and from the spiritual Pharao, the devil. And when you shall be demanded, what you mean by this eating and drinking, you shall say: We were, through the sin and transgression of the first man Adam, made bondmen and captives to the devil; out of which bondage we could by no means be delivered, till it had pleased God the Father to send his only-begotten Son to take our nature upon him, that he might die, and be an acceptable sacrifice to pacify the Father's wrath."

Wherefore, the night before he suffered, he declared unto us by these visible signs, what communion we have in him of all that ever he deserved for us. And then he commanded us to use the same; because we should be always put in remembrance of that our redemption and deliverance, none otherwise than Moses did to the Israelites, the night before he did by the wonderful might of God bring them out of the great captivity, wherein they were holden in Egypt. The words of Saint Paul to the Corinthians do teach no less than I have here written. For he saith: "So often as you eat this bread, and drink this cup, you shall declare the death of the Lord till he come. And therefore, whosoever eateth of this bread, or drinketh of this cup unworthily, doth eat and drink his own damnation." Here is a plain declaration of the end and purpose of Christ, when he instituted this most sacred sacrament: forsooth, to keep in remembrance his most dolorous death, and precious blood most plenteously shed upon the cross. And whosoever eateth and drinketh it unworthily, that is to say, for any other purpose than for the same it was ordained for, the same eateth and drinketh his own damnation. I think not contrary, but that most men will think this a strange interpretation of this place; forasmuch as the most ancient, yea, all the doctors that make any mention of this place, and Calvin himself in this book which I have translated, do apply the unworthiness in receiving of this sacrament to the unpenitent heart of the person which receiveth it. And in very deed, such one is far unworthy to receive so worthy a sacrament; forasmuch as he is not the member nor servant of Christ, but a member of the devil, and servant to sin. And this interpretation is no less godly than fruitful. For thereby are the members of Christ put in fear to presume to come to the table of the Lord, unless they have first examined and found themselves the true members of Christ, endued and adorned with perfect faith, hope, and charity. But if we will go to the native sense of the text, we shall perceive, that in this place Paul speaketh of the small regard the Corinthians had to this most sacred sacrament, not using it with so much reverence as they ought to do. For he addeth these words, "Putting no difference of the Lord's body:" as he should have said, esteeming it nothing better than the common bread wherewith they fed their bodies. The phrase of speaking giveth this interpretation; for if I say, This man was not worthily entertained, I mean not, that the party which entertained him was not worthy to entertain so noble a man; but that he was not used, as was beseeming for such a man to be used. So that to receive the sacrament unworthily is to receive it otherwise, or for another purpose, than it ought to be received for; that is, after any other form, or for any other purpose, than the words of the first institution do declare. For when the use of good things is altered from the purpose and end they were first ordained for, then are they unworthily handled. All they therefore, which do privately receive the sacrament, either to merit themselves, or other; that do make it a sacrifice for the redemption of sin; or to pacify God's wrath in any condition, or after any other form, or for any other purpose than is declared in the words of the first institution, do receive it to their damnation; putting no difference of the Lord's body, but using it as a matter of merchandise, or occupation to get their living upon. They only receive it worthily, which receive it as a most worthy sacrament and sign, representing unto us the communion and participation we have in all that ever Christ did or purchased for us by taking our nature, and suffering therein all manner of most miserable afflictions, and finally by his most cruel and dolorous death. Therefore to hoise it over their heads, to dance it over the cup, to carry it in the streets with great pomp and glory, to bow their knees, and to knock their breasts before it, and to lock it up in a pix, to have it ready to serve at all hours all such chapmen as shall call for it, is but a politic cast of the merchants, which display and set abroad to be seen such merchandise as they would fainest sell. As they do offend, which neglect and common this most holy mystery, esteeming it no better than the common bread wherewith our bodies be fed; so do they also offend, which honour it with divine honour, making it thereby an idol of all other most to be abhorred, both for that, as they use it, it is a plain antichrist, spoiling Christ of his victory achieved by the once offering of himself for all; and also for that it pulleth the believers thereon from the true adoration of God the Father, and maketh them to honour, for the invisible, immense, and eternal God, that visible, measurable, and corruptible bread and wine. Yea, as they use it, it is not the communion of Christ's body and blood at all, but a fond invention of their own. For Christ did not make so many crossings and blessings, and then eat up all himself; but we must believe that they receive it for us, and in all our names. Well, I shall remit the faithful readers to the author of this little book, most humbly beseeching the Lord our God plenteously to pour out of his spirit of knowledge upon us all, that we may daily more and more find out the hid and secret abominations, to the utter extirpation and routing out of the same. And in the mean time let us pray together, that it may please the Lord to augment the number of his faithful, turning Sauls into Pauls, that the hard hearts may be mollified by hearing the persecutors preach Christ, whom they persecuted. The Spirit of truth be with you all! So be it.

It is the Spirit that quickeneth; the flesh profiteth nothing at all.
John vi.

[COVERDALE.]

FORASMUCH as the most holy supper of our Lord Jesus Christ hath of long time been wrapped up in manifold and great errors, and even of late days wrapped in many opinions and contentions, nothing so quiet as was beseeming; no marvel though certain weak conscienced persons cannot well determine what thing they ought chiefly to follow, but do with indifferent and suspensed mind look, when the servants of God, setting all contention apart, shall agree among themselves, and bring the matter to some concord and unity. And seeing that such kind of doubt hath no small incommodity annexed, and that it is a thing most dangerous to have no certain determination of that mystery, the knowledge whereof is so necessary to our salvation; I have thought it a thing most profitable, briefly to speak of the chief sum of the matter, and yet plainly to declare, what thing we ought chiefly to stick unto therein. Moreover, certain honest men, perceiving the matter to require no less, desired me earnestly to take it in hand; whose request I could by no means deny, unless I would have been slack in doing my duty. And that the difficulty thereof may the more easily be opened, it is needful to declare what order we intended to follow herein.

First, I shall declare, for what cause and to what end the Lord hath instituted this most holy sacrament.

Then, what fruit we take thereof; and herein I will declare, how the body of Christ is given us in it.

Thirdly, what is the right use thereof.

Fourthly, I shall rehearse the errors and superstitions, whereby it hath been defaced; and so will I declare, how the servants of God ought to differ from the papists.

Finally, I will declare the original of that contention, which hath been so earnestly maintained even of the same men, which in our time have applied all their study to bring the gospel to light again, to replenish again the congregation, and to restore the sincere and pure doctrine.

As concerning the first, when it pleased the Almighty, our God, by baptism to choose us into the congregation, that is to say, into his house, which he will nourish and defend; and that he hath received us, not only as household servants, but also as his children; it behoveth him, if he will play the part of a good father, to bring us up, ministering unto us all things necessary to food and clothing.

But as concerning the things that pertain to the education of the body, because they be common to all men, so that as well the evil persons as the good be partakers thereof, they are not to be taken for things appertaining to his household only. No doubt, in that he feedeth and defendeth our bodies, and whiles we be partakers of all those good things which he most plenteously and liberally giveth us, is declared a great token of his fatherly goodness towards us. But in like manner as the life wherein he hath regenerate us is spiritual, so is it needful that the meat, wherewith we should be sustained and strengthened, be also spiritual. For we must understand, that we are not called to possess the celestial inheritance in time to come only; but that through hope we are in manner set in possession thereof already: so that he hath not only promised us life; but delivering us from death, he hath already led us into it in very deed. And this thing obtained we, when he begat us anew with the seed of immortality, that is to say, his word, which through the Holy Ghost he hath printed and fastened in our hearts. That we therefore may defend and sustain this life, we must not seek the caducal and corruptible meats wherewith the belly is fed; but we must provide for our souls much better and more excellent food. And the whole scripture witnesseth, that the selfsame word, whereby the Lord hath begotten us anew, is the spiritual bread whereby our souls are sustained and fed: the reason is this, because in it Christ our only life is given and ministered unto us. For when God would that all abundance of life should remain in Christ, to the intent that by him he might make us partakers thereof, he ordained the word also, whereby Christ and all his mercies might be ministered unto us. This sentence therefore is infallibly true, that our souls are fed and nourished with none other food than Jesus Christ.

Wherefore the heavenly Father, being careful for our education, gave us none other food; yea, rather he committed this unto us singularly. And forasmuch as it is sufficient enough for the recreation and sustenance of our souls, he willed us to content ourselves therewith, and that our souls should rest together therein; because we may by no means be without that food, which being taken away, none other can be found. Now do we perceive, after what sort Christ is the only food wherewith our souls be fed; but because he is distributed unto us by the word of the Lord, as by the instrument appointed for the same purpose, he is named bread and wine.

And that which is spoken of the word, appertaineth also to the sacrament of the supper, whereby the Lord leadeth us unto the partaking of Christ. For because we be so weak and feeble, that we cannot with unfeigned trust of mind receive him, when he is offered unto us in the bare preaching of the doctrine; the Father of mercy, willing to accommodate himself unto our infirmity therein, hath joined unto the word a sign to be seen with the eyes, whereby he might represent unto us the very substance of his promises, that, all doubt and wavering taken away, we might be confirmed and strengthened in him.

Seeing therefore this mystery is high and hard to attain to, and that we cannot by wit comprehend, or by study understand, how the body and blood of Christ may be communicated unto us; and that we be so rude and ignorant, that we understand not the very least of the divine matters; it was needful to declare and open this mystery after such sort as the ability of our wit might away withal.

And for that cause did the Lord institute the supper, that he might print in our consciences those promises, wherewith he hath in the gospel promised to make us partakers of his body and blood; and that he might establish us in this persuasion, our spiritual life to be remaining in him, that we, receiving so noble a pledge, may conceive a sure hope of salvation. Furthermore, that we should be exercised in acknowledging his great goodness towards us, and in celebrating and setting forth of the same with all laud and praise. Thirdly, that we should be provoked to embrace holiness and innocency, forasmuch as we acknowledge ourselves to be the members of Christ; and that above all other we set forth and maintain friendship and brotherly concord, whereof we have an especial commandment. When we have well and diligently marked these three causes, (to which no doubt the Lord had respect, when he instituted the supper,) an entry shall be opened unto us, that we may the better understand, what fruit we receive thereby, and by what mean we may use it aright.

We must therefore now come unto the second part, that we may declare, what wholesome fruit the supper of the Lord bringeth unto us, so we will understand and gather the same. And that shall we know, when we will diligently perpend our own great lack which it succoureth. No remedy we must needs be vehemently troubled and vexed in mind, so often as we consider what we are ourselves, and when we examine all that is in us. For there is not one of us, that can find so much as one little crumb of justice in himself; but contrariwise, we are defiled with so many vices and wicked deeds, stuffed full of so great a multitude of sins, that there needeth none other accuser than our own conscience; neither needeth it to seek for any other judge to give sentence against us. Whereof it followeth, that the ire of God is stirred against us, and that none of us can be able to escape the judgment of eternal death.

And unless we will be very dreamers and blockheads, no remedy but we shall through that horrible cogitation be vexed and troubled, as it were with a continual hell-fire; for we cannot remember the judgment of God, but incontinent our own damnation is before our eyes. We are therefore already swallowed up by the devouring sink of death, were it not that Almighty God delivereth us. And what hope of resurrection may we have, when we consider our own flesh, so rotten and full of all corruption? And therefore, whether we consider body or soul, nothing can be more miserable than we are, so long as we shall consider but ourselves only; and whiles we perceive so great miseries, no remedy we must needs be miserably tormented and affected with extreme heaviness. That the heavenly Father therefore might succour this our calamity, he gave unto us the supper, as a glass wherein we might behold Christ crucified and raised again: crucified, that our sins might be forgiven; raised again, that we, delivered from corruption and death, might be restored to the heavenly immortality. This singular consolation take we of the Lord's supper, that it directeth and leadeth us unto the cross and resurrection of Christ; that we may know for certainty, that we, although we be wicked and unclean, be acknowledged and received of the Lord, yea, and taken for just; and that by him we are restored to life, notwithstanding that we be hedged in within all kinds of death; and that we be replenished with all kinds of felicity, notwithstanding that we be miserable and full of calamity. Or to make the thing more plain, when there is no goodness at all remaining in us, neither any one thing of those things which should help to the obtaining of salvation, the supper doth abundantly witness unto us, that we have obtained all things profitable and wholesome, in that we be partakers of the death and passion of Christ. Wherefore we may affirm, that whiles the Lord admitteth us into the fellowship of the goods and riches of Christ, he openeth the treasury of his mercies. Let us remember therefore, that in the supper is given unto us as it were a glass, wherein we may behold Christ crucified, to deliver us from death and damnation, and raised up again, to justify us and give us life everlasting: And albeit that the same mercy is given unto us in the gospel, yet for that in the supper we have more certainty and fuller fruition, we can do no less but acknowledge that we receive this profit thereof.

But for because the mercies of Christ appertain nothing unto us, unless he himself be ours before, it is most expedient, that in the supper he be given unto us, that those things whereof we have spoken may in very deed be performed in us. And therefore I have used to say, that Christ is the matter and substance of the sacraments, and that the mercies and benefits which we get by him are the efficacy and strength thereof.

To conclude, the whole strength and energy of the supper consisteth in this thing, to confirm the reconciliation with God made by the death and passion of Christ; to certify us, that our souls be washed in his blood, and that we be made just through his obedience; and, to conclude, to print surely in our minds that hope of salvation, which we have in all those things that he hath done for us.

Upon this must we necessarily conclude, that there is a substance annexed unto this virtue; otherwise should we have no stedfastness or certainty therein. We must therefore conclude, that in the supper are given unto us two things; that is to say, Christ, as fountain, origin, and matter of all good things, and the fruit and efficacy of his death and passion: which thing even the very words that be spoken in the supper do abundantly declare. For when he bade us eat his body and drink his blood, he addeth, that his body was given for us, and his blood shed for the remission of our sins: wherein he doth first declare, that his body and blood is not simply without any other consideration communicate unto us, but that we must also consider the fruit that cometh unto us by his death and passion. In fine, how may we be able to come to the fruition of so exceeding good things, unless we be partakers of the body and blood of him that hath produced these things, and given them unto us?

Now enter we into that question, which hath been so greatly tossed, both in time past and in these our days also; how those words are to be understood, wherein Christ calleth his body bread, and his blood wine. Which words may easily be opened, if we keep in memory those principles which I have before set forth; that is to say, that all the fruit we seek for in the supper is brought to nought, unless Christ be given unto us therein, as the foundation and substance of all the whole matter. And if we once grant this thing, then no doubt we shall grant also, that there is given unto us nought else but an unprofitable and vain sacrament, if we deny that in it is given unto us the very participation of Christ; which thing were execrable and shameful blasphemy. Furthermore, if the manner of the communion with Christ be such, that we be partakers of all the mercies and benefits which he gat for us by his death, then are we not partakers with the spirit only, but with the manhood also, wherein he performed perfect obedience to God the Father, to the intent he might pay our debts; although, to say the truth, the one cannot be without the other: for when he giveth himself unto us, he doth it to the intent we should possess him whole. And therefore, as I have said that his Spirit is our life; even so doth he with his own mouth declare, that his flesh is our food, and his blood our very drink. If this be not spoken in vain, no remedy our life must needs consist in him, and our souls be nourished with his flesh and blood, as with their proper and peculiar food.

Of that thing have we testimony in the supper; when it is said of the bread, that we should take it, and eat it, and that it is his body; and of the cup, that we drink it, and that it is his blood: there are the body and blood named, to the intent we should learn to seek the substance of our spiritual life therein. Now if any man would demand of me, whether the bread be the body of Christ, and the wine his blood, thereto would I answer, that the bread and wine are visible signs, representing unto us the body and blood of Christ; and that they be called the body and blood, because they be as it were instruments, whereby the Lord Jesu Christ distributeth them unto us. This form of speaking agreeth very well with the thing.

For notwithstanding that our eyes, no, nor our wits cannot comprehend the communion that we have in the body of Christ, yet is it there openly shewed before our eyes. We have in a like thing an example very fit for the purpose. When the Lord would that his Spirit should appear in the baptism of Christ, he shewed him under the shape of a dove. John the Baptist, receiving that history, saith that he saw the Holy Ghost descending. But if we mark it well, we shall find that he saw nought else but a dove: for the substance of the Holy Ghost is invisible. But for that he knew that vision to be no vain figure, but the most sure token of the presence of the Holy Ghost, he doubted nothing at all to affirm that he saw him; because he was represented unto him under such sort, as he was able to abide. Even so must we say, as concerning the communion that we have in the body and blood of Christ. It is a spiritual mystery, which can neither be seen with the eyes, neither comprehended with the wit. Therefore, as the weakness of our nature requireth, it is set forth with visible figures and signs; but yet under such sort, that it is not a bare and simple figure, but joined unto his verity and substance. The bread therefore is not unworthily called the body; forasmuch as it doth not only represent it unto us, but also bring unto us the same thing. I can be right well content therefore to grant that the name of the body of Christ be transferred unto the bread, because it is the sacrament and figure thereof.

But this one thing will I add, that the sacrament of the Lord ought by no means to be separate from his substance and verity. And yet is it not only meet, but also very necessary, so to set them asunder, that they be not confounded: but to divide them so, that the one should be made perfect without the other, is most unseemly. When we therefore do behold the visible sign, we must consider what it representeth, and who gave it us. For the bread is given to the intent that it should be the figure of the body of Christ, and we are commanded to eat it. It is given, I say, of God, the certain and unchangeable Verity. If so be that God can neither deceive nor lie, it followeth that he doth in very deed perform and fulfil all that he doth there signify. No remedy therefore, we must needs unfeignedly receive the body and blood of Christ in the supper; forasmuch as the Lord offereth unto us therein the communion of them both. For what should this mean, that we should eat bread and drink wine, to the intent that they should declare unto us that his flesh is our meat, and his blood our drink, if he, letting the spiritual verity pass, should give us nought else but bread and wine? Had he not then instituted this mystery feignedly and in vain, and, as we say in the French tongue, under deceivable signs? And therefore must we needs grant, that if the representation which the Lord giveth in the supper be no feigned thing, that then the inward substance of the sacrament is annexed to the visible signs; and that in like manner as the bread is distributed in the hand, so is the body of Christ communicate unto us, to the intent we should be partakers thereof. And doubtless if there were no more but this one thing, yet ought it to satisfy us abundantly; forasmuch as we understand, that in the supper Christ giveth unto us the very substance of his body and blood, that we may with full right possess him, and in possessing him be called into the society of all his good things. For in that we possess him, all the treasures and heavenly goods which be secretly laid up in him are set out unto us, to the intent that they should be ours, and that we should enjoy them with him. Briefly therefore to define the profit of the supper: we may say, that in it Jesus Christ is offered unto us, that we may possess him himself, and in him abundance and plenty of all the mercies and benefits that the mind can desire. Which thing is an exceeding great help unto us, in stablishing our consciences in that trust which we ought to have in him.

Another utility is, that by it we are more stirred and admonished to acknowledge the benefits which we have and do daily receive of the Lord Jesu Christ, that we may give unto him honour and glory; and that, as meet is, we celebrate his most holy name with continual praises. For by nature we are very negligent in the remembrance of the goodness of our God, neither do we think thereon at any time, unless he do awake our sluggishness, and provoke us to our duty. And with sharper pricks can we not be pricked, than in that he compelleth us, as it were, to see with our eyes, and to handle with our hands, yea, openly to know and perceive the greatness of the inestimable benefit, in that he feedeth and refresheth us with his own proper substance; which thing he would should be declared and made open unto us, in that he biddeth us declare his death till he come. If so be that it be a thing so necessary to salvation, not to be unmindful of the mercies and benefits that God hath shewed unto us, but rather diligently to call them again to memory, and to extol them greatly to other men, that we may by mutual admonitions be stirred up, we see therein a singular commodity of the supper; which calleth us back from the vice of unthankfulness, and suffereth us not to forget that great benefit which Christ shewed us, when he died for our sakes; but it bringeth us to this pass, that we give thanks unto him, and do as it were with an open testimony confess how much we are bound unto him.

The third kind of utility consisteth in this thing, that we be thereby more vehemently stirred up to sanctimony and purity of life, and are with more force of persuasions driven, chiefly and before all other, to keep charity and friendship among ourselves. For seeing that we be made the members of Christ, being graffed into his body, and are joined together with him, as with our head; it is but meet that we chiefly be fashioned after his purity and innocency, and that there be especially such concord among us, as ought to be among the members of one body. Although, to have the true understanding of this utility, we ought not to think, that the Lord doth only exhort and stir us up either inflame us with an external sign. For this is the chief thing, that he with his Spirit worketh entirely in us, to add force and efficacy to his ordinance, which he hath appointed as it were an instrument, serving entirely to this purpose, that he might accomplish and finish his work in us. Therefore, because the power of the Holy Ghost is coupled with the sacraments, when they be received so as they ought to be, we ought to hope and trust, that they be an help unto us, that we may go forward in holiness of life, and especially in charity.

Now must we come to the third of the chief parts, which we have purposed in the beginning of this little book, that is to say, to the right use; that we may reverently observe the institution of the Lord. For whosoever cometh unto this sacrament with a certain contempt, negligently, or without regard, nothing careful to hold his purpose, and to persevere in that wherein the Lord hath called him, he doth frowardly abuse it, and in abusing filthily contaminate it. But to contaminate and pollute the thing that God hath so holily consecrated, is a great and intolerable sacrilege. Neither is it in vain that Paul declareth so grievous and cruel damnation to all them that receive it unworthily. For if there be nothing, either in heaven, either in earth, that is more worthy than the body and blood of the Lord; it is no small fault[1] to despise it, and to receive it without consideration, and to come thither not well and diligently prepared. Furthermore, he doth advertise us to prove ourselves, that we may use it even as the thing requireth. If so be that we understand what probation that ought to be, we shall also perceive what use that is which we look for; but great and wise circumspection must be had in this thing. For as we cannot be too diligent in examining ourselves, as the Lord hath commanded, even so did the sophistical doctors, whiles they required I cannot tell what kind of probation and diligence in examining of a man's self, such as never man could be able to perform, held the miserable consciences too much perplex, casting them into wonderful dangerous anxiety, yea, rather into horrible torments. And to be delivered from these inrollings of perturbations, we must, as I have said before, reduce all things to the institution of the Lord, as to the rule, which if we

[[1] Old edition *aute*; but the Latin is, *Culpa non minima est*.]

follow, we shall neither slide nor err. And following it, we ought to consider, whether we feel in ourselves unfeigned repentance and faith; which two are so joined between themselves, that it is not possible that the one can by any means consist without the other. For if we do suppose that our life remaineth in Christ, then must we acknowledge, that in ourselves we are dead.

If we seek our force and strength in him, then must we understand, that we destituted of all strength do faint. If we put all our felicity in his mercy, we must needs perceive, how great our misery is, when that is away. If our quietness and tranquillity be reposed in him, then must we feel nought else in ourselves, but unquietness, troublesome cares, and solicitudes. And such affection cannot be in us, but it will engender in us a certain displeasance of our whole life, besides the carefulness and fear, and at the last, the love and desire of justice. For he that knoweth the filthiness of his sin, and the misery of his estate, whiles he is exiled from God, is so greatly abashed, that he is constrained to be out of conceit with himself, to condemn himself, and for very dolour of heart to weep and sigh. To these things is the judgment of God objected incontinent, which thrucheth the conscience of the sinner in wonderful straits, when he perceiveth, that he can by no means escape, and that there is no place of defence remaining. When we, acknowledging our own misery after such sort, are able to taste of the goodness of God, then do we desire to direct all the order of our life unto his will; that, abjecting the things which we followed before, we may in him be made a new creature. If we therefore will have that communion which is beseeming for us to have, the communion of the most holy supper of the Lord, let us with a firm confidence of mind take Christ for our justice, life, and health: let us embrace his promises, supposing them to be certain and constant: let us renounce all succours to the contrary, which strive therewith, and all confidence of the same; that we, distrusting ourselves and all other creatures, may be quiet in him only, and content ourselves with his only mercy: which thing because it cannot be done, unless we know how much need we have of help and succour, no remedy we must needs be most sharply pricked and digged, as it were with a goad, through the feeling of our misery, that we, as men half famished, may desirously look for him. For how fond a thing were it to seek for meat without any manner of appetite! And to get an appetite to meat, the next way is to have an empty stomach; but in such taking that it may admit meat. Of this it followeth, that it behoveth our souls to be hungry, and fervently to desire meat, that they may in the supper of the Lord find their nutriment.

Furthermore, it is to be noted, that we cannot desire Christ, unless we do aspire to the justice of God, which consisteth in the denial of ourself, and the obedience that ought to be given unto him. For it can by no means agree, that we should be of the body of Christ, living in the mean time filthily, voluptuously, and without rule. Seeing that in Christ is nought else but all purity, continence, gentleness, sobriety, verity, humbleness, and all other like virtues; it behoveth us, if we will be members of his body, to be clear from all voluptuousness and riot, from arrogancy, intemperance, vanity, pride, and other vices; for we cannot mingle those with him, without great shame and reproach. It behoveth us alway to remember, that there is no more concord between him and iniquity, than is between light and darkness. Lo, by what means we may come to perfect repentance; by appointing our journey so, that our life be fashioned after the example of Christ. But although this thing be common to all parts of the life, yet take they place chiefly in charity, which in this sacrament is singularly commended unto us; by reason whereof it is also called the bond thereof. For as the bread, which for the use of all men is there sanctified, is made of many grains so compact together, that one cannot be separate and discerned from the other; even after the same rate ought we to be joined together with the indissoluble bond of friendship. And so do we all receive one body of Christ, to the end we may be his members[1]. But if we be full of discords and dissensions, we do, as much as in us lieth, tear Christ, and pull him in sunder; neither shall we be guilty of smaller sacrilege than if we had done the thing in deed. Let us not therefore be

[1 The sentiment contained in this passage appears to be borrowed from Augustine, Expos. in Evang. Joannis Tractatus xxvi. de cap. vi. Opera, Tom. ix. p. 50. G. Ed. 1541. See above, pp. 419-20.]

bold to come thither, if any hatred or evil will towards any man, and chiefly a Christian, and joined to the unity of the church, do remain in us. We must also, for the keeping and following[1] of the order of the Lord, bring with us another affection, that is to say, that we confess with mouth, and declare in very deed, how much we are bound to our Saviour; and that we may give thanks unto him; not only that we may give glory to his name, but that we may also instruct one another, and that our neighbours may through our example learn what they ought to do.

But for that there can no man be found, that hath so profited in faith and sanctity of life, but that he lacketh yet very much; it were danger lest very many godly consciences should be troubled with those words that I have spoken; unless I would return, mitigating those precepts which I have given of faith and repentance. For that kind of teaching is very dangerous, wherein some men, leaving[2] the perfect trust and repentance of the mind, will that all men which be not endued with such things be excluded: for so should all men be excluded, not one man excepted. And to prove that thing to be true, who can boast that he hath no point of diffidence in him, and that he is depraved with no spot of mind or with no kind of weakness? Certes, the children of God have such faith, that it is needful for them always to pray unto the Lord, that he be present and help their incredulity. For this disease is so fast rooted in us, that we can by no means be healed, before we be delivered out of the bonds of this body. Yea, the holiness of our life is such, that we must needs pray daily to get remission of sins and grace to amend. And although some be more imperfect than some, yet is there no man but he faileth in many things. Yea, the justice of man is such, that the wise man compareth [Isai. lxiv.6.] it to a defiled cloth, which is no less than if he had said with the psalmist: "All have fallen, they are made altogether unprofitable; there is none that doth good, not one." There is none, that hath not need to say with David: "Lord, who is able to know the greatness of sin? do thou, good Lord, cleanse me from my sins, the magnitude whereof I am not able to comprehend." And therefore, if that integrity of

[1 Old edition, *swoloyng*. Latin, *teneamus et sequamur*.]
[2 Latin, *requirentes*.]

faith and life be required, wherein wanteth nothing at all, the supper should not be only unprofitable unto all men, but also very hurtful: which thing no doubt is most wide from the mind and purpose of the Lord, which gave unto us his congregation nothing more wholesome than that.

When we therefore shall feel in ourselves a faith not yet perfect, and shall not be endued with so pure a conscience, but that it accuse us of many vices; that ought not to let us for coming to the Lord's sacred table, so be that we, void of all hypocrisy and simulation, do in that weakness trust for health in Christ, willing to direct our life after the rule of the gospel. But namely I say, that there be none hypocrisy: because very many do deceive themselves with vain flatterings, persuading themselves, that it is sufficient if they condemn their vices, although they do nourish the same; or else it sufficeth, if they abstain from them for a time, and intend to return to the same again incontinent. But the true repentance is firm and constant. And therefore it bringeth to pass, that we strive against the evil that we ourselves carry with us, not for a few days or months, but through all the time of our life, without any manner intermission. When we feel that vices do so displease us, and that the unfeigned hatred of them, proceeding from the fear of God, is graffed in us, and that we be also led with the desire to live well and holily, we are apt and meet to receive the supper of the Lord, although there be yet remaining in us very many fragments of infirmities. Yea, unless we were weak, subject to diffidence and unperfect life, the sacrament were unprofitable for us, and the institution thereof had not been necessary.

Seeing therefore it is the remedy wherewith God would succour our weakness, strengthen our faith, increase our charity, and set us forward in sanctity of life, we ought so much the rather to use it, how much more grievously we feel ourselves oppressed with the magnitude of the disease. Much less ought it to be an impediment unto us. For if we do lie for excuse, that we be yet weak in faith and not of life perfect enough, to the intent we may withdraw ourselves from the use of the supper, it were even like as if a man would abstain from physic, because he were sick.

The weakness therefore of faith, and the vices of our lives, ought to admonish us to come to the supper, as to the chief remedy, that they might be amended and corrected; so that we come not void of all faith and repentance: whereof the first is hid in the mind, and therefore our conscience must bear us witness before God; the latter is declared in action and work, and therefore it is requisite that it appear in our life.

As concerning the time of celebrating the supper, it may not be appointed and prescribed unto all men. For there is no man, but he shall sometime have such private impediments as may excuse a man, though he abstain. Besides that we have no precept, whereby all men be compelled to use it so oft as it may be offered unto them. But yet, if we have respect unto the end whereunto the Lord leadeth us, we shall know, that the use thereof ought to be much more common, than it is commonly among many men. For look how much more we be oppressed with weakness, so much the more often ought we to be exercised in it; because it may and ought to be profitable unto us, both for the confirmation of our faith, and also for the setting forward of the holiness of life. Wherefore in all congregations well ordered ought to be such custom, that the supper be celebrate so oft as may be, and so much as the people shall be able to receive. And every private person ought, so much as in him lieth, to be ready to receive it so often, as it shall be celebrate in a common assembly, unless he be by very urgent causes constrained to abstain. For albeit that the time is not assigned, nor the day expressed by any precept or commandment; yet ought this thing to suffice, that we know it to be the Lord's will we should use this sacrament oftentimes. Otherwise we know not the profit that cometh unto us thereby. The excuses that some men lay are void and vain. Some say, they are not worthy; and by that pretext they abstain all the year. Others do not only consider how unworthy they be; but they do also lay for them, that they cannot communicate with such as they see come thither unprepared. Also, other suppose, that the oft use of it is superfluous; neither do they think that it ought to be so often iterated and repeated, after that we have once received Christ.

I ask of those first, which lay for themselves their own unworthiness, how their conscience can sustain so great misery more than an year; and dare not call upon the

Lord accordingly? For they will grant it to be a point of rashness to call upon God as a Father, unless we be the members of Christ; which thing cannot be done, unless the substance and verity of the supper be fulfilled in us: and if we have the verity itself, we are, with much better reason, meet to receive the same. Whereby we perceive, that they which would exempt themselves from the supper as unworthy, do rob themselves of that great commodity of invocating and praying to God. But I would not compel them, whose consciences be troubled and feared by any religion, to the intent they should intermingle themselves rashly. But rather I counsel them to tarry for a season, until the Lord shall vouchsafe to deliver them from that anxiety. In like manner, if there be any other cause, I do not deny but it is lawful to defer. I do only purpose to declare, that no man ought to continue long in this thing, that he may abstain for his unworthiness. For so is the congregation robbed of the communication, wherein all our health consisteth. Let him rather endeavour to fight against all the impediments which the devil casteth against him, lest he be excluded from so great a good thing, and consequently robbed of all the benefits together.

The other men's reason is more apparent, because they use this reason: that is to say, if it be not lawful to eat common bread with them that name themselves brethren, and do yet nevertheless live filthily and licentiously, much less that bread which is consecrated for this intent, that it may represent and give unto us the body of the Lord.

But it is no hard thing to make answer to these also, that it pertaineth not to every private person to judge and discern, who ought to be admitted, and who to be depelled, but to the whole congregation, either else the shepherd and elders, whose help he ought to use in the ordering and governing of the congregation. For Saint Paul commandeth us not to examine other, but ourselves. It is our duty to admonish them that live viciously; and, if they will not hear us, to make relation to the shepherd, that he may finish the matter by the authority of the congregation. But we may not so withdraw ourselves from the company and assembly of the wicked, that we forsake the communion of the congregation. Besides these things, it shall oft times chance, that the crimes be not so manifest,

[COVERDALE.]

that it may be lawful to proceed to excommunication. For although the shepherd shall in his mind judge any man to be unworthy, yet may he not pronounce him to be such a one, or prohibit him the supper, unless he have convicted him by the judgment of the congregation: which thing when it chanceth, there remaineth none other remedy, but that we desire God, that he will deliver his church from all offences in this mean time, whiles we look for the day of judgment, wherein the chaff shall be severed from the good grain.

The third have no kind at all of the likeliness of the truth. For this spiritual bread is not given unto us, to the intent we should be glutted incontinent; but rather that, tasting the sweetness thereof, we should hunger the more after it, and use it as often as it should be proffered unto us. This is the thing that I have expounded before, that Jesus Christ is never so communicate unto us, so long as we be in this mortal life, that our souls may be satiate with him, but that he may be an accustomed nourishment unto them.

To come to the fourth part. When the devil perceived, that the Lord left to the congregation nothing more profitable than this sacrament, he did after his accustomed manner employ himself, even incontinent upon the first institution, to contaminate it with divers errors and superstitions, to the intent he might corrupt and destroy the fruit thereof; neither did he cease to labour his purpose, until he had put away the institution of the Lord, and turned it into a lie and vanity. It pertaineth not to my purpose to assign, in what time every deceit and error had his beginning. It shall be sufficient for me particularly to note errors that the devil hath invented, which we must beware of, if we will have the supper of the Lord uncorrupted. First therefore, when the Lord gave the supper unto us, to the intent it should be distributed among us, that it might represent unto us the communion which we have in his body, and also that we might be partakers of that sacrifice which he offered unto his Father, to purge our sins; men have, on the contrary, by their own wits commented, that it is a sacrifice whereby we obtain of God remission of sins. Which thing is detestable sacrilege, and not to be suffered by any means. For unless we acknowledge and believe stedfastly, that the death of the Lord Jesu Christ is the only sacrifice, whereby he reconciled us to God the Father, putting away all the sins whereof we were guilty in his judgment, we overthrow and destroy his force and efficacy. Unless we grant, that Christ is the only priest, by whose intercession we are come again into favour with his Father, we rob him of his honour, and do him great injury. Seeing therefore that that opinion which feigneth that the supper of the Lord is a sacrifice, whereby we get and obtain remission of sins, fighteth against the same, it must be taken away and condemned as devilish[1]. That it repugneth is most certain: for how can these things agree, That Christ in dying offered sacrifice to the Father, whereby once for all he obtained pardon and remission of all our sins; and, that we must sacrifice again daily, that we may obtain that thing which is to be sought in his only death?

This error was not at the highest incontinent upon the beginning; but increasing by little and little, it was at length brought to this point. It is manifest that the fathers of old time called the supper a sacrifice. But they shew a reason why; because the death of Christ is represented therein[2]. Their saying, therefore, is to this purpose: that because the supper is the memory of that only sacrifice, wherein we ought utterly to content ourselves, therefore is that name attributed. Neither can I blame[3] the custom of the old congregation, because they did in their gesture and rite figurate a certain image of a sacrifice with the same ceremonies in manner, that were in use under the old law, this one thing excepted, that instead of a beast they used bread for their sacrifice; which thing, for that it pricketh too near the Jewish mark, and is not agreeable to the institution of the Lord, I do not allow it.

[1 Old edition, *as it must be taken away and condemned devilish.* The Latin, tollenda ipsa et ut diabolica damnanda est.]

[2 So Augustine: Sacrificium ergo visibile invisibilis sacrificii sacramentum, id est, sacrum signum est. Augustin. de Civitate Dei. Lib. x. cap. v. Opera. Vol. v. p. 82. C. Ed. 1541; and also Chrysostom, in Epist. ad Hebr. Hom. XVII: Τί οὖν; ἡμεῖς καθ' ἑκάστην ἡμέραν οὐ προσφέρομεν; προσφέρομεν μὲν, ἀλλ' ἀνάμνησιν ποιούμενοι τοῦ θανάτου αὐτοῦ... κ. τ. λ. Opera. in Nov. Test. Comment. Tom. VI. p. 856, Ed. 1663. And that this is the doctrine of the ancient liturgies, is shewn by Medé, Christian Sacrifice, chap. ix. Works. pp. 478, &c.]

[3 Neque possum .... *excusare*, is the Latin. Perhaps we should read, *Neither can I but blame.*]

For in the old Testament, the time of figures, the Lord instituted such ceremonies to be observed, until that sacrifice were celebrated in the flesh of his most dear beloved Son, which was the truth of them all. Seeing, therefore, all this is finished, there remaineth no more but that we use the communion thereof. It is therefore superfluous to declare that thing with figures. Therefore by the institution of Christ we are not commanded to offer a sacrifice, but to take and eat the thing that is already offered and sacrificed. And although the ancients did somewhat offend in that observation, yet was not the impiety so great as that which did afterward creep in. For the thing that was proper and peculiar to the death of Christ, was utterly transposed to the mass, that it might satisfy to God for our offences, and that we might be reconciled by it. Besides these things, that office which was Christ's, was attributed unto them which called themselves priests, that they might sacrifice unto God, and that they might pray before him with their sacrifices, to obtain pardon and remission of our sins. I will not dissemble this solution, which the enemies of the truth do bring in this matter, that the mass is no new sacrifice, but the application of that only sacrifice whereof I have spoken. Although they go about to cover their abomination with some manner of colour, yet doth it manifestly appear to be a mere cavillation. For it is not only said that the sacrifice of Christ is but one, but also that it ought not to be iterate, seeing that the force and efficacy thereof is perpetual. It is not said that Christ was once offered up to the Father, that other should afterward use the same oblation, that they might apply unto us the force of his intercession; but that he is entered into the sanctuary of heaven, and that he appeareth there, to the intent he may make the Father merciful unto us through his intercession. As concerning the application of the merit of his death, that we may feel the fruit thereof, that is done, not after such sort as they of the popish church think it to be done; but when we receive the tidings of the gospel, even such as the ministers, whom God hath ordained as ambassadors, do in their preaching protest, yea, such as he hath sealed with sacraments, as with seals. All, as well teachers as pastors, have allowed this opinion of the common people, wherein they supposed that man to deserve mercy and justification, even for the work's sake, which would hear or buy a mass. But I say, that if we will take any profit of the supper, we must bring thither nothing of our own, to the intent to deserve the thing that we look for; but that we must only receive with faith the mercy that is in it offered unto us. And yet doth not that mercy remain in the sacrament; but as it cometh from the cross of Christ, even so it sendeth us back again to the same. Nothing therefore is so contrary to the true understanding of the supper, as to make thereof a sacrifice. For it will not suffer us to acknowledge the death of Christ to be the only sacrifice, which shall continue for ever. These things well understand, it shall be evident that all those masses, wherein is no such communion of the supper as the Lord instituted, are nought else, but very abomination. For the Lord did not ordain, that the priest only should severally satisfy himself after he had finished this sacrifice; but his will was, that this sacrament should be distributed in an open assembly, like unto the first supper which he celebrated with his apostles. But after that this detestable opinion was invented, this unhappy custom proceedeth out of it, as out of an hell-mouth, wherein the people contenting themselves with being present at the action, as though they should thereby obtain some great merit, do in the mean time abstain from the communion, because the priest boasteth, that he offereth sacrifice for all, and chiefly for them that be present. I let pass the deceits and illusions, wherein is so much unseemliness that they are not to be spoken of, as to attribute to every little saint his appropriate mass, and to transfer unto Wat and Will, as we say in the French proverb, the thing that is spoken of the supper of the Lord: also to make merchandise thereof; with the other puddle of filthinesses, which have sprung of this name sacrifice.

Another error followeth, which the devil hath sown, to the intent to corrupt this holy mystery; that is to say, in that he commented the transubstantiation of the bread into the body, and of the wine into the blood of Christ, after the words should be pronounced with the intent to consecrate[1].

[[1] With regard to the necessity of the intention of the priest to the essence of the sacraments, this opinion was delivered by pope Eugenius, in the council of Florence, in the year 1438, and adopted

First, that comment hath no foundation at all in the scripture, neither hath it any testimony of the old congregation; and therefore can it by no means agree or stand with the words of the Lord. Is not such an interpretation too violent and too much wrested, to say, that when Christ shewing bread, calleth it his body, the substance of the bread is consumed, and that the body of Christ succeedeth in the place thereof? But it needeth not to call the matter into question, seeing that the bright and splendiferous verity is of itself able to confute so absurd a vanity. I let pass infinite testimonies, both of the scripture and of the fathers also, wherein the sacrament is called bread. I say this only, that the nature of the sacrament requireth, that the material bread remain for the visible sign of the body. For it is a general rule among the sacraments, that the signs which we see in them, ought to have some similitude with the spiritual thing that they represent. As we are therefore in baptism certified, that our souls be inwardly washed, when the water that washeth the filth of the body is poured upon us, to declare the same thing; even so there needs must be in the supper material bread, that it may be declared unto us, that the body of Christ is our food. For what declaration were it, if the quality, whiteness, should represent unto us that body? We know therefore manifestly, that unless the substance do there remain, all the representation which the Lord, willing to accommodate himself to our infirmity, gave unto us, doth utterly decay and perish.

For the words which the Lord spake, sound no less than if one would say: In like manner as man's body is nourished and sustained with bread, so is my flesh the spiritual food, wherewith the souls be quickened. Besides these things, for what purpose doth Paul propone that similitude? As one loaf is made of many grains mingled and joined together one with another, even so we, (forasmuch as we take part all of one bread), ought to be fast joined together one with another. And if the whiteness only should remain without the substance, were it not a thing to be laughed at, to hear a man speak as Paul doth? Wherefore without any doubting at

by the council of Trent. See Sess. vii. Can. 11, 12, and Sess. xiv. chap. 6; and the Catechism, Part ii. 23; and Hey and Burnet on the twenty-sixth Article.]

all, I conclude that this transubstantiation is the devil's interpretation, to deprave the truth of the supper.

Many doating casts have followed of this lie; and would God they had not been more than doating casts, and that they had not been also horrible imaginations! For men, imagining I cannot tell what manner of placely presence, have taught that both the divinity and the humanity of Christ are fastened unto the whiteness, nothing considering, what inconveniences followed upon the same. Although the old doctors of Sorbonne have reasoned very subtilly, how the body and blood is joined with the signs; yet can it not be denied, but that in the popish church was received both of high and low, and is at this day with fire, sword, murder, and all kinds of torments cruelly defended and holden, this opinion, that Christ is contained under these signs, and that we ought to seek him there: which opinion if they will maintain, no remedy they must also grant, that the body of Christ, as a thing infinite, is contained in no place, either else that it is in divers places at once. And in the affirming hereof, they came at length to this pass, that it differeth nothing at all from a fantastical apparition. To appoint therefore such kind of presence, inclosed in a place wherein the body of Christ should be included in, or as they say, locally joined to the sign, is not only a thing foolish, but also an execrable error, diminishing the glory of Christ, and utterly destroying all that ought to be believed as concerning his human nature. For the scripture teacheth in every place, that like as in earth Christ took our humanity, even so he plucking the same out of this mortal estate, and yet nothing changing the nature thereof, carried it up into heaven. And for this cause ought we, when we speak of the humanity of Christ, to consider two things: the first, that we diminish nothing of the verity of his nature; the other, that we derogate nothing of his glorious estate. And to do this thing in his kind, we must lift up our minds into heaven, that we may seek our Redeemer there. For if we will cast him from us under the corruptible elements of this world, we shall both destroy those things which the scriptures do witness as concerning his human nature, and also bring to nought his most glorious ascension. But because many men have abundantly handled this matter, I had rather let it pass, than to wade farther therein. My mind was to note by the way this thing only, that to think that Christ is shut up under the bread and wine, either else to join them so together, that our mind cleave fast there, and is not erected into heaven, is a devilish dotage; which thing I shall also touch in another place.

And when this perverse opinion was once received, it engendered many other superstitions. First, that carnal adoration, which is none other thing than mere idolatry. For if a man would prostrate himself before the bread, and honour Christ there, as if he were there present, contained therein, were not that the setting up of an idol instead of the sacrament? For we were not commanded to honour, but to eat. We ought not therefore so rashly to attempt that thing. Furthermore, this was an observation in the old congregation, to admonish the people, before the supper should be celebrated, that they lift up their hearts, to the intent they should understand, that they ought not to stick in the visible sign, if they would honour Christ aright[1]. But we shall not long contend as concerning this article, if the presence and conjunction of the verity with the sign be well understand; whereof I have already spoken, and will hereafter declare at large. Out of the same fountain are sprungen the residue of the superstitious ceremonies; as to carry the sacrament through the streets once in the year, as it were in a pomp;

[[1] That this was the practice in the African churches as early as the third century, we have the testimony of Cyprian, who thus writes: Quando autem stamus ad orationem, fratres dilectissimi, vigilare et incumbere ad preces toto corde debemus. Cogitatio omnis carnalis et secularis abscedat, nec quidquam tunc animus quam id solum cogitet quod precatur: ideo et sacerdos, ante orationem præfatione præmissa, parat fratrum mentes dicendo, *Sursum corda;* ut dum respondet plebs, *Habemus ad Dominum*, admoneatur nihil aliud se quam Dominum cogitare debere. Cyprian. de Orat. Dom. p. 152, Oper. ed. Fell. And Augustine, at the beginning of the fifth century, speaks of these words as being used in all the churches: Quotidie per universum orbem humanum genus una pene voce respondet, *Sursum corda se habere* ad Dominum. Augustin. de Vera Relig. c. 3. Opera. Vol. I. p. 158, C. Ed. 1541. The same thing is true of the liturgies of Antioch and Cæsarea, Constantinople and Rome, Africa, Gaul, and Spain; and from them these sentences have descended into our own Liturgy. See Palmer's Origines Liturgicæ, Vol. II. pp. 110—113.]

another season to set up a tabernacle for it, and to keep it all the year long shut up in a pix, or case, that the people may give heed thereunto, as unto God: which things, because they are all not only invented by man's wit, without the word of God, but also plain repugnant to the institution of the supper, they ought of all Christians utterly to be rejected.

I have declared whence this calamity in the papistical church, that the people doth all the year long abstain from the communion of the supper, had his beginning; because it is counted as a sacrifice, which one man must offer up in the name of the whole multitude.

But although we may use it but once every year, yet is it then miserably pulled in sunder, as it were torn in pieces. For whereas the sacrament of the blood ought to be distributed to the people, as it appeareth by the express commandment of the Lord, they decree that the people ought to be contented with the one half part. So are the miserable Christians by most wicked guile robbed of the benefit that God gave them; neither is it any small benefit to have the communion of the blood of the Lord to nourish us withal: and it is too much cruelty to take that thing violently from them, unto whom it belongeth of right.

Wherein we may easily perceive, with what foolhardiness and frowardness the pope hath exercised tyranny against the congregation of God, after time that he only held the imperie, when the Lord had commanded his disciples to eat the bread that was sanctified in his body, and then coming to the cup, he said not only, 'Drink ye,' but he added expressly, *all*. Would we have a thing spoken more openly? He biddeth us eat the bread, using no universal word therein; but of the cup he biddeth us *all* drink. Whence cometh this difference, but that he intended thereby to prevent this malice and subtilty of the devil? Nevertheless the pope is of such arrogancy and pride, that he dare be bold to command to the contrary, Look that ye do not all drink. And that he may declare himself to be wiser than God, he saith, it is right and agreeable to reason that the priests have some prerogative more than the people, to the end that the dignity of a priest should be honoured. As though the Lord had not been of sufficient discretion, nor had considered, after what sort the one ought to be known from the other! Besides this, he objecteth the dangers that might befal, if the cup should be given commonly unto all men. Some drop, forsooth, might chance to be shed: as though the Lord had not foreseen that thing! Doth not he lay negligence to the Lord's charge, that saith he confoundeth the order that he should observe, and that he hath cast his people into this danger without any manner of reason? And that they may declare that there ensueth no great incommodity upon this change, they say, that the whole is comprehended under one kind, because the body cannot be separated from the blood. As though the Lord had dissevered[1] them, the one from the other! For if the one part may be left as superfluous, it had been foolish and vain for both to be distinctly and severally given unto us.

But some of the pope's band, perceiving that this so great abomination could not otherwise be defended than impudently, went about to cover it by some other means. They say, that when Christ had instituted this sacrament, he spake unto his apostles only, whom he had as then promoted to the order of priesthood. But what answer will they make to Paul, which saith, that he hath taught the christian people the thing that he learned of the Lord, that every one should eat of the bread, and drink of the cup? But who hath revealed unto these men, that Christ gave the supper unto his apostles, as unto priests? The words sound to the contrary, in that he doth afterwards command that they, following his example, should do the same. He prescribeth therefore a rule, which he would should continue in his church for ever. And this rule was in the ancient time observed, unto such time as Antichrist, ruling alone, advanced himself and stretched up his horns against God's verity, to the intent to destroy it utterly. We see therefore, that it is intolerable frowardness so to divide and tear this sacrament, that those parts should be dissevered which God hath joined.

That I may conclude the more briefly, I will comprehend in one chapter the thing that else might have been denied; that is to say, that the devil hath without any doctrine of the supper, brought in this manner of celebrating, setting up in the stead of the doctrine ceremonies, some filthy, some unprofitable, some also noisome and dangerous, whereof have ensued very many evils; insomuch that the mass, which is

[1 Old edition, *discovered*. Latin, *distinxisset*.]

used in the popish church instead of the supper, if I should define it aright, is none other thing than a mere apish emulation and disguised masking. I call it an apish emulation, because that like as apes do play the wantons in imitating rudely and without reason the works of men; even so do they imitate the Lord's holy supper in such wise, that with their preposterous inventions they corrupt the whole truth thereof. And to declare this to be true, is not this the chief thing that the Lord left with us, that we should celebrate this mystery with perfect and true understanding? Whereupon it followeth, that the substance thereof consisteth in doctrine; and that once taken away, there remaineth nought else but a ceremony, cold, and without virtue or strength. Not only the scriptures are witnesses to this thing, but also the pope's own laws; wherein there is a sentence alleged, in which Augustine asketh: "What other thing baptism should be without the word, than a corruptible element? With the word (as he addeth incontinent), not in that it is pronounced, but because it is understand[2], &c." Whereby he declareth, that the sacraments do take their force and energy of the word of the Lord, when it is preached after such sort as it may be understand. The residue is not worthy the name of a sacrament. But in the mass it is so far unlike that any doctrine should be intelligibly heard, that contrariwise all the whole mystery is thought to be profaned, unless all things be said and done privily and covertly, to the intent nothing may be perceived or understand. So that their consecration differeth nothing from a kind of enchantment: for after the manner of an enchanter, they think that with whisperings and divers gestures they bring Christ out of heaven into their hands. Whereby we perceive, that the mass so ordained is rather a manifest and open profanation of the supper, than the observation thereof; and that the peculiar and chief substance of the supper wanteth, which consisteth in this thing, that the mystery be truly opened to

[[2] Quare non ait, Mundi estis propter baptismum, quo loti estis; sed ait, Propter verbum quod locutus sum vobis; nisi quia et in aqua verbum mundat? Detrahe verbum, et quid est aqua, nisi aqua? Accedit verbum ad elementum, et fit sacramentum, etiam ipsum tanquam visibile verbum......Unde ista tanta virtus aquæ, ut corpus tangat, et cor abluat, nisi faciente verbo? Non quia dicitur, sed quia creditur." Expos. in Evang. Joannis. Tract. LXXX. do Cap. xv. Tom. IX. p. 96.]

the people, and the promises rehearsed with open voice; not that the priest, without either reason or understanding, should stilly whisper out an humming that cannot be understand. I call it a play or masking, because there is nought else seen, but the foolishness and gestures of players; which things would become a play much better than the sacred supper of the Lord.

No doubt the sacrifices of the old testament were celebrated with divers ornaments and ceremonies. But because they had a good signification, and were all ordained to instruct and exercise the people in godliness, they were far unlike unto these, which serve for none other purpose at all, but that without any manner profit they may occupy and hold suspense the mind of the people. To conclude, because these mass-mongers, (if I may so call them,) do allege this example of the old testament for the defence of their ceremonies, it shall be good to note, what difference is between that which they do, and that which was by God commanded to the Jewish people. For if I lay for me this one thing, whatsoever was then done was founded in the commandment of God, and that their foolish trifles have none other foundation than in man's invention, were not there a great difference? But I have things to disprove them, which be much greater than this be. For it was not for nought that the Lord preserved such a form for a time, to the intent that at the length it should have an end and be abrogate. No doubt, because he had not as then declared his doctrines so plainly, he would so much the rather that his people should be exercised in figures, that the thing which wanted in that testament, might be repaired in the other. But since that Christ appeared in the flesh, look, by how much more the doctrine is lightened, so much are the figures diminished. Seeing therefore we have the body, we must leave the shadows. For if we will replenish the abolished ceremonies, we shall patch again that veil that Christ brake in sunder by his death; and so shall we obscure and darken the light of the gospel. Thus do we perceive, that this multitude of ceremonies which is seen in the mass, is the form of the Jewish law, utterly contrary to the christian religion. I am not of that mind, that I would disprove all ceremonies which do serve to honesty and a public order, whereby the more reverence is given to the sacrament; so that they do well agree to the purpose, and be sober. But that unmeasurable labyrinth may by no means be suffered; forasmuch as it hath engendered infinite superstitions, and made the people as it were amused without any manner edification.

By this it may easily be perceived, wherein those unto whom God hath opened the understanding of his truth ought to differ from the papists. First, they shall be out of doubt, that it is abominable sacrilege to count the mass as a sacrifice, whereby remission of sins may be obtained; either to repute the priest for a mediator, which may apply the merits of Christ's passion unto them that buy masses, or be present at the doing of them, or do with devotion worship them. But they shall rather believe, that the death and passion of Christ is the only sacrifice, whereby the ire of God is pacified, and perpetual justice gotten unto us; and besides these things, that the Lord Jesus is entered into the celestial sanctuary, that he may there shew himself for us, and by the virtue of his sacrifice pray for us. But yet they shall easily grant, that the fruit of his death is communicate unto us in the supper, not by the merit of the work, but for the promises that are made unto us therein, so that we embrace them with faith. Furthermore, they ought in no case to grant, that the bread is transubstantiated, as they say, into the body of Christ, or the wine into blood; but they must in that thing constantly believe, that the visible signs do retain his[1] substance, that they may represent unto us that spiritual verity whereof I have spoken before. Thirdly, although they ought to be surely persuaded with themselves, that the Lord doth in very deed give the same thing that he doth represent, and so, that we do unfeignedly receive the body and blood of Christ; yet shall they not seek it as included under the bread, or fastened, as they say, locally unto the visible sign. Much less ought they to honour the sacrament; but to stretch up the mind into heaven, that they may there receive and honour Christ.

Hence shall it come to pass, that they shall despise and condemn for idolatry all those superstitious ceremonies, as well of the carrying forth of the sacrament in pomp and processions, as of the building up of those tabernacles where-

[1 Signa veram substantiam suam retinere: *their substance.*]

in it is set forth to be honoured. For the promises of the Lord stretch no further, than to that use which he committed unto us. Furthermore they shall judge the institution of the Lord to be violated and broken, in that the people is robbed of the one part of the sacrament; and that it is necessary that both parts be wholly distributed, if it should be observed aright. In fine, they shall suppose that it is not only superfluous, but also dangerous, and that it becometh not the christian religion, to use so many ceremonies taken of the Jews, more than the simplicity wherein the apostles instructed us. They shall also judge, that it is even of an ungodly frowardness so to celebrate the supper with gestures and maskers' movings, that no doctrine at all may there be heard, but is rather buried, as though it were a certain kind of magical art.

To conclude at the last, we must now come to the last of the chief parts; that is to say, to that contention which in our time is stirred in this matter: which forasmuch as no doubt it was of the devil's stirring upon, to let, or rather to break the course of the gospel, I would wish it to be forgotten for ever; much less can I be delighted in the rehearsing of the same. But because I do perceive very many godly minds, which know not whither to turn themselves, I will briefly say the thing that I shall think necessary, to declare how they may deliver themselves.

First, I desire and beseech all faithful persons, even for the name's sake of the living God, that they be not greatly offended, because this controversy is moved among them, that were the chief captains in restoring and bringing in again of the doctrine of the gospel. For it is no new thing for the Lord to suffer his servants to be ignorant in some things, and suffer them to contend among themselves: not that he would suffer them to err continually, but for a time, to the intent he might make them more humble. And no doubt, if all things had chanced prosperously to this day, and had flowed according to our will, perhaps men would have forgotten themselves, either else the mercy of God should not have been so much known as it ought to be. And therefore the Lord's will was to take away from men all occasion of glorying, that glory might be given unto him only.

Furthermore, if we consider with how great darkness the world was beset, when they which moved this controversy began to lead us back again to the light of the verity, indeed we will marvel nothing at all, though they knew not all things from the beginning. It is rather a notable miracle of God, that they in so little space of time were so illumined, that they themselves might escape, and lead other, out of that sink of errors wherein we had been so long time drowned.

But there is no better way than to rehearse the matter itself, even as it was done. For thereby it shall appear, that there is not so much matter of offence in this behalf, as is commonly supposed to be.

When Luther began to teach, he handled the matter of the supper so that, as concerning the corporal presence of Christ, he seemed to leave it such as all men did then conceive. For condemning transubstantiation, he said, that the bread was the body of Christ, because it was joined together with him; besides this, he added certain hard and gross similitudes. But that he did by compulsion, because he could not otherwise declare his mind. For it is a hard thing to expound so hard a matter, and not to use some things not all of the fittest for the purpose. After this did Zuinglius and Œcolampadius begin to grow: which when they considered the guile and deceit that the devil had brought in in establishing that carnal presence, which had been taught and believed for six hundred years before, they supposed it wickedness to dissemble a matter of so great importance; and chiefly, because there was annexed unto this error an execrable idolatry, that Christ should be worshipped, as included under a piece of bread. But because it was very hard to pull back this opinion, which had been long and deeply rooted in the hearts of men, they applied all the force of their wit to impugn the same, teaching that it was a most gross and absurd error not to acknowledge those things which be throughout the whole scripture testified of the ascension of Christ; that he in the nature of man is received into heaven, and that he shall tarry there until he descend to judge the world. But whiles they were very much bent unto this purpose, they omitted to declare, what presence of Christ in the supper we ought to believe, and what communion of his body and blood is there received: insomuch that Luther supposed them willing to leave nought else but the bare signs, void of the spiritual substance; and therefore he began to resist openly, insomuch that he declared them worthy to be counted for heretics. And after the contention waxed once hot, in progress of time it was so increased and inflamed, that it was too fiercely stirred to and fro about a fifteen years together; during which time neither party would with indifferent and quiet mind hear other. For although that they did once confer between themselves, yet was there so great alienation of minds, that they departed, the purpose not brought to pass. For when they should have come to some concord, they recoiled more and more, minding nought else but to defend their opinion, and to confute the contrary.

We perceive therefore, in what thing Luther erred, and also wherein Zuinglius and Œcolampadius did err. It was Luther's duty, at the beginning to admonish that it was not his purpose to stablish such a local presence as the papists do dream; also, to protest that he sought not in this place to have the sacrament honoured as God; thirdly, to abstain from those rude similitudes, most hard to be understanded, or else to use them moderately, and to interpret them so that they might not have been cause of any offence. To conclude, since that contention was moved, he passed all measure, both in declaring his opinion, and also in rebuking other with too much rigour of words. For when he should have expounded his mind, so that it might have been received; according to his accustomed vehemency, to the intent to impugn them that held the contrary, he used incredible forms of speaking, which could not well be suffered of them, whose minds were but slenderly appointed to give credence to him. The other also offended, in that they did stick so stiffly in the impugning of that superstitious and fantastical opinion of the papists, as concerning the placely presence, and the adoration that followed thereof, employing their diligence to the rooting out of vices, rather than to the establishing of that thing which was profitable to be known. For notwithstanding that they denied not the verity, yet did they not teach it openly, as was beseeming. This do I understand, that whiles they gave themselves studiously and diligently to affirm that the bread and wine were called the body and blood of Christ, because they be the signs thereof, they thought not that they ought in the mean time to do this thing also, to add to that, 'they are the signs after such sort that the verity is nevertheless joined unto them. Neither did they declare that they went not about to deface the true communion which the Lord giveth us in his body and blood.

Of truth, neither of them was unworthy blame, forasmuch as they did not sustain to hear one another; that, all affection laid apart, they might follow the verity, on which side soever it should appear. But yet ought not we therefore to let pass our duty towards them, lest we forget the mercies and benefits which God gave unto them, and distributed unto us by their hands. For unless we be unthankful and unmindful of those things which we owe unto them, abstaining from all reproach and evil report, we shall easily forgive these and much greater things. To conclude, seeing that we know they were both of godly conversation and excellent doctrine, and that they also which at this day be on-live[1] be no less, we ought neither to speak nor judge of them otherwise than with great modesty and reverence. And chiefly, because it hath pleased our Lord God so, that after he had by this means instructed them to humility, he made an end of this unhappy contention, or at the least qualified it for the time, so that in the mean season it might be finished.

This have I spoken, because there is as yet no order published, wherein that concord is appointed; which thing were very necessary. But this thing shall be, when God will that all they which should set an order in these things do agree in one. In the mean time this ought to suffice you, that there be a brotherly friendship and conjunction between the congregations, as belongeth to the christian communion. With one voice therefore we all confess, that when we do, according to the institution of the Lord, receive the sacrament with faith, we are undoubtedly made partakers of the substance of the body and blood of Christ. How this thing should be done, some men can better define, and more plainly expound, than some. But this thing is chiefly to be remembered, that we exclude all carnal imagination, and that the mind ought to be erected up into heaven, and that we think not our Lord Jesu Christ to be so vile that he may

[1 On-live: alive. Old edition, *on lyue*.]

[COVERDALE.]

be contained in corruptible elements. Again, lest the force
of this most sacred mystery should be diminished,
we must think that it is wrought by the secret
and wonderful power of God, and that his
Spirit is the bond of this partaking,
which is for that cause
called spiritual.

FINIS.

THE

ORDER OF THE CHURCH IN DENMARK,

AND IN MANY PLACES OF GERMANY,

FOR THE

LORD'S SUPPER, BAPTISM, AND HOLY WEDLOCK.

# The order that the chur=
che and congregacion of Chryst in Denmark,
and in many places, countres and cities of Ger=
many doth vse, not only that the holy
supper of the lorde, but also at
the ministracion of ye bles=
sed Sacrament of
Baptisme & ho=
ly Wedlo
cke.

### Set forth by Myles Couerdale.

Non possumus que audiuimus et vi-
dimus non loqui. Acto. 4.

THE

## ORDER OF THE CHURCH IN DENMARK,

AND IN MANY PLACES OF GERMANY,

## FOR THE LORD'S SUPPER, BAPTISM, AND HOLY WEDLOCK.

To all them that hunger and thirst the glory of God and wealth of their neighbours, be grace, mercy, and peace, from the same everlasting God our most dear Father in heaven, through our Lord and only Saviour Jesus Christ.

It were to me a singular comfort, my right dear and entirely beloved brethren and sistern in Jesu Christ, if I might be with you myself continually, and communicate unto you some part of little taste which I have received of the Lord my God for your sakes. And all the lawful ways that I could devise, have I sought this great while to obtain licence of the higher powers for the same purpose.

But it will not be. Wherefore, though I be hindered and kept from you by all the means that Satan and his members can imagine, yet shall ye have my poor heart; yet will I not cease to wish you good; yet will I do the best for you that I can, although it be but with my pen.

In token whereof I have set forth unto you the order and manner, that many which have received God's word unfeignedly do use, not only at the most holy supper of our Lord, but also at the ministration of the blessed sacrament of baptism, and when any couple of persons are joined into holy wedlock. And this have I done to the intent, that when ye have spied and do see that this order is agreeable unto God's word, not varying from the most wholesome doctrine thereof, ye may wish in your hearts to have God's truth prosper likewise among you in the realm of England, and pray unfeignedly with me and all other sinners, that the Father of mercy and God of all comfort will so lighten and illuminate the hearts of our rulers, that they may follow the earnest monition of the second psalm, and be no more without understanding, but be wise betimes, and embrace the Son of God, while he offereth himself unto them; and not only to suffer the word of God to have the upper hand above all other doctrines, but also themselves to lay to their hands in abolishing the blasphemous and damnable abuses, that are here as yet suffered about the foresaid three principles of Christ's religion. Wherefore, dear brethren, when ye compare this order underwritten, which is the doctrine of God's word and practice of the primitive church, to the vain ceremonies used here yet, after the church of Rome, lift up your hearts to Almighty God, and beseech him that for Christ's sake he will once grant that these three, his holy supper, holy baptism, and holy wedlock, may be truly and sincerely ministered and practised also among us, to the glory of his blessed name, and increase of his kingdom for ever. Amen.

## ¶ THE ORDER TAKEN FOR THE DUE MINISTRATION OF THE HOLY SUPPER OF THE LORD.

For thy better instruction thou shalt first understand, that the blessed sacrament of the body and blood of the Lord, the worthy memorial of our redemption, is at no time denied to any christian man, when God's word is truly preached, if he lawfully require it. And as none doth minister it save the priest, which is the officer appointed thereto ; so is it not ministered but when there be other present to receive it as well as the priest. Now because that where God's word is truly preached, men do see the fruit of the said holy sacrament, therefore resort they the oftener to the same holy supper of the Lord, and delight the more therein. But specially to see what a number come to it on the Sunday, and how reverently, it would do one's heart good. And because they may the more fruitfully be partakers thereof, therefore on the Saturday, when the preaching is done (for every day they have a sermon), all such as are appointed in themselves to be partakers of the Lord's Supper, come one after another to the priest ; of whom they learn, not only what the sacrament is, and the right use thereof, but also they being repentant and sorry for their sins, and professing amendment, receive there God's promises for their absolution, to the singular comfort of their conscience, and are exhorted by the priest to do against the morrow as the holy apostle Paul biddeth them ; that is, even to try, examine, and prove themselves, whether they can be content unfeignedly in their hearts to take better hold on the kingdom of God, than they have done in times past; to be more stedfast in faith and hope toward God and his promises ; to be more fervent in prayer and love toward God, and for his sake to shew unfeigned love toward every man ; to forgive heartily, as they would be forgiven ; to mortify their flesh daily more and more, by reasonable abstinence and godly exercises of the spirit, and virtuous occupation of the body ; to be glad in distributing the works of mercy to the poor, &c. And when the priest, preacher, or curate (for all is one thing) hath given every one this, or such a like exhortation, and enjoined each one his penance according to his estate, (as subjects to be true and obedient to their rulers, servants to be faithful and diligent in waiting on their masters' commandment, children to honour and obey their parents, and to learn virtue while they be young, householders to keep their houses in the fear of God, and so forth;) when the priest (I say) hath enjoined them thus to live and to increase in the same well-doing, he committeth them to God and to the word of his grace. And so they depart.

¶ On the Sunday in the morning (at six of the clock in summer, and at seven in winter) the bell ringeth, and the people prepare themselves to the church, so that soon after the bell hath rung the second time, the church is almost full of men, women, and children. Then a little afore the hour is expired, they ring the bell the third time, which ceaseth not till the hour strike. And at the quire door, beside the table of the Lord, stand two good sober singing men, which (commonly a quarter of an hour afore the sermon) begin a psalm; and all the people, both old and young, with one voice do sing with them, after such a fashion that every note answereth to a syllable, and every syllable to one note commonly, and no more, so that a man may well understand what they sing. But first, for the most part, they sing the Paternoster in their mother tongue, and then the psalms, sometimes more, sometimes fewer, according as the time requireth, but all in their own language. Now, when the clock smiteth (which is commonly seven in summer, and eight in winter), the superattendent, or chief curate, cometh into the pulpit, and first of all he wisheth unto his audience and to himself grace, mercy, and peace from God the Father, through his blessed Son Jesus Christ our Saviour. And to the intent that their hearts may be opened to the true understanding of the gospel which he is about to preach unto them, he exhorteth them to call for help to the Holy Ghost. So after that the two foresaid men (or at the least one of them) hath orderly begun, all the church followeth, and sing with one voice unto the Holy Ghost this song, *Veni, sancte Spiritus*[1], &c. or such another like it, in their mother tongue.

[1 The following is the original of this ancient hymn, a translation of which was adopted in the service of the Ordination of Priests in the first Liturgy of Edward the Sixth, and afterwards, in the shorter form in which it is now found, on the review of the Liturgy in the reign of Charles the Second:

Veni, Creator Spiritus,
Mentem tuorum visita:
Imple superna gratia
Quæ tu creasti pectora.

Qui Paraclitus diceris,
Donum Dei altissimi,
Fons vivus, ignis, caritas,
Et spiritalis unctio.

¶ Then the preacher taketh the gospel of that present Sunday (or some other place of the scripture that he is appointed to declare), and expoundeth it clearly by the other manifest places of the bible, noting in it such lessons, such consolations, and such ensamples, as are for the edifying of his audience.

¶ Commonly, at the latter end of the sermon, he maketh a pretty short rehearsal of it, by the way of exhortation to the people, or prayer toward God. And then requireth he them to confess and knowledge their sins unto God with him, every man in his own conscience, and to say such or like words in his heart, as I have plurally expressed in the general confession, that I humbly offered to the king's most honourable council for the edifying, anno 1539. When the priest hath prayed for all estates, and made this or such like confession in their name, he prayeth God to be merciful to them, to bless them, to shew the light of his countenance over them, and to have mercy on them.

Then giveth he them this, or such a like absolution, and saith :

To all them that repent and are sorry for their sins, detesting and abhorring their old wicked life ; if they be hungry and thirsty for God's mercy in Christ, believing surely to have forgiveness only by him, purposing to forsake all abomination of living, and from henceforth to live in the fear of God, and unfeignedly to keep his commandments ; to all such (by the virtue of God's word and commission

> Tu septiformis munere,
> Dextræ Dei tu digitus;
> Tu rite promissum Patris,
> Sermone ditans guttura.
>
> Accende lumen sensibus,
> Infunde amorem cordibus,
> Infirma nostri corporis
> Virtute firmans perpetim.
>
> Hostem repellas longius,
> Pacemque dones protinus.
> Ductore te sic prævio
> Vitemus omne noxium.
>
> Per te sciamus da Patrem,
> Noscamus atque Filium :
> Te utriusque Spiritum
> Credamus omni tempore.
>
> Sit laus Patri cum Filio,
> Sancto simul Paraclito ;
> Nobisque mittat Filius
> Charisma Sancti Spiritus. Amen.]

of the same) I pronounce and warrant free remission and clean forgiveness of all their sins. To the other, that will not repent, but still harden their hearts against God's truth, continually abiding in the blindness of false doctrine and filthiness of wicked living, having no purpose nor mind to come to repentance; to all such (by the virtue of the same word and commission thereof) do I pronounce damnation, and the terrible wrath of God, until they amend.

¶ So after that he hath wished the peace of God unto his audience, he cometh down. Then all the congregation and church in manner aforesaid do sing the creed or belief in their own mother tongue. And when that is done, the Curate, or else his coadjutor, standeth up afore the table of the Lord, and requireth all such as are appointed then to be partakers thereof, to be well ware what they do, and make a just account with themselves after what manner they have proved and tried their own consciences, whether it be done unfeignedly and in an earnest manner, and whether[1] they be at one with all men, and so forth. If it be so indeed, he giveth God thanks for it. If no, he prayeth them right gently, that they will think no shame to absent themselves from this holy supper, till the reconciliation be made, lest they come to it unworthily. And then giveth he them this exhortation, or else another such like:

## AN EXHORTATION AT THE SUPPER OF THE LORD.

DEAR friends, we are all baptized into the death of our Lord Jesu Christ: wherefore after holy baptism we must all the days of our life fight and strive in continual battle and war against sin, death, and the devil; and so bear about with us in our bodies the passion and death of our Lord Jesu, and must prove by experience, that the enemies whom we have to do withal are neither weak nor feeble, but mighty and valiant, to whose power men are naturally subdued, so that upon earth there is none so mighty as to resist this power of darkness through his own strength; so feeble and weak is all our ability in comparison thereof. For the which cause God the Father, through Christ his dear Son, hath ordained another power and kingdom, in the which is righteousness and life; and through his death and blood hath he delivered us, and brought us from sin to righteousness, from death to life, from the devil to God; and hath included the kingdom of his

[1 Old edition, *whē* (*when*).]

grace in the preaching, believing, and following of his word; which, being begun in the holy Christianity, shall go forth until the last day; that we which receive, believe, and do after the same word, by the merits of Christ, our reconciler and Saviour, should be and continue for ever his dear children, and heirs of the kingdom of grace, that is to say, of everlasting salvation; forasmuch as we through such faith do eat continually his flesh and drink his blood, that is to say, abide in him, and he in us.

To the intent now that this so great goodness, declared by the word of God, might daily among us be practised, distributed, and exhibited; therefore hath the gracious and merciful Lord Jesus Christ instituted and ordained a remembrance of this his wonderful work, and commanded that we at his supper in the sacrament should eat his very body and drink his very blood; whereby the hearts of all such as are faithful believers and fear God, might be assured of this same grace of God and everlasting salvation: and also that in the holy congregation and church his glorious remembrance might be kept, that is to say, to give him thanks and praise, to sing, speak, preach, and read thereof; to exhort and comfort one another among ourselves: and finally, with all faithfulness one to shew toward another such love and favour, as we ourselves have received of our dear Lord Jesus Christ.

¶ And forasmuch as we now are happened into these later days, in the which this so precious treasure is unhallowed and wickedly abused, this holy sacrament shall (for the necessary causes now rehearsed) be to us also a testimony of this present time before God and the world[1], that we do utterly both in word and deed refuse and forsake all the deceitfulness of the papistry, and that we faithfully with all our hearts submit ourselves under the gospel of Jesus Christ.

¶ Wherefore, ye dearly beloved in the Lord, forasmuch as this matter is so weighty, even God's own institution and ordinance, yea, and his commandment also, that we should do it; and likewise, seeing the necessity which should cause us to accomplish the same is so great, specially on our behalf toward God (to whom we owe a long *Deo gratias*, and

[1 Old edition, *word*.]

thanks), we ought in no wise to refrain ourselves from it, neither suffer ourselves to be kept back therefrom; but ofttimes with repentant hearts to seek this our soul's medicine and comfort of our conscience, believing what Christ saith to us herein, and doing as he commandeth us.

And as for those that seek no such repentant hearts, faith, and comfort herein, but live in open blasphemy, continuing in sin and wicked life, they shall know, that they are unworthy of this holy supper, and also excommunicate, till they amend.

But to the intent that the unrepentant may through the grace of God be lightened, and that we ourselves may fruitfully enjoy this supper to the amendment of our lives, and also that all Christendom generally may become the better, and be edified; therefore let us heartily make our prayer to God the Father of all mercy, believing assuredly that he will graciously hear us through our Lord Jesus Christ, who commanded us to pray, and promised us, saying: "Ask, and ye shall have; seek, and ye shall find; knock, and it shall be opened to you."

Wherefore, in consideration of the same commandment and promise, lift up your hearts, and say thus with me in your prayer:

O Lord God, our Father in heaven, we thy miserable children upon earth beseech thee, that thou wilt mercifully look on us, and lend us thy grace; that thy holy name may be sanctified among us and in all the world, through the pure and sincere teaching of the word, and through earnest charity in our daily living, and our conversation. Seclude thou graciously all false doctrine and evil living, whereby thy worthy name might be blasphemed and slandered.

¶ O let thy kingdom come, and be great. All sinful, blind people, and such as are holden captive of the devil in his kingdom, those bring thou to the knowledge of the true faith in Jesus Christ thy Son.

¶ Strengthen us, Lord, with thy Spirit, to do and to suffer thy will both in life and death, in weal and woe; that our will may alway be broken, offered up, and mortified.

¶ And give us our daily bread. Preserve us from covetous desire, and carefulness of the belly; that of thee we may be assured to have abundance of all good things.

Forgive us our trespass, as we forgive them which offend us; that our heart may have a sure and glad conscience, and that we never fear, nor be afraid for any sin.

Lead us not into temptation, but help us through thy Spirit to subdue the flesh, to despise the world with his vanities, and to overcome the devil with all his crafty assaults.

And finally, deliver thou us from all evil, both bodily and ghostly, temporal and eternal. Amen.

They that earnestly desire all this, let them say, Amen; believing without any doubt, that it is granted and heard in heaven, according as Christ promised us, saying, When ye pray, believe assuredly that ye shall have it, and it shall come to pass. Amen.

> Then rehearse he the words of the holy supper out of three evangelists, Matthew, Mark, and Luke, and also out of Saint Paul, Cor. xi. saying:

¶ THE Lord Jesus, the same night wherein he was betrayed, took bread, and giving thanks, brake it, and said: Take ye, and eat; this is my body, which shall be given for you. This do in the remembrance of me. In like manner, when supper was done, he took the cup also, saying: This cup is the new testament in my blood. As oft as ye drink this, do it in the remembrance of me.

> This done, the whole church, in the manner abovesaid, do sing a psalm or two of thanksgiving for this blessed sacrament. And in the mean season, they that are appointed then to sup with the Lord, come soberly and with great reverence one after another (the men first, and then the women,) to the table of the Lord, where they kneeling (one, I say, after another) receive at the hand of one of the priests the sacrament in form of bread. And then goeth he with like reverence to the other end of the table, and at the hand of another of the priests (which standeth there ready for the same purpose) he kneeleth down, and receiveth it also in the form of wine; and all the other follow reverently, and do the same. If one of the priests, or both, be disposed likewise as then to sup with the Lord, [he] kneeleth down, and his companion serveth him.

And even so doth he also to his fellow, in like manner and reverence.

> If the communicants, and they that receive then the sacrament, be many, they sing the more psalms of thanksgiving; else sing they the fewer.

When this holy supper is done, and the partakers thereof that were appointed thereto, one of the ministers standeth up, and exhorteth the people to give earnest thanks to God, with this or such a like prayer:

O ALMIGHTY God, most merciful Father, thou that openest thy gracious hand, whereby all things living have their food in due season; we give honour, praise, and thanks unto thee for all thy benefits, both ghostly and bodily, which thou hast richly poured upon us, without any of our deserving; but specially we thank thee for this worthy memorial of our redemption, wherein thou hast nourished and fed our souls with the body and blood of thy dear Son, our Saviour Jesus Christ, blessed for ever. Amen.

### Another.

O LORD Jesu Christ, our Redeemer, honour and praise be alway given unto thee for feeding our souls with this spiritual and heavenly food. And we beseech thee for thy tender mercy, that as thou hast given it us for a sacrament of continual thankfulness, of daily remembrance, and of charitable unity; even so, most merciful Saviour, lend us alway thy grace to be thankful unto thee for it, and not only by it to be continually mindful of our redemption, purchased through thy death and blood-shedding, but also in consideration thereof to increase in love toward thee, and all mankind for thy sake.

### Another.

O LORD God Almighty, we thank thee with all our hearts, that thou hast fed our souls with the body and blood of thy most dear Son. And we beseech thee unfeignedly so to illuminate our minds with thy holy Spirit, that we may daily increase in strength of faith to thee, in assuredness of hope in thy promises, and ferventness of love toward thee and our neighbours, to the glory and praise of thy holy name. Amen.

Thus the priest concludeth, and endeth the office of this present mystery, and blesseth the people, rehearsing these words of scripture. Numbers vi.

¶ THE Lord bless you and preserve you: the Lord shew his face to you, and have mercy on you: the Lord turn his countenance unto you, and give you peace. Amen.

And so they depart.

---

## ¶ THE ORDER TAKEN[1] FOR THE DUE MINISTRATION OF THE BLESSED SACRAMENT OF BAPTISM.

ON the Sunday, at one of the clock after noon, they have a sermon of an hour long, with like ringing and singing of psalms afore in their mother tongue, as they had in the morning, to the which pracing[2] the people come as thick as they did then. And as they sing a psalm for grace to the Holy Ghost in the morning, so do they here also at every sermon, where or whensoever it be made. And like as in the morning, when the sermon is done, the preacher exhorteth them to confess their sins with him in their hearts, and thereupon doth absolve them by the power and authority of God's word; so doth he here also in like manner, and in every sermon. Then sing they a like song of thanksgiving, as they did in the morning, and as they be accustomed to do after every preaching.

In the mean season, while this psalm of thanksgiving is sung, (or else afore,) the font is prepared: the midwife is there present with the child, or more midwives, if there be more children to be christened, (as there be commonly), with a fair company of honest, sober women. And when the psalm is sung out, the minister, being there ready at the font, readeth a lecture of the bible; and when he hath declared it compendiously to the edifying of the congregation, he exhorteth them, that forasmuch as all men are conceived and born in sin, and that seeing it is unpossible for a man to come into the kingdom of God, except he be born anew and regenerate, they will shew and declare their godly love, and call upon God the Father, through Jesus Christ, and in his name, that he will mercifully baptize that child (or those children) with the Holy Ghost, and receive him (or them) to grace.

Upon the same exhortation they make their hearty prayer, beseeching God to have mercy on the child; and then addeth he this, or such a like petition in their name, saying:

O ALMIGHTY God, which in commanding us to pray hast assured us that we, believing stedfastly in thy promise, shall have all that we desire, specially concerning the soul;

[1 Old edition, *for taken*. Compare pp. 470, 480.]

[2 preasing, or pressing, Nares: but qu. *preaching*. Old edition, *paceing*.]

wherein we seek thy glory and the wealth of our neighbours; our humble petition to thee, O most dear Father, is, that forasmuch as this child is not without original sin, thou wilt consider thine own mercy, and according to thy promise send this child thy good Spirit, that in thy sight it be not counted among the children of wrath, but of light and grace, and become a member of the undefiled church espoused to Christ, thy dear Son, in faith and love unfeigned, by the means of the same Jesus Christ our Lord. Amen.

Another prayer.

O ALMIGHTY eternal God, most merciful Father, forasmuch as the just liveth by faith, and unpossible it is for any man without belief to please thee; we beseech thee, that thou wilt grant to this child the gift of faith, wherein thou wilt seal and assure his heart in the Holy Ghost, according to the promise of thy Son; that the inward regeneration of the Spirit may be truly represented by the outward baptism; and that the child may be buried with him into death, and be raised up by him from death again, to the praise of thy glory and edifying of his neighbour. Amen.

¶ Sometime also the priest readeth this parcel of the x chapter of St Mark's gospel, saying:

AND they brought little children to him, that he should touch them. And his disciples rebuked those that brought them. But when Jesus saw it, he was displeased, and said unto them, Suffer little children to come to me, and forbid them not; for of such is the kingdom of God. Verily, I say unto you, whosoever receiveth not the kingdom of God as a child, shall not enter therein. And he took them up in his arms, and put his hands upon them, and blessed them.

> Then the godfather, if it be a man child, (or the godmother, if it be a woman child,) holding the child in his arms, cometh and standeth by the priest, who asketh him, on the child's behalf, if he forsake the devil and all his works? He saith, Yea; and upon the priest's interrogation, he confesseth his faith in the face of the church. So the priest taketh the child in his left hand, and with his right hand he poureth water on his head, calling him by his name (as he did afore), and baptizing him in the name of the Father, and of the Son, and of the Holy Ghost.

Finally, the minister committeth the children to the prayers of the congregation, and exhorteth the godfathers and godmothers most earnestly to see that the children be brought up and instructed in christian knowledge and virtue, the glory of God, and edifying of the commonwealth.

Then sing they a psalm that either concerneth some thanksgiving to God for his word, or else some necessary petition.

*And so they depart.*

Now in like manner as thou seest this blessed sacrament ministered on the Sunday, even so with like reverence do they use it at the same hour on those week-days that the congregation, in the authority of their head rulers, hath appointed to that use. And if the children in the mean time be in any danger, then the midwives baptize them. And as the congregation and multitude of the people is great at the ministration of holy baptism on the Sunday, so is it also on the other appointed days, though they be work-days. Whereby it is to be noted, that the institution and ordinance of God is in great reputation among them: for as it is ministered reverently, so is it heard with great devotion and ferventness; and though there be always some unthankful livers, yet the flock of Christ be ever bringing forth good fruits, and follow the word of life in their conversation.

---

## THE ORDER TAKEN FOR THE DUE MINISTRATION OF HOLY WEDLOCK.

As touching God's holy institution of marriage, thou shalt understand, that privy contracts be avoided as much as may be; and young folks are so well brought up in the fear of God, and instructed in the knowledge of his word, that they will not lightly be enticed to run on head, and marry without the honest consent of their parents and tutors. Again, the fathers and mothers which have young folks apt to marriage, are circumspect, not suffering their sons and daughters to go long beyond their time unmarried; but both for the avoiding of uncleanly conversation in their children, and also for their own discharge, they provide them honest marriages meet for them. Which thing to do they are not only [moved] in the daily sermons that they hear, but also by the old godly practices of such holy men as was Abraham, and Isaac, &c. Neither do the two young persons come together after a light or indiscreet manner; but even at their hand-fastening, (when the knot of holy wedlock is fast knit,) there are present the father and mother of the parties, or else (if they be dead, or absent,) their nighest kinsfolks and tutors; and so is also some honest discreet preacher or curate of theirs, who to the edifying of them maketh a godly collation out of God's word, for their example, learning, and comfort in holy wedlock.

So when the time approacheth that they shall be married openly in the face of the church, the curate, in the presence of the whole congregation, giveth warning certain days afore, and requireth that if any man know some lawful impediment to hinder the said marriage, he will notify it at his monition. If no hinderance be made, then at the day appointed the bridegroom, having a company of honest men with him, and likewise the bride, having an honest company of women with her, come to the sermon in the morning, (which, as I said afore, is every day at seven of the clock in summer, and at eight in the winter,) and after that the preaching is done, and the sacrament ministered in the manner aforesaid, they come both before the preacher: in the mean time the whole church in their mother tongue do sing the 106th [128th] psalm, *Beati omnes qui timent Dominum, &c.*

Then the preacher speaketh to them both by name, and asketh them saying: *M.* and *N.* are ye minded to live together in holy wedlock, and to testify and confirm that same your purpose here in the presence of this congregation? They answer, Yea. Then (saith he) I take you all here that stand by to witness, requiring you to record the same, and to remember it: and saith moreover, If there be any man here that knoweth a lawful impediment by God's word, that these two persons may not proceed forth together in marriage, let him speak now. So if there be none to make impediment, then the preacher saith: Forasmuch as here appeareth no hinderance to the contrary, but that ye may go forth together in holy wedlock, I pray God stablish the thing he hath wrought in you: seeing also that both your consents are knit in holy wedlock, and ye confess the same here openly before God and the world, I declare and pronounce you to be married together, in the name of the Father, and of the Son, and of the Holy Ghost. And in so saying, he joineth their hands together, and addeth moreover: Let not man therefore separate them asunder, whom God hath coupled together.

This done, he exhorteth them to remember, how that God hath joined them in holy marriage, and (according to the commandment of God) to love one another, and so to keep their household, and to bring up their children (when God sendeth them) in the fear of God, that their whole living may redound to the glory of his holy name and edifying of the commonwealth.

Then rehearseth he this (or such another) prayer in the name of the whole church and congregation :

O ALMIGHTY God, Father of heaven, forasmuch as it hath pleased thee to call these new-married folks unto holy wedlock, like as at the beginning thou sawest it not good for a man to be alone; for the which cause thou madest him an helper like to himself, and so ordainedst that they two should be as one person; we beseech thee, that unto these new-married folks thou wilt grant thy holy Spirit, whereby they

[COVERDALE.]

living in holy wedlock, may still trust in thy goodness, overcome all temptation, and lead a godly honest life, to the edifying of every man. Bless them also, that in the fruit of their body they may praise thee, and so bring up the same, that it may be to thy glory and profit of the commonwealth. Amen.

Then the church singeth a psalm of thanksgiving, and so departeth.

## THE CONCLUSION OF THIS LITTLE BOOK.

THOU seest now, what order is kept in the ministration and use of the foresaid three holy ordinances of God; concerning the which I write here nothing of 'had I wist[1],' nor of uncertainty, but even as I know, and as I have not only seen with mine eyes and heard with mine ears, but been present also long and many a day at the execution, practice, and experience thereof: which things as I write to give all good hearts occasion of fervent prayer to God, that he will grant his word to grow likewise among us; even so in the virtue of God's holy name, and for that precious blood sake of his most dear Son, I admonish and exhort all subjects to be patient, to avoid all kind of sedition, to commit the reformation of all errors, superstitions, ceremonies, vain traditions, wicked laws, and unjust statutes of men, even unto God the author of peace, and to the working of his Spirit in those princes and rulers whom he hath called to office for the same purpose. Let no man be slack in his duty, but give God that which is his, and to the king the things that belongeth unto him, according as Christ commandeth, Matt. xxii., and as St Paul exhorteth, Romans xi.

This I say, to stop the mouths and the blasphemous tongues of such as will not cease to rail on men, and to slander me (yea, even to the king's majesty), as though I were a perverter of common order, or took upon me to change the laws and to make new statutes. Nay, ye ungodly hypocrites, not so: but as I am sure that there is heavy damnation laid up for all such subjects as rebel or make

[1 'Had I wist,' a colloquial expression of doubt and uncertainty: q. d. 'If I had known, I would have told it;' which would imply that he did not know.]

sedition against the prince, or disobey the least commandment of God in their sovereign; even so am I assured, that there is no less damnation prepared for those rulers or heads that make unjust laws and cruel statutes to maintain their own lusts, and oppress the poor. I report me to the tenth chapter of Esay, the second and third of Micheas, and to the latter end of the fifth chapter of the prophet Hieremy. Let all rulers therefore beware, that they make no acts of parliament nor statutes against God's word, and let all subjects learn of St Peter (1 Pet. ii.) to be obedient. And not only that, but if they be commanded any unlawful thing, then let them learn of the same St Peter (Acts iv.) to obey God more than men.

In the mean time, till God's blessed word only be ruler among us, and till all wicked inventions of men be abolished, let those that fear God unfeignedly be fervent in their prayers, and increase in all thankfulness and virtuous living towards God and men. Let no man, woman, nor child of God be slack in his duty; but let faith increase in strength, let hope be evermore assured of God's promises, let charity always love God and her neighbour, and leave no good work undone, that may be to God's glory and man's profit. And then shall we be known not only readers and hearers of the truth, but true disciples of the same. And though we cannot attain to the perfectness of that commonwealth, which I spake of afore, (where God's ordinances are so reverently ministered, the poor so richly provided for, and youth so virtuously brought up;) nevertheless we, doing our best, and begging strength of God to do more than we can do of ourselves, shall not only be allowed and accepted in his sight, but also have the continual assistance of his holy Spirit, whereby we sufficiently harnessed and armed against all temptations of sin, hell, devil, and our own flesh, shall as well have the upper hand of them, as we have (through the only power of God) overcome so many stormy winds and tempests of adversity in time past, and as we hope to escape these present troubles by the help of Jesus Christ, whose name be blessed for ever! Amen.

## A LITTLE COMPLAINT, WITH A SHORT EXHORTATION, MADE UNTO ALL THEM THAT ARE NO DISSEMBLERS WITH GOD'S WORD, BUT UNFEIGNEDLY LIVE THEREAFTER.

LIKE as God (according to his most blessed nature) ever loving, gracious, merciful, and true, doth alway send his word afore he plague the world, and giveth us warning afore the destruction come, willing us to convert unto him, to forsake our own evil ways, and to lay hand on eternal life; even so contrariwise the devil, the father of falsehood and lies, envying man's salvation, casteth ever one bone or other in the way, to hinder the glory of God, to stop his word, to keep back his truth, lest through the stedfast believing and following thereof his own kingdom should be minished, God's amplified and increased. Sometime, to hinder the gospel of the glory of the great God, he stirreth up tyranny and cruelness, moving some rulers or great men of the world to take part against it, to persecute it, to trouble and vex them whom God hath called unto it. Ensample whereof ye see in Pharao, in king Achab, in Antiochus, in Herod, and in those great prelates that shewed their hot charity upon our Saviour Christ and his apostles. The devil also, to set up his kingdom the better, getteth him chaplains for his own tooth, (such as were Baal's prophets, 3 Regum [1 Kings] xxii.) that they may ever, either in confessions or otherwise, move kings and princes to take part against their own salvation, and to trouble such as tell them no dreams nor phantasies, but even the very word of God; as the prophet Micheas did.

Sometime (I say), lest the truth should be believed, the devil, as he is the father of lies, so getteth he false witnesses to testify even against Christ, and against poor Stephen and Paul, his servants; yea, and to preach, that their doctrine is naught, seditious, new learning, and heresy, Matt. xxvii. Matt. ii. Acts vii. xxiv.; that they will destroy good works, Romans iii.; that they will keep no holy day, Matt. xii. John v.; that they will not fast, Matt. ix. Mark ii. Luke v. Thus (I say) is the devil ever about to overthrow Christ's kingdom, and to set up his own. And because his lying chaplains should the better fight against Christ, he teacheth them to go craftily to work, to lie and spare not, to call the disciples of Christ new fellows, to say that they care neither for fasting, nor praying, for alms-deed, nor for good work; yea, make the world believe (saith the devil) that they care neither for one ceremony, nor either for one sacrament nor other. Such lying lessons doth the devil teach his scholars; and not only this, but also to wrest and wring the scripture from the manifest understanding of it: of the which juggling cast he hath given them an example in the fourth chapter of Matthew and fourth of Luke.

Who now, considering this great decay of godliness, that the devil hath brought into the world (partly through the tyranny that he hath stirred up in great men, partly through the false witness-bearing of hypocrites and lying teachers), hath not cause to mourn in this behalf? Who will not be sorry to see God's holy word thus persecuted, thus exiled, thus evil reported, thus belied?

Nevertheless all this evil doth not the devil think sufficient: he cannot herewithal be content; but he entereth in also among them that profess the name of Christ, that are called his brethren and disciples, that pretend to love and favour his truth; and among them, look who is meet for his purpose, most inconstant, and least regardeth Christ's words in his heart, of him he maketh either an whoremonger, a deceiver of his neighbour, or a follower of other vices of his own carnal lusts, robbing him utterly of that most holy, most stedfast, and living faith that Christ taught, and also of those worthy fruits of the Spirit of God, repentance and works of light, which the scripture speaketh of: by the means whereof, and because he bare the name of a christian brother, therefore, even as he behaveth himself now, and as he liveth, so must we be reputed of the ungodly, and such livers must we be called. If he be a breaker of peace, a maker of sedition, a drunkard, a false buyer and seller, a follower of filthy lusts, a bringer up of sects (as God ever suffereth them to be deceived that will not abide the order of his word); then must we also be called breakers of common order, railers, makers of insurrection, drunkards, false dealers with our neighbours, heretics, followers of fleshly and carnal liberty. Yet though all our teaching, writing, talking, and living, be to the contrary, yet bear we the blame: so blind is this wicked world in judgment, and so unthankful in their living, are a great number of them that are called christian men (as I understand) on the other side.

Wherefore to you, dearly beloved in God, elect and chosen to an high vocation in Jesus Christ, even to be flesh of his flesh, and bone of his bones, to be citizens with the saints, and of the household of God, to you I make this my moan afore rehearsed; trusting, that though neither the world, nor those false brethren, which, because they were not of us are gone from among us, 1 John ii., and are fallen in love with the world, after the example of Demas, 2 Tim. iv.; though neither of them both, I say, will hearken to the voice of God while it is called to-day, but still harden their hearts against God's truth; my trust is, as I said before, that ye will hold your hand still on the plough, that ye will walk honestly now, while the mercy of God lendeth you the daylight. Ye know that our Lord said, "The night shall come, in the which no man shall be able to work." Ye see how our "adversary the devil goeth about like a roaring lion, seeking whom he may devour." Ye see what a number of great men on the one side have girded their swords about them, and stand even in complete harness to fight against the manifest word of God: ye see what swearing, what blaspheming of God's name, what pride, what excess, what filthiness of body; and idleness is used, practised, and daily maintained in their houses; ye see how they cannot abide the hearing of God's word, but blast and blow against it, persecute it, and exile it, as much as in them lieth.

On the other side ye see, what a number of hypocrites, antichrists, false prophets, and flattering chaplains, are not only about great men, but everywhere in manner roar, and cry, and stamp against our Lord's doctrine, keep the people still in blindness, and feed them with draff and dregs instead of God's word.

Thirdly, ye see what a number here be in the world, which, pretending to love God's word by their outward hearing, reading, and talking of it, live clean contrary against it, bring not forth the worthy fruits of repentance, are as great swearers, as filthy, as idle, as covetous, as deceitful in bargaining, as unapt to all good works, as they were afore they knew the truth: and by this means is it come to pass, that through such unchristian living the good word of God is more suppressed than either through the cruelty of tyrants or flattering lies of hypocrites : all which three sorts of enemies, because they are not of us, but without, therefore will I have the less to do with them.

But of you, dearly beloved, will I be bold to exhort you, for the tender mercy of God, that, in consideration of the premises, ye will walk godly and worthily in this wicked world, continuing (as I trust ye do) in stedfastness of the christian faith, in ferventness of love toward God, and toward your very enemies for his sake, in looking assuredly for his promises, being patient and joyful in trouble, earnest in prayer at all times; ready into true obedience, to keep all good order, to be exercised in all good works, every man according to the estate that God hath called him unto. As many of you as are called to office and common authority, to bear rule, or to give judgment in causes of the commonwealth, be diligent in your office, Romans xii.; punish the evil, and maintain the good[1], 1 Pet. ii. Roma. xiii.; accept no person in judgment, allow no false accusation, shed no innocent blood, Exod. xxiii.; and hear the small as well as the great, Deut. i.

As many of you as are called to the office of preaching, follow the apostle's counsel: "Take heed unto yourselves, and to all the flock, in the which the Holy Ghost hath appointed you to be overseers, to feed the congregation of God," &c. Acts xx. "Feed Christ's flock which is among you, and take the oversight of them, not as though ye were compelled, but willingly; not for the desire of filthy lucre, but of a good mind; not as lords over the parishes, but to be an ensample unto the flock." 1 Pet. v. "To cast away unghostly and old wivish fables, to be unto them that believe an ensample in the word, in conversation, in love, in the spirit, in faith, in pureness; to give attendance unto reading, to exhortation, to doctrine." 1 Timoth. iv. "Study to shew yourselves to God laudable workmen, which need not to be ashamed." 2 Tim. ii. All other estates among you I heartily exhort and require, every one to do their duty; as subjects to be obedient and true to their princes and higher powers, Romans xiii. 1 Pet. ii. Tit. iii.; men to love their wives heartily, as they are taught, 1 Pet. iii. 1 Thess. iv. Ephe. v.; wives so

[1 Old edition, *God*.]

to "behave themselves as it becometh women that profess godliness through good works," 1 Tim. ii.; that their chaste conversation may win the wicked, 1 Pet. iii.; men to deal gently with their servants, Ephe. vi. Coloss. iii.; to bring up their children in the nurture and doctrine of the Lord, Ephe. vi. Deut. iv.; servants to be faithful, true, and obedient to their masters, Ephe. vi. Coloss. iii. 1 Pet. ii.; that they may do worship to the word of God in all things, 1 Timo. vi. Tit. ii.

And if we thus behave ourselves, every one in his calling, then shall it come to pass, that even they which now blaspheme us as evil-doers shall at the last be ashamed of their part, and convert from their own evil ways to the true faith and living which is taught in the word of God; to whom, for his infinite grace and gifts thereof, be honour and praise now and evermore. Amen.

FINIS.

# A Shorte Re-Capitulation or Abrigement

of Erasmus Enchiridion brefely comprehendinge the summe and contentes thereof very profitable and necessary to be rede of all trew Christen men.

Drawne out by M. Coberdale,
Anno. 1545.

Timo. vi.
Suffer afflictions as goode and feathful sowdgars of Jesu Christ.

Job vii.
Syeng the lyffe of man, ys but
A battell or warfarr upon the earthe.

## EPHES. VI.

Be strong in the Lord and in the power of his might. And put on the armour of God, that ye may stand stedfast against the crafty assaults of the devil. For ye must not wrestle against flesh and blood, but against rule, against power, and worldly rulers of the darkness of this world, against spiritual wickedness, for heavenly things.

## II. COR. X.

Let not your weapons pertaining to this battle be carnal things, but mighty in God, able to cast down strong holds and overthrow the imagination of man, and every high thing that exalteth itself against the knowledge of God, and bring into captivity all understanding to the obedience of Christ our Lord and God.

---

[This Treatise, as the title expresses, is an abridgement of a small work of Erasmus, entitled, "Enchiridion militis Christiani, saluberrimis præceptis refertum, authore D. Erasmo Roterodamo, cui accessit nova mireque utilis Præfatio;" but divested of much of its controversial and learned matter, and retaining all which is most spiritual and practical in the original. This edition is printed from a copy of Bishop Coverdale's work belonging to the Library of Sion College, London.]

# THE SUM OF THE PROLOGUE.

THE preface, prologue, or long epistle, written to the right virtuous and sage Father, Paulus Wolzius[1], (whom Almighty God even now this last year hath delivered out of this wretched world,) declareth evidently, that though some men have even married themselves to the vain pastimes and pleasures of the world, yet God through adversity (as his accustomed manner is) nurtureth and teacheth his own, chasteneth them, and calleth them to a christian life. To the furtherance whereof, like as every one of us is bound to bestow all his labour and study, so is not he to be cast away, that being weak and frail, not only desireth to be virtuous, but also is fervent in learning the way of godliness; whereof they are the best teachers, that, avoiding the tediousness of huge and great volumes, do instruct men rather to live godly, than to waste their hours in long and vain disputations. For how few soever they be that give themselves to sound doctrine, yet the fear of God, the fruit whereof is eternal salvation, appertaineth unto all men. Neither doth any man attain so nigh unto wisdom, as he that is in love withal, and appeareth not so much learned himself, as he is studious to allure all others, (yea, as well friend as foe, as well Turk as Christian,) to godliness; and is not himself overcome with evil, but rather overcometh evil with good. For as it is a christian man's part to save, and not to destroy, so hath the same right true and effectual divinity subdued more people in times past to the kingdom of Christ, than any other artillery, weapon, or ordnance of war. Yea, like as our most cruel enemies may be mollified and won with benefits and kindness, when we seek nothing so much as their health; even so, in seeking their destruction, we may sooner turn into Turks ourselves, than that we shall cause them to become christian men.

*God through adversity calleth his own children to repentance.*

*Who is most and best learned.*

[1] The following is the inscription of the dedication referred to: "Reverendo in Christo Patri ac D. D. Paulo Volsio religiosissi: Abbati Monasterii, quod vulgo dicitur Curia-Hagonis, D. Erasmus Rotero."

*The corruptness of the world.*

Now to consider the corruption of this world, and how far it is out of frame; the darkness, the troublous ruffling, the great tyranny, avarice, and iniquity thereof unpunished; how cold men are in charity, and how greatly given to ambition and lucre; who, lamenting the same, doth not see thousands of occasions for us all to take better hold of Christ's doctrine, and to have recourse thereunto? Specially considering, that the cruel Philistines prevail so greatly, and cease not, even now in our time, to stop it up, wringing and wresting it to their filthy purposes; yea, babbling and carping so sore against it, that from fear men dare not drink the living water thereof, but must be fain to take such corrupt liquor as come out of their all-to broken cisterns, even earthly things for heavenly, pelfary of men's inventions instead of God's holy commandments: which trifles yet shall easily of themselves vanish away, if the light of faith be so kindled in our minds, that we lose not the rule and pattern of Christ's love and charity. And doubtless, it shall further the gospel most notably, if they that teach it do excel in the knowledge and life thereof; and if princes, establishing no laws for their own pleasure, delight more to reform their people with mercy than with cruelty, rather to defend them than to oppress them. As for princes, they should without doubt use less oppressing of their people, less warring one against another, and less shedding of blood, if bishops and priests that be about them were not readier to flatter them, than they are sincerely to instruct them in Christ's doctrine; which as it manifestly rebuketh covetous Pharisees, hypocrites, and proud rich folks, so doth it openly teach us to do good, and to be meek and gentle of mind even to our enemies. Now though princes make many laws, whereof Christ is not the author, yet as they are to be obeyed when they command that which is just and right, so is it best to suffer them, even when they be evil. As touching the common people, though their estate be low, their understanding gross and weak, and they of devil bound to obey; yet forasmuch as they pertain to the mystical body of Christ, they must be nourished, forborne, and cherished after a fatherly manner, until they wax more strong in Christ. For every one is not like perfect in the kingdom of God. Wherefore he

*Our Philistines.*

*Priests.*

*Princes.*

*The common people.*

that is called to more excellent of gifts, ought, after the manner of the highest elements, to draw others unto him, and to help, that his inferiors may be transformed into his nature, and not, under the pretence and cloak of virtue, to disagree from the learning of Christ, which is the only mark every man ought to shoot at, and in no wise to change it; to enforce himself to come as often as he can: which, as it is the highest perfection allowed of God, so consisteth it not in the manner or kind of living, not in garments, meats, or drinks, but in the affections and mind.

And like as there is no estate of living, but there be some dangers whereinto it may fall; so ought no man to be displeased, but rather to take it in right good worth, when he is warned thereof: neither is he a condemner of other men, that faithfully sheweth them their duty. And yet can there nothing be free from the cavillation of lewd persons; but whatsoever is spoken, yea, even to the praise of virtue against vice, that same is taken in the most, and judged of them to be of a wrong and sinistral opinion. Yea, of so corrupt and perverse judgments are some, that they count it, even in priests, to be but a small vice, which is most abominable; and also esteem it to be an high virtue, which hath but only the visor and appearance of godliness; thinking themselves better for the ceremonies, rules, and trifles of men's invention, and yet having no conscience at all to slander other men. Neither need men to fear, that the reproving of such abuses doth either subvert religion, or hinder true obedience. For whomsoever the Holy Ghost inspireth, is of his own accord, without any manner of compulsion, ready to obey, yea, even those rulers that be sharp and rough; who nevertheless should no more abuse the obedience of their inferiors, than any man should make his liberty a cloak or cover to his carnal living: which though some do, yet ought not other men therefore to be locked, as Jews, in the bondage of ceremonies. For the more a man is religious, and given unto true godliness, the less he yieldeth to the ceremonies of men's invention; wherein if no man were snared till he were of perfect experience, then, like as the fewer should be deceived, even so doubtless, according to the desire of all them that be good, the religion of the gospel should be so pleasant unto every man that

*Nothing is free from the cavillation of lewd persons.*

*The Holy Ghost is the author of obedience.*

they should be heartily well content therewith without any other.

And reason it is, that all things give place to the glory of Christ; wherewith Moses rejoiced, that his own honour was defaced and minished, like as also the religions of men should be, if they that profess the gospel did live thereafter. For as they whom we now call religious are nothing like them of the old time, but drowned in hypocrisy and worldly business, yea, nothing better than other temporal men, save only in appearance; even so shall the vows of chastity, poverty, and obedience be better kept of him that observeth the profession of holy baptism, than they be of them.

The rest is then, that seeing the confidence in ourselves is most dangerous, we neither disdain them that be feeble, nor foolishly stand in our own conceit, for no diversity of living from other men: but rather, following the counsel of Christ, let us even from our hearts confess, when we have done our best, that "we are but unprofitable servants." And to the intent that we may be obedient unto Christ himself, let us be ready, not only to hear them that call us unto him, but also to tolerate and suffer the evil; nevertheless in such sort, that if they command things wicked and contrary to the doctrine of Christ, we rather obey God than men.

## THE FIRST CHAPTER.

HOW WE MUST WATCH AND LOOK ABOUT US ALWAY WHILE WE BE IN THIS LIFE.

WHOSO will escape the danger of sin, and prosperously go forward in the way of godliness, must alway consider that this life of man is a perpetual warfare; and must be circumspect, that the world with his delusions and flattering pleasures juggle not his mind from watching, or make him too careless, as though he had already conquered his enemies. Who, considering that they be so many, as namely, the wicked and crafty devils above us, the world afore and behind us, yea, on the right hand and on the left, as well shaking the wall of our souls with the guns of adversity, as prompting us unto evil with his vain promises; not only because the slippery and crafty serpent layeth a wait, even by our own affections and sensuality to entice and draw our minds unto mortal and deadly pleasures, but also, while we ourselves bear about with us the old earthy Adam, our own most perilous enemy; considering, I say, we have so many deadly enemies, ought we not therefore still to be weaponed and alway to watch? Why sleep we then so fast, giving ourselves to idleness, to pleasure, to revellings, as though we should rather live in banqueting than in warfare against such enemies? Why will we rather make truce with vice and sin, than with God, with whom the wicked can have no peace, namely, they that not only take part with sin, but unkindly also and wickedly break their appointment made with him? Have we not in holy baptism professed and bound ourselves to fight faithfully ever under the standard of Christ our captain, to whom we owe more than we have to pay? Do not the badges and signs of baptism in us testify, that we are sworn unto him never to forsake him? Whereof the name of Christ also ought to put us in remembrance. Why are we then such renegades, that we not only take part against him which bestowed his own life for us; but do it also in a filthy quarrel, to obtain no other reward than the very death of our souls? If in these mad wars of men the miserable soldiers do jeopard their lives, are pricked and stirred up into courage through the greatness of the pay,

*The life of man is but a warfare.*

*Enemies at hand.*

*We have promised in baptism to fight alway under the standard of Christ.*

through the comfort of the captain, through the cruelness of the enemies, through shame of cowardice, or desire of praise; how much more then should the hope of reward kindle us to have lusty stomachs, when he that shall quit our pain, if we win the field, beholding us, doth not only comfort us in our labours and travails, while we are yet fighting, but also giveth us such reward as excelleth all the senses and wits of man, even blessed immortality and heaven itself! The hope of which reward should by reason inflame the quick courage of gentle stomachs, seeing he that hath promised can never lie nor deceive. And considering he beholdeth us that seeth all things, like as very shame of cowardice at the least way should move us to be lusty in this battle; even so, forasmuch as to be praised of him is very felicity, why jeopard we not our lives to have this praise?

Seeing now we are so circumspect in avoiding the dangers and death of the body, why perceive we not the death of the soul, which is much more cruel? Now even *Tokens that the soul is sick.* as the body is out of temper when it will keep no meat, so when the word of God seemeth bitter unto us, if our mind rise up against it; if our memory keep it not; if we think not upon it, nor work thereafter; if our soul grudge, or be weak and faint to work the deeds of mercy, to suffer trouble or loss; if the eyes of our mind be waxen so dim, that they see not the clear light of the truth; if our inward ears hear not the voice of God; summa, if we lack all our inward feeling and perceiving of the knowledge of God, it is an evident token, not only that our soul is crazed, but also dead; because God, which is the life thereof, is away. For feeling is a token of life; and like as the body is not alive, if he feel not the pricking of a pin, even so when we are wounded in our soul, and have committed evil, [if] it grieve us not, then is not our soul alive, but dead. For the which cause also Christ called the Pharisees painted sepulchres, namely, because they bare dead souls about with them. Wherefore, considering that the bodies of good men are the temple of the Holy Ghost, and forasmuch as according to the gospel the mouth speaketh out of the abundance of the heart, no doubt we would speak the lively words of God and work his deeds, if he, our life, were present within our hearts.

*Causes of consolation.* Thus, though we fight in strange and wonderful jeopardies, with many violent and subtle adversaries, yet have we causes sufficient to be of good comfort; for though our enemies be grievous, yet have we present help at hand. Though they be many against us, what matter is it, when God is on our side? If he stay us, who can cast us down? As for our enemy, he is no new soldier, but one that was overcome many years agone, and overthrown by the might of Jesus Christ; and he shall now also be subdued in us by the same power, if we, as lively members, remain in Christ our head. For though we be not strong in our own strength, yet in him we shall be able to do all things. If the end and victory of our war depended of fortune, then might we doubt thereof; but it is certain and sure, namely, in the hands of our protector, whose benignity never faileth man. Wherefore, if we being thankful unto him, that for our salvation first oppressed the tyranny of sin; if we be not careless nor negligent, but with all diligence do our part again, and be of good comfort, we, I say, fighting in this manner, do follow his ensample; neither bearing us to hold upon the grace of God, as they do that be careless, neither casting away the confidence of mind, as do they that mistrust his mercy; then, through his strength, we shall be sure in conclusion to win the field.

## THE SECOND CHAPTER.

### WHAT MEANS ARE TO BE USED IN THE WAR OF A CHRISTIAN MAN.

WHEREAS nothing pertaineth more to the war of a christian man, than to know with what weapons he must fight, and to have the same always ready at hand; even so, considering the adversary is never idle, we ought not to cease from war; but if we will fight against the multitude of vices, we ought alway to watch, to have our mind armed, and to take the weapons of defence; but specially to provide us of two, namely, prayer and knowledge, which be the chief armour of a christian man. Perfect prayer lifteth up the mind unto God; knowledge armeth the mind with wholesome precepts and honest opinions. These two cleave so together, *Two weapons.*

[COVERDALE.]

that the one cannot lack the other: for as the one maketh intercession, so the other teacheth how we ought to pray, namely, in the name of Jesu; and what we ought to desire, even that which is wholesome for our soul's health. Now though prayer be more excellent, because she talketh familiarly with Almighty God, yet is knowledge no less necessary: which as it ought not to be imperfect, so ought not prayer to be faint, slack, or without quickness; neither can we well perform the great journey that we have to go, without the aid and help of these two means. The use of prayer is not to mumble and babble much, as they do that are not ripe in God's Spirit. For five words spoken in knowledge are better than ten thousand babbled with the mouth. Neither is it the noise of our lips, but the fervent desire of the mind, that God alloweth. Which fervent prayer, with like study or meditation of the holy scripture, is able as well to put aback the great violence of our enemies, as to make easy our grievous adversity. If we with this heavenly manna and food of God be refreshed in the furtherance of our journey, it shall make us bold and strong to buckle with our enemies. For the doctrine of God, as it only is pure and undefiled, contrary to the nature of men's doctrines; even so to them that, spiritually understanding it, may abide the hearing thereof, there is nothing sweeter nor more pleasant, and therefore the more worthy to be searched and well pondered. This is the river of comfort, the fountain of ease, the well that refresheth the weary, the water of Siloe, where the blind receive their sight: to the study whereof if we apply ourselves wholly, that is, if we exercise our minds continually in the law of God, we shall be so armed, that we need not to fear any assault of our enemies.

*The use of prayer.*

*The doctrine of God.*

Touching the heathen poets and philosophers, if we taste of them measurably, so that we wear not old nor die in them, they are not utterly to be disallowed. Yea, whatsoever they teach well, ought no more to be despised, than was the counsel of Jethro, whom Moses followed. As for such as write uncleanly, we ought either not to touch them, or else not to look too far in them. To be short, all manner of learning should be tasted in due season and measure, with good judgment and discretion, under the correction of Christ's doctrine; so that the wisdom of God be above all other, our

*Liberal sciences are not to be despised.*

best beloved, our dove, our sweetheart: which may not be *With reverence ought we to come to the word of God.* touched, but with clean and washen hands, namely, with high pureness of mind and due reverence. For so coming unto it, we shall see the pleasures, delicacies, and dainties of our blessed spouse, the precious jewels of rich Solomon, even the secret treasure of eternal wisdom. Wherefore, considering the verity of God neither deceiveth, nor is deceived, we ought to give more credit thereunto, than to anything that we do bodily either see or hear.

As considering the interpreters of the holy scripture, we ought not to choose them that teach to brawl and contend, but such as go farthest from the letter; whose godliness and holy life is known, whose learning is more plenteous, and whose exposition is most agreeable to God's word. Now as we ought to grow unto perfectness and strength in the knowledge thereof, and not still to be children; even so, if we will have it to be savoury unto us and to nourish us, we must not read without understanding, as cloisters do, but break the rod, and taste of the sweetness therein; specially considering, that as it is the spirit and not the flesh that quickeneth, so will the Father of heaven be worshipped in the spirit, and not in the bark of the letter. Wherefore though we should not despise the weak, yet ought we to make speed unto more secret mysteries, and to stir up ourselves thereunto by often prayer, till it please God through his Son Jesus Christ to open it that yet is shut unto us. *Expositors of scripture.*

Now to[1] our purpose: if we, wandering through all doctrines, pick and choose out the best, and by the example of the bee refuse the poison, and suck out only the wholesome and sweet juice, it shall arm our minds the better to a virtuous conversation. But that divine harness, which with no weapon can be pierced, is fetched only out of the armoury of holy scripture, wherewith our David, Christ Jesus, brake the forehead of our adversary. Wherefore if we list to go unto the store-house of God's scripture, we shall there find the true armour of this war, valiant in God not only to destroy fortresses, and counsels, and every high thing that exalteth itself against the doctrine of God; but also to resist in the day of adversity, and to quench all the hot and fiery weapons of our cruel enemy. Such weapons or armour of *In the armoury of God's word are the best weapons.*

[1 Old edition, *though.* Erasmus, *Ut ad institutum revertamur.*]

light, though we be the refuse and outcasts of the world, hath Almighty God given us, to make us stout and lusty in his wars. For in his armoury find we the harness of justice and verity, "the buckler of faith, the helmet of health, and the sword of the Spirit, which is the word of God:" wherewith if we be diligently covered and fenced, there shall no tribulation, straitness, hunger, nakedness, persecution, &c., separate us from the love of God. Such armour, I say, shall holy scripture minister abundantly unto us, if we occupying our time therein do use the same wisely.

## THE THIRD CHAPTER.

### HOW THAT THE FIRST POINT OF WISDOM IS A ZEAL TO KNOW HIMSELF. OF TWO MANNER OF WISDOMS, THE TRUE AND THE APPARENT.

IF we thus war now, intending to obtain the peace which Christ only giveth, we must strongly fight against our own vices, with whom God, our only peace and felicity, is at variance. Of the which felicity they are utterly void, yea, very wretches, filthy and unhappy, that, lying still in the night of ignorance and foolishness, are destitute of his wisdom. If we be wise, we shall be conquerors of the enemy. Wherefore, like as worldly wisdom is foolishness before God, even so if we be wise in him, it ought not to dismay us, when the world judgeth us to be fools, to be deceived, to doat, and to be mad bedlames, because we intend to depart towards Christ. Is not this a miserable blindness, sore to be mourned, when in trifles and things of no value, yea, unto filthiness, and in evil only, we are clear witted, and in things concerning salvation, and in goodness, not to have much more understanding than brute beasts? O how good a thing is it to have knowledge, to be willing to learn and to be obedient unto the truth! Contrariwise, a very cruel thing is it to lack knowledge; yea, as he is good for nothing which hath no wisdom, so is it a worse thing to disdain to learn. But to withstand and impugn the truth is worst of all, and farthest from grace; namely, when we despise the wisdom of God, and think scorn

*Worldly wisdom.*

*To withstand the truth is worst of all.*

to be taught of it. For the which cause he himself shall utterly forsake them, and rejoice in their destruction. For to count it madness, when one liveth godly, is a very beastly and devilish wisdom; after the which followeth presumption, blindness of mind, rage and tyranny of affections, and finally, the whole heap of all vices, and liberty to do what one listeth, yea, custom of sin, dazing[1] of the wits, bodily death, and afterward death everlasting. Thus we see that the mother of extreme mischief is worldly wisdom.

But contrariwise, of the wisdom of God come all good things, specially soberness, meekness, the secret joy of a clear conscience, which vanisheth not away, but groweth to eternal gladness and mirth. This wisdom must we require only of God, with fervent prayer, out of the veins of holy scripture. The chief part of it is to know ourselves, which we shall do the better, if we well consider what we be inward and within our skins. *The fruits of God's wisdom.*

## THE FOURTH CHAPTER.

### OF THE OUTWARD AND INWARD MAN.

ALMIGHTY God made man at the first of diverse parts, coupled with blessed concord; but the serpent, the enemy of peace, put them asunder again with unhappy discord, sowing the poison of dissension between them that were honestly agreed: insomuch that now neither the mind can rule the body without business, neither will the body obey without grudging. For whereas in man there should be such an order, that like as in a prosperous commonalty, for avoiding of debate and strife, the wisest bear most rule, and the subjects obey their officers; this original decree of nature and first example of honesty notwithstanding, the order in man is so troubled, that the subjects will not obey the prince; yea, the corrupt affections and appetites of the flesh strive to be more master than reason itself: which unquiet affections whoso overcometh, the same liveth a blessed life, mounting up to celestial things, and as a king endowed with wisdom, willing

[1 Dazing: dazzling, confusion.]

and purposing to do nothing amiss, nothing against the judgment of reason, nothing inordinately, nothing frowardly, nothing corruptly.

## THE FIFTH CHAPTER.

#### OF THE DIVERSITY OF AFFECTIONS.

THE eternal law, which God hath created in the right reason of man, teacheth him to abhor all corrupt affections, and not to live after them; which thing even the heathen philosophers do also confess. Now, as we are bound surely to know what motions we be most inclined unto, so ought we to understand, that through right reason (which is the power of God's holy Spirit) the most violent of them may either be repaired, or else turned into virtue. Truth it is, that as some man is more prone unto virtue than some, either by reason of the influence of the celestial bodies, or else of our progenitors, or else of the bringing up in youth, or of the complexion of the body; even so some vices follow the countries, some the complexion of the body, some the age of man; some be appropriated unto kind; and sometime an evil disease of the man is recompensed with another certain contrary good gift or property. As for the vices that are nighest unto virtues, we must amend them and turn them into that virtue which they most nigh resemble. For let a man that is soon provoked unto anger refrain his mind, and he shall be nothing faint-hearted, but bold, yea, and free of speech without dissimulation. The niggard, by the exercise of reason, shall be thrifty and a good husband; the flatterer shall through moderation be courteous and pleasant; the obstinate may be constant, solemnness may be turned to gravity, one full of foolish toys may become a good companion. But in any wise must we beware, that we put not the name of virtue to any manner of vice; as to call cruelty justice, envy zeal. The way then to felicity is, first, to know ourselves; secondly, to do all things after the judgment of reason, whose mouth must not be out of taste, but without corruption. Now as there is no greater reward than felicity; even so that which unto our

*Some man is more prone to virtue than some.*

*The way to felicity.*

only strength is hardest of all to do, is most easy, if we look unto God our helper. Wherefore if we, grounding ourselves upon a sure promise of a perfect life, do forthwith set upon it, and go lustily unto it, no doubt we shall be able to bring it to pass; for to be willing to be a christian man is a great part of Christianity. And though the beginning of a thing be never so hard, yet the way of virtue in process doth wax easy. Shall beasts be more ready to be tamed than we in our minds? Shall we, for the health of our bodies, be ruled by the counsel of a physician, being a man, and not master of our own affections, at the commandment of God himself, to have a quiet conscience all our whole life? Shall we do more to save our bodies from sickness, than to deliver both body and soul from eternal death?

A good will doth much.

## THE SIXTH CHAPTER.

### OF THE TWO PARTS OF MAN PROVED BY HOLY SCRIPTURE.

A SHAME it is, that in this war men be so rude and unexercised, that they know not the diversity between reason and affections. For that the philosophers call reason, the same doth St Paul sometime call the spirit, sometime the inward man, sometime the law of the mind. That they call affection, calleth he sometime the flesh, sometime the body, sometime the outward man, the law of the members, and the body of death. And thus our war is peace, life, and liberty of the soul; but death and bondage of the flesh with all his lusts. Now whereas Plato put two souls in one man[1], St Paul in one man maketh two men so coupled together, that neither without other can be either in heaven or hell; and

What reason is.

[1 The passage, to which allusion is here made, is found in the Timæus, c. 44; in which Plato, after stating that the Deity, having himself first of all created the heavenly beings, committed to them the creation of mortals, adds: οἱ δὲ μιμούμενοι, παραλαβόντες ἀρχὴν ψυχῆς ἀθάνατον, τὸ μετὰ τοῦτο θνητὸν σῶμα αὐτῇ περιετόρνευσαν, ὄχημά τε πᾶν τὸ σῶμα ἔδοσαν, ἄλλο τε εἶδος ἐν αὐτῷ ψυχῆς προσῳκοδόμουν τὸ θνητόν, δεινὰ καὶ ἀναγκαῖα παθήματα ἔχον, πρῶτον μὲν ἡδονήν, μέγιστον κακοῦ δέλεαρ, ἔπειτα λύπας, κ.τ.λ. ...ξυγκερασάμενοι τ᾽ αὐτὰ ἀναγκαίως τὸ θνητὸν γένος ξυνέθεσαν.]

again so separated, that the death of the one must be the life of the other. This is the old debate between the two twins, Jacob and Esau, which, or ever they come to light, wrestle together within their mother's womb. Between these two brethren is never joined perfect concord. For Esau hateth Jacob, who, having Esau ever suspected, dare not come within his danger. Which thing should teach us to suspect our own sensual flesh, and alway to eschew the counsel thereof. Yea, meet is it and convenient, that the woman be obedient to the husband, that Isaac be more set by than Ismael, that grace increase, and tyranny of the flesh minish. For when carnal affections wear old, then springeth up the blessed tranquillity of an innocent mind, and sure quietness of the spirit. Let no Ismael therefore, the child of the flesh, deceive us with his pastime and pleasures; but let our Isaac always suspect him, and flee the occasions of sin. For full wild is the flesh; so that the trouble thereof is expedient to the exercise of virtue, to the custody of humility, to nurture us, and to teach us, when we are tempted, first to desire help of God; secondly, that if we be his, no temptation can be dangerous unto us; and finally, against all vain-glory, against so wild and manifold affections to be ever still wrestling. For by such victory we shall be sure of the blessing of God, and obtain grace to be at another time much more surely armed against our enemies; namely, if we halt not on both sides, but lean more to the Spirit of God than to our own carnal affections; which if we manfully subdue unto the end, we shall be sure after these troublous storms to have true quietness, even to see the Lord, to taste and feel how sweet and pleasant he is, and to obtain eternal consolation in him.

---

## THE SEVENTH CHAPTER.

### OF THE THREE PARTS OF MAN.

MAN, after the mind of Origen, is made of three parts[1]. The first part is the flesh, wherein the malicious serpent

[[1] Paulus non solum adorat in spiritu, verum etiam deservit in spiritu. Nam adorare quis potest et sine affectu; deservire vero ejus

through original trespass hath written the law of sin, whereby we be provoked unto filthiness and coupled unto the devil, if we be overcome. The second part is the spirit, wherein *The spirit.* we represent the similitude of the nature of God; who after the eternal law of his own mind hath graven therein the law of honesty, whereby we be knit into God, and made one with him. The third part is the soul, partaker of the *The soul.* sensible wits and natural motions, which if she, forsaking the flesh, cleave unto the spirit, becometh spiritual; but if she follow the corrupt affections of the flesh, then joineth she herself unto an harlot, and is made one body with her that, being an evil, strange, flattering, foolish, and babbling woman, breaketh her promise, and forsaketh the husband of her youth. Wherefore if we incline unto the spirit, it maketh us not only blessed, religious, obedient, kind and merciful; but also teacheth us to desire celestial and necessary, pure, perfect, and godly things, to obey God more than men, and though some affections be disguised with visors of virtue, yet not to be deceived with them. If we incline to the flesh, it maketh us beasts, despisers of God, disobedient, unkind, and cruel; yea, and causeth us to desire delicate, pleasant, and filthy things. The rule of true god- *The rule of true god-liness.* liness therefore is to lean so nigh unto the spirit, that for any good inclination or virtue we ascribe nothing to ourselves; that we do nothing for our own pleasure or advantage; that for observing of outward things we judge not ourselves better than other men; that we regard more our neighbours' necessity, and be readier to help them, than to keep men's traditions; that our love be chaste and spiritual, and that nothing be so dear unto us as Christ himself.

est, quem constringit affectus. Deservit ergo apostolus Deo, non in corpore, neque in anima, sed in meliore sui parte, id est, in spiritu. Hæc enim tria esse in homine designat ad Thessalonicenses scribens, [1 Thess. v. 23.], cum dicit: *Ut integrum corpus vestrum, et anima, et spiritus in die Domini nostri servetur.* Origen. Commentariorum in Epistolam ad Romanos, Lib. I. Opera, Tom. IV. p. 468, col. 2. Ed. Paris. 1759. See also ib. p. 473, col. 2.]

## THE EIGHTH CHAPTER.

### CERTAIN GENERAL RULES OF CHRISTIAN LIVING.

Now to guide and convey us out of the blind errors of this world unto the pure and clear light of spiritual living, we must of virtue and godliness make even a craft and occupation; the rules whereof if we do follow and manfully exercise ourselves therein, the Holy Ghost shall bring our purpose forward. These precepts shall do us much good against blindness, against the flesh, and against our own weakness, namely, three evils, that proceeding of original sin remain still in us, to nurture us, and for the increase of virtue. For whereas blindness, cankered with corrupt and evil bringing up, lewd company, froward affections, darkness of vices, and with custom of sin, dimmeth the judgment of reason; so that in the election of things we be deceived, and instead of the best follow the worst: *Three necessary points.* the first point is therefore, that we have knowledge to discern what is to be refused or clean abolished, and what is to be accept. Secondly, whereas the flesh draweth us to inordinate affections, we must hate that which we know to be evil, and love that which is honest, wholesome and good. Thirdly, whereas infirmity overcometh us, either with tediousness or temptation, we must be of good courage, and so continue in the things which we have well begun, that we faint not, and that after we have set our hand to the plough, we look not backward, until we have obtained the crown promised.

## THE NINTH CHAPTER.

### AGAINST THE EVIL OF IGNORANCE.

#### *The First Rule.*

*We must judge well of scripture, not doubting in the promises of God.* THE first rule must be, that we so judge both of Christ and of his holy scripture, that we be sure how that it greatly pertained to our health, and that though the world be against it, yet nothing that we perceive with our natural senses is or can be so true as it there is read in the scripture, inspired of God himself, brought forth by so many prophets, approved with the blood of so many martyrs, with the consent of all good men so many hundred years, with the doctrine and life of Christ himself, with so many oracles, &c.; which scripture is so agreeable to the equity of nature, and every where so like itself, so ravisheth, reneweth, and altereth the minds of them that take heed thereunto; yea, and telleth of so many great, wonderful, and true things, that if we oft consider the same, it shall stir us up unto more ferventness, both of faith, prayer, and virtue; being sure, that as the reward of vice and of these momentary pleasures is both vexation of mind and eternal punishment, so unto good men shall be given an hundredfold joy of a pure conscience, and finally, everlasting life.

## THE TENTH CHAPTER.

### The Second Rule.

As the first rule is then, not to doubt in the promises of God, so is the second rule, that we enter in the way of salvation gladly, boldly, and with a good courage; that we be alway ready for Christ's sake to lose both life and goods; that we be not negligent, but fervent; that we suffer not the affections of our lovers, the pleasures of this world, the care of our household, the chain of worldly business, to hold us back from the kingdom of heaven. For we must forsake Egypt, that we turn not again to the flesh-pots thereof; so haste out of Sodom, that we look not back; so flee out of Babylon and from the vices thereof, that we do it speedily, without prolonging of the time; that we trust no longer to ourselves, but commit us wholly unto the Lord; that we serve him altogether, and no other master, that we halt not on both legs. For the Lord is so jealous over our souls, that he will have all that he hath redeemed with his blood, and cannot suffer the fellowship of the devil, whom he once overcame by his death. So be there but two ways only; the

*[margin: With a good courage must we enter in the way of salvation.]*

*[margin: Two ways only.]*

one of salvation, the other of perdition. The strait way is that we must walk, whereinto though few do enter, yet must we consider, that we are as much bound as other men to lead a christian life, to take Christ's cross upon us, and to follow him. For if it belong unto us to live with Christ, and to rise again to eternal life; then belongeth it also unto us to die with him, and to be crucified with him, as touching the world, sin, and carnal desires. Which as it is a hard thing and known unto few, so is it the common and general profession of all christian men, sworn and promised in baptism, the most holy and religious vow of all. And though there be never so few that perfectly follow the head, yet must we all enforce ourselves to come thereto. For of all christian men they are the best, that with stedfast heart and purpose are still minded so to be.

## THE ELEVENTH CHAPTER.

### *The Third Rule.*

<small>We must despise whatsoever leadeth from the way of Christ.</small> THE third rule is, that we utterly despise and count for thing of nought whatsoever would force us from the way of virtue and of Christ. Which as it is of all other lives the most commodious, so even at the first ceaseth it to be sharp, and in process is made easier, pleasant, and delectable; whereby we go with sure hope, and that without labour, to eternal felicity: whereas these mad men of the world, with their own extreme labour, purchase eternal death. Now though the way of godliness were much more laborious than the way of the world, yet the hope of reward and the comfort of God assuageth the tediousness thereof, and of bitter maketh it sweet. But in the way of the world one care and sorrow <small>Nothing worse than to be servant unto sin.</small> springeth of another without any quietness. For nothing is filthier or more laborious than the bondage of Egypt, nothing more grievous than the captivity of Babylon, nothing more intolerable than the yoke of Pharao and Nebuchodonosor. But Christ's yoke is pleasant, his burthen is light. Summa, there lacketh no pleasure where a quiet conscience is; no misery, where an unquiet conscience crucifieth the mind. They

that out of the vices of Babylon are converted unto the Lord, have experience hereof, and can tell us, that nothing is more grievous than vice, nothing more easy, more cheerful, or more comfortable than is virtue. Nevertheless, though both the reward and labours of virtue and vice were like, yet were it better to be vexed with Christ, than to swim in pleasure with the devil; which is so filthy, cruel, and deceitful a master, that every man should flee out of his service, wherein is nothing but grievous labour in purchasing, sorrow and thought in losing, yea, many thousand jeopardies, miserable care, perpetual torment, mischance, labour spent in vain, much grief of heart and mind. But whoso endeavoureth himself with sure purpose to come from a vicious world to a good conversation in Christ, obtaineth that he seeketh, changeth trifles with things of more value, yea, silver for gold, flint for precious stone; findeth better friends, for outward pleasures and riches of the body enjoyeth such as be inward, better, purer, and more certain. So that his loss shall be turned to advantage, adversity to solace, rebuke to praise, vexation to comfort, bitter things to sweet, evil to good. *What they obtain that convert unto God.*

## THE TWELFTH CHAPTER.

### *The Fourth Rule.*

THE fourth rule is, that we have none other mark and ensample of living, save only Christ: who is nothing else save charity, simplicity, innocency, patience, cleanness, and whatsoever himself taught; to whom we direct our journey, if we be so given only unto virtue, that we love and desire nothing but either Christ, or else for Christ; hating, abhorring, flying, and avoiding nothing but only sin, or else for sin's sake. And thus if our eye be pure, all our body shall be bright; for that whatsoever honest or indifferent thing we take in hand, it shall turn to our wealth. As for filthy things, neither advantage; nor punishment should make us to commit them. Mean things, verily, and indifferent ought no further to be desired than they are profitable to a christian living. As for example, conning or learning must *Christ only must be the mark and ensample of our living.*

be loved for Christ's sake; so that when we know him and the secrets of his scripture, we love him in such sort, that opening him unto other, we both take fruit of him ourselves; and if we have knowledge of other sciences, we use them all to his honour. For better is it to have less knowledge and more love, than much to know, and not to love. Thus every thing, so far forth as it helpeth most unto virtue, ought chiefly to be applied. But rather ought we to lack them, than that they should hold us back from Christ; unto whom we ought to haste so fervently, that we should have no leisure to care for other things, whether they be given us, or taken away from us; but even to use the world as though we used it not. After this rule if we examine all our studies and acts, then like as having a craft or occupation, we will not labour to defraud our neighbours, but to find our households and to win them unto Christ; even so, when we fast, pray, or use any such like, we shall not do it for any carnal purpose, but proceed on still, till we come unto Christ; neither going out of the way, nor hoping or suffering any thing that shall not minister unto us some occasion of godliness.

*Marginalia: Love is more excellent than knowledge.*

## THE THIRTEENTH CHAPTER.

### The Fifth Rule.

THE fifth rule is, that we count it perfect godliness alway to apply ourselves to ascend from things visible to things invisible: which if we do not, then are we no true honourers of God, but plain superstitious. And yet, being strangers in this visible world, whatsoever offereth itself to our sensible powers, we considering it, ought to apply the same either to the world angelical, or else to manners, even unto God, and to the invisible portion of ourselves. And thus the thing that we perceive by our sensible wits shall be unto us an occasion of godliness[1]. Yea, by the light of this

*Marginalia: We must ascend from things visible to things invisible.*

[1 The following is the language of the original, which the statement contained in this passage is intended to express: In mundo visibili quoniam peregrini sumus, nusquam oportet conquiescere; sed quicquid occurrit sensibus, id apta quadam collatione vel ad mundum

visible sun we shall learn that great is the pleasure of the
inhabitants of heaven, upon whom the eternal light of God is
ever shining: and likewise, by the dark night we shall think
how horrible it is, a soul to be destitute of the light of God;
and that if the beauty of the body be pleasant, the beauty of
the soul is much more honest. For the less feeling we have *The less delight we have in earthy things, the more pleasure have we in heavenly.*
in things transitory and of the body, and the less we are
moved therewith, the more sweetness we find in things pertaining to the Spirit, and the better are we acquainted with
things eternal; to the love whereof we ought to arise from
things temporal, and in comparison of the other even to
despise them, and more to fear the disease, poison, and death
of the soul than of the body, flee the wrath of God more
than any thunder or lightning. The mystery therefore in
all things ought to be looked upon, as well when we consider the outward creatures and works of God, as in the
study of his holy scriptures: the spirit whereof, and not the
bare letter, must specially be searched out, and the allegories *Allegories.*
handled, not dreamingly or unfruitfully, neither with subtle
disputations, (after the manner of our divines that are too
much addict to Aristotle,) but well favouredly, after the ensample of the old doctors. For inasmuch as it is the Spirit
that giveth life and liberty, therefore in all manner letters,
and in all our acts, we must have respect to the Spirit and
fruits thereof, and not to the flesh and his fruits; wishing
rather to be privily allowed in the sight of God, than openly
in the sight of man; rather to worship God in spirit and *In spirit and verity will God be worshipped.*
verity, than otherwise; rather to eat Christ's flesh and drink
his blood spiritually, than only with the mouth: rather to be
quickened, and to have life in the Spirit, than, hanging St
John's gospel or an *Agnus Dei* about our necks, to rejoice
in any carnal thing, where the Spirit is not present; rather
to be one spirit with the Spirit of Christ, to be one body
with his, to be a quick member of his church, than without

angelicum, vel (quod est utilius) ad mores, et ad illi respondentem
hominis partem, referre. .... Ergo quicquid in eo vides, immo quicquid
in hoc crassiore mundo, qui constat ex elementis, quem nonnulli a
reliquis distinxere; denique quicquid in crassiore tui parte, id assu-
escas ad Deum atque invisibilem tui portionem referre. Ita fiet, ut
quicquid usquam se sensibus objecerit, id tibi fiat occasio pietatis.
Militis Christiani Enchiridion, Canon v. p. 51.]

fruit to say or hear many masses; rather to have a clean and sunny mind, and to study to walk with Christ in new life, than to have the body washed, touched with salt, anointed, or sprinkled with holy water; rather to represent and follow the virtuous and blessed doctrine of saints, yea, to counterfeit Christ in them, than to rejoice in touching their relics, to honour their bones, or to be buried in a grey friar's coat; rather to express the lively and very image of Christ, set forth in his own doctrine and living, than to creep to the cross, or to have at home a piece of the wood that it was made of; rather to ascend to more perfectness of the Spirit, to grow in perfect love and charity, and to offer an humble and contrite heart unto God, than to have confidence in carnal things, or superstitious ceremonies, traditions, and inventions of men; rather to do the things that the eyes of God require, than to please the eyes of men; rather to procure the quietness and innocency of the mind, and to seek the nourishment thereof by the true hearing, seeing, and feeling of the word of God on the soul, than by the outward senses of the body; rather with inward medicines to heal the hurts of the soul, and by the wings of love to fly up to the Spirit, than, creeping on the ground with unclean beasts, to be still unlearned in the mysteries of Christ, or to be destitute of the sweet liquors that cometh of him.

*We must follow Christ in his saints.*

## THE FOURTEENTH CHAPTER.

### *The Sixth Rule.*

*We must vary from the common people.*

THE sixth rule is, that varying as much as possible both from the deeds and opinions of the common sort of men, we fit the example of godliness at none, save only at Christ himself, the only true pattern and form of living, the only true path and right high-way. For like as are the opinions wherewith our minds be instructed, such are also our manners and conversation. And therefore christian men, in bringing up their children, should chiefly care, that even from the cradle they be christianly persuaded; and not to learn to sing filthy or wanton songs, to wail or wring their hands for the loss of worldly goods, to recompense evil for evil: for tow is not readier to catch fire than man is disposed unto vice; which chiefly proceedeth of evil opinions, when instead of a sweet thing we embrace that which is sour, and when for it that might do us good we follow our own damage or loss. Wherefore, considering that the common sort of people and their manners now-a-days be most corrupt, and seeing there is no worse author of living than they be; forasmuch, I say, as the flock of good men is but small, yea, vice more regarded than virtue; no estate, no opinion, no name or person of man should move us to tread one path from Christ's truth, or from the life of virtue; whereof now-a-days men are more ashamed than were the heathen in times past: yea, to be a right christian man is accounted every where a very vile thing; so vain is the world, and in so great reputation have they it, to be born of noble blood, to be rich, to have their pleasures, to be strong and valiant, to be praised of the world, to be accounted worldly-wise; when in very deed the chiefest nobility of all is to be the child of God, the chiefest riches is to possess him in whom are all things; the chiefest pleasure of all is so to delight in Christ, that we be moved with the love of none other lust; the chiefest strength is, when a man hath so overcome himself, that he can find in his heart to despise all injuries, to recompense good for evil, to pray for them that curse him; the chiefest praise of all is, for godliness' sake to be mocked and laughed at of evil men, and to be approved of Christ; the chiefest wisdom of all is, to be circumspect in providing for the life to come. Summa, we must not conform ourselves to this world, but so alter our minds, that we hearken and approve not what is the will of men, but what is the good, well-pleasing, and perfect will of God. For if we move not the eyes of our heart from Christ, but follow his verity, we shall not go out of the way. If we walk after his light, so that it shine unto us, we shall neither stumble in darkness, nor fall into the blind errors, opinions, or sects of the world.

*Nothing should make us to go from the truth.*

*True nobility.*
*True riches.*
*True pleasure.*
*True strength.*
*True praise.*
*True wisdom.*

## THE FIFTEENTH CHAPTER.

#### OPINIONS MEET FOR A CHRISTIAN MAN.

*We are not born for ourselves.*

THIS excellent learning then of Christ must be established in us, that we think us not to be born unto ourselves, but to the honour of God and wealth of all men: so that, loving him again which bestowed himself on us altogether for our redemption, we also for his sake love other men, and abhor their vices; having not only respect to their need, and what we are able to do for them, but also remembering the manifold causes, that by reason should move us to love them, to tender them, to be at one with them, and not to account them as strangers, or to hate them for any alteration of vesture, or of any such trifle; yea, in no wise to despise them, but esteeming their hurt our own; to consider that, whatsoever we have received, it is given us to bestow upon them, and to increase in edifying of them in charity. This learning will induce men to desire no vengeance, but to be the sons of their Father in heaven, to overcome evil with good, to suffer hurt rather than to do it, to forgive other men's offences, to be gentle in manners; if they be cunning, to forbear and amend the ignorance of the unlearned; if they be rich, to be circumspect in distributing the goods that God hath given them; in poverty, to be as well content as other men; in

*Offices of christian men.*

office, to be more careful and diligent in considering their charge, in noting the manners of evil persons, yet not to despise the profession of virtue; in labouring for a common office, or in executing of the same, to do it alway for the profit of the common, and not for their own singular wealth, being ready, even with the loss of their own life and goods, to defend that which is right; being loth to have pre-eminence, which if it chance unto them, yet to think that they also have a Lord and Master in heaven, even Jesus Christ, and that no man is bound to follow his doctrine more straitly than they; that he will of no man ask more strait accounts than of them; that they lean not to their own wills; that they flatter not themselves in evil; that their manners be such as deserve riches, honour, reverence, dignity, favour, and authority; that they themselves be not guilty in the offences which they do punish in others; that they despise no man in comparison of themselves; that in bearing rule they would not so much to excel as to profit all men; that they turn not to their own profit the things which are common, but bestow that they have, yea, and themselves also, upon the commonwealth; that in their titles of honour they refer all such things unto God; that in ministering their office they fetch not example of their predecessors or of flatterers, but only of Christ; that they be ready rather to lose their dominions than Christ, who hath a far better thing to give them. For nothing is so comely, so excellent, so glorious to kings, princes, and rulers, as in similitude to draw nigh unto the highest, greatest, and best king, even Jesus Christ; instead of violence to exercise charity, and to be minister unto all men. In conclusion, we must so cleave unto the learning of Christ, and be so circumspect therein, that we cloak not our own vices with other men's faults. *We may not cloak our own vices with other men's faults.* For though holy men have sometime done anything not to be followed, (as David, when he committed adultery and murder; Solomon, when he had so many queens and concubines; Noe, when he was drunken; Lot, when he lay with his own daughters; Mary Magdalene, when she sinned so sore[1]; Peter, when he denied the Lord; Paul, when he persecuted the church of God;) yet ought we to do nothing that varieth from Christ; but as we have been like other men in sin, so should we be companions and partners also with them that repent and turn unto God. And as for other men's deeds, we ought not churlishly so much to bark against them, neither with cruelness to fear them, as with softness and apt means to amend them, and allure them unto Christ.

## THE SIXTEENTH CHAPTER.

### *The Seventh Rule.*

THE seventh rule is, that studying diligently to draw on still as nigh as we can to the beholding of heavenly things, *We must still be climbing up unto godliness.*

[1 See above, p. 329.]

we turn our minds so fervently thereunto, that the very love of Christ cause us to hate all transitory and filthy things, which shall wear the more vile unto us, the more we set by things invisible. Therefore ought we so to press unto the best, that though we be not so perfect in all things as we should, our mind yet be not defiled with grievous offences, but more receivable of the benefits of God. And though we cannot do so well as holy and blessed men have done before us, yet let us commit no worse things than the heathen, who, though they had no perfect knowledge of God, yet was honesty dearer unto them than either fame, goods, life, or any thing else in the world. And doubtless it shall notably withdraw us from sin, if we ponder well in our minds the incommodities thereof, as infamy, poverty, loss of goods, wasting of time, the hate of good men, grief of mind, miserable unquietness of conscience, with thousands more such like inconveniences. Wherefore better it is that our youth believe this to be the property of sin, than with woeful experience to learn it in themselves. And though we cannot attain to the most excellent virtue, yet shall it profit much, if we, being but in civil or moral virtues, run not headlong into all kind of vices. Notwithstanding, forasmuch as that is not the resting-place and quiet haven of felicity, but a shorter journey thereunto, we must pray still unto God, that he will vouchsafe to pluck us up to better things.

*We must ponder the incommodities of sin.*

## THE SEVENTEENTH CHAPTER.

### *The Eighth Rule.*

THE eighth rule, that when the storm of temptation riseth against us, we be not discontented with ourselves, as though God cared not for us, or favoured us not; but rather give him thanks, because he instructeth us [as] his own heirs, chasteneth us as his own most singularly beloved children, and proveth us[1] as his own assured friends: which is a token that he loveth us, as he did the apostle Paul, blessed Job, and other holy saints, who, being both great and many, have suffered troubles as well as we. Why should we then be

*We may not despair in God.*

*Temptation is a sign that God loveth us.*

[1 Old edition, *to us.* Original, *Ut amicum explorat.*]

discouraged, or fall in despair; and not rather do our best to overcome, as they did, considering that we have a faithful God, that will not forsake us, nor suffer us to be tempted above our strength, but make us able to endure?

## THE EIGHTEENTH CHAPTER.

### The Ninth Rule.

THE ninth rule is, that our mind be alway watching and circumspect against the sudden assault of our enemy; that his temptation, suggestion, and first motion unto sin may be holden down at the beginning, while it is fresh, and be put back to his confusion. For more easily or more surely is he never overcome, than by that means. *(margin: We must ever keep watch.)*

## THE NINETEENTH CHAPTER.

### The Tenth Rule.

THE tenth rule is, that whatsoever the enemy tempteth us, we straightway either hate, abhor, and defy him; or else pray fervently, or get us to some holy occupation, setting our whole minds thereupon; or else to answer the tempter with words of holy scripture: whereof to have some certain sentences ready against those inconveniences that we are most inclined unto, is very profitable in all temptations. *(margin: Remedies against temptation.)*

## THE TWENTIETH CHAPTER.

### The Eleventh Rule.

THE eleventh rule is, that in temptation we neither give up our hold, neither, when we are comforted, wax wanton, or stand in our own conceits; but when our enemy stirreth us unto filthy things, to behold not our own feebleness, but *(margin: We must neither be faint-hearted nor presumptuous.)*

to remember that we may do all things in Christ, who biddeth us be of good cheer, for he hath overcome the world. Again, when we have overcome our enemy, or done some good work, we must beware that we ascribe nothing thereof to our own merits, but thank only the free benevolence of God, of whom we receive all things. Thus against this double mischief we shall find double remedies, if we not only in temptation, despairing in our own strength, and trusting in the benevolence of Christ, do flee for succour unto him, but also in our spiritual consolation, humbly confessing our own unworthiness, immediately give him thanks for his benefits.

## THE TWENTY-FIRST CHAPTER.

### *The Twelfth Rule.*

*Of temptation must we alway take an occasion of virtue.*

THE twelfth rule is, that when we have avoided the stroke of our enemy, we take his weapon from him, and smite him with his own sword; so that when we are provoked unto evil, we do not only abstain from sin, but thereof also take an occasion of virtue, grow stronger in courage, know our own weakness the better, increase the more in good deeds, and humble ourselves the more in all things. And thus shall temptations be ever the renewing of our holy purpose, and increase of godliness and virtuous living: thus shall we not only vanquish our enemy, but if he begin with us again afresh, he himself shall minister unto us an occasion of godliness.

## THE TWENTY-SECOND CHAPTER.

### *The Thirteenth Rule.*

*We must be bold and after one temptation ever look for for another.*

THE thirteenth rule is, that in the conflict and battle we be bold and behave ourselves so manfully, as though we should never fight more. Nevertheless, when we have overcome, we must alway after one temptation look for another, never departing from our harness, but always watch and keep our standing, as long as we are in this body.

## THE TWENTY-THIRD CHAPTER.

### The Fourteenth Rule.

THE fourteenth rule is, that we favour not ourselves in any one vice, be it never so small. For if we with christian hatred abhor one, we must needs abhor all. Yea, if true charity have once possessed our hearts, we shall indifferently hate the whole host of evil things, and not flatter ourselves so much as in the least. For though we cannot as yet pluck up the whole generation of vices, nevertheless we must alway, day by day, withdraw somewhat of our evil conditions, and be ever adding something to good manners.

<small>Into smallest faults of all must we not favour ourselves.</small>

## THE TWENTY-FOURTH CHAPTER.

### The Fifteenth Rule.

THE fifteenth rule is, that in the conflict of temptation we compare not only the bitterness of the fight with the pain which followeth the sin, but also the present sweetness of the sin that enticeth us with the pleasure of the victory hereafter, and with the tranquillity of mind that followeth the same. For as, if we be overcome, there followeth us a more painful and longer grief than we should have had in time of fight, if we had won the victory; even so, if we be conquerors, there followeth us a more great and longer pleasure than was it that carried us into sin, which was overcome. Which thing he shall lightly[1] judge that hath had experience of both. Wherefore, if we prove sometime what it is to overcome, the oftener we do it, the more pleasant shall the victory be unto us.

<small>The bitterness of the fight must we compare to the pain that followeth the sin.</small>

<small>Let us prove what it is to overcome.</small>

[[1] Lightly: easily. Original, *facile*.]

## THE TWENTY-FIFTH CHAPTER.

### The Sixteenth Rule.

*We may not despair though we be under.* THE sixteenth rule is, to have our minds so armed aforehand, that though we be fallen into sin and overcome, we yet despair not, but take thereby occasion of greater courage to wrestle more strongly, to come again quickly to ourselves, to take a good heart unto us, to repair again the rebuke and shame of the fall with new courage and lustiness of virtue, after the ensample of David, Solomon, Peter, Paul, &c., whom God no doubt suffered to fall, lest we, after we are fallen, should despair. Wherefore, if we rise up quickly with a lusty courage, and go to it afresh, both fiercer and more circumspect, our deadly offences shall grow in us to a living of godliness, while we love more fervently, that erred afore most shamefully.

## THE TWENTY-SIXTH CHAPTER.

### The Seventeenth Rule.

*We must exercise ourselves in the cross of Christ.* THE seventeenth rule is, that against all manner weapons and darts of our most wicked enemy we cast the cross of Christ, and exercise ourselves diligently therein; not after the common manner slenderly, repeating the story of his passion, or honouring the image of the cross, or with a thousand signs of it arming all our body round on every side, or laying up at home some piece of that holy tree, or weeping for sorrow that Christ suffered so great wrong; but, as lively members of our head, to mortify our own affections, and so recording the mystery of the cross, that if we be tickled with ambition, ashamed to be set at nought in this world, tempted with envy, with gluttony, with filthy pleasure, with covetousness, we consider to what vileness Christ our head humbled himself; how kind, loving, and good he is, even to the worst; how he drank eysil[1] and gall; how full

[1 eysil: vinegar.]

of temptation and grief all his whole life was; how poor he became for our sakes. Thus in all temptations shall it not be grievous, but pleasant and delectable unto us, to have oppressed our own affections.

## THE TWENTY-SEVENTH CHAPTER.

### *The Eighteenth Rule.*

THE eighteenth rule is, that when any affection moveth us to iniquity, we consider the filthiness of sin and the great dignity of man. For seeing that in other trifles we take advisement with ourselves, reason it were that, or ever we consent unto the fiend, we pondered well this most weighty matter, who made us, in how excellent a state we are set, with how exceeding great price we are bought, to how great felicity we are called, how that for man's sake only God hath forged the marvellous building of this world, brought us into the company of angels, made us his own children, heirs of immortality, members of Christ and of his church, our bodies the temple of the Holy Ghost, our minds the images and habitation of God. On the other side, to consider, that sin is the most filthy pestilence and consumption both of the mind and body, even the deadly poison of the most filthy serpent, and the prest wages of the devil's most miserable service. This, if we take good advisement, we shall see, it were not wisely done, for a momentary and poisoned little short pleasure of sin, to fall from so great dignity into so vile estate.

*[margin: We must consider the filthiness of sin and the dignity of man.]*

## THE TWENTY-EIGHTH CHAPTER.

### *The Nineteenth Rule.*

THE nineteenth rule is, that we still have in mind the eternal beneficence of God, and the wicked noisomeness of the devil; namely, with what goodness Almighty God hath made us, with what mercy redeemed us, with what liberty endued

*[margin: We must still have in mind the goodness of God and the malice of the devil.]*

us, with what tenderness he daily suffereth and sustaineth us wretched sinners, patiently looking for our amendment; with what joy he receiveth us, when we turn again: contrarily, with how natural hate and envy the cruel father of all mischief did long ago lay wait to our health, into what grievous temptation he hath cast us, imagining daily to draw us into eternal mischief. Thus being mindful of Almighty God and his manifold benefits, we shall not unkindly depart from so noble, so loving, and so beneficial a Father, to make ourselves wilfully bound unto the devil, that most filthy and cruel master.

## THE TWENTY-NINTH CHAPTER.

### *The Twentieth Rule.*

<small>The diversity of rewards.</small>

THE twentieth rule is, that we forget not, but alway remember, what great difference is between the reward of virtue and the reward of sin; yea, even in this world are the fruits of them unlike. For like as the end of faith is eternal salvation in heaven, and the reward of sin is everlasting death in hell; even so here in this life godliness bringeth tranquillity and quietness of mind, even a blessed joy of pure and clean conscience, a thing more precious and pleasant than all the world: and contrariwise, a perpetual grief, unquietness, and gnawing of the mind, with a thousand other evils, accompanieth sin and wickedness even in this life.

## THE THIRTIETH CHAPTER.

### *The Twenty-first Rule.*

<small>We must behold the misery of this present life.</small>

THE one-and-twentieth rule is, that we consider how full of grief and misery, how short and transitory, this present life is; how on every side death lieth in wait against us, and suddenly catcheth us; how unsure we are of one moment of life; how great peril it is to continue that kind of life, wherein if sudden death should take us, as it often fortuneth, we were but lost for ever.

## THE THIRTY-FIRST CHAPTER.

### *The Twenty-second Rule.*

THE two-and-twentieth rule is, that we, fearing the extreme mischief of impenitency, ponder well, how few of them which have prolonged their lives in iniquity, be truly converted from sin and with due repentance reconciled unto God again. Therefore is it meet that we, being monished, do remember how easy it is to fall into sin, but hard to turn back again.

*Mark what extreme mischief followeth when men will not repent.*

## THE THIRTY-SECOND CHAPTER.

REMEDIES AGAINST CERTAIN VICES; AND FIRST, AGAINST BODILY LUST.

To resist the lust of the body if we will be well weaponed, we must consider the incommodities thereof; namely, how filthy and beastly it maketh us, how momentary and bitter it is, how it pulleth us from our good name and fame, consumeth our goods, killeth the strength and beauty of the body, decayeth and hurteth health, causeth innumerable and filthy diseases, disfigureth youth, hasteth age, dulleth the wit and sight of the mind, withdraweth us from all honest studies, taketh away the use of reason. Likewise by the hurt that we have seen other have through their voluptuous pleasures, should we learn to avoid the same; and as well by the ensamples of them that are virtuous, as by the great commodities of chastity, to be pure and clean, both in body and mind: considering to how many vain offices they be subject, that put their heads under the girdle of filthy lust; how it is alway coupled with those sins that be greatest, and most in number; how this life vanisheth away faster than smoke; how many that follow such things are taken away by sudden death; how sharp the extreme judgment of God is; how the joy of a pure mind is much sweeter than the pleasure of sin; how great benefits the Lord hath heaped upon us, and all to make us refrain from deadly and mortal pleasures; how he

*The incommodities of bodily lust.*

alway beholdeth us, whatsoever we do or think; how greatly obstinacy and frowardness of mind springeth of bodily lust; what great sorrow followeth thereafter; how the more that we are consecrated unto God, yea, the more learned we be, and the more we have received of his gifts, the more unmeet and the more shame it is for us to abuse ourselves, what estate or kind soever we be of.

## THE THIRTY-THIRD CHAPTER.

### A SHORT RECAPITULATION OF REMEDIES AGAINST THE FLAME OF LUST.

*We must avoid occasions.*

IN conclusion, if we will be sure from the enticings of lust, we must be circumspect, avoiding all occasions; moderate in eating, drinking, and sleeping; abstain from pleasures, regard our own death, behold the death of Christ, live with such as be uncorrupted, eschew the communication of wanton persons, flee idle solitariness and sluggish idleness, exercise ourselves in the meditation of celestial things and honest studies, specially of holy scripture, giving ourselves oft and purely unto prayer, most of all when we be tempted.

## THE THIRTY-FOURTH CHAPTER.

### [AGAINST THE VICE OF AVARICE.]

To resist the vice of covetousness, we must call to remembrance the dignity of the estate of man, to the use whereof Almighty God hath created all things. And though we possess riches, yet must we despise them: yea, so far must we be from all carefulness of our living, that we cloak not our covetousness with the name of necessity; but first seek the kingdom of heaven, and be sure that he, which maketh provision for the lilies of the field and birds of the air, will not suffer us to lack. And as we must abhor wilful begging, even so, possessing money, we must set no store thereby, nor love it, but be faithful dispensers of it, and of all that God hath committed unto us: yea, though we lose them, yet not to be sorry therefore; for they are but a burthen, and though they be accounted among good profitable things, yet are they of the lowest sort, and help not unto virtue, whereof the reward is true honour, and not riches; wherewith if any friendship, honour, or pleasure be gotten, it is but false and feigned. Somewhat therefore shall it move us the less to desire them, if we consider the great incommodities of them; namely, with how sore labour and jeopardy they are gotten, with how great thought and care they are kept, with how great sorrow they are lost, how they are even but sharp thorns, how hard it is for the rich to enter into heaven; how that riches be commonly either unjustly gotten, or else unjustly kept; and how that avarice is plain idolatry before God, whom no man can please that setteth his heart upon mammon. *The incommodities of riches.*

## THE THIRTY-FIFTH CHAPTER.

### A SHORT RECAPITULATION OF REMEDIES AGAINST THE VICE OF AVARICE.

In conclusion, if we will resist the vice of avarice, then as we must discern true things from apparent, true commodities from false, so must we with our inward eyes behold Almighty God, who only satisfieth the mind of man. We must remember, not only that we came naked out of our mother's womb, and shall naked go thither again, but also that this present life with all his riches is uncertain; and therefore should we turn our minds from the corrupt manners of the common sort, and rather content ourselves with poverty, considering the fearful woe that Christ threateneth the rich men of this world. *Naked we came, and naked shall we go.*

## THE THIRTY-SIXTH CHAPTER.

### AGAINST AMBITION OR DESIRE OF HONOUR.

If ambition vex our minds, we must be surely persuaded, that only to be honour which springeth of virtue, yea, that to be the chief and only honour which is praised of God; and again, that to be no honour, but rebuke, which is given of an ungodly person, for an ungodly person, for a dishonest thing. For the more honour we deserve, the less we desire it, *Honour springeth of virtue only.*

being content with the conscience of well-doing. As for the honours that the common people desire so greatly, they be but vain, because that, as they are given of them that put no difference between honesty and dishonesty, so are they given oft for mean and filthy things, and that to the unworthy. Now if any honour be given unto us, we ought to refer all unto God. Therefore, as nothing is more full of pricks, cares, perils, and sorrows, than the life of great men, so is nothing better than a quiet mean life. For seeing all honour is coupled with great charge, better is it for us, humbling ourselves, to be partakers of mercy, than by ambition to be excluded from the succour of grace. Wherefore, if the ensample of Christ stick fast in our minds, we shall learn the better to despise all worldly honour, and to rejoice only in the cross of Christ. For if we be despised of God and abhorred of his angels, what good shall worldly honours do unto us?

*Nothing better than a quiet mean life.*

## THE THIRTY-SEVENTH CHAPTER.

### AGAINST PRIDE OR SWELLING OF THE MIND.

We shall not swell in our minds, if we know ourselves, and account what good thing soever we have to be the gift of God, and not of us; ascribing all evil only unto ourselves. We must remember, how filthy we were conceived and born; how naked, needy, wretched, and miserable we crept into this light; how many diseases, chances, cumbrance, griefs, and troubles this wretched body is in danger unto. For a surer proof of incurable foolishness and lack of understanding is not, than if we stand greatly in our own conceit. Wherefore, if for honour, beauty, cunning, or any such thing, we be moved unto pride, the best is to humble ourselves before God, and to consider our own deformities. In conclusion, it shall chiefly refrain us from pride, if we ponder well, not only what we are in ourselves, how filthy in our birth, and as a bubble of water in all our life, yea, even worms' meat when we die, but also what Christ became for us.

*We must know ourselves.*

*We must consider our own deformities.*

## THE THIRTY-EIGHTH CHAPTER.

### AGAINST WRATH AND DESIRE OF VENGEANCE.

WHEN grief of the mind moveth us to be avenged, we must remember that wrath is no manliness, but a very childish, feeble, and vile thing is it to desire vengeance. As for another man's folly, we must little regard it; yea, and beware, lest in avenging his lewdness we become lewder ourselves. For by revenging is no injury eased, but augmented, and the longer it endureth the more incurable it is. But softness healeth it, and of an enemy maketh a friend. For no man can be hurt of us, except we will[1], or except we follow the grief of our own minds: yea, we will not stick to forgive him, if we think not scorn to consider the infirmities that moved him to offend us; or if we will do any thing for love or authority of the person, or compare that his offence with his former benefits; or consider how sore and oft we ourselves trespass against God, who shall even as much forgive us as we remit unto our brethren. Which thing if we do, it is a readier way to obtain remission of our sins, than for absolution to repair to Rome, to sail to St James, or to try most large pardons. Wherefore by the ensample of Christ, that suffered so much for us, being his enemies, we should suage our own minds, and pardon other men, yea, even the unworthy. And though we be angry and grieved with another man's vice, yet should we love the person, and harden not our minds against him, but against wrath; being so temperate in ourselves, that we suffer not our own affections to rule us, but overcome evil with goodness, malice with kindness, which is even to follow the perfect love of Christ Jesu. For as it is the property of a wise man to suppress all displeasure, even so to follow the appetite of wrath is not the point of a man, but plainly of beasts, and that of wild beasts: which thing we shall evidently perceive, if we behold our own countenance in a glass when we be angry.

In conclusion, to what evil soever we perceive ourselves to be specially inclined or stirred, whether it be through

*Wrath is a childish thing.*

*As we forgive, so shall we be forgiven.*

[1] Original: Hominem homini nocere non posse, si nolit, nisi in his quæ sunt extraria bona.

vice of nature, custom, or evil bringing up; against the assault of such enemies, as against the vice of backbiting, filthy speaking, envy, gluttony, and other like, there must be certain rules written in the table of our mind, which for forgetting must now and then be renewed. And we, as Christ's soldiers, must have our mind armed long aforehand with prayer, with noble sayings of wise men, with the doctrine of holy scripture, with ensamples of devout and holy men, and specially of Christ: and in what persons soever we find or perceive the image of Christ, with them to couple ourselves, withdrawing us from the company of other, and making our special and familiar acquaintance with holy St Paul and his doctrine.

<small>Our minds must be armed with prayer, with holy scripture, and with examples of holy men.</small>

Imprinted at Ausborch by
Adam Anonimus,
in the moneth of May,
Anno 1545.

[Since the foregoing pages were printed off, the Editor has met with a copy of the second edition of the Treatise on the Lord's Supper, with the Order of the Church in Denmark, &c., in the possession of Dr Thackeray, Provost of King's College, Cambridge; by whose kindness he is enabled here to supply the part of the Epistle to the Reader which was added in that edition, together with the title-page and colophon.]

# A Faythful

and moost Godlye treatyse concernynge the most sacret Sacrament of the blessed body and bloude of oure sauioure Christe, compiled by John Caluyne, a man of no lesse lernyng and literature, then Godlye studye, and example of liuynge. And translated into Latyne by Lacius a man of lyke excellencie. And nowe laste of all, translated into Englyshe by a faythfull brother, no lesse desirous to profyt the weake brothers then to exercise the talent of the Lorde to this honoure and glorye. In declaration whereof, he hath set before this litle booke an Epistle to the reader much more effectuous then in the fyrst ediciom.

☞ Wherunto the order that the Churche and congregation of Christ in Denmarke doth vse at the receiuinge of Baptisme, the Supper of the Lorde, and Wedlocke; is added.

☞ Myles Couerdale.

Luke xix. Chapter
☙ Be doyng till I come.

---

✠ Imprinted
at London by John Day and Wyllyam Seres, dwellynge in Sepulchres Parish at the signe of the Resurrection a litle aboue Holbourne Conduite.

Cum gratia & priuilegio ad imprimendum solum.

[After the words, "and in all our names," p. 433, line 29, instead of the concluding lines which there follow, the second edition has the following pages:]

We must believe that their receiving of it is the application of Christ's merits to us. We must believe that they can thereby relieve the souls in the bitter pains of purgatory. We must believe that our being present at this their sacrifice, (as they call it), shall give us good speed in all our affairs, be they never so devilish. We must believe that a priest, (being never so ungodly in his living, never so much subject unto sin, never so much the devil's member), is the minister of God, and that his prayer and sacrifice in the mass is acceptable to God. In fine, we must believe that their masses be of strength to purchase the assistance of God in all dangers, and a present remedy against plague, penury, and all diseases both of man and beast, against wars, robberies, and all incursions of enemies, both bodily and ghostly. How can these assertions stand with the communion of Christ's body and blood? Did Christ shew the bread to his apostles, and then eat it himself, to certify their consciences thereby? Did he bid any one of them take bread and wine, and shew them to the residue of the faithful, so oft as they would communicate his body and blood, and then eat and drink all himself, instead of all the faithful that should be present? I think no man is so much without shame once to think it. But I know the root of their error. They say, that as Christ was the high priest or bishop to minister unto his apostles the communion of his body and blood, which he did indeed offer on the cross to his Father; so did he ordain his apostles, and in them all that should succeed them, priests to offer up the selfsame, (say they), to apply the sacrifice done by Christ with the merits of the same to them that are present thereat, or that shall by any means have it done for them. Oh, blind bussards! Where are your spiritual eyes become? Did Christ, being the high priest, distribute the bread to his apostles, to the intent that they, and all other their successors, should shew the bread and wine to the people, and then eat and drink all themselves? A man that hath so much ghostly knowledge as the grain of a mustard-seed, would not fail to say, that Christ meant rather that the apostles and priests should distribute the bread and wine among the faithful people, willing them to certify themselves thereby, that they are partakers of the body and blood of Christ. For what saith the text? "So oft as ye shall do this, ye shall do it in the remembrance of me." But what was it that they should do in the remembrance of him?" Forsooth, divide bread and wine amongst them. The private receiving of the bread and wine therefore can by no means stand with the institution of Christ, which was, that according to his example we should, by the dividing of bread and wine amongst us, certify ourselves that we are all partakers with Christ in his redemption, through the ransom that he paid for us on the cross. How standeth this with our hearing of mass, to the intent to speed the better thereby, when we go about our worldly business, be they honest or unhonest, godly or ungodly? Forsooth, I suppose, even as much as the carrying of bread in a man's purse in the night-time, or in a tempest, serveth to keep him from blasting with evil airs. So that I dare be bold to affirm, that this hearing of mass is no better than mere superstition, and the mass itself so far from the institution of Christ, that it seemeth not to be any part of the commemoration of Christ's passion; but a mere invention of man, crept into the church by the subtle suggestion of our most cruel and malicious enemy the devil, who hath always endeavoured to poison all the wholesome food of man's soul, as it appeareth right well by the great abuse that this most sacred sacrament is grown unto. This was and ought to be so necessary a food to the soul, that without it no Christian can tarry in Christ, neither have Christ tarrying in him; whereby it is plain, that without this food no soul hath any life in it. For Christ is the life that is in the christian soul. No less necessary therefore is this food to the souls of the congregation, than the sinews be to the body to hold the joints together. Our adversary therefore could in no case be quiet, till he had poisoned this so necessary food, corrupting therein the virtue and strength to unite and knit the Christians to Christ their head, making it of force to draw them quite from him by putting their confidence in it, trusting to redeem their sins by oft offering up thereof; insomuch that they fell to founding of abbeys, chantries, and anniversaries for the salvation of their souls: for so was it always specified and conditioned in the writings made between the founders of such abbeys, chan-

34—2

tries, and anniversaries, and the receivers of the yearly rents given to that use, yea, rather abuse. And in this miserable estate hath it continued even these six hundred years, poisoning the souls of them that should have been fed thereby.

But here must I beware, that our enemy do not poison these words of mine also, causing men to understand me as one that would deny it to be possible for any man to tarry in Christ, or to have Christ tarrying in him, unless he receive these visible sacraments or signs, bread and wine. No doubt, christian reader, the belief and trust in Christ is the mean whereby Christ tarrieth in us, and we in him. But the belief and trust are established and confirmed by the use of these visible signs. As this belief and trust therefore are necessary to the abiding in Christ, so is the use of these holy sacraments also, for that it is the establishment and confirming of the said belief and trust. To all them, therefore, to whom this belief and trust are necessary, are these sacred sacraments also necessary. Whereupon I conclude, that all Christians, which are of age and discretion to discern the faith in Christ, ought also to use these most holy sacraments to establish and confirm this faith withal. And Christ knowing the weakness of man, and how hard it was to beat into his head the understanding of the high mystery of the participation and communion that all faithful should have in his merits, used these visible signs, that we might in them even with our senses perceive this wonderful distribution of the body and blood of Christ among his faithful, which our gross nature could no more compass without these visible signs, than the carnal and fleshly Jews could, when Christ told them of the eating his flesh and drinking of his blood, by believing in him. To help our weakness therefore, it pleased the almighty wisdom of the Lord to declare unto us by our senses the thing that the same senses caused the Jews to abhor: the manner, I say, of our participation and communion in Christ, and all that ever he deserved for us. For even as we see, that we, being many, are partakers of one loaf of bread by eating thereof, and of one cup of wine by drinking thereof; so are we certified by that participation, that we, being many, believing in Christ, are by that belief made partakers of Christ, and with Christ in all that is his, none otherwise than all the members of one body be partakers

of all joys and pleasures that chance to the head. For as
the loaf whereof we eat is made of many grains, and the cup
of wine whereof we drink is made of many grapes, and yet
is but one cup of wine, and the loaf but one loaf; even so are
we that believe in Christ but one body with him, and he our
head, notwithstanding we be many in number, and of divers
nations, estates and conditions. For as in the body be divers
members serving to divers uses, so are there in the congregation of Christ, which Paul calleth the body of Christ, divers
estates; "some apostles, some preachers, and some teachers." 1 Cor. xii.
And as in the body is no member, whereunto is not appointed
his peculiar and necessary office; so in the congregation of
Christ is there none estate or condition, but it is profitable,
yea, necessary to the other.

"This is a great mystery," saith Paul, "the mystery, I Ephes. v.
say, of Christ and his congregation;" for it is his body, of his
flesh, and of his bones. Not that the congregation or church is
that natural body that died on the cross, nor we, the members
of the same church, the flesh and bones of the same: but for
that it was that congregation, it was we, the members of this
church, that caused Christ to take our nature upon him, that
therein he might satisfy for our sins, making us partakers
with him in this satisfaction; and so are we his body and
members, that is to say, his body and members were and are
the price wherewith we were redeemed out of the captivity
and thraldom that we were in. This mystery is great, and
far above the beastly man's capacity. But if we will be given
to the Spirit, the Spirit shall minister unto us abundantly the
understanding thereof. For it is a common phrase or manner
of speaking amongst us: when any hath bestowed his money
upon any kind of merchandise, we say, Lo, here is my xx *li.*
or here are his hundred marks; shewing forth the wares that
were bought with my xx *li.* or his hundred marks, so that
here the thing bought beareth the name of the price. In
like manner doth Paul call the congregation redeemed by
Christ's body, his very body, his flesh, and his bones, because
it is the merchandise that was bought with his body, his flesh,
and his bones. The most sacred sacraments also of the body
and blood of Christ are called his body and blood, because
they declare unto us what the body and blood of Christ be
unto us, none otherwise than I call this book the supper of
the Lord, because it declareth the supper of the Lord. So

that here thou mayest see, gentle reader, wherein thou hast been so far and so long deceived. Forsooth, in that thou hast not known nor considered the causes, why these most holy sacraments bear the names of that they represent, shew, or declare unto us; but hast grossly persuaded thyself with the carnal and fleshly Jews, that Christ spake carnally, minding to turn the substance of the bread and wine into the substance of his body and blood, when he said unto his disciples, "This is my body." But doubtless, good christian brother, our most cruel enemy hath in this point uttered even the greatest part of his malicious practice. He hath not failed always to beat into our heads the omnipotency of God, who could by his word make all things of nought; his verity, which will not suffer him to leave ought undone that he saith is or shall be done; and then his words at his last supper, "This is my body," &c. Here laboureth he with tooth and nail, as they say, to keep us in the plain letter, that we measure not these words by the scriptures of like phrase. The verity itself, saith he, hath spoken it; wherefore it cannot be otherwise. The only Almighty, which created all things by his word, hath said it: it is not therefore impossible that it should be so. Thou art a christian man, and hast professed to believe all the words of Christ to be true, though thy reason cannot comprehend the manner how. And wilt thou, with the carnal and fleshly Jews, doubt in the performance of the words that thy Saviour shall speak? He said that a virgin should bring forth a child: and wilt not thou believe it, because thou canst not by reason be persuaded that it is possible for a virgin to bring forth a child? What could the obstinate Jews do more, than blindly and obstinately say, "How can this man give us his flesh to eat, and his blood to drink?" And wilt thou be as obstinate as they, and think it impossible for him to give thee his flesh, (yea, his very natural flesh), and blood under the form of bread and wine? Oh, subtle serpent! Oh, crafty dissembler! Now changest thou thyself into an angel of light. Thou madest the Jews abhor Christ's words, because the law, which they professed, taught them that it was abominable to eat the raw flesh, or drink the blood of any beast, much more of a man. And because they should not consider and understand the spiritual eating of his body, and drinking of his blood by faith, thou puttest them in mind of the corruptible manna that the

*Note the subtlety of the devil.*

fathers did eat in wilderness; and that, notwithstanding that bread came from heaven, yet was it not of such lively force that it might preserve the eaters thereof from death. Yea, thou heldest them in opinion, that it was not possible for Christ to give them his flesh to eat, and his blood to drink, after such sort that their stomachs might away withal. Wherefore they said: "How can this fellow give us his[1] flesh to eat, and his blood to drink?" But here thou comest unto us with the contrary. Thou biddest us believe, that he was able to change bread and wine into his flesh and blood, that we might thereby away with the devouring thereof. Thus thou playest on both hands; with them, because they should not look for any spiritual eating or drinking of Christ's flesh and blood; and with us, that we should not regard the spiritual eating and drinking, but that we should most regard the fleshly devouring of the bread and wine: so that neither the Jews neither we can come to the[2] true eating of Christ's flesh and drinking of his blood by unfeigned faith in him and his merits.

Here mayest thou plainly see, most dearly beloved in the Lord, by what means our ghostly enemy hath spoiled us of the use of these most precious jewels, the sacraments of Christ's body and blood; and how he laboureth daily in his members, the wicked papists, to withhold from us the knowledge of the spiritual eating and drinking of Christ, which beginneth now to spread the world over all. Let us run, therefore, unto our present and only succour in this great danger. To Christ, I say, let us run, most humbly beseeching him, our Saviour and Redeemer, plenteously to pour out of his Spirit of knowledge upon us all, that we may daily more and more find out the hid and secret abominations, to the utter extirpation and rooting out of the same. And in the mean time let us pray together, that it may please the Lord to augment the number of his faithful, turning Sauls into Pauls, that the hard hearts may be mollified, by hearing the persecutors preach Christ whom they persecuted. The Spirit of truth be with you all! So be it.

It is the Spirit that quickeneth, the<br>flesh profiteth nothing<br>at all. John vi.

[1 Old edition, *this*.]      [2 Old edition, *be*.]

# ERRATA.

PAGE LINE
134, 4, for *timorously* read *temerously*.
137, 4, for *Nebuchadnezzar* read *Nabuchodonosor*.
138, 3, after *felt* insert *no*.
160, 19, for *Joshua's* read *Josue's*.
185, 11, dele *in a while*.
222, 4, *to be very good indeed:* so the old edition; but it should evidently be, *to be very God indeed*.
257, 23, for *take upon* read *take upon him*.
443, 34, for *held* read *hold*.

# INDEX.

## A.

ABEL, in what sense he is said to have offered a more excellent sacrifice than Cain, 27, 8; the first martyr, 29.

Advocate, Christ our, 384, 5.

Affections in man, diversity of, 502.

Affliction and trouble cometh from God, 95; sent for the punishment of our sins, 97; less than our sins, 100; sent by God of a loving and fatherly mind towards us, 103; God for Christ's sake, of mercy, love, and favour, doth correct and punish us, 105; Christ in what he suffered hath blessed and sanctified affliction, 106; God sendeth it for our good, 110; seeketh our reformation, 111; proves us with afflictions, 116; afflictions further us to the knowledge of God and ourselves, and to wisdom, 119; further us to the knowledge of our sins and to repentance for them, 121; and to the exercising and increasing of our faith, 123; give occasion to pray unto God, and to praise him, 127; further us in virtue and godliness, 129; help and further us toward the fear and love of God, 134; teach men patience, meekness, and lowliness, 136; teach men pity, compassion, and patience toward other, 138; trouble and affliction maketh men hard and strong, 139; teacheth men to despise the world, 140; help to much quietness and commodity in the world, 142; a furtherance to eternal life, 145; effect of on the unfaithful, 147; how it may be overcome, 153; support in adversity, 156; duty of faith, hope, and confidence toward God in adversity, 164; of prayer in adversity, 166; of repentance and amendment of life in adversity, 168; examples of patience in adversity out of scripture, 169; other examples, 174.

Agony of our Saviour, considerations from, 256, &c.; proof from, that he did not suffer by compulsion, but willingly, 257; intended to declare unto us the weakness and feebleness that our flesh receiveth at the sight of adversity, *ib.*; because he would take upon him a true man, who felt our adversity in his own flesh, and so could have pity on us, *ib.*; that he might teach us, to whom our weakness ought to resort for comfort and help in trouble, *ib.*; an evidence that he is man, 260; to prove to us that when he sends to us affliction, it is not always in anger, 262; but he sendeth us his own help and comfort, *ib.*; that we might derive comfort in trouble, when we consider that our heavenly Father bringeth his own Son into such trouble for our sakes, 262.

Altar, one, what it signifieth, 45.

Apostles, preached salvation by Christ, 77; declared by preaching of the word and ministration of the sacraments, *ib.*

Aread, explained, 277.

Aristotle, opinion of, in what true blessedness consists, 175, 6.

Ark, the, a type of Christ, 32.

Ascension of Christ, considerations on, 380, &c.; he ascended, not after his Godhead, but after his manhood, 382.

Assyria, kingdom of, 34.

Augustine, quoted, 128, 141, 199, 203; says that the wicked do not spiritually eat the flesh of Christ and drink his blood, 427; states the difference between the sacrament and the thing itself, *ib.*; referred to, 445 *n.*; speaks of the Lord's supper as a sacrifice, and in what sense, 451 *n.*; referred to, 456 *n.*; declareth that the sacraments do take their effect of the word of the Lord, 459, 60.

### B.

Babylon, kingdom of, 34; captivity at, a figure of the captivity of sin, 400; deliverance from, what signified by, *ib.*

Baptism, instituted by Christ, and enjoined on his Apostles, 78; Christians planted in the church by baptism, 370; through baptism we receive Christ, 410; we receive Christ, and have forgiveness of our sins through the grace and gift of Christ, *ib.*; the water in baptism cannot cleanse the soul from sin, 411; not instituted by Christ in vain, *ib.*; not neglected by the faithful, *ib.*; in baptism we professed and bound ourselves to fight under the standard of Christ, 495; the badges and signs of baptism testify that we are sworn unto him never to forsake him, *ib.* See SACRAMENTS.

Belief, nature and condition of true belief, 344; true believers partakers of everlasting life, 249; keep God's commandments, *ib.*

Bernard, quoted, 120, 165, 181.

Bread and wine anciently offered in the Lord's supper, 451; not agreeable to the institution of Christ, *ib.*

Bull, Bishop, on the opinions of the Docetæ, referred to, 21 *n.*

Burial of Christ, reflections on, 316—21; the description of by the Evangelists, necessary for the assurance of our belief in his death and resurrection, 317; his burial must needs be honourable, foretold by Isaiah, *ib.*; we must learn with Christ to die from the world, and to be buried in his death, 318, 19; what we may learn from the conduct of the women, who brought spices for the burial of our Saviour, 320, 1.

### C.

Caii Fragmenta, referred to, with regard to the death of Peter, 362 *n.*

Casaubon adv. Baronium, quoted with regard to the meaning of τὸ τέλειον, as applied to the Eucharist, 203.

Ceremonies, outward of the Jews, sacraments of heavenly things, 445; why God ordained them, 447; no ground for the abuses introduced by the Romanists into the Lord's supper, 461; not all ceremonies to be disapproved, which serve to honesty and public order, whereby the more reverence is gained to the sacrament, *ib.*

Checkmate, to set at, explained, 50 *n.*

Christ, the seed of the woman, explained, 21; all true Israelites trusted in Christ, 50; all holy prophets point unto Christ, 59; all God's elect saved by, 70; the only salvation of all the world, 72; temptation of in the wilderness, 73; Christ's doctrine, special points of, 74; the patient suffering of, 75; the fruit of Christ's death, *ib.* 220; his power saveth all, 77; held nothing back from his Apostles, *ib.*; our example, 201; the true paschal lamb, 211; the bread of life, which came down from heaven, 212; we must learn humbleness from the example of, 213; foreknowledge of Christ exemplified in his prediction of the treachery of Judas, 214; we must learn patience from the example of, 219; meekness, *ib.*; Christ, the only way, 221; divinity of, proved by his doctrine and miracles, 222; testified by the scriptures of the Old and New Testament, *ib.*; by his own declaration, that we must believe on him, *ib.*; because he was before Abraham, *ib.*; because he hath all power in heaven and earth, *ib.*; from the declaration of Thomas, My Lord and my God, *ib.*; because he created all things, *ib.*; because he came in the flesh, *ib.*; because he took on him the seed of Abraham, 223; because he was in the bosom of the Father, *ib.*; because he came down from heaven, *ib.*; because he is declared by St John to be God, *ib.*; and the true God and eternal life, *ib.*; comfort from the ascension of, 229; with the faithful in adversity, 230; our great high-priest, 247; the way to God, 248; proved to be God from his resurrection, 346, 348, 406; why it behoved Christ to die and to rise again, 368, 9; sitteth at the right hand of God, King and Lord of all things, our faithful Advocate and Mediator, 384, 5; sendeth his Spirit to his church, 385; that Christ is the Saviour of the world, is the sum of the christian faith, 408; proved from his ascension up to heaven, and sending the Holy Spirit, 407, 8; all things should give way to the glory of, 494.

Christian living, rules of, 506; we must judge well of Scripture, not doubting the promises of God, *ib.*; we must with a good courage enter into the way of salvation 507; two only ways, of salvation and perdition, *ib.*; we must despise whatever leadeth from the way of Christ, 508; Christ must be the end and mark of our living, 509; we must ascend from things visible to things invisible, 510; we must follow Christ in his saints, *ib.*; we must not go back from the truth, 513; in Christ is found true nobility, pleasure, strength, praise, and wisdom, *ib.*; we must be climbing up unto godliness, 515; we may not despair in God, 516; we must ever keep watch, 517; we must neither be faint-hearted nor presumptuous, 518; we must of temptation take occasion of virtue, *ib.*; we must compare the bitterness of the fight with the pain that followeth sin and the sweetness of the victory, 519; we must exercise ourselves in the cross of Christ, 520; we must consider the misery of sin and the dignity of man, 521; we must consider the goodness of God and the malice of the devil, *ib.*; we must consider the end of faith, present tranquillity and quietness of mind, and everlasting salvation in heaven, 522; also of sin, perpetual grief and disquietness of soul in this life, and everlasting death in hell, *ib.*

Christian man, opinions meet for, 514.

Chrysostom, quoted, 356*n.*; speaks of the Lord's supper as a sacrifice, and in what sense, 451*n.*

Church, division of members by Augustine, 202—6; tried by affliction, 128; four marks of, 412—20.

Cicero quoted, 177.

Clemens Alexandrinus quoted, 21*n.*, 203*n.*

Consolation, grounds of, in our spiritual trials, 496, 7.

Creation, the, 14.

Cyprian referred to, 456*n.*

### D.

David, a prophet, 53; his faith in Christ, *ib.*

Death, in us the punishment of sin, in Christ, obedience and love, 230.

Death of Christ, considerations on, 308 —10; concluded and determined in the counsel of God, 403; yet the Jews not less guilty in putting him to death, 404.

Desert or dizzard explained, 4, 284.

Denmark, account of the reformation of Church in, 424; order in for the administration of the Lord's supper, 470—8; mode of consecration of elements, 476; received kneeling, *ib.*; order for ministration of baptism in,

478, 9 ; administered publicly in the congregation, *ib.*; order for the ministration of holy wedlock, 480.

Devil's chaplains, 484.

Docetæ, their opinions stated, 21 *n.*

Doctrine of Christ's faith no new thing, 4 ; foolishness to those that perish, 5 ; to those who are saved the power of God, *ib.*; we must put on the nature of Christ's doctrine, 10.

E.

Egypt, deliverance out of, a type of our redemption by Christ, 39.

Elect, all God's saved by Christ, 70.

Ephesians, Epistle to, chap. iv. 8, explained, 407.

Eucharist, called τὸ τέλειον, 203 *n.*

Eusebius says that the old Fathers, as pertaining to the religion and substance, were all christian, 14 ; referred to on the death of Peter, 362 *n.*

Eutychians mentioned, 455.

F.

Faith, christian, antiquity of, 4, 14 ; foundation of, 18 ; older than the Jewish faith, 35.

Faith defined, the substance of things hoped for, the evidence of things which do not appear, 5 ; the scripture hath imputed unto it our justification before God, *ib.*; not without other virtues following, but without any other work or deed justifying, 6 ; of Adam, 25 ; of Noah, 32 ; of Abraham, 34, 5 ; of Isaac and Jacob, 36 ; of Moses, 38 ; necessary for the reception of the sacraments, 80 ; support of in adversity, 102 ; confirmed and increased in adversity, 125 ; power of in adversity, 173 ; strengthened in affliction, 317 ; nature of true faith explained, 344, 5.

Fall of man, 17.

Fathers, the, looked beyond the sacrifices to Christ, 46 ; saved by Christ, 72.

Forgiveness of sins explained, 375.

G.

Godliness, the rule of true, 505.

H.

Ham, the first idolater after the flood, 34.

I.

Inheritance, the eternal, to be attained through the cross and trouble, 340.

Irenæus referred to, 21 *n.*

Isaiah, testimony of Jerome concerning, 66.

J.

Jerome says that Isaiah is not only a prophet, but an evangelist, 66.

Joel, prophecy of, contained in chap. ii. 28—32, explained, 399, &c.

John the Baptist foretold, 63 ; mission and preaching of, 74.

Joshua, a type of Christ, 50 ; in the destruction of the heathen nations acted by the command of God, 51.

K.

Keys (Matt. xvi.), meaning of, 373, 4.

L.

Lamb, passover, a type of Christ, 39, 211.

Law of Moses leadeth unto Christ, 37 ; giving of the law, 39 ; the deliverance out of Egypt a type of the redemption by Christ, *ib.*; that contained in the Ten Commandments required of the fathers before the law, 40 ; the law, why given, 43 ; given to further the promise, *ib.*; laws ceremonial, 47 ; judicial, *ib.*

Laws given to Noah, 33.

Life of man a warfare, 495.

Love, evidence of faith, 234 ; the commandment of Christ, 236 ; the be-

-ginning and end of the commandments of Christ, 417.

Luther, review of the controversy between Luther, Zuingle, and Œcolampadius on the Lord's supper, 463—5.

## M.

Magdalene, Mary, whether the person mentioned in Luke vii. considered, 329, n.

Man, two parts of, 503; three, 504.

Manichees and Anabaptists, their opinions considered, 51 and n.

Mede, Joseph, referred to, 451 n.

Mediatorial kingdom, when Christ will resign it, 385.

Melchisedec, a type of Christ, 55, 6.

Ministers, necessity of prayer for, 250; importance of their office, ib. 359.

## N.

Name of the Lord, to call on, explained, 402.

## O.

Œcolampadius, his controversy with Luther on the Lord's supper, 463—6, his opinions with regard to the presence of Christ in, 465.

Origen says that man consists of three parts, the flesh, the spirit, and the soul, 504.

## P.

Palmer, his Origines Liturgicæ referred to, 452 n.

Passion, our Saviour's, consideration of, 279.

Patience in adversity, 169.

Pearson, Bishop, referred to, 21 n., 50 n.

Pentecost, day of, described, 388, 9; Peter's discourse on, reflections upon it, 397, &c.

Perfection, christian, explained, 203, 5; in what sense the word is used by Augustine, ib.

Peter, denial of Christ, considered, 272—4.

Pharaoh, his impenitence, 118.

Plato put two souls in one man, 503.

Pliny, the younger, quoted, 101.

Prayer, duty of in adversity, 125; Christ an example of prayer to faithful believers, that they in all afflictions should have recourse to the Father of heaven, 247; after what sort we ought to pray, ib.; for ourselves and for all that are given and committed to us of God, ib.; how we ought to pray, ib.; especially we ought to pray, that our heavenly Father may be glorified, ib.; for the ministers of the word, 250; we ought to pray that God would make us one by his Holy Spirit in the faith, 253; that he will defend us from the evil, ib.; that he will sanctify our bodies, our souls, and our whole lives to his service, ib.

Prophecy, the prophets preached the old faith, 62; all holy prophets point to Christ, 59, &c.; the prophets allow the righteousness of God by faith, 62; speak of the Godhead and manhood of Christ, 63; of the office of Christ, 64; of the kingdom of Christ, ib.; of the sacrifice, death, burial, resurrection, and ascension of Christ, 65, 6; and of the calling of the heathen, 66; the prophets sought salvation in Christ, 67; prophecy of Daniel, chap. ix. considered, 67, 8.

Psalm, the hundred and tenth, exposition of, 53—58; the sixteenth, 8—11; prophecy contained in, explained, 406, 7.

## R.

Reformers, described by Augustine, 205.

Repentance followeth from the preaching of the word, 409; fruit of the Holy Spirit, ib.

Resurrection of Christ, doctrine of, 76; described by the Evangelists, 322;

for the strengthening and stablishing of our faith in Christ, 323.; why they do not speak all alike, *ib.*; whoso truly believeth the resurrection of Christ is prepared to believe all that concerneth Christ, *ib.*; what is signified by the earthquake which accompanied the death and resurrection of Christ, 324; why the Evangelists so distinctly describe the resurrection of Christ, 327; why Christ at first permitted his disciples to doubt his resurrection, *ib.*; why Christ led them gradually to the belief of his resurrection, 328; why Christ would not suffer Mary to touch him after his resurrection, 330; why he appeared to them so often after his resurrection, 343; the resurrection a proof that he is the true Messiah, 405; a strong argument to prove his Godhead, *ib.*; why Christ ate bread before them, 343; what we learn from the doubting and confession of Thomas, 345; our Saviour's appearance to the disciples at the sea of Galilee after his resurrection, 348, &c.; reflections, 349, &c.; what instructions we derive from the miracle wrought by him on that occasion, 351, &c.; what instruction the ministers of the gospel derive from his discourse with Peter, 355—61.

## S.

Sacraments, special, instituted by Christ, baptism, and the supper of the Lord, 79; to set before our eyes his heavenly and invisible grace, *ib.*; with these outward sacraments it pleased him to set forth his grace and loving-kindness, *ib.*; cleanseth and nourisheth our souls with his flesh and blood, *ib.*; is at one with us, and we with him, 80; must be used with faith, *ib.*; it was the will of Christ, through preaching of the word and ministration of the sacraments, to gather his church together, *ib.*; instituted them for a remembrance of his gifts, *ib.*; exterior signs of his grace, that his people might be associated together in the unity of faith, 345; the grace not to be ascribed to the outward elements, *ib.*; those who are moved by the Holy Spirit do not despise the outward sacraments, 411; to use them without faith profiteth not, *ib.*; visible evidences of the promise and grace of God, *ib.*; by whom used devoutly and reverently, *ib.*

Sacrifice, divine origin of, 27; sacrifices figures of the sacrifice of Christ, figures of things to come, 28; sacrifice of Abel considered, *ib.*

Salvation by grace, 42.

Sciences, liberal, not to be despised, 498; all manner of learning shall be tasted under the correction of Christ's doctrine, *ib.*

Scripture, original of, 48; given that man might be led to salvation, 394; expositors of, which to be preferred, 499.

Serpent, curse upon, 19; brasen serpent a type of Christ, 44.

Sin, we must flee the occasions of, 504; remedies against sins, 523; against bodily lust, *ib.*; against avarice, 524; against ambition, 525; against pride, 526; against desire of vengeance, 527.

Spirit, Holy, office of, 226; qualifications necessary for receiving, 227; all reading and doctrine in vain without it, 228; peace of God through the Spirit, 229; prayer to God for, 239; office of described, 239, 40; promise of described, 383, 388; earnest of our inheritance, 384, 8; sending of described, 387, &c.; how fully given, after our Lord's ascension, *ib.*; time of giving, 388; place where given, 389; manner of giving, *ib.*; explanation of the miracle, *ib.*; life given by the Holy Spirit, 392; the image of God restored by, 392, 3; given to those who in fervent love and unity are gathered together, 393;

the fountain of unity, *ib.*; given not only to the learned, but to the simple and unlearned, 398; was before in the godly, but more fully given after the ascension of Christ, 399; sending of, proof of our Saviour's ascension, 407; granted to prayer, 420; the author of obedience, 493.

Spiritual things, represented by outward and visible tokens, 390; the gifts of the Spirit thus signified, *ib.* 390; also by outward tokens in the supper are represented the body and blood of Christ, *ib.*

Supper of the Lord, institution of, 79; qualifications for approaching, 202 —6; the faithful receiveth in his soul through faith the body and blood of Christ, 207; Christians strengthened by it to eternal life, 211; meaning and importance of the outward signs, 330, 1, 340; when we eat Christ's flesh and drink his blood, 212, 331; the faithful Christian must lift up his soul from the outward elements to Christ, who feedeth the soul to eternal life, 351; grace worked in the hearts of the true believers, which in faith at the supper receive the true body and blood of the Lord, 352; breaking of bread in the supper, the token of the new covenant confirmed by Christ on the cross, 418; instituted by Christ, that by outward signs he might make his church mindful of his death, *ib.*; to gather together and unite the church into one communion and fellowship in Christ, *ib.*; bread and wine are signs, not bare signs, but seals of his covenant, to declare that all blood for sin is only in Jesus Christ, 419; abused by the Papists in offering it up as a sacrifice for the redemption of the souls of the church, 426, 451; explanation of our Saviour's words in the institution of, 429—31; unworthiness in receiving, explained, 432; in what sense persons said to receive to their own damnation, *ib.*; those who privately receive the sacrament to merit themselves or other; who make it a sacrifice for the redemption of sin, *ib.*; who are they that receive it worthily, viz. those who receive it as a most worthy sacrament or sign representing all that Christ did or purchased for us by his death, 433; they offend which honour the bread with divine honour, spoiling Christ of the victory achieved by the once offering of himself for all, *ib.*; Christ did not eat up all himself, but they require us to believe, that the priest receives it for us, and in our names, *ib.*; worthy receiving explained, *ib.*; for what cause and to what end Christ instituted this sacrament, 436; the fruit which the supper of the Lord bringeth to us, 437—9; in what sense the body and blood of Christ are given to us in the Lord's supper, 440; the sacrament of the Lord ought not to be separated from his substance and verity, 439, 440; we are stirred up by it to consider the benefits we receive of our Lord Jesus Christ, 442; we are more vehemently stirred up to holiness of life, *ib.*; the right use thereof, 443; how we ought to approach the Lord's table, 446, 7; plea of unworthiness considered, 448, 9; in what sense the fathers spoke of the Lord's supper as a sacrifice, 451; Romish opinion of the Lord's supper as an actual sacrifice for sin opposed to the sufficiency of the sacrifice of Christ, 453; refusal of the cup in the Lord's supper by the Romanists opposed to the institution of Christ, 459, 60; the fruit of Christ's death communicated to us in the Lord's supper, not on account of the merit of the work, but for the promises that are made to us therein, 461; substance of our belief, that when we do, according to the institution of the Lord, receive the sacrament with faith, we are undoubtedly made partakers of the substance of the body and blood of Christ, after a spiritual manner, 465, 6; in the mass, we are required to believe that the priests' receiving of the bread and wine is the application of Christ's merits to us, 530; that they can relieve souls in purgatory, *ib.*; that being present at this their sacrifice, as they call it, will give us speed in all our affairs, *ib.*; that their masses purchase the assistance and favour of God, *ib.*; these assertions cannot stand with the communion of Christ's body and blood, *ib.*; the private receiving of the bread and wine can by no means stand with the institution of Christ, 531; the mass is so far from the institution of Christ, that it seemeth not to be any part of the commemoration of Christ's passion, but a mere invention of man, *ib.*; this sacrament so necessary a food to the soul, that without it no Christian can tarry in Christ, or have Christ tarrying in him, *ib.*; belief and trust in Christ confirmed by the use of these visible signs, 532; Christ gave them to help our weakness, 532.

T.

Τέλειος, τελειόω, and τελείωσις, used by the fathers to express the religious condition of the more advanced Christian, 203 *n.*; illustrated from Clemens Alexandrinus, *ib.*; the term τὸ τέλειον applied to the Eucharist, and in what sense, *ib.*; applied to the illustration of the language used by Coverdale (205, 206), with regard to the peculiar consolations which the faithful derive from the Lord's supper, *ib.*

Tertullian referred to, 21 *n.*, 55 *n.*

Testament, old, not to be refused, 71; declared by the new, *ib.*

Thief, penitent, considerations from the history of, 301, 2.

Tongues, fiery, meaning of, 389.

Transubstantiation, doctrine of, considered, 453, 4; doctrine of the Council of Trent on, *ib.*

Truth, the danger of withstanding the, 501.

U.

Unbelief, the origin of all vices, 240.

Unity and brotherly love in the church, prayer for, 385.

V.

Veil in the Temple, rending of, what signified by, 75.

*Veni Creator*, hymn, an account of, 471.

W.

War of a christian man, the two weapons necessary in, prayer and knowledge, 497; the use of prayer, 498; of knowledge, *ib.*; our weapons must be fetched out of the storehouse of God's word, 499.

Water and blood from Christ's side, what signified by, 75.

Wicked, God withholdeth his grace from, 255.

Winchester, Gardiner, Bishop of, his book on the Sacrament noticed, 429.

Wisdom, worldly, foolishness before God, 500.

Wisdom of God, source of all good things, 501; to be obtained by prayer, *ib.*

Word of God, we must come with reverence to, 499.

World, corruption of, 492.

Z.

Zuinglius, his opinions on the Lord's supper, 463—6.

www.ingramcontent.com/pod-product-compliance
Lightning Source LLC
Chambersburg PA
CBHW052044290426
44111CB00011B/1610